Sociology of

DEVIANT BEHAVIOR

15.2   Divorces and Divorce Rates in Relation to Population, United States, 1890–1957 (Rates per 1000 of mid-year Population)   437

15.3   The Nature of Marriage   456

16.1   Percentage of Population Aged 45 Years and Over in the Labor Force, 1890–1954   470

16.2   Percentage of Population 65 Years of Age and Over in Eight Western Countries   477

16.3   Population of the United States, by Age, 1960, 1950, and 1900   477

17.1   Racial Minorities in the United States, 1960   504

17.2   Number and Percentage of Nonwhite Population in Some Southern States and the District of Columbia, 1960   505

17.3   Number and Percent of Nonwhite Population in Selected Large Cities, 1960   506

17.4   Location of the Negro Population, by Region, 1790–1960   507

17.5   States with Largest Indian Populations, 1960   515

17.6   Estimated Spanish-Speaking Population of the Southwest, 1950   522

17.7   Jewish Population, by Continents   531

17.8   Jewish Population by Cities of the World, 1960   531

19.1   Number of Juvenile Delinquency Cases Disposed of by 56 Courts Serving Areas with Populations of 100,000 or More, 1938–1945   574

19.2   An Analysis of 1912 Studies Made by the American Social Hygiene Association, January 1, 1940, to March 31, 1945, in Communities Adjacent to Military Installations   582

19.3   Suicide Death Rates per 100,000 Population, United States, 1938–1947   586

21.1   Resident Patients by Type of Hospital, 1955–1959   633

Figures

1. The Growth of a City   88

2. Interaction of Factors that Produce Deviant Behavior   121

3. Selected Types of Delinquent and Criminal Behavior   211

4. Changing Proportion of Age Groups in the Population, 1900–1960   478

5. Percentage of Nonwhite Population in Counties of Southern States   503

6. Percentage of Negroes in Schools with Whites, May 1961   545

7. Hospital Status Hierarchy   637

PART

I

Social Deviation

Tables

1.1 Social Groups Which May Be Based on Interests 7

3.1 Estimated Proportion of Population Living in Cities of 100,000 or More 62

3.2 Cities over 100,000 Population in Major Regions of the World, 1950 63

3.3 The Fourteen Largest Urbanized Areas in the United States 64

3.4 Growth of the Urban Population in the United States 1790–1960 65

3.5 Schematic Version of Urbanism as a Way of Life 66

3.6 Internal Migration in the United States 71

3.7 Rates per 100,000 Population for Crimes Known to the Police in Rural and Urban Areas, United States, 1960 79

3.8 Rates per 100,000 for Crimes Known to the Police by City Size, United States, 1960 84

3.9 Estimated Rates of Chronic Alcoholism in the Adult Population by Sex and Population Size Groups, United States, 1940 85

3.10 Distribution of Meat Black-Market Offenders According to Desirability of Residence 92

5.1 The Scale for Temperament 122

7.1 Percentage of 1698 Persons Who Had Committed Offenses 169

8.1 Major Crimes Reported to the Police in the United States During 1960 206

8.2 Number and Percentage of Crimes for Which Women Were Arrested in Cities with 25,000 Population and Over, 1952 207

8.3 Number and Percentage of Arrests of Persons under 18, under 21, and under 25 Years of Age, 1960; in 2460 Cities over 2500 in Population 208

9.1   Motivation of Murderers   238

11.1   Drugs Used First and Last, and Drug Preferred by 1036
       Patients at the United States Public Health Service Hos-
       pital at Lexington   294

11.2   Rates of Arrest for Narcotic Drug Law Violations (Chicago)
       per 10,000 Population for Different Age Groups   296

11.3   Age at Beginning of Addiction of 1036 Patients at the
       United States Public Health Service Hospital at Lexington   297

11.4   Length of Addiction among 1036 Patients at the United
       States Public Health Service Hospital at Lexington   298

11.5   The Percentage Distribution of Arrests for the Most Seri-
       ous Types of Offenses in the Narcotic Bureau and the
       Chicago Police Department, 1951   312

12.1   The Effect of Alcoholic Beverages   323

12.2   Apparent Consumption of Alcoholic Beverages, per capita
       (Aged 15 and Over), United States, 1850–1960, in United
       States Gallons   333

12.3   Proportion of United States Population Twenty-one and
       Over Who Drink Alcoholic Beverages   333

12.4   Drinking Frequency by Percentage of Drinkers, Washing-
       ton, 1951   334

12.5   Incidence of Drinking, by Type of College   337

12.6   Frequency of Drinking During Past Year   337

12.7   The Iowa Scale of Preoccupation with Alcohol   340

12.8   Estimated Rates of Alcoholism in Various Countries   341

12.9   Symptoms and Mean Onset Ages (Years) of 13 Selected
       Symptoms in a Wisconsin Study Group of 252 Alcoholics,
       1955   342

14.1   Number and Rate of Suicides per 100,000 Population,
       United States, 1950–1960   404

14.2   Suicide Rates for Selected Countries, 1958   407

14.3   Suicides by Sex by Country, 1958, 1959   413

14.4   Suicide Rates in the United States, by Age, 1959   416

15.1   Interpersonal Relations in Modern Marriage   433

Contents xiii

Social Differentials in Suicide   412

The Suicide Process   419

Suicide and Mental Disorder   425

Suicide and Status   426

15. CONFLICTS IN MARITAL AND FAMILY ROLES   430

Concept of Marital and Family Conflict   430

The Process of Family Disintegration   433

Desertion   435

Divorce   436

Conflicting Roles and Role Expectations in the Family   441

Conflicts Involving Cultural Background and Interests   447

Psychological Characteristics and Marital Interaction   448

Social Participation and Marital Happiness   450

Marital Happiness, Companionship, and the Sexual Relation   451

Economic Problems and Marital Stability   452

Marital Stability and Social Structure   453

16. ROLE AND STATUS CONFLICT IN OLD AGE   460

Physiological Changes   460

Psychological Changes   463

Changes in Social Roles and Status   464

Increases in Aged Population   476

Old Age and Mental Disorders   480

Social Participation of the Aged   484

Social Adjustment of the Aged   486

17. MINORITY GROUPS   491

The American Creed   491

The Concept of a Minority Group   501

Minorities in the United States   503

18. DISCRIMINATION AND PREJUDICE   534

Forms of Discrimination   535

Relation of Discrimination to Prejudice   553

Cultural Factors and Prejudice   554

Prejudice and Personality Needs   561

Prejudice and Economic Factors   564

Prejudice and the Minority   567

19. THE EFFECT OF WAR ON DEVIANT
BEHAVIOR   570

War and Social Change   571

War and Social Deviation   572

PART III.   *Deviant Behavior and Social Control*

20. THE REDUCTION OF DEVIANT BEHAVIOR:
GENERAL PROGRAMS   593

Moral and Ameliorative Problems   596

Organized Public Education   597

Preventive Agencies   607

21. THE REDUCTION OF DEVIANT BEHAVIOR:
THE USE OF INSTITUTIONS   621

Prisons   621

Mental Hospitals   632

22. THE GROUP APPROACH TO SOCIAL
REINTEGRATION   644

Group Approaches to Alcoholism   647

Group Methods with Drug Addicts   653

Group Methods in Reintegrating the Mentally Disordered   655

Group Methods in Reintegrating the Aged   663

Group Methods with Delinquent and Criminal Offenders   664

INDEX TO AUTHORS   673

INDEX TO SUBJECTS   685

Television, Motion Pictures, Radio, and Comic Books   178

Neighborhoods and Occupations   181

Associates   184

Delinquent Gangs or Subcultures   186

The Family   196

Alcohol and Delinquency or Crime   200

8. TYPES OF DELINQUENT AND CRIMINAL OFFENDERS   204

Type of Crime   204

Sex of Offenders   206

Age of Offenders   207

Delinquent and Criminal Behavior Systems   210

Personality Traits and Criminal Behavior   216

Types of Delinquents   219

Vandalism   219

Automobile Theft by Juveniles   228

9. TYPES OF OFFENDERS: MURDERERS AND SEX OFFENDERS   231

Murderers   231

Sex Offenders   240

10. CAREER CRIMINALS   257

Occasional Property Offenders   257

The Habitual Petty Offender   258

White-Collar Offenders   261

Ordinary Criminal Careers   270

Organized Crime   273

The Professional Offender   284

11. DRUG ADDICTION   292

The Effect of Drugs   293

Extent of Addiction   295

Age and Length of Addiction   297

Education and Occupation of Drug Addicts   298

The Process of Opiate Addiction   301

The Process of Using Marihuana   303

The Culture of Drug Addiction   305

Delinquency, Crime, and Drug Addiction   310

Treatment   313

The Control of Drug Addiction   314

12. ALCOHOL DRINKING AND ALCOHOLISM   318

Physiological Effects of Alcohol   321

Drinking as a Social Phenomenon   325

Public Drinking Houses and Society   327

Extent of Drinking in the United States   332

Types of Drinkers   337

The Alcoholic Process   341

Personality Traits and Excessive Drinking   346

Group and Subcultural Factors in Alcoholism   347

13. THE FUNCTIONAL MENTAL DISORDERS   362

Problems of Definition   363

Extent of Mental Disorders in the United States   367

Trends in Mental Illness   370

Organic Mental Disorders   371

Functional or Nonorganic Mental Disorders   373

Mental Disorder as a Process   379

Cultural Factors in Mental Disorders   394

Social Stratification and Mental Disorders   396

Heredity and Schizophrenia   398

14. SUICIDE   403

Suicide and Cultural Norms   404

Variations by Country   406

Suicide and the Law   407

Suicide and the Type of Society   408

Contents

PREFACE   vii

PART I.   *Social Deviation*

1. SOCIAL DEVIATION   3

Society and Group Relationships   4

Culture and Social Norms   8

Social Differentiation and Subcultural Norms   10

Social Stratification and Deviant Behavior   13

Social Deviation and Societal Reaction   17

The Social Visibility of Deviant Behavior   20

Deviant Behavior   22

Types of Deviant Behavior   23

The Scientific Study of Deviant Behavior   31

2. DEVIANT BEHAVIOR AS SOCIAL BEHAVIOR   36

Biology and Social Behavior   38

Social Nature of Man   45

Social Roles   49

3. URBANIZATION, URBANISM, AND DEVIANT BEHAVIOR   60

The Growth of World Urbanization   60

Urbanization in the United States   63

Urbanism as a Way of Life   65

Decline in Intimate Communication and Modification of Mechanisms of Informal Social Control   74

ix

Urban Characteristics a Matter of Degree   76

Comparisons of Certain Forms of Deviant Behavior in
Rural and Urban Areas   78

Social Deviation and City Size   83

Distribution of Deviant Behavior within a City   87

Explanation of Distributions of Deviant Behavior
within Cities   94

4. ECONOMIC AND TECHNOLOGICAL FACTORS
IN SOCIAL DEVIATION   99

Poverty and Deviant Behavior   99

Fluctuations in the Business Cycle and Deviation   105

Technological Development and the Cultural Lag   105

Substandard Housing and Deviant Behavior   110

5. CONTROVERSIAL THEORIES OF
DEVIANT BEHAVIOR   116

Deviant Behavior and Feeble-Mindedness   116

Deviant Behavior and Body Type   119

The Psychiatric Theory of Deviant Behavior   125

The Psychoanalytic Explanation of Deviant Behavior   126

General Evaluation of the Psychiatric and
Psychoanalytic Explanations   136

PART II.   *Deviant Behavior*

6. THE NATURE OF DELINQUENCY AND
CRIMES   145

The Scientific Study of Criminal Behavior   145

Crime and Social Control   148

What Is a Crime?   152

7. SOURCES OF DELINQUENT AND CRIMINAL
ATTITUDES   167

The General Culture   168

Preface

    Some five years have elapsed since this book first appeared. It has been gratifying to learn that it has been well received. In this revision I have followed essentially the approach of the original work: namely, the analysis of certain behavior in terms of deviations from norms. I have felt, however, that a text book not only should "grow" with the literature but also reflect changes in the author's thinking. Consequently, substantial revisions have been made in nearly all chapters. Four chapters have been almost completely rewritten. In each case I have included significant recent research and the latest statistical data, including 1960 United States Census figures. Two chapters have been added: Chapter 8, which emphasizes types of juvenile delinquents; and Chapter 21, which presents the sociological aspects of the prison and the mental hospital. More material has been included on juvenile delinquency.

    Moreover, in this revision I have placed more emphasis on process in the analysis of deviant behavior and less on mere description or isolated facts. In line with more recent developments in sociology, I have added considerable comparative materials on deviant behavior from other societies. It is hoped that this material will place a number of issues presented here in a wider perspective.

    This book is written as a text for courses designated as "social disorganization," "social problems," "social pathology," "deviant behavior," or some similar term. As its title suggests, I have tried to deal with certain deviations from social norms which encounter disapproval and to which theory and concepts derived from sociology and social psychology may be applied. Consequently, "problems" primarily of concern to economics, political science, or public health are not discussed.

    The book has been organized in three parts: Social Deviation, Deviant Behavior, and Deviant Behavior and Social Control. Part I presents a general approach to social deviation, describing and defining various forms, introducing a number of sociological and sociopsychological concepts, and discussing the effects of contemporary urbanism. In addition, various theories of deviant behavior, such as those stressing poverty, cultural lag, and the psychiatric and psychoanalytic explanations of deviant behavior are presented in Part I rather than throughout the book, thus avoiding repetition. Part II presents a detailed analysis of a considerable number of forms of deviant behavior. In Part III, various types of proposed solutions are dealt with at one time rather than after the analysis of each form of deviant behavior, so that the similarity of various approaches may be seen. Chapter 22, for example, deals with various group approaches, such as group therapy, and their application to such fields as alcoholism, mental disorder, drug addiction, and criminal behavior.

In Chapters 1 and 2, I have explained, in terms of deviant behavior, various concepts which are applied throughout the book. They have included social norms and values, subcultural groups, social differentiation, social structure, societal reaction, socialization, social status, self-conception, social roles, and the definition of the situation. In particular, I have stressed role theory. The wide use of these concepts is based on the premise that deviant behavior is social behavior, to which the same concepts can be applied as to nondeviant behavior. It is hoped that the opening chapters will help those who have not previously had an introductory course in sociology; for those who have, it will serve as a transition and review. Except for the first chapter each one ends with a summary and all conclude with an annotated list of selected readings. Extensive case material and personal documents are included throughout.

I have appreciated the help and suggestions of several persons who have read parts of the original or revised text, particularly Frank E. Hartung, Kingsley Davis, Arnold W. Green, Lyle W. Shannon, Simon Dinitz, Michael Hakeem, David Mechanic, Thomas J. Scheff, Eugene A. Friedmann, Orville G. Brim, Jr., Ersel E. Le Masters, Alfred Kadushin, Leslie A. Osborn, Donald W. Olmstead, Andrew L. Wade, and Torgny Segerstedt. My research assistant on the revision, Virginia M. Lambert, has been particularly helpful to me. Several of my graduate teaching assistants have also furnished useful comments. I should like to acknowledge especially the help of my wife, Ruth, who has spent many long hours typing, retyping, and editing both editions of this book.

M. B. C.

Madison, Wisconsin
January, 1963

To my children

from whom I have learned a great deal

MARSHA, STEPHEN, and LAWRENCE

REVISED EDITION

Sociology of
DEVIANT BEHAVIOR

Marshall B. Clinard

University of Wisconsin

HOLT, RINEHART AND WINSTON, INC.

New York — Chicago — San Francisco
Toronto — London

Social Deviation

Man's achievements in the area of social relationships have not equaled his achievements in physical science and technology. Within a few centuries man has solved many of the mysteries of the world around him. His endeavors have progressed from the realm of folklore and magic to that of science. His knowledge of the earth and all its resources, and even the vast areas of outer space, surpasses the wildest speculation of primitive man, medieval philosophers, or the early American colonists. The tremendous information he has amassed has enabled him to build great dams and irrigation projects to prevent catastrophic floods and droughts and open up marginal lands to cultivation. He has learned to control pestilence and many diseases so that his expected life span is greatly increased. In large parts of the Western world, at least, modern technical skills have provided food, clothing, and shelter for most of the population, and scientific research today increasingly deals with such intricate problems as nuclear fission, electronics, and changes in the human cell.

Unfortunately these technological advances have not brought with them a comparable degree of conquest over man's problems of relationships with other persons. His success in social relationships generally has not approached his progress in his physical environment. Although the physical scientists have fathomed the very structure of energy and have produced means of travel in outer space, man has been increasingly plagued with difficulties in his personal relationships.

Just as man has had to cope with mysticism and dogma in his understanding of the physical world, similar stumbling blocks have stood in his path as he has attempted to deal with problems in social relationships. Unscientific observations and theories of the behavior of man are as rampant today as they were concerning the physical world in the medieval ages. Many falsely consider the behavior of man, his achievements as well as his problems, as a product of individual strength or perversity. The behavior of persons who constitute problems to themselves and to others is falsely attributed to individual biological weaknesses in inheritance, to feeblemindedness, to body type, or even to racial origin, or is explained as the product of poverty or simply of the "moral" weakness of the individual.

3

Most people fail to realize that the scientific study of society, social behavior, and the social problems associated with them is fairly recent, though the basic discoveries which have culminated in the advances in the physical world go back many centuries. In fact, the basic knowledge for man's dramatic control of physical phenomena, resulting in the discovery of atomic energy, is the outcome of mathematical and other learning accumulated over at least two thousand years. Until fifty to a hundred years ago scientific methods were applied for the most part to the physical world only, whereas human personality and group behavior were left chiefly to philosophical and moral speculation. Scientific efforts in the latter areas have required the development of concepts and research tools for the study of human behavior. Some of the more important of these concepts will be discussed briefly in the following sections.

Society and Group Relationships

From birth man must depend upon other human beings. Physically and economically he is dependent upon others for his survival and, socially, he relies upon his fellow human beings for his personal development and his satisfactions. Man alone lives in true social groups. Like man, most animals form groups, and there may even be prolonged association, mutual dependence, and cooperation toward biologically common goals. The term *society or social group,* however, can be applied to no animal other than man, for the ties which bind a human group together are not merely biological needs but abstract social relationships. Shared sets of common meanings or symbols, feelings of unity, and systems of mutual obligation characterize man's social groups. Some may attempt to read human counterparts into the life of other animals, but man alone has such social institutions as a political state, an economic system, and religion. He alone has laws and moral judgments.

Social groups are more than simply a group or collection of persons. In a social group several persons are in interaction, there are social relationships among the persons, and, finally, there is a degree of consensus or concerted action. Social groups exist when there are *social relationships* among a number of persons. Social relationships, in turn, are a consequence of recurring or repeated *social interaction* between two or more persons. An individual, in his actions, takes into account what he considers to be the expectation of others, and his behavior, in turn, means that he expects others to act toward him in a certain way. These mutual expectations and a person's evaluation of them represent his *social role,* a term which will be more fully discussed in the following chapter.

> Sociology is the study of groups. There are many kinds of groups, and one inclusive way of conceiving of them is in terms of concerted action. All joint enterprises involve some kind of social differentiation and an integration

of the various contributions, and such coordination is facilitated when there is consensus. . . . From birth to death each human being is a participant in a variety of groups, and neither he nor anything he does or experiences can be understood when separated from the fact of such participation. As John Donne so eloquently expressed it, "No man is an island, entire of itself." Human conduct is continually subject to social control. What one does often depends more upon the demands he imputes to other people than it does upon his own preferences.[1]

As a result of his group experiences, a human being becomes dependent on others. The importance of this dependence on groups, and man's need for human group relationships, can be demonstrated in situations where group contacts are removed. For example, prison officials have learned that solitary confinement, with its almost complete isolation from human relationships, is one of the most severe forms of punishment for any human being. A few days of this type of treatment usually will render the most defiant prisoner tractable. Admiral Byrd voluntarily isolated himself for several months in the uninhabited polar regions of Antarctica more than a hundred miles from the nearest human being of his expedition. He described his experiences of being alone and vividly showed how dependent the individual is on social groups when he is removed from such contacts.

10 P.M. Solitude is an excellent laboratory in which to observe the extent to which manners and habits are conditioned by others. My table manners are atrocious—in this respect I've slipped back hundreds of years; in fact, I have no manners whatsoever. If I feel like it, I eat with my fingers, or out of a can, or standing up—in other words, whichever is easiest. What's left over, I just heave into the slop pail, close to my feet. Come to think of it, no reason why I shouldn't. It's rather a convenient way to eat; I seem to remember reading in Epicurus that a man living alone lives the life of a wolf.

A life alone makes the need for external demonstration almost disappear. Now I seldom cuss, although at first I was quick to open fire at everything that tried my patience. Attending to the electrical circuit on the anemometer pole is no less cold than it was in the beginning; but I work in soundless torment, knowing that the night is vast and profanity can shock no one but myself.

My sense of humor remains, but the only sources of it are my books and myself, and, after all, my time to read is limited. Earlier today, when I came into the hut with my water bucket in one hand and the lantern in the other, I put the lantern on the stove and hung up the bucket. I laughed at this; but, now when I laugh, I laugh inside; for I seem to have forgotten how to do it out loud. This leads me to think that audible laughter is principally a mechanism for sharing pleasure. . . . My hair hasn't been cut in months. I've let

---

[1] Tamotsu Shibutani, *Society and Personality: An Interaction Approach to Social Psychology*, p. 61. © 1961. Prentice-Hall, Inc., Englewood Cliffs, N.J.

it grow because it comes down around my neck and keeps it warm. I still shave once a week—and that only because I found that a beard is an infernal nuisance outside on account of its tendency to ice up from the breath and freeze the face. Looking in the mirror this morning, I decided that a man without women around him is a man without vanity; my cheeks are blistered and my nose is red and bulbous from a hundred frostbites. How I look is no longer of the least importance; all that matters is how I feel. However, I have kept clean, as clean as I would keep myself at home. But cleanliness has nothing to do with etiquette or coquetry. It is comfort. My senses enjoy the evening bath and are uncomfortable at the touch of underwear that is too dirty.[2]

In social groups, as well as in the larger society, there are social structures involving systems of relationships among the members. Members have definite reciprocal rights and duties which are the result of each person's *social status* or social position. An individual's definition of the world around him depends largely upon his social status, such as the class and subgroups to which he belongs. These interrelated status positions are based on such criteria as sex, age, race, family, and achievement. When status is based on one's position in the social structure at birth, regardless of personal attributes, it is referred to as *ascribed status*. When a person's social position is the product of achievement it is termed *achieved status*. In former times a person's status and role were clearly defined, and were largely fixed for life at the time of birth. In contemporary society it is possible that one's position at birth can be much altered through achievement. Changes in statuses and roles may give rise to conflicts within the person as well as among groups, a situation which we shall discuss frequently later.

Many people are as unaware of the great diversity and specialization among groups in modern society, and of the variations in their effects upon individual persons, as is a fish of the water around him. Groups, such as the neighborhood, village, or city, are based on physical proximity, and others, such as the family and larger groups of relatives, are based on kinship. Still others are based on congeniality, or on economic, technological, or other interests. The group nature of man is well indicated in Table 1.1, a list of groups based on interest.

Some social groups are informally organized and temporary, whereas others are highly formal and stable in their structure and in the specific duties and obligations of each member. The relatively permanent, stable, uniform, and formal manner in which social groups are interrelated produces what are termed *social institutions*. In addition, social institutions are generally distinguished by the fact that they encompass activities which are regarded as vital to certain ends, or as worthy in themselves by the

---

[2] Richard E. Byrd, *Alone* (New York: G. P. Putnam's Sons, 1938), pp. 139–140. Reprinted by permission of the publishers.

society in which they exist.[3] For example, government, which is a social institution, is regarded as vital for the maintenance of order or peaceable relations in society. Other institutions include the family, and the economic, religious, and educational institutions. The *social structure of an institution*

Table *1.1. Social Groups Which May Be Based on Interests*

Interests	Groups
Congeniality	Friendship groups Social clubs Taverns Purely social groups, boys' gangs, etc.
Economic interests	Corporations, partnerships Professional societies Associations of commerce Labor unions
Technological interests	Crafts Some athletic associations and teams Police departments
Religious interests	Churches Sects and other organizations
Aesthetic interests	"Schools" of painting, sculpture, literature, etc. Bands, orchestras, choirs, etc.
Intellectual interests (science, philosophy, the intellectual aspects of the humanities, etc.	Research groups Learned societies
Educational interests	Schools Universities Study groups, etc.
Political interests	Political parties and machines Taypayers' associations, etc.
Recreational interests	Philatelists' societies Yacht clubs Bridge clubs Some sport teams and clubs, etc.
Ameliorative interests	Charitable societies Community welfare organizations Alcoholics Anonymous Minority group associations, etc.

SOURCE: Adapted from John L. and John P. Gillin, *Cultural Sociology* (New York: The Macmillan Company, 1948), pp. 291–292. These groups may arise through other factors than interests alone.

[3] See George C. Homans, *Social Behavior: Its Elementary Forms* (New York: Harcourt, Brace & World, Inc., 1961), p. 5.

or other stable group consists of shared understandings concerning the duties and obligations of participants, the ways in which activities are to be carried out, the proper order of activities, ideas about what is desirable and undesirable or good and bad, and evaluations of the relative importance of the contributions of given participants and of the deference to be accorded by one participant to another. In addition, there are usually prescribed methods for recruiting participants, for training or indoctrinating them, and for expelling them.

Stated most simply, the social structure of an institution is merely the form in which group activities are to be carried out. However, the form is not "visible" or "tangible," but consists of systems of shared understandings in the minds of human beings as to their obligations, as in the case of the family. The *function of a social institution,* on the other hand, is generally described as its central activity or purpose, as this is defined by the society in which the institution exists. Thus, the family may be viewed as primarily concerned with the rearing and care of children. In some societies the procreation of the family may be stressed as contributing to the strength of the state; whereas in others it may be stressed as an agency which contributes to the fulfillment of personal happiness. Changes in the specific functions and structures of institutions and in the relationship of one institution to another have an important bearing on social problems. The stability of any society depends greatly on the functioning of its institutions and on their ability, through formal and informal means, to maintain social control.

Culture and Social Norms

The concept of *culture* is closely related to the concept of social group, and others mentioned thus far, in that each of these concepts refers to phenomena which are constituted of the same basic social ingredients.[4] Culture may be distinguished from another concept, society, as involving primarily *normative standards* for conduct, rather than interaction and social relationships. Like society, culture arises out of the need of people to communicate about the meaning of things and to regulate social life. Culture is a system of symbols or meanings with three distinct properties. It is *transmittable, learned,* and *shared.* The fact that it is transmittable means that it is passed from one generation to another. The fact that it is learned means that it is not an innate or biological quality of persons, but that it is acquired and participated in by persons through association with others. The fact that it is shared means that there is a fair degree of consensus among a number of persons concerning what is proper and im-

---

[4] See Talcott Parsons, *The Social System* (New York: The Free Press of Glencoe, 1951), especially Chaps. 1 and 12.

proper behavior, what meanings are to be attached to objects, situations, or events. It is only when such consensus exists that a group of persons can be said to be members of a "culture." Thus, it is evident that culture has existed before the individual's birth and will continue, though probably with modifications, beyond his lifetime. It is more than merely a description of ways of acting. It is a system of standards and evaluations of how to act. Culture is a "blueprint for behavior," telling what a person must do, ought to do, should do, may do, and must not do.[5]

Social relationships and behavior are regulated through *social norms,* often referred to as standardized ways of acting, or expectations governing limits of variation in behavior. Some social norms may be fairly widespread, whereas others are not. Some are temporary, and some are more permanent. Some may have considerable force to support compliance with them, whereas others have very little. Among the more universal and permanent social norms are many of those associated with institutions. Many *institutional norms,* but by no means all, are supported by a high degree of consensus and an intense reaction when violated.

Social values are simply those things to which a society or cultural group attaches value, worth, or significance.[6] Social values are described by some as the goals or objectives of a given society or culture. They are not only shared; they are regarded as matters of collective welfare to which is often attached a high degree of emotional belief that they are important. The distinction between social norms and social values can be illustrated by the criminal law. Although criminal laws are simply legal norms regulating various types of behavior and are enforced by the coercion of the state, certain values or basic goals are involved in some of them. Murder, manslaughter, bigamy, rape, theft, and burglary are violations of legal norms, but the social values involved include the protection of human life, the protection of sexual and family life, and the protection of property.[7] Among the value orientations which Williams feels are the objectives of such a complex society, as, for example, American society, are achievement and success, activity and work, efficiency and practicality, progress, material comfort, humanitarianism, equality, nationalism-patriotism, and democracy and individual personality.[8]

Rarely are individuals consciously aware of the often arbitrary nature of the social norms and social values of a culture or subculture, for they are introduced to them in the ongoing process of living. Social norms are transmitted from one generation to another through groups, and each

---

[5] Robin M. Williams, Jr., *American Society* (New York: Alfred A. Knopf, Inc., 1954), p. 23.

[6] Homans, *op. cit.,* Chap. 3.

[7] Hermann Mannheim, *Criminal Justice and Social Reconstruction* (New York: Oxford University Press, 1946). He also included the values of protection against property, protection of labor, and protection against labor.

[8] Williams, *op. cit.,* pp. 388–442.

individual largely incorporates into his life organization the beliefs, ideas, and language of the groups to which he belongs. Men thus come to see the world around them not with their eyes alone, for if they did they would see the same things, but rather through their cultural and other group experiences. Even the moral judgments of man are not generally his alone, but those of the group or groups to which he belongs.

In the following passage Ellsworth Faris has brilliantly pointed out the significance of seeing the world through group experiences:

> For we live in a world of "cultural reality," and the whole furniture of earth and choir of heaven are to be described and discussed as they are conceived by men. Caviar is not a delicacy to the general. Cows are not food to the Hindu. Mohammed is not the prophet of God to me. To an atheist God is not God at all. Objects are not passively received or automatically reacted to; rather is it true that objects are the result of a successful attempt to organize experience.[9]

The process by which persons learn and incorporate cultural meanings and values is called *socialization*. The process of socialization continues throughout life. Rarely are individuals consciously aware of the often arbitrary nature of the social norms and social values of a culture, for they are introduced to them in the ongoing process of living. Social norms are transmitted from one generation to another through groups, and each individual largely incorporates into his life organization the beliefs, ideas, and language of the groups to which he belongs. Man develops a set of social norms and values as he develops a social environment, which consists of people with whom he comes into contact first in the family, then in his neighborhood and school, and later in his economic, religious, or educational groups, and his social class.[10]

Social Differentiation and Subcultural Norms

Among more homogeneous peoples, such as primitive or folk societies, most norms and values are perceived in a somewhat similar, but by no means entirely so, way by various members of a society. Because of this fact members of the society come to share many common objectives and meanings. Modern societies are more complex and there is much *social differentiation*. In a highly differentiated society relatively distinct clusterings or groupings of persons will arise which have in common some socially assigned attribute or quality. Social clusterings arise around such attributes as race, occupation, ethnic background, religion, political party, residence,

---

[9] Ellsworth Faris, *The Nature of Human Nature* (New York: McGraw-Hill Book Company, Inc., 1937), pp. 150–151.
[10] Muzafer Sherif, *The Psychology of Social Norms* (New York: Harper & Row, Publishers, 1936), p. 46. For a general discussion of norms, also see Torgny T. Segerstedt, "The Uppsala School for Sociology," *Acta Sociologica* (Scandinavian Review of Sociology), 1:85–119, No. 2 (1955).

and many others. Modern societies are greatly differentiated by social class and into age or peer groups, into thousands of different occupational groups, often into a large number of religious groups, and even into rather distinct regional and neighborhood groups.

Sometimes social groupings which arise in the manner described may develop and share a set of values and meanings which are distinctive to some degree from the values and meanings shared by the society of which they are a part. When this occurs such a group may be called a *subculture*. A subculture is, simply speaking, a "culture within a culture." This implies that the subcultural group participates in and shares the "larger" culture of which it is a part, but also shares some meanings and values which are unique. A subculture is not necessarily in opposition to the larger culture, even though some conflict may arise between it and the larger culture.

Large modern societies consist of a variety of subcultures and social groups, each often with its own set of norms and values not only as to what constitutes proper conduct but also even as to the goals of life itself. Cohen has suggested that subcultures emerge in a highly differentiated society when, in effective interaction with one another, a number of persons have similar problems.[11] Sociological research has shown the existence of pronounced differences in normative structures of subcultures involving persons of different age groups, social classes, occupations, racial, religious, and ethnic groups, neighborhoods, and regions. In addition, there are some even more limited subcultures such as those among teen-age gangs, prostitutes, alcoholics, drug addicts, homosexuals, and professional and organized criminals. Even institutions for the treatment of deviants, such as prisons, actually develop subcultures with their own social systems.[12] In fact, so diverse are the subcultural norms of most large societies that there are probably only a few norms which are accepted as binding on *all* persons.

An American child raised as a member of another culture, whether Eskimo, Chinese, or Hottentot, would adopt the norms and values of that culture, just as the immigrants to America adopted the more general norms and values of American culture. Similarly, a person in modern society tends to acquire the norms of those subcultural groups of which he is a part. Although a modern society has certain common norms and values, there are many differences in norms and values.[13] As one writer has stated, "Within such complex aggregates as modern nations many norms are

---

[11] See, for example, Albert K. Cohen, *Delinquent Boys: The Culture of the Gang* (New York: The Free Press of Glencoe, 1955), p. 59.

[12] See Donald Clemmer, *The Prison Community* (rev. ed.; New York: Holt, Rinehart and Winston, Inc., 1958). Also see Donald R. Cressey ed., *The Prison: Studies in Institutional Organization and Change* (New York: Holt, Rinehart and Winston, Inc., 1961), and Richard A. Cloward, Donald R. Cressey, George H. Grosser, Richard McCleery, Lloyd E. Ohlin, Gresham M. Sykes, and Sheldon L. Messinger, "Theoretical Studies in Social Organization of the Prison" (Pamphlet 15; New York: Social Science Research Council, March, 1960).

[13] Frank E. Hartung, "Common and Discrete Values," *Journal of Social Psychology*, 38:3–22 (August, 1953).

effective only within limited subcultures, and there are wide differences in individual conformity and conceptions of normative structure." [14]

The norms and values of *peer groups*—persons of similar generations or ages—also may differ considerably. For example, a peer group, such as teen-agers in modern urban societies, often has standards of conduct and even goals which are quite different from those of other peer or age groups, and these may lead to misunderstandings and conflicts. The teen-age subculture is characterized by particular norms of dress, music, language, sexual activity, ways of regarding society and adults, and recreation.[15] Sometimes stealing, car theft, and vandalism become accepted norms among certain parts of the teen-age subculture.

Racial and religious discrimination may be greater in one part of a society than in another, depending on subcultural regional norms. Neighborhoods in the larger American cities often have distinct behavioral norms and values. The social norms and values in one neighborhood may contribute to the development of stealing by teen-age boys as a form of recreation and status, whereas in another the norms and values may encourage teen-age participation in scouting programs and similar forms of community-directed youth activities which lead toward nondelinquent behavior. Neighborhood norms may define policemen in one area as "enemies" and in the other as symbols of respect for law. Similarly, prostitutes, professional criminals, drug addicts, organized criminals, and similar groups may have a series of social norms and values distinct from those of the larger society. An understanding of this condition of highly differentiated and often conflicting norms as part of the way "modern" societies are organized is essential to a meaningful analysis of social deviation. A set of norms is not always supported in the same way by different subcultural groups.

There is a tendency for diversity of norms between groups to increase in a highly differentiated society. Often groups in such a society do not develop norms which are radically different from one another; the norms simply differ in emphasis. Nevertheless, if a person belongs to a number of groups in such a society, and if each group either holds different norms or emphasizes them differently, considerable personal conflict may ensue. The norms and social roles a person secures from the family group may not necessarily always agree with the norms and social roles of the play group, age or peer group, work group, or political group. Certain groups may become more important to an individual's life organization than

---

[14] Williams, *op. cit.*, p. 30.

[15] See, for example, "The Teen-Age Culture," *The Annals*, Vol. 338 (November, 1961), for a description of the characteristic norms of teen-agers in our culture as well as those of teen-agers in Europe. There is also a discussion of the Italian-American, Jewish, and Negro teen-age cultures. See also James S. Coleman, *The Adolescent Society* (New York: The Free Press of Glencoe, 1961).

others and, consequently, he may tend to conform to the norms of the groups with which he is more closely identified. The family, while important, is only one of many groups which may be related to a person's behavior, whether deviant or nondeviant. Among other important sources of norms and social relationships are social class, occupational, neighborhood, school, and religious groups, and the gang or clique.

All this means three things: (1) that within a modern society there may be almost as pronounced differences among various groups about the norms of accepted behavior as there are between large cultures; (2) that to explain logically how members of certain deviant subgroups in a society come to act the way they do can be explained in the same way, for example, that an Eskimo becomes culturally an Eskimo; and (3) that even when we speak of the norms of a given family we are likely to be referring actually to the social class, occupational, or some other subcultural group to which the family belongs.

Social Stratification and Deviant Behavior

Modern societies are socially differentiated in many ways: probably none is greater than the variations in behavior among the social classes in a society. Social class can be viewed as a hierarchical system by which large groups of families in society are ranked according to a social position of inferiority, equality, or superiority. Ranks may be based on six levels of stratification: prestige, occupation, possessions, interaction, class consciousness, and value orientations.[16] Studies of class structure have shown how value orientations, patterns of family life, and behavior in general not only represent but serve actually to integrate class ways of life.

So different are the social norms and other behavior of, for example, American social classes, that these differences are probably actually greater than those between members of the same social class but, say, from some other Western European or even Asiatic societies. The norms of longshoremen, for example, may differ markedly from those of doctors or professors. The norms and values of the middle class and lower class have been characterized in the studies by Miller and Cohen.

Kinsey and others, for example, have shown the existence of great class differences in sex behavior and even in the nature of the sex relation itself. Studies by Green,[17] Davis,[18] and others have shown that even family rearing patterns of the lower and middle classes are greatly different. The

---

[16] Joseph A. Kahl, *The American Class Structure* (New York: Holt, Rinehart and Winston, Inc., 1957), pp. 8–13.

[17] Arnold W. Green, "The Middle-Class Male Child and Neurosis," *American Sociological Review*, 11:31–41 (February, 1946).

[18] Kingsley Davis, "Mental Hygiene and the Social Structure," in Arnold Rose ed., *Mental Health and Mental Disorder* (New York: W. W. Norton & Company, Inc., 1955).

Lower Class (Miller) [a]	*Middle Class* (Cohen)
Concern with "trouble" involving official authorities or agencies of middle-class society	Cultivation of manners and courtesy
Toughness such as physical prowess, masculinity, fearlessness, bravery, daring	Control over physical aggression
Ability to outsmart others and to gain money by "wits"	Respect for property of others
Excitement of thrills, risk, and danger	Desire for wholesome recreation
Belief that people are favored by fate, fortune, and luck	Ambition; postponement of immediate goals for long-term objectives
Resentment of external controls of authority but at the same time dependence on them	Individual responsibility

[a] Although a useful characterization of general lower-class norms and values, particularly in larger cities, there are great variations within this broad category. The way of life of many lower-class families resembles, to some extent, middle-class norms and values.

SOURCES: Walter B. Miller, "Lower Class Culture as a Generating Milieu of Gang Delinquency," *Journal of Social Issues*, 14:5–19, No. 3 (1958); and Albert K. Cohen, *Delinquent Boys: The Culture of the Gang* (New York: The Free Press of Glencoe, 1955), pp. 88–91.

use of physical punishment, for example, is an acceptable form of disciplining children in lower-class families. The middle-class boy is more likely to be whipped if he fights; the lower-class boy if he does not, or if he loses. Studies have shown great differences in the norms, behavior, and family structure of teen-age youth by social class.[19]

Much of this research has directly or indirectly contributed to the understanding of deviant behavior. There are great differences in the incidence and nature of different types of deviant behavior by social class. Behavior may be approved in one class and disapproved in another. Class status may represent, for the individual, different neighborhood norms and different patterns of interpersonal relations, particularly between parents and children.[20] The greater incidence of juvenile delinquency among the lower class has been shown in many sociological studies.[21] Sociological investigations have suggested that auto theft is more likely to be a middle-

[19] August B. Hollingshead, *Elmtown's Youth* (New York: John Wiley & Sons, Inc., 1949). Also see Coleman, *op. cit.*

[20] The social behavior of particular adolescents was found to be largely a result of the social class they belonged to, according to one study in which adolescents were divided by class. Hollingshead, *op. cit.*

[21] See, for example, Terence Morris, *The Criminal Area: A Study in Social Ecology* (London: Routledge and Kegan Paul Ltd., 1957). Also see Albert J. Reiss, Jr. and Albert Lewis Rhodes, "Delinquency and Social Class Structure," *American Sociological Review*, 26:720–733 (October, 1961).

class juvenile offense.[22] The type and nature of sex offenses by juveniles appears to be related to social class.[23] The rates for adult crime in general are higher in lower-class areas. Nearly all crimes of violence, such as murder, are committed by lower-class adults, and the nature of lower-class sub-culture and family life seems to offer an explanation of the origin of most murders.[24] Prostitution appears to be consistently more prevalent among the lower classes. The more overt types of crime, such as burglary, are rare among members of the middle and upper classes, who become more often involved in types of crime to which the term "white-collar crime" has been applied. Sociological studies have shown the existence of wide-scale viola-tions of law by persons in the upper and middle classes, politicians, govern-ment officials, businessmen, labor union leaders, doctors, and lawyers.[25]

Probably in no area has social class shown more pronounced differences than in the area of mental disorder. Faris and Dunham demonstrated years ago, in their Chicago study of the residences of public and private mental patients, that mental disorder was generally greater in the lower class.[26] More recently another study has revealed great differences in the relative incidence and nature of neuroses and psychoses by social class.[27] Schizophrenia, a common form of mental disorder, was nine times more prevalent among those of the lowest social class. There were even class differences in the type of the neuroses.

The incidence of suicide is related to occupation and social class. This has been established by many studies, including Sainsbury's study of Lon-don suicides.[28]

Merton has explained all deviant behavior in terms primarily of social structure, particularly social class. He suggests that all forms of deviant behavior result from differentials in the access to the success goals of a society by *legitimate* means.[29] Deviations are thus symptoms of dissociation

[22] William W. Wattenberg and James Balistrieri, "Automobile Theft: A 'Favored-Group' Delinquency," *American Journal of Sociology*, 57:575–579 (May, 1952).

[23] Albert J. Reiss, Jr., "Sex Offenses: The Marginal Status of the Adolescent," *Law and Contemporary Problems*, 25:309–334 (Spring, 1960).

[24] Henry Allen Bullock, "Urban Homicide in Theory and Fact," *Journal of Criminal Law, Criminology, and Police Science*, 45:565–575 (January–February, 1955); and Marvin E. Wolfgang, *Patterns in Criminal Homicide* (Philadelphia: University of Pennsylvania Press, 1958).

[25] Edwin H. Sutherland, *White Collar Crime* (New York: Holt, Rinehart and Winston, Inc., reissue 1960), and Marshall B. Clinard, *The Black Market: A Study of White Collar Crime* (New York: Holt, Rinehart and Winston, Inc., 1952).

[26] Robert E. L. Faris and H. Warren Dunham, *Mental Disorders in Urban Areas* (Chicago: The University of Chicago Press, 1939).

[27] August B. Hollingshead and Frederich Redlich, *Social Class and Mental Illness* (New York: John Wiley & Sons, Inc., 1958). Also see Jerome K. Myers and Bertram H. Roberts, *Family and Class Dynamics in Mental Illness* (New York: John Wiley & Sons, Inc., 1959).

[28] Peter Sainsbury, *Suicide in London* (London: Chapman & Hall, Ltd., 1955).

[29] Robert K. Merton, *Social Theory and Social Structure* (rev. ed.; New York: The Free Press of Glencoe, 1957), pp. 131–194.

between culturally prescribed aspirations and socially structured ways of realizing them, or a situation of *anomie,* meaning in general "normlessness." [30] According to this theory, modern urban societies emphasize such status goals of competitive success as material gain and higher education, but provide limited means for everyone to achieve these goals legitimately because of the great differentials by age, sex, ethnic status, and particularly social class. "It is only when a system of cultural values extols, virtually above all else, certain *common* success-goals for the population at large while the social structure rigorously restricts or completely closes access to approved modes of reaching these goals *for a considerable part of the same population,* that deviant behavior ensues on a large scale." [31] Consequently, other means, some *illegitimate,* may be used to achieve, for example, the goal of material gain. Several categories or adaptations of behavior may emerge to achieve such goals—conformity, innovation, ritualism, retreatism, and rebellion.[32] A particular adaptation is dependent on the individual's acceptance or rejection of cultural goals and on his adherence to, or violation of, accepted norms.

The greatest pressure for deviation arises among the lower socioeconomic groups, where opportunities to acquire material goods are fewer and the level of education is lower. Innovation through ordinary stealing, vice, or organized crime may be ways of achieving goals of wealth and power. Retreat from the goal is still another possible reaction to a situation where a discrepancy exists between the goals and the means of achieving them. This may result in frustration and internal conflict and lead to the development of psychoses, neuroses, chronic alcoholism, or drug addiction.[33]

A reformulation of Merton's theory of anomie has been made by

[30] *Ibid.* Also Robert K. Merton, "Social Problems and Sociological Theory," in Robert K. Merton and Robert A. Nisbet, *Contemporary Social Problems* (New York: Harcourt, Brace & World, Inc., 1961), pp. 697–737. Also see Parsons, *op. cit.,* pp. 256–267. The concept of *anomie* was originally formulated by Émile Durkheim in *Suicide* (originally published 1896; tr. John A. Spaulding and George Simpson; New York: The Free Press of Glencoe, 1951).

[31] Merton, *Social Theory and Social Structure,* p. 146.

[32] Several other forms of adaptation have been added by Dubin. See Robert Dubin, "Deviant Behavior and Social Structure: Continuities in Social Theory," *American Sociological Review,* 24:147–164 (April, 1959).

[33] Although the theoretical statement of the relation of anomie to deviant behavior has been widely quoted, little research has been done to establish its validity. Theoretically it is a general explanation at the level of social structure rather than at the sociopsychological level of the individual. The success-goal aspirations of a society which are not achieved by the deviant are not clear or specific. Moreover, it does not adequately explain why, in American society, most lower-class males do not go beyond institutional goals to achieve them. Likewise, it does not explain deviant behavior in societies where "esteemed goals" are not thought of as available to everyone, i.e., where there is generally ascribed rather than achieved status. Nor does the theory, based primarily on American goal orientation, explain, for example, why subcultural delinquency is becoming a nearly world-wide phenomenon.

Cloward to include not only differentials in the availability of legitimate means, but variations in the access or opportunity for illegitimate means.[34] Within this context he has sought to explain delinquency, crime, alcoholism, drug addiction, mental illness, and suicide. In much the same way delinquency has been said to arise from the disparity between what lower-class youths are led to want and what is actually available to them. Desiring such conventional goals as economic and educational success, they are faced with limitations on legitimate avenues of success to these goals. Being unable to revise their goals downward, they experience frustration and turn to delinquency if the norms or opportunities are available to them.[35]

Cohen has stated a theory of gang delinquency which has a general approach similar to Merton's anomie but is considerably more specific.[36] Delinquent gangs, he suggests, arise as a consequence of the class structure of American society. Delinquent gang behavior is a product of group solutions to the status problems, needs, and frustrations of the American lower-class system in a world of predominantly middle-class values and virtues.

Social Deviation and Societal Reaction

Reactions to deviations from social norms can vary in the direction of approval, tolerance, or disapproval. Modern societies encourage a certain amount of nonconformity, provided it is in an approved direction. Deviations which society approves may be rewarded by admiration, prestige, money, or other symbols. Some deviations in the form of new mechanical inventions, new styles in architecture, painting, literature, music, and fashions may, on occasion, meet with general approval. Approved deviations may also include behavior which is more industrious, ambitious, pious, patriotic, brave, or honest than is called for by the norms of a particular situation. Everyone is supposed to be a careful driver, for example, but rewards are sometimes given for the driver who has never had an accident over a long period of years. A certain degree of heroism is expected of everyone, civilian or soldier alike, but medals or other forms of recognition are given to soldiers, and occasionally to civilians, who are particularly heroic and risk their own lives.

In general, however, a society is probably more concerned with punishing disapproved deviations from norms than with rewarding compliance with norms. Deviations may be reacted to with varying degrees of disapproval. What specific behavior is disapproved, and the point at which disapproval will be expressed, depends largely on the content of the norms

---

[34] Richard A. Cloward, "Illegitimate Means, Anomie, and Deviant Behavior," *American Sociological Review*, 24:164–176 (April, 1959).

[35] Richard A. Cloward and Lloyd E. Ohlin, *Delinquency and Opportunity: A Theory of Delinquent Gangs* (New York: The Free Press of Glencoe, 1960).

[36] Cohen, *op. cit.*

of the given society in question. Deviations which are disapproved may be reacted to with disgust, anger, hate, gossip, isolation, and ostracism, or even physical punishment. Deviations from orthodox political and religious thinking, approved sexual behavior, or certain legal codes may encounter strong disapproval.

Generally speaking, the norms of a given society or group may be known not only by observing what people do, but by observing when and how sanctions, both positive and negative, are applied. It is by observing what behavior is socially punished that we learn what behavior is disapproved and is therefore in violation of the norms. By observing what behavior is socially rewarded, or esteemed, we learn what behavior more nearly expresses the ideals embodied in the norms. Thus it is by observing the operation of sanctions, or in other words, *social control,* that we can infer the nature and the limits of acceptable and nonacceptable behavior implicit in given norms.

> In speaking of social control, then, reference is being made to the fact that men interact with one another in regularized ways as they cooperate to accomplish collective goals. In organized groups the activities of the participants are curtailed by the conventional roles that they play. But such control is not restricted to formalized settings. Participants in lynching mobs are not free to do as they wish; a man who is not in sympathy with the prevailing mood may be torn to pieces if he tries to assert his opposition. Even those who are physically alone often take into account what the reactions of other people are likely to be if they should find out about what he is doing. *Social control refers to the fact that human behavior is organized in response to expectations that are imputed to other people.* This does not necessarily involve coercion; various constraints are placed upon the things men do by virtue of their participation in groups.[37]

Behavior which is disapproved at one time may later become approved. This implies that ideas of what is proper or improper normative behavior may change. Over the years scientists who have challenged traditional beliefs have been scorned, ridiculed, ostracized, or even punished. Copernicus, Galileo, and many others who were regarded as deviants in their day would undoubtedly be regarded today with the same approval as was accorded Einstein. Within comparatively recent times there was strong disapproval of women's smoking, drinking alcoholic beverages, particularly in public, using make-up, wearing one-piece bathing suits, or engaging in political activity. Many religious offenses of various types, such as engaging in recreation on the Sabbath, were formerly considered crimes. Professional boxing matches or "prize fights" were generally a criminal offense during most of the nineteenth century in the United States. New York, for example, did not legalize prize fighting until 1896 and subse-

---

[37] Shibutani, *Society and Personality,* pp. 60–61. Italicized in the original.

quently changed the law several times so that present legalization of professional fighting actually dates from as late as 1920.

> It was a crime in Iceland in the Viking age for a person to write verses about another, even if the sentiment was complimentary, if the verses exceeded four strophes in length. A Prussian law of 1784 prohibited mothers and nurses from taking children under two years of age into their beds. The English villein in the fourteenth century was not allowed to send his son to school, and no one lower than a freeholder was permitted by law to keep a dog. The following have at different times been crimes: printing a book, professing the medical doctrine of circulation of the blood, driving with reins, sale of coins to foreigners, having gold in the house, buying goods on the way to market or in the market for the purpose of selling them at a higher price, writing a check for less than $1.00. On the other hand, many of our present laws were not known to earlier generations—quarantine laws, traffic laws, sanitation laws, factory laws.[38]

This means, of course, that the norms which define deviant behavior are not necessarily the same in various cultures, nor are they the same in a given culture over a period of time. Homosexual behavior, prostitution, or drunkenness does not constitute deviant behavior in some societies today. Some Scandinavian countries, for example, have such different interpretations of sexual norms that many delinquent and criminal acts in American society would not be regarded as such there. Changed attitudes in the United States over the past fifty years toward tobacco smoking by juveniles and young adults is an indication of how normative standards can be redefined in time. Formerly there was great preoccupation with smoking among younger groups, laws were passed forbidding it, and often were strictly enforced. Smoking was thought to be related to a variety of other social problems.

Deviations vary in the *intensity* of the reaction to the deviation, as well as in the *direction* of approval or disapproval. Some deviations from norms in a society are not only approved but encouraged. Likewise, disapproved deviations may encounter various degrees of sanction, varying all the way from a certain amount of tolerance to mild and even strong disapproval. Certain behavior of the "idle rich," of actors, musicians, and artists, or of extreme religious sects, although not approved, may be tolerated. Deviations from norms of politeness, dress, table manners, cleanliness, and the telling of risqué stories in public may encounter mild disapproval in the form of ridicule or scorn. Lying and malicious gossip may be more strongly disapproved, while certain behavior such as murder, burglary, and robbery may be punished by the political state through fine, imprisonment, or even death.

---

[38] Edwin H. Sutherland and Donald R. Cressey, *Principles of Criminology* (6th ed.; Philadelphia: J. B. Lippincott Company, 1960), p. 15.

Norms have varying degrees of strength, or "resistance potential," in the event of a disapproved deviation from them, "a power which may be measured in degrees of what the group regards as the severity of the sanction." [39] Each norm can be thought of as having a *tolerance limit,* that is, the ratio between violations of the norm and a society's willingness to tolerate it or suppress it.[40] Deviations from sexual norms, for example, have different tolerance limits, depending on the society. Over the centuries, prostitution has been approved, tolerated, or disapproved, depending on cultural norms. In certain Near Eastern countries and in ancient Greece prostitution was approved, and in Paris today it is not extensively suppressed. Some communities in the United States tolerate prostitution either by ignoring its presence and not enforcing the laws or by allowing a "red-light district" to exist. Other communities may take a strong position and attempt to wipe it out.

The concept of "tolerance limit" is in some respects, however, misleading, for it implies that there is a definite and absolute point at which norm violations will involve a reaction. Actually the relation between norm violation and the societal reaction is not as simple as this and may depend on the nature of the situation or on the social status of the deviant.

The Social Visibility of Deviant Behavior

Wide variations exist in the "social visibility" of negatively regarded deviations, that is, the extent to which behavior comes to the attention of people within a society and the acts are defined as "deviant." Certain crimes, such as kidnaping, violent sex offenses, murder, lynching, and armed robbery, for example, are highly visible and create much comment and action. Other offenses, such as white-collar crime, abortions, blackmail, rape, homosexuality, and petty theft, are not as socially visible; moreover, some of these are not even likely to be reported to the police.

Many reasons might be cited for this lower social visibility and the failure to report many of these crimes: (1) The offended person often fears unfavorable publicity and embarrassment if he is involved in blackmail, abortion, or sex offenses. (2) For other reasons he may not wish the offense to be discovered. In a case of theft he might not wish to have the police investigate because of his own illegal behavior or the nature of the stolen property. (3) The offense may be of a petty nature involving, for example, the theft of an article of little value and the victim may not take the time to report it. (4) Some offenses are known only to the offender and

---

[39] Thorsten Sellin, "Culture Conflict and Crime" (Bulletin 41; New York: Social Science Research Council, 1938), p. 34.

[40] Courtland C. Van Vechten, "The Tolerance Quotient as a Device for Defining Certain Social Concepts," *American Journal of Sociology,* 46:35–44 (July, 1940).

he would hardly report himself. These offenses would include vagrancy, disorderly conduct, or carrying concealed weapons. (5) Witnesses to a crime may not wish to report it because of fear, inconvenience, or embarrassment. (6) Friends and relatives may try to protect the offender or the victim and therefore do not report the offense.[41]

Symptoms of mental disorder are not always interpreted as such and so do not become visible to members of a society. In some instances the mentally ill person is considered simply as "eccentric," "odd," or "difficult." This is particularly true of many neurotic symptoms. In other cases interpretations may make the behavior less socially visible. Certain persons who are mentally ill may become members of a religious sect and claim to experience trances and visions without provoking much comment. In a society which emphasizes orderliness and cleanliness a neurotic with certain compulsive symptoms in this direction may not be conspicuous. Manic behavior is less visible in a dynamic society like America, whereas symptoms of mental depression or social withdrawal have a high degree of visibility. Mental illness is also less visible among some occupational groups than among others; manic behavior in certain salesmen is an example.

Generally, the physical symptoms of intoxication tend to be visible, as the intoxicated person usually displays such physical symptoms as thickened speech, flushed face, and unsteady gait, although certain physical illnesses may produce similar symptoms. It is the social behavior of the intoxicated person, however, which attracts the most attention from others and brings about the strongest reaction. Some persons can actually be quite intoxicated without exhibiting noticeable behavior patterns, but others may become quarrelsome, noisy, loquacious, silly, depressed, or otherwise annoying to other people so that the drunken behavior becomes even more conspicuous than the physical symptoms.

A person's status may largely determine whether or not deviant activity on his part is interpreted by others as deviant and, therefore, as disapproved behavior. In many instances deviant acts may be interpreted as attributes associated with the status the person occupies, and therefore not perceived as "deviant," with all that implies.[42]

The social visibility of many forms of deviant behavior varies by social class and by racial characteristics. Among the lower classes, or among a group of homeless transients, for example, drunkenness may

---

[41] Thorsten Sellin, "Research Memorandum on Crime and the Depression" (Bulletin 27; New York: Social Science Research Council, 1936), pp. 69–70.

[42] For further elaboration see Edwin M. Lemert, *Social Pathology* (New York: McGraw-Hill Book Company, Inc., 1951), Chaps. 2, 3, and 4. Also see Homans, *Social Behavior*, pp. 349–359 and S. Kirson Weinberg, *Social Problems in Our Time* (Englewood Cliffs, N.J.: Prentice-Hall, Inc., 1960).

provoke little comment, and an alcoholic may at times go largely unde-
tected. On the other hand, drunkenness or alcoholism in a middle-class
group may stand out like a fire on a hillside.

Deviant Behavior

Deviations from norms which are tolerated or which provoke only
mild disapproval are obviously of little concern to a society. Only those
situations in which behavior is in a disapproved direction, and of sufficient
degree to exceed the tolerance limit of the community, constitute *deviant
behavior* as it will be used here. This includes such deviations from norms
as delinquency and crime, drug addiction, alcoholism, mental disorders,
suicide, marital and family maladjustment, problems of old age, and
discrimination against minority groups. Obviously the extent and degree
of disapproval in a particular instance are dependent on the nature of the
situation and the community's degree of tolerance of the behavior involved.

Deviant behavior and *social problems* are not necessarily the same
thing. Not all social problems are instances of deviant behavior. For
example, soil erosion, flood damage, and forest destruction have for
decades been considered as social problems. Yet these problems can
hardly be considered as instances of deviant behavior. To be sure,
soil erosion may exemplify a variation from ideal standards of soil pro-
ductivity, yet this variation is not a consequence of social behavior. The
same could be applied to social problems involving disease or physical
handicaps, such as cancer, heart disease, blindness, and crippling.[43]

Some writers refer to the existence of what has been described here
as deviant behavior as *social disorganization* and the society as being
"disorganized." A state of disorganization is often thought of as one in
which there is a "breakdown of social controls over the behavior of the
individual" and a decline in the unity of the group because former patterns of behavior and social control no longer are effective.[44] There are
a number of objections to this frame of reference. (1) Disorganization is
too subjective and vague a concept for analyzing a general society. Effective use of the concept, however, may be made in the study of specific
groups and institutions. (2) Social disorganization implies the disruption

---

[43] Such conditions, when dealt with in textbooks on "social problems," are completely
in order. It is only suggested here that they are not instances of deviant behavior within
the definition stated above.

[44] Contemporary use of the concept "social disorganization" comes largely from
W. I. Thomas and Florian Znaniecki, *The Polish Peasant in Europe and America* (New
York: Alfred A. Knopf, Inc., 1927). For criticisms of this concept see John F. Cuber,
Robert A. Harper, and William Kenkel, *Problems of American Society* (New York: Holt,
Rinehart and Winston, Inc., 1956), Chap. 22; Lemert, *op. cit.*, Chap. 1; and Hartung,
"Common and Discrete Values," *loc. cit.*

of a previously existing condition of organization, a situation which generally cannot be established. Social change is often confused with social disorganization without indicating why some social changes are disorganizing and others not. (3) Social disorganization is usually thought of as something "bad," and what is bad is often the value judgment of the observer and the members of his social class or other social groups. For example, the practice of gambling, the patronage of taverns, greater freedom in sex relations, and other behavior do not mean that these conditions are naturally "bad" or "disorganized." (4) The existence of forms of deviant behavior does not necessarily constitute a major threat to the central values of a society. The presence of suicide, crime, or alcoholism may not be serious if other values are being achieved. American society, for example, has a high degree of unity and integration despite high rates of deviant behavior if one considers such values as nationalism, highly developed industrial production, and goals of material comfort. (5) What seems like disorganization actually may often be highly organized systems of competing norms. Many subcultures of deviant behavior, such as delinquent gangs, organized crime, homosexuality, prostitution, and white-collar crime, including political corruption, may be highly organized. The slum sex code may be as highly organized and normative regarding premarital relations in one direction as the middle-class sex code is in the other.[45] The norms and values of the slums are highly organized, as Whyte has shown in his *Street Corner Society*.[46] (6) Finally, as several sociologists have suggested, it is possible that a variety of subcultures may contribute, through their diversity, to the unity or integration of a society rather than weaken it by constituting a situation of social disorganization.[47]

Types of Deviant Behavior

In the chapters which follow, a number of types of deviant behavior or, as they have been termed, "strongly disapproved deviations," are discussed. The following discussion presents a brief description of each of these types of deviant behavior, including the nature of the norms involved, the extent of the violation, and, in some cases, definitions of a few important concepts which are necessary to understand the deviation.

Most sociologists are skeptical of loose terms, such as "socially maladjusted," "antisocial," "emotionally disturbed," "abnormal," "mentally

---

[45] William F. Whyte, "A Slum Sex Code," *American Journal of Sociology*, 49:24–32 (July, 1943).
[46] William F. Whyte, *Street Corner Society* (Chicago: The University of Chicago Press, 1943).
[47] See Robin Williams, Jr., "Unity and Diversity in Modern America," *Social Forces*, 36:1–8 (October, 1957).

ill," "sexually deviant," and even an omnibus category, such as "delinquency," unless the norms are stated. The definition of excessive drinking and alcoholism, for example, involves norms, such as the amount of alcohol consumed, the purpose and meaning of the drinking, the social handicap to the individual, and the degree of inability to refrain from excessive drinking. Even the norms involved in mental disorder need to be so stated that we can determine with some precision who is mentally ill and who is not, whom we are to treat, and whom not to treat.

DELINQUENCY AND CRIME

Among the norms whose violation usually exceeds the tolerance limit of the community in even a highly differentiated society are the legal norms. To emphasize their importance and to force compliance with them, a series of penalties has been established by the political state. Enacted laws represent varying degrees of tolerance for the behavior outlawed. Some legal norms forbidding certain behavior are supported by nearly all segments of a society, the behavior in question being regarded as inimical to group welfare, whereas norms embodied in other laws have little support. Deviant behavior, such as murder, kidnaping, sexual abuse of young children, or incest, may be overwhelmingly and strongly disapproved. Other behavior, while disapproved legally, may have less public disapproval. Although persons differ about the validity of individual legal norms, there may be agreement that there is need for "obedience of the law" in general.

Most criminal behavior represents a conflict of the norms of particular groups or individuals against those norms which the law represents. Much juvenile delinquency, organized prostitution, gambling, traffic in narcotics, and homosexuality, for example, arise from the growth of subgroups which, although in physical contact with the rest of the society, may have different norms. Norms of subgroups which conflict with legal norms may be those of certain age groups, social classes, occupations, neighborhoods, or regions.

The exact amount of law violation in American society today is unknown, but the evidence points to its extensive nature. During 1960, 1.9 million serious crimes were reported to the police in the United States. Because some offenses, such as rape, are not frequently reported to the police, obviously more crimes were committed than these figures reveal. Reported to the police during 1960, according to the Federal Bureau of Investigation, were an estimated 432,906 cases of burglary, 88,970 robberies, usually with a gun, and 321,400 automobile thefts. There were 9140 murders and cases of nonnegligent manslaughter, 15,560 rape cases, and 130,230 cases of aggravated assault.

Property crimes, such as larceny, burglary, automobile theft, and robbery, constituted 91.7 percent of all crimes reported to the police in the United States in 1960. Murder and nonnegligent manslaughter, which are *personal crimes,* accounted for only 0.5 percent of the total. There is also a large group of *offenses against public order,* including vagrancy, disorderly conduct, prostitution, and gambling.

Certain types of offenses are often not included in the statistics for ordinary crimes. *White-collar crimes* are violations of laws by businessmen, professional men, and politicians in connection with their occupations. Their consequences are not usually tabulated as crimes, even though their effect on society as a whole may be far more serious than that of a typical burglary. These offenses include embezzlement and other trust violations, falsified income tax returns, political corruption, violations of food and drug laws, violations of banking and security laws, fee splitting by doctors, and violations of countless other regulations affecting persons of the white-collar class.

Antisocial acts committed by persons under a certain age, usually sixteen to eighteen, which are considered to be injurious to the person or society are classified as *juvenile delinquency.* Generally "delinquents" are not punished by the criminal law but are treated in other ways. Antisocial acts of juveniles include not only those which would be crimes if committed by adults but many other offenses which are peculiarly juvenile, such as truancy, incorrigibility, and vandalism. Although these latter acts are disturbing to community norms and are of increasing concern to American society, they are not generally included in national figures of "crimes" which have been committed.

In 1960 approximately 514,000 juvenile delinquency cases, involving about 443,000 children aged ten through seventeen, were handled by juvenile courts in the United States. These children represented about 1.8 percent of all children in this age group in the country, and represented a 6 percent increase over 1959 cases, in contrast to only a 2 percent increase in the child population. In addition, about 306,000 traffic cases were disposed of by juvenile courts in 1960, involving roughly 264,-000 different children, or about 1.0 percent of the child population.

DRUG ADDICTION

The use of such drugs as morphine, heroin, opium, cocaine, and marihuana, other than for medicinal purposes, is considered as a deviation from cultural or legal norms not only in the United States but also in many other Western societies. The use of drugs is disapproved because most of them are habit-forming. Their use tends either to decrease mental or physical activity or to overexcite and sustain such activity. Where a habit has been established, there may be excruciating physical and mental symptoms when the drugs are not used. Furthermore, drug addiction may become extremely expensive for a person who has been addicted for some time and has built up an increased tolerance for the drugs. Some addicts even commit thefts or engage in prostitution to finance their addiction.

ALCOHOLISM

The use of alcohol as a beverage is widespread in Western civilization and, by the majority of the population at least, its use in moderation is generally approved. Where alcohol is consumed mainly for purposes of conviviality or ceremony it is termed *social or controlled drinking*. The *social drinker* is able to control his drinking and rarely becomes intoxicated. Drinkers who deviate from the norms of the drinking patterns of a culture, and from such legal norms as those prohibiting drunkenness and driving while intoxicated, are referred to as *excessive drinkers*.

Excessive drinkers use alcohol for purposes of intoxication and some may even become completely dependent upon its effects. The *heavy drinker* uses alcohol more frequently than does the social drinker. He has occasional sprees of drunkenness, but in general his drinking does not seriously deviate from drinking norms. *Alcoholics* are those excessive drinkers who deviate markedly from drinking norms by the frequency and quantity of their consumption of alcohol and by the unconventional times and places selected for the drinking. Such excessive consumption of alcohol tends to disturb their interpersonal relationships in their family, occupational, and social groups. The alcoholic is unable to control consistently, or stop at will, either the start of drinking or its termination once started. Most deviant of all are those whose alcoholism has become chronic. *Chronic alcoholics* almost completely lose control over their drinking and become "compulsive" drinkers. They become so dependent upon alcohol that they live to drink and drink to live. Some of their characteristics are solitary drinking, morning drinking, and general physical deterioration.

In 1960 there were, in the United States, an estimated 4,470,000 alcoholics, which is equivalent to a rate of 4000 alcoholics per 100,000 adults aged twenty years and over. Of these alcoholics it was estimated that about a fourth were chronic alcoholics, or those alcoholics with complications.

MENTAL DISORDERS

When an individual's behavior patterns in interpersonal relationships persistently deviate from certain cultural norms to the extent that a society considers his conduct to be a nuisance, a danger, or a handicap to himself, the behavior is often regarded as deviant and the person as mentally disordered. Mentally ill persons have difficulty in relating to others and in sharing the norms and objectives of others in given situations. Every society tolerates a range of behavior and a certain amount of eccentricity, but mental disorders often exceed the "limits of eccentricity."

In its extreme form, behavior in mental disorders not only is disapproved but often is also unintelligible to others.[48] Violations of legal norms, on the other hand, are likewise disapproved, but criminal behavior is generally intelligible to others. Psychotic persons, for example, may exhibit hallucinations, delusions, losses of memory, peculiar construction in language, and inappropriate emotional responses. They may be unnecessarily seclusive, overexcited, extremely aggressive, or depressed. Psychotic individuals disturb other persons since it is difficult to interact with them, and the individual with a severe mental disorder may find it increasingly difficult to participate at all in a society.

Psychoses are of two types, organic and functional. *Organic psychoses* are presumed to have some connection with disturbances in the physical organism. They include the senile psychoses or mental disorders of old age; alcoholic psychoses, which are related to alcoholism; and paresis, which is caused by syphilis. The *functional psychoses* are those in which the mental disorder cannot be attributed to organic disturbances. The chief disorders of this type are schizophrenia, characterized by withdrawal from reality, hallucinations, and delusions; manic-depressive psychoses, with symptoms of extreme elation, deep depression, or both; and paranoia, characterized by illusions of grandeur and extreme beliefs of persecution. That these types are not disease entities in the sense of physical illness is shown by the fact that psychiatrists vary in their diagnoses of cases.

Traditionally psychiatrists have classified mental disorders into the neuroses and the psychoses. Neurotic conditions are not as noticeable to other persons generally as is psychotic behavior. In mild forms they may even be recognized as a problem only by the individual, his immediate family, or his friends. Consequently, deviations from cultural norms are less clear with neurotic than with psychotic behavior. Neurotic conditions include hypochondria, compulsions, phobias, and hysteria. Compulsive disorders comprise repetitive or ritualistic behavior, such as excessive hand washing or dressing in a precise manner. Phobias represent obsessive fears about something, such as high places, death, the loss of one's mind, or illness. If the individual is a hypochondriac he is unduly, and usually needlessly, concerned about the state of his health. Hysterical symptoms—which are without a physical basis—include fainting spells, tics or tremors, or the loss of sight or hearing or, for example, the ability to write.

It has been estimated that there are about 2 million psychotic persons

[48] Robert E. L. Faris, *Social Disorganization* (2d ed.; New York: The Ronald Press Company, 1955), p. 324.

in the United States and over 4 million so severely neurotic as to need psychiatric treatment. One study concluded that the probabilities are that about one person in twenty, by the age of forty-five, and one in ten, by the age of sixty-five, will develop a serious mental illness, either an episodic or a continuing one.[49] In 1959 there were 616,964 mental patients in long-term mental hospitals, about 88 percent of them in public mental hospitals, state, county, or city. Actually the total is much higher in view of the fact that the movements of patients in and out of these hospitals during a given year is extensive. From 1955 to 1960 there has been a slight decline in the resident population of these hospitals. In 1960, 235,-231 patients were admitted to state and local mental hospitals for the first time, and about 100,000 were admitted who had previously been in mental hospitals. In addition, many persons are treated outside a mental hospital by psychiatrists, clinical psychologists, social workers, counselors, and ministers.

The economic costs of mental disorders in terms of loss of earnings are extremely large. Losses in 1952, for all patients resident in mental institutions in the United States, were estimated at $700 million in one year.[50] The estimated losses during the first year for first admissions in 1954 were $160 million. Estimated present value of all future earnings of first admissions to public prolonged-care hospitals was $1.9 billion. First admissions (1954), based on probable discharge and death rates (but not including readmissions) will lose 556,000 labor-force years in their remaining years of life, or equal to a present value of $800 million.

SUICIDE

Many persons in Western civilization take their lives each year, but in no Western society is this action approved. There may be feelings of sympathy for the personal difficulties in certain cases of suicide, but this sympathy does not constitute approval. Norms opposed to suicide have a long historical background, including particularly strong attitudes against it in Christian theological doctrine. Also a factor is the general implication of cowardice in retreating from life through suicide and of disgrace to the family and even the associates of the suicide. Attempted suicide is even a crime in several countries and in a few states in the United States. This extreme and complete form of social withdrawal has long interested social scientists and others who consider suicide to be a reflection of difficulties in interpersonal relations.

During 1959 in the United States there were 18,330 deaths officially

[49] Herbert Goldhamer and Andrew W. Marshall, *Psychoses and Civilization* (New York: The Free Press of Glencoe, 1953), p. 11.
[50] See Rashi Fein, *The Economics of Mental Illness* (New York: Basic Books, Inc., 1958), p. 87.

reported as suicides, or a rate of 10.4 per 100,000. Many more suicidal deaths undoubtedly occur but are not recorded as such because of the disgrace involved. The Metropolitan Life Insurance Company has estimated that more than 100,000 persons annually attempt suicide.

CONFLICTS IN MARITAL AND FAMILY ROLES

All societies recognize the importance of marriage and family relationships. Although great variations exist in marital and family systems, it is generally assumed in most Western European societies that marriage and family relationships have a high degree of permanence and are capable of satisfying the expectations of the marital partners. Marriage and family unity prevail where the roles and expectations of the members are satisfactorily achieved. If conflicts in marriage or family roles develop, the marital or family relationship is impaired.

Separation, desertion, and divorce, as they represent varying degrees of dissolution of the family, are generally strongly disapproved in Western societies. So also is wife beating or similar forms of physical violence. As scientific research and marriage counseling have advanced in recent years, the concept of marital maladjustment has been broadened. Increasingly it is being regarded as embracing those situations in which the marital partners display little marital affection, slight dependence on one another, and no sharing of satisfactions and decision making. Where these are present there may be indifference, dissatisfaction, and incompatibility between the marital partners and a situation deviating from the behavior expected by each partner in marriage.

Obviously the actual extent of the breakdown of interaction in the marital or family situation cannot be determined. Generally divorce statistics are cited as an objective, though limited, indication of the extent of role conflicts in marriages. The United States ratio is about one divorce to every four marriages; in 1959 about 1,500,000 marriages to about 400,000 divorces, affecting about 4 percent of all children under eighteen. In addition, many families are broken by legal separation or by desertion, either temporary or permanent, of one or the other marital partner, more frequently the husband. Even these figures on broken homes, however, do not indicate the full extent of marital and family role conflicts in the United States. Studies of married persons have revealed that a considerable proportion of marriages in certain samples are unhappy even though the marriage has not been physically or legally dissolved.[51]

---

[51] See Ernest W. Burgess and Paul Wallin, *Engagement and Marriage* (Philadelphia: J. B. Lippincott Company, 1953); Harvey Locke, *Predicting Adjustment in Marriage* (New York: Holt, Rinehart and Winston, Inc., 1951); and L. M. Terman, *Psychological Factors in Marital Happiness* (New York: McGraw-Hill Book Company, Inc., 1938).

ROLE AND STATUS CONFLICT IN OLD AGE

In growing older a person is faced with making adjustments so that his expectations and his evaluations of his social roles are in harmony with those of the persons with whom he interacts. The roles of the aged are not clearly defined in contemporary society, and often the aged person experiences conflicts where his expectations are based on roles which were formerly appropriate. To the extent that the aged person's behavior exhibits conflicting roles which are unsatisfactory to himself and to society it is deviant. This definition of certain behavior among the aged as social deviation is admittedly weak. A more precise statement is difficult until the status and roles of the aged in contemporary society are more clearly defined. Deviant behavior among older persons includes feelings of lowered social status, loneliness, unhappiness, or rejection.

As childhood and other diseases have been controlled and as man's life span has continued to increase, the proportion of older men and women in the United States has become significantly greater. At present in the United States 9.2 percent of the population is sixty-five or over. It might be supposed that technological developments and this increased life expectancy have added much to a fuller enjoyment of life by these older people. Unfortunately, many old people in the United States are unhappy in their daily living, feel frustrated in their relationships with other persons, and may even develop senile psychoses.

DISCRIMINATION AGAINST MINORITY GROUPS

Over the past few centuries a set of norms has evolved relating to certain rights for persons regardless of their race, creed, or ethnic derivation. These norms include political equality, due process of law and equal justice, freedom of opportunity to achieve economic and political success, and the right to express one's religious beliefs. A Universal Declaration of Human Rights embodying these norms was approved by the United Nations in 1948. A similar group of norms and values constitutes what is termed the American Creed.[52]

These norms and values in the United States developed out of the philosophy of the Enlightenment and the English, American, and French revolutions, with their emphasis on the importance of the individual; the traditional judicial procedures of English justice; Christianity, with its concept of universal brotherhood; capitalism, with its belief that individual success is based on individual initiative; and, finally, American na-

---

[52] Gunnar Myrdal, *An American Dilemma* (New York: Harper & Row, Publishers, 1944), Chap. 1.

tionalism itself, with its emphasis on the racial, religious, and ethnic diversity of America. These values are reflected in the Declaration of Independence, in the Constitution and its amendments, and in numerous decisions of the Supreme Court, particularly those in recent years dealing with the illegality of laws upholding segregation or denying equal citizenship rights to all persons.

When a group is placed in a lower status on the basis of race, religion, or ethnic background, the action is considered discrimination. It takes many forms and involves suffrage and public office, the administration of justice, employment and business opportunities, education, public accommodation and housing, and every form of social participation. Social norms and values sanctioning discrimination, such as beliefs about racial superiority and anti-Semitism, have a long history. Such discriminatory norms are derived from various subcultural groups and in some historic periods or in certain areas have even been enacted into law.

In the United States discrimination in varying degrees is directed at 18,000,000 or more Negroes, or approximately one in every ten Americans; at over 5,500,000 Jews; at over 3,500,000 Spanish-speaking people, primarily the Mexicans and Spanish-Americans of the Southwest and the Puerto Ricans of New York City; at over 500,000 Indians; and at over 700,000 of Japanese and Chinese origin.

The Scientific Study of Deviant Behavior

Many people believe that deviant behavior cannot be studied scientifically because scientific methods cannot be applied to them in the same manner as in the case of the physical sciences. Human behavior, they claim, is not the proper field for scientific research. This skepticism about the effectiveness of the social sciences is due, in large part, to the extreme complexity of the data which the research worker in these fields must use. In fact, the nature of human behavior is thought by some to be so different from other data that they would restrict the term "science" to the so-called exact or physical sciences such as biology, chemistry, and physics. They would even deny the use of the term "science" to such social or behavioral sciences as sociology, social psychology, anthropology, economics, and political science, upon which the solution of problems of deviant behavior ultimately depends. As Sellin has indicated, however, these, "are important considerations, but they do not permit us to assume that social facts cannot be studied scientifically and laws of social life gradually established. They merely recognize that the social scientist has great hazards to overcome." [53]

Part of this confusion is a result of failure to consider the nature of

---

[53] Sellin, "Culture Conflict and Crime," pp. 12–13.

scientific methods. The scientific study of human behavior assumes that the criteria of science can be applied to the data involved. This means that human behavior can be studied as a *natural process,* or as a sequence of events in which certain events follow from other events, in much the same way as the process through which a disease develops or a chemical process occurs. Whether events which follow are "caused" by preceding events cannot be determined by observing the order of occurrence of the events alone; they must be subjected to scientific investigation.

The scientific study of deviant behavior, like the scientific approach to any data, is an attempt to describe the *processes* associated with the behavior. Generalizations as to cause and effect relationships in such processes are the purpose of science. Such generalizations, if eventually achieved, are usually stated in terms of probabilities. A criminal career, for example, is generally found to have followed a long series of circumstances and incidents, usually beginning with juvenile delinquency and progressing to more serious acts. Likewise, the admission of a psychotic patient to a mental hospital is not the result of one experience but rather may be the culmination of many experiences. The series of steps which precede the chronic alcoholic's admission to the alcoholic ward may extend back for many years. A divorce is seldom the product of a single argument.

A science also tries to put some order into a series of heterogeneous data by reducing them to *types,* as, for example, when the zoologist or botanist classifies animals or plants into species. The scientific study of "criminals" has resulted in the discovery that not all criminals have the same characteristics, but instead that there are various types of criminal careers. Similarly, excessive drinkers are of various types. People suffering from mental disorders and suicides can also be subdivided into a number of types. Generally, such types or classifications are given names or terms in order to facilitate or simplify the manipulation of the mass of data involved in each type.

The social scientist, as contrasted with those who make unscientific claims about human behavior, is willing to do three things. First, he is willing to subject his hypotheses to tests. Second, he avoids making generalizations which are not based on empirical studies. Third, he will state his confidence in a proposition according to the degree to which it has been verified by a test using experimental or empirical data.

Scientific method is nothing more than a description or guide to the logic of scientific inquiry. It is generally stated as a series of steps, which in its simplest form involve:

1. the formulation of a hypothesis referring to the phenomenon to be studied;
2. the observation and collection of data which will test the hypothesis;
3. the classification and analysis of the data obtained; and
4. the arrival at conclusions as to whether, from the results of the analysis, the hypothesis is confirmed or not confirmed.

A *hypothesis* is a statement of a relationship that appears to exist, as, for example, "Delinquency is produced by crime stories on the radio and television." In this hypothesis the social scientist would define how he uses such terms as "delinquency," "crime stories," and other variables. In order to *test* such a hypothesis, however, it would have to be stated in a form which is testable, as "A significantly greater proportion of juveniles who listen to or watch crime stories on radio and television also have been legally classified as delinquent than have those who do not listen to or watch such crime stories." He then *observes* as much as he can of the relevant data, using the *research techniques* most appropriate to the data studied. It is usually not feasible for the social scientist to use mechanical instruments similar to those used in the physical science laboratories. Instead, he may rely on questionnaires and interviews, case histories, and personal documents, such as diaries. In other types of studies he may use ecological techniques, such as spot-mapping, community studies, and, finally, the comparative studies of people living in different cultures.

The social scientist in his research must see that the group he uses for study is representative of the phenomena he is studying. In most instances he also compares the group he is studying with a control group. For example, in testing the hypothesis about the relation of delinquency to crime stories on radio and television, the social scientist must select a *representative sample* of all juvenile delinquents. Since only relatively few juvenile delinquents are sent to correctional institutions, he might decide to select a random sample of those who had been arrested or had appeared before a juvenile court. It also would be necessary, as in most research studies on behavior problems, to compare the delinquents, or the *experimental group,* with a sample of nondelinquents, or a *control group,* in order to discover to what extent the latter also listen to or watch crime stories.

This hypothesis would be partially *verified* if the delinquents, or a statistically significant proportion of the experimental group, listened to or watched crime stories and the nondelinquents did not. The hypothesis would be rejected if no differences were found, or if the control group were discovered to have been listening to or watching crime stories as much as or more than the experimental group. Even after the conclusion of this study, a generalization could not be established until the study had been repeated on other samples of the delinquent and nondelinquent population.

Advances in any physical or social science are often made through efforts to predict or control real phenomena. Such efforts may reveal the inadequacies of scientific knowledge when applications fail to produce the expected results. Applications may also confirm and even extend scientific knowledge. In the physical world, for example, the application of astronomy to the problems of sea and air navigation resulted in improvements in both the theory of astronomy and the techniques of navigation. Efforts to control criminal behavior contribute not only to the field of criminology but also to the broader study of human behavior and society in general.

On the other hand, emphasis on the application, rather than the discovery, of basic scientific knowledge can be carried too far. Generally speaking, application of knowledge is not the *goal* of the science, but rather a by-product of or consequence of scientific discovery.[54] Preoccupation with social welfare and social legislation, where it has not been simultaneously concerned with scientific study of deviant behavior, has often hindered the development of basic knowledge in this area.[55] Unfortunately, attention has often been concentrated on the control of delinquency and crime, alcoholism, discrimination, mental illness, and marital difficulties without the accumulation and study of concepts, theories, and research upon which to base such a program of control.

The primary motivation of most scientists studying deviant behavior today, as of the physical scientist in his laboratory, is scientific curiosity. This does not mean that most social scientists who attempt to understand human behavior are uninterested in its practical application or that the two are necessarily opposed. Rather, students of society, as scientists, are interested chiefly in the discovery of knowledge.

Increasing recognition is being given to the importance of systematizing knowledge about deviant behavior, for without this systematization knowledge cannot be effectively utilized in social control. The mere description of the characteristics of deviants is of little use without some explanation of the development of their behavior. With the extension and systematic application of scientific knowledge, there appears to be no reason why many types of deviant behavior cannot be solved.

Selected Readings

The Annals. November, 1961, issue on "The Teen-age Culture." A series of articles dealing with the norms of a particular peer group subculture, namely, teen-agers. Includes a discussion of Italian-American, Jewish, and Negro subcultures in our society and also in several foreign countries.

GOODE, WILLIAM J., and PAUL K. HATT. *Methods in Social Research.* New York: McGraw-Hill Book Company, Inc., 1952. An excellent discussion of the scientific method in the study of human behavior. Discusses scientific design and the techniques used primarily in sociological research.

HOMANS, GEORGE C. *Social Behavior: Its Elementary Forms.* New York: Harcourt,

---

[54] In a similar way modern-day space explorations involve applications of previously discovered basic knowledge in sciences such as physics or astronomy, which, however, have been added to by testing this knowledge through space explorations.

[55] Edwin H. Sutherland, "Social Pathology," *American Journal of Sociology*, 50:429–436 (May, 1945).

Brace & World, Inc., 1961. An analysis of social behavior based on data obtained from observations of behavior in small groups in industry, in laboratory settings, and in communities. The social behavior of given group members is seen to depend upon a number of variables, such as their status, their role, the probability of rewards for given acts, and so forth.

JAHODA, MARIE, MORTON DEUTSCH, and STUART W. COOK. *Research Methods in Social Relations.* 2 vols. New York: Holt, Rinehart and Winston, Inc., 1952. An introductory statement of the basic processes and selected techniques in social research. Illustrative material primarily deals with the study of prejudice.

KAHL, JOSEPH A. *The American Class Structure.* New York: Holt, Rinehart and Winston, Inc., 1957. An analysis of the norms and behavior patterns of American social classes.

LEMERT, EDWIN M. *Social Pathology.* New York: McGraw-Hill Book Company, Inc., 1951, Chaps. 1–3. Discusses the nature of deviation and the societal reactions to deviations from norms. There is also an analysis of the concepts of social visibility as well as mention of the tolerance quotient.

MILLER, WALTER B. "Lower Class Culture as a Generating Milieu of Gang Delinquency," *Journal of Social Issues,* 14:5–19 (1958). A well-known description of some of the norms of the lower class in America.

SELLIN, THORSTEN. "Culture Conflict and Crime." New York: Social Science Research Council, Bulletin 41, 1938. Deals with the relation of science to criminology and presents a well-known discussion of the concept of "norms" in relation to crime and human behavior in general. Conduct norms have a varying degree of "resistance potential"; hence norms can be classified on this basis.

SUTHERLAND, EDWIN H. "Social Pathology," *American Journal of Sociology,* 50:429–436 (May, 1945). A theoretical survey of fifty years of research on deviant behavior.

Deviant Behavior
as Social Behavior

Many people look upon such deviants as delinquents, criminals, mental patients, suicides, and alcoholics as strange varieties of human beings whose behavior arises in an entirely different way from that of the more balanced and respectable members of society. It is true that deviant behavior is one kind of human, or social, behavior, just as conforming behavior is another kind. However, the difference between conforming and deviant behavior does not mean that there are different physical or psychological qualities which the deviant, as compared with the conformist, possesses. This assertion is alien to the thinking of many persons. We often learn to look upon those who behave differently from the way "we" behave as possessing individual qualities unlike our own. We tend, furthermore, to believe that these "qualities" are the "causes" of the behavior involved. Thus, we say a person is an alcoholic, or "drinks" excessively because he is "weak," "has no character," "has no will power," or has "bad heredity." We tend, therefore, to believe that the excessive drinking of which we disapprove is due to some lack of "character" within the person. In the same way, we attribute excessive "sex drives" to the sex offender and prostitute, or we say that they are "emotionally insecure" and are attempting to find love and affection in sexual release. We describe delinquents as "having a need to rebel," or as "releasing aggressive drives which they have suppressed too long," or as "having hostile, aggressive, and rebellious personality traits." [1]

In various ways, therefore, our mode of perceiving and interpreting the world and the things about us is conditioned by meanings and categories with which our culture has provided us. As noted in the previous chapter, we see our world through a cultural mesh, and nowhere is this truer than in our perception of social deviants.

This attitude that deviants are inherently different is built upon a

---

[1] See Edwin H. Lemert, *Social Pathology* (New York: McGraw-Hill Book Company, Inc., 1951), Chaps. 3 and 4 for further elaboration on this problem.

series of false assumptions, for *all deviant behavior is human behavior.* By this is meant that the same fundamental processes which produce the "normal" person also produce the "abnormal," for both of them are human beings. If certain basic processes underlie the development of the normal person, the same processes and structures must be sought in the deviant. Common components of human nature are found in all types of normality and abnormality.

> One implication of the sociological approach to the study of human behavior is that men are always participants in joint enterprises of one sort or other and that all individualistic explanations of the things men do are necessarily incomplete. Men are rarely isolated and acting purely as independent agents. Respiration is essentially an involuntary organic process, but even that is subject to social control. Men deliberately check their panting if they do not wish to appear cowardly or weak, or they may sigh to indicate hopelessness. Even passive acquiescence and failure to act are social to the extent that such hesitation arises from the anticipated reactions of other people. Each person is involved in many transactions to which he may contribute and thereby modify but only in his capacity as a participant in them. This means that what a man does cannot be explained exclusively in terms of his personality traits, his attitudes, or his motives. People frequently do things they do not want to do. Human behavior is something that is constructed in the course of interaction with other people, and the direction it takes depends upon the inclinations of others as well as those of the actor.[2]

Differences in subprocesses exist; if they did not there would be no way to account scientifically for deviant behavior. The subprocesses affecting deviants, however, must operate within the general framework of a theory of human nature. The units of analysis, as well as the fundamental social processes in all human conduct, are the same whether the end products are inmates of correctional institutions or wardens, mental patients or psychiatrists, habitual criminals or ministers. Brown writes that abnormal behavior is not something outside nature: "It is a naturalistic phenomenon, socially defined as undesirable, but nevertheless a naturalistic phenomenon that developed as all other human nature developed." [3]

Moreover, there does not appear to be any general personality pattern of conformity or nonconformity with social norms or values.[4] Persons may

---

[2] Tamotsu Shibutani, *Society and Personality: An Interaction Approach to Social Psychology,* p. 60. © 1961. Prentice-Hall, Inc., Englewood Cliffs, N.J. By permission.

[3] Lawrence Guy Brown, *Social Pathology* (New York: Appleton-Century-Crofts, Inc., 1946), p. 62. This quotation has been used by permission of the publisher.

[4] Many psychiatrists and psychologists believe, however, that there is such a relationship. Talcott Parsons, a sociologist, has also suggested, without supporting evidence, that there is a relationship between a nonconformist personality pattern and deviant behavior. —*The Social System* (New York: The Free Press of Glencoe, 1951), Chaps. 7–9, and particularly pp. 256–267.

deviate from certain norms and comply with others.[5] Those who deviate from sex norms may not steal, for example, and many white-collar offenders may have a rigid sexual code. In most cases strongly disapproved deviations may be but a small proportion of a person's total life activities. Even where the deviations constitute a more organized subculture, as in certain types of crime, accepted conduct may coincide at many points with the norms and values of the larger community.[6] In the case of professional crime, for example, personal honor and "honesty among thieves" may be a reality because it would generally be inappropriate to depend on the police or other outside agencies for support.

Further confusion arises in the minds of some observers when they perceive that certain factors are associated with the occurrence of deviant behavior. They often jump to the conclusion that two phenomena are related when they may have no connection. When it is noted, for example, that delinquency and bad housing are often associated, a causal relationship may be presumed to exist. Others may perceive that delinquents read comic books, so they conclude that comic books cause delinquency. In both instances, the observer has failed to take into account how such situations may cause delinquency. Most important, however, they may have failed to observe that these same factors—bad housing and comic books—affect a large proportion of our population without necessarily producing deviant behavior. Although most delinquency occurs in so-called slum areas, where housing is poor, the relation has little direct connection with any theory of human behavior and must be discounted as an error in perception. Moreover, delinquency does occur in areas of good housing; hence, if the same logic is used, this situation might be attributed to the adequacy of the housing situation. In studying deviant behavior it is always necessary to consider whether similar influences are affecting nondeviants; therefore, some *theory of human behavior* must be devised which will account for the differential effects, if they exist.

With this statement of the thesis that, fundamentally, both deviant and nondeviant persons have essentially the same components, some further discussion of these components is necessary. Here the interest is not so much in society, culture, or the group as in the individual. The discussion will begin by analyzing what relation a person's biological structure has to his actions and what the differences are between the biological nature of man and that of other animals.

Biology and Social Behavior

Man has a biological nature and a social nature, but it is obvious that without a biological nature there could be no human nature. There is an

---

[5] Robert Harper, "Is Conformity a General or Specific Trait?" *American Sociological Review*, 12:81–86 (February, 1947).

[6] Lemert, *op. cit.*, p. 49.

interplay between the two rather than opposition. Man is an animal who must breathe, eat, rest, and eliminate. Like any other animal, he requires calories, salt and other chemicals, and a particular temperature range and oxygen balance. Man is an animal who is dependent upon his environment and limited by certain of his biological capacities. "Social influences profoundly affect the ways in which human bodies behave . . . but human bodies never cease to be animals." [7]

In the past it was customary for social scientists to engage in lengthy debates as to whether the social behavior of man was in any way biological. Modern social scientists are more likely to begin with the assertion that biology is of little relevance to social or symbolic behavior.[8] There are no physical functions or structures, no combination of genes, and no glandular secretions which contain within themselves the power to direct, guide, or determine the type, form, and course of the social behavior of human beings. Physical structures or properties set physical limits on the activities of persons, but whether such structures will set *social* limits depends on the way in which cultures or subcultures symbolize or interpret these physical properties.

INSTINCTS

Certain writers on deviant behavior, particularly psychoanalysts, have erroneously stressed the animal nature of man, especially with reference to the existence in man of an "unrepressed primitive" animal nature.[9] It is said that man has instincts and that many contemporary difficulties in social relations result from man's inability to overcome his real or original nature. Man has no primitive instinctive nature, however, for there are no universal or instinctive patterns of behavior common to all men and transmitted biologically from one generation to another. Man does not have instinctive patterns of behavior. Hunger can be satisfied with a variety of foods, many of which are injurious to men. Sex acts have no particular season, there is no inborn pattern of courtship, and no "natural" way of sexual intercourse. There is no instinct which makes man religious or irreligious, kind or cruel, a killer or a pacifist.

HEREDITY AND DEVIANT BEHAVIOR

If human behavior is to be inherited, it must have a direct connection with the biological structure, such as the tissue of the brain, the nervous

---

[7] Theodore M. Newcomb, *Social Psychology* (New York: Holt, Rinehart and Winston, Inc., 1950), p. 48. Copyright 1950 by Holt, Rinehart and Winston, Inc. The quotations from this book are reprinted by special permission.

[8] For further discussion see, for example, Alfred R. Lindesmith and Anselm L. Strauss, *Social Psychology* (rev. ed.: New York: Holt, Rinehart and Winston, Inc., 1955), Chaps. 1 and 2.

[9] See the discussion of psychoanalysis, pp. 126–139.

system, the glands, or the blood. Moreover, the specific factor or factors must be present when the ovum is fertilized by the spermatozoon. An inherited quality must be reasonably specific, and must be stable enough that it might be able to affect all members of the species. Regardless of these prerequisites, some biologists still believe that crime, alcoholism, certain types of mental illness, and certain sexual deviations can be carried as specific unit factors in biological inheritance. According to this biological theory, certain specific deviant behavior can be inherited in much the same manner as eye or hair color, through the genes and the chromosomes, at the time of the fertilization of the ovum. Persons with this scientific orientation speak of "born criminals," "born alcoholics," or "inherited insanity."

The evidence today is overwhelmingly against such a view. For example, the following conclusion about criminal behavior has been reached.

> It is obviously impossible for criminality to be inherited as such, for crime is defined by acts of legislatures and these vary independently of the biological inheritance of the violators of the laws. If persons with certain inherited traits are more likely to commit crimes than persons with other inherited traits, these traits have not been identified and their connection with criminal behavior has not been demonstrated. Anyone who speaks of the direct or indirect inheritance of criminality except in the senses stated in the first two propositions in this paragraph is speaking from his preconceptions and assumptions and not from factual evidence.[10]

Although the evidence is incomplete and contradictory, the numerically important types of mental disorder do not appear to be biologically inherited.[11] The evidence on the inheritance of alcoholism was surveyed by Jellinek, a biologist, who combined fifteen studies of heredity made of 4372 clinical alcoholics, of whom, 2799, or 52 percent, were found to have had at least one inebriate parent. He found that the estimates of the several investigators as to the percentage of alcoholics who had a possible history of hereditary factors varied from a high of 83 percent to a low of 23 percent. In his conclusions Jellinek, having left out some of the studies which dealt exclusively with persons suffering from alcoholic psychoses in which other factors besides alcoholism might be present, stated that the studies surveyed showed that "the incidence of hereditary taint in the total group of alcoholics probably does not exceed 35 percent. This leaves us with a large alcoholic population in which inebriety has developed independently of any hereditary liability." [12] This is far too cautious a state-

---

[10] Edwin H. Sutherland and Donald R. Cressey, *Principles of Criminology* (6th ed.; Philadelphia: J. B. Lippincott Company, 1960), p. 90.

[11] This will be discussed in Chapter 13, "The Functional Mental Disorders."

[12] E. M. Jellinek, "Heredity of the Alcoholic," in *Alcohol, Science, and Society* (New Brunswick, N.J.: Quarterly Journal of Studies on Alcohol, 1945), p. 109.

ment, for the presence of an alcoholic parent by no means represents necessarily a biological rather than a social influence.

In order to prove that crime or other deviant behavior is inherited, the nature of the inheritance must be stated in such precise terms as to suggest what part of the physical organism is affected or how the organism as a whole is affected. This has not been done. Since attitudes derived from the norms of the culture cannot be inherited, deviant attitudes derived from other sources cannot be inherited. Likewise, deviant behavior cannot be hereditary because such a theory assumes that what constitutes disapproved behavior is the same in all societies, which is not necessarily the case.

What many persons confuse as inheritance in behavior is the social transmission of somewhat similar ways of behaving from one generation to another in a culture, or from one family to another. Actually none of this is hereditary, for there is no way in which so-called family traits or culture can be inherited through the genes. The inheritance of eye color is one thing; the inheritance of thousands of social norms and values is another. Anthropologists have demonstrated conclusively that there is no connection between the biological features of race and culture. A typical American Negro, for example, would have little in common culturally with an African Negro. The American Negro has no appreciable vestige of his African culture left today. The social organization, the language, the African gods, the witchcraft, the food habits have all been supplanted by a Western European culture. The complexity of gene structure which would be required to transmit a culture as part of the biological heritage would be inconceivable.

One of the reasons for the belief in constitutional differences was the error in perceiving the reasons for resemblances and differences in the trait structures of father and son, mother and daughter, and brothers and sisters. The experiences of no two children are exactly the same even for an hour or a day, let alone a month, a year, or more. The child learns to adapt to the world around him and to the people in the world. Thus it can be understood that the experiences of two brothers, particularly if there is a considerable age disparity, may be even more distinct than the experiences of friends of either one. Among these differences in experiences are obviously the addition of siblings to the family, playmates, school classes, and teachers. If the family has moved during the childhood of two brothers, as many families do, the neighbors and the general environment may be quite different. What is probably most important is the change in attitudes of the father and mother with additional children, and changes in social status and possibly in occupation. The method of treating an older and a younger child may be quite different because of changes in the parents' social situation.

The relevance of all this discussion to deviant behavior should be clear.

If one can inherit only something which is carried physiologically, and none of the social norms or values of one's culture or subculture are thus transmitted, much of what are termed "family traits" are eliminated. It is obvious, however, that behavioral traits can be passed on from grandfather to father and son through sharing common experiences and attitudes without recourse to inheritance. Likewise, there is no way in which such deviant attitudes as disrespect for laws, sexual licentiousness, or, in mental illness, for example, difficulties in interpersonal relations such as fear of other people, can be inherited. It is intriguing to consider what might happen in each instance if it were possible to cross such traits. Such possibilities include crossing a shoplifter's genes with a forger's genes, the genes of a person who likes people with those of one who does not, or those of a teetotaler with those of an alcoholic.

Neither moral behavior nor immoral behavior is biologically inherited. This would be impossible, for, as we have said above, the definitions of what constitutes such behavior vary not only among societies, but, as Kinsey showed about sex behavior, primarily by social class within a society. Morality also varies by generation, as illustrated by the changes in norms designated in the criminal code each year. Thus the gene structure would have to be extremely variable to keep up with these changes in moral definitions. Moreover, as indicated before, any propositions about the inheritance of deviant behavior would have to apply as well to the non-deviant.

GLANDS

Some writers have sought a more specific explanation of certain forms of deviant behavior in the malfunctioning of certain glands of the human body, particularly the endocrine glands. Berman suggested that persons who are criminal, irresponsible, and unable to adjust to society have disturbances in the thymus gland.[13] Schlapp and Smith explained criminal behavior as being due to malfunctioning of the glands,[14] a theme which has become a particular favorite of many European, particularly Italian, criminologists. Efforts have also been made to trace some forms of mental disorders and alcoholism to the improper functioning of certain glands, particularly the thyroid and adrenal glands.[15] Others have suggested that malfunctioning of the gonads and abnormal secretion of the sex hormones

[13] Louis Berman, *The Glands Regulating Personality* (New York: The Macmillan Company, 1922).

[14] Max Schlapp and E. H. Smith, *The New Criminology* (New York: Liveright Publishing Corporation, 1929).

[15] J. M. Nielsen and George N. Thompson, *The Engrammes of Psychiatry* (Springfield, Ill.: Charles C. Thomas, Publisher, 1947), pp. 357–362.

produce not only the effeminate homosexual and the oversexed personality types but the prostitute.[16]

In spite of these claims, research on glandular structure has as yet produced no conclusive explanations in any area of deviant behavior, with the possible exception of certain unique cases. Part of this inability to prove a relationship can be attributed to the fact that little is known about the relationship of endocrine glands to disorders in behavior.[17] In fact, very little is known about the functioning of glands among nondeviant persons. Ashley-Montagu states unequivocally that "not one of the reports on the alleged relationship between glandular dysfunctions and criminality [has] been carried out in a scientific manner, and that all such reports are glaring examples of the fallacy of false cause." [18] Somewhat similar statements have been made about efforts to relate schizophrenia or the manic-depressive psychoses to endocrine disturbances.[19]

Even if there were evidence that disturbances in the endocrine glands were related to certain forms of deviant behavior, it would be difficult to establish the fact that the glandular disturbances preceded the deviant behavior. Incarceration in a prison or a long period of mental illness might upset the glandular functioning of an individual. The association of glandular deficiencies with the development of alcoholism is even more difficult, for alcoholics may consume large quantities of alcohol over long periods during which their diet is anything but balanced. It is likely that glandular secretions occasionally may affect a personality, but there seems to be no general correlation between certain behavioral characteristics and endocrine disturbance. Further research using control groups is imperative in order to pass beyond speculation to facts in this area.

PHYSICAL CHARACTERISTICS AND DEFECTS

Some persons claim that certain antisocial behavior is often produced by poor health or disease. In particular, there has been an interest in the relation of deviant behavior to brain pathology, infectious diseases, heart lesions, and such foci of infection as tonsils or teeth.[20] Crossed eyes, facial

---

[16] See, for example, A. Myerson and R. Neustadt, "Bisexuality and Male Homosexuality," *Clinics*, 1:956 (December, 1943).

[17] R. G. Hoskins, *Endocrinology: The Glands and Their Functions* (New York: W. W. Norton & Company, Inc., 1941).

[18] Montague Francis Ashley-Montagu, "The Biologist Looks at Crime," in J. P. Shalloo ed., "Crime in the United States," *The Annals*, 217:55 (September, 1941).

[19] See Roy M. Dorcus and G. Wilson Shaffer, *Textbook of Abnormal Psychology* (3d ed.; Baltimore: The Williams & Wilkins Company, 1945), p. 307. Also see Kimball Young, *Personality and Problems of Adjustment* (New York: Appleton-Century-Crofts, Inc., 1947), p. 743.

[20] H. Cotton, *The Defective, Delinquent and Insane: The Relation of Focal Infections to Their Causation, Treatment, and Prevention* (Princeton, N.J.: Princeton Uni-

deformities such as large nose or acne, and other physical defects, such as clubfeet, have also been said to have an important relationship to delinquency and crime.[21] There is, however, no one-to-one relationship between physical defects and social maladjustment. There are undoubtedly criminals, for example, who are physically weak, have infected tonsils, or are cross-eyed, but there are many persons with these characteristics who are not criminals, and the incidence of these conditions may be even greater among the noncriminal population.

Some biological or physical characteristics, while not having a direct effect on social behavior, may have some indirect effect. "It has been said that if Cleopatra's nose had been a half inch longer, she would have had a different kind of influence on history. Certainly physique, including health, appearance, physical strength and coordination, skin pigmentation, growth rate, height, weight, etc., are important factors in developing the kind of attitudes that a person has about himself." [22] What is important is the individual's conception of people's attitudes toward his appearance. A physical handicap, such as crossed eyes, may cause a person *indirectly* to seek certain antisocial contacts and participate in criminal activity. The expected social roles of women are different, however, and the chance of their participation in serious crime for this reason may be limited. The fact that a male has what appear to be feminine characteristics may make his indulgence in homosexual practices more likely, even though homosexual behavior does not appear to be inherited. Finally, a person who has a dark skin or other Negroid features is forced to assume a series of subservient roles in a culture and often must live in city slums where criminal norms are more prevalent, and where there is greater temptation to adopt delinquent and criminal patterns of behavior.

INTELLIGENCE

Although the limits of intelligence are probably set at birth, the development of intelligence is greatly dependent on such variables as social experience, language, and education. Intelligence tests measure only intelligence as liberated through specific environmental forces. They do not measure innate intelligence, for such a form exists only in the abstract. Intelligence existing in any individual (which present intelligence tests attempt to measure) is a product of both environment and potentialities.

---

versity Press, 1921); and W. Hunter, "Chronic Sepsis as a Cause of Mental Disorder," *Journal of Mental Science,* 73:549–563 (October, 1927). Formerly case histories of deviants often included a question about whether there had been a difficult pregnancy or a traumatic birth.

[21] See, for example, Ralph S. Banay, "Physical Disfigurement as a Factor in Delinquency and Crime," *Federal Probation,* 7:20–24 (January–March, 1943).

[22] Richard Dewey and W. J. Humber, *Development of Human Behavior* (New York: The Macmillan Company, 1951), p. 87.

A succeeding chapter will present a discussion of intelligence and deviant behavior with largely negative conclusions.[23]

Social Nature of Man

Despite the fact that man is an animal, little that has a meaningful relationship to the essential qualities of human behavior can be derived from the study of lower forms of animal life. No matter how anthropomorphic we are in seeing human qualities in ants, bees, mice, dogs, and horses, there are extremely important differences that cannot be bridged. The behavior of lower forms of animal life is largely controlled by a series of innate reflexes and instincts, whereas man's behavior patterns are transmitted by culture from one generation to another. Man alone among the animals possesses language with which to convey abstract meanings. He alone has the language and intelligence needed to convey highly technical ideas, such as mathematical concepts. Man alone has a self, plays a variety of social roles, and makes moral distinctions. Lower animals are not nearly as dependent on others of their kind as is man. The limitations on the possibility that animals can approach human beings in their behavior far outweigh the few similarities. Even some comparative psychologists have pointed out the fallacy of trying to derive valid knowledge about human beings from experiments on animals. Hilgard, a well-known psychologist, has summed it up as "the price paid for overmuch experimentation with animals is to neglect the fact that human subjects are brighter, are able to use language—and probably learn differently because of these advances over lower animals. . . . Only if a process demonstrable in human learning can also be demonstrated in lower animals is the comparative method useful in studying it." [24]

LANGUAGE

Without language there can be no abstract reasoning, no social interaction, no self or conception of self; without language the human animal cannot play social roles. The possession of language is the most important distinguishing characteristic separating man from other animals. No matter how many experiments reveal subhuman or pseudohuman qualities in the learning process of rats and apes, the dividing line between the two groups is impossible to bridge without language. Language enables the human being to deal with norms and values. Scientific, moral, and religious ideas are carried and expressed through language. "The absence of morality, religion, conscience, etc., among both adult apes and human infants is

---

[23] See Chapter 5.
[24] Ernest R. Hilgard, *Theories of Learning* (New York: Appleton-Century-Crofts, Inc., 1948), p. 329.

based upon the same inability to represent to oneself in terms of a human language, one's own goals, purposes, or principles." [25] Even terms like "criminal," "drunk," "mental patient," "Negro," or "Jew" take on abstract or stereotyped meanings in common language.

A child acquires the language of his parents; he also acquires cultural meanings or evaluations which are communicated principally through language.[26] Conceptual categories are merely our general modes of viewing or relating to things, but our more specific modes of perceiving and feeling are closely aligned with the linguistic categories we have acquired. For example, the white child who learns that "dirty Negro" refers to dark-skinned persons will probably perceive or see a dark-skinned person as "dirty" whether he actually is dirty or not. In addition, the child may thus learn to have a feeling of revulsion or disgust when he sees a Negro.

The human infant, whether he turns into a criminal or a noncriminal, is born into this world the most plastic of all animals. A few reflexes, some drives, such as hunger and sex, and a potentiality for human behavior are about all he has. In turn, a human being requires a longer time to mature than any other animal. The child becomes socialized through the use of language. In communication through language with others over a long infancy, childhood, and young adulthood the human being interacts with others and both his and other personalities become modified. One social psychologist has defined *social interaction* as the "process by which an individual notices and responds to others who are noticing and responding to him." [27] This reciprocal process of interaction with other persons and through them with culture and subculture enables the child or adult to develop a unique personality, whether deviant or not.

CONCEPTION OF SELF

Man is the only animal who has a "self" in the sense that he conceives of himself as a separate being, has an understanding of who and what he is, and is even able to talk to evaluate himself in ways which are sometimes laudatory and at other times reproving. The human being is not born with a self; he acquires one through social interaction.[28] Like other, but mature, animals, a young infant cannot distinguish between himself

---

[25] Lindesmith and Strauss, *op. cit.*, p. 25.

[26] Should the student doubt this he might ask himself how often he has heard the following phrases: "She's a nice prostitute," "He's a kind murderer," or "He's a very sincere thief." Such phrases have a peculiar sound—the adjectives "kind," "nice," and so on, are incongruent with the invidious images portrayed by the nouns "prostitute," "murderer," or "thief."

[27] Newcomb, *op. cit.*, p. 21.

[28] Perhaps some persons would rush to defend a pet dog and say that he not only conceives of himself as a separate being, but when punished he has been observed to sulk. We would be the last to disturb such a pleasant fantasy, but it might be well to

and others. He and everything else in the world are part of a confusing hodgepodge with little meaning except in the immediate present. As speech develops, he realizes that he has a self separate from others. He acts out roles or parts, such as a cowboy, a fireman, an Indian chief, a policeman, his father or his mother. In this role playing it is not someone else who does the things that the child does, but he himself. This constitutes the "play stage" of personality growth where dolls, toys, and other similar objects become an indispensable part of this acting process. Later the child develops a further conception of self through playing games of various types where there must be an ability to shift roles by playing the parts of the other players. The growing child learns to internalize the roles of others and in so doing to distinguish his own role from that of others. When the internalization of these roles has been sufficiently developed to give the child a conception of a generalized "other" person to whom he can respond, he has also achieved what might be referred to as a generalized self. As George H. Mead has written: "No hard-and-fast line can be drawn between our own selves and the selves of others, since our own selves exist . . . only insofar as the selves of others exist." [29]

As the child learns that he is a separate person, that is, as he learns to think of himself as "Johnny" and not as Billy, Fred, or Daddy, he also learns that "Johnny" has certain attributes. He learns this not from himself alone, but from the reactions of others toward him, and eventually from these actions plus his interpretations of them. In effect, Johnny learns to apply to himself both the words and the attitudes of others. He may become unhappy because the words "bad boy" conjures up a thought image of something he has learned to dislike and fear, and the idea of "Johnny, you are bad" which occurs in the momentary reflection of himself as others see him arouses a feeling of fear, shame, and dislike all at once. This is what we mean when we say that the child's self-concept develops as he, by means of language, takes the attitude of others toward himself and then calls out in himself (in his symbolic response) the attitude of others. This process is instantaneous and is not at all prolonged, as our description might suggest.

The three steps involved in each phase of this process, from the standpoint of the individual, are

Perception: Attending to the other's action
Interpretation: Attribution of meaning to the other's action
Response: Acting or feeling on the basis of the meaning attributed [30]

---

suggest the absence of two elements that make this improbable, namely, that a dog has no way to refer himself to himself and, second, he possesses no words with which to talk to himself about the errors of his ways.

[29] George H. Mead, *Mind, Self, and Society* (Chicago: The University of Chicago Press, 1934), p. 164.

[30] *Ibid.*, Chaps. 1 and 2. Actually, the three steps above characterize all social behavior, in the sense that all action (or response) which is social is preceded by perception and interpretation (or definition).

The normal person is able to call out the same responses in himself that he calls out in others. An organized and integrated self permits him to put himself in the place of another, while still maintaining his own identity. This growth of self-realization can be illustrated by the development of children's moral ideas. In a study of lower-class children in Switzerland, Piaget showed that a child's ideas of fair play move from self-centered judgments to seeing them through the eyes of others.[31] Until about the age of five a child has an absolute idea of right and wrong, and from then until about the age of ten the child comes to realize that moral ideas are not real in themselves but are related to numerous group ideas. Finally, the child learns that the group can make exceptions to rules and that new ones can be made by the group. In this way the child learns to acquire abstract, generalized ideals. He is not born with "natural" moral judgments; instead, children in the early grades have "abstract conceptions of justice and 'fairness' [which] are not yet very clear." [32]

The self-concept is not static, but is subject to change and modification throughout a person's life. It changes as the others with whom one identifies change, or as the expectations of these others alter. The concept of self which one has as a child will be decidedly different from one's concept of self as an aged person.[33]

> In recent years more and more students of human behavior have come to recognize the importance of personal identity, for what a man does or does not do depends in large measure upon his conception of himself. Each individual is tied to a pattern of communal life by the manner in which he is identified. By virtue of being who he is, he assumes status in a group. He can locate himself and is recognized by others, and his relationship to each of the others is thereby defined. Far from being creatures of impulse, men generally inhibit their organic dispositions in order to live up to the standards of conduct that they set for themselves. They are constantly responding to what they believe themselves to be. . . . Many of the distinctive features of human behavior arise from the fact that men orient themselves within a symbolic environment and strive to come to terms with what they believe themselves to be. Men give their lives willingly for a variety of worthy causes; they deny themselves many joys in order to build gigantic political or industrial empires; they build up social barriers to protect their progeny against miscegenation; they plot vengeance for a wrong suffered long ago by their ancestors; they create monuments in their own honor; they push their children to "make a name" for themselves; lovers commit suicide when they are denied the right to marry; artists paint happily for "posterity," serenely indifferent to the fact that their contemporaries regard them as mad. Al-

---

[31] Piaget, *Moral Judgment of the Child* (London: Routledge and Kegan Paul Ltd., 1932).

[32] Gardner and Lois Murphy and Theodore Newcomb, *Experimental Social Psychology* (New York: Harper & Row, Publishers, 1937), p. 650.

[33] See, for example, Zena S. Blau, "Changes in Status and Age Identification," *American Sociological Review*, 21:198–203 (1956).

though men take these activities for granted as a part of human life, no other animal is known to engage in such conduct. It is unlikely that any creature without self-conceptions would do any of these things. Human behavior consists of a succession of adjustments to life conditions, but each man must come to terms with himself as well as with other features of his world. To understand what men do we must know something about what each person means to himself.[34]

The self-conception, therefore, is an important aspect of the person, and whether one is dealing with deviant or nondeviant behavior it is necessary to recognize this. It is the image in our minds of the "self" (ourselves) that we try to enhance and defend whether we are a judge or a criminal. When this self-image gets out of line with the conception which others have of a person, the result may even be the "great inventor" or similar figures found in mental hospitals. As a person's conception of himself changes, so may a large part of his personality, as is indicated in what is termed the "successful treatment" of mental patients, alcoholics, and delinquents. What, in part, happens is that the deviant comes to view himself differently, placing new expectations on his conduct, as well as new demands.

Social Roles

Up to now the discussion has been about the fact that all social behavior is human behavior and that people have language and a conception of self that other animals do not have. This leads us to a further discussion of why people act the way they do. Social behavior has to be acquired. It is not there at birth but develops through experiences. Behavior becomes modified in response to the demands and expectations of others. Personality, or a person's general *pattern* of behavior, is produced by social interaction in the sense that practically all behavior is only in relation to other people. Terms like "honesty," "friendliness," "shyness" have meaning only in relation to other people. Even expressions of emotionality, such as anger or depression, although they have physiological concomitants, are mostly the expressions of social reactions. They can be expressed, controlled, or accentuated according to a variety of social and cultural definitions.

The process described in the development of the self is also descriptive of the process involved in the development of other social behavior. Social behavior develops not only as we respond in relation to other people, but also as we anticipate the responses of other people to us and incorporate them into our conduct. When two people converse, both are more or less aware of the fact that each is evaluating the other's behavior. In

---

[34] Shibutani, *op. cit.*, pp. 247–248.

this process each person evaluates his own behavior as well as the behavior of other persons. The person's behavior, based on his estimate of how he should act, is called *role playing,* and his idea of the other person's behavior is called *role taking.* A *social role* more specifically involves four parts: (1) the person's identification or conception of himself; (2) the appropriate behavior he displays according to his conception of the situation; (3) the roles which are acted out by other persons in response to his role; and (4) the evaluation by the individual of these roles.[35] The activities of a human being in the course of a day can be regarded as the performance of a series of roles which he has learned and which others expect him to fulfill. The most important part of this process is role taking. Through role taking, or assuming the attitudes of others toward ourselves, we not only gain an idea of what kinds of persons we are, but also of what other persons expect of us. When we direct our actions according to these expectations we are, in effect, engaging in *self-control. Social control,* on the other hand, becomes possible through the fact that persons acquire the ability to behave in a manner consistent with the expectations of others.[36]

Like the actor who plays many stage parts, even though they are exaggerated, all persons fill numerous roles. A person's social roles are linked with his position in society. There are age roles, sex roles, social class roles, occupation roles, and family roles. Such roles are, for example, those of an old or a young person, a man or a woman, a husband or a wife, a parent or a child, a doctor, a lawyer, or a salesman. The student and the professor play a series of roles in the lecture room, in the office discussing a subject or bargaining for a grade, and often in their greeting and demeanor toward one another on the campus. Negroes, in their relations with whites, often act out roles, and the problems arising from these interacting roles are an important aspect of what are called race relations. For example, in the South, there is often a "continued flow of agreement by the Negro while a white man is talking, such as 'Yes, boss,' 'Sho nuff,' 'Well, I declare' and the like." [37]

It is through the expectations of others that persons are assigned roles and statuses and are expected to engage in the behavior prescribed for these roles and statuses. The status and role (or roles) which a person is assigned cannot be easily changed by his own desires: whether a person plays the role which society has assigned to him or not, his behavior is still interpreted by society as consistent with this role and its corresponding status. For example, the behavior of the ex-inmate of a prison in his home

---

[35] Lindesmith and Strauss, *op. cit.,* p. 166.

[36] Shibutani, *op. cit.,* pp. 118–121, 197. Self-control is, in essence, social control, for persons see themselves from the standpoint of the group and thus they try to maintain self-respect through achieving social respect by meeting the group's expectations. Also see S. F. Nadel, "Social Control and Self-Regulation," *Social Forces,* 31:265–273 (1953).

[37] John Dollard, *Caste and Class in a Southern Town* (New Haven, Conn.: Yale University Press, 1937), p. 180.

community may be interpreted in a manner consistent with real or imagined criminal "tendencies," even if he is making a determined effort to "go straight." The power of community interpretations in perpetuating a person's occupancy of a criminal status and role may have several consequences. Sometimes such persons will "give in" to the societal definition and actively play the role which has been expected of them. In other cases, such persons may move to different communities where presumably their past experiences are unknown, and where their noncriminal behavior may provide the basis for assignment of a conventional and "respectable" status and role.[38]

On the basis of social roles, deviants can be distinguished as to whether they represent primary or secondary deviation.[39] Persons may engage in deviant behavior but continue to occupy a conventional status and role. Such deviant behavior constitutes *primary deviation* when it is rationalized and considered as a function of a socially acceptable role. On the other hand, deviant actions may be reacted to by arrest, imprisonment, or other sanctions; the deviant then becomes officially labeled as such and may even be socially isolated as a deviant. Consequently the deviant has less opportunity to play conventional roles and comes to incorporate a societal image of himself as a deviant. When this occurs there is *secondary deviation.* "When a person begins to employ his deviant behavior or a role based upon it as a means of defense, attack, or adjustment to the overt and covert problems created by the consequent societal reaction to him, his deviation is secondary." [40]

Thus persons may commit delinquencies and crimes without becoming secondary deviants and without being regarded as "delinquents" and "criminals." Women may engage in sex acts under conditions similar to that of the "prostitute" but do not consider themselves as one. There are persons who engage in homosexual acts but are not "homosexuals" in the sense of secondary deviation. A person may be a heavy drinker and not be designated a "drunk." But once the label of "deviant" has been given a person it may have important consequences for further deviant behavior.

Human behavior fundamentally represents a series of social roles which may be deviant or nondeviant. Professional thieves, for example, play a variety of roles. Punctuality in keeping appointments with partners and the code of not "squealing" on another thief are of particular importance in their profession. Social status or position among thieves is based on their technical skill, connections, financial standing, influence, dress, manners, and wide knowledge. Their status is also reflected in the attitudes which ordinary criminals have toward them as well as the attitudes of lawyers, the police, court officials, and newspaper reporters. The profes-

---

[38] See Shibutani, *op. cit.,* and Lemert, *op. cit.*   [39] Lemert, *op. cit.,* pp. 75–76.
[40] *Ibid.,* p. 76.

sional criminal may likewise play different roles toward victim, friend, wife, children, father, mother, grocer, or minister.

Most of the "script" for these deviant roles, as for nondeviant ones, is derived from group experience and cultural or subcultural situations. On occasions, however, where appropriate roles are not provided they may be unique to the individual's own life experience. The diversity of social roles in modern urban society, as will be indicated later, is an important factor in the extent of social deviation of modern society. Because of this diversity and lack of coordination of social roles, the actual behavioral responses of persons to certain situations fail to conform to what would ordinarily be expected. A person's own evaluation of his role is often not the same as that of others.

THE DEFINITION OF THE SITUATION

A *definition of a situation* is merely an anticipation of action in a given situation.[41] In defining a situation one assumes the standpoint of real or imagined others and imaginatively rehearses the action expected by these others of oneself. Role taking, or assuming the attitude of others, is the elementary process involved in defining a situation.

> In the drama of life, as in the theater, everyone performs for some kind of audience. In a small community the observers are easy enough to find; but in our complex, pluralistic society the people in whose eyes a person seeks to preserve and enhance his status are not so apparent. Much depends upon the communication channels in which he regularly participates. . . . The comprehension of what a man does requires a record of (1) his definition of the situation, (2) the kind of creature he believes himself to be, and (3) the audience before which he tries to maintain his self-respect.[42]

The definition of the situation is essentially a means by which an individual organizes his behavior. In order imaginatively to rehearse his own action, he takes into account the anticipated responses of others and organizes them into his own behavior.[43] In defining situations with which we are unfamiliar, we often look for "cues" which allow us to assess the present circumstances in terms of contexts with which we are more familiar. For example, in meeting a stranger, as on a train, we usually inquire as to his destination, where he is from, and what he does for a living. With such questions, we are actually trying to determine the stranger's social status. We do this because if we know what his status is, we can anticipate much of his behavior, and much about his life circumstances as well. If the stranger is an unemployed, poorly dressed man of middle age, we make

---

[41] William I. Thomas and Florian Znaniecki, *The Polish Peasant in Europe and America* (New York: Alfred A. Knopf, Inc., 1927), II, 1846–1849.

[42] Shibutani, *op. cit.*, p. 279.   [43] *Ibid.*, pp. 118–119.

certain assumptions about him, and base our own responses to him on these assumptions. We may define him as "not in our class," and thus treat him in a way such as to keep interaction at a minimum. Or we might make an entirely different definition.[44]

The particular definition a given individual makes will be influenced by all that he has known and experienced until that time. The latter would include the set of attitudes, norms, and values which the person has acquired or known, the particular set of statuses and roles he has occupied, or is familiar with, and the particular cumulation of experiences and situations he has known of or participated in. For example, if a teen-ager perceives a set of keys left in a car he may interpret the situation as an opportunity to steal it; another may pay no attention to the same situation. A difficult situation may be perceived one way by a person contemplating suicide, and a completely different way by someone else.

ATTITUDES

Certain definitions of situations are relatively conventional or stabilized. These will be referred to as *attitudes*.[45] Every individual has literally thousands of such attitudes which provide the basis for his actions in many situations. On the basis of acquired attitudes a flavored solution of a chemical called alcohol may be regarded as a delectable beverage by a habitual drinker, whereas that same chemical may not only taste highly disagreeable to a teetotaler but be regarded as poisonous and sinful to drink. A Negro may be thought of as quite similar in his personality to most white men or he may be thought of as shiftless, immoral, oversexed, and naturally superstitious, thus causing behavior with reference to the Negro to vary correspondingly. Objects or social norms in our culture are defined by a person's experiences, as the following case illustrates.

> A novel example is furnished by Fung Kwok Keung, born Joseph Rinehart of American parents living in Long Island, New York. At the age of three, his parents deserted him, and he was adopted by Chinese, taken to China and reared there for nineteen years. Recently he returned to the United States. He is Chinese in manner, speech, habit, outlook—in all ways but appearance.[46]

---

[44] See Erving Goffman, *The Presentation of Self in Everyday Life* (New York: Doubleday Anchor Books, 1959), Chap. 1.

[45] "Attitudes denote these [states of readiness] which are learned [formed] in relation to definite stimuli [objects, persons, situations, values, or norms] and which are more or less lasting."—Muzafer Sherif, *An Outline of Social Psychology* (New York: Harper & Row, Publishers, 1948), p. 207.

[46] Quoted in William F. Ogburn and Meyer F. Nimkoff, *Sociology* (Boston: Houghton Mifflin Company, 1946), p. 8. As the groups to which a person belongs differ, then so do his attitudes.

Most attitudes are developed through group associations rather than as a result of individual experience. Inasmuch as people are all, in one way or another, members of groups, attitudes generally represent shared meanings. Hence most attitudes are derived from cultural norms. Groups, then, to which the individual may belong serve as a frame of reference and undoubtedly influence his attitudes. A group in terms of whose norms a person orients his behavior is a *reference group*. Such groups are not necessarily the same as *membership groups* to which a person is recognized as belonging.[47] A delinquent gang may be the reference group of a delinquent rather than such membership groups as family, church, and similar groups.

Although cultural experiences are often superficially similar, they are not the same in detail, nor are they experienced in the same way by two individuals. As mentioned above, attitudes are derived from social experiences, and thus may differ according to such variables as the country or part of the country in which we live, the part of the city or town in which we have been raised, the social class and occupation to which we belong, and the amount of our education. These differences in attitudes have been reflected in numerous surveys of public opinion. People have been shown to differ a great deal in their attitudes toward things simply on the basis of their religious training. The attitudes of a slum neighborhood toward crime, delinquency, the police, gambling, premarital sex relations, and prostitution are often much different from those held in middle-class residential areas. To the average white man in Iowa a Negro is not quite the same person that he is to the average white man in Mississippi.

Of fundamental importance in the development of attitudes are those groups which are described as "primary." Primary groups include the family, the neighborhood, and various friendship groups such as high school cliques and boys' gangs—all groups from which basic attitudes are acquired, particularly those attitudes involving social values. These *primary groups* are extremely important because social interaction tends to be intimate and "face to face," which makes a greater impression on the person than the less intimate type of group. These primary groups affect the individual early in life, presenting the child with the first ways of acting, and with the only possible "right" conception of a situation. Early attitudes become important whether they are about foods, manners, and religion or about Negroes, Jews, and honesty. These attitudes are called primary not only because they develop first but because they have attached to them strong personal ties which are more difficult to modify later in life. Among deviants, for example, the corner gang may supply the child with a view of the world in general, including conceptions of such broad

[47] Newcomb, *op. cit.*, p. 225.

categories as the police and schoolteachers, or stealing and truancy in particular. Likewise, another boy may secure many different definitions of behavior from his family, the YMCA, and his Cub Scout den.

As distinguished from "primary group attitudes," there is another source, called *secondary groups*. These are somewhat later associations based on common interests, abilities, roles, and status position and include occupational groups, labor union or professional groups, church, tavern, club, or lodge. Members of these groups are not emotionally tied together, and the members might not even know each other well. The norms which are present usually refer to a specific area of life and may not be those of all the members. It is in this sense that it is often possible to speak of a person as belonging to such a secondary group without really becoming a part of it. Although a person undoubtedly acquires many attitudes from secondary groups, they are not likely to be the first presented to him on such important questions of behavior as racial or sexual attitudes. Oftentimes primary groups, such as the family, tend to channel persons, particularly when young, into secondary groups with similar norms, and in such circumstances what may appear to be a continuous hold of the family on the individual turns out to be a partial illusion.

Although people secure most of their attitudes from the general culture and from subcultural situations that differ according to region, neighborhood, class, occupation, religion, and education, some attitudes are the result of unique personal experiences. An example is the favorable change in attitudes toward Negroes that sometimes occurs among soldiers under battle conditions. This method of acquiring attitudes through unique experiences is not common, but probably everyone has had such experiences. Most attitudes involving disrespect for law are acquired through group experiences but some persons who have had particularly brutal experiences in a correctional institution or in a so-called reformatory may have attitudes of disrespect turn into hatred for law and law officers, as happened to John Dillinger.

A differential process of acquiring attitudes has been suggested by Sutherland, particularly in connection with his fourfold theory of criminal behavior.[48] The theory can be applied in general, however, to the acquisition of many other forms of deviant behavior involving cultural norms. He has suggested that variables such as the following would account both for the difference in the development and for the continuance of delinquent and criminal deviant attitudes: (1) How early in life did the association with a certain deviant norm begin? (2) How many and how extensive were the facets of the person's life associated with the deviant behavior? Did the definition of a social situation include only one social role or all the per-

---

[48] Sutherland and Cressey, *op. cit.*, Chap. 4.

son's activities? (3) How continuous was the contact with the deviations? Did the association continue over a period of years, or was it limited to only a brief period? (4) How important was the association with the person who furnished a deviant model? In this connection, how much did the person identify himself with the deviant model, whether it was a companion, a member of the family, a play group, or other models? [49]

Research on attitudes has brought out the fact that, while they may be relatively stabilized definitions of situations, they can and do change. Among the more important variables which change attitudes appear to be such factors as the following: first, the strength of a particular attitude in the presence of external influences; second, increased familiarity due to firsthand experience; and third, the prestige of the model presenting a given attitude. These three ideas can be illustrated by the resistance to the influence of crime stories on the part of a middle-class boy who has attended a high school where there is little deviant behavior, who has been an active Boy Scout, and who has conceived of himself as a "model boy." Suppose that a boy who has long been a delinquent moves into his neighborhood. Under the personal influence of this boy the first youngster may tend to alter his attitudes. If the new boy is someone with considerable prestige and one whom he admires, there is an increased possibility that he himself may engage in delinquent behavior. If the prestige model in this example were reversed the delinquent boy might well become nondelinquent.

In summary, then, the definition of a situation which a person makes is, in part, dependent upon his past experiences and learning. It is also dependent on the responses of others in the immediate situation, for it is these responses which the individual takes into account in defining the situation and organizes into his own behavior. Consequently, no two individuals, not even identical twins, could be expected to perceive and define all situations in precisely the same way. The assumption that, if persons have been reared in the same home and have had the same general experiences, their definitions should be uniform in all situations is naïve. Of course, however, greater similarity would be expected among such persons than among those having had dissimilar general experiences.

Some tend to attribute socialization primarily to early childhood, and particularly to experiences in the family. It is argued that, since the first experiences of the child with others are within the family group, trait structures arising there form the basis for the entire structure of personality. The evidence about this stability or the all-important emphasis on the family is not conclusive. Much of the research on personality to date

---

[49] For an application of these ideas as applied to delinquent and criminal behavior, see pp. 184–186.

has been concerned primarily with the family and has not taken sufficiently into account the play group and other influences which the child encounters in early life, particularly in street play in urban areas and in preschool and kindergarten activities.[50]

Even so-called *motives* are acquired as the result of social experience. They are socially molded, usually in accord with the prevailing norms of particular groups to which the individual belongs. For example, the possession of an automobile and the status it would give might be so important a goal to a delinquent boy that he would steal one. If his goals were directed toward a status based on higher grades in school or on some conventional hobby the end results would be different. Reference groups to which an individual belongs or from which he wishes to gain acceptance have an important bearing on the attitudes of a person. If the group is important to him he will often do everything demanded of him to secure or maintain acceptance. If a delinquent gang is important to him, a boy will do all he can to conform to the gang, whereas a boy in a Scout troop may have entirely different demands placed upon him. The negative attitudes of a group of teetotalers toward liquor may be as strong as the positive attitudes of a group of regular tavern patrons. Thus people tend to respond to the attitudes of the group to which they belong.

Persons appear to vary in their emphasis on given motives, depending on cultural and subcultural norms, the definition of the situation, and the life organization of the individual. In the process of reaching goals, deviants and nondeviants may adopt what might appear to be different patterns of behavior, but in reality they may be achieving similar goals in their own way. Some boys may have fun playing baseball or indulging in other sports, whereas others may find even more fun in stealing automobiles, slashing tires, wrecking a school, or beating up a stranger. Some may find companionship in a delinquent gang rather than in a Boy Scout troop; some people may prefer the fellowship of drinking companions in a tavern to the fellowship offered by a church. A young "punk" in a city slum may seek to gain a status of a far different kind from that sought by a college student. Some men would probably prefer to have the prestige and acclaim accorded them in an organized criminal syndicate or in professional crime than be president of a university. Businessmen and politicians have engaged in illegal behavior in order to secure funds with which to buy material goods which, in turn, bring them greater recognition in society.

---

[50] Likewise, research has not stressed experiences in later life as factors in personality orientation. Most studies of personality traits have been based on evidence derived from memories in which childhood experiences, particularly in the family, are likely to be recalled without their necessarily having much bearing on why a person acts as he does later in life.

Social roles weld themselves into a continuous pattern of behavior, referred to as *life organization*. Thus it is possible to speak of the life organization of a college professor, an alcoholic, a suicide, a professional criminal, or any person, whether he is deviant or nondeviant. This life organization is unique to each individual, although much may be derived from the general culture, subculture, and unique experiences. The life organization of some persons results in a well-integrated personality, whereas in that of others there may be conflicting elements. The life organization of some types of deviants is often well integrated, as is true of organized and professional criminals. Conflicts within the life organization, on the other hand, play an important part in the development of mental illness, alcoholism, or suicide. Such difficulties in life organization may develop when there are marked discrepancies between the person's appraisal of various situations and the interpretation by other persons of his behavior. This conflict may be seen in an individual who becomes mentally ill when faced with a variety of conflicting roles involving his parents, wife, wife's family, employer, and his own friends. Conflicts between role expectations and evaluation are also important in marital maladjustment.

Summary

The same fundamental processes are involved in deviant and nondeviant behavior. Differences in subprocesses exist; if they did not, there would be no way to account for deviant behavior. The biological structure of man is of little importance in accounting for deviant or nondeviant behavior. He does not have instincts which could account for such behavior. Deviant behavior cannot be inherited, and there is no evidence that glandular malfunctioning is involved in the great majority of cases. Physical defects do not distinguish the deviant from the nondeviant. Physical characteristics are not directly important, although they may have an indirect influence in some cases of deviant behavior.

It is the social rather than the physical nature of man which is important in studying deviant and nondeviant behavior. This includes attitudes, social roles, and life organization. The fact that man has language and a conception of self makes him different from other animals. Attitudes are important components of personality or behavior and are acquired primarily through relations with others. Attitudes are secured from primary and secondary groups and from unique experiences.

All persons play a variety of social roles which involve the way a person conceives of himself, the behavior he displays according to this conception, the roles acted out by others in response to his behavior, and his evaluation of his role. Deviants as well as nondeviants play social roles, and this fact must be understood in analyzing such behavior. The organization of social roles is called a person's life organization. A well-integrated life organization may characterize some deviants, whereas others may be the product of conflicting roles. Persons tend to define a given social situation in terms of past experiences.

Selected Readings

CAMERON, NORMAN. *The Psychology of Behavior Disorders.* Boston: Houghton Mifflin Company, 1947. An analysis of mental disorder primarily in terms of difficulties in role playing and self-conception.

CLINARD, MARSHALL B. "Criminal Behavior Is Human Behavior," *Federal Probation,* 13:21–26 (March, 1949). A discussion of the importance of considering criminal and noncriminal behavior within the same frame of reference and with the same concepts.

CRESSEY, DONALD R. *Other People's Money.* New York: The Free Press of Glencoe, 1953. This study is a sociopsychological analysis of embezzlement emphasizing particularly self-conception.

GOFFMAN, ERVING. *The Presentation of Self in Everyday Life.* New York: Doubleday Anchor Books, 1959. A discussion of the self and its importance in social interaction with others.

LEMERT, EDWIN H. *Social Pathology.* New York: McGraw-Hill Book Company, Inc., 1951, Chap. 4, "Sociopathic Individuation." This is an excellent application of the concept of social role to the study of deviant behavior.

LINDESMITH, ALFRED R. *Opiate Addiction.* Bloomington: University of Indiana Press, 1947. A sociopsychological interpretation of opiate addiction using many of the concepts presented here.

LINDESMITH, ALFRED R. and ANSELM L. STRAUSS. *Social Psychology.* Rev. ed. New York: Holt, Rinehart and Winston, Inc., 1955. Discusses human nature, language, the self, and social roles. Chapter 13, "Deviant Behavior," is a sociopsychological discussion of a number of areas.

SHIBUTANI, TOMATSU. *Society and Personality.* Englewood Cliffs, N.J.: Prentice-Hall, Inc., 1961. Discusses the fundamental processes and concepts involved in socialization. An unusually clear and interesting discussion of social behavior.

Chapter 3

Urbanization, Urbanism, and Deviant Behavior

City living has characterized some areas for centuries, but has spread with such acceleration over the past century as to encompass hundreds of millions of people throughout the entire world. This process of urban life has produced what some have called the "Mass Society." Urban life has greatly increased social differentiation, the clash of norms and social roles, and the breakdown in interpersonal relations among persons. Modern urban life has presented opportunities for the development of such a "way of life" on a tremendous scale.[1]

The Growth of World Urbanization

Cities first appeared in the Near East, in Mesopotamia, in the region between the Tigris and Euphrates rivers, about 3500 B.C.[2] A few centuries later they also appeared in the Nile Valley of Egypt and the valley of the Indus River, in what is now West Pakistan. The emergence of the earliest cities, according to Sjoberg, required (1) that the surrounding region have a climate and soil sufficiently favorable to support a large population, (2) relatively speaking, an advanced technology in both agricultural and non-agricultural spheres, and (3) a complex social organization, particularly in political and economic spheres.[3]

Thus cities have existed for thousands of years. Some cities, such as those of the Orient, were of considerable size. In general, however, only a small proportion of the people lived in them, as compared with urban populations today, and few cities had over 100,000 persons. Athens, at its

---

[1] Rose Hum Lee, *The City: Urbanism and Urbanization in Major World Regions* (Philadelphia: J. B. Lippincott Company, 1955). Also see special issue, "World Urbanism," *American Journal of Sociology*, Vol. 60 (March, 1955), and Nels Anderson, *The Urban Community* (New York: Holt, Rinehart and Winston, Inc., 1959).

[2] Gideon Sjoberg, *The Preindustrial City: Past and Present* (New York: The Free Press of Glencoe, 1960), pp. 25–51. Also see Kingsley Davis, "The Origin and Growth of Urbanization in the World," *American Journal of Sociology*, 40:429–437 (March, 1955).

[3] Sjoberg, *op. cit.*, p. 27.

peak in the fifth century B.C., was estimated to have had between 120,000 and 180,000 persons; Rome had several hundred thousand; Florence in 1338, 90,000; and London in 1377, 30,000.[4]

Life in the large cities of several hundred years ago, both in Europe and in the Orient, was quite different from life in the same cities today. There were no forms of rapid or extensive communication and transportation, nor were there the means of distribution and preservation of food which modern inventions have made possible. Consequently, cities, even though large, tended to be actually clusters of villages. Urban populations were much more permanent and settled than they are today, there was less migration into the cities from rural areas, and because of this and because of the absence of media of mass communication as we have them today, people were able to know one another much better than they do now.

In 1800 only about 3 percent of the world's estimated population of 906 million lived in places of more than 5000 persons. By 1950 this percentage had increased to about 30 percent. Whereas the world population had increased by nearly 165 percent during these one hundred and fifty years, the urban population of the world had risen by 2535 percent to what has been termed not merely a population explosion but a world "urban explosion." In 1800 the proportion of the world's population living in cities of 20,000 or more was 2.4; in 1950 it was 20.9 percent.[5] Cities of 100,000 or more were 1.7 percent of the total world population in 1800; in 1950 they were 13.1. In 1800 there were fewer than 50 cities in the entire world with 100,000 or more inhabitants and none with a million persons, a figure which is smaller than the number of cities in the million class today.

The increase in the proportion of urban population in the underdeveloped areas of the world, such as those in South America, Africa, and Asia, has been particularly great. In India, for example, which is thought of as a rural nation, 8.2 percent of the population in 1941 lived in cities of 20,000 or more, whereas in 1961, 17.8 percent lived in cities of that size. This amounts to over 75,000,000 urban persons in India in 1961, or a number larger than the population of most countries of the world. Only 2 Indian cities had over a million population in 1941; by 1961 there were 6, and Davis estimates that by 1970 there will be 10.[6] In 1951 there were 77 cities with 100,000 or more persons; in 1961 there were 121.

Australia leads the world in the proportion of its population living in cities of 100,000 or more. (See Table 3.1.) The United Kingdom with 51.0, Japan with 41.2, and Argentina with 39.5 percent follow in that

[4] Davis, "Origin and Growth of Urbanization," loc. cit.   [5] Ibid.
[6] Kingsley Davis, "Urbanization in India: Past and Future," in Roy Turner ed., India's Urban Future (Berkeley: University of California Press, 1962), p. 25.

order. The United States has 28.4 percent of its population living in cities of this size.

Table 3.1. Estimated Proportion of Population Living in Cities of 100,000 or More

Country	Percent
Australia (1959)	57.4
United Kingdom (1958)	51.0
Japan (1959)	41.2
Argentina (1958)	39.5
Israel (1959)	34.3
Denmark (1958)	34.2
West Germany (1959)	30.7
United States (1960)	28.4
Union of South Africa (1960)	25.4
Sweden (1959)	24.7
Italy (1959)	23.9
USSR (1959)	23.5
United Arab Republic (1958)	22.2
Brazil (1959)	17.6
France (1954)	16.8
Indonesia (1959)	9.4
Ghana (1960)	7.3
India (1951)	6.6
Congo (1959)	5.9
Burma (1958)	5.3

SOURCE: Prepared from *United Nations Demographic Yearbook, 1960* (New York: 1960).

The number of large cities in the major regions of the world is shown in Table 3.2. In 1950, there were over nine hundred cities of 100,000 or more persons and over forty-nine cities with more than a million inhabitants. Twenty percent of the world's population lived in cities of 20,000 or more, and 13 percent in cities of 100,000 or over. Asia has the largest number of cities with a population of 1 million and over. According to 1960 estimates, Tokyo is the largest city in the world, with nearly 10 million persons, or one in ten persons in Japan.

Behind this growth of modern urbanization, particularly in the Western European world, have been many forces which can only be listed here: the breakdown of the feudal system with its loss of prescribed duties and obligations and integrated way of village life; the Commercial and later the Industrial Revolution, which produced a wide dispersion of the population, particularly to cities; the development of the factory system of production, and extensive occupational differences; the development of science, which brought a secular way of life by destroying many age-old traditions of thought, also produced new forms of transportation as well as improvements in agriculture so that millions of people were freed from immediate dependence on the land, and enabled to work and live in cities. The virtual disappearance of the large family and with it the loss of many family functions and responsibilities further weakened the ties of family members to the land. All these forces produced drastic changes in the interpersonal relations of those who moved to cities.

Table 3.2. Cities over 100,000 Population in Major Regions of the World, 1950

Area	1,000,000 and over	500,000 to 1,000,000	250,000 to 500,000	100,000 to 250,000	Total cities over 100,000
Africa	1	3	6	27	37
Asia (excludes USSR) (includes Near East)	20	22	43	178	263
Europe	14	28	46	187	364
USSR (1939 figures)	2	9	20	58	89
North America	7	15	27	91	140
Oceania	2		3	5	10
South America	3	4	11	26	44
Total	49	81	156	572	947

SOURCE: Rose Hum Lee, *The City: Urbanism and Urbanization in Major World Regions* (Philadelphia: J. B. Lippincott Company, 1955), p. 55. Data secured by Lee from *United Nations Demographic Yearbook, 1952*, Table 8, pp. 202–214.

Also essential for this growth of modern cities are more specific conditions. The level of agricultural production must be sufficiently high to provide a surplus which will allow people to concentrate in areas for non-agricultural production. Sources of power, such as coal, electricity, or oil, are also necessary to provide large concentrations of persons with the means of industrial production. Electricity, for example, has become essential not only in such production but as part of mass communication through the telephone, radio, and television.

Urbanization in the United States

The United States, following the Civil War, changed from a society of rural communities to one of the most urbanized in the world. So rapid and extensive has been this urbanization that it is now possible to refer to America as an "urban society." As Table 3.4 shows, in 1790 only 5.1 percent of the population lived in cities. By 1880 this proportion had increased to 28.2 and in 1920 approximately half the people were urban. Using a slightly different definition, in 1950 the urban population of the United States was 64 percent of the total, and in 1960, 69.9. In 1960 this amounted to 125,268,750 persons. In nine states the percentage of urban population exceeds 75: in order they are New Jersey, Rhode Island, New York, Massachusetts, Illinois, Connecticut, Hawaii, and Texas.

Perhaps even more drastic has been the increase in the United States in the number of places with 2500 population or over—from 236 in 1850 to 2262 in 1910. By 1940 this figure had increased to 3464, and by 1950 to 4284, although the latter figure represented, in part, a change in the definition of an urban place. The number of cities, however, gives no idea of the increasing concentration of population in and around a small number of places. The 132 cities of 100,000 persons and over contained more than one fourth (28.4 percent) of the total population of the United States in 1960. One out of ten Americans lives in a city of one millon or more. A measure of urbanization, namely "urbanized areas," which includes cities with a population of 50,000 or more and those persons residing in certain contiguous areas which are not part of the city, is now used. The fourteen largest urbanized areas in the United States in 1960 are shown in Table 3.3.

Table 3.3. The Fourteen Largest Urbanized Areas in the United States

Area	Population in millions
New York—northeastern New Jersey	14.1
Los Angeles—Long Beach area	6.5
Chicago—northwestern Indiana	6.0
Philadelphia—New Jersey area	3.6
Detroit	3.5
San Francisco—Oakland area	2.4
Boston	2.4
Washington–Md.–Va.	1.8
Pittsburgh	1.8
Cleveland	1.8
St. Louis, Mo.–Ill.	1.7
Baltimore	1.4
Minneapolis—St. Paul	1.4
Milwaukee	1.1

SOURCE: *United States Census of Population, 1960. Summary of Number of Inhabitants* (Washington, D.C.: Bureau of the Census, 1961), pp. 1–50.

Slightly more than one half of the total, and more than three fourths of the urban, population of the United States in 1960 was living in 213 urbanized areas. Of the 95.8 million persons living in urbanized areas, 58.0 million lived in the 254 central cities and 37.8 million lived in the urban-fringe area outside the city. The 16 urbanized areas with more than 1 million inhabitants had a combined population of 51.7 million, or more than half of the 213 urbanized areas.

Table 3.4. Growth of the Urban Population in the United States,
1790–1960

Year	Percent urban	Percent rural
1790	5.1	94.9
1800	6.1	93.9
1810	7.3	92.7
1820	7.2	92.8
1830	8.8	91.2
1840	10.8	89.2
1850	15.3	84.7
1860	19.8	80.2
1870	25.7	74.3
1880	28.2	71.8
1890	35.1	64.9
1900	39.7	60.3
1910	45.7	54.3
1920	51.2	48.8
1930	56.2	43.8
1940	56.5	43.5
1950	64.0	36.0
1960	69.9	30.1

SOURCE: *United States Census of Population, 1960. Summary of Number of Inhabitants* (Washington: Bureau of the Census, 1961), pp. 1–4. The definition of "urban" changed in 1950, so that the comparable figure for that year was 59.6, and in 1960, 63.1.

Urbanism as a Way of Life

The growth of modern cities has meant the development of a way of life much different from that of the rural world. Urbanism as a way of life is often characterized by extensive conflicts of norms and values, by rapid social change, by increased mobility of the population, by emphasis on material goods and individualism, and by a marked decline in intimate communication.[7] The relation of these factors to the size, density, and heterogeneity of an urban area can be seen in the schematic presentation in Table 3.5.

[7] See Louis Wirth, "Urbanism as a Way of Life," *American Journal of Sociology,* 44:1–24 (July, 1938). Wirth's statement was based in part on Georg Simmel, "The Metropolis and Mental Life," in Paul K. Hatt and Albert J. Reiss, Jr. eds., *Reader in Urban Sociology* (New York: The Free Press of Glencoe, 1951), pp. 563–574; Robert E. Park, *The City* (Chicago: The University of Chicago Press, 1925); Anderson, *op. cit.;* and Kingsley Davis, H. C. Bredemeier, and Marion J. Levy, Jr. eds., *Modern American Society* (New York: Holt, Rinehart and Winston, Inc., 1949). Other terms, such as "mass society" or "secular," have been used which in general reflect the same process. For a discussion of secular societies, see Howard Becker, *Man in Reciprocity* (New York: Frederick A. Praeger, Inc., 1956), pp. 169–197.

Table 3.5 Schematic Version of Urbanism as a Way of Life

Size An increase in the number of inhabitants of a settlement beyond a certain limit brings about changes in the relations of people and changes in the character of the community	Greater the number of people interacting, greater the potential differentiation (mobility). Dependence upon a greater number of people, lesser dependence on particular persons. Association with more people, knowledge of a smaller proportion, and of these, less intimate knowledge. More secondary rather than primary contacts—increase in contacts which are face to face, yet impersonal, superficial, transitory, and segmental. More freedom from personal and emotional control of intimate groups. Association in a large number of groups, no individual allegiance to a single group.
Density Reinforces the effect of size in diversifying men and their activities, and in increasing the structural complexity of the society.	Tendency to differentiation and specialization. Separation of residence from work place. Functional specialization of areas—segregation of functions. Segregation of people: city becomes a mosaic social world.
Heterogeneity Cities products of migration of peoples of diverse origin. Heterogeneity of origin matched by heterogeneity of occupants. Differentiation and specialization reinforces heterogeneity	Without common background and common activities premium is placed on visual recognition: the uniform becomes symbolic of the role. No common set of norms and values, no common ethical system to sustain them; money tends to become measure of all things for which there are no common standards. Formal controls as opposed to informal controls. Necessity for adhering to predictable routines. Clock and the traffic signal symbolic of the basis of the social order. Economic basis: mass production of goods, possible only with the standardization of processes and product. Standardization of goods and facilities in terms of the average. Adjustment of educational, recreational, and cultural services to mass requirements. In politics, success of mass appeals—growth of mass movements.

SOURCE: Schematic version by E. Shevky and W. Bell, *Social Area Analysis* (Stanford, Calif.: Stanford University Press, 1955), pp. 7–8, derived from Louis Wirth, "Urbanism as a Way of Life," *American Journal of Sociology*, 44:1–24 (July, 1938). Copyright 1938 by The University of Chicago.

Cities vary in the extent or degree to which they are characterized by urban qualities. Some cities have much less norm conflict, social change, mobility, individualism, and impersonality than others. Likewise, great variations in such characteristics often exist among local areas of a given city. Moreover, certain cultural values in a society may increase the effects of urbanization. If a culture emphasizes material possessions as a central value, the impersonality of urban life will tend to increase that emphasis. Furthermore, in a culture where people are formal in their behavior and where the people are, as a cultural pattern, more self-contained, the impact of urban life may further intensify impersonality in relationships.

All too frequently the shortcomings of urban life are emphasized. Cities have several advantages over rural areas. Certainly they have been the centers of industrial production and distribution and as such have contributed much to higher standards of living. Cities, to a greater degree than rural areas, have been centers for inventions and the modification of cultural patterns. This is partly due to the anonymity of the city and its diversity of cultural patterns which provide more freedom for creative thought than do rural areas. As a result, artistic and intellectual centers have developed in many larger cities. Cities have also been the centers of great public health advances, particularly in sanitation and the prevention of disease. In fact, without good sanitation it would be difficult for many cities to exist. City living, as a way of life, is associated with many aspects of "civilization."

> What we call civilization as distinguished from culture has been cradled in the city; the city is the center from which the influences of modern civilized life radiate to the ends of the earth and the point from which they are controlled; the persistent problems of contemporary society take their most acute form in the city. The problems of modern civilization are typically urban problems.[8]

City living does not, of course, directly result in deviant behavior, but many of the conditions associated with city life are, to a preponderant degree, conducive to deviation.[9] It should be kept in mind, however, that the set of variables associated with the concept of urbanism may be found independent of city environments. In other words, "urbanism" is not synonymous with "city." Whereas "city" refers to an area distinguished principally by population size, density, and heterogeneity, "urbanism" refers to a complex of social relationships. Although urbanism may more fre-

---

[8] Louis Wirth, "The Urban Society and Civilization," *American Journal of Sociology*, 45:744 (March, 1940).

[9] For a discussion of rural and urban ways of life and the manner in which they may lead toward or away from various forms of deviation, see Eleanor Leacock, "Three Social Variables and Mental Illness," in Alexander H. Leighton, John A. Clausen, and Robert N. Wilson eds., *Explorations in Social Psychiatry* (New York: Basic Books, Inc., 1957), pp. 308–338.

quently arise within city environments, this does not mean that it is limited to them. Rural areas are also becoming "urbanized" as their way of life is experiencing such changes. Some of these changes represent the spread of behavior patterns emanating from cities, but much of the change in rural areas has come about as the result of new relations among people who live in these areas. Some of the conditions of an urban way of life will be discussed in the following sections.[10]

NORM AND SOCIAL ROLE CONFLICTS

A major characteristic of urbanism is the diversity of interests and backgrounds of persons who at the same time live in close contact with one another. People living in urban communities vary in age, race, ethnic background, occupation, interests, attitudes, and values. Moreover, urban life is characterized by contrasts in wealth, abilities, and class structure. "Cities generally, and American cities in particular, comprise a motley of peoples and cultures, of highly differentiated modes of life between which there is often only the faintest communication, the greatest indifference and the broadest tolerance, occasionally bitter strife, but always the sharpest contrast." [11] Large cities, in particular, have generally been cities within cities in the form of areas with subcultures, religious affiliations, or racial characteristics. These are often groups with different customs as well as separate languages. Although in the United States there is the idea that eventually these will disappear as separate areas, in cities in other parts of the world the existence of such diverse areas has been, and is often expected to continue as, a "natural" part of city existence.

Urban life attracts people with varying values and ideologies, and it also fosters the growth of differences. Because of the greater density of the population and increased mobility, individuals under urban conditions are exposed to a great variety of social contacts. Media of mass communication, such as the newspaper, radio, and television, constantly bring individuals in an urban world into contact with divergent ideologies. Furthermore, the relative impersonality of city life permits the development of special-interest groups, whether a racketeering political machine or a Society for the Prevention of Cruelty to Animals.

The heterogeneity of the population, the complex division of labor, and the class structure existing in the larger communities generally result in divergent group norms and values and conflicting social roles. In

---

[10] See Charles T. Stewart, Jr., "The Urban and Rural Dichotomy: Concepts and Uses," *American Journal of Sociology*, 64:152–158 (September, 1958) and Richard Dewey, "The Rural–Urban Continuum: Real but Relatively Unimportant," *American Journal of Sociology*, 66:60–66 (July, 1960). Also see Paul Hatt and Albert J. Reiss, Jr. eds., *Cities and Society* (New York: The Free Press of Glencoe, Inc., 1957), especially pages 35–45, and Anderson, *op. cit.*

[11] Wirth, "Urbanism as a Way of Life," *loc. cit.*, p. 20.

modern urban societies, so differentiated and so conflicting have become the ends sought by different groups that individuals are often in the position of not knowing in many areas of life exactly what are the conventional ways of behaving and the proper social roles. Persons who are conventional in their sexual behavior live alongside those who are sexually promiscuous. The city harbors those who respect the law and are honest in most of their social relationships as well as those who have little respect for laws, officials, or property. Variations exist in religious beliefs, family systems, and the means of achieving satisfying human relationships.

At the same time the impersonality of urban life tends to foster increased individual freedom. This freedom in a mass society, as Rose has pointed out, means that "there are fewer standards to which the individual must conform and the concepts of 'right' and 'good' are relative. To an individual without the training to make up his mind on such ethical matters, or the strength of character to conform to standards which he thinks proper, freedom may be demoralizing." [12]

Norm and role conflicts, or diversities of norms and behavioral standards, create a situation where no single standard is likely to be upheld and where deviation from it is not met with penalizing sanctions. Individuals who have been taught to accept the supremacy of a single rule may become skeptical of its validity when they discover, under urban conditions, that breaking the rule does not bring about social ostracism or censure as supposed.

RAPID CULTURAL CHANGE

Rapid social and cultural change, disregard for the importance of stability of generations, and untempered loyalties also generally characterize urban life. New ideas are generally welcome, inventions of mechanical gadgets are encouraged, and new styles in such arts as painting, literature, and music are often approved. Becker has characterized urban society as a secular one or "one in which resistance to change is at a minimum or, to say the very least, where change in many aspects of life is quite welcome." [13] Consequently, elements which are traditional, or "sacred," dwindle in importance and "cynicism with reference to the alleged values of contending groups and skepticism with reference to the alleged truths have become marks characteristic of the modern [urban] sophisticated man." [14]

Urban life itself also tends to facilitate changes in norms and ideol-

[12] Arnold Rose, "The Problem of a Mass Society," in Arnold Rose, *Theory and Methods in the Social Sciences* (Minneapolis: University of Minnesota Press, 1954), p. 37.

[13] Howard Becker, *Through Values to Social Interpretation* (Durham, N.C.: Duke University Press, 1950), p. 67.

[14] Louis Wirth, "Ideological Aspects of Social Disorganization," *American Sociological Review*, 5:482 (August, 1940).

ogies, as well as systems of behavior, which may greatly alter the nature of the social structure and the relationships of people to one another. Sometimes these changes appear to result partly from the practical exigencies of urban life; at other times they seem to be outgrowths of the failure of informal controls to uphold and maintain the older values and ideologies. Urban living has brought such great changes in the modern family, for example, that it has come to be called the urban family. The reduced size of the modern family has been both a characteristic and a result of urban life. Urban life has developed the concept of the equality of the sexes in marriage, a concept which has caused considerable conflict with rural definitions of family roles. The structuring of urban society into often fairly distinct peer groups has resulted in the magnification of age differences and the widening of the gap between teen-age persons and older generations. Likewise, the emphasis on youthful values in urban life has meant that as people grow older they are faced with new definitions of roles which may necessitate considerable readjustment.

MOBILITY

An urban population exhibits considerable horizontal and vertical mobility. Horizontal mobility involves physical movement in connection with occupation and other activities, or it may mean change of residence within a community or to another. Vertical mobility involves changes in occupational and social status.

Modern transportation, particularly in urban areas, enables persons to move about rapidly and to come into frequent contact with many different people. It has been said that less than a century ago a man might live a lifetime without ever going far from his home, and without seeing more than a handful of strangers.

One writer has stated that speed is the most common characteristic of urban life.[15] Time has become an extremely important factor, and it is seldom possible for urbanites to relax. Transportation, job, meetings, recreation, home—all move in response to the clock. Even children learn to hurry at an early age. They must get to school on time, be dismissed on the minute, and head toward home on some sort of transportation which often leaves "on the dot." When they arrive home they rush out to play and then run home to dinner. "In spite of many time-saving gadgets and devices invented to leave more and more minutes free from some drudgery or operation, the urban day is still too short." [16]

Figures of the United States Census Bureau reveal how frequently families move in contemporary society. Less than 2 percent of the adult population in 1952 could be called "old-timers" in their communities in

---

[15] Lee, op. cit., p. 459.   [16] Ibid.

that they had always lived in their present homes. The number of persons who move each year is approximately one in five. Each year about 30 million persons move (see Table 3.6), and of this number about 5

Table 3.6. Internal Migration in the United States

Year	Total number of persons	Persons moving their home Within same state	From one state to another
1948–49	27,127,000	22,783,000	4,344,000
1949–50	27,526,000	23,637,000	3,889,000
1950–51	31,158,000	25,970,000	5,188,000
1951–52	29,840,000	24,728,000	5,112,000
1952–53	30,786,000	25,264,000	5,522,000
1953–54	29,027,000	23,993,000	5,034,000
1954–55	31,492,000	26,597,000	4,895,000
1955–56	33,098,000	28,045,000	5,053,000
1956–57	31,834,000	26,758,000	5,076,000
1957–58	33,263,000	27,679,000	5,584,000

SOURCE: U.S. Bureau of the Census, *Current Population Reports; Population Characteristics.* October 13, 1958, Series P-20, No. 85, pp. 8–9.

million cross county lines. Another 5,000,000 move across state lines. Two out of five move across regional lines as well, many of them one or two thousand miles. Younger persons are more mobile than older persons; yet a large number of persons age sixty-five and over also move. During the years 1951–1952, 38 percent of those between twenty and twenty-four changed their places of residence, and the proportion was almost as great for those between twenty-five and twenty-nine. Nearly 9 percent of those sixty-five and over changed their residence during this period.

Although urban societies generally tend to regard mobility favorably, such frequent moves may have unsatisfactory effects. They tend to weaken attachments to the local community, particularly among primary or face-to-face contacts, to make persons less interested in maintaining certain community standards, and to increase contact with secondary groups of diverse patterns, "thus weakening the bonds which provide the basis for social control among members of local groups." [17] As a person becomes more mobile he comes into contact with many different norms and comes to understand that other codes of behavior are different from his own. Mobility often means the loss of personal relationships, such as kinship ties, neighbors, and close friendships. For child and adult alike, it may be

[17] Paul H. Landis, *Rural Life in Process* (New York: McGraw-Hill Book Company, Inc., 1940), p. 320.

necessary to acquire new friends and new norms, to change social roles, and to reconcile old norms and roles with new ones.

As close relations with neighbors and relatives are severed, there is less control over the mobile person's behavior and a decline in the importance to him of having a "good reputation" in the eyes of these persons. Too, the standards by which reputation is judged may become more diverse and may depend less upon the specific ethical and moral qualities of the person than upon the "general impression" of him as a person. Children may have increasingly fewer contacts with their grandparents and other relatives. Largely because of this mobility it is likely that a large proportion of young people today, living under urban conditions in America, cannot give the names of great-grandparents on either side of the family. The identification of third cousins usually becomes impossible.

As an illustration of the role mobility may play in some types of criminal behavior, in a study of farm, village, and city offenders in Iowa and in a replication of this study in Iowa and one in Sweden, mobility was found to play an important part in the development of criminal behavior.[18] Those from rural areas were found to have had extensive contacts with persons outside their home communities. This mobility, as measured by changes in residence and the frequency of outside contacts, was greater than that of a group of nonoffenders from the same area. It was also greater than that of their parents.

MATERIALISM

External appearances and material possessions become of primary importance in an urban society, where people are more often known for their gadgets than for themselves. People increasingly come to judge others by how well they display their wealth, a display which Veblen has called "conspicuous consumption." Under urban conditions the type of clothes a man wears or the automobile he drives, the costliness of his home and its furnishings, the exclusiveness of the club or association to which he belongs, and the knowledge of his salary or the amount of his financial assets are often the sole means others have of judging him or his success in life. It is on the basis of readily "visible" criteria such as these that status is assigned. Some persons emphasize the importance of "status symbols" in urban society.[19]

---

[18] Marshall B. Clinard, "The Process of Urbanization and Criminal Behavior," *American Journal of Sociology*, 48:202–213 (September, 1942). Also see his "Rural Criminal Offenders," *American Journal of Sociology*, 50:38–45 (July, 1944) and his "A Cross-Cultural Replication of the Relation of Urbanism to Criminal Behavior," *American Sociological Review*, 25:253–257 (April, 1960). Also see Harold D. Eastman, "The Process of Urbanization and Criminal Behavior: A Restudy of Culture Conflict." Unpublished doctoral thesis, University of Iowa, Iowa City, 1954.

[19] See Erving Goffman, *The Presentation of Self in Everyday Life* (Edinburgh: University of Edinburgh Social Science Research Center, 1956), especially Chap. 1. Also see Vance Packard, *The Hidden Persuaders* (New York: Pocket Books, Inc., 1958).

INDIVIDUALISM

In modern urban societies two almost contradictory trends are taking place which affect the position of the individual. On the one hand, the focus is on the individual, as urban persons have more and more come to regard their own interests as paramount in their social relationships.[20] Thus "I" feelings come to replace much of the cooperation characteristic of rural life. People feel that they must look after their own interests and increase their status through their own efforts. The urban person's strong belief in hedonism or personal happiness as the goal of life is increasingly reflected, for example, in modern marriage, the function of which is thought to be primarily personal happiness, all other functions being regarded as subordinate.

As individualism in urban society has increased, competition has also been intensified. Each individual may feel that he is in ceaseless competition with the remainder of society, or at least with that part of the society in which he operates. The intensity with which the goals are striven for is, generally, in proportion to the values attached to them and the extent to which they can satisfy socially induced needs of the individual.

The role of this individual competition in modern urban societies is difficult to evaluate. Ordinary competition has many favorable aspects. Where it is fair it minimizes such factors as favoritism, prejudice, or other bias in the struggle for status in social life. Competition can also serve as an important dynamic force for production, as laboratory experiments have shown. Competition can also, on the other hand, make the desire to achieve social status through the acquisition of wealth and other means assume an importance out of all relation to other factors. It often condemns the loser to a feeling of failure and frustration or it may force him to resort to unconventional methods of achieving status. One psychiatrist has pointed out the effect of competition in the development of mental illness: "Some of our mental breakdowns are caused by the kind of society in which we live—a highly competitive society in which there are few winners and many losers. Everyone is in competition with everyone else—not only for economic gain, but for esteem, love, respect, and recognition." [21]

On the other hand, there is a contrary stress in the modern urban world away from this type of individualism and aptly referred to by

---

[20] There is much emphasis on individualism within contemporary economic, political, religious, and philosophical thinking. This individualism is also related to the Protestant Reformation, the seventeenth- and eighteenth-century political revolutions of England, America, and France, and the development of the American frontier. For some examples see Abbott P. Herman, "Our Values of Individualism," in *An Approach to Social Problems* (Boston: Ginn and Company, 1949), Chap. 8.

[21] George Thorman, "Toward Mental Health" (No. 120; New York: Public Affairs Pamphlets 1946), pp. 19–20.

Riesman as "The Lonely Crowd." [22] According to him, there are three types of personalities in modern societies, each one "directed" in a different way. The "tradition-directed" type almost unthinkingly conforms to the norms of his culture. "Inner-directed" persons have some degree of independence in their actions. Regardless of conflicts with society, such individuals do not necessarily follow what others do but try to ignore the environment or shape it to fit their needs. The third type is what might be thought of as the modern urban type of personality, who loses his individuality and constantly follows the dictates of others. He wishes to conform and to be like others, and consequently becomes what Riesman has termed an "other-directed" person, his actions being directed not by himself but by others.

Decline in Intimate Communication and Modification of Mechanisms of Informal Social Control

Central to the problem of urbanization is the decline in intimate communication among the members of society. Urbanized areas, particularly those where the population is dense and mobile, tend to create an extensive area of impersonality for their residents. Associations among people are not so much on the basis of knowing each other's total personality as acquaintance with particular social roles. Human beings tend to be regarded categorically much as other physical objects, often to be "manipulated" without much feeling and, primarily, for personal satisfaction. Most urban associations with people are brief and fragmentary, and tend to be stereotyped because of the impossibility of dealing with each association individually. Max Weber suggested that density and the presence of large numbers of persons decrease the possibility of mutual acquaintanceships between individuals.[23]

Although a person meets many people face to face in his daily contacts, these contacts in the city are, nevertheless, often "impersonal, superficial, transitory, and segmental." [24] The urban world is one of anonymity where there are few ties or interests to bind a person to others. Urban conditions generally do not provide means for getting psychologically "close" to other persons, and the so-called blasé, sophisticated attitude of many big-city dwellers represents in part a way of protecting their privacy from the intrusions of others. When they encounter difficulties in their inter-

---

[22] David Riesman, *The Lonely Crowd: A Study of Changing American Character* (New Haven, Conn.: Yale University Press, 1950).

[23] Max Weber, *Wirtschaft und Gesellschaft* (Tübingen, Germany: Mohr, 1925), Pt. II, p. 514.

[24] Wirth, "Urbanism as a Way of Life," *loc. cit.*, p. 12. There is often a tendency to overlook the fact that intimate contacts may exist in a city. See, for example, William F. Whyte, *Street Corner Society* (Chicago: The University of Chicago Press, 1943).

personal relations they consequently must often turn to professional counselors or psychiatrists. In many of the transitory relationships encountered,
the only things of interest are those directly pertaining to the situation; for
example, whether a man will "stand" for a round of drinks, is a "good
talker," or has a new car or some new and expensive gadget. This has
helped to produce the loneliness of the urban world so well described by
Auden:

> . . . This stupid world where
> Gadgets are gods and we go on talking,
> Many about much, but remain alone,
> Alive but alone, belonging—where?—
> Unattached as tumbleweed.[25]

This decline in close personal relations is reflected in contemporary
American films about urban life where the hero and heroine are usually
not identified with strong family ties and often are even without any strong
attachments.[26] This is in marked contrast to the close personal contacts of
the less urbanized small town where the townspeople may know large
numbers of people by name or sight and know many of them even intimately.[27] Generally speaking, under the urban conditions of a larger city
a person may be "acquainted" with many more people than he would
under rural conditions, but a rural person may "know" more people intimately than does an urban individual.

Whereas "anonymity" is virtually impossible in a rural society, it
is the "norm" in a predominantly urban society. This is why, in the
absence of intimate personal acquaintances, a person's status and character are judged by others from his "self-presentation," or the external
indices of that self. Thus symbols of wealth, sophistication, or other
forms of influence are of special significance to urban society.[28]

Many of those who migrate to our larger cities pride themselves on the
fact that "Now, thank God, I don't *have* to know my neighbors, go to Rotary,
belong to a church, or participate in an annual Community Chest drive!" And
the big city does little to disabuse them of this attitude. Individuals can and
do live comfortably in our large cities with no formal ties between themselves
and the structures of the culture save the money tie between them and their

---

[25] W. H. Auden, *The Age of Anxiety* (New York: Random House, 1946), p. 44.
Reprinted by permission of the publisher.

[26] Martha Wolfenstein and Nathan Leites, *Movies: A Psychological Study* (New
York: The Free Press of Glencoe, 1950).

[27] Albert Blumenthal, *Small-Town Stuff* (Chicago: The University of Chicago Press,
1932). For example, in Mineville the average person knew nine tenths of the townspeople by sight or name and a large number intimately.

[28] See Goffman, *op. cit.* for a discussion of the way in which personal impressions
are formed in a mass society. See also C. Wright Mills, *The Power Elite* (New York:
Oxford University Press, 1956), especially pp. 71-93, for a discussion of "elites" (high-
status persons) in modern society.

jobs. One may or may not elect to exercise one's political right to vote; one may or may not own property, marry, or belong with anybody else to anything; but one must tie into the structure to the extent of getting money regularly. . . .

Urban folk delay marriage and in some cases elect not to marry; and kinship ties are narrowing and attenuating. Citizenship ties are weakening in our urban world to the point that they are largely neglected by large masses of people. Neighborhood and community ties are not only optional but generally growing less strong; and along with them is disappearing the important network of intimate, informal social controls traditionally associated with living closely with others.[29]

Generally speaking, where intimate group participation languishes, the incidence of social deviation is high.[30] Others have suggested that the breakdown of intimate communication in an urban society lies at the center of social problems in that the individual finds that he cannot easily communicate with his fellows and thus cannot orient his own values or put himself into harmony with the group.[31]

It has been said that as urbanism has increased, as man's behavior has become more individual, competitive, and materialistic, and as his conformity to social norms has become less affected by informal group controls, greater opportunities and inducements appear to develop for behavior which deviates from accepted norms.

Urban Characteristics a Matter of Degree

The description of the characteristics of the urban way of life which has been presented here should be considered only as an abstract ideal type which can be compared with the characteristics of rural society. It does not mean that the life of all persons in a city is so characterized. One may have considerable personal relationships, for example, with others in a city. Limited studies have shown that primary group life survives in urban areas and is effective over considerable segments. For example, a Detroit study of family patterns found that neighborliness was widespread, with about 75 percent reporting that they got together with neighbors as well as with relatives; 55 percent got together with "other friends" once or twice a week or a few times each month.[32] In addition, only 11 percent had no relatives at all in the Detroit area, and 54 percent

[29] Robert S. Lynd, *Knowledge for What?* (rev. ed.; Princeton, N.J.: Princeton University Press, 1946), p. 83.

[30] Stuart A. Queen and Jeannette Gruener, *Social Pathology: Obstacles to Social Participation* (rev. ed.; New York: Thomas Y. Crowell Company, 1948).

[31] Rose, *op. cit.*, p. 25.

[32] Cited in Harold L. Wilensky and Charles N. Lebeaux, *Industrial Society and Social Welfare* (New York: Russell Sage Foundation, 1958), p. 122. Also see Whyte, *op. cit.* Sjoberg has stated that preindustrial cities of underdeveloped countries do not have as much of the characteristics of urbanism. While there is a difference in degree,

saw one or more related units of the family once or twice a week. Other studies in Chicago have shown that customer-clerk relations in smaller city stores can be quite intimate.[33]

As one study has suggested, the role of mobility and impersonality in urban life should not be overstated either in the local community or in the factory and other work situations.

> Whatever the mobility of the population, intimate contacts with relatives, neighbors, and friends are a universal feature of urban life at home and in the local community (as indeed they were in an earlier day among the Little Polands and Little Sicilies of the slum). Such contacts are also a universal feature of life at work. Even in the huge workplace where many thousands mass for the daily routine, the informal workgroup seems destined to go on performing its usual functions of controlling the workpace, initiating new members, deciding how far to go along with the boss, and making work a bit more like play. There is no evidence that human relations are any more atomized at work than in the local community and neighborhood, though the liveliness of informal groups may, of course, vary from place to place.[34]

Although the life of suburbia has been described among the young upwardly mobile middle class as often a transient superficial life,[35] others have pointed out that areas with single-family dwellings, particularly those with more factory workers, have considerable stability in their family life and local community relations.[36] Even where people move within the city some retain active friendships over the city in neighborhoods where they once lived. "Spatial mobility makes for city-wide ties; stability makes for local area ties; and most urban residents have both." [37]

Certainly a degree of intimate life does exist in any city, in both the local community and the work place, but it is not anywhere near the same as it is in the villages or rural areas. Moreover, in the city a person experiences almost daily large areas of impersonal relations where his personal identity is not recognized. To admit the need for exercising caution in order to avoid overstating the universal presence of urban characteristics does not minimize, however, their importance as a framework for understanding much of contemporary life and deviant behavior.

---

the characteristics of an urban way of life can be found in cities like those of India. See Marshall B. Clinard and B. Chatterjee, "Urban Community Development in India: the Delhi Pilot Project" in Turner, *India's Urban Future*, pp. 71–93.

[33] Gregory P. Stone, "City Shoppers and Urban Identification: Observations on the Social Psychology of City Life," *American Journal of Sociology*, 60:36–45 (July, 1954).

[34] Wilensky and Lebeaux, *op. cit.*, p. 124.

[35] See William F. Whyte, Jr., *The Organization Man* (New York: Simon and Schuster, Inc., 1956).

[36] Flint City—Fringe Survey. Social Science Research Project, University of Michigan, Ann Arbor, 1955, as cited in Wilensky and Lebeaux, *op. cit.*, pp. 126–127.

[37] Joel Smith, William H. Form, and Gregory P. Stone, "Local Intimacy in a Middle-Sized City," *American Journal of Sociology*, 60:284 (November, 1954). See also Peter H. Rossi, *Why Families Move: A Study in the Social Psychology of Urban Residential Mobility* (New York: The Free Press of Glencoe, 1956).

The discussion to this point has been in terms of the world-wide growth of urbanization and the development of urbanism as a way of life. If it can be demonstrated that this frame of reference is useful in explaining the incidence of deviant behavior, it will furnish overwhelming evidence against the contention that deviant behavior is the product of biological or individual psychological forces. It will also help to explain the rising problems of deviant behavior, such as crime and delinquency, in underdeveloped countries undergoing rapid industrialization and urbanization.[38] The following section will compare the incidence and prevalence of certain forms of deviant behavior in rural and urban areas, between cities of various sizes, and within areas of a city. Such material should furnish some evidence for the contention that urbanization and urbanism are related to the extent and increase of deviant behavior in modern societies.

Comparisons of Certain Forms of Deviant Behavior in Rural and Urban Areas

For centuries writers have been concerned about the debauchery and moral conditions of the cities and have generally praised rural life. Hesiod, for example, wrote about the corrupt justice of the cities.[39] The Greeks and Romans compared the city with agricultural areas, noting the greater evils and sources of criminality in the cities. One of the first systematic comparisons of rural and urban peoples was made by Ibn Khaldun in the fourteenth century. This famed Arab historian compared life in the city with that among the nomadic tribes. He found that the nomads had good behavior, whereas evil and corruption were abundant in the city; that honesty and courage were characteristic of the nomads, whereas lying and cowardice were prevalent in the city; and that the city caused decay, stultified initiative, and made men depraved and wicked. In general, rural life has been, and still largely is, a world of close personal relationships which Burgess has thus described:

> But the main characteristics of small-town life stand out in clear perspective: close acquaintanceship of everyone with everyone else, the dominance of personal relations, and the subjection of the individual to continuous observation and control by the community. . . . This fund of concrete knowledge which everyone has of everyone else in the small town naturally em-

---

[38] See J. J. Panakal and A. M. Khalifa, *Prevention of Types of Criminality Resulting from Social Changes and Accompanying Economic Development in Less Developed Countries*, Reports on the Second United Nations Congress on the Prevention of Crime and the Treatment of Offenders, London, August, 1960 (New York: United Nations Department of Economic and Social Affairs, 1960).

[39] See Pitirim Sorokin, Carle Zimmerman, and Charles Galpin, *A Systematic Sourcebook in Rural Sociology* (Minneapolis: University of Minnesota Press, 1930), pp. 27–52, 54–68.

phasizes and accentuates the role of the personal in all relationships and activities of community life. Approval and disapproval of conduct, likes and dislikes of persons, play correspondingly a tremendous part in social life, in business, in politics, and in the administration of justice.[40]

DELINQUENCY AND CRIME

The types, incidence, and reactions to rural crime, as with urban crime, are a function of the type of life and the various norms and values of the communities. Delinquency and crime rates today are generally much lower in rural areas than in urban. In general, the differences between rural and urban property crimes are greater than the differences in crimes against the person.

Some delinquent and criminal acts committed in rural areas are dealt with informally and not officially reported, and there are undoubtedly more opportunities to commit offenses in urban as compared with rural areas. The differences between rural and urban rates, however, are so great that differential reporting or opportunity could, at most, account for only a small part. Also, there is little evidence to support the theory held by some that the city attracts deviants from rural areas.[41]

As Table 3.7 shows, burglary rates in the United States, as a whole,

Table 3.7. *Rates per 100,000 Population for Crimes Known to the Police in Rural and Urban Areas, United States, 1960*

	Rate	
Offense	Urban	Rural
Murder and nonnegligent manslaughter	4.9	6.4
Forcible rape	10.3	6.8
Robbery	70.7	11.9
Aggravated assault	88.7	42.2
Burglary—breaking or entering	568.9	210.9
Larceny—theft ($50 and over)	340.8	102.8
Automobile theft	243.7	42.1

SOURCE: Derived from Federal Bureau of Investigation, *Uniform Crime Reports* (Annual Bulletin, 1960; Washington, D.C.: Government Printing Office, 1960), p. 33. The population figures used were based on the 1960 census. Rates for the above are based on 1960 census data. "Urban areas" include Standard Metropolitan Statistical Areas.

are generally almost three times as great in urban areas as in rural, larceny is over three times as great, and robbery over six times.[42] The rates for burglaries known to the police per 100,000 population in 1960

[40] Ernest W. Burgess, in Blumenthal, *op. cit.*, pp. xii–xiii.   [41] See page 95.
[42] In such countries as France, Belgium, Switzerland, Holland, Germany, Sweden, Finland, Denmark, and Italy the incidence of urban offenses, crimes known, and con-

were, for example, 568.9 in urban areas and 210.9 in rural areas. Crimes such as murder, which are relatively infrequent as compared with property crimes, are about the same, with a somewhat higher rate in rural areas, where the rate is 6.4 as compared with 4.9 in urban. Rape rates are much higher in urban areas, 10.3 in urban as contrasted with 6.8 in rural.

Specific studies, rather than statistical comparisons, also seem to support the thesis that the urbanization of rural areas and an increase in crime go hand in hand. A study of the southern mountain villages showed that as the hill country was opened to outside contacts criminal activities increased.[43] The most important factor associated with this increase was the growing lack of community identification on the part of individuals as the villages became more urbanized. A study of rural inmates in an Iowa reformatory revealed that characteristics associated with an urban way of life played a significant role in their criminal behavior.[44]

MENTAL DISORDERS

Most contemporary data on mental disorders, but not all, show that the rates are generally higher in urban than in rural areas. As with crime, many writers feel that the expansion of urbanism is significant in the production of mental illness in our society.[45] One writer has stated that "the data also show that insanity is much more prevalent in urban than in rural areas, a fact of no little significance for the student of rural sociology. . . . there seems to be no doubt of the association between urbanity and insanity." [46] After a study of the prevalence of mental disorder among the urban and rural populations of New York State, Malzberg concluded that

victions per population have been reported as generally higher than among rural areas. In Finland, for example, during the years 1930–1933 there were approximately seven times as many property crimes known to the police in urban areas as in rural.—Hans H. Burchardt, "Kriminalität in Stadt und Land," *Abhandlungen des Kriminalistischen Instituts an der Universität Berlin* (4. Folge, 4 Bd., 1. Heft [1936]). Louis Wirth and Marshall B. Clinard, "Public Safety," in *Urban Government*, Supplementary Report of the Urbanism Committee to the National Resources Committee (Washington, D.C.: Government Printing Office, 1939), I, 247–303. Also see Sorokin, Zimmerman, and Galpin, *op. cit.*, II, 266–302, 315–329.

[43] M. Taylor Mathews, *Experience Worlds of the Mountain Peoples* (New York: Columbia University Press, 1937).

[44] Clinard, "Rural Criminal Offenders," *American Journal of Sociology*, 50:38–45 (July, 1944). A replica of Clinard's study made several years later found that these characteristics also played a role in the lives of offenders.—Eastman, "The Process of Urbanization and Criminal Behavior: A Restudy of Culture Conflict," cited above.

[45] For an over-all picture of the general distribution of mental disorder, see Stuart A. Queen, "The Ecological Study of Mental Disorder," *American Sociological Review*, 5:201–209 (April, 1940); Robert E. L. Faris, "Ecological Factors in Human Behavior," in James McV. Hunt ed., *Personality and the Behavior Disorders* (New York: The Ronald Press Company, 1944), pp. 736–757; C. W. Schroeder, "Mental Disorders in Cities," *American Journal of Sociology*, 47:40–47 (July, 1942); and Abraham Myerson, "Review of Mental Disorders in Urban Areas," *American Journal of Psychiatry*, 96:995–999 (January, 1940).

[46] T. Lynn Smith, *The Sociology of Rural Life* (New York: Harper & Row, Publishers, 1940), p. 125.

the rural regions of the state had less mental disorder than the urban.[47]

In another study, Texas rates for all persons who became psychotic for the first time were found to be two and a half times greater in urban areas than in rural, a difference which was statistically significant.[48] The same differential held for the sexes with an average annual rate per 100,000 for males in urban areas of 76 in contrast with 44 in rural areas; for females an even greater difference—99 as compared with 36. Even the age-specific psychoses rates were consistently higher in urban areas than for the same rural age group. The disparity between rates for rural and urban areas increased with advancing age. Jaco has summarized the results of the Texas study as follows: "In examining the overall results concerning the incidence rates of mental disorders in the rural and urban areas, no significant evidence was found to support the notion that the large rate differentials between urban and rural areas were due to differences in accessibility to psychiatric treatment facilities or to the type of psychiatric facilities available in the two areas." [49]

Not all the evidence supports the conclusion that the incidence of mental illness is much less in rural areas. The differences may actually be smaller than they now appear to be because of the likelihood that rural families may keep mentally disturbed members at home rather than hospitalize them. A study made in Tennessee concluded that mental health in rural areas is not necessarily as good as the smaller number of commitments to mental institutions might indicate, for almost half the psychotic individuals in rural areas were found to be cared for by their families.[50] For this reason it is possible that mental deviants in urban society may be somewhat more socially visible, and that both unofficial and official tolerance of the deviation will be less.

ALCOHOLISM

The chances that rural persons will become chronic alcoholics are less than half as great as those for urban dwellers, according to estimates made by Yale University's Section on Alcohol Studies. In 1940 the rate per 100,000 adult population in areas of less than 2500 population was 474 as compared with 972 in cities of 100,000 population or over. There were 821 male alcoholics for every 100,000 rural males, as compared with 1894 in large cities; the difference between rural and urban women, com-

[47] Benjamin Malzberg, "The Prevalence of Mental Disease among the Urban and Rural Populations of New York State." *Psychiatric Quarterly* 9:55–88 (January, 1935).

[48] E. Gartly Jaco, *The Social Epidemiology of Mental Diseases* (New York: Russell Sage Foundation, 1960). Also see Leacock, "Three Social Variables and Mental Illness," *loc. cit.*, p. 314.

[49] Jaco, *op. cit.*

[50] William F. Roth, Jr., and Frank H. Luton, "The Mental Health Program in Tennessee," *American Journal of Psychiatry*, 99:662–676 (January, 1943). A study of the Eastern Health District of Baltimore found that one fourth of the rural psychotics were not hospitalized.

puted on a standardized population, is somewhat less. The rates of reported deaths from alcoholism per 100,000 adults in 1940 was nearly twice as great in cities of over 100,000 as in rural areas.[51] Urban commitments for alcoholic psychoses are reported to be three and a half times the rate for rural areas.[52]

The principal reasons for this lower rate of alcoholism in rural areas are the social norms and the amount of social control at the personal level over drinking or excessive drinking. Farm people in the United States are much less likely to drink alcoholic beverages than are city dwellers. One half of the rural people are abstainers, but this proportion decreases as the size of the city increases, until in cities with a population of over 500,000 only one fourth do not drink. Both farm rearing and farm residence are associated with lower proportions of heavy drinkers. A recent Iowa study showed that 58 percent of drinkers in the city were either moderate or heavy drinkers as compared with 43 percent of the farm drinkers.[53] Moreover, the extent of drinking increased among the farm-reared who had migrated to the city but this increase was in moderate rather than heavy drinking.

SUICIDE

On the whole, persons living on farms and villages either in Europe or in America are much less likely to take their lives than persons living in cities. In London the standardized rate, expressed as a percentage of that for the whole of England and Wales, is 115, for the county boroughs 106, for other urban districts 97, and for rural districts 88.[54] In Sweden, Denmark, and Finland wide differences exist between farm and city in the suicide rates, in Finland the urban rate being over twice as high.[55] A detailed study of suicide in France showed that the chances that farm people and persons living in places of less than 2000 population would take their lives were considerably less than for city people.[56] Only in the Irish Free State and the Netherlands have suicides been reported to be greater in rural than in urban areas.[57] This has been partially explained as being due to the large number of old persons in rural areas who, feeling useless from an economic point of view, commit suicide.

---

[51] E. M. Jellinek, "Recent Trends in Alcoholism and Alcohol Consumption," *Quarterly Journal of Studies on Alcohol*, 8:23 (June, 1947).

[52] Landis and Page, *op. cit.*

[53] Harold A. Mulford and Donald E. Miller, "Drinking in Iowa. II. The Extent of Drinking and Selected Socio-cultural Categories," *Quarterly Journal of Studies on Alcohol*, 21:34–35 (March, 1960).

[54] Figures cited in Peter Sainsbury, *Suicide in London: An Ecological Study* (New York: Basic Books, Inc., 1956).

[55] Louis I. Dublin and Bessie Bunzel, *To Be or Not to Be* (New York: Harrison Smith and Robert Haas, 1933), p. 82.

[56] Maurice Halbwachs, *Les Causes du Suicide* (Paris: Librairie Félix Alcan, 1930).

[57] Dublin and Bunzel, *op. cit.*, pp. 82–83.

The suicide rate in cities of the United States of a population of over 10,000 has generally been almost twice as great as that in smaller cities and rural areas. A student from a small western Kansas town has written of suicides in his community over the past twenty years.

> I know of only four suicides in the last twenty years in the town and its agricultural hinterland. Two of these are dramatic memories of my childhood and occurred in 1932. Both suicides were men (one the president of the Citizens State Bank and the other the county treasurer) who had become involved in dishonest financial affairs. The other two suicides were individuals past middle age and without kinship or community ties. One, a man, whose wife had died several years previously and who was without children, had spent his savings in an attempted rejuvenation. The other suicide, a woman, was separated from her husband and son and was shunned by the women of the community because she talked incessantly. One of the local ministers created a sensation in connection with this woman's funeral sermon—he accused the women of the town of murdering the woman who had committed suicide by refusing to associate with her. To my knowledge, no farmers have committed suicide in this area in the last twenty years.[58]

The differential in rural and urban suicide rates appears to be declining because of the tendency for an urban way of life to characterize rural areas. An analysis of 3081 cases of suicide in Michigan between 1945 and 1949 revealed that rural males exhibited higher suicide rates than urban males.[59] Although "farmers and farm managers" had a high suicide rate in Michigan, the majority of "rural" males who committed suicide were engaged in urban occupations and resided in urbanized fringe areas. It is possible that the high rural rate in this sample was due to two factors: as urban values become more widely disseminated in rural areas they create an intense personal conflict because of the disparity between urban and rural values as they affect behavioral alternatives; and the occupations of rural males who committed suicide are characteristic occupations of urban groups, thus suggesting exposure to conflicting values and norms. Although they lived in the country, these people were oriented to an urban way of life.

Social Deviation and City Size

The higher incidence of certain forms of deviant behavior in urban communities has been, in general, demonstrated by a comparison of urban with rural rates, but several questions remain to be answered: (1) If urban rates for certain forms of deviation are, in turn, analyzed by the size of the community, is there a proportional increase as one proceeds from the small city to the great metropolis? (2) Do deviation rates vary according to

---

[58] From an unpublished personal document.
[59] W. Widick Schroeder and Allan J. Beegle, "Suicide: An Instance of High Rural Rates," *Rural Sociology*, 18:45–52 (March, 1953).

the distance from a large community? (3) Within any city are there variations in the rates of deviation according to the degree of urbanism of the
area?

CRIME RATES BY CITY SIZE

Comparisons in the United States of crime rates by city size show
some startling differences and, in most crimes even a continuous progression in rates as the size of the city increases.[60] (See Table 3.8.) In 1960

*Table 3.8. Rates per 100,000 for Crimes Known to the Police
by City Size, United States, 1960*

	Population	Murder—Nonnegligent manslaughter	Manslaughter by negligence	Forcible rape	Robbery
I	Over 250,000	6.8	4.4	15.2	117.6
II	100,000–250,000	5.6	4.1	7.6	57.5
III	50,000–100,000	3.3	2.9	5.5	36.6
IV	25,000– 50,000	2.9	2.3	4.7	22.6
V	10,000– 25,000	2.4	1.5	4.0	15.7
VI	Under 10,000	2.7	1.3	3.3	12.8

	Population	Aggravated assault	Burglary—Breaking or entering	Larceny $50 and over	Larceny Under $50	Auto theft
I	Over 250,000	154.1	742.1	477.5	1,070.8	368.8
II	100,000–250,000	83.3	668.3	371.2	1,322.6	288.2
III	50,000–100,000	58.9	512.8	343.1	1,107.9	199.0
IV	25,000– 50,000	39.9	433.0	282.9	1,057.7	154.1
V	10,000– 25,000	35.2	347.9	200.1	923.3	112.8
VI	Under 10,000	28.9	288.9	140.8	650.0	82.1

SOURCE: Federal Bureau of Investigation, *Uniform Crime Reports* (Annual Bulletin,
1960; Washington, D.C.: Government Printing Office, 1961), pp. 81–82. Included in this
report were 49 cities over 250,000 population; 80 cities from 100,000 to 250,000; 189 cities
from 50,000 to 100,000; 379 cities from 25,000 to 50,000; 880 cities from 10,000 to 25,000;
and 1789 cities under 10,000. Population figures on which these rates are based are those
included in the 1960 census reports.

[60] Durkheim in France, some fifty years ago, maintained that crime increases directly with the volume and density of the population. A later study by Burchardt concluded that crime rates in European cities generally increase directly with the size of
the city. The only exceptions which he found were in the Netherlands and Austria,
where the largest cities have the least crime, a situation which he explained as due to
unique factors. A comprehensive study of crime in France and Belgium has shown
major differences in rates of urban and rural areas, and in those of cities of different
sizes. The study found, however, that such rates are affected by the extent of industry
and other social factors. See Denis Szabo, *Crimes et Villes* (Louvain: Catholic University
of Louvain, 1960).

the rate per 100,000 population for burglaries reported to the police, for example, which is probably the best comparable index of crime, rose steadily from cities of less than 10,000, with a rate of 288.9, to cities over 250,000 population, with a rate of 742.1, or over twice as great.[61] Robbery rates were nine times as great in the larger cities as compared with the smaller ones.

It is interesting to note that rates by city size are often affected, however, by the cultural factors in the area in which the cities are located.[62] In fact, the regional location of a city seems often to be more related to the crime rate than is the extent of urbanization in the state. Some states, such as California, with a large proportion of urban population, also have high crime rates, whereas Massachusetts, which is also heavily urbanized, has a comparatively low rate. It is likely that the urban "way of life" in a more recently developed area like California is characterized by norm conflicts, rapid change, and other unsettling conditions, whereas in older areas, such as New England, these aspects of urbanism may be somewhat attenuated.

ALCOHOLISM

Although cities with a population over 100,000 have estimated rates for chronic alcoholism which are considerably higher than the rates for cities up to 10,000 population, as shown in Table 3.9, the progression

Table 3.9. Estimated Rates of Chronic Alcoholism in the Adult Population by Sex and Population Size Groups, United States, 1940

Population size group	Males per 100,000 adult males	Females per 100,000 adult females	Both sexes per 100,000 adult population
Places of 100,000 and over	1,894	294	972
Places of 10,000 to 100,000	1,422	190	727
Places of 2,500 to 10,000	1,428	217	743
Rural (less than 2,500)	821	154	474

SOURCE: E. M. Jellinek, "Recent Trends in Alcoholism and Alcohol Consumption," *Quarterly Journal of Studies on Alcohol*, 8:23 (June, 1947). Reprinted by permission of the Journal.

[61] Federal Bureau of Investigation, *Uniform Crime Reports* (Annual Bulletin, 1960; Washington, D.C.: Government Printing Office, 1961). pp. 81–82. The rates for reported burglaries appear to decline in cities of 500,000 or more population, which may be due to a saturation point in urbanization above which size burglary rates do not materially increase.—Wirth and Clinard, "Public Safety," *loc. cit.*, p. 265.

[62] Wirth and Clinard, "Public Safety," *loc. cit.*, p. 265. Also see Lyle Shannon, "The Spatial Distribution of Criminal Offenses by States," *Journal of Criminal Law, Criminology and Police Science*, 45:264–274 (September–October, 1954).

by city size is not continuous. A suggested explanation is that cities of from 10,000 to 100,000 contain many suburban areas where the rate of alcoholism may be high. This irregular progression in rates for alcoholism is in contrast to the continuous increase in the percentage of drinkers as the size of the city increases.[63]

SUICIDE

Suicide rates appear to increase with the size of the community, until cities of 500,000 and over are reached. The suicide rate per 100,000 population during 1927–1933 ranged from 15.9 in cities of 10,000 to 25,000 population to 19.9 in the 250,000 to 500,000 group, with the rates in cities of over half a million population declining slightly.[64] It has been noted that fast-growing cities tend to have a higher suicide rate.[65]

RACIAL DISCRIMINATION

In larger urban communities, where contacts between racial groups become more impersonal and segmental, there is often a decline in discrimination in some areas and an increase in others. Compared with smaller communities there is likely to be less emphasis on patterns of subservience or etiquette and less segregation of facilities such as parks, libraries, and the like, which serve to symbolize status differences. Often the enforced segregation in social contacts of a small community are replaced by "voluntary" segregation or social separation of the races. After examining the correlation of various indices of urbanization with discrimination it was found that while the relative gain from urbanization for nonwhites may be substantial, because of a low starting point, the absolute differences may be maintained so that urbanization does not mean the lessening of all types of discrimination.[66]

On the other hand, urban racial social violence has occurred in every geographic region in the United States, including such cities as Chicago, Detroit, Tulsa, New York, Washington, East St. Louis, and Atlanta. There are four patterns of urban racial violence: [67]

1. Spontaneous brawls over an immediate disturbance, among bystanders.
2. The "mass, uncoordinated battle" occurring when groups of one race

---

[63] American Institute of Public Opinion Survey, December, 1947.
[64] Wirth and Clinard, "Public Safety," *loc. cit.*, p. 271.
[65] Henry Wechsler, "Community Growth, Depressive Disorders, and Suicide," *American Journal of Sociology*, 67:9–17 (July, 1961).
[66] H. M. Blalock, Jr., "Urbanization and Discrimination in the South," *Social Problems*, 7:146–152 (Fall, 1959).
[67] See Allen D. Grimshaw, "Urban Racial Violence in the United States: Changing Ecological Considerations," *American Journal of Sociology*, 66:110 (September, 1960).

attack usually isolated members of the other. Mobs of one race seldom engage mobs of the other race in open battle.

3. The "urban pogrom," which is the full-scale assault of one group, almost always white, upon Negroes, and which has occurred particularly where whites have assumed the tacit approval of local government. These "pogroms" have resulted in the flight of large numbers of the minority community.

4. Stray assaults and stabbings on the part of individuals or small groups of one race upon individuals of the other.

Distribution of Deviant Behavior within a City

According to the most generally accepted theory, the characteristic spatial pattern of cities is a series of concentric circles, with each circle having certain distinctive characteristics moving out from the central business district into increasingly better areas of housing.[68] The ecological pattern of the city in terms of concentric zones leading out from the first circle are Zone I, the central business district; Zone II, an area known variously by a number of names such as the slums, zone in transition, or interstitial area; Zone III, an area of two- and three-family flats or dwellings; Zone IV, an area of single-family dwellings; and Zone V, the suburban or commutation area. These circles can be thought of as undergoing constant movement in the form of expansion outward, much like the movement taking place on the surface of water when a pebble is dropped into it. The central business district is constantly expanding into the slum much as many persons living in each successive zone may eventually move outward to another area.

Although this theory implies equal expansion in all directions, few cities ever completely approximate a series of concentric circles. Rivers, mountains—or a lake, as in the case of Chicago—interfere with this natural growth. Even so, there are some cities, such as Rochester, New York, which closely resemble this pattern.[69] This abstraction of concentric circles is no different from the law of falling bodies wherein the principle of an equal rate of fall between an iron ball and a feather is valid only if both are in a vacuum.

---

[68] Ernest W. Burgess, "The Growth of the City," in Robert E. Park and Ernest W. Burgess, *The City* (Chicago: The University of Chicago Press, 1925). Later theory based on city growth is that cities have a pattern of sectors like pieces of a pie. According to this theory, industrial areas follow river valleys, water courses, and railroad lines out from the city and become surrounded by workingmen's housing, with factories tending to locate even along the outer fringe of the city. According to the sector view, the best housing then does not fringe the entire city but only parts of it. The main industrial areas of the future may well be located on the outskirts of cities in new industrial towns and suburbs as is now taking place.—Homer Hoyt, *The Structure and Growth of Residential Neighborhoods in American Cities* (Washington, D.C.: Federal Housing Administration, 1939), pp. 75–77, and his "The Structure of American Cities in the Post-War Era," *American Journal of Sociology*, 48:475–481 (January, 1943).

[69] William Ogburn and Meyer Nimkoff, *Sociology* (Boston: Houghton Mifflin Company, 1946), pp. 414–416.

The slum is an area of particular interest to sociologists. It is an area of high land values but cheap rents. This curious contradiction is the result of such land being held "in pawn," so to speak, on the assumption that the central business district will expand into the area and will bring its business firms, manufacturing establishments, and high-priced rental units such as hotels and apartment hotels. The landowners, who seldom live in the area, do not wish to improve slum housing since it will eventually be torn

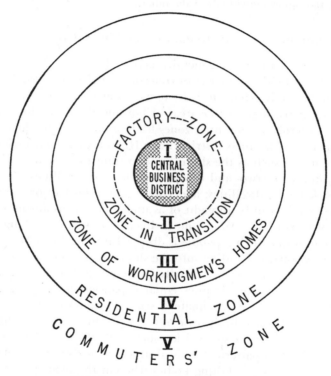

FIGURE 1.—The Growth of a City

SOURCE: Adapted from Burgess, "The Growth of a City," in Park and Burgess, *The City*.

down. This fact and the rather undesirable location make for cheap rentals. Yet the land remains so high-priced that when an occasional apartment hotel is erected in the area, as in the case of Chicago's Gold Coast, it must be of skyscraper proportions to be profitable. Zorbaugh has described the slum of Chicago in this way:

> One alien group after another has claimed this slum area. The Irish, the Germans, the Swedish, the Sicilians have occupied it in turn. Now it is being invaded by a migration of the Negro from the South. It has been known successively as Kilgubbin, Little Hell, and, as industry has come in, as Smoky

Hollow. The remnants of these various successions have left a sediment that at once characterizes and confuses the life of this district. . . .

It is an area in which encroaching business lends a speculative value to the land. But rents are low; for while little business has actually come into the area, it is no longer desirable for residential purposes. It is an area of dilapidated dwellings, many of which the owners, waiting to sell the land for commercial purposes, allow to deteriorate, asking just enough in rent to carry the taxes. . . .

The city, as it grows, creates about its central business district a belt of bleak, barren, soot-begrimed, physically deteriorated neighborhoods. And in these neighborhoods the undesirable, and those of low economic status, are segregated by the unremitting competition of the economic process in which land values, rentals, and wages are fixed.[70]

In each section of the city there are wide variations in age, sex, nationality and racial origins, occupation, social class, homeownership, condition of housing, literacy, and education. Differences in social class are one of the most important characteristics of various areas of a city. The shifting of persons under *ecological* pressures brings about an association of like with like and a tendency for population specialization in certain areas.[71]

The central business district and the "zone in transition" have accentuated urban characteristics. The population of these areas is heterogeneous. The residents are chiefly unskilled workers and their families, and include migrants from rural and other areas, and various nationality and racial groups. People tend to move in and out of the areas with great frequency. For a long period of time prostitutes, vagrants, homeless men, delinquents, and criminals have often been concentrated in these areas. The norms and values of these areas, consequently, do not always agree with those of the more stable areas of the city. The residents of these areas are often more likely than those of other areas to regard delinquency and crime without as much disfavor as other areas of the city and to have different norms about sexual behavior,[72] political honesty, or similar behavior. Considerable differences also exist in other social norms and values of various individuals and groups who live there. Patterns of parent-child relation-

---

[70] Harvey Zorbaugh, *The Gold Coast and the Slum* (Chicago: The University of Chicago Press, 1929), pp. 127–129.

[71] For many years botanists and geologists have been interested in studying the pattern of distribution and movement in space of plant and animal life, which they call plant and animal ecology. Following this, interest grew in human ecology, or the study of the distribution of man and his institutions in space, which includes the study of rural-urban differences as well as differences in city size and within cities. The study of the ecology or distribution of deviant behavior has largely developed in the past forty years.

[72] The sex code of these areas, while often different from that of the middle-class regarding, for example, premarital sex relations, is just as highly organized.—William F. Whyte, "A Slum Sex Code," *American Journal of Sociology*, 49:24–32 (July, 1943).

ships of persons residing there and in Zone III may be considerably different from those in the middle-class areas of Zones IV and V.[73]

This does not mean that the slum is "disorganized," for about some norms and values there may be considerable agreement among all groups; moreover, each group may have a high degree of organization of its own. Whyte, in a study of an Italian slum of a large American city, found that both formal and informal groups among the Italians generally had a complex and well-established organization.[74] Nationality and racial groups, however, tend to live in close association with one another even though there may be considerable social isolation from a different group living geographically close. This means in general that few close interpersonal relationships are developed among the diverse groups constituting the population of these areas.

Zone III has a more stable population, more skilled workers, and fewer foreign-born or racial groups. Second-generation immigrant groups moving out of the slum generally move here first. Zones IV and V largely consist of apartment houses, single-family dwellings, and commuters' houses, which means that they are chiefly upper-middle and upper class.

Over a century ago a few studies were made of the distribution of deviant behavior within a city,[75] but most of this type of research began with the stimulation of sociological studies by Park, Burgess, and their students of the Chicago community in the 1920's. The spot-mapping of deviants by place of residence has revealed that, on the whole, certain types of social deviation tend to be concentrated in specific areas. For example, conventional crime, delinquency, mental illness in general and schizophrenia in particular, suicide, prostitution, vagrancy, dependency, illegitimacy, infant mortality, as well as associated problems such as high death and disease rates, have been found to vary with the areas of the city. The highest rates are in Zones I and II, and become successively lower out from this area. The evidence on alcoholism and the manic-depressive psychoses does not show quite this pronounced pattern for, although there are probably higher rates in Zones I and II, the differences are not as marked from one part of the city to another. White-collar crime, on the other hand, is greater in Zones IV and V of the city. Gambling and prostitution are prevalent not only in Zone II but sometimes beyond the suburban fringe of the city.[76]

---

[73] Arnold W. Green, "The Middle-Class Male Child and Neurosis," *American Sociological Review*, 11:31–41 (February, 1946).

[74] Whyte, *Street Corner Society*.

[75] Yale Levin and Alfred Lindesmith, "English Ecology and Criminology of the Past Century," *Journal of Criminal Law and Criminology*, 27:801–816 (March–April, 1937), and Alfred Lindesmith and Yale Levin, "The Lombrosian Myth in Criminology," *American Journal of Sociology*, 42:653–679 (March, 1937).

[76] Walter C. Reckless, *Vice in Chicago* (Chicago: The University of Chicago Press, 1933).

Delinquent gangs were found by Thrasher to be largely concentrated in the zone of transition.[77] The spot-mapping of some 60,000 cases of delinquency, truancy, and crime by Shaw and McKay showed a close correlation among the rates of all three groups, with wide variation in their distribution among the local communities of the city.[78] The slum area near the centers of commerce and industry had the highest rates, whereas those in outlying residential communities of higher economic status were uniformly low. In a later study of some 25,000 juvenile court delinquents, distributed over thirty-three years, Shaw and McKay reported additional evidence of the consistency of high rates of delinquency in Zone II.[79]

Findings similar to those in Chicago have been reported for eight other large metropolitan cities and eleven other cities, all widely separated geographically, including Boston, Philadelphia, Cleveland, Richmond, Birmingham, Omaha, and Seattle.[80] Higher rates of delinquency were found in the inner zones and lower rates in the outer zones, and in all nineteen cities, except for Boston, Birmingham, and Omaha, the rates also declined regularly from innermost to outermost zones. Even in these cities where rates in the outermost zones were somewhat higher than in the intermediate, as in Boston, the explanation may possibly be the fact that the industrial areas are near the periphery as well as the differences in the policies of the courts in the various areas. A study of Croydon, a large English city near London, revealed that the highest rates for delinquency were concentrated in areas of the city populated by unskilled and semiskilled workers' families.[81]

The correlation of delinquency rates with economic factors should not be interpreted as indicating any direct relation to poverty or bad housing, as Shaw and McKay have indicated. They point out that in rural areas there may be poverty but little delinquency. Poverty, moreover, does not produce a tradition of delinquency because of a lack of money in itself; rather, it may interfere with the realization of status or prestige. The explanation of delinquency, they believe, is to be found in the general social situations in delinquency areas.

The rate of arrests of adults per 10,000 population seventeen years of age and over was more than ten times as great in the central areas of Chi-

---

[77] Frederic M. Thrasher, *The Gang* (Chicago: The University of Chicago Press, 1927).

[78] Clifford R. Shaw and Henry D. McKay, *Delinquent Areas* (Chicago: The University of Chicago Press, 1929). Jonassen has criticized the limitations of data, the methodology, and the internal consistencies of the data.—Christen T. Jonassen, "A Re-evaluation and Critique of the Logic and Some Methods of Shaw and McKay," *American Sociological Review*, 14:608–614 (October, 1949).

[79] Clifford R. Shaw, Henry D. McKay, *et al.*, *Juvenile Delinquency and Urban Areas* (Chicago: The University of Chicago Press, 1942).

[80] *Ibid.* Automobile theft may often be somewhat of an exception to the generalization that delinquency tends to be concentrated in areas such as these.

[81] Terence Morris, *The Criminal Area: A Study in Social Ecology* (London: Routledge and Kegan Paul Ltd., 1958).

cago as in the outlying areas of the city.[82] The rates for nearly all 29 types of crimes known to the police in Seattle, and arrests for these crimes during the period 1949–1951 showed a decline as one moved out in six one-mile concentric zones from the highest land value in the central business district.[83] There was a tendency for 23 out of the 29 types of crime known to the police to decrease more or less in direct proportion from the center of the city, in particular shoplifting, theft, arson, rape, sodomy, and burglary. Bicycle theft was the only crime known to the police which had a higher rate in Zone VI (149.5) than in Zone I (65.3). The differentials between inner and outer zones were relatively small for Peeping Toms, obscene telephone calls, indecent liberties, and carnal knowledge. Not a single category in the arrest series showed a higher rate in the peripheral zones. Arrest rates for fraud, rape, prostitution, lewdness, robbery, gambling, and common drunkenness showed the greatest difference, while auto theft and indecent exposure showed the least.

White-collar crime, as one might expect, follows a reverse pattern, with concentration in Zones IV and V of the city. In a study of wartime black-market offenders in the wholesale meat industry in Detroit, Hartung found that more than 80 percent of them lived in the most desirable areas of the city. (See Table 3.10.) Of the ten who lived in the least desirable areas (4 and 5), three lived in good downtown hotels.

Table 3.10. Distribution of Meat Black-Market Offenders According to Desirability of Residence

Residentially de-sirable quintile	Number of personal defendants	Percentage of total
1	62	48.4
2	41	32.0
3	15	11.7
4	4	3.1
5	6	4.7

SOURCE: Frank E. Hartung, "A Study in Law and Social Differentiation: As Exemplified in Violations of the Emergency Price Control Act of 1942 and the Second War Powers Act, in the Detroit Meat Industry." Unpublished doctoral dissertation, University of Michigan, Ann Arbor, 1949, p. 221. Index of residence desirability constructed by Detroit Bureau of Governmental Research on the basis of twenty criteria.

[82] Ernest R. Mowrer, *Disorganization, Personal and Social* (Philadelphia: J. B. Lippincott Company, 1942), p. 143.

[83] Calvin F. Schmid, "Urban Crime Areas: Part II," *American Sociological Review;* 25:655–678 (October, 1960). There also appears to be a remarkable constancy and uniformity in the spatial patterning of crime by gradients. A comparison of two series of offenses known to the police in Seattle, 1939–41 and 1949–51, shows a close correspondence with high correlations for burglary and robbery.—*Ibid.,* p. 669.

MENTAL DISORDERS

Over fifty years ago British writers raised the question as to why, if there was a specific diathesis (condition in the body) governing insanity, there should be such vast differences in its geographical distribution.[84] Recent ecological research in urban areas has similarly raised some important questions concerning the connection between social relationships in local urban communities and mental disorders. Such ecological research on the distribution of mental illness dates from the 1939 study of Faris and Dunham in Chicago and Providence, in which the residences of 34,864 cases admitted to state and private mental hospitals during a thirteen-year period were spot-mapped.[85] Subsequent research in seven other cities has largely substantiated their findings.

At the present time the evidence derived from these studies indicates that mental illness within a city increases, in general, with the degree of urbanization of the area.[86] There are three major conclusions. (1) All types of mental disorders show a marked concentration in Zones I and II, and the rates successively decline in all directions as one goes out from the center of the city. Faris and Dunham have reported that the highest average annual rate per 100,000 population in Chicago was 499, occurring in the central business district, which includes the hotel and homeless-men area. The next highest rate of 480 was found in other vagrant and rooming-house areas. Lowest in the incidence of mental disorder was the outlying residential district, with a rate of 48, or only one tenth that of the highest areas. (2) The rates of schizophrenia follow the same pattern of distribution as for all psychoses. The highest rates are found in the rooming-house areas, where impersonality and social isolation are most pronounced. In the Chicago study the differences between the rates for schizophrenia in the rooming-house areas and those in the better residential area ranged from fivefold to ninefold. (3) As opposed to the pattern of schizophrenia, the manic-depressive rates show a much wider distribution within the city and do not follow the concentric pattern closely.

Interpretations of the significance of these distributions, particularly with reference to the difference in the distribution of schizophrenia and manic-depressive psychoses, have suggested the hypothesis that the former is a product of residence in areas of extensive social isolation, whereas the latter is related to too intense social contacts in a society. Evidence of this

[84] W. R. MacDermott, "The Topographical Distribution of Insanity," *British Medical Journal*, September 26, 1908, p. 95.

[85] Robert E. L. Faris and H. Warren Dunham, *Mental Disorders in Urban Areas* (Chicago: The University of Chicago Press, 1939).

[86] H. Warren Dunham, "Current Status of Ecological Research in Mental Disorders," *Social Forces*, 25:321–327 (March, 1947).

relationship to schizophrenia is suggested by the fact that persons—Negroes are an example—residing in areas not primarily populated by those with similar ethnic or racial backgrounds, show a higher incidence of such a disorder than those who live in areas in which they are more integrated. The variations in rates among the Negroes of Chicago, according to the type of area in which they lived, were greater than the differences, however, between all Negroes and all whites.

Explanation of Distributions of Deviant Behavior within Cities

Some have suggested that the explanation of variations in deviant behavior within cities is differential reporting in various areas to authorities. Actually, however, the official rate differences between various areas of a city are so marked, often being, two, five, and even ten times as great, that even if reporting errors were overcome the rates probably would be little changed. As Schmid has written after studying the spatial distribution of crime in Seattle, "In spite of crime statistics and distortion in the derivation of rates resulting from differentials in population mobility and composition, there is still a very considerable portion of the high incidence of crime in the central segment of the city that must be explained on grounds other than these circumstances." [87]

There have been various explanations of these variations in the distribution of deviant behavior within a city. Some authorities explain the variations as the result of the greater number of urban characteristics in the areas closest to the center of the city.[88] Different areas certainly exhibit considerable variations in such factors as ethnic and racial diversity, differential norms, social cohesion, family life, socioeconomic status, physical deterioration of the area, and population mobility.

The differences in social class subcultures in each of the areas may account in large part for the variations in the incidence of deviant behavior. The subculture of lower-class urban areas is characterized by norms conducive to high delinquency, crime, prostitution, drug addiction, and other deviant behavior. Thus Miller explains the high concentration of delinquency and crime in certain areas as a product of lower-class culture which contrasts sharply with middle-class legal values, characterized particularly by values of toughness, "smartness"—mainly to outsmart or dupe someone—and excitement.[89] If this type of explanation is general, it would mean that the different systems of norms, values, and social relation-

[87] Schmid, "Urban Crime Areas: Part II," *American Sociological Review*, 25:675 (October, 1960).

[88] Some have referred rather to the "social disorganization" in each area with much the same meaning.

[89] Walter B. Miller in W. C. Kvaraceus and W. B. Miller, *Delinquent Behavior: Culture and the Individual* (Washington, D.C.: National Education Association, 1959), pp. 8–13.

ships which are associated with the different social classes may directly influence the degree of deviant behavior. Or it could mean that whatever the differences in the values and norms of the different classes, the deviant actions of persons in certain social classes, particularly the lower classes, are more likely to be noticed and to be dealt with officially.

It has also been suggested that certain areas of the city attract rather than produce deviants, and that those who are economically poor, or who are physically or socially deficient, tend to go from rural areas to the more urbanized area of the city.[90] If one considers the "skid row" concentration of alcoholics, criminals, prostitutes, and drug addicts there may be some justification for the view, since the way of life in these areas tends to enhance such concentration. As one writer has stated: "No doubt, the clustering of arrestees charged with drunkenness, vagrancy, prostitution, lewdness, disorderly conduct, and similar crimes in Seattle's Skid Road can be explained in part by the drift hypothesis."[91] This "drift" hypothesis is supported by little evidence as far as other areas of the city are concerned. People may migrate because of differences in economic or educational status or because their friends migrated and told them about a new place to live, but there is little evidence to indicate that persons migrate because they are deviant. For example, there is no indication of selective migration of deviants to Harlem in New York City, which has a high delinquency and crime rate. Furthermore, there are indications that deviant behavior is as common among those who were reared, for example, within certain areas of a city as among those who were migrants to them. Faris has this to say about the theory that persons with mental illness in a large city have migrated there:

> It has been contended that persons who are mentally abnormal tend to fail in their economic activities and as a consequence drift into the slum areas, from which they are eventually committed to a hospital. The concentration of rates, therefore, would represent not the areas in which mental illness develops, but areas to which persons drift after they became abnormal. An unpublished study of the Chicago cases of catatonic schizophrenia, however —a group sharply concentrated in the foreign-born and Negro slum areas— found that most of the patients were born and brought up in the areas from which they were committed and had not drifted into these areas. Rate computations were also made separately for younger (twenty-nine years and less) and older (thirty and over) schizophrenics of both the paranoid and the catatonic types, and of first commitments and recommitments. If drift were important, there should be a sharper concentration of older cases and of recommitted cases, for these would have had more time to fail and to drift to the slums. The findings, however, were that the amount of concentration was

---

[90] See, for example, Donald R. Taft, *Criminology* (New York: The Macmillan Company, 1950).
[91] Schmid, "Urban Crime Areas: Part II," *loc. cit.*, p. 676.

approximately the same, except for some indications of a drift of some of the catatonic schizophrenics from one low-income area to another, that is, from foreign-born slum areas to hobo areas. Their highest rates, nevertheless, were in the foreign-born areas. . . .

Once more it may be pointed out that the contrast between distributions of different mental disorders is inconsistent with the hypothesis that a drift to the slums as a result of economic failure is the principal cause, for there is no reason to assume that the drift would follow such precise patterns.[92]

It seems more likely that the distribution of deviant behavior, with high and low rates in certain areas, has suggested possible factors for such distribution since it furnishes us with leads as to the social factors which may produce given forms of deviant behavior. Consequently, treatment and prevention might be concentrated in certain local areas where the rates are highest in much the same way as public health officers concentrate their work in certain areas of the city. The latter often use spot maps of the city showing typhoid, scarlet fever, poliomyelitis, and similar contagious diseases and, with this information, concentrate on measures like vaccination, quarantine, and control of carriers, the elimination of outside toilets, and the institution of better hygienic practices. A similar approach to deviant behavior would not eliminate the problem but would tend to lower the overall urban rate.[93]

Present-day trends in city growth emphasize suburbanization and decentralization, particularly in the location of plants outside the city. The factors contributing to this growth have been stated by Harris as (1) the greater mobility made possible by automobiles, (2) lower taxes on the periphery, and (3) a greater number of small dwelling units due to the decrease in the size of the family.[94] These general changes in city patterns are bound to influence current theories on the concentration of deviant behavior. Through decentralization, contacts with deviant forms of behavior may become less intensive, and clusters of deviation may come to assume different patterns.

Summary

Urbanism, with its mobility, impersonality, individualism, materialism, norm and role conflicts, and rapid social change, appears to be associated with higher incidence of deviant behavior. Some evidence has been presented here about the comparative incidence of crime, mental illness, alcoholism, and suicide in rural and urban areas, in cities of different size, and within cities.

---

[92] Robert E. L. Faris, *Social Disorganization*, 2d ed., pp. 337, 339. Copyright 1955, The Ronald Press Company.

[93] John B. Martin, "New Attack on Delinquency," *Harper's Magazine* 189:97–109 (July, 1944).

[94] Chauncy D. Harris, "Suburbs," *American Journal of Sociology*, 49:1–13 (July, 1943).

Delinquency and crime rates, as computed from official statistics, are almost universally lower in rural as compared with urban areas. Other forms of deviant behavior also tend, in general, to be statistically more frequent in urban areas. There are also regional and area variations in rates. Although considerable variation in urban characteristics exists from one area of a city to another, further research may possibly indicate that some of the variation may arise from differences in the way of life of social classes residing in each area.

Some persons have attempted to explain these differences in the extent of deviant behavior as being almost entirely due to differences in reporting or opportunity. Others have suggested that the inner zones of the city attract deviants from the other zones or from rural areas, but little evidence exists for either of these contentions. Obviously, these great differences are not due to variations in the biological constitution of individuals. Consequently, the variations among the zones can be thought of as important in suggesting social and cultural explanations for deviant behavior as well as indicating what areas should receive the greatest attention in any effort to reduce it.

Selected Readings

ANDERSON, NELS. *The Urban Community: A World Perspective.* New York: Holt, Rinehart and Winston, Inc., 1959. A view of the impact of urbanism in a world-wide perspective, including a discussion of the characteristics of urbanism, its effect on the family and other groups, and a discussion of social change and conformity under urbanism.

BURGESS, ERNEST W. "The Growth of the City," in Logan Wilson and William Kolb, *Sociological Analysis.* New York: Harcourt, Brace & World, Inc., 1949, pp. 407–414. This is a reprint of the original article, which described the concentric patterns of the city using data from Chicago.

CLINARD, MARSHALL B. "The Process of Urbanization and Criminal Behavior," *American Journal of Sociology,* 48:202–213 (September, 1942). A study of the incidence of the urban characteristics of mobility, impersonality, and contacts with differential norms among farm, village, and city criminal offenders.

CLINARD, MARSHALL B. "Urbanization, Urbanism, and Criminal Behavior," in Ernest W. Burgess and Donald Bogue eds., *Research Contributions to Urbanism.* Chicago: The University of Chicago Press, 1962.

DUNHAM, H. WARREN. "Current Status of Ecological Research in Mental Disorders," *Social Forces,* 25:321–327 (March, 1947). A survey of all ecological studies of mental illness up to that time and an evaluation of the ecological research technique in this area.

MALZBERG, BENJAMIN, and EVERETT S. LEE. *Migration and Mental Disease.* New York: Social Science Research Council, 1956. A study of the extent of migration among all admissions to hospitals for mental disorder in New York during a three-year period. Includes an excellent introduction by Dorothy I. Thomas, summarizing and evaluating other similar research, including ecological studies and other studies of mental illness among migrants and nonmigrants.

MORRIS, TERENCE. *The Criminal Area: A Study in Social Ecology.* London: Routledge & Kegan Paul Ltd., 1957. An ecological study of crime and delinquency in an English city. Has an excellent survey and critique of nearly all studies of the ecology of delinquency both in America and in foreign countries.

RIESMAN, DAVID. *The Lonely Crowd: A Study of Changing American Character.* New Haven, Conn.: Yale University Press, 1950. An important discussion of "tradition-directed," "inner-directed," and "other-directed" personality patterns. He states that the modern urban person is losing his individuality and tends to conform to the dictates of others.

ROSE, ARNOLD. *Theory and Methods in the Social Sciences.* Minneapolis: University of Minnesota Press, 1954, "The Problem of the Mass Society," pp. 25–49. This is a discussion of the relation of social problems to the rise of urban or the "mass society" of today. There are also some suggestions for the solution of some of the difficulties presented by a "mass society."

SCHMID, CALVIN F. "Urban Crime Areas: Parts I and II." *American Sociological Review,* 25:527–542 and 655–678 (August and October, 1960). A detailed ecological study of urban crime areas in Seattle involving 20 crime variables and 18 social, economic, and demographic indices for 93 census tracts. Contains several maps showing distribution of crimes.

SHAW, CLIFFORD, HENRY D. MC KAY, *et al. Juvenile Delinquency and Urban Areas.* Chicago: The University of Chicago Press, 1942. A series of studies of the ecological distribution of juvenile delinquency in twenty large American cities.

SJOBERG, GIDEON. *The Pre-Industrial City.* New York: The Free Press of Glencoe, 1960. A discussion of the historical development of the city and the differences between preindustrial cities of the past as well as those of underdeveloped areas today and the industrial city.

WILENSKY, HAROLD L., and CHARLES N. LEBEAUX. *Industrial Society and Social Welfare.* New York: Russell Sage Foundation, 1958. Contains an excellent statement of the nature of urban-industrial society and its effects, particularly on juvenile delinquency.

WIRTH, LOUIS. "Urbanism as a Way of Life," *American Journal of Sociology,* 44:1–24 (July, 1938). Probably the best statement of the characteristics of the urban way of life.

Chapter 4

Economic and Technological
Factors in Social Deviation

Economic distress has long been considered as the basic cause of society's ills. Economists and others, including some sociologists, have contributed many studies attempting to show that the underlying basic factors in social deviation originate in economic forces. Among the approaches which might be termed economic are those relating social problems to the lag of nonmaterial parts of culture behind technological development, to the depressed phase of the business cycle, to the economic strength of a given area, and to poverty and substandard housing. Many of these writers have recognized the fact that economic factors are extremely important in social life and that most modern societies are built around an essentially economic ideology. They believe that the explanation of deviant behavior lies in the malfunctioning of the technological and economic system, the failure to control the machine age and to provide adequate goods and services for everyone in a society. Thus it has seemed reasonable to them to correlate the incidence of social deviation with various economic indices.

There have been exclusively economic explanations of delinquency and crime, alcoholism, prostitution, mental illness, race prejudice, and other social problems. Implicit in all these studies is the assumption that if "poverty" could be abolished, the business cycle eliminated, technological developments properly controlled, and "adequate" housing provided for everyone, we would then enter a social millennium largely devoid of social deviation.

Poverty and Deviant Behavior

Since the great economic writings of Adam Smith economic explanations of deviant behavior have been advanced by many students of social problems. Such spokesmen of the classical economic theory as Smith, Ricardo, and others discussed the degrading role of poverty. Alfred Marshall, in the introduction to his now historic work in the field of capitalist economic theory (1891), wrote:

And very often the influence exerted on a person's character by the amount of his income is hardly less, if it is less, than that exerted by the way in which it is earned. . . . It is true that in religion, in the family affections and in friendship, even the poor may find scope for many of those faculties which are the source of the highest happiness. But the conditions which surround extreme poverty, especially in densely crowded places, tend to deaden the higher faculties. Those who have been called the Residuum of our large towns have little opportunity for friendship. . . . No doubt their physical, mental, and moral ill-health is partly due to other causes than poverty, but this is the chief cause.

. . . Although then some of the evils which commonly go with poverty are not its necessary consequences; yet, broadly speaking, "the destruction of the poor is their poverty," and the study of the causes of poverty is the study of the causes of the degradation of a large part of mankind.[1]

Writers who mentioned social problems in the nineteenth and early twentieth centuries often stressed the need for socioeconomic surveys, settlement houses, philanthropy, and other economic uplift procedures, as well as socialism or even communism, to deal with the moral decay of society. Writers such as Henry George, Karl Marx, Charles Booth, Jacob Riis, Jane Addams, and William Bonger felt that we should concentrate our efforts on correcting the maldistribution of income and overcoming economic fluctuations, not only because they were bad in themselves but because they produced most of the vices and evils besetting the world.[2]

Marx felt that crime, prostitution, vice, and moral evils were primarily due to the poverty produced by the capitalistic system, with its ownership of the means of production by a few, the general maldistribution of wealth, and an inevitable class struggle. The solution to these problems would eventually come in the establishment, first, of a dictatorship of the proletariat (i.e., world-wide communism), and, later, of a classless society in which each person would contribute according to his ability and receive according to his needs.[3] Many writers of Marx's day were socialists and were thus strongly influenced by the classic statement of Marx. Today, this general position has swelled into a dynamic communistic doctrine carrying an economic explanation of the world's difficulties into the farthest corners of the globe.

Every person who subscribes to the paramount importance of economic factors in societal development is by no means a communist. In fact, ardent believers in capitalism imply another materialistic emphasis by insisting

---

[1] Alfred Marshall, *Principles of Economics* (8th ed.; London: Macmillan & Co., Ltd., 1936), pp. 1–3.

[2] See Charles Booth, *Life and Labour of the People in London* (London: Macmillan & Co., Ltd., 1892).

[3] Karl Marx, *Das Kapital* (S. Moore and E. Aveling, trans.; F. Engels, ed.; Hamburg, Germany: Otto Meisner, 1890). See also Karl Marx and Friedrich Engels, *The Communist Manifesto* (F. Engels, ed.; London: 1848).

that a higher standard of living will lead to the elimination of most social difficulties. The same line of reasoning prompts philanthropists to assume that merely by distributing some of their wealth among the poor they will eliminate much deviant behavior.

Many studies have tried to show that poverty is the basic cause of social deviation. Probably the most widely known of all exponents of the view was William Bonger, a Dutch social economist who used European data to ascribe practically every social problem to poverty.[4] He attempted to develop the thesis that the mental state of criminals is an outgrowth of economic degradation on the one hand and class cleavage on the other. One of his most common devices was to compare fluctuations in the price of grain with fluctuations in the amount of crime. Other later investigations have attempted to show that most delinquents or criminals and other deviants come from the unskilled, poor population.

EVALUATION OF POVERTY AND DEVIANT BEHAVIOR

Without question poverty has serious consequences for health, the cultural quality of family life, and educational opportunity. Above all, it limits social participation, particularly in the political, social, and economic sphere. There are a number of objections, however, to poverty as a basic explanation of deviant behavior: the meaning of the concept of poverty itself is relative; studies of poverty have been derived from biased samples; noneconomic factors are often of primary importance in deviation; and, finally, deviation may be reduced without a great deal of change in economic conditions.

1. The entire emphasis on "poverty," "lower economic group," or "minimum standard of living" can be challenged by questioning the meaning of these expressions. They cannot be regarded as absolute and timeless designations in terms of either money or material goods. If poverty is regarded as a relative term, both from the standpoint of other cultures and in time, it has little utility as a universal explanation of deviant behavior. A poor person in America may have infinitely more material goods than a poor person in India or China; a relatively poor family today may have technological possessions and education superior even to those of the upper classes of the American Revolutionary period. Poverty must be defined in terms of the aspirations and expectations of a culture and its capacity to produce these goods. Thus radio, television, electricity, inside plumbing, central heating, an old car or a washing machine, canned foods, and so on, are material possessions which the poor generally have in this country today but which would have been considered luxuries years ago. In fact, it is of

---

[4] William A. Bonger, *Criminality and Economic Conditions* (Henry P. Horton, trans.; Boston: Little, Brown & Company, 1916).

interest that even though there has been a constant increase in the living standards of Western European countries over the past century, there is no indication that deviant behavior has decreased.

Many studies of the economic background of deviants represent biased samples. Most economic studies, for example, have neglected to indicate that a considerable proportion of our nondeviant population also has a low income and also is poorly housed. A considerable number of American families in recent years have had an income below the minimum standards recommended for health and welfare by the Bureau of Labor Statistics.

It is likely that the proportion of deviants from lower socioeconomic groups would generally be much smaller if the samples were more representative. Probably a greater proportion of deviants among the lower socioeconomic group comes to the attention of authorities, both in detection and in commitment, than the proportion of deviants from the wealthier classes. Delinquents among the higher economic groups, for example, are often dealt with by informal means. Crime of the white-collar type among the upper classes is seldom prosecuted, and few persons of this group are imprisoned for it. After surveying the extent of crime among business and professional men, Sutherland has written:

> The theories of criminologists that crime is due to conditions statistically associated with poverty are invalid because, first, they are derived from samples which are grossly biased with respect to socio-economic status; second, they do not apply to the white collar criminals; and third, they do not even explain the criminality of the lower class, since the factors are not related to a general process characteristic of all criminality.[5]

Alcoholics and mental patients from the upper socioeconomic groups are less likely to be included in many studies of alcoholics who come to the attention of public agencies, for they are often treated privately either by psychiatrists or in private clinics or hospitals. A study of 2023 male patients from the Connecticut outpatient alcoholism clinics which were created in recent years tends to contradict previous impressions of the alcoholic population.[6] According to this study, rather than being "alcoholic bums" and derelicts, "nearly two-thirds of the men were gainfully employed when they first came to the clinic; 56 per cent were known to have held steady employment on one job for at least 3 years; 25 per cent for at least 10 years. At least seven out of ten have held jobs involving special skills or responsibility." Sex deviants such as prostitutes likewise appear to exist among all classes; yet those arrested for sexual promiscuity are more likely to be from the poorer classes.

2. Several investigations have indicated that poverty is by no means

---

[5] Edwin H. Sutherland, "White-Collar Criminality," *American Sociological Review* 5:1–12 (February, 1940).

[6] Robert Straus and Selden D. Bacon, "Alcoholism and Social Stability," *Quarterly Journal of Studies on Alcohol,* 12:231–260 (June, 1951). Quotation from page 259.

the only factor accounting for the deviant behavior. Poverty alone does not explain the hobo and the migratory worker, the shelter-house man, and even the beggar. Anderson has presented several other factors of importance, including personality defects.[7] Certain crises, such as family conflict, feelings of failure, disgrace, or embarrassment, and fear of punishment might cause a man to desert his home or community. In some cases racial or national discrimination has resulted in a man's becoming a tramp (one who won't work) or a hobo (one who works only occasionally). In still other situations the longing for new experiences has led a man to develop wanderlust and join the ranks of the homeless man.

After studying 20,000 occupants of shelter houses, Sutherland and Locke also indicated that economic destitution is not the only factor.[8] Many others besides strictly economic considerations were found to be significant in the development of a homeless man. Most of these men had never been really part of any community. More than half of them had been primarily engaged in transient or seasonal labor during most of their lives. Others had moved, before the depression, from one job to another. Few of them had had close relations with their families even when they were young men. Only one third had ever married, and nearly all of these were either divorced, separated, or widowed. Rarely had any of them been connected with a church, and in general they had few personal friends. Thus the road to dependency generally involved not only such factors as prolonged marginal dependency or a long period of economic deterioration, but marital and sexual problems, excessive drinking, cultural conflicts, detachment from family and personal friends, and personal crises.

On the whole, the helpless, ragged shelter-house man has become so demoralized that he is not generally what would be termed a beggar. The latter capitalizes on the contrast between his appearance and that of others, appeals to pity, and generally exploits his lowered economic status. In fact, it is questionable whether an economic factor such as poverty alone explains the beggar seen on the streets of many cities. In a detailed study of beggars, Gilmore found that begging is generally a highly organized activity with general acceptance of a role of begging rather than working. Professional beggars know what types of begging are most productive, such as exhibiting deformities or "hitting" for a handout young people on dates, and where to beg, as in crowds of persons in the theater district or going to or from church. Careful attention is paid to styles of dirty dress and the use of certain words and signs. Some of this knowledge is transmitted from

---

[7] Nels Anderson, *The Hobo* (Chicago: The University of Chicago Press, 1923; reissued by Phoenix, 1961); pp. 72–86.

[8] Edwin H. Sutherland and Harvey J. Locke, *Twenty Thousand Homeless Men* (Philadelphia: J. B. Lippincott Company, 1936). Also see H. Warren Dunham, *Homeless Men and Their Habitats: A Research Planning Report* (Detroit: Department of Sociology and Anthropology, Wayne University, 1953).

generation to generation in begging families; where begging is organized in teams, as in the following case, it distinguishes the professional from the amateur:

> An organization of beggars formerly had their headquarters in the rear of a saloon run by Joe Thomas on a side street just off the central business section. In this back room the beggars kept a supply of old clothes, crutches, false legs, collodion to put in the eyes to make "blind men," acid to make "jiggers" on the arms, and other articles needed in their make-up. They would come here in the morning dressed in their regular street clothes and would change to their "begging" togs. At the end of the day, they would return to head-quarters and change back to their street clothes. There were usually about 70 members of this gang, including ten or twelve women. They were in charge of a precinct captain for an alderman who was a political friend of a state senator. For protection each paid $1.50 to $4.00 per day depending on his "stand." This protection consisted of security from police interference and assurance that other beggars would not be allowed in the loop area.[9]

In the cities of India a common feature in many bazaar areas, as well as in the central shopping areas, temples, and railway stations, is the inevitable beggar who makes his rounds daily. Although a certain type of mendicancy, such as religious begging, has long been common in India, professional begging has become an urban phenomenon for the simple reason that it is a lucrative "trade." [10] One survey reported that in the city of Bombay alone there are about 10,000 beggars, some 47 percent of whom are able-bodied. The total beggar population of Delhi has been estimated at about 3000, 44.5 percent of whom are able-bodied. Many beggars "earn" more than the daily wage of nonbeggars.

3. There are indications, moreover, that the social integration of an area can be improved without major material changes. For example, the Chicago Area Projects, where neighborhood councils in the slums have dealt with problems of delinquency, appear to have made a reduction in these rates without changing either economic or housing conditions.[11] Treatment in general and group methods in the treatment, in particular, of mental disorder, crime, and alcoholism, for example, through Alcoholics

---

[9] Harlan W. Gilmore, *The Beggar* (Chapel Hill: University of North Carolina Press, 1940), p. 117.

[10] M. V. Moorthy ed., *Beggar Problem in Greater Bombay* (A Research Study; Bombay: Indian Conference of Social Work, 1959), p. 14, and *The Beggar Problem in Metropolitan Delhi* (Delhi: Delhi School of Social Work, 1959).

[11] H. L. Witmer and E. Tufts, *The Effectiveness of Delinquency Prevention Programs*, Children's Bureau, United States Department of Health, Education, and Welfare, Publication 350 (Washington, D.C.: Government Printing Office, 1954), p. 15. Also see Solomon Kobrin, "The Chicago Area Project: A 25 Year Assessment," *The Annals*, 322:19–29 (March, 1959), and Anthony Sorrentino, "The Chicago Area Project After 25 Years," *Federal Probation*, 23:40–45 (June, 1959).

Anonymous, do not necessarily require marked changes in the economic status of the individual.[12]

Fluctuations in the Business Cycle and Deviation

Modern society has been characterized by recurrent fluctuations in economic conditions, fluctuations commonly referred to as prosperity, recessions, and depressions. During periods of recession or depression there is an increase in unemployment and poverty, along with a general decline in morale. It is believed by some people that these conditions are associated with increased juvenile delinquency, crime, prostitution, mental disorder, marital maladjustment, suicide, and racial tensions. On the other hand, many believe that prosperity is accompanied by "high" living and increased alcohol consumption. In the scientific study of these relationships, different rates of deviant behavior have been compared with various economic indices, generally utilizing measures of statistical correlation.

From the evidence available it can be concluded that the business cycle has little or no direct relation to most forms of social deviation with the exception of suicide. The processes of urbanism and norm conflicts must be regarded as the more basic factors in producing social deviation. Whereas deficiencies in given economic processes may intensify urbanism, they certainly are not the prime causes of our contemporary difficulties. It is likely that a balanced economic system would still have most of our contemporary problems since most of them involve conflicts in norms and difficulties in interpersonal relations rather than technological or strictly economic issues.

Technological Development and the Cultural Lag

The machine age and all of its complexity have been blamed by a number of scientists, including sociologists, for the confusion and deviation of the world in which we live. Their ideas have been reflected in the beliefs of many laymen that if we could only master the machine we would be able to build a world free of crime and other social problems. This theory, with different solutions proposed for the problems, has wide acceptance both in the West and in the communist countries. The idea has been illustrated in countless cartoons, such as those showing a complex machine and a socially incompetent modern "caveman."

In fact, no explanation of social deviation has enjoyed a popularity equal to that of the scientific theory based upon the "cultural lag," a con-

---

[12] Marshall B. Clinard, "The Group Approach to Social Reintegration," *American Sociological Review*, 14:257–262 (April, 1949).

cept first suggested by Ogburn in 1922.[13] All social problems, according to him, resulted basically from social change, which creates maladjustments among various parts of a culture. Today, the term is part of everyday speech, and many editorials and cartoons dwell on the theme. A survey of the literature of social science indicates that practically every conceivable problem at one time or another has been considered to be a cultural lag. "At the basis of all social problems are culture lags. . . . The maladjustments create confusion and inject uncertainties in the relations of individual to individual, individual to group, and group to group." [14] A text on social problems stated that the cultural lag concept is as basic to sociology as the theory of gravitation is to physics:

> Although mankind has become adapted to the new tempo of living and has accepted and exploited scientific and technological achievements, it has failed to adjust the social structure—economic, political, and social ideas and institutions—to the new pattern of material culture. Indeed, men are trying to manage the new world of machines with the ideas and institutions of horse-and-buggy days and, in some cases, of the Stone Age. This failure to modernize social ideas and institutions has produced the serious "cultural lag" that confronts our society and causes most of our social problems.[15]

Such unrelated social problems as unemployment and labor conflicts, congestion and insufficient housing construction, inadequate medical care, educational problems, traffic casualties, juvenile delinquency, crime, mental illness, moral conflicts, the costs and destruction of war, and adolescent instability have been attributed to technological maladjustments. Other studies have ascribed the decline of family ethics to a lag behind technological advance. Some would explain increased crime as partly due to the lag in the number of police behind the more rapid growth in population, as well as to the failure of modern mechanical devices for dealing with criminals to keep pace with the growth of crime.[16] One writer has well summarized the impact of this materialistic interpretation of human history:

---

[13] William F. Ogburn, *Social Change* (New York: The Viking Press, Inc., 1922). For further elaboration of his theory, see William F. Ogburn ed., *Recent Social Trends in the United States* (New York: McGraw-Hill Book Company, Inc., 1933); National Resources Committee, *Technological Trends and National Policy* (Washington, D.C.: Government Printing Office, 1937); William F. Ogburn, *The Social Effects of Aviation* (Boston: Houghton Mifflin Company, 1946); and William F. Ogburn and Meyer Nimkoff, *Sociology* (Boston: Houghton Mifflin Company, 1940). An earlier writing by the sociologist Charles Cooley stated the somewhat similar view that social problems grew out of the "formalism" of certain social institutions which became ossified or fixed, while others undergo transformations.—Charles Cooley, *Social Organization: A Study of the Larger Mind* (New York: Charles Scribner's Sons, 1919).

[14] Elio Monachesi, "Sociology and Culture," in Emerson P. Schmidt ed., *Man and Society* (Englewood Cliffs, N.J.: Prentice-Hall, Inc., 1938), p. 46.

[15] Harry Elmer Barnes and Oreen M. Ruedi, *The American Way of Life* (2d ed.; Englewood Cliffs, N.J.: Prentice-Hall, Inc., 1950), pp. 2–3.

[16] Ogburn and Nimkoff, *op. cit.*, pp. 886–887.

Anyone who fondly retains his foreign language, who doesn't believe in divorce, who bakes his own bread, or who is slow to accept the technological improvements of his business competitor, these are all "in lag." Circumstances such as the congested condition of the streets, the regular delay in the appearance of subject matter in secondary texts after its general acceptance, and scores of other cases, are also "evidence of lag" and have been uncritically classified under that omnibus rubric.[17]

According to the cultural lag thesis, various parts of modern culture are not changing at the same rate. Some parts, the technological, are changing more rapidly than the nontechnological aspects of society, such as the family, religion, and the political system. Since there are a correlation and an interdependence of parts among all social institutions, a rapid change in one part of a culture requires readjustments through changes in the various other correlated parts. Technological changes eventually cause alterations in other parts of the culture, but corresponding changes in the nonmaterial culture do not occur simultaneously with the changes in the material sphere.[18] This differential time sequence results in the cultural lag.

The nonmaterial aspects of culture change much more slowly than the material for several reasons: (1) there is more emotional opposition to change in the former; (2) improvements resulting from changes in the material culture are more readily received since they are more observable; (3) a materialistic emphasis is itself a supreme value in our society; and (4) habit, vested interests, and ignorance all combine to favor the maintenance of the *status quo* in the nonmaterial sphere. "Social problems arise, and existing problems are aggravated, when a society creates or accepts instruments of change, yet fails to understand, anticipate, or deal with the consequences of such action." [19]

Most so-called "lags" are thought to indicate that certain technological revolutions have far outsped economic and other social changes, thus creating maladjustments. Not only are adherents of this approach certain that a lag can be shown to exist in social areas but also that the extent of the lag and the severity of the maladjustment can be measured. With the present-day emphasis on machines and the rapidity with which these ma-

---

[17] John H. Mueller, "Present Status of the Cultural Lag Hypothesis," *American Sociological Review*, 3:320 (June, 1938).

[18] Ogburn, as well as others, in more recent writings has tried to place less stress on technological changes and has implied that lags could take place between any two parts of the culture even if both were adaptive: "The strain that exists between two correlated parts of culture that change at unequal rates of speed may be interpreted as a lag in the part that is changing at the slowest rate, for the one lags behind the other." In another connection Ogburn has written that "the lag of social changes behind technological progress is simply a special case of the general phenomenon of unequal rates of change of the correlated parts of culture."—Ogburn and Nimkoff, *op. cit.*, pp. 886, 893.

[19] Abbott Herman, *An Approach to Social Problems* (Boston: Ginn and Company, 1949), p. 51.

terial aspects are changing, the lag between the technological and the adaptive culture has become increasingly great. Steam power replaced hand power; electrical power and electronics, together with the gasoline engine, have made great inroads into the use of steam power; and now nuclear fission has become a source of power.

AN EVALUATION OF THE CULTURAL LAG THEORY
OF DEVIANT BEHAVIOR

Regardless of whether cultural lag is restricted to the material-non-material definition or is described as a lack of synchronization in social institutions in the general culture, those who hold this theory believe that social problems can be explained by cultural lags, that they have been constantly increasing rather than decreasing, and that the most important factors are technological and economic. The proposed solution to the problem of cultural lag obviously lies in social planning in order to restore balance within the culture. Such planning would include a study of past changes in the material culture and a prediction of future changes and of the resistances in a society which prevent adjustment to technological change.

The cultural lag explanation impresses many students of social problems, for it focuses attention on culture as a unified whole and stresses the interdependence of institutions in a society. In fact, properly employed, the cultural lag concept is extremely useful as a theoretical instrument to explain some disunities in a culture that are primarily economic. The cultural lag hypothesis may even have some predictive value, primarily in economic areas. For example, Ogburn has demonstrated how future consequences of technological devices can be predicted, making it possible for society to avoid many of the dislocations of the past.[20]

Despite the wide following that the cultural lag theory has had among social scientists interested in problems of deviant behavior, however, there are a number of serious objections to it. These include the fact that norms and values, other than technological and materialistic ones, are often involved in deviant behavior; moreover, consideration of the individual is omitted, and the term "cultural lag" is loosely used.

1. The problems of modern society involve, fundamentally, conflicts of norms and values which are many and of diverse origins. The cultural lag theory, even though there have been recent attempts at modification, is essentially an overstatement of the role that technological and economic

---

[20] Ogburn, *The Social Effects of Aviation*. See also "National Policy and Technology," in *Technological Trends and National Policy*, Pt. I, sec. 1; and William F. Ogburn ed., *Technology and International Relations* (Chicago: The University of Chicago Press, 1949). Also see Charles R. Walker ed., *Modern Technology and Civilization* (New York: McGraw-Hill Book Company, Inc., 1962).

forces play in conflicts in a society. It assumes that the norm conflicts disturbing a society are largely derived from these sources. Undoubtedly some social change does originate in technological factors, but much social change has been brought about by ideas not connected with material culture. They include Christianity and other great religious doctrines, the growth of secularism, democracy, the humanistic philosophy, communism, individualism, equal rights for women, and the English concept of justice in law. Questions involving the use of alcoholic beverages and conflicts stemming from racial and religious discrimination disturb modern societies a great deal, but only by the widest stretch of the imagination can they be brought within the lag concept. Actually most social change is a product of inextricably connected forces, both material and nonmaterial. Wallis puts it thus: "It seems to us unwarranted and also historically inaccurate to say that society must always hop when technology swings the rope." [21]

2. Attitudes, motivations, and social roles of the individual person are of little consequence because impersonal forces far more basic are said to be in operation. The cultural lag theory falsely implies that the person is an automaton, controlled almost entirely by impersonal forces, largely technological and economic.

3. "Cultural lag" is used so loosely that it often has little meaning. Instead of a single concept to be applied indiscriminately to all types of change, Mueller, for example, has suggested two types of lags: those that are really delayed responses and those that are spurious, that is, are actually not lags at all.[22] Most of the applications of the social lag concept turn out on close analysis to be spurious lags. Examples of true lags are seen in the workmen's compensation laws, which followed considerably behind the development of machine technology, and the development of other measures to deal with unemployment arising from new inventions. In cases of this type the relation between the variables, between one cultural element and another, can be established. Many supposed lags are not lags at all because the variables assumed to be closely related are actually not. It would be impossible to relate, for example, divorce rates as measures of marital difficulties and industrial production or other similar economic indices unless one had a rather unusual concept of what basically were the causes of such marital maladjustment.

Actually, the existence of a lag and its direction rest inevitably on a question of values. What is a lag to one scientist may not be to another.[23] A large percentage of women working in industry may suggest that the family system is lagging behind the industrial system and that later adjust-

---

[21] Wilson D. Wallis, in Letters to the Editor, *American Journal of Sociology*, 43:807 (March, 1938).
[22] Mueller, "Present Status of the Cultural Lag Hypothesis," *loc. cit.*, p. 320.
[23] *Ibid.*

ments will take women out of the economic system and back into the home. On the other hand, the same facts might as plausibly suggest that more industrial work should be provided for women because of equalitarian treatment of women, because of the decline of various functions of the family, and because some psychiatrists might believe it good mental hygiene to provide useful tasks for women who have little to do in modern urban society. Similarly, how can we be assured, as some have suggested, that contemporary marriage ethics and sexual morals are lagging behind industrial development, and if they are, is it known how much they lag? Persons with opposite value systems might reach opposite conclusions. Mumford, too, has pointed out that the idea implies that man must always make an adjustment to the machine, whereas on occasions what may be required is adjustment away from the machine: "In truth, interactions between organisms and their environments take place in both directions, and it is just as correct to regard the machinery of warfare as retarded in relation to the morality of Confucius as to take the opposite position." [24]

Substandard Housing and Deviant Behavior

Probably few people believe that inadequate housing, by itself, is a cause of deviant behavior, but many consider it to be one of the major causes. Considerable evidence has been submitted to indicate that substandard housing plays a major role in deviant behavior.[25] In Detroit fifteen times as many criminals per unit of population came from a blighted area as from a normal residential area. In Cleveland 21 percent of the murders and 26 percent of the vice centers were in a deteriorated housing area representing only 1 percent of the land area and 2.5 percent of the population. A study of Jacksonville, Florida, showed that the cost of police protection in blighted areas was twelve times more per unit of area than in the remainder of the city. An Indianapolis study of census tracts (enumerative areas in a population census) near the center of the city, where the housing had deteriorated, showed that whereas only 10.4 percent of the city population lived there, these people utilized some 30 percent of the city hospital service and made up 24 percent of the cases in the venereal disease clinics and 19 percent of the patients in mental hospitals. Almost 25 percent of the cost to the city of arresting, trying, and imprisoning misdemeanants and 36 percent of the cost of felony cases involved residents of this area. In addition, this district accounted for 16.7 percent of the city's fire cost.[26]

---

[24] Lewis Mumford, *Technics and Civilization* (New York: Harcourt, Brace & World, Inc., 1934), p. 317.

[25] S. E. Sanders and A. J. Rabuck, *New City Patterns* (New York: Reinhold Publishing Corporation, 1946), p. 12.

[26] R. Clyde White, "The Relation of Felonies to Environmental Factors in Indianapolis," *Social Forces*, 10:498–509 (May, 1932).

A study by a federal housing agency indicated that poor housing is an important element in nearly all phases of social deviation, particularly juenvile delinquency. The relation of housing to delinquency was indicated as follows: (1) Physically deteriorated areas in which there is much congestion, together with many pool halls, beer taverns, and houses of ill repute, have larger proportions of delinquency. (2) Because of overcrowding at home, young boys and girls have to share rooms with adults, not always members of their own families, adolescents of different sexes have to share rooms, and there may be three or more individuals sleeping in the same room. (3) Those places in the city characterized by land crowding, inadequate recreation areas, and buildings so crowded that there is inadequate light and ventilation often have more than their share of delinquents. (4) Homes from which come delinquent children are usually found to be substandard from the standpoint of physical conditions and modern facilities.[27]

Research in the fields of racial, ethnic, and religious prejudice has consistently indicated three major effects of segregated housing in deteriorated areas: (1) It represents symbolically in an observable form the subordination of certain peoples to those with more adequate housing. (2) It perpetuates intergroup tensions, prejudice, and stereotypes by largely eliminating the opportunity for personal contacts among members of different groups. When certain minority groups attempt to move into areas populated by a dominant group the resistance of the latter may increase tension and prejudice and even result in vandalism or race riots. (3) It makes for serious health problems, and some claim it directly or indirectly affects other problems of a more social nature, such as juvenile delinquency.

The exceptionally bad housing among Negroes may have an effect on their family system. Because of the Negroes' economic situation, two or more families may occupy the same set of rooms without any semblance of privacy. When the family lives separately, it may take in lodgers, a practice that is more frequent when the household is headed by a woman. These living arrangements may seriously affect family morale and sex patterns. Bad housing "probably explains why so many Negroes congregate on the streets of Negro neighborhoods. So far as the children are concerned, the house becomes a veritable prison for them. There is no way of knowing how many of the conflicts in Negro families are set off by the irritations caused by overcrowding people, who come home after a day of frustration and fatigue, to dingy and unhealthy living quarters." [28]

Conclusions about Housing and Deviant Behavior. A more careful

---

[27] Federal Emergency Administration of Public Works Housing Division, "The Relation between Housing and Delinquency" (Research Bulletin 11; Washington, D.C.: Government Printing Office, 1936), p. 40.

[28] E. Franklin Frazier, *The Negro in the United States* (rev. ed.; New York: The Macmillan Company, 1957), p. 636.

analysis of the high deviation rates of the slums does not indicate that either low economic status or bad housing is the explanation. Rather, low economic status or racial prejudice forces persons to reside in low-rent areas which are characterized by the presence of accentuated urban characteristics and norm conflicts. Although it is true that sociological studies of the ecological distribution of delinquency and of mental illness within cities have indicated that such deviation and poor housing are correlated, this fact in itself is not the important variable. Rather, the explanation of the deviation appears to be a product primarily of the social conditions and the extensive urbanism of the area. One comprehensive report on housing lists as a popular fallacy "that substandard housing is the direct cause of delinquency and crime and that its elimination would result in a crimeless world." [29]

Part of the difficulty in attempting to show such relationships has been the research techniques employed. Such studies are based merely on large statistical comparisons, disregarding for the most part individual case studies where the meaning of the economic factors could be better understood. Summarizing available evidence and suggestions, Chapin has concluded that adequate housing can neither produce new and desirable personality traits nor cure mental disorders.[30]

What sometimes appears to be significant is often a crude relationship at best. Some studies have attempted to prove that when housing is improved, general social conditions, including the incidence of delinquency, also improve. It has been claimed, for example, that the juvenile delinquency rates in one particular housing development dropped from 3.18 per 100 children to 1.64 [31] as a result of changes in housing facilities. A study of 171 relocated families in Minneapolis revealed that families which moved to less crowded quarters gained in five out of eight indices of social conditions.[32] As compared with the children of a control group, there was a decline in juvenile delinquency among the children of a group of Negro families in Newark who were rehoused during World War II.[33] There is some question, however, as to whether in such situations housing accounted for the decline or whether it was due to changes in social conditions. A New York study compared the housing facilities of 277 delinquency cases from 196 city blocks in East Harlem with the homes of more than 31,000

[29] Quoted in Edith Elmer Wood, *Introduction to Housing: Facts and Principles* (Washington, D.C.: U.S. Housing Authority, Federal Works Administration, 1939), p. 55.

[30] F. Stuart Chapin, "Some Housing Factors Related to Mental Hygiene," in "Social Policy and Social Research in Housing," *Journal of Social Issues*, Nos. 1 and 2 (1951).

[31] Naomi Barer, "Delinquency before, after Admission to New Haven Housing Development," *Journal of Housing* 3:27 (December, 1945–January, 1946).

[32] F. Stuart Chapin, "The Effects of Slum Clearance and Rehousing on Family and Community Relationships in Minneapolis," *American Journal of Sociology*, 43:744 (March, 1938).

[33] Housing Authority of the City of Newark, *The Social Effects of Housing* (Newark, N.J.: 1944).

nondelinquent children of the same age in the area.[34] The study found no relationship between the physical aspects of bad housing and juvenile delinquency as revealed by court records, although the social relationships connected with housing were found to be important. Finally, it has not always been demonstrated that the families which moved into a housing project had previously lived in the area. After studying an English city Morris concluded that physical characteristics of an area are of little relevance to crime and delinquency, except as an indirect determinant of the social status of the area. Even after the construction of new government housing projects the high rates of delinquency remained.[35]

Summary

In the light of all this evidence it appears that it is not poverty, the amount of income, or economic factors generally which are crucial for understanding the dynamics of social and personal deviation. The relation of economic factors to deviant attitudes, social roles, and life organization must be demonstrated before much reliance can be placed on explanations based on economic factors. Although no one would imply that economic factors are not significant, they must have a demonstrated meaningful relationship to human behavior if they are to be considered as basic.

What is important is the urbanized setting in which economic factors function, and the interpretation given by the person and the group to the economic situation in which they find themselves. Poverty and deprivation, prosperity and depressions are important only in terms of the aspirations, needs, socially defined status, and cultural conditionings of the person. A sudden improvement in earning power may have as much of a disorganizing influence on a person as a decrease, but a different kind of deviant behavior will result.

Countries with much material welfare, such as the United States, have some of the highest deviation rates in the world, and these rates are extremely high during times of great economic prosperity. Comparisons of rural and urban deviation rates in most societies, including America, indicate much lower rural rates even though tenant farmers and farm laborers often may be generally poorer and live under housing conditions almost as unsatisfactory as those in large urban centers.

There is some indication that juvenile delinquency, rather than being a product of poverty, may, if anything, be related to "the affluent society." Certainly there is some evidence for this in the increasing delinquency of Western society and, in particular, in such countries as the United States

---

[34] Wood, *op. cit.*, p. 56.
[35] Terence Morris, *The Criminal Area: A Study in Social Ecology* (London: Routledge & Kegan Paul Ltd., 1957).

and Sweden. Writing of the relation of juvenile delinquency to American prosperity of recent years, Galbraith has stated:

> Thus an aspect of increasing private production is the appearance of an extraordinary number of things which lay claim to the interest of the young. Motion pictures, television, automobiles, and the vast opportunities which go with the mobility, together with such less enchanting merchandise as narcotics, comic books, and pornographia, are all included in an advancing gross national product. The child of a less opulent as well as a technologically more primitive age had far fewer such diversions.[36]

Speaking of communities where private consumer goods are far more developed than public services, such as the school, Galbraith says:

> Here, in an atmosphere of private opulence and public squalor, the private goods have full sway. Schools do not compete with television and the movies. The dubious heroes of the latter, not Miss Jones, become the idols of the young. The hot rod and the wild ride take the place of more sedentary sports for which there are inadequate facilities or provision. Comic books, alcohol, narcotics, and switchblade knives are, as noted, part of the increased flow of goods, and there is nothing to dispute their enjoyment. There is an ample supply of private wealth to be appropriated and not much to be feared from the police. An austere community is free from temptation. It can be austere in its public services. Not so a rich one.[37]

Actually the basic process through which social deviation increases appears to lie in the urban way of life which is found today in all communities, regardless of the economic system. Urbanism is present whether a society is capitalist, democratic socialist, communist, or fascist. Forces tending to emphasize urban ways of life are present in all systems, and their influences range from New York City and Chicago to Moscow, Madrid, Stockholm, and the islands of Indonesia. This emphasis on urbanism rather than the economic system as the basic problem for society does not imply that a given economic system may have no relation to the characteristics of urbanism which we have described. All society is an interrelated whole, and each institution, whether it be the economic, religious, or family system, may affect the central ideologies of a society. Consequently, one economic system may accentuate urban ways of life while another may help to minimize them. An economic system which does not protect the individual from depressions, unemployment, and lack of social security in childhood and old age, or which stresses individual materialistic success at the expense of others will accentuate urban characteristics of individualism, materialism, and the role of competition. An economic system which so regulates all phases of the individual's life that he becomes dependent upon, and subservient to, the central political organization will result in great empha-

[36] John Kenneth Galbraith, *The Affluent Society* (Boston: Houghton Mifflin Company, 1958), pp. 256–257. Used by permission of the publishers.
[37] *Ibid.*, pp. 257–258.

sis on impersonality in social relations and upon the importance of technology and the state rather than human welfare. Such an economic system will emphasize not only materialism and striving for individual advantage through special rewards and favors but also self-interest through the growth of the fear and helplessness of the individual in the face of impersonal and bureaucratic forces.

Selected Readings

ANGELL, ROBERT C. *The Family Encounters the Depression*. New York: Charles Scribner's Sons, 1936. The effect of the depression on the family was not primarily one of economic insecurity.

CAVAN, RUTH S., and KATHERINE H. RANCK. *The Family and the Depression*. Chicago: The University of Chicago Press, 1938. A study of the effect of the depression on a group of families.

GALBRAITH, JOHN K. *The Affluent Society*. Boston: Houghton Mifflin Company, 1958. A somewhat different view of the role of economic factors and social problems, namely, that affluence, rather than poverty, is important.

GILMORE, HARLAN W. *The Beggar*. Chapel Hill: University of North Carolina Press, 1940. A study of begging as a highly organized activity and not one primarily arising from economic need.

MORRIS, TERENCE. *The Criminal Area: A Study in Social Ecology*. London: Routledge & Kegan Paul Ltd., 1957. An analysis of crime and delinquency areas in an English city, with one conclusion being that physical deterioration or new housing has, on the whole, little direct relation to crime.

MUELLER, JOHN H. "Present Status of the Cultural Lag Hypothesis," *American Sociological Review*, 3:320–327 (June, 1938). An excellent criticism of the cultural lag theory in which he distinguishes particularly between "spurious" and true lags.

OGBURN, WILLIAM F. *Social Change*. New York: The Viking Press, Inc., 1950. This book is the classic statement of the cultural lag theory. Originally published in 1922, it was reprinted again in 1950 with a supplementary chapter.

STRAUS, ROBERT, and SELDEN D. BACON. "Alcoholism and Social Stability," *Quarterly Journal of Studies on Alcohol*, 12:231–260 (June, 1951). This study of 2023 male alcoholics who visited outpatient clinics for treatment, indicated that many alcoholics come from the middle class.

SUTHERLAND, EDWIN H. "White-Collar Criminality," *American Sociological Review*, 5:1–12 (February, 1940). In this well-known presidential address to the American Sociological Society, Sutherland stated that crime cannot be explained by poverty, for it occurs among the middle and upper socioeconomic groups as well. Criminological research should be conducted on broader samples of criminal offenders.

WALKER, CHARLES R. ed. *Modern Technology and Civilization*. New York: McGraw-Hill Book Company, Inc., 1962. This book of readings explores the relationship between man and the machine, and assumes that the future of all civilizations is closely linked to the manner in which man may either use or misuse modern technology. It also explores the human problems and promises of the machine age in which man now lives.

Chapter 5

Controversial Theories
of Deviant Behavior

Approaching the problem of deviant behavior—either the general problem or specific types of behavior—with a background of particularistic knowledge derived from their own specialties, some scientists have on occasion shown little or no grasp of the principles of human behavior. In this chapter the following theories will be discussed: that deviants are feeble-minded, have certain body types, or can be explained entirely by psychiatric or psychoanalytic principles.

Deviant Behavior and Feeble-Mindedness

In the past, and to some extent today, constitutional inferiority in the form of subnormal intelligence has been frequently advanced as one of the principal causes of certain forms of deviant behavior. Hundreds of studies of intelligence have been made of juveniles and criminals, prostitutes, alcoholics, and hoboes. The assumption has been made that either low intelligence and deviant behavior are directly associated, or that low intelligence is likely to lead a person into patterns of such behavior.[1]

The theory that there is a relationship between intelligence and deviant behavior is now on its way out of accepted literature. The reasons for this are based on actual intelligence scores of deviants, on the fact that certain data are largely derived from biased samples, and on the fact that a direct relationship between intelligence and deviant behavior is simply an assumption.

More careful study of the empirical evidence has not substantiated earlier beliefs about subnormal intelligence. Not only are there wide variations in the intelligence scores of deviants, but in general their scores do not appear to differ too much from those of the general population. Sutherland examined 350 studies of the intelligence of some 175,000 criminals

---

[1] Goddard was one of the earliest writers to advocate this theory. See Henry H. Goddard, *Human Efficiency and Levels of Intelligence* (Princeton, N.J.: Princeton University Press, 1922), pp. 72–73.

and delinquents and found such great variations in the percentage of offenders diagnosed as feeble-minded that any relationship had little meaning. In the period 1910–1914 the feeble-minded so diagnosed averaged 50 percent; between 1925 and 1928 they were 20 percent.[2] He also found that if allowances were made for selective factors in conviction and imprisonment the scores did not differ materially from those of the general population. Zeleny, too, found that a comparison of scores of inmates of correctional institutions with those of the general population showed little difference, the ratio being only 1.2 to 1.0.[3] Another study covering some 10,000 Illinois prisoners found that their intelligence scores differed little from those of the normal population.[4]

Several wartime studies of prostitutes for the United States Public Health Service have failed to confirm the belief that girls from such groups are necessarily feeble-minded.[5] The Kinsey report, as well as other similar studies which have indicated widespread sexual deviation on the part of the general population, would serve to confirm the idea that sexual promiscuity certainly cannot be directly associated with intelligence scores.[6]

Now that more extensive studies have been made of alcoholism and mental disorder in all social groups, the intelligence quotient is no longer considered to be significant in their etiology. One test group of 47 compulsive drinkers had a mean I.Q. of 114.9, which is somewhat above the average, their standard deviation was 14.3 and their range was 73–139 on the Wechsler-Bellevue Adult Intelligence Test. Halpern, who made the study, said: "In general, then, this group of alcoholic subjects showed no characteristic organization of mental abilities which would serve to distinguish them either from normal subjects or from other clinical groups. For this group there was no evidence of mental impairment or deterioration." [7] Bühler subsequently corroborated these findings in her study of 100 alcoholics. They had an average I.Q. score of 103.2, or well within the normal range.[8]

---

[2] Edwin H. Sutherland, "Mental Deficiency and Crime," in Kimball Young ed., *Social Attitudes* (New York: Holt, Rinehart and Winston, Inc., 1931), pp. 357–375.

[3] Leslie D. Zeleny, "Feeble-Mindedness and Criminal Conduct," *American Journal of Sociology*, 38:564–578 (January, 1933).

[4] Simon H. Tulchin, *Intelligence and Crime* (Chicago: The University of Chicago Press, 1939).

[5] H. L. Rachlin, "A Sociological Analysis of 304 Female Patients Admitted to the Midwestern Medical Center, St. Louis, Mo.," *Venereal Disease Information*, U.S. Public Health Service, 25:267 (September, 1944).

[6] Alfred C. Kinsey, Wardell B. Pomeroy, and Clyde E. Martin, *Sexual Behavior in the Human Male* (Philadelphia: W. B. Saunders Company, 1948).

[7] Florence Halpern, "Psychological Test Results," in Jane F. Cushman and Carney Landis, *Studies of Compulsive Drinkers* (New Haven, Conn.: Quarterly Journal of Studies on Alcohol, 1946), p. 83.

[8] Charlotte Bühler and D. Welty Lefever, "A Rorschach Study of the Psychological Characteristics of Alcoholics," *Quarterly Journal of Studies on Alcohol*, 8:197–260 (September, 1947).

EVALUATION OF DEVIANT BEHAVIOR AND FEEBLE-MINDEDNESS

Most of the studies of the intelligence of deviants have been based on institutional populations or detected deviants, and the fact that the studies sometimes indicate that deviants may have a low intelligence may simply mean that the samples are biased. Various investigators agree that there are fewer mental defectives among randomly chosen school children than among the delinquents who get caught, and that institutionalized delinquents have an average I.Q. below that of school children.[9] If professional and white-collar criminals, persons who are seldom detected or go to prison, were added to the sample of persons in penal institutions, the intelligence scores would undoubtedly increase. There may be, however, a relation between intelligence and certain types of offenses, with the habitual petty offender generally having a lower intelligence than the white-collar or professional criminal. If alcoholics from the more educated groups were added to drunks tested in Skid Rows, the I.Q. distribution would be skewed upward.

No one knows the actual components of innate intelligence because the effect of social experience on the latter is such that it appears to be impossible to measure.[10] It is now generally agreed that the so-called intelligence test measures only "test intelligence" and not innate intelligence. Moreover, there is increasing evidence that the I.Q. can be somewhat modified by social experience.[11] On logical grounds, moreover, there is nothing in the nature of subnormal intelligence that implies a relationship with either social attitudes or social roles. The idea that persons with low intelligence are likely to engage in deviant behavior must be regarded simply as an assumption, since one might also argue that low intelligence could lead to rigid compliance with traditional ways of acting and higher intelligence could be associated with deviant behavior when traditional values are violated. Although studies have not been made, the great proportion of persons with low intelligence scores undoubtedly are nondeviants, whereas there are large numbers of persons with above normal intelligence who are.

A feeble-minded boy may associate with a delinquent group and engage in delinquencies much as would a boy of normal intelligence. It is conceivable that where the deviant actions require skill and initiative the feeble-minded person might, however, be excluded. On the other hand,

---

[9] Maud A. Merrill, *Problems of Child Delinquency* (Boston: Houghton Mifflin Company, 1947), p. 162.
[10] See George L. Stoddard, *The Meaning of Intelligence* (New York: The Macmillan Company, 1943).
[11] *Ibid.*

without the acquisition of deviant attitudes and certain social roles the feeble-minded boy might never become a deviant. In terms of human behavior the concept of feeble-mindedness has little significance. After surveying various delinquency studies Merrill has stated: "As measured in terms of I.Q., intelligence has little relation to the choice or persistence of a criminal career. Of young people who break the law, we have more opportunities to observe the behavior of the less intelligent than of the more intelligent." [12] In the total pattern of personality, intelligence may in a given case have some relation to delinquent behavior but the degree of intelligence alone does not account for the delinquency.

Deviant Behavior and Body Type

In the past the writings of Lombroso on crime and Kretschmer on mental illness—and in more recent years of Hooton on crime and of Sheldon on mental illness, crime, and alcoholism—have tried to correlate deviant behavior with certain body types. These studies have aroused great controversy among those interested in deviation and have captured the imagination of many laymen. The public has been quick to accept these ideas, for carried in the folklore of our culture is a common belief in the direct relationship between physiognomy and personality. Crippled hunchbacks appear in literature as stereotypes of evil or as court jesters, fat persons are presumed to be jolly, thin persons are sad and melancholy, and the red-haired are hot-tempered. Commonly cartoons and literature picture the criminal, for example, as of middle age, hard in appearance and often with a malformation in the ear and in general facial structure. The myth of racial superiority and inferiority has served to perpetuate in the popular mind these ideas about differences in the physical appearance of deviants.

Lombroso, in the latter part of the nineteenth century, made studies to show that most criminals were characterized by certain physical characteristics.[13] On the basis of his studies in Germany in the 1920's, Kretschmer believed that he could classify human beings into three rather distinct physical types which were differently associated with certain forms of mental illness.[14] The asthenic type, who had a thin, narrow build, particularly in the shoulders and chest, long thin arms and delicately shaped hands, was associated with schizophrenia, as was the athletic type. The

---

[12] Merrill, op. cit., p. 180.   [13] See Chapter 6.

[14] E. Kretschmer, Physique and Character (London: Routledge & Kegan Paul Ltd., 1925). Although Mohr and Gundlach, attempting to test Kretschmer's body types, found some agreement in their study of Illinois prisoners, they found the same distribution of physical traits among the noncriminal population.—George J. Mohr and Ralph H. Gundlach, "The Relation between Physique and Performance," Journal of Experimental Psychology, 10:117–157 (February, 1927).

latter, as the name indicates, was a strong, muscular, well-developed physical type with broad shoulders and a thick chest. The pyknic type, on the other hand, was round and fat in appearance and was associated with the manic-depressive psychoses.

Somewhat later, Hooton, a physical anthropologist, made an elaborate study in which he compared several thousand prisoners with a control group.[15] He attempted to revive in many respects the Lombrosian theory—which started the science of criminology—that most criminals are some sort of atavistic, "primitive" men with observable physical features. Hooton reported that criminals are more likely to have long thin necks and sloping shoulders, low and sloping foreheads, thinner beard and body hair, more red-brown hair, thin lips, compressed jaw angles, and a small, extremely protruding ear. He stated, in addition, that certain body types are connected with certain types of crime, tall, thin men tending to murder and rob; tall, heavy men to kill and commit forgery and fraud; undersized men to steal and to commit burglary; and short, heavy persons to assault, rape, and commit other sex crimes.

Von Hentig went even further and suggested, on the basis of a study of Western outlaws, that criminals who committed frontier depredations were primarily red-haired and that red-haired persons are physiologically more active, impulsive, and with "accelerated motor innervation." Hence he concluded "that the number of red-headed men among the noted outlaws surpassed their rate in the normal population." [16] Another writer has presented contrary evidence, indicating that of fifty-eight frontier bad men only two were red-haired.[17]

The general thesis of Lombroso, Kretschmer, and Hooton has been elaborated since 1940 by Sheldon into a much more complex theory. Sheldon is a medically trained psychologist who for several years has been Director of the Constitution Laboratory and Professor of Medicine at Columbia University. His studies have been widely publicized and have come to the attention of millions of persons both here and abroad.[18] His thesis that a human being's behavior and personality are closely related to the structure of his body has been set forth in three volumes.[19] Sheldon has

---

[15] E. A. Hooton, *Crime and the Man* (Cambridge, Mass.: Harvard University Press, 1939), and *The American Criminal: An Anthropological Study* (Cambridge, Mass.: Harvard University Press, 1939).

[16] Hans von Hentig, "Redhead and Outlaw," *Journal of Criminal Law and Criminology*, 38:6 (May–June, 1947).

[17] Philip J. Rasch, "Red Hair and Outlawing," *Journal of Criminal Law and Criminology*, 38:352–356 (November–December, 1947).

[18] See, for example, Robert Coughlan, "What Manner of Morph Are You?" *Life*, 30:65–66 (June 25, 1951).

[19] William H. Sheldon, S. S. Stevens, and W. B. Tucker, *The Varieties of Human Physique* (New York: Harper & Row, Publishers, 1940); William H. Sheldon and S. S. Stevens, *The Varieties of Temperament* (New York: Harper & Row, Publishers, 1942); and William H. Sheldon, *Varieties of Delinquent Youth* (New York: Harper & Row, Publishers, 1949).

offered, in terms of his system, an explanation of mental illness, crime, delinquency, and, indirectly, homosexuality.

Sheldon has attempted to isolate three poles of physique, through the use of numerous anthropometric measurements and profile photographs delineated as the somatotypes or body types of the endomorph, mesomorph, and ectomorph, which correspond roughly to the pyknic, athletic, and asthenic types of Kretschmer.[20] These types—which may be thought of as the round, soft, and fat type, the muscular and big-boned type, and the thin, small, bony type—are by no means the distinct entities that they were to some of his predecessors. Rather, persons possess all three components, which are indicated by a subjective rating scale of 1 to 7. Thus the endomorph might be a 5–3–1 with 5 parts of endomorph, 3 of mesomorph, and 1 of ectomorph. Sheldon, moreover, goes far beyond either Kretschmer or Hooton in attempting to correlate psychological or temperamental factors with each body type. A body type of endomorphy is correlated with what he calls a psychological temperamental type of viscerotonia, mesomorphy with somatotonia, and ectomorphy with cerebrotonia. The somatotype, psychological characteristics, and the culture interact to produce deviant behavior (see Figure 2).

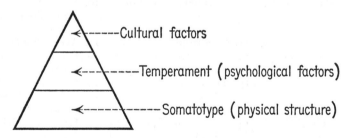

FIGURE 2.—Interaction of Factors That Produce Deviant Behavior

The characteristics of each type of temperament are indicated in the scale in Table 5.1. Round types, for example, tend to like people, muscular types to be aggressive, and thin types to avoid people.

Generally, the mesomorphs with psychological characteristics of somatotonia do not fare well. Sheldon's more recent work has dealt with a study of 200 delinquent boys in the Hayden Goodwill Inn, a Boston social agency. According to his findings, delinquents and criminals are heavy, insensitive, aggressive mesomorphs.[21] In a study of 312 psychotic cases Sheldon found that endomorphy and mesomorphy are correlated with manic-depressive behavior reactions, that mesomorphy was also associated with paranoid reactions, and that ectomorphy was related to certain schizo-

---

[20] He also refers to a T component of thoroughbrededness or "fine breeding."
[21] Sheldon, *Varieties of Delinquent Youth.*

Table 5.1. The Scale for Temperament

I Viscerotonia	II Somatotonia	III Cerebrotonia
1. Relaxation in Posture and Movement	1. Assertiveness in Posture and Movement	1. Restraint in Posture and Movement, Tightness
2. Love of Physical Comfort	2. Love of Physical Adventure	2. Physiological Overresponse
3. Slow Reaction	3. The Energetic Characteristic	3. Overly Fast Reactions
4. Love of Eating	4. Need and Enjoyment of Exercise	4. Love of Privacy
5. Socialization of Eating	5. Love of Dominating, Lust for Power	5. Mental Overintensity, Hyperintentionality, Apprehensiveness
6. Pleasure in Digestion	6. Love of Risk and Chance	6. Secretiveness of Feeling, Emotional Restraints
7. Love of Polite Ceremony	7. Bold Directness of Manner	7. Self-Conscious Motility of the Eyes and Face
8. Sociophilia	8. Physical Courage for Combat	8. Sociophobia
9. Indiscriminate Amiability	9. Competitive Aggressiveness	9. Inhibited Social Address
10. Greed for Affection and Approval	10. Psychological Callousness	10. Resistance to Habit, and Poor Routinizing
11. Orientation to People	11. Claustrophobia	11. Agoraphobia
12. Evenness of Emotional Flow	12. Ruthlessness, Freedom from Squeamishness	12. Unpredictability of Attitude
13. Tolerance	13. The Unrestrained Voice	13. Vocal Restraint, and General Restraint of Noise
14. Complacency	14. Spartan Indifference to Pain	14. Hypersensitivity to Pain
15. Deep Sleep	15. General Noisiness	15. Poor Sleep Habits, Chronic Fatigue
16. The Untempered Characteristic	16. Overmaturity of Appearance	16. Youthful Intentness of Manner and Appearance
17. Smooth, Easy Communication of Feeling, Extraversion of Viscerotonia	17. Horizontal Mental Cleavage, Extraversion of Somatotonia	17. Vertical Mental Cleavage, Introversion
18. Relaxation and Sociophilia under Alcohol	18. Assertiveness and Aggression under Alcohol	18. Resistance to Alcohol, and to Other Depressant Drugs
19. Need of People When Troubled	19. Need of Action when Troubled	19. Need of Solitude When Troubled
20. Orientation toward Childhood and Family Relationships	20. Orientation toward Goals and Activities of Youth	20. Orientation toward the Later Periods of Life

SOURCE: William H. Sheldon, *Varieties of Delinquent Youth* (New York: Harper & Row, Publishers, 1949), pp. 26–27. Reprinted by permission of the publishers.

phrenic responses.[22] Neurosis was explained by Sheldon as a conflict arising primarily from a person's attempting to be different from what is expected "normally" from his somatotype and temperament.

He has also associated physique with certain degrees of alcoholism. According to Sheldon, alcohol agrees with fat, soft persons and they seldom become addicted to it. Even a moderate quantity of alcohol serves, however, to accentuate the personality traits of persons who are of a hard, athletic body build. In conjunction with other situational components, individuals with such a body type become chronic alcoholics. Finally, those persons who are primarily thin and who have flat chests and a generally weak physical constitution find alcohol unpleasant, for it increases strain and brings on fatigue and dizziness. Consequently, they generally dislike alcohol and avoid its use.

The Gluecks employed the logic of Sheldon and Lombroso in their study of physical types and delinquency in 1956.[23] In their study approximately 60 percent of a group of 500 delinquent boys in a correctional training school were classified mesomorphs, and with traits of temperament and character associated with this body type, as compared with 30 percent of 500 boys in a control group. They thus suggested that "some body types have a greater delinquency potential than do others," implying that a mesomorphic body build may have etiological significance in the commission of delinquent behavior. This study seems to indicate little more than that these boys, most of whom belonged to delinquent groups and who were in correctional institutions, tended to be more muscular than other boys, which is what one might expect and proves nothing more than that about the relation of delinquency and body type. From these figures it is somewhat difficult, however, to explain any actual connection because of the overlap in body types, including mesomorphs, between the two groups.[24]

EVALUATION OF DEVIANT BEHAVIOR AND BODY TYPE

These studies of the relation of physique to deviant behavior have been attacked on numerous grounds:

---

[22] Phyllis Wittman, William H. Sheldon, and Charles J. Katz, "A Study of the Relationship between Constitutional Variations and Fundamental Psychotic Behavior Reactions," *Journal of Nervous and Mental Diseases,* 108:470–476 (December, 1948).

[23] See Sheldon and Eleanor Glueck, *Physique and Delinquency* (New York: Harper & Row, Publishers, 1956).

[24] See also Eleanor Glueck, "Body Build in the Prediction of Delinquency," *Journal of Criminal Law, Criminology and Police Science,* 48:577–579 (March–April, 1958). For a more recent study of the relation of appearance and criminal behavior, see Raymond J. Corsini, "Appearance and Criminality," *American Journal of Sociology,* 65:49–51 (July, 1959). Corsini found that the most physically attractive sex offenders tended to be those whose crimes had involved having sexual relations with adults (rape), while the least attractive sex offenders tended to be those who had victimized children (pedophilia).

1. They have not actually demonstrated the relation between physique and behavior. Hooton and Sheldon both tried to suggest that criminal types are the result of the selection of organically inferior types by the environment. Inferiority is judged by the presence of deviant behavior. Even if an association were proved statistically between constitutional features and behavior, before the theory could be accepted, there would still be need for an adequate general theory of human nature which would incorporate such findings.[25] The jump from body type to temperament is similarly assumed rather than explained. Even if high statistical correlations were to be found, and they were not, the correlations in themselves would not prove the meaningful association of such variables.

2. Most of the argument involves, in general, jumping from certain anatomical characteristics to deviant behavior. In nearly all such studies cultural factors either are not considered at all or occupy a position subordinate to physical factors. All these three studies deal with undefined, unstable, and relative terms, such as "crime" and "delinquency," which involve value judgments, and attempt to relate them to a more stable factor, such as physique. Although Sheldon considers the family, he leaves out for the most part such factors as the neighborhood and the community.

3. The contention that certain physical characteristics are by their very nature inferior is simply an assumption and nothing more. The physical appearance of the organism is naturally neither "good" nor "bad." It is significant that Hooton and Sheldon reach opposite conclusions as to what is "inferior." According to the former the criminal is an inadequately developed, runty physical type, whereas Sheldon finds the criminal and alcoholic inferior because they are a husky, athletic type.

4. None of these studies have used adequate control groups. Sheldon, for example, used no control group in his study of 200 delinquents, and Hooton compared 4200 native white prisoners with 300 noncriminals—150 Nashville firemen and 150 others, including outpatients of a Boston clinic, militiamen, and patrons of a bathhouse. Neither firemen nor militiamen belong in a control group because they are selected on the basis of a physical examination. Nevertheless, the statistical differences between Hooton's criminal and control groups were insignificant; moreover, comparisons of the Nashville and Boston control groups showed greater differences than those between the criminal and control groups. In Hooton's study the physical differences among these various types of offenders, such as robbers and burglars, were almost infinitesimal and generally statistically insignificant.

5. These studies have been largely conducted on institutionalized populations, or very select groups, such as Sheldon's, which probably do

[25] Edwin H. Sutherland, "A Critique of Sheldon's *Varieties of Delinquent Youth,*" *American Sociological Review,* 16:10–13 (February, 1951).

not represent a normal sample of the total population. This is particularly true of persons who are imprisoned, for they are not representative of all criminals.

The Psychiatric Theory of Deviant Behavior

In recent years the theory that deviant conduct is a result of child-hood experiences in the family has gained great popularity. This theory is shared by representatives of many academic disciplines and laymen. It is the view of causation which is most frequently displayed in popular magazines, the press, and other mass media of communication, and pro-pounded by most social welfare workers and psychiatrists and many psychologists.

To a great extent this theory owes its ascendancy to the dissemination of psychiatric and psychoanalytic thought over the past several decades.[26] Yet it could be said that both this idea and, indeed, psychiatric thought itself derive from more fundamental values which are rooted in the traditions of our culture. Prominent among these values are the beliefs in the responsibility of parents for the training and preparation of children for adult life, and the relation between early training and adulthood.

Undoubtedly there is much solid common sense in the idea that child-hood experiences may influence later behavior—*if* childhood is regarded as the primary arena in which culture is acquired. Robert Merton has sug-gested that whatever prominence childhood and family experience may be assigned is due to the fact that the family is the principal transmitting agency of culture to the child.[27]

While many would agree with Merton, there are others who imply that *certain childhood experiences have effects which transcend all other social and cultural experiences*. These proponents suggest that certain childhood incidents or family relationships lead to the formation of certain types of personalities which contain within themselves seeds of deviant or conforming behavior, irrespective of culture. Thus childhood is the arena in which personality traits toward or away from deviance are developed, and a person's behavior after the childhood years is fundamentally the act-ing out of tendencies formed therein. Thus essentially these proponents offer the following formula.

---

[26] Psychiatrists are medical doctors who have had specialized training beyond their M.D. degree in a medical school, generally from other psychiatrists. Psychoanalysts are nearly always medically trained persons who have received special training, usually in a psychoanalytic institute. The differences in psychiatric thinking are great and the discussion here does not deal with those psychiatrists who take a nearly biochemical or organic approach to human behavior.

[27] See Robert K. Merton, "Social Structure and Anomie: Revisions and Extensions," in Ruth N. Anshen, *The Family: Its Function and Destiny* (rev. ed.; New York: Harper & Row, Publishers, 1959), p. 275.

1. All deviant behavior is a product of something in the individual, such as personal disorganization or "maladjusted" personality. Deviants are individuals who are psychologically "sick" persons. Culture is seen not as a determinant of deviant and conforming behavior but rather as the context within which these tendencies are expressed.

2. All persons at birth have certain inherent basic needs, in particular the need for emotional security.

3. Deprivation of those universal needs in men during the early years of childhood leads to the formation of given personality types of structure. The degree of conflict, disorder, retardation, or injury to the personality will vary directly with the degree of deprivation.

4. Childhood experiences, such as emotional conflicts, will determine personality structure and thus the pattern of behavior in later life.

5. Family experiences of the child almost exclusively determine the pattern of behavior in later life, whether deviant or nondeviant, by affecting the personality structure of the child. The need for the mother to provide maternal affection is particularly stressed.

6. A high degree of certain so-called general personality traits, such as emotional insecurity, immaturity, feelings of inadequacy, inability to display affection, and aggression characterize the deviant but not the nondeviant. Such traits are the product of early childhood experience in the family. It is argued that, since the first experiences of the child with others are within the family group, traits arising there form the basis for the entire structure of personality. Deviant behavior is often a way of dealing successfully with such personality traits, for example, "immature" persons may commit crimes or "emotionally insecure" persons may drink excessively and become alcoholics.

This, then, is the theoretical framework with which psychiatry largely explains deviant behavior. Each year are published many books and articles written by psychiatrists who attempt to explain such diverse problems as stealing, murder, sex offenses, delinquency, alcoholism, narcotic addiction, marital difficulties, and the psychoses and the neuroses, as well as racial and religious prejudice.

The Psychoanalytic Explanation of Deviant Behavior

One part of the general field of psychiatry is called psychoanalysis, which has in addition to the psychiatric frame of reference its own particular system of explaining deviant behavior. This, as we shall shortly point out, involves what psychiatrists call conflicts between the id and the superego; the masculinity-femininity conflict, infantile regression, and parent fixation. We shall discuss this approach in detail because its followers publish widely on deviant behavior and their approach has greatly affected not only American psychiatry in general but many social workers and others who deal with deviants.

Because of their emphasis on sex and symbolism, psychoanalytic works in particular make fascinating reading for both professional people and laymen, with the result that probably no approach to deviant behavior has a wider audience. Sigmund Freud, the Viennese psychiatrist who died about twenty years ago, founded psychoanalysis, which has become an important part of the contemporary vocabulary and thinking of Western Europeans.

According to psychoanalytic writers, the chief explanation of behavior disorders must be sought in an analysis of the *unconscious mind,* which consists of a world of inner feelings that are unlikely to be the obvious reasons for behavior or to be subject to recall at will. Antisocial conduct is a result of the dynamics of the unconscious rather than of the conscious activities of mental life. Much of the adult's behavior, whether deviant or nondeviant, owes its form and intensity to certain instinctive drives and to early reactions to parents and siblings. A leading analyst once stated this in emphatic terms: "One thesis is that the child's relation to his family remains throughout life the prototype of its relation to its fellows in general, that this exercises the profoundest influence on its character and conduct." [28]

METHOD

Psychoanalysts generally rely on the use of lengthy free association and the analysis of dreams to infer unconscious experience and motivations. The analyst listens, often taking notes, while the patient, usually in a reclining position, rambles on, presumably verbalizing all his thoughts. Through this "free association" the patient is thought to be able to reveal words, phrases, and ideas ordinarily excluded from consciousness. The same principle holds in hypnosis, which is sometimes used, but the latter technique has many physical disadvantages over free association.

Dreams are supposed to have an obvious meaning as well as a hidden one. That part of the dream which one can recall is its obvious content, whereas the unconscious processes which give rise to the dream are its hidden meanings. Since the latter are generally not acceptable to the dreamer, they must be transformed in some symbolic way to be made acceptable. The "censor," a mechanism of importance in this scheme, decides what may come to the dreamer's conscious mind and what may not. It also transforms, condenses, elaborates, and dramatizes the hidden content, through symbols, into the obvious content. These symbols often have sexual connotations. In dreams the father may be said to be symbolized as

[28] E. Jones, "Relationship of Psychoanalysis to Sociology," in E. Jones ed., *Social Aspects of Psychoanalysis* (London: Williams & Norgate, Ltd., 1924), p. 37.

a king and/or various animals, the mother thought of as nature, and pro-creation by sowing or tilling.

CONFLICTS OF THE ID AND THE SUPEREGO

In the psychoanalyst's scheme, personality is thought of as composed of three parts: the primitive animal *id*, the *ego*, and the *superego*. Psycho-analysis assumes that the conscious self is built over a great reservoir of biological drives. Although biology, in the form of basic animal drives, plays an important part in psychoanalytic theory, these drives are present in everyone and do not necessarily represent individual biological differ-ences.

1. The *id* is the buried reservoir of unconscious instinctual animal tendency or drive. From the Freudian standpoint these instincts are of two major types: the *libido*, including chiefly sexual drives, but not exclusively limited to this drive, and the love or life-trend instincts; and the sadistic or destructive instincts. These instincts operate in every activity.

2. The *ego* is elaborated from the large tract of instinctual tendencies as a result of the contact of the individual with the outer social world. Freud postulated here a dualistic conception of mind: the "id" or internal unconscious world of native or biological impulses and repressed ideas, and the "ego," the self, operating on the level of consciousness. These two may sometimes be compatible but more often are incompatible, unless adjusted through some psychological mechanism. There may be constant conflict between the "ego," the conscious part of the mind representing the civilized aspect of man, and the "id," the unconscious or "primitive" in man.

3. The *superego*, on the other hand, is partly conscious, partly un-conscious, and it is the conscious part which corresponds to the conscience. It is man's social self, derived from cultural definitions of conduct, the mores.

Some writers on psychoanalysis have made almost synonymous with criminal behavior the unresolved conflicts between the primitive id and its instinctive drives and the requirement of society. According to this view, crime arises out of inadequate social restrictions which society has placed on what psychoanalysts assume to be the original instinctive, unadjusted nature of man, which is savage, sensual, and destructive. Criminal behavior is thought of as an almost necessary outcome or expression of the personal-ity, and hence does not always necessitate contacts with a "criminal" cul-ture. According to Karpman, all persons are born criminals in the sense that they come into the world unconditioned and unrepressed. Society, therefore, is the mechanism through which we are conditioned so as to re-press our criminal tendencies: "To put it in other words, we are born selfish, hateful, spiteful, mean; and it is the culture that makes us devoted, loving, kind and sympathetic. . . . criminality . . . [is viewed] as being expressive of the anti-social feelings that each of us carries within him. And it is out of this criminal basis our normal citizenry carried that our criminal population is evolved." [29] Zilboorg writes that crime results from the temporary overcoming of the resistance of the superego and then the ego by instinctive drives from the id.[30] After the discharge of such impulses and the consequent silencing of id drives, the superego reasserts itself and a sense of guilt is felt. According to Abrahamsen, murder arises from the expression of the individual's natural aggressions: "Murder has psychological root in the person's aggressions related to attack and defense. These are expressions of his fight for survival or may be due to an erotic drive, no matter how distorted or concealed it may be." [31]

Psychoanalytic writers dealing with the problems of suicide have stressed the polarity principle of the life (love) and death (hate) instincts of the id.[32] According to this view, there is a strong desire in the id for self-destruction, such as mutilation or suicide, and at the same time a desire for self-preservation. The superego, in turn, contains various social and moral restrictions on personal violence or self-destruction. The forces pulling toward self-destruction and self-preservation are in constant interaction, and when the former overcomes the latter, self-inflicted death ensues. In the course of normal mental development toward maturity, the destructive drives are directed outward in the form of aggression or are sublimated. Failure to direct these tendencies outward results in the individual's fighting or destroying himself.

Psychoanalysts often find hidden motives behind suicides as, for example, self-mutilation or self-destruction in place of injury to another person. Menninger has described three varieties of suicide: the wish to kill; the wish to be killed, which may take the form of hypochondria or alcoholism, or exposure of oneself to diseases; and the wish to die. According to him, the death wish, which is part of the id, may occur in alcoholics where chronic drunkenness is in a sense a slower method of self-annihilation than some of the others customarily employed. Alcoholism may also be a means of self-punishment, the desire for which stems from guilt feelings created by incessant war between the id and the superego.

Some psychoanalysts have suggested that the conflicts between the id

---

[29] Ben Karpman, *The Individual Criminal: Studies in the Psychogenetics of Crime* (Washington, D.C.: Nervous and Mental Diseases Publishing Co., 1935), p. ix.

[30] Gregory Zilboorg, *Mind, Medicine and Man* (New York: Harcourt, Brace & World, Inc., 1943).

[31] David Abrahamsen, *Crime and the Human Mind* (New York: Columbia University Press, 1944), p. 148. Also see Karl Menninger, "Verdict Guilty—Now What?" *Harper's Magazine* 210:60–64 (August, 1959).

[32] Karl Menninger, *Man against Himself* (New York: Harcourt, Brace & World, Inc., 1938).

and the superego explain prejudice. In our modern complex society the natural drives and personal wishes of the id meet all varieties of blocks in the path of achievement. More and more frustrations being forced upon individuals result in greater inner tensions and anxieties. Yet there are no standard cultural means of relieving this pressure. Tensions must somehow be relieved, either directly or through "free-floating aggression" against persons and groups. Just as the mother or other disciplinarian becomes the object of conscious or unconscious hatred and hostility of the child, so "out-groups" and other people with assumed or real divergences in physical or other characteristics become objects of hate through the displacement mechanism, i.e., hatred is shifted from the persons and groups who stand in the way of one's fulfillment of goals to a more convenient object.

As a consequence of these frustrations of the id the hostility toward the Jew in the world today may emanate from a transference of the hatred of Christians for Christ and Christianity itself. According to this explanation, Christ, a Jew, gave the world a morality which curbed the id impulses of Western mankind. But since men do not relish these restrictions on their material desires, they unconsciously fear and hate not only Christ but his doctrines as well. On the one hand they overcompensate these feelings by strict adherence to the church, and on the other by sympathizing unconsciously with all those persons who do not uphold this morality. The Jews serve as the objects of hate because it was they who produced a religious leader who introduced this hard morality. The Jews, in other words, are hated because they gave the world a Christ. This theory of prejudice is called Christophobia, meaning an irrational fear of Christ.[33]

Prejudice against the Negro has been explained as resulting from the white man's desire for sexual relations with Negroes or from his envy of their so-called hypersexuality. According to this explanation, white people believe that Negroes are less inhibited and more passionate sexually, that colored males have larger sexual organs than do white males, and that colored females can experience more orgasms than can white women. White persons who do not have sexual relations with Negroes feel that they must repress their desires, whereas those who do have relations with Negroes experience marked guilt feelings.[34] McLean believes that southern whites think themselves somewhat lacking in sexual expression, while the Negro has a superabundance of such feelings. Their jealousy of the Negroes and the need to repress the id desires toward them result in prejudice. She says that as whites are "devoid of the capacity for the expression of genuine warmth unconsciously they feel that the Negro has what they lack. They anxiously search for something which will give meaning to their lives

---

[33] For a description of this explanation of anti-Semitism see Maurice Samuel, *The Great Hatred* (New York: Alfred A. Knopf, Inc., 1940), pp. 105–115.

[34] See discussion of this theory in Arnold and Caroline Rose, *America Divided* (New York: Alfred A. Knopf, Inc., 1948), p. 290.

through their contacts with the Negro. These contacts, however, are fraught with the terror of the forbidden. Their inflexible consciences, in seeking a victim to punish for all manner of forbidden impulses, must keep in subservience those who represent the temptation." [35]

MASCULINITY-FEMININITY CONFLICT

Every person, psychoanalytically, has both masculine and feminine tendencies or, to put it another way, is naturally bisexual with homosexual and heterosexual components. Within each individual this fact results in a certain amount of conflict. Many psychoanalytic writers have emphasized the conflict of the masculine and feminine components which are a part of everyone's original make-up, the one being aggressive and the other passive. The rapist, for example, has a feeling of inferiority and fear of sexual inadequacy which prevents normal permanent sexual alliances. Murder may even be a defense against "feminine" traits which are abhorred by the murderer.

Some psychoanalytic writers believe that alcoholism in the male represents the direct expression of his homosexual drives. Drinking often enables him to be in male company exclusively, particularly in bars and taverns, and it also enables him to overcome his feeling of sexual impotency. Eventually the inebriate substitutes the consumption of alcohol for heterosexual contacts. After analyzing the hangovers of seven men and seven women alcoholics, Karpman has concluded that they reflect guilt over homosexual feelings.[36]

INFANTILE REGRESSION

Psychoanalysts think of a normal personality as having developed through a series of four stages. The development of personality involves shifting interests and changes in the nature of sexual pleasure from the oral and the anal preoccupation of infant life, to love of self, love of a parent of the opposite sex, and, finally, love of a person of the opposite sex and other than one's parent. Some of these stages overlap and may go on simultaneously. Some persons do not progress through all these stages, have conflicts, and develop personality difficulties.

According to psychoanalysts, the newborn individual operates on a pain-pleasure principle, and the environment is viewed merely as consisting of desirable objects which serve to bring about bodily comfort and satisfaction, such as oral gratification through nursing and preoccupation with

---

[35] Helen V. McLean, "Psychodynamic Factors in Racial Relations," *The Annals*, 244:164 (March, 1946).
[36] Ben Karpman, *The Hangover* (Springfield, Ill.: Charles C Thomas, Publisher, 1957).

activities of elimination. This stage, from the point of view of the affectional or libidinal development, is one of preoccupation with one's own body. From the start, however, this interest becomes increasingly blocked by cultural controls and restrictions. The adult world insists on adjustment to social patterns and an increasingly greater restriction on freely expressed biological drives and fantasies.

Many psychoanalysts stress the fact that deviants are immature persons who have not developed into fully socialized adults. The activities of deviants unconsciously represent unresolved infantile desires to which they have returned. Others believe that the type of crime, the type of objects involved in the crime, and the person from whom something was stolen often indicate infantile regression. Stealing from superiors, for example, may be symbolic of original childhood envy of adult sexual organs. Burglary has been traced by one psychoanalyst to fixation in the oral stage of development, and arson has been explained as a regression to an infantile stage of development.[37] Foxe has even classified various types of crime in terms of trauma and fixation in childhood. Automobile theft is due to regression to the early oral stage; burglary, forgery, and embezzlement are due to regression to the late oral stage; and armed robbery and swindling are due to regression to the late anal.[38]

> Earliest training leaves its impress upon one's constitution and character and so it is not surprising that so many individuals in whom the training deviated considerably from average showed strong marks of primitive infantile patterns [anal-oral stage]. . . . That even crime should show such impression —the tooth-like dagger of the assaulter and the tooth-like sadistic pen of the forger, the anal explosiveness of the gun-holding robber—is not at all remarkable.[39]

Many psychoanalysts have concluded that the etiology of schizophrenia lies in the regression of the total personality to the stage in life in which the ego is not completely molded. It is, therefore, a retreat to a form of infantilism. The alcoholic has often been characterized by psychoanalysts as a passive, insecure, dependent, "oral" personality of an infantile type, with his latent hostility being thereby obscured.

PARENT FIXATION AND CONFLICTS

Generally psychoanalysts regard patterns of behavior as having been formed in the early years, in many before five years, in nearly all before

---

[37] Otto Fenichel, *The Psychoanalytic Theory of Neurosis* (New York: W. W. Norton & Company, Inc., 1945).

[38] Arthur N. Foxe, "Classification of the Criminotic Individual," in Robert M. Lindner and Robert V. Seliger eds., *Handbook of Correctional Psychology* (New York: Philosophical Library, Inc., 1947).

[39] Arthur N. Foxe, "Criminoses," in V. C. Branham and S. B. Kutash eds., *Encyclopedia of Criminology* (New York: Philosophical Library, Inc., 1949), p. 117.

adolescence. Normal psychic development involves not only the question of normal affectional development but also a gradual emergence from a condition of dependence on parental authority and care to one in which the individual achieves a greater degree of independence. Failure to do so results in a socially inadequate adult personality.

In infancy the mother becomes definitely an object of the child's libido. She is the first object to whom love impulses are directed, but since she is the first person who restricts pleasure she is also one to whom hate is first directed. Based on this early attachment to the mother, there arises an *Oedipus phase* in libidinal development in which the male child unconsciously becomes a rival of his father for the mother's sexual affections and, therefore, comes to hate his father. In the case of girls, the conflict with the mother over the father is called the *Electra complex*.[40] Psychoanalytic writers have tried to show that many social phenomena can be understood only when viewed in the light of the Oedipus complex, which produces significant manifestations in almost every sphere of human activity.

An outstanding example of this approach is the view held by many, but not all, psychoanalysts, that the Oedipus complex is universal in all cultures.[41] Sexual adjustments become heterosexual, with the love object outside the family. With the deviant, however, this conflict is not solved; there are guilt feelings over the incestuous desires for the parent of the opposite sex, and an unsatisfactory shift to other heterosexual persons. These guilt feelings are relieved by deviant behavior or by the punishment that arises from antisocial behavior.

Criminals and neurotics have much in common, for example, for both feel that they need punishment to relieve guilt feelings arising from an Oedipus situation. The individual may feel a need for punishment because of the hostility he has harbored against a member of his family. He may commit a crime and seek punishment by society, whereas another may seek self-punishment through a neurosis. Self-destructive tendencies may result in a murder's being committed in order to receive punishment.

Many psychoanalysts believe that the behavior difficulties associated with alcoholism lie in various Oedipus or Electra conflicts. Alcoholism is interpreted as an escape valve from these intolerable inner battles.

Homosexuality in a man has been explained as a result of over-attachment for the mother in an unresolved Oedipus complex which results in his rejecting sex relations with other women. Psychoanalytic theories of prostitution often explain it as caused by the individual's failure

---

[40] Another conflict may result from overattachment to the mother, which turns to violent dislike and is called the *Orestes complex*. All these terms have their origin in the characters and plots of the classic Greek plays.

[41] Many psychoanalysts use the Oedipus complex symbolically but do not regard it as universal.

to reach sexual maturity. Some psychoanalysts characterize the prostitute as a person who has been denied sufficient parental love, affection, and security in childhood and who therefore establishes liaisons because she wants to feel that she is wanted and needed. She also suffers from, or has never outgrown, her Electra complex for her father, and is often incapable of receiving real sexual gratification.

SOME SPECIFIC CRITICISMS OF PSYCHOANALYTIC THEORY

1. *Contrary to psychoanalysis, evidence suggests that human behavior is a product of social experience and that it is not determined by an innate reservoir of animal impulses termed the id.* Depending upon his social and cultural experiences, a man can be either cruel or gentle, aggressive or pacifist, sadistic or loving. He can be either a savage Nazi Jew-baiter or a compassionate and tender human being like Albert Schweitzer or Mohandas Gandhi. No detailed refutation is necessary, therefore, to disprove a psychoanalytic theory that some forms of criminality, for example, should be envisaged as outbursts of unsocialized original animal impulses. What constitutes criminal behavior is a matter of social determination, and impulses secure their social meaning only through the medium of social interaction. There is no savage man lurking under a veneer of socialization. This belief in something resembling human instincts, which was common until the 1920's, has been completely refuted by a large number of studies by social psychologists, psychologists, and anthropologists. It is no longer even a debatable subject.

2. *There is no evidence to support the theory that sex represents an all-inclusive factor which explains a host of mental conflicts.* The psychoanalytic emphasis on sexual eroticism is a great overstatement of an important aspect of human behavior. As Horney has indicated, conflicts can arise in many areas of human experience, particularly through excessive competition.[42] Likewise, religion, the achievement of status, and various conflicts in social roles—all constitute wide areas of possible mental conflict.

3. *The entire psychoanalytic scheme is bodily conscious rather than primarily socially conscious for the child's development is greatly influenced by social relationships which have little or no connection with bodily functions.* The evidence does not support the view that these rather presocial experiences involving oral and anal stimulation affect the entire course of human life. The idea that frustrations of the libidinal infantile drives universal in all human beings will necessarily affect personality has been rejected by Orlansky after an extensive survey of anthropological literature. In a study of various societies he considered the effects on personality of different methods of nursing, mothering, bowel training, and

---

[42] Karen Horney, *New Ways in Psychoanalysis* (New York: W. W. Norton & Company, Inc., 1939).

restraint of motion, and reached negative conclusions about their "specific invariant psychological effect upon children." [43] He concludes that parental attitudes which are derived from the culture are the chief variables. Sewell, likewise, has concluded from a study of 162 farm children that different methods of infant breast feeding, weaning, and bowel training have practically no subsequent effect on personality.[44]

4. *Psychoanalytic theory has assumed certain universal uniformities in human behavior as arising from the assumed uniformities in human biological drives, irrespective of cultural influences, or historical eras, or of variations in social structure.* Actually "drives," if they exist, have no inherent direction or aim; but the complex behaviors necessary to relieve the physical tensions, which we term "drives," are learned through social experiences. For example, the stomach contractions which we refer to as "hunger" do not in themselves explain why Americans eat hamburgers, Koreans prefer rice, and Eskimos prefer seal blubber. The kinds of food eaten and the methods of obtaining and preparing them are culturally learned.

An outstanding example of this approach is the view that the Oedipus complex is universal in all cultures. One survey of Freudian concepts has stated that "Freud assumed the Oedipus relationship to exist universally, and while other investigations have found instances of it, no indications of a universal cross-sex parental preference have been discovered in either children or adults." [45] It appears that Freud overrated the uniformity of family patterns and failed to perceive that sexual definitions are products of the child's social relationships. Even in our culture families do not exhibit a similar culture pattern, and there is considerable variability in the specific behaviors expected of persons in their family roles. In turn, if various family patterns throughout the world are examined, these patterns and roles become even more variable.

> It is a truism today that adult behavior is a function of the culture in which it was learned. Psychiatric thought had not gone so far at the beginning of the century, however, and Freud's notion of the universal Oedipus complex stands as a sharply etched grotesquerie against his otherwise informative description of sexual development. From the analysis of data relating to object choice, it is apparent that in this matter perhaps more than in any other the nature of the chosen object and the reactions to other similar or dissimilar objects are dependent on the early home environment of the child. So far we are in agreement with Freud. But, beyond this, Freud seeks a common or typical pattern of development. If such existed, it should come only from a

---

[43] Harold Orlansky, "Infant Care and Personality," *Psychological Bulletin,* 46:1–48 (January, 1949).
[44] William H. Sewell, "Infant Training and the Personality of the Child," *American Journal of Sociology,* 58:150–159 (September, 1952).
[45] Robert R. Sears, "Survey of Objective Studies of Psychoanalytic Concepts" (Bulletin 51; New York: Social Science Research Council, 1943), pp. 134–135.

common culture pattern, i.e., from a constant situation in which learning could take place in a uniform way.[46]

General Evaluation of the Psychiatric and Psychoanalytic Explanations

Psychiatry and psychoanalysis have a large following in present-day society and their literature is extensive. Psychoanalysis has emphasized the meaningfulness of subjective experience and as a theory it has contributed to the understanding of various psychological processes through which the mind avoids certain painful experiences. The emphasis on the unconscious, on symbolic expressions, and on mental conflict has been noteworthy, even if overstressed in the explanation. Some have increasingly recognized the importance of the larger world of cultural definitions and interpersonal relationships in the development of deviant behavior. Moreover, the remarks presented here are focused on the *theoretical explanation, and not on therapy.* Certainly some favorable therapeutic results are achieved by psychiatrists and psychoanalysts working with deviants. Therapy, however, does not necessarily always follow the theory but may be improvised to fit an individual case. Moreover, the results achieved by therapy may be due to other factors, such as the intimate social relationship between practitioner and patient.

1. *Psychoanalytic as well as psychiatric theory has all too frequently assumed that adult behavior and personality are almost wholly determined by childhood experiences, most of them in the family, whereas the overwhelming bulk of evidence suggests that behavior varies according to situations and social roles and that personality continues to develop throughout life.* Such early family influences have probably been greatly overemphasized, sometimes to the virtual exclusion of the effect on personality of other groups such as the peer group, occupation, neighborhood, marriage, and other later social situations. Even in early life the socialization of the child is greatly influenced by the play group, by street play in urban areas, by preschool and kindergarten activities, and by neighbors and others, such as relatives. Largely on the basis of current anthropological studies, Orlansky has concluded that "the rigidity of character structure during the first year or two of life has been exaggerated by many authorities and that the events of childhood and later years are of great importance in reinforcing or changing the character structure tentatively found during infancy." [47] This seems plausible, for life must be regarded as a continuous experience of social interaction which cannot be arbitrarily divided between infancy, childhood, and adult experience. To psychiatrists and

---

[46] *Ibid.*, p. 136.   [47] Orlansky, "Infant Care and Personality," *loc. cit.*

psychoanalysts, events occurring at forty years of age, for example, may be explained by some occurrence at age four. The theory of predetermination of adult behavior on the basis of heredity has largely disappeared; in its place is predetermination based on early family interaction. For the most part, the sociological approach to deviant behavior, while certainly recognizing the importance of the family, does not agree with this theory in even paramount or exclusive emphasis on the family or on parental models as necessarily the determinants of either deviant or nondeviant behavior.

2. *Despite their claims, the explanations of psychiatrists and psychoanalysts and their proponents concerning deviant behavior have not, for the most part, been scientifically verified.* Psychiatrists and psychoanalysts have generally failed, and even have often refused, to use experimental or more verifiable situations, or other more rigorous and controlled techniques, to test their hypotheses.[48] For evidence, there is reliance on verbal recall of childhood experiences, which are interpreted by the psychiatrist or psychoanalyst. Much of that evidence is derived from memories in which childhood experiences, particularly in the family, are likely to be recalled without their necessarily having much bearing on why a person acts as he does in later life. Much of this type of activity has been criticized for using imagination and guesswork too freely. Another person going over the same material might find some other equally valid and significant explanation which did not employ the theory, for example, of psychoanalysis.[49] Most psychiatric and psychoanalytic studies have been concerned only with deviant persons, and only a few studies have employed control groups of nondeviant persons. This is understandable if one considers that they specialize in treatment, but they frequently generalize without utilizing accepted scientific procedures, such as samples of sufficient size or representativeness. One important psychoanalytic volume, for example, covered only six cases and yet was called *Roots of Crime*.[50]

3. *Psychiatric and psychoanalytic explanations of deviant behavior exemplify a blurring of the line between "sickness" and simply deviations from norms.* According to these explanations the presence of mental aberra-

---

[48] See, for example, Lyle W. Shannon, "The Problem of Competence to Help," *Federal Probation*, 25:32–39 (March, 1961). He suggests a number of positive criteria in evaluating a professional person's ability to deal effectively with deviant behavior: (1) the ability to predict human behavior, (2) the ability to control or modify human behavior, and (3) the existence of a body of scientific research which tends to support the explanation of the professional group in question and with which the therapy in question appears to be consistent.

[49] Sears, "Survey of Objective Studies of Psychoanalytic Concepts," p. 133. Some psychoanalysts maintain that successes in therapy are proof of the validity of their theoretical systems. This is no more proof than the "cures" of patent medicine. Other factors, such as the subject's belief and acceptance of the interpretation, as well as his personal relations with the analyst, also enter into the so-called successful treatment.

[50] Franz Alexander and William Healy, *Roots of Crime* (New York: Alfred A. Knopf, Inc. 1935).

tions explains the occurrence of certain antisocial actions, such as crime. Thus, criminal or socially deviant behavior is itself made the criterion for the diagnosis of mental abnormality. In this sense deviations from norms of "sinful behavior," such as delinquency and crime, are used as the basis for inferring the presence of "sickness" or mental aberration. This tendency is similar to older attempts to link behavioral deviations with "possession by devils." [51]

4. *Some writers, after extensive investigations, have concluded that psychiatric and psychoanalytic diagnoses are unreliable, and that there is absence of agreement among psychiatrists themselves concerning what objective criteria are to be employed in assessing degrees of mental well-being or mental aberration.*[52] To a great extent it is the very absence of objective criteria of either mental illness or mental health which is responsible for the psychiatrists' and psychoanalysts' tendencies to equate "sickness" and, for example, delinquency and crime. This is because, lacking such criteria, there is no way of distinguishing between those whose criminal acts are excusable on the basis of mental disorder from those who, though committing criminal acts, are not mentally disordered. Finding themselves unable thus to distinguish "mentally healthy" criminals from "mentally unhealthy" ones, criminal behavior itself is used as a criterion of mental disorder, or of other abnormalities within the person. This dilemma, in essence, underlies the psychiatric explanation of deviant behavior and the psychiatric view concerning the treatment of deviants.[53]

5. *No evidence has been produced, despite these claims, that so-called personality traits are associated with deviations from disapproved norms.* Comparisons with control groups have revealed that no series of traits can distinguish deviants from nondeviants in general.[54] Some de-

---

[51] Barbara Wootton, *Social Science and Social Pathology* (New York: The Macmillan Company, 1957), p. 207.

[52] See Wootton, *op. cit.*, especially Chap. 7; Michael Hakeem, "A Critique of the Psychiatric Approach to Crime and Corrections," *Law and Contemporary Problems.* 22:681–682 (Autumn, 1958); Michael Hakeem, "A Critique of the Psychiatric Approach," in Joseph Roucek ed., *Juvenile Delinquency* (New York: Philosophical Library, Inc., 1958), pp. 79–112; Arthur P. Miles, *American Social Work Theory* (New York: Harper & Row, Publishers, 1954), pp. 122–130; Percival Bailey, "The Great Psychiatric Revolution," *American Journal of Psychiatry*, 113:387–406 (November, 1956); Marshall B. Clinard, "Contributions of Sociology to Understanding Deviant Behavior," *British Journal of Criminology*, in press; Thomas S. Szasz, "Malingering: Diagnosis or Social Condemnation?" *American Medical Association Archives of Neurology and Psychiatry*, 76:432–438 (1956); and Thomas S. Szasz, *The Myth of Mental Illness* (New York: Paul B. Hoeber, Inc., 1961).

[53] See Wootton, *op. cit.*, and Hakeem, "A Critique of the Psychiatric Approach to Crime and Corrections," *loc. cit.*, for further elaboration of this problem.

[54] See, for example, Karl F. Schuessler and Donald R. Cressey, "Personality Characteristics of Criminals," *American Journal of Sociology*, 55:476–484 (March, 1950), and Edwin H. Sutherland, H. C. Schroeder, and C. L. Tordella, "Personality Traits and the Alcoholic: A Critique of Existing Studies," *Quarterly Journal of Studies on Alcohol*, 11:547–561 (December, 1950). Also see Leonard Symes, "Personality Characteristics and

viants are "emotionally insecure," but some nondeviants are also "emotionally insecure." On the other hand, some deviants are "emotionally secure." One is never sure whether given personality traits were present before the deviant behavior developed or whether experiences encountered as a result of the deviation produced the traits. Thus the fact that a boy or a girl in a correctional institution is "emotionally insecure" is no proof that he or she was so prior to commitment to the institution or prior to the first delinquency. The alcoholic who is "emotionally insecure" may have developed this trait as a result of reactions of others during a long period of alcoholism. Moreover, a personality trait does not indicate how a person will act in a given situation or explain how specific definitions of situations, such as techniques of stealing, are acquired. Part of the difficulty has arisen from the fact that psychiatrists, being practitioners, see deviants almost entirely and obviously do not have an opportunity to study many nondeviants. They erroneously assume, therefore, that such traits as they find characterize only deviants.

Summary

In this chapter three theories of the cause of deviant behavior—feeblemindedness, body type, and childhood experiences (the psychiatric and psychoanalytic explanations)—have been discussed. Although these theories have much support, for a number of reasons they do not offer a valid explanation of deviant behavior. Much of the inadequacies in their explanations can be attributed to the training and background of the investigators. Since deviant behavior is seen and experienced from this frame of reference, more often than not the facts are manipulated to fit the theory, rather than altering the theory to fit the facts. This is particularly true of psychoanalysis.

On the whole, these theories tend to be explanations of the social behavior of human beings without full consideration of the social nature of man. That consideration is necessary if one is to attempt to explain behavior as it actually occurs within society, instead of in what Planck has called the "picture world," or the world of "other things being equal."

Satisfactory control groups of nondeviants have not been utilized in most of the studies. Explanations have been largely based on the analysis of deviants only, such as delinquents, criminals, or alcoholics, without reference to other persons who do not exhibit this behavior.

Many of the concepts of psychiatry and psychoanalysis have been valuable contributions to a science of human behavior. Despite the vociferous claims of the psychiatrists and the psychoanalysts, however, that their *general theory* offers a solution to deviant behavior, they are more a system of beliefs than scientifically verified bodies of knowledge. Until psychiatry and psychoanalysis are supported by extensive research using accepted scientific methods they will continue to remain largely a body of intriguing speculation.

Superficially, these three theories seem to be simple ways of dealing with deviant behavior. It is fortunate that there is so little validity in the theories, however, for they would mean that it would be virtually impossible ever to control deviant behavior effectively. If feeble-mindedness or body type were associated with certain deviations, control would have to be through selective eugenic breeding and sterilization. Both methods may be applicable to other animals, but for man it would be virtually impossible because of the extensive nature of deviations, the possibility of biological inheritance through recessive characteristics, the relatively free marriage selection system in modern society, and the democratic rights of each individual. The application of psychiatric and psychoanalytic principles on a large scale and the use of psychiatry and psychoanalysis as treatment devices for millions of deviants would be an extremely complex solution.

Selected Readings

BAILEY, PERCIVAL. "The Great Psychiatric Revolution," *American Journal of Psychiatry*, 113:387–406 (November, 1956). The many conflicting approaches to treatment of specific forms of deviant behavior by psychiatrists are a cause of concern, according to this well-documented article.

GLUECK, SHELDON, and ELEANOR GLUECK. *Physique and Delinquency*. New York: Harper & Row, Publishers, 1956. A study of the physique of 500 delinquent boys in a correctional training school, as compared with a control group of boys.

HAKEEM, MICHAEL. "A Critique of the Psychiatric Approach," in Joseph Roucek ed., *Juvenile Delinquency*. New York: Philosophical Library, Inc., 1958, pp. 79–112. A critical appraisal of the methods and evidence on which psychiatric theory is based.

MONROE, RUTH L. *Schools of Psychoanalytic Thought*. New York: Holt, Rinehart and Winston, Inc., 1955, Chaps. 2, 3, 5, and 7. A comprehensive description of the concepts and methods of psychoanalysis with critical comments. Chapter 7 deals with the theoretical explanations of certain deviant behavior and the use of psychoanalysis in treatment.

ORLANSKY, HAROLD. "Infant Care and Personality," *Psychological Bulletin*, 46:1–48 (January, 1949). A study of whether any universal findings could be established when psychoanalytic theory was applied to a large number of primitive societies.

SCHUESSLER, KARL F., and DONALD R. CRESSEY, "Personality Characteristics of Criminals," *American Journal of Sociology*, 55:476–484 (March, 1950). A survey of all studies which sought to differentiate the personality traits of delinquents and criminals, with a control group. The survey concluded that such differences have not been established.

SEARS, ROBERT R. "Survey of Objective Studies of Psychoanalytic Concepts." New York: Social Science Research Council, Bulletin 51, 1943. This well-known critique of psychoanalysis criticizes writers in this field for not generally employing scientific methods of proof.

SEWELL, WILLIAM H. "Infant Training and the Personality of the Child," *American Journal of Sociology*, 58:150–159 (September, 1952). An attempt to test empirically the effect of certain child-rearing practices on personality emphasized by the Freudians. The conclusions were negative.

SHANNON, LYLE. "The Problem of Competence to Help," *Federal Probation*, 25: 32–39 (March, 1961). A discussion of the positive and negative criteria which should be used in evaluating a professional person, such as a psychiatrist, on his competence to help a deviant.

SUTHERLAND, EDWIN H. "A Critique of Sheldon's *Varieties of Delinquent Youth*," *American Sociological Review*, 16:10–13 (February, 1951). An excellent criticism of one of the leading books dealing with the relation of body type and deviant behavior.

SZASZ, THOMAS S. *The Myth of Mental Illness*. New York: Paul B. Hoeber, Inc., 1961. A psychoanalyst states the view that what is considered to be mental illness has come to be defined as whatever psychiatrists say it is, and that psychiatry has, with increasing and misplaced zeal, called more and more kinds of behavior "illness."

WOOTTON, BARBARA. *Social Science and Social Pathology*. New York: The Macmillan Company, 1959. Includes an appraisal of current psychiatric beliefs and concludes that there is little evidence that antisocial attitudes are due to lack of maternal affection in infancy. She particularly condemns the blurring of the line between "sickness and sin" for which she holds contemporary psychiatry responsible.

PART

II

Deviant Behavior

Chapter

6

The Nature of Delinquency
and Crimes

In the previous discussions, which have covered many forms of deviant behavior, the air has been cleared of some fundamental misconceptions about deviant behavior in general; urbanization has been found to be a profitable over-all frame of reference for the analysis of deviant behavior; and, finally, several key concepts of considerable utility have been presented. They include the society, culture, groups, social norms, values, attitudes, conception of self, and social roles. Beginning with crime and criminal behavior, these concepts will be applied more specifically to a number of important forms of deviant behavior.

For many hundreds of years men have been intrigued with crime and criminals, if numerous songs, poems, and stories in the literature of many cultures are any indication of this interest. Ballads dealing with thieves and highwaymen, gaols and sheriffs, have been passed down from generation to generation. Today this interest in criminal offenders has come into even greater prominence as evidenced in the subject matter of many contemporary novels, newspapers, magazines, radio and television plays, and motion pictures. In fact, so large is the proportion of popular mass communication devoted to criminal behavior that one is tempted to speculate about the content of fictional literature in that millennium of a crimeless society.[1]

The Scientific Study of Criminal Behavior

Despite these centuries of interest in crime, it is only within the past seventy-five years that men have sought to study scientifically the factors underlying criminal behavior. Previously there had been considerable writing and speculation about the nature of crime, but little interest in the criminal. Near the end of the eighteenth century, several writers, notably Cesare Beccaria in Italy and Jeremy Bentham in England, suggested that

---

[1] So much space is devoted to the reporting of various crimes in the daily press of Western society that the difference between most papers and one like the *Christian Science Monitor*, which seldom prints crime news, is striking.

a crime was simply an act wherein the pleasure derived from illegal behavior exceeded the possible pain that might consequently be imposed as punishment. This conception of crime was based on the principles of hedonistic psychology, which assumed that the behavior of all persons was completely a matter of individual responsibility and that their misbehavior was motivated by pain and punishment.

Basing his ideas on this belief, but with no actual studies of criminals and noncriminals to prove it, Beccaria expressed his views in a famous essay on crime and punishment. He suggested that there should be uniform penalties for given crimes but that they should vary according to the severity of the crime.[2] Crimes were punished differently by various judges, with little or no punishment for a nobleman and great severity for a serf; hence Beccaria's idea was revolutionary at that time. His conception of punishment, with so many years for burglary and so many more for robbery, still underlies the criminal law of nearly all countries today.

It was not until 1876, however, that there was any really scientific study of criminals. It was begun by Cesare Lombroso, an Italian army doctor. The abstract methods of studying crime did not appeal to him; instead, he began the study of the anatomy of various criminals. Lombroso was influenced by some work he had done in taking various physical measurements of patients in mental hospitals and by the still controversial Darwinian theory of evolution, and its corollary, that contemporary man had antecedents in various forms of primitive man.[3] While he was dissecting the famous brigand Vilella, Lombroso discovered a distinct depression in the back part of the skull similar to one he had found in lower animals. Becoming convinced that some criminals were characterized by certain physical features, he later classified criminals into two additional categories, insane and criminaloids, persons who were not born with physical stigmata but who actually had innate tendencies toward crime. Lombroso vividly describes his findings:

> This was not merely an idea, but a revelation. At the sight of that skull I seemed to see all of a sudden, lighted up as a vast plain under a flaming sky, the problem of the nature of the criminal—an atavistic being who reproduces in his person the ferocious instincts of primitive humanity and the inferior animals. Thus were explained anatomically the enormous jaws, high cheekbones, prominent superciliary arches, solitary lines in the palms, extreme size of the orbits, handle-shaped or sessile ears found in criminals, savages, and apes, insensibility to pain, extremely acute sight, tattooing, excessive idleness, love of orgies, and the irresistible craving for evil for its own sake, the desire

---

[2] Cesare Beccaria, *An Essay on Crimes and Punishments* (New York: Stephen Gould, 1809).

[3] Cesare Lombroso, *L'uomo delinquente* (Turin: Bocca, 1896–1897). Also see Gina Lombroso Ferrero, *Lombroso's Criminal Man* (New York: G. P. Putnam's Sons, 1911); and Cesare Lombroso, *Crime, Its Causes and Remedies* (H. P. Horton, trans.; Boston: Little, Brown & Company, 1912).

not only to extinguish life in the victim, but to mutilate the corpse, tear its flesh, and drink its blood.

I was further encouraged in this bold hypothesis by the results of my studies on Verzeni, a criminal convicted of sadism and rape, who showed the cannibalistic instincts of primitive anthropophagists and the ferocity of beasts of prey.

The various parts of the extremely complex problem of criminality were, however, not all solved hereby. The final key was given by another case, that of Misdea, a young soldier of about twenty-one, unintelligent but not vicious. Although subject to epileptic fits, he had served for some years in the army when suddenly, for some trivial cause, he attacked and killed eight of his superior officers and comrades. His horrible work accomplished, he fell into a deep slumber which lasted twelve hours and on awaking appeared to have no recollection of what had happened. Misdea, while representing the most ferocious type of animal, manifested in addition, all the phenomena of epilepsy, which appeared to be hereditary in all the members of his family. It flashed across my mind that many criminal characteristics not attributable to atavism, such as facial asymmetry, cerebral sclerosis, impulsiveness, instantaneousness, the periodicity of criminal acts, the desire of evil for evil's sake, were morbid characteristics common to epilepsy, mingled with others due to atavism.[4]

In developing their theories, Lombroso and his followers, Garofalo and Ferri, who modified his theory, measured thousands of offenders. The work of the Italian school of criminology aroused world-wide interest in the study of criminals. Although some accepted the idea that a criminal was characterized by innate stigmata and did further research and writing along these lines, others were convinced that the idea was sheer nonsense. Goring in England led the main attack with a study which found no appreciable physical difference, except in weight, between a large group of university students and inmates of English prisons.[5]

In the early part of this century, the two main developments in criminology were Gabriel Tarde's theory of imitation and crime and the theories based on the mentality of criminals. Tarde, a French judge and later a professor, had worked out a theory which, being sociopsychological rather than biological, was the complete opposite of Lombroso's. He believed that crime resulted from the imitation of antisocial behavior in others.[6] This idea came to him when, as a French judge, he sentenced fathers, then sons, and sometimes even an older brother, and later a younger brother. His general ideas of social factors in crime were in advance of his time, although they were not valid with respect to his theory of imitation.

---

[4] Gina Lombroso Ferrero, *Lombroso's Criminal Man* (New York: G. P. Putnam's Sons, 1911), pp. xiv–xvi. Reprinted by permission of the publisher.

[5] Charles Goring, *The English Convict* (London: His Majesty's Stationery Office, 1913). He offered an explanation that offenders inherited an inadequate personality.

[6] Gabriel Tarde, *Penal Philosophy*, tr. by Rapelje Howell (Boston: Little, Brown & Company, 1912).

Americans have played an important role in the development of criminology. Goddard and others stressed mental deficiency as the explanation of crime. In 1915, William Healy, a psychiatrist, published his famous volume, *The Individual Delinquent,* which, in addition to presenting material on delinquents, for the first time offered detailed case studies of individuals with an emphasis on their personality traits. Sutherland, beginning in 1924, eventually developed the important sociological theory that differential association with criminal norms is the cause of criminal behavior.[7] Criminological theory in America and Europe has increasingly emphasized social and group factors in the explanation of delinquency and crime.[8] European criminologists in general, however, consider biological factors as much more important than do American writers.[9]

Crime and Social Control

All societies and groups develop ways of dealing with behaviors which fall outside the range of tolerance of given societal or group norms. These methods are ordinarily called "negative sanctions" because they impose penalties on those whose behavior has transcended the range of tolerance of the norms. "Positive sanctions," on the other hand, consist of special rewards, such as praise, recognition, or prestige which are bestowed on persons whose behavior has conformed, or has exceeded conformance, to prescribed norms.

Both negative and positive sanctions are categories of social control. Social control may, in turn, be classified as either "formal" or "informal." In general, formal controls are the *official* actions of a group or society in response to the behavior of group members, whereas informal controls such as gossip or ostracism consist of *unofficial* group actions. Official actions or formal controls, such as the criminal law, derive from the official group machinery set up to carry out the functions of the group or agency. These controls are, in effect, imbedded in the formal structure of the group. However, these formal controls are generally backed by certain beliefs, ideals, customs, convictions, attitudes and opinions which in

---

[7] Edwin H. Sutherland, *Principles of Criminology* (Philadelphia: J. B. Lippincott Company, 1924, and subsequent revisions of 1934, 1939, 1947, 1955, and 1960). Also see Marshall B. Clinard, "Sociologists and American Criminology," *Journal of Criminal Law and Criminology,* 41:549–577 (January–February, 1951).

[8] See Albert Geis, "Sociology and Crime," in Joseph S. Roucek ed., *Sociology of Crime* (New York: Philosophical Library, Inc., 1961), pp. 7–33, and Clinard, "Sociologists and American Criminology," *loc. cit.*

[9] See, for example, Stephan Hurwitz, *Criminology* (Elsie Giering, trans.; London: George Allen & Unwin Ltd., 1952), and Olof Kinberg, *Basic Problems of Criminology* (Copenhagen: Levin and Munksgaard, 1935). Not all European criminologists take this position. See Hermann Mannheim, *Group Problems in Crime and Punishment* (London: Routledge & Kegan Paul Ltd., 1955). Also see Wolf Middendorff, *Soziologie des Verbrechens* (*Sociology of Crime*) (Dusseldorf: Eugen Diederichs Verlag, 1959).

themselves are actually informal controls. Thus, in this sense, informal and formal controls cannot be considered as completely discreet categories.[10]

The use of penalties through the criminal law is, therefore, but one of the formal methods of control, and it is a small part of the total system of social controls which operate to create and maintain order in society. Likewise, crime, which is behavior that is defined by law or legal norms, is nevertheless relative to the legal norms of a given area, community, state, or nation.

> What is crime to one city, county, or nation may not be to another. What was crime yesterday may not be today, and what people consider crime today may not be tomorrow. . . . Moreover, laws are but one facet of the regulations we impose on individuals which may vary all the way from ordinary customs, social conventions such as good manners, rules and regulations of a church or lodge, the mores, to other rules such as those called public regulations and laws. All of them represent simply variations in norms and are all part of a continuum. Sometimes, in fact, we may punish some acts which are not crimes more severely than if they were. Examples of such are public reactions to some unconventional manners, the punishment of illegitimacy, or the religious penalty of excommunication.[11]

No effort is required on the part of the group to secure compliance with most of our group norms, for they are the spontaneous and unconscious ways of acting which characterize the bulk of the customs of any culture. Generally speaking, mechanisms of control, such as customs, mores, traditions, beliefs, attitudes, and ideals, are taught through prolonged interaction between persons. Likewise, *informal control* of behavior may be observed in specific behaviors, such as gossip, ridicule, reprimands, praise, criticism, gestural cues, glances of approval or disapproval, emotional expressions, denial or bestowal of affection, ostracism, verbal rationalizations, verbal expressions of opinion, and many other methods. These specific modes of responding to the behavior of group members are generally learned without conscious awareness through group participation. Moreover, because they have been incorporated into their behavior systems and outlooks they are used in a way which seems "natural" or "spontaneous" to the persons involved. Unlike formal controls, informal controls are not exercised through official group mechanisms. Gossip, as an example of an informal social control, is undoubtedly one of the most effective instruments yet devised for disciplining people. These controls are extremely important in any society, for they bulwark the more formal

[10] See Paul H. Landis, *Social Control* (rev. ed.; Philadelphia: J. B. Lippincott Company, 1956).
[11] Marshall B. Clinard, "Criminal Behavior Is Human Behavior," *Federal Probation*, 13:24 (March, 1949).

controls of law. They are extremely effective in a folk society and in rural neighborhood situations of primary personal relationships.

To summarize, the difference between formal and informal controls does not depend on the specific behavior necessary for their operation, but depends instead on the source of origin of societal reaction to such behavior, whethey they derive from formal machinery and relationships or from informal personal relationships.[12]

FORMAL CONTROLS

Formal controls involve organized systems of specialized agencies and standard techniques. There are two main types: those instituted by agencies other than the state, and those imposed by the political state. Rules of a more abstract nature are formulated and authority is given such agents as the clergy or police for their interpretation and application.

A series of specific actions is established to punish the transgressor and to reward those whose compliance with the norms is regular or beyond the expectation of the group. Curiously, nonpolitical agencies, such as business concerns and professional, religious, or social groups, probably use rewards more than penalties, which is just the reverse of formal governmental controls. Through promotions, bonuses, or some token of merit, business organizations frequently reward those who have made an outstanding contribution to the firm, who have never been absent, or who have an unusual safety record. Professional groups often reward outstanding service with election to office or some citation. Religious groups reward faithful adherents by promises of a future state of euphoria, by positions of leadership, and by pins or scrolls given for faithful attendance at Sunday school or similar activities. Clubs, lodges, fraternities, and sororities likewise offer a large number of prestige symbols for those who walk the path from neophyte to full-fledged member without reflecting dishonor on the group. Recognition of a type similar to military rewards is given to a small number of civilians each year in the United States through the Carnegie awards for outstanding heroism.

Nonpolitical groups also impose penalties, some of which may be more severe than punishments imposed for crimes. A business concern may fire a man from his job, and a professional group or a union may suspend a member or even expel him from the group, which may mean a loss of livelihood. Baseball players who do not obey the rules of the league or the ball club are usually fined $50 or $100 for an infraction and they may be suspended. Religious organizations may demand penance or withhold

---

[12] See Landis, *op. cit.*, and Robert Bierstedt, *The Social Order* (New York: McGraw-Hill Book Company, Inc., 1957), pp. 188–189.

certain religious services such as the wedding privilege or religious service at death. They may even use what is, to members of a particular faith, the most drastic punishment of all—excommunication from the church. Clubs and similar groups generally utilize a scale of fines, withdrawal of membership privileges, or even expulsion as formal means of controlling their members.

The other type of formal control is exercised by the state through its political and legal institutions. Unfortunately, this control is seldom exerted through positive sanctions or rewards. Some cities occasionally give publicity to safe and courteous drivers, but the reward is seldom more than a pleasant notoriety. The Mr. Milquetoast who goes through life obeying nearly all the requirements imposed upon him by law seldom receives any rewards. Of course, a man's good reputation may be of benefit to him in connection with certain occupational or community responsibilities, and if he should be apprehended for violation of law his past conduct may mitigate the punishment. An important exception to this failure of the state to use rewards as a means of control is the practice in our armed services of giving good-conduct ribbons, medals, or special leaves for faithful adherence to duty or for outstanding bravery, even though every soldier is supposed to do his duty.

Social control of civilians is characterized by a variety of punishments which may be imposed by the state. If a person is below the legal adult age, he comes under the jurisdiction of the courts as a "delinquent." If the offender has reached the legal age of adulthood he is subject to punishment under the criminal law. He can be put on probation, fined, imprisoned, or even condemned to death. The state of Delaware still flogs persons for certain offenses, and in the past various other cruel and inhumane methods of punishing criminals have been authorized by governments.

The measures at the disposal of the state for the control of violations by its members are not confined to the penalties available through the criminal law. The state has many ways of compelling individuals, business concerns, and labor unions to obey the law. It may withdraw a doctor's, lawyer's, or druggist's right to practice, and it may suspend a tavernkeeper or a restaurateur from doing business for a few days, a year, or even permanently. If an individual or a company makes a product illegally, such as alcohol, or if a concern manufactures foods in violation of pure-food laws, the products may be seized and destroyed by the government without compensation. In settling claims for back payment of taxes or fraudulent returns on taxes, the government may require an additional payment which may be quite a severe penalty. If a business concern or a union is defying a law, the government may institute an injunction "to cease and desist" from further violations, and if further violations occur, contempt of court proceedings may be instituted. Many other examples of government penalties could be cited to indicate that the criminal law is not the only sanction used by political institutions to secure compliance with conduct norms.

What Is a Crime?

The nature of a criminal act may be considered from two points of view, either as a violation of the criminal law or as a violation of any law punished by the state, depending upon the particular assumption with which illegal behavior is approached.

A CRIME AS A VIOLATION OF THE CRIMINAL LAW

First, from a strictly legal position, an act is a crime only when the statutes so specify. These statutes, and the subsequent interpretations of them by the court, constitute the criminal law. Most of the conventional crimes, such as burglary and robbery, were crimes under the common law long before the enactment of any legislation.

At one time or other beliefs of all kinds have been punished by the state under the criminal law, which has developed as a result of legislative and court action. Violations of the criminal law have included such behavior as engaging in recreational activities on the Sabbath, practicing witchcraft, smoking, failing to show proper respect to a noble, wearing one-piece bathing suits, listening to illegal radio programs, and selling alcoholic beverages. Slavery was at one time supported in the United States by laws which severely punished any person opposing slavery or aiding slaves to escape. In 1931 a study of the inmates of the prisons of the federal government showed that, primarily because of the Prohibition laws, 76 percent of them had been convicted of crimes which were not crimes sixteen years earlier.[13]

On the other hand, many parts of the criminal law today, such as the laws against armed robbery, have a long history of being regarded under the common law as antisocial. When written criminal codes came into being, sanctions against these acts were included, since many of them had their origin in institutional norms and values. Even though at one time they were primarily settled through fights or duels, murder, libel, and assault, for example, became crimes largely because private settlements of such disputes tended to disorganize the stability of social relationships. Occasionally one sees the continuation of this process when a relative of a victim takes the law into his own hand. Violations of these laws, which have their origin and partial support in the mores and are offenses bad in themselves, are referred to by lawyers as *mala in se.*

---

[13] George W. Kirchwey, "The Prison's Place in the Penal Systems," *The Annals,* 157:13–22 (September, 1931).

Certain types of behavior which constitute a considerable portion of the criminal law have no such basis in the mores or common law. Lawyers refer to this general group of criminal offenses as *mala prohibita,* or bad simply because they have been prohibited. Most of these offenses have grown out of more recent technological and cultural changes in society. Many are associated with the automobile, with building codes, with hygiene, and with foods and drugs. Other acts have become crimes because of the activities of some pressure group. Types of behavior which have been so outlawed through this means include the sale of alcoholic beverages, unfair trade practices, cruelty to animals, and the teaching of evolution. Other behavior which has become criminal under changing social conditions includes misuse of trademarks, false advertising, the manufacture of impure foods and drugs, acts in restraint of trade, fraudulent or negligent acts of bank officials resulting in insolvency of banks, sale of fraudulent securities, and improper conduct of labor relations.

In order to deal with crime effectively it is necessary not only to get people to modify their ideas about the extreme seriousness of certain crimes but more frequently to get society to take a stronger view toward certain acts which are not regarded as serious even though they are prohibited. Sutherland summarized the problem in this manner: "Laws have accumulated because the mores have been weak and inconsistent; and because the laws have not had the support of the mores they have been relatively ineffective as a means of control. When the mores are adequate, laws are unnecessary; when the mores are inadequate, the laws are ineffective." [14]

The Criminal Law in Practice. A number of misapprehensions about the nature of the criminal law should be removed before criminals are discussed. Since people are often confused by what they hear about criminal behavior, a few general principles or observations about the criminal law are presented below.

1. The first common misapprehension involves the distinction between two commonly used terms, *felonies* and *misdemeanors.* In general, felonies are offenses which are punished by a sentence of one year or more to a state prison or reformatory. Misdemeanors, on the other hand, are generally dealt with under municipal or county ordinances and involve sentences of less than a year in local institutions. Actually there are few clear-cut distinctions between the two in relation to the acts involved. Often the decision is quite arbitrary, so that a theft of an article worth over $50 is a felony, whereas a theft of one of less value is a misdemeanor. Many offenses, such as burglary and assault, involve various degrees of seriousness, some of which arbitrarily constitute felonies and others misdemeanors. In fact, studies have shown that a felony in one state is often considered a mis-

---

[14] Edwin H. Sutherland and Donald R. Cressey, *Principles of Criminology* (6th ed.; Philadelphia: J. B. Lippincott Company, 1960), p. 11.

demeanor in another, and vice versa. At the discretion of the prosecuting attorney misdemeanant categories, such as "disorderly conduct," can be used to cover a variety of offenses which would otherwise be felonies. This is particularly true of many sex and assault cases.

2. Many people assume that a crime always involves a question of *intent*. Although this is generally the case, there are many exceptions. Statutes are increasingly being enacted which do not incorporate this element. In many states today the criminal law provides that persons may be convicted for crimes, such as adultery, bigamy, selling mortgaged property illegally, and passing bad checks, without criminal intent being established. People have also been convicted of injuring someone because of negligence or because of driving in an intoxicated condition; yet in none of these cases did the person have intent, unless one were to assume that he intended to be negligent or to get drunk in order to harm someone.

3. Only a person who is *competent* can commit a crime. In most states he cannot be adjudged a criminal if he is suffering from a psychosis. Also, the individual must be of legal age. This age is usually eighteen, although in the case of certain felonies there may be concurrent jurisdiction at sixteen, and in the case of murder the act may constitute a crime from the age of twelve. Although a person below the age of eighteen is generally regarded as a delinquent rather than a criminal, it would be an error to assume that all or even a large part of delinquency is comparable to adult criminality, or that boys and girls who are picked up for delinquency or are sent to our state training schools are always "junior criminals."

Actually the behavior covered by the term "delinquency" goes beyond any definition of crime; many acts, if committed by adults, would not even appear before the courts. The delinquent child is not technically prosecuted, nor is there a formal trial with a prosecutor and a defense attorney, or a list of witnesses testifying either against or for someone. There are no specific penalties for delinquent acts, and the judge is permitted great latitude in his judgment, although this latitude is not permitted beyond the delinquent's twenty-first birthday. In Wisconsin, for example, a delinquent child is "any child under the age of eighteen years who has violated any law of the state or any county, city, town or village ordinance, who by reason of being wayward or habitually disobedient, is uncontrolled by his parent . . . who is habitually truant from home or school, who habitually so deports himself as to injure or endanger the morals or health of himself." [15] The following are some of the offenses for which juveniles are apprehended, a list which should certainly remove the erroneous impres-

---

[15] *Wisconsin Laws Relating to Juvenile Delinquency* (Madison: State Department of Public Welfare, Division for Children and Youth, March, 1952). For a discussion of the legal aspects of juvenile delinquency, see Donald J. Newman, "Legal Aspects of Juvenile Delinquency," in Joseph S. Roucek ed., *Juvenile Delinquency* (New York: Philosophical Library, Inc., 1958), pp. 29–56.

sion that boys and girls picked up for delinquency or committed to training
schools are all "junior criminals."

1. Violates any law or ordinance
2. Engages in immoral or indecent conduct
3. Knowingly associates with vicious or immoral persons
4. Knowingly enters or visits house of ill repute
5. Patronizes gambling establishments
6. Patronizes a tavern where intoxicating liquor is sold
7. Uses intoxicating liquors
8. Patronizes a public poolroom
9. Smokes cigarettes around public places
10. Is habitually truant from school
11. Is incorrigible and will not obey parents
12. Absents self from home without consent
13. Wanders in streets at night, not on lawful business (curfew)
14. Habitually wanders about railroad yards or tracks
15. Begs or receives alms
16. Engages in an illegal occupation
17. Is in occupation or situation dangerous to self or others
18. Deports self so as to injure self or others
19. Habitually uses vile, obscene, or vulgar language in public places
20. Jumps train or enters car or engine without authority

4. An *attempt* to commit a crime is also punishable under many circumstances, although usually in a lesser degree, on the theory that the act
was intended even though it did not occur. This includes, for example,
attempted murder or rape, or the carrying of a concealed weapon, which
has been changed from a misdemeanor to a felony on the assumption that
the possession of a concealed weapon implies an intent to commit a crime.

5. Under most criminal laws an *accomplice* is considered equally guilty
in the commission of an offense. If a group of persons robs a filling station
and the operator is shot and killed in the process, not only is the person
who held the gun liable for prosecution for murder but all the others, including the lookout, are liable. In a recent English case a man was executed
for the killing of a police officer even though at the time of the murder he
was being physically held by the arresting officers while his accomplice did
the shooting.

6. The criminal law contains no implication that differentials exist
in the treatment of crime on the basis of social class, race, and sex. Actually
the differences are so great that one criminologist has even questioned the
possibility of determining the causes and processes of crime.[16] There are
certainly marked differences in the arrests of lower- and upper-class persons

---

[16] Walter C. Reckless, *The Crime Problem* (3d ed.; New York: Appleton-Century-
Crofts, Inc., 1961), Chap. 3. He would substitute for causes "categoric risks" of getting
arrested and involved in the administrative process.

for the crimes they commit, a fact which will be discussed in more detail later. Likewise, Negroes are more likely to be arrested, convicted, and sentenced to prison than will a comparable group of white offenders. Although the ratio of crimes committed is lower for women than for men, a large proportion of crime committed by women is not reported or prosecuted. This is particularly true of women shoplifters, who are often not reported. When women are involved in offenses with men, as they often are, they are seldom prosecuted and even if convicted are rarely sent to prison. A woman committing murder is seldom given the death penalty.

Trends in the Criminal Law. There are a number of significant trends in the development of the criminal law. Some of them represent improvements; others do not.

1. There has been a trend toward the wider use of probation, the suspended sentence, and the indeterminate sentence, rather than imprisonment. The former method of a flat sentence of so many years for certain crimes is being replaced by the use of indeterminate sentences of, for example, from one to ten years, one to twenty years, or one to life, depending upon the offense. Most criminologists believe that an indeterminate sentence makes it possible for an administrative board, rather than the judge, to study the offender and determine how long an offender should stay in prison, how best to rehabilitate him and at the same time protect society.

2. There has been a marked increase in the use of compulsory psychiatric examinations of offenders for purposes of informing the court in certain sex or personal offenses, or in cases of previous felony conviction. A somewhat similar trend has been the widespread enactment of sex-deviate laws which require the psychiatric examination of certain types of offenders and their indefinite detention for treatment.

3. Physical punishment for crimes has been decreasing. A study of history will reveal that there are probably few methods of physical punishment which have not been used to enforce the criminal law. Men have been tortured and maimed in a variety of ingenious ways; they have been forced to man galleys or transported overseas to penal colonies; they have been executed by various devices. Beginning with the end of the eighteenth century, offenders were more likely to be imprisoned, fined, or placed on probation. These forms of punishment are now almost the only methods that our society uses to punish criminal offenders.

Physical punishment has constituted such a large part of the criminal law in the past that we should examine the philosophies which have been advanced to support it. According to one view, physical punishment exacts retribution; here we have *lex talionis* and vengeance, or an "eye for an eye and a tooth for a tooth." The offender should pay his debt to society. Another view, similar to Beccaria's idea of long ago, is that the punishment of an offender deters others from similar acts. Then there is the concept that punishment restores the social equilibrium, which has been upset by certain crimes. In such cases the offender might be considered to expiate his offense through suffering. Finally, in addition to these theories of punishment, some people have felt that punishment reforms, something it obviously cannot do. On the contrary, physical punishment, whether by imprisonment or otherwise, appears to produce a number of harmful effects.[17]

1. It tends to isolate the individual. Some have remarked that what society holds against a man is not the crime he committed but the fact that he has been physically punished, as by imprisonment.

2. Punishment may simply develop cautious actions in the individual so that instead of changing his attitudes he may simply try harder not to be apprehended again.

3. It frequently creates new and undesirable attitudes in the individual, such as fear, and lack of self-confidence.

4. Punishment may even give the offender status. Delinquents and adults who have been punished often occupy a higher position in the eyes of other deviants and sometimes even in the eyes of the general public simply because of this fact.

5. Any attempt to reform an individual must be a constructive process, but physical punishment is the opposite of this. In fact, in many instances the application of force may stop any efforts on the part of the individual to change his personal behavior voluntarily.

The death penalty has been rapidly declining as a form of punishment. At the end of the eighteenth century it could be employed in at least 240 crimes in England, and there were almost as many capital crimes in the United States. With the development of the idea of prisons, the wider extension of equality before the law affecting noble and serfs alike, and the greater respect for human life, there has been a gradual trend toward the abolition of capital punishment.[18]

Many countries have abolished the death penalty during peacetime: Belgium, Denmark, Holland, Iceland, Italy, New Zealand, Norway, Portugal, Sweden, Switzerland, Argentina, Brazil, Colombia, Peru, Uruguay, Venezuela, and Costa Rica. Although in the Soviet Union the death penalty had been reserved for cases of high treason, espionage, sabotage, terrorist acts, banditry and premeditated murder under certain aggravated circumstances, it was announced in May, 1961, that the death penalty might be applied to large-scale embezzlers of state property and to counterfeiters. The death penalty, all executions being by a firing squad, was also sanc-

---

[17] Sutherland and Cressey, *op. cit.*
[18] See George Rusche and Otto Kirchheimer, *Punishment and Social Structure* (New York: Columbia University Press, 1939).

tioned for especially dangerous habitual offenders and for prisoners who committed violence in their place of confinement.[19] In 1962 the death penalty was further extended to certain public officials who receive bribes, to those who make attempts "under aggravating circumstances" on the life of a policeman or a citizen-volunteer charged with maintaining public order, and to those who commit some types of forcible rape.[20]

― After discussions going back over many years, the English Parliament passed the Homicide Act of 1957 which restricted the number of cases in which the death penalty could be imposed.[21] At the time of the passage of this act it was anticipated that the number of executions would be reduced about five sixths, and so far this estimate has been proved to be substantially accurate.

In the United States persons can still be executed for such crimes as murder, kidnaping, treason, rape, and for armed robbery in many southern states. Of the 42 states with capital punishment in 1960, 24 of them use electrocution, 11 lethal gas, 6 hanging, and in 1 state, Utah, the prisoner has the choice of shooting or hanging. During the twenty-four-year period, 1930 through 1953, a total of 3281 persons were executed by civil authorities, 87.0 percent of them for murder and 11.4 percent for rape. There has been a marked decline in the use of capital punishment in the United States, from an annual average of 167 between 1930 and 1939 to 80 per year for the period 1950–1953. In the calendar year 1960, 57 prisoners were executed in this country, somewhat above the figure of 49 for each of the years 1958 and 1959, which was a record low. Twenty states with capital punishment conducted one or more executions in 1960, five of them accounting for 37 executions: California with 9, Arkansas and Texas 8 each, and Georgia and New York 6 each. Of all the executions, 45 were for murder, 8 were for rape, 2 were for kidnaping, 1 was for robbery, and 1 was for aggravated assault by a life prisoner.

A number of arguments can be advanced against capital punishment: (1) There appears to be little evidence that capital punishment has a deterrent effect. Homicide rates in the United States are generally much lower in the states which have abolished capital punishment than in those which have not. This may simply mean that the presence or absence of capital punishment has no relationship to the homicide rate and that the entire question probably rests on more basic factors in the social environment. Vermont, for example, has a mandatory death penalty; yet it has one of the lowest homicide rates in the country. There are such marked differ-

---

[19] As reported in *The New York Times*, May 7, 1961, p. 28.

[20] As reported in *The New York Times*, February 28, 1962, pp. 1, 5.

[21] For example, treason, piracy, killing of a law officer, and murder connected with the commission of another crime such as robbery would be subject to the death penalty. For a complete discussion of the history of capital punishment in Great Britain and this new law, see Gerald Gardiner, "Criminal Law: Capital Punishment in Britain," *American Bar Association Journal*, 45:259–261 (March, 1959).

ences in the homicide rates within a state that the deterrent effect of the death penalty is doubtful. (2) The abolition of the death penalty has resulted in no consistent reaction. Sometimes there has been an increase in murder and sometimes not. (3) Moreover, evidence indicates that juries are less willing to convict a person when the penalty is death. (4) Another argument against capital punishment is that if an injustice has been done it can never be remedied. (5) A disproportionate number of persons executed are Negroes, young people, and the poor. Of those persons executed for rape from 1930 to 1960, for example, 89.9 percent were Negroes. Over 60 percent of all those executed during 1960 were Negroes, and of these over three fourths were under thirty-five. (6) Finally, there is the debasing effect of executions on societies where the taking of human life is contrary to most religious and social beliefs. It is not in line with contemporary scientific thinking, which emphasizes the treatment and rehabilitation of criminals.

Although there has been a trend away from the use of physical punishments, greater severity in the use of imprisonment has developed in two directions. In response to public hysteria, particularly in the case of certain crimes of violence and sex offenses, penalties of imprisonment up to 199 years have been provided by some states. This sentence is more severe than even a so-called life sentence, since a person becomes eligible for release from prison after serving about one third of his sentence. In the case of life imprisonment this period is from eleven to fifteen years, a figure based on approximately a forty-five-year life expectancy beyond the average age at commission of the crime. The second direction has been the passage of habitual-criminal laws (sometimes called Baumes Laws, after the first one passed in New York), which often require incarceration for life, with no parole, after four felony convictions.[22] On the whole, criminologists look with disfavor on both these trends because they emphasize the crime and not the possible rehabilitation of the offender, and because they often remove all hope from him. Thus not only is further rehabilitation almost impossible: the individual becomes a difficult custodial problem in a correctional institution.

An interesting and significant trend has been the expansion of federal criminal law, which has resulted in making many crimes national crimes. Some of these laws which have developed during the past half century follow:

1910 The White Slave Act (Mann Act)
1925 National Motor Vehicle Theft Act (Dyer Act)
1932 Extortion Act (prohibition of the sending of such notes through the mails)

[22] Great Britain uses preventive detention of from five to fourteen years for habitual criminals. Norval Morris, *The Habitual Criminal* (Cambridge, Mass.: Harvard University Press, 1951).

1934   Kidnaping Act (Lindbergh Act)
1934   National Firearms Act (registration and taxation of machine guns and
      similar weapons)
1934   National Bank Robbery Act (robbery of banks connected with the
      Federal Reserve System or insured by the federal government)
1934   National Stolen Property Act (transportation in interstate commerce
      of stolen articles worth more than $5000)
1934   Anti-Racketeering Statute (prohibition of racketeering in interstate
      commerce)
1951   Slot machines and other gambling devices (machines cannot be moved
      in interstate commerce)
1951   Occupational tax on gamblers ($50 tax on bookies)

Federal laws of this type have been enacted primarily because of the difficulty in dealing with crime on a restricted political basis when criminals, like other persons, move freely and rapidly across state lines. Without the authority provided by a federal law, officers must depend upon the cooperation of officials in other states. Moreover, the cost of extraditing an offender from one state to another has discouraged the prosecution of many crimes. The Bank Robbery Act was enacted in 1934 when the Federal Deposit Insurance Corporation began to insure deposits in most banks, many of which are also members of the Federal Reserve System. Robberies of these banks actually constitute robbery of the federal government.

Although there will probably be further federal expansion of such specific laws in the future, most of them will be restricted to interstate commerce. Other expansion of the enforcement of federal laws has come from more general federal laws, such as postal regulations and tax laws of the Internal Revenue Service.

WHITE-COLLAR CRIME

The definition of a crime solely in terms of the criminal law seems to be too restrictive, however, for the adequate explanation of criminal behavior. Many students of the problem, particularly scientists with a broad point of view, feel that a crime should be defined not only in terms of the criminal law but in broader terms as any act punishable by the state, regardless of whether the penalty is a criminal one or is administrative or civil in nature. They believe that the strict legal definition of a crime is too limited and biased and does not include what has been termed "white-collar crime."

Lawbreaking is often divided into two neat categories: the conventional crimes, such as larceny, burglary, and robbery, which are usually punished under the criminal law; and those violations of law which have come to be known as "white-collar crimes" and which are seldom punished in this way. They include violations of law by businessmen, politicians and government employees, labor union leaders, doctors, and lawyers.[23]

Many investigations by governmental committees, both state and federal, have revealed that white-collar crime among business concerns is extensive. These investigations have covered banking operations, the oil industry, stock exchanges, public utilities, munitions, real estate, insurance, and railways. Violations of law by businessmen include the illegal activities of reorganization committees in receiverships and in bankruptcies; restraint of trade such a monopoly, illegal rebates, infringements of patents, trademarks, and copyrights; misrepresentation in advertising; unfair labor practices; financial manipulations; and wartime crimes, such as black marketeering.[24]

Employers seem to have extensively violated federal laws regulating wages, hours, and public contracts, as well as labor relations and trade practices.[25] A study covering seventy large corporations which, with two exceptions, are included among the two hundred largest nonfinancial institutions in the United States, found that they had had 980 decisions rendered against them for violations of government regulations, an average of 14 per corporation.[26] Sixty corporations had had decisions against them for restraint of trade, 53 for infringement of patents, 44 for unfair labor practices, 28 for misrepresentation in advertising, 26 for rebates, and 43 for miscellaneous offenses. Sixty percent of these adverse decisions were rendered during the ten-year period 1935–1944, during which time there was increased government enforcement of business regulations. After a careful analysis Sutherland concluded that although 158 cases were dealt with by the criminal courts, in actuality crimes were committed in 779 out of the 980 cases, 583 being decisions by civil courts. Even if the analysis were restricted to the criminal courts, it would show that almost two thirds of the corporations had been convicted at one time or another and had an average of 4 convictions each.

Various offenses of a white-collar nature are committed by politicians and government employees. They include direct misappropriation of public funds or the illegal acquirement of these funds through padded payrolls, through relatives illegally on the government payroll, or through

---

[23] One might ask about college professors. There is the possibility of accepting bribes for higher grades, but this has never been a part of the pattern of college teaching. If it was, the results would be as chaotic as politics are.

[24] See Frank Gibney, *The Operators* (New York: Harper & Row, Publishers, 1960) for an account, with many case histories, of unethical and illegal practices in business and politics.

[25] Robert A. Lane, "Why Business Men Violate the Law," *Journal of Criminal Law, Criminology, and Police Science*, 44:151–165 (July–August, 1953).

[26] Edwin H. Sutherland, *White Collar Crime* (New York: Holt, Rinehart and Winston, Inc., 1949, reissued 1960), p. 20.

monetary "kickbacks" from appointees. Usually, however, the illegal activities are more subtle. Politicians and government employees may gain financially by furnishing some favor to business firms or to criminal syndicates. Favors for which politicians may be rewarded by certain businessmen include illegal commissions on public contracts, issuance of licenses or certificates of building or fire inspections, and tax exemptions or lowered tax valuations. Criminal syndicates may share the proceeds of gambling or other profits with public officials who give protection from arrest.

Labor union officials may engage in a variety of criminal activities, such as the misappropriation or misapplication of union funds, defiance of the government by failure to enforce laws affecting their labor unions, collusion with employers to the disadvantage of their own union members, and the use of fraudulent means to maintain their control over the union.[27]

Certain activities in the medical profession are not only unethical but illegal. They include giving illegal prescriptions for narcotics, performing illegal abortions, making fraudulent reports and giving false testimony in accident cases, and fee splitting. Fee splitting, in which a doctor splits the fee he charges with the doctor who referred the case to him, is against the law in many states because of the danger that such referrals will be based on the size of the fee rather than on the proficiency of the practitioner. This practice actually involves the very life of the patient if a doctor refers him to an inferior surgeon in order to secure a part of the surgeon's fee. One study reported that two thirds of the surgeons in New York City split fees.[28] Dr. Paul R. Hawley, Director of the American College of Surgeons, declared that the American people would be shocked at the extent of this practice as well as at the amount of unnecessary surgery performed on patients throughout the country.[29]

Lawyers engage in such illegalities as misappropriating funds in receiverships, securing perjured testimony from witnesses, and "ambulance chasing" in various forms, usually to collect fraudulent damage claims arising from an accident. When cases of these types are discovered the offender is more apt to be disbarred from practice than prosecuted.

The consideration of only conventional crimes gives an erroneous impression of the extent and effects of crimes on society as well as of the nature of criminals.[30] Persons sentenced to prison are usually rather poor

---

[27] Malcolm Johnson, *Crime on the Labor Front* (New York: McGraw-Hill Book Company, Inc., 1950). See also Robert Kennedy, *The Enemy Within* (New York: Harper & Row, Publishers, 1960).

[28] Cited in Sutherland, *White Collar Crime*, p. 12.

[29] "Too Much Unnecessary Surgery," *United States News & World Report*, 34:47–55 (February, 1953). Also see H. Whitman, "Why Some Doctors Should Be in Jail," *Collier's*, 132:23–27 (October, 1953).

[30] Frank E. Hartung, "White Collar Crime: Its Significance for Theory and Practice," *Federal Probation*, 17:31–36 (June, 1953). See also Donald J. Newman, "White-Collar Crime," in *Law and Contemporary Problems*, 23:735–753 (Autumn, 1958).

and relatively uneducated, whereas white-collar criminals are usually in the higher income brackets and are better educated. There is considerable difference in the effect on society of ordinary crimes as compared with white-collar offenses. Sutherland has made these comparisons:

> The financial loss to society from white-collar crimes is probably greater than the financial loss from burglaries, robberies, and larcenies committed by persons of the lower socio-economic class. The average loss per burglary is less than one hundred dollars, a burglary which yields as much as fifty thousand dollars is exceedingly rare, and a million-dollar burglary is practically unknown. On the other hand, there may be several million-dollar embezzlements reported in one year. Embezzlements, however, are peccadilloes compared with the large-scale crimes committed by corporations, investment trusts, and public utility holding companies; reports of fifty-million-dollar losses from such criminal behavior are by no means uncommon.[31]

Many people believe, however, that white-collar crimes are not crimes, and that "crime" and "criminal" should be arbitrarily restricted to the more overt acts of ordinary criminals which fit the common stereotype and which they themselves would never do. This arbitrary distinction is made not on the basis of illegal behavior but on the basis of how the judicial process—namely, the criminal law—reacts to it. Sociologically a crime is any act which is considered socially injurious and which is punished by the state, regardless of the type of punishment. The difficulty in limiting the definition of a crime in terms of the criminal law becomes evident when one compares the punishment of a fine, jail sentence, or probation given an apprehended burglar or bank robber with the different kind of punishment often given a person of white-collar status who violates the law. A doctor who violates the law might be punished by having his license revoked, a lawyer by being disbarred, or a businessman by being enjoined by the government, being required to pay civil damages, having his license to do business suspended, or, in some cases, having his product seized and destroyed. Several factors may enter into the decisions on the dispositions of tax violations which are ordinarily settled by an additional payment of money rather than by criminal prosecution. Tax cases involving large sums of money and flagrant law violations may sometimes be handled administratively, such as being "settled," or by criminal prosecution.

The reports of the Federal Food and Drug Administration carry evidence of widespread violations of laws whose purpose is to safeguard the nation's health and welfare. Such cases include selling various types of food contaminated by filth, hair, and rodents; misrepresenting products, such as selling horse meat as beef, mixing mineral oil with salad oil, or

---

[31] Edwin H. Sutherland, "Crime and Business," *The Annals*, 217:113 (September, 1941). Also see Marshall B. Clinard, "Corruption Runs Far Deeper Than Politics," *The New York Times Magazine*, August, 1952, p. 21.

mixing ground chick-peas or cereal with coffee; short-weighting or using deceptive containers; and, occasionally, selling products which contain physically harmful ingredients. These violations may result in a variety of possible actions: issuance of a civil court injunction to cease further violations; seizure and destruction of the product; and, in the case of the federal law, a fine of up to $5000 and imprisonment of up to five years. It seems logical to regard these violations as crimes, whether or not those responsible for them appeared in the criminal courts. All these sanctions imply that this behavior is socially injurious, that punishment is involved, and that the offender is being stigmatized by society.

Sutherland has shown that unless a more inclusive concept of what constitutes "crime" is used, it is impossible to deal analytically with the different illegal activities which are punished according to occupation and social class.[32]

> White-collar crime is real crime. It is not ordinarily called crime, and calling it by this name does not make it worse, just as refraining from calling it crime does not make it better than it otherwise would be. It is called crime here in order to bring it within the scope of criminology, which is justified because it is in violation of the criminal law. The crucial question in this analysis is the criterion of violation of the criminal law. Conviction in the criminal court, which is sometimes suggested as the criterion, is not adequate because a large proportion of those who commit crimes are not convicted in criminal courts. This criterion, therefore, needs to be supplemented. When it is supplemented, the criterion of the crimes of one class must be kept consistent in general terms with the criterion of the crimes of the other class. The definition should not be the spirit of the law for white-collar crime and the letter of the law for other crimes, or in other respects be more liberal for one class than for the other.[33]

Why White-Collar Crime Is Punished Differently. Punishments for white-collar crimes vary considerably, and are in a striking contrast to the punishment for ordinary crimes. There are several reasons for this difference. First of all, many acts of businessmen which are socially harmful were not made illegal until rather recent times. Embezzlement and some forms of fraud, for example, were not designated as crimes until late in the eighteenth century, and it was not until after the beginning of the nineteenth century that the following acts were outlawed in this country: restraint of trade, false advertising, insolvency of banks due to fraud or negligence of officials, sale of fraudulent securities, and misuse of trade-marks. This slow development was partly due to the fact that the philosophy of laissez faire

---

[32] This sociological conception of crime does not include as crime behavior which is solely antisocial, injurious to society, unfair, greedy, but not necessarily illegal.

[33] Edwin H. Sutherland, "White Collar Criminality," *American Sociological Review* 5:5 (February, 1940), and Hartung, "White Collar Crime," *loc. cit.* Also see Marshall B. Clinard, *The Black Market: A Study of White Collar Crime* (New York: Holt, Rinehart and Winston, Inc., 1952), pp. 226–262.

and *caveat emptor* ("let the buyer beware"), which characterized our general social, political, and economic thinking, prohibited the development of certain needed legal prohibitions regardless of occupation or social class.

Second, there has been little organized public resentment against many socially injurious white-collar crimes, and without great public pressures it has been difficult to get criminal laws passed against this behavior. As one writer has pointed out, white-collar crime differs from other crime, not only in the methods of dealing with it but in the status of the offender, the toleration of the public, and the support which offenders may receive from other groups in the society.[34] This confusion over white-collar crime is a reflection of the diversity of status systems in present-day society. White-collar crimes are usually more complex and are often diffused over a longer period of time than are simple and overt crimes, such as burglary, a fact which tends to obscure the essential criminality of the acts.[35] Furthermore, white-collar crimes are publicized differently from ordinary crimes; consequently, they usually arouse less public resentment.

Summary

A crime may be defined broadly as any act punishable by the state or, in a restricted fashion, as any act punishable by the criminal law. The former definition would include as white-collar crime a host of offenses against the law which are socially injurious but not often punished with a criminal penalty. In either case the use of formal punishment by the state is only one way in which society seeks to secure support for its social norms. What situation is defined as a crime may be relative to both place and time. The criminal law has been characterized by a number of trends, including the wider use of probation, compulsory psychiatric examinations for certain offenses, the decreasing use of the death penalty, and, unfortunately, a trend toward severe penalties for particular types of offenses and for repeaters. Society should more properly consider the offender and not merely the criminal act.

Selected Readings

CLINARD, MARSHALL B. *The Black Market*. New York: Holt, Rinehart and Winston, Inc., 1952, Chaps. 1, 2, and 9. An analysis of price and rationing violations during World War II. Chapter 9 discusses white-collar crime and, in particular, whether black-market activities were crimes.

FULLER, RICHARD C. "Morals and the Criminal Law," *Journal of Criminal Law and Criminology*, 32:624–630 (March–April, 1942). A discussion of the relation of social norms and values to ordinary crimes and to white-collar crimes.

---

[34] Vilhelm Aubert, "White Collar Crime and Social Structure," *American Journal of Sociology*, 58:263–271 (November, 1952).

[35] See Sutherland, *White Collar Crime*, pp. 50–51.

HARTUNG, FRANK E. "White Collar Crime: Its Significance for Theory and Practice," *Federal Probation,* 17:31–36 (June, 1953). This article surveys the research on white-collar crime and suggests its theoretical and practical implications.

NEWMAN, DONALD J. "Legal Aspects of Juvenile Delinquency," in Joseph S. Roucek ed., *Juvenile Delinquency.* New York: Philosophical Library, Inc., 1958, pp. 29–56. A discussion of the difference between delinquency and crime and of some of the important issues in dealing with juveniles as delinquents and not criminals.

NEWMAN, DONALD J. "White-Collar Crime," *Law and Contemporary Problems,* 23:735–753 (Autumn, 1958). A survey of the literature and discussion of the definition and legal basis of white-collar crime and the positive and negative view of whether white-collar violations are crime and white-collar violators criminals.

SUTHERLAND, EDWIN H. *White Collar Crime.* New York: Holt, Rinehart and Winston, Inc., 1949, reissued 1961, Chaps. 1–3. The first comprehensive work dealing with white-collar crime. Chapter 3 is a discussion of the problem of whether such crime is actually crime.

SUTHERLAND, EDWIN H., and DONALD R. CRESSEY. *Principles of Criminology.* 6th ed. Philadelphia: J. B. Lippincott Company, 1960, Chap. 1. This chapter presents some of the essential aspects of the criminal law which are necessary for the study of criminology.

TAPPAN, PAUL W. "Who Is the Criminal?" *American Sociological Review,* 12:96–103 (February, 1947). The position of this article is that the definition of crime in criminology should be restricted to the criminal law and that to include white-collar crime is confusing.

Chapter 7

Sources of Delinquent and
Criminal Attitudes

Thus far this discussion of crime has attempted to clarify the nature of delinquent and criminal acts. It has shown that behavior becomes criminal because it is socially harmful and subject to punishment by the state. This chapter will focus attention on the sources of various conflicting norms which either are in opposition to laws forbidding certain behavior or fail to support them.

Criminals and delinquents develop attitudes and definitions of situations through group association in the same fashion as do noncriminals and nondelinquents. This group experience involves not only the family about which we now hear so much, but also the play group, the school, the neighborhood, clubs, church, marriage, occupation—in fact, all life in its interaction with culture and subculture. Both criminality and noncriminality are "natural" in the sense that they are the outgrowths of processes of social definitions.

First of all, in a consideration of these group experiences, some of the factors in the general culture should be examined, including cultural ideologies which might enhance criminal behavior, the effect of law-enforcement agencies on criminal behavior, and the effects of such secondary influences as motion pictures, radio, television, newspapers, and comic books. The role of the neighborhood or occupational group, the subculture of delinquent companions and gangs, and the role of the family will also be discussed. All these areas, it is contended, are potential sources of criminal attitudes and thus should be considered in developing any program to control delinquency or crime.

Although there is evidence which seems to indicate that certain types of neighborhoods are one of the most important bases for an attack on delinquency, efforts at control should go beyond the neighborhood. The larger society, as it impinges on the community as well as on the adult and the juvenile, must be dealt with in any realistic analysis of delinquency and criminal behavior. Moreover, the attempt to draw a line between the world of the juveniles and young adults and the larger world of the adult is theoretically indefensible, for both groups secure deviant and non-deviant norms within the social framework of our general culture.[1]

The General Culture

Great Britain, New Zealand, and the Scandinavian countries appear to have much lower crime rates than does the United States. This fact is significant, for even a superficial comparison with these countries reveals some striking differences. Several characteristics of American culture undoubtedly account for its high rate of crime. Taft has suggested the following as characteristic aspects of American culture and significantly related to its high crime rate.

1. American culture is dynamic.
2. American culture is complex.
3. American culture is materialistic.
4. American culture is individualistic.
5. American social relations are increasingly impersonal.
6. American culture fosters restricted group loyalties.
7. American culture encourages survival of frontier values.
8. American culture lacks the viewpoint of social science.
9. American culture has faith in law without expecting or even approving obedience to all laws.[2]

Although several of these characteristics have already been discussed in the analysis of the role of urbanism in producing deviant behavior, some need further elaboration in the sections which follow. They will include the general disobedience to law, the selective obedience to law, the illegal behavior of law-enforcement officers, and the relation to delinquency and crime of such secondary media of communication as the press and its treatment of crime and motion pictures, television, radio, and comic books and their treatment of crime.

GENERAL DISOBEDIENCE TO LAW

Although American culture professes obedience to law, there is extensive flaunting of these taboos on the part of the general adult population. There are indications that disobedience to law is far more widespread than reports of crimes committed show; indeed, Reckless has asserted that many violations of the criminal code are not officially known.[3]

Several studies have been made of the extent of unreported delin-

---

[1] Marshall B. Clinard, "Secondary Community Influences and Juvenile Delinquency," *The Annals*, 261:42–43 (January, 1949).

[2] Adapted from Donald R. Taft, *Criminology* (3d ed.; New York: The Macmillan Company, 1956), pp. 38–43. Item 4 has been added by the author.

[3] Walter C. Reckless, *The Crime Problem* (3d ed.; New York: Appleton-Century-Crofts, Inc., 1961), pp. 23–25.

quency and crime. A comparison of a group of 337 Texas college students with a group of 2049 delinquents who came to the attention of the Fort Worth juvenile court revealed that the delinquent acts of these college students had been as serious, although probably not as frequent, as those of the delinquents.[4] Although the college students had rarely appeared in court except for traffic offenses, everyone had committed other offenses for which he could have been charged. For example, on the average every 100 male students committed 116 precollege thefts and 36 thefts during college. Of 49 criminology students at a midwestern university, 86 percent had committed thefts, and about 50 percent had committed acts of vandalism.[5]

An interesting study was made of criminal behavior among the general adult population in metropolitan New York City.[6] Of 1698 persons who answered a questionnaire anonymously, 91 percent stated that they had committed one or more crimes after they were sixteen years of age. (See Table 7.1.) Sixty-four percent of the men and 29 percent of the women

Table 7.1. Percentage of 1698 Persons Who Had Committed Offenses

Offense	Men	Women
Malicious mischief	84%	81%
Disorderly conduct	85	76
Assault	49	5
Auto misdemeanors	61	39
Indecency	77	74
Gambling	74	54
Larceny	89	83
Grand larceny (except auto)	13	11
Auto theft	26	8
Burglary	17	4
Robbery	11	1
Concealed weapons	35	3
Perjury	23	17
Falsification and fraud	46	34
Election frauds	7	4
Tax evasion	57	40
Coercion	16	6
Conspiracy	23	7
Criminal libel	36	29

SOURCE: James S. Wallerstein and Clement J. Wyle, "Our Law-Abiding Law-Breakers," *Probation*, 25:112 (April, 1947).

[4] Austin L. Porterfield, *Youth in Trouble* (Fort Worth, Tex.: Leo Potishman Foundation, 1946), pp. 32–35.
[5] Unpublished material collected by the author.
[6] James S. Wallerstein and Clement J. Wyle, "Our Law-Abiding Law-Breakers," *Probation*, 25:107–112 (April, 1947). The immediately following statistics are from this study.

could have been convicted of felonies. The mean number of offenses committed by the men in adult life (over sixteen years of age) was eighteen and ranged from 8 percent for ministers to 20 percent for laborers. Between eight and nine in every ten men and women had stolen things; one in four of the men admitted stealing an automobile; and one in ten of this group had robbed someone. From this study it was concluded that "the number of acts legally constituting crimes are far in excess of those officially reported. Unlawful behavior, far from being an abnormal social or psychological manifestation, is in truth a very common phenomenon."

The types of violation varied greatly according to occupation: "Businessmen and lawyers were highest in perjury, falsification, fraud and tax evasion; teachers and social workers in malicious mischief; writers and artists in indecency, criminal libel and gambling; military and government employees in simple larceny; mechanics and technicians in disorderly conduct; farmers in illegal possession of weapons; laborers in grand larceny, burglary and robbery; students in auto misdemeanors."

Many different reasons were given for the violations of law. A doctor, for example, admitted taking a car without permission, explaining it as an "emergency." A laborer who had broken in and taken property said that he "put it back later."

> Several persons stated that they had had to falsify their religion to get a certain job, others reporting violation of birth control or gambling laws regarded the laws themselves as stupid and therefore they saw nothing wrong in violating them. Larceny of objects under $100 in value covered such items as towels, a bathmat, a spoon and stamps. One man asserted that his high bill gave him at least a moral right to steal from the hotel where he was staying. Another excused himself for stealing from his employer by observing, "My boss is a jerk." A mechanic who falsified to get someone to sign a document explained that the paper in question was his marriage license. Another man learned that crime did not pay when he used a falsehood in the matter of signing a document. He added to his admission, "My uncle's will, but got nothing, anyway." A farmer faced with the issue of whether or not he had been guilty of assault without provocation wrote "no" in the designated space, but added the comment, "Thrashed a lot of men in my time but they all jolly well deserved it." A woman artist decided to call herself guilty of assault but with the qualifying phrase "Threw ash tray at an unbearable cad." A self-styled criminologist over sixty gave up after reading the questionnaire and returned it with the sweeping comment, "Too much trouble, I've done them all."

The Kinsey report on sexual conduct in American society—although the sample used is only partially representative—revealed the startling presence of serious violations of criminal law of which the public had not been aware.[7] The study revealed that nearly all men with less than an

---

[7] A. C. Kinsey, W. B. Pomeroy, and C. E. Martin, *Sexual Behavior in the Human Male* (Philadelphia: W. B. Saunders Company, 1948). This study has been criticized for the lack

eighth-grade education and about three fourths of those with a college training had had premarital intercourse, an offense which is punishable in every state as fornication, about one third of the sample had had homosexual experiences, and nearly three fourths had had relations with prostitutes. There were extramarital relationships in a third of the marriages, a violation of our laws relating to adultery. Kinsey concluded that "the persons involved in these activities, taken as a whole, constitute more than 95 per cent of the total male population. Only a relatively small proportion of the males who are sent to penal institutions for sex offenses have been involved in behavior which is materially different from that of most of the males in the population." [8]

Few evidences of our lawless behavior would be more startling to people of another culture than the widespread indirect association of the American people with organized crime through their participation in organized gambling. In 1951 the Kefauver Committee found that widespread illegal gambling was being practiced in nearly every city of any size in the United States. People illegally bet billions of dollars through organized racketeers on policy and numbers rackets as well as on the outcome and point range of many amateur and professional athletic contests. Within recent years some athletes have become involved with the law either because they did not report an offer of a bribe or because they accepted one. From 1956 through 1961 twenty college basketball players were paid $44,500 in bribe money to fix forty-four games, according to statements and indictments by prosecutors in New York and North Carolina. Another six players were charged with accepting money in "softening-up" cash, as potential or actual contact men.[9]

——This public lawlessness undoubtedly has its effects on other criminals as well. Ten years ago Senator Paul Douglas made some significant remarks on the effects of this and other types of illegal behavior upon American society.

> Other events during the year [1951] have also shown that the evils which have been revealed are far more pervasive than we should like to believe. They go deep into our social life and are not confined to politics. Thus, large numbers of players on leading college basketball teams have confessed to accepting money from gamblers in order to "fix" the point score in games. Further inquiry has developed that the colleges themselves were not guiltless, since they have allowed both the sport and the players to be professionalized. It has also been revealed that the major portion of the football team at the United States Military Academy—an institution which has prided itself upon its honor—

of representativeness of the sample and for the inaccuracy of some of the data furnished by some of the subjects as well as for other flaws. See Paul Wallin, "An Appraisal of Some Methodological Aspects of the Kinsey Report," *American Sociological Review*, 14:197–211 (April, 1949).

[8] Kinsey, *et al., op. cit.*, p. 392.

[9] See Tim Cohane, "Behind the Basketball Scandal," *Look*, 26:85 (February 12, 1962).

systematically cheated in their examinations in order to maintain their eligibility. Informal polls of the student bodies of a number of colleges have indicated that cheating is apparently a widespread practice while the professionalization of college football has become more and more evident. In one FBI district alone, the number of cases of embezzlement from banks by trusted officials has reached a startling figure. These and other developments are symptoms of ethical weaknesses which permeate wide sections of our society from which we had expected higher standards. They have brought a feeling of disgust to most Americans and have made them skeptical about the existence either of integrity in active life or of any real professional virtue.[10]

In 1959 the shock of television scandals on several nationally televised "quiz shows" swept through the American public, an estimated fifty million of whom, in 1958, had been watching the three leading quiz programs. A number of programs were found to have been rigged by feeding the contestants answers in advance. On this basis one contestant, whose father and uncle each had won a Pulitzer Prize in literature, defeated thirteen opponents and therefore won $129,000. Others confessed to winning large amounts fraudulently, as much as $237,500 in one case and $98,500 in another. Altogether, ten contestants were brought before the courts on charges of perjury since they had denied the charges under oath before a grand jury. They were given suspended sentences, but were allowed to keep their "earnings."

SELECTIVE OBEDIENCE TO LAW

Much more common than general disobedience to law is the tendency in American culture for persons to obey laws on a selective basis. Instead of obeying all laws one disregards those types of law which directly affect his own occupation and social class. Sutherland, as well as others, emphasized this public attitude that one can use his own discretion as to which laws he must obey. Some laws are obeyed, others are not, according to a person's own beliefs rather than the general welfare.[11]

Many businessmen believe that such laws as those regulating securities and banking procedures, tax collections, restraint of trade, labor relations, wartime price control and rationing, and others of a similar nature, are not as binding on the individual as are our burglary and robbery laws. Some labor leaders see no reason for obeying laws prohibiting labor "racketeering" or laws affecting the conduct of labor relations and strikes if it is to their advantage to break them. Farmers have been known, too, to disobey the law selectively; examples include their failure to pay proper income

---

[10] Paul H. Douglas, *Ethics in Government* (Cambridge, Mass.: Harvard University Press, 1952), pp. 9–10. Also see "Ethical Standards in Public Life," *The Annals,* Vol. 280 (March, 1952).

[11] Edwin H. Sutherland and Donald R. Cressey, *Principles of Criminology* (6th ed.: Philadelphia: J. B. Lippincott Company, 1960), p. 86.

taxes, their intimidation of farm auctioneers, and their dumping of milk trucks to keep up the price of milk in the depression of the thirties.[12] Government officials operate in a situation where bribes and favors are on occasion offered by businessmen and where politicians, including congressmen, may exert influence in behalf of special interests. A political scientist has this to say about political corruption:

> The record indicates that the political morality reflects, rather than shapes, the society in which it operates and that, more pertinently, it is naïve in the extreme to expect from politicians a far different ethical standard from that which prevails throughout the country. Indeed, were today's politicians to adopt such a standard they would almost certainly be rejected by the voters as idealists, dreamers, crackpots, or visionaries.[13]

The implications of selective obedience to law can be seen more clearly if ordinary crimes are considered. Many persons who engage in such crimes as robbery and burglary consider some of our laws unjust and too severe, and they often have a number of rationalizations for these attitudes. They point to the general dishonesty of the public, the brutality of the police, and the corruption of public officials, including those in the courts. A professional confidence man who is smart enough to outtrick a "sucker" may contend that the law should not punish him, or in any event not as severely as it does. A man with a prison record who has a dependent family, whose wages are too low, and whose record interferes with employment possibilities may advance such arguments as rationalizations for thefts or burglaries. Certainly ordinary criminals are acquainted with the effects of this selective obedience to law, and this attitude presents a major problem in the rehabilitation work of our correctional institutions. As the warden of one of our prisons said in 1946, "What am I supposed to do, retrain people to be honest in a dishonest world of black markets and frauds?" Perhaps Willy Sutton, a well-known professional bank robber, put it best when he told a group of New York reporters some years ago: "Others accused of defrauding the government of hundreds of thousands of dollars merely get a letter from a committee in Washington asking them to come in and talk it over. Maybe it's justice but it's puzzling to a guy like me."

Great inconsistency exists in modern urban society between the behavior required of a child and that of an adult, and these differences are not clearly defined as a correlate of age. In fact, adults are permitted increasing transgressions of the conduct norms, whereas juveniles are expected to conform to ideals. In many simpler societies the situation is reversed. It is the juveniles who have considerable freedom, whereas the behavior of

---

[12] James O. Babcock, "The Revolt in Iowa," *Social Forces*, 12:369–373 (March, 1934).
[13] H. H. Wilson, *Congress: Corruption and Compromise* (New York: Holt, Rinehart and Winston, Inc., 1951), p. 234.

adults is one of rigid conformity.[14] The inconsistent value patterns of the adult world constitute one of the chief moral hazards to the juvenile in the modern world. The relation between the differing degrees of latitude allowed in the behavior norms of the adult and the juvenile worlds can best be illustrated by the fact that if we were to insist on the same, or comparable, behavior standards among our adults as among our juveniles, our police, jails, or courts could not possibly deal with the consequent avalanche of cases. There are few adults, particularly in large urbanized areas, whose conduct would approach the standards set by that ideal for juveniles, the Boy Scout Code.

THE BEHAVIOR OF LAW-ENFORCEMENT OFFICERS AND AGENCIES

The general attitude of the American public toward law-enforcement officers is certainly not conducive to obedience. The American people generally do not have the same degree of respect that the English have for their "bobbies," barristers, and judges. In general, legislative bodies, considered as corporate bodies and not as individuals, are regarded with suspicion and distrust, and the police are looked upon as harsh, corrupt, and inefficient. There is a more favorable public attitude toward the courts, but the higher courts are often ridiculed because of their corporate inefficiency; the lower courts, for their inefficiency and dishonesty.

Although there is much evidence of this disrespect for law-enforcement agencies, it is possible that it may represent simply a vicious circle in that what the American people expect their law-enforcement officers to be is actually what they often are. Certainly, numerous studies have indicated that the police and other law-enforcement agencies, instead of preventing the development of criminal attitudes and acts, actually constitute one of the chief sources of indoctrination in attitudes of disrespect for law.[15] The all too common practice of employing police personnel and electing judges who in no way exemplify the type of conduct required of those charged with enforcing the law adds both directly and indirectly to the production of delinquency and crime. Far too many police officers, both urban and rural, are simply political appointees. Many are intellectually unfit, inefficient, brutal in making arrests and securing evidence through the third degree, and frequently willing to accept bribes even from juveniles. In

---

[14] For example, see Margaret Mead, *Coming of Age in Samoa* (New York: William Morrow & Company, Inc., 1928), and the works of Bronislaw Malinowski on the Trobriand Islanders.

[15] William Westley, "Violence and the Police," *American Journal of Sociology*, 59:34–41 (July, 1953). Also Ernest J. Hopkins, *Our Lawless Police* (New York: The Viking Press, Inc., 1931).

some instances police officers may even go further than this, as in the case of several Chicago policemen who in 1961 were convicted of collaborating with criminals in a number of burglaries.[16] Such behavior does not encourage respect for law nor aid in the prevention of delinquency or the rehabilitation of offenders.

Many judges also do not merit the respect of juveniles, for their attitudes on the bench and the general atmosphere of their courtrooms often seem to indicate a lack of understanding. This situation is understandable when one realizes that most law schools and the legal system itself do not provide adequate, or indeed, any training for lawyers or judges in juvenile or adult rehabilitation work. Very few jurists apply scientific knowledge in the treatment of crime in the courts. Cases of political influence, bribery, and outright violations of law by jurists occur in American society in sufficient numbers partially to endanger the concept of "justice" which has come over to us from English law. In 1949, a police judge in Newark pleaded guilty to stealing over $630,000 through a rigged-up series of fictitious mortgages. He had used the money to cover his losses in horse racing bets. The serious injuries in such cases lie not only in the crime but in its effects on other offenders.

The Kefauver Committee found that organized crime in American cities could not exist or flourish without extensive bribery of politicians, public officials, sheriffs, police officers, and others. As Tannenbaum has stated, "He who would ask the question 'Why have we as much crime as we do have and why do we have this kind of crime?' must first be asked to answer the larger question, 'Why do we have the kind of political life that we do have in our larger cities?' " [17] A Scandinavian criminologist once wrote the author that bribery of police and judicial officials is almost nonexistent in Sweden. Yet in the United States the "fix" is so common that Sutherland's comment about it is no different from that of others who have studied the relation between crime and law enforcement in this country:

---

[16] See Virgil W. Peterson, "The Chicago Police Scandals," *The Atlantic,* 206:58 ff. (October, 1960). See also Barron Beshoar and George Harris, "How Denver's Cops Turned Burglar," *Life,* 51:18 ff. (November 3, 1961).

[17] Frank Tannenbaum, *Crime and the Community* (Boston: Ginn and Company, 1938), pp. 150–151. Reprinted by permission of the publishers. "The evidence . . . is perhaps sufficient to indicate that a considerable portion of crime in our larger cities, and also its character, are reflections of, and are intimately bound up with, the kind and character of the political organizations that exist in these cities. The political machine, the gamblers and the gangsters, the police and the local ward heelers, the city magistrates and the court clerks, the lawyers who practice in the courts, the bondsmen, the local attendants, the 'fixers,' the hangers-on, the good fellows about the political clubs, the dispensers of favors and the securers of jobs, the people willing to 'go to the front' for the less fortunate who have been arrested, the givers of political jobs to honest political workers, are all intertwined into a system, or still better, a way of life, for that part of our community which occupies itself with the business of governing under the conditions that make this kind of governing both possible and necessary."—*Ibid.*

When one is caught the problem is to "fix" things. This occurs very commonly in the so-called law-abiding groups in relation to traffic violations, gambling, smuggling liquor, and certain other crimes. In other circles it occurs in relation to shoplifting, picking pockets, robbery, burglary, and murder. There is a prevalent belief among prisoners that their own cases could have been "fixed" if they had had sufficient money. According to that belief the only reason for being arrested or convicted is poverty. It is probable that no part of the population is better acquainted with the corruption and graft in the legislative, judicial, and police systems, so far as they exist, than are the professional criminals.[18]

The methods of dealing with crime often constitute little subcultures for the transmission of criminal norms.[19] According to reports of state and federal inspectors, many American jails fail to meet standards of health and welfare. Conditions in many of our boys' training schools, our reformatories, and our prisons are not much better. The large number of criticisms of such institutions can be summarized by stating that most of them, as now constituted, probably produce more crime in a society than they eliminate.[20] Although there are small islands of exceptions in the correctional systems, scientific studies, reports of inmates and wardens, the high percentage of repeaters, and the frequent prison riots by outraged inmates —all justify this conclusion.

The prisoners' idle hours are primarily devoted to conversations about crime and sex. The more sophisticated offenders provide tutelage for the naïve in both the techniques and the philosophy of crime. Fellow inmates of detention houses and cell mates tutor others in how to "strip" a car properly, how to "blow" a safe or successfully counterfeit money; moreover, there is frequently indoctrination in homosexual practices. Most prisons are far too large to deal with human beings on a personal basis, the strict discipline antagonizes men, the one-sex community stimulates unhealthy sex attitudes, the supervisory personnel is often inferior, and there is all too frequently little that is rehabilitative. Since the bulk of the several hundred thousand persons in our jails and prisons annually receives these experiences, they represent a contribution of the general culture to the American crime problem.

Fortunately, there is evidence that this situation is changing. More often than in the past policemen are being selected on a merit basis and given training in proper police conduct. Some judges receive training at professional institutes which deal with delinquency and crime. Jail and prison conditions are slowly being improved, although most of them still have a long way to go to achieve recommended standards.

---

[18] Sutherland and Cressey, *op. cit.*, p. 198.

[19] Donald Clemmer, "Observation on Imprisonment as a Source of Criminality," *Journal of Criminal Law and Criminology*, 41:318 (September–October, 1950).

[20] For a complete discussion of prisons see Chapter 21.

THE NEWSPAPER AND CRIME

The press has been charged with generally promoting and glorifying crime because of the volume of its news items and its continual elevation of so-called public enemies by building them up as success stories: "When a newspaper carries the story that a certain criminal is the worst, or the best, or the most dangerous, or some other superlative appellation, it is one of the few consolations this criminal will have, in case of conviction, while he is in prison." [21]

Unusual events are newsworthy and gain ready access to the printed page, for the urban American reader is little concerned with the ordinary happenings in everyday life. Only the unusual, the different, and the new attract his attention. He dotes on war, rape, murder, and crime. The breaking of the law is an event that captures reader interest. The amount and prominence of space devoted to crime in the newspapers and the amount of conversation based on these stories present a bewildering picture of immortality in our society. By continually playing up crime, it is likely that newspapers are important in making us a crime-centered culture. As a result, crime often seems more frequent than it really is. Perhaps to some, crime stories resemble the folk tales of frontier bad men. They provide vicarious emotional thrills which are seldom derived from conventional institutions. The newspapers also provide information about the techniques of committing crime, although this is probably not too important in individual cases.

There is a difference between reporting a crime in simple, verifiable factual statements, as is often done in many countries, and loading a long, detailed crime story with emotionally charged words. Crime receives particular prominence in American newspapers because of the amount of space given to crime stories and because of their position on the front page. The proportion of crimes stories to the rest of the news is not an adequate basis for comparison, for the front page sells the paper. Even a reader on his way to the comic section cannot help noticing front-page crime stories and pictures. If he misses it there he is sure to hear it included in the dinner-table conversation. Under the guise of supplying what the reader demands, crime is not merely made prominent: it is supplied to the reader in colorful exposition and frequently with "on the scene" lurid photographs. A person is not merely murdered or slain; he is brutally slain with a blunt instrument. The suspect does not merely attempt to escape capture; the desperate killer, his cunning increased by his emotional stimulation, gives the inept police a terrific run for their money.

There is general indifference on the part of the newspapers to the

---

[21] Sutherland and Cressey, op. cit., p. 211.

serious moral implications of this almost universal practice. Admittedly such a statement raises the problem of the function of the newspapers. On the one hand, the concept of free enterprise condones the collection of sordid tales as a valuable vehicle for selling advertisements; on the other, the concept of social responsibility suggests that some newspapers might re-evaluate their role in a society.

Television, Motion Pictures, Radio, and Comic Books

The great interest of juveniles and adults in television, motion pictures, the radio, and comic books has caused some people to overestimate their importance, whereas others tend to discount them in their explanations of delinquency and crime. It is conceivable, however, that even if all these media were to disappear from our culture we probably would still have almost as much delinquency and crime as we now have. Certainly we had delinquency and crime before any of them were considered of consequence.

A recent survey of television, covering such questions as types of programs, time spent watching television, and the like, was conducted by a research team at the Stanford University Institute for Communication Research.[22] The findings of this survey were based on responses from 6000 children, 2000 parents, and 300 teachers. It was found that from the age of three to sixteen the average child devotes about a sixth of his waking hours to watching television, and more than half the children studied watched "adult" programs, such as crime plays, westerns, and shows featuring emotional problems. The investigators analyzed 100 hours of programs in the so-called children's hours, the period from 4:00 to 9:00 P.M. In those 100 hours they counted twelve murders, sixteen major gun fights, twenty-one persons shot, twenty-one other violent incidents in which one person slugged another, an attempted murder with a pitchfork, two stranglings, one stabbing in the back with a butcher knife, three successful suicides (and one unsuccessful suicide), four people pushed over a cliff, two attempts made to run over persons with automobiles, a raving psychotic loose in an airliner, two mob scenes (in one the wrong man was hanged), a horse grinding a man under his hoofs, two robberies, a woman killed by falling from a train, a tidal wave, an earthquake, a hired killer stalking his victim, and, finally, one guillotining. Although admitting the disturbing effects of such violence on children, they concluded that almost invariably delinquent children who blamed television for their crimes had something seriously wrong with their lives quite apart from watching television and that with few exceptions these problem children had problems before they learned anything about crime from television.

[22] Wilbur Schramm, Jack Lyle, and Edwin B. Parker, *Television in the Lives of Our Children* (Stanford, Calif.: Stanford University Press, 1961).

There has also been much public indignation against the misnamed "comic" books, particularly their vicious crime content. It is reported that over fifty cities have taken steps to ban objectional ones. After studying some delinquents and the contents of comic books, a psychiatrist concluded that comic books produce a great deal of serious delinquency.[23] In his opinion, comic books suggest delinquent ideas to children, stimulate unwholesome fantasies, suggest sexually abnormal behavior, emphasize deceit and cruelty, and supply techniques for committing delinquencies. Most of the material he presents is based on a few cases, little of it is of a scientific, factual nature, and he does not make any study of the effect of comic books on nondelinquents.

It is doubtful if many cases can be found where, even though there was no evidence of prior deviant behavior, such behavior could be attributed only to reading comic books. Much of the material represents fantasy and makes no attempt at reality. To those already delinquent, comic books may furnish techniques and even additional reasons for committing an offense.[24] One psychiatrist, in suggesting a cautious approach to the problem of comic books, has summarized what appears to be a realistic view:

a. No one has conclusively demonstrated that the comic books are detrimental in any way.

b. Campaigns to eliminate them are useless and serve only to release the aggressive feeling of the crusaders.

c. No normal child under the age of 12 is likely to be harmed by them. Neurotic children need treatment and would be equally affected by the movies or the radio.

d. Normal adolescents may be harmed by certain types of comics, especially the "jungle adventure" type.

e. Parents are the best judges of what their children should read. If parents supervise their children's reading of comics the undesirable ones would soon disappear.

f. The argument that children waste time on the comics, which could be better spent, needs further study.

g. More study should be devoted to eliciting the facts about the comics.[25]

Research indicates that although both delinquents and nondelinquents attend motion pictures, the delinquents attend more often and exhibit greater interest in them. In some studies marked differences were noted between delinquents and their control groups in this regard. Although this

---

[23] Frederic Wertham, *Seduction of the Innocent* (New York: Holt, Rinehart and Winston, Inc., 1953).

[24] In his study of 1313 delinquent gangs in Chicago, Thrasher found that comic strips in the newspapers did influence these groups and their activities. Not only did many of the gangs obtain their names from the comic strips but suggestions for vandalism and other destructive activities were directly traceable to this source.—Frederic M. Thrasher, *The Gang* (rev. ed.; Chicago: The University of Chicago Press, 1936), p. 113.

[25] John R. Cavanagh, "The Comics War," *Journal of Criminal Law and Criminology,* 40:34–35 (May–June, 1949).

fact may have significant implications, careful additional study would be required to ascertain them.[26] There is no question that the motion picture often presents a version of our culture emphasizing wealth, materialism, and immoral conduct, both criminal and sexual, which, as far as juveniles are considered, furnishes them approved models conducive to delinquency. Approximately half of the motion pictures produced during 1948 dealt with murder or the activities of criminals.[27]

A realistic appraisal of these forms of entertainment indicates, therefore, that on the whole their direct influence on the juvenile only serves to aggravate whatever existent deviant attitudes and personality traits there may be. Schramm has stated that children both learn and are influenced by the various media of mass communication, but that what they receive from the mass media is first passed through another set of influences, such as family, school, and church, before it becomes a very important guide to actions. "We might say that what television does to children is less significant than what children do with television; and what children do with television . . . depend[s] on their homes, their schools, their peer group relations, and many other factors quite outside the mass media." [28]

This does not mean, however, that such media have no effect. In 1961 a Senate committee looked into the problem of the large proportion of television programs dealing with crime and violence. In general, the conclusion was reached that this material might have an indirect effect on many youths by presenting a distorted picture of approved American values. The vivid pictures of juvenile delinquents and criminal offenders presented on television serves to perpetuate a stereotyped picture, in the minds of the public, of all delinquents and criminals as tough and vicious. Consequently, this makes it difficult to bring about changes in the punitive aspects of the criminal law and correctional programs and to utilize measures to bring about reformation. From such a view, television programs may be thought of more directly as increasing, in the long run, the seriousness of delinquency and crime.

It is unfortunate that few actual scientific investigations have been made of the influence of these various forms of entertainment on delinquency and crime. Certainly there has been only limited investigation of

---

[26] See Maud A. Merrill, *Problems of Child Delinquency* (Boston: Houghton Mifflin Company, 1947), p. 91. Also see William Healy and Augusta F. Bronner, *New Light on Delinquency and Its Treatment* (New Haven, Conn.: Yale University Press, 1936), p. 72. In a study made almost thirty years ago Blumer and Hauser found that motion pictures represented important factors in only about one in ten of the delinquent boys and one in four of the delinquent girls. See Herbert Blumer and Philip M. Hauser, *Movies, Delinquency and Crime* (New York: The Macmillan Company, 1933), p. 198.

[27] For this reason, in Sweden, children under fourteen are not permitted to see most motion pictures, which are primarily American; moreover, certain crime films are censored for adults.

[28] Wilbur L. Schramm ed., *Mass Communications* (Urbana: University of Illinois Press, 1960), p. 466.

the millions of nondelinquent juveniles who avidly attend crime movies, nightly watch several television programs dealing with crime and violence, or read comic books regularly. In most cases the result of the preoccupation of the public with the effect on juvenile delinquency of television, motion pictures, radio, and comic books is merely to release the feeling that something should be done. The deeper question of why juveniles are interested in this entertainment raises issues which adults often do not wish to face because of their own interests in similar material. Likewise, this problem is evidence of a reluctance on the part of the adult world to deal effectively with factors basic to it—general disobedience to law, the presence of disorganizing influences in local neighborhoods, political corruption, and certain emphases in our culture, such as materialism and extreme individuality. The existence of gangs of delinquent boys is a more important and more difficult immediate problem than television, motion pictures, radio, or comic books, but few communities have the necessary vision to attack it. In dealing with social difficulties the public tends to take the easiest course.

Neighborhoods and Occupations

So far these comments about the inconsistency of cultural norms have referred to the social heritage as a whole. This section will describe the role of neighborhoods and occupations in transmitting criminal norms. The neighborhood or local community is one primarily of personal relationships, where people live and where their local institutions are located. It is an area of more personal social participation in which the activities of child and adult tend to be organized around agencies, such as the local stores, the school, the church, playgrounds, and sometimes even a motion-picture theater. This local world may include taverns, lodges, gangs, athletic teams, and sports organizations. The members of the neighborhood tend sometimes to share in other activities, such as weddings and funerals, picnics and carnivals. It is a world of meaningful experiences to the individual. At the same time, the neighborhood reflects some of the norms and evaluations of the outside world. A child who lives "back of the yards" or "across the tracks" develops a conception of himself as being different from children in other neighborhoods. As a recent major work on delinquency concluded, "the major effort of those who wish to eliminate delinquency should be directed to the reorganization of slum communities." [29]

Neighborhoods often differ as to social class, in the variety of the

---

[29] Richard A. Cloward and Lloyd E. Ohlin, *Delinquency and Opportunity: A Theory of Delinquent Gangs* (New York: The Free Press of Glencoe, 1960), p. 211. They point out that whereas slum areas used to be organized, they are now becoming "disorganized" because of such factors as the decline of the local political power structure and new housing developments.

composition of racial, ethnic, and religious groups, and in the stability of the population. Even more important, there may be pronounced differences in the social norms of the local community. There are local areas which are organized principally around conventional norms, and there are other areas in which unconventional standards predominate. In either instance no local community has norms exclusively of one type or another; rather, conflicting standards are present in varying proportions. A person in a delinquent area may have close associations with persons who engage in, or encourage him to engage in, delinquency and at the same time have similar contacts with law-abiding persons.

Some local communities maintain the middle-class virtues of pride in family status, of obedience to the sexual mores, of respect for the police and law, at least insofar as the more overt crimes are concerned. These local communities have considerable stability and relatively little racial and ethnic diversity. These areas do not tolerate such establishments as taverns, houses of prostitution, gambling, and "fences" for the disposal of stolen goods. Most of the boys and girls belong to such traditional groups as the Scouts, and the adults are actively organized in conventional groups like the parent-teacher association. Other groups are patterned along conventional ways, engaging in woodcraft, hikes, and games. Occasionally there is some vandalism but there is little theft. The social norms of the community are largely conventional, and conventional institutions exist to support these norms. The moral responsibilities of the outside world and general culture are continually brought into the lives of juvenile and adult alike.

Many local communities have norms so different from those of middle-class neighborhoods that they might be a part of a separate culture. A considerable proportion of our population lives in these areas. They are represented by Zone I and mainly by Zone II of our large cities, and by an area "back of the tracks" in our smaller cities and towns.[30] The moral values in these areas are reflected in the types of recreational facilities, consisting of places of prostitution, strip-tease joints, burlesque shows, public drinking places, and taxi dance halls. Many of the taverns permit gambling and sell liquor to minors and drunks. There are secondhand stores which often dispose of shady merchandise, and "fences" and junkmen who foster

---

[30] See pages 87–90. In some places our farming areas are characterized by these pockets of moral deterioration, as has been satirized in *Tobacco Road*, and suggested by differentials in the moral standards of owners and some farm labor. Farming districts and small towns probably do not have nearly as distinct local areas as do the large urban communities, because of personal relationships which transcend the immediate neighborhood. A study of one small city showed that although counterparts to delinquency areas in large cities produced crime, localizations of deviant values were not entirely confined to a neighborhood but rather were associated with membership in certain families and small groups with deviant attitudes.—Donald R. Taft, "Testing the Selective Influence of Areas of Delinquency," *American Journal of Sociology*, 38:699–712 (March, 1933).

delinquencies and crimes because of their willingness to purchase stolen goods. Premarital and extramarital relations are common, many girls are expected to engage in such relations or in sexual promiscuity, and many girls and boys believe that such conduct is proper.

The norms of conventional society are not nonexistent in these areas, however, and they include some traditional organizations such as youth groups, lodges, and churches. There are families who have traditional virtues, and there are persons who live in the area but whose standards are not part of it. On the whole, however, these conventional organizations are not too effective. These neighborhoods are often insulated from much of conventional society and its norms.[31]

Far too often the "big shots" of these areas are successful young "punks," criminals, shady politicians, or owners of vice resorts. Their position of high social status is a demonstration that participation in the activities of conventional society is not the only way to achieve success. This world with prestige values different from other neighborhoods has been described by two delinquents.

> Every boy has some ideal he looks up to and admires. His ideal may be Babe Ruth, Jack Dempsey, Al Capone, or some other crook. His ideal is what he wants to be like when he grows up and becomes a man. When I was twelve years old we moved into a neighborhood where there lived a mob of gangsters and big crooks. They were all swell dressers and had big cars and carried "gats." Us kids saw those swell guys and mingled with them in the cigar store on the corner. Jack Gurney was the one in the mob that I had a fancy for. He used to take my sis out and that was how I saw him often. He was in the stick-up racket before he was in the beer racket and was a swell dresser and had lots of dough. He was a nervy guy and went in for big stuff. He was a mysterious fellow and would disappear sometimes for several days but always came back. He was looked up to as the leader of his mob and anybody would gladly be in his place.

> Naw, I don't wanna be a big lawyer or business man, I wanna amount to something. I wanna be a big shot, like "P.J." [well-known beer baron]. Have all the guys look up to me, and have a couple of Lincolns, lots of molls, and all the coppers lickin' my shoes.[32]

Similar to the impact of neighborhood norms on the individual are those of certain occupations. In some, norms may be law-abiding, whereas in others they may not be. This will be discussed in detail in a more extensive presentation of white-collar crime in a later chapter.

---

[31] Sutherland and Cressey, *op. cit.*, pp. 160–161.
[32] Chicago Area Project, "Juvenile Delinquency," A Monograph Prepared by the Institute for Juvenile Research and the Chicago Area Project (rev. ed.; Chicago: 1953), pp. 8–9.

Associates

The role of cultural, neighborhood, and occupational norms and values in the development of criminal attitudes has been discussed, but the method of transmittal to the individual delinquent or criminal has not been indicated. These attitudes are primarily acquired through companions and by participation in small intimate groups in much the same manner as law-abiding norms are transmitted. Companions who play a major part in the acquisition of these norms include the play group or gang, siblings in the family, associates in one's occupation, and other persons. Popular thinking about delinquency and crime is, for once, quite correct in its emphasis on the role of "evil companions" in this behavior.

Most delinquents are arrested in company with others, and it can be safely assumed that those who had no companions at the time of their arrest had had at least one in the beginning of their delinquency.[33] In one study of 5480 Chicago delinquents Shaw found that 81.8 percent of those brought into juvenile court had one or more companions.[34] Considering those with one or more companions, he found that 30.3 percent had one companion, 27.7 percent had two, 10.8 had three, 7.1 had four, and 5.9 percent had five or more.

In one of their studies Healy and Bronner found that two thirds of a group of 3000 Chicago and Boston delinquents had had bad companions. In another of their studies 70 percent of the delinquents were found to have had delinquent companions.[35] After comparing 500 delinquents with an equal number of nondelinquents, the Gluecks reported that "delinquents almost without exception chummed largely with other delinquents while the nondelinquents, despite the fact that they too lived in the slums, had few intimates among delinquents."[36] Although 98.4 percent of the delinquents associated with other delinquents, only 7.4 percent of the nondelinquent group had done so. Two previous studies of the Gluecks had revealed a similar picture, with 70 percent of a group of 1000 Boston delinquents and 60 percent of a group of Massachusetts reformatory men having committed their offenses with companions.[37]

---

[33] For a current survey of various findings, see Thomas G. Eynon and Walter C. Reckless, "Companionship at Delinquency Onset," *British Journal of Criminology*, 2:162–170 (October, 1961).

[34] Clifford R. Shaw and Henry D. McKay, "Social Factors in Juvenile Delinquency," National Commission on Law Observance and Enforcement, *Report on the Causes of Crime* (Washington, D.C.: Government Printing Office, 1931), II, 195–196.

[35] Healy and Bronner, *op. cit.*, p. 52.

[36] Sheldon and Eleanor T. Glueck, *Delinquents in the Making* (New York: Harper & Row, Publishers, 1952), p. 89. Also see their original study, *Unraveling Juvenile Delinquency* (Cambridge, Mass.: Harvard University Press, 1950).

[37] Sheldon and Eleanor T. Glueck, *One Thousand Juvenile Delinquents* (Cambridge, Mass.: Harvard University Press, 1934), p. 100, and their *Five Hundred Criminal Careers* (New York: Alfred A. Knopf, Inc., 1930), p. 152.

Some persons are critical of the emphasis on neighborhood and associational factors on the ground that generally only about one fourth of the boys even in the worst delinquency areas have appeared before the juvenile courts. One writer has attempted to answer this by pointing out that official delinquency, as measured by juvenile court statistics, represents only a small proportion of actual offenders.[38] If police records in Chicago are used, this figure increases to nearly two thirds. Boys in areas of high delinquency simultaneously exhibit socially approved and disapproved behavior; hence the term "nondelinquent" becomes a rather meaningless one and represents middle-class standards of behavior. A substantial number of boys who engage in juvenile delinquency, however, presumably grow up to be law-abiding persons.

This view that most crime and delinquency arise from the adoption of deviant norms, particularly through the tutelage of others, has been supported by other studies of petty thievery, of highly organized thievery, of organized crime, and of white-collar crime.[39]

NONGANG COMPANIONS

Most persons who consider the role of companions in crime have in mind only juvenile gangs or the more organized criminal syndicate. A great deal of this type of juvenile association, however, is not with organized groups but instead with one or two companions. In a large study of 4663 Chicago delinquents who had been brought before the juvenile court for committing thefts, 33 percent had only one companion and 31 percent had two companions.[40] Although seven in every ten of a group of 1000 Boston delinquents had committed offenses with companions, less than one in ten (7.3 percent) belonged to a gang.[41] Another study found that approximately only half of the delinquents who had delinquent companions belonged to gangs.[42]

It is possible, of course, that some nongang offenders at one time had an association with a gang; yet many of the nongang associates are undoubtedly those who have acquired deviant attitudes through other sources, particularly through contact with someone who has been in a correctional institution. Differential association with criminals or delinquents by means

[38] Solomon Kobrin, "The Conflict of Values in Delinquency Areas," *American Sociological Review*, 16:653–661 (October, 1951).

[39] Clifford R. Shaw and Henry McKay, *Juvenile Delinquency and Urban Areas* (Chicago: The University of Chicago Press, 1942); Edwin H. Sutherland, *The Professional Thief* (Chicago: The University of Chicago Press, 1937); Edwin H. Sutherland, *White Collar Crime* (New York: Holt, Rinehart and Winston, Inc., 1949, reissued 1961), and Clinard, *The Black Market*.

[40] Shaw and McKay, "Social Factors in Juvenile Delinquency," *loc. cit.*, p. 196.

[41] Glueck and Glueck, *One Thousand Juvenile Delinquents*, p. 94.

[42] Glueck and Glueck, *Unraveling Juvenile Delinquency*, pp. 163–164.

of contacts with one or two persons appears to be more characteristic of rural and village areas than of urban ones. In urban areas larger group patterns of delinquency are the more typical method of association. In rural areas these companions are more often chance acquaintances. A study of rural offenders found that almost two thirds of them had not been associated with groups of boys who stole, and if this category is restricted to those who committed serious thefts, 87 percent had never had such previous association.[43] This apparent difference in the pattern of associates is due to the existence of a predominant measure of personal relations and informal social control in farm and village areas.

Delinquent Gangs or Subcultures

Many studies have shown the high incidence of gang membership among youthful offenders. Approximately two thirds, for instance, of a sample of Iowan and Swedish criminal offenders had belonged to a group of boys who stole.[44] During later childhood and early adolescence nearly all normal children associate in groups for play, religious activities, or other special interests. Some of these groups develop into conflict groups or gangs in the sense that they are in conflict with some other groups in society. Some of these gangs turn from mere conflict with other gangs, the family, or the school to conflict with the police, property owners, and certain moral standards of a society. Our interest here is not in the gang but in the delinquent gang. Thrasher has described the emergence of such a gang:

> Natural leaders emerge, a relative standing is assigned to various members and traditions develop. It does not become a gang, however, until it begins to excite disapproval and opposition, and thus acquires a more definite group-consciousness. It discovers a rival or an enemy in the gang in the next block; its baseball or football team is pitted against some other team; parents or neighbors look upon it with suspicion or hostility; "the old man around the corner," the storekeepers, or the "cops" begin to give it "shags" (chase it); or some representative of the community steps in and tries to break it up. This is the real beginning of the gang, for now it starts to draw itself more closely together. It becomes a conflict group.[45]

Gangs grow out of the play activities and come to acquire a definite organization. They tend to reflect neighborhood values. If located in cer-

---

[43] Marshall B. Clinard, "Rural Criminal Offenders," *American Journal of Sociology*, 50:38–45 (July, 1944).

[44] Marshall B. Clinard, "A Cross Cultural Replication of the Relation of the Process of Urbanism to Criminal Behavior," *American Sociological Review*, 25:253–257 (April, 1960). Also see Marshall B. Clinard, "The Relation of Urbanization and Urbanism to Criminal Behavior," in Ernest W. Burgess and Donald J. Bogue eds., *Research Contributions to Urban Sociology* (Chicago: The University of Chicago Press, 1962).

[45] Thrasher, *op. cit.*, p. 30.

tain areas, primarily middle-class, the members of the play groups may engage in harmless club activities. In other areas, on the other hand, gangs may bring the delinquent norms of these areas into intimate contact with the individual. Such gang delinquency, in the form of stealing and vandalism, may be regarded as a natural adjustment not only to the social roles, behavior patterns, and norms of the group but to those of the neighborhood of which the group is a part.

Many delinquent groups in the more urban areas in America have a past history; some have been in existence for many years, long enough so that their members may have older brothers or even fathers who were once members. Gangs which have directed their activities toward crime and delinquency for some time have an opportunity to furnish excellent training in criminal techniques. They teach new members how to empty slot machines, shoplift, obtain junk illegally, open freight cars, snatch purses, "roll" drunks, secure skeleton keys, purchase guns, steal automobiles, engineer holdups, sell stolen goods to "fences," and, finally, bribe a policeman or otherwise "fix" a case. New members may progress from truancy and stealing petty objects and junk to the more serious activities of breaking into freight cars, purse snatching, jack-rolling drunks, burglaries, automobile thefts, and even armed robbery.

When the gang develops considerable skill and the individual stays with it for a long enough period of time, he may acquire a considerable knowledge of crime, moving from the more simple offenses to the serious rackets. Many gangs furnish the training in techniques, the rationalizations, and the social status that accrue to those who have developed skill in crime. The following account of the "copper-wire" gang is typical of a large city gang.

> Police held 10 Milwaukee boys Sunday night on suspicion of stealing 42 cars and forging near-perfect street car passes in water colors. The "copper-wire gang," so-called because it used copper wires to "jump" cars' ignitions, was taken into custody when a 16-year-old member was picked up in a stolen car, police said. Authorities said they would be charged with stealing 42 cars over a two months' period. Two 18-year-olds were being held by police and the eight younger members were at the detention home. The 16-year-old who was arrested Friday had two guns in the car with him, police said. They believed they were to be used in holdups. They said the 16-year-old had perfected the copper-wire technique and taught it to the others. Donald H_____, 18, was accused of counterfeiting street car passes in water color so well they could hardly be distinguished from the originals. He allegedly produced as many as 40 a week and sold them for a quarter apiece.[46]

The effectiveness of delinquent gangs in disseminating knowledge of crime lies in the fact that through mutual excitation the gang makes illegal

---

[46] *Milwaukee Journal*, March 27, 1950.

acts attractive to the individual. In this sense gangs represent the spontaneous development of a form of group life to satisfy needs for new experiences, response, security, and recognition which are not met by conventional institutions, such as religious organizations, youth activities, and clubs. Members enjoy the thrill of common intimate participation in interests involving conflict.

> When we were shoplifting we always made a game of it. For example, we might gamble on who could steal the most caps in a day or who could steal in the presence of a detective and then get away. We were always daring each other that way and thinking up new schemes. This was the best part of the game. I would go into a store to steal a cap, by trying on one and when the clerk was not watching walk out of the store, leaving the old cap. With the new cap on my head I would go into another store, do the same thing as in the other store, getting a new hat and leave the one I had taken from the other place. I might do this all day and have one hat at night. It was fun I wanted, not the hat. I kept this up for months and then began to sell the things to a man on the west side. It was at this time that I began to steal for gain.[47]

—Each gang is a social system. Many common symbols and activities hold it together, and each of its members is assigned a social status or position. Common symbols include gang names such as the Dirty Dozen, the Purple Gang, So So's, the Onions, the Torpedoes, the Wolves, White Rocks, the Murderers, Bat-Eyes, Dukies, and the Hawthorne Toughs. They have their own universe of discourse and argot, as well as songs and stories which have become traditional with them. Common activities of various types hold them together: gang fighting, raiding, robbing, defending a hang-out, getting "shagged" (group sexual activities), holding smut sessions, drinking, playing games and pranks, maintaining clubrooms, gambling, and committing acts of vandalism.[48] These common activities give a gang unity in its endeavors, and *esprit de corps*. Part of its integration comes from warfare with other groups which have different names and territories, or which are organized along different racial, religious, or ethnic lines. Gangs develop common traditions not only through conflict with other gangs but through warring with the police, who represent more conventional norms. Many juvenile gangs in New York City have terms for various forms of gang fighting:

Sounding: A dirty or questioning look.
Roughing: A jostling of one member of a gang by a rival gang member.
Fair one: A fist fight between two boys.
Rumble: A gang fight of the less serious kind, sometimes produced by a "sounding."

---

[47] Chicago Area Project, *op. cit.*, p. 5.   [48] Thrasher, *op. cit.*, p. 277.

Stomping: A gang fight in which the enemy is knocked to the ground and kicked while down.

Burn, waste, or go down: To hold a gang fight in which "blades" [knives] and "pieces" [guns] are used.

Call it on: To hold a prearranged grudge fight in which anything goes.[49]

The position or social status of gang members is measured in ways entirely different from those used by such conventional groups as the YMCA or the Boy Scouts. A gang member achieves high status by displaying courage and skill in the commission of a crime, by having a long record of delinquencies, and, better still, by having been incarcerated in a correctional institution. Each boy comes to be designated by a nickname which is somewhat indicative of his social status in the gang.

> When I was 8 years old I did my first job in the racket. This job was the biggest thrill I ever got in my life. . . . When it got too dark to play ball we all went into the alley to have a smoke and tell stories. The big guys got talking about stealing, and my brother said he had a good place spotted where we could get some easy "dough." The place was a butcher shop on Thirty-first Street. The big guys planned everything, and I only listened. These guys were seven or eight years older than me and had pulled off a lot of big jobs before. They would never let me go with them on big jobs; this night I went along and they didn't say a word. . . .
>
> Everything was locked tight. The owner lived over the butcher shop, so we couldn't make much noise by breaking the glass or jimmying the door. We all went up to the back door, and then my brother got a box and stood on it and tried the transom—and it opened. It was too little for my brother or the other guys to get through. Then I was thrilled when they said I'd have to crawl through the transom. That was the kick of my whole life. I was only 8 and always very little so I could get through the transom easy. I was scared but made up my mind to go through anyway. I was too thrilled to say no.
>
> My brother lifted me up on his shoulders and I crawled through the transom. I hung down on the inside and stood on an ice-box and then crawled down on the floor. The door was locked with a padlock and chain, but I was able to unlock the window and let the big guys in that way. The big guys looked for money first and found $22. Then we all got everything we wanted to eat and several cartons of cigarettes and ditched the place. When we got out, my brother divvied up everything and I got $4 and a lot of cigarettes. I felt like a "big-shot" after that night because the big guys said I could go with them every time they went robbin', and many times I had to crawl through transoms and one time through an ice-box hole. That's why the big guys called me the "baby bandit." [50]

As a result of participation in gang behavior its members develop fairly uniform attitudes toward "opposition to authority, contempt for the

---

[49] *The New York Times,* May 15, 1955, sec. 4.
[50] Chicago Area Project, *op. cit.,* pp. 7–8.

traitor, recognition and prestige through delinquency, hero-worship, stigma of petty stealing, and control of the gang over its members." [51] Nowhere are these values of the gang better seen than in the gang leader who comes to exemplify them. His control over the gang depends on such qualities. It is he who helps to invoke the code of the gang and to punish and ridicule those who do not live up to the standards of conduct the gang demands. One leader of a delinquent gang has written:

> The boys I ran around with were just like me, steal anything they get their hands on. One boy would make plans for stealing money, and we would give him jiggers and help him out if he needed help, and the other boys would do the same. We would meet every Saturday night in the pool room and set down in the pool room and plan our schemes out for the following week. The leader of each group was supposed to be tough. He would take most of the money and split the rest of it with the rest of the boys. I was leader, and never did cheat the other fellows out of a dime, and they had me for their leader until I was sent to Eldora Training School. The gang then got them a different leader, and they continued to take part where I left off. Then in Eldora they came and seen me and told me I could be their leader when I was released, but I said I wasn't going to be another leader, and they called me names such as coward. Well, I couldn't very well take those names, so I was their leader again when I was released, but I wished I wouldn't of for it got me only in trouble again, while the other boys was released on probation. It didn't offer me nothing but bad luck.[52]

Some boys' gangs disappear after a while, and others continue for many years. Although there is no hard-and-fast line of demarcation between a gang of younger offenders and one of older offenders, the latter tend to drift into more serious crimes. The membership of older criminal gangs appears to be drawn chiefly from those juveniles who have had a record of incarceration in correctional institutions. Criminal gangs become tied up with politics and organized criminal rackets. They develop connections as part of criminal syndicates, work with political machines, and specialize in types of rackets.

TYPES OF DELINQUENT SUBCULTURES

— Five types of delinquent subcultures have been distinguished by Cohen and Short: the parent male subculture, the conflict-oriented subculture, the drug-addict subculture, the semiprofessional theft subculture and the middle-class delinquent subculture.[53] (1) The parent male subculture is the more common, involving a small gang whose behavior is nonutilitarian, malicious, negativistic, versatile and characterized by short-

---

[51] *Ibid.*, p. 5.   [52] From a personal document.
[53] Albert K. Cohen and James F. Short, Jr., "Research in Delinquent Subcultures," *Journal of Social Issues*, 14:20–37, No. 3 (1958).

run hedonism and group automony. These characteristics form the common core from which the other types develop, hence the idea of "parent." (2) The conflict-oriented gang may be a much larger group with a high degree of organization and a definite territory, and in readiness to engage in physical conflict and "rumbles" with other gangs. (3) The drug-addict subculture centers around the use of narcotic drugs and a distinct way of dress; its members are often referred to as the "cats." (4) Semiprofessional theft has a utilitarian, systematic, and pecuniary character using strong-arm methods and is characterized by the sale of stolen articles. (5) The middle-class delinquent fosters "the deliberate courting of danger (suggested by the epithet 'chicken') and a sophisticated, irresponsible 'playboy' approach to activities symbolic, in our culture, of adult roles and centering largely around sex, liquor, and automobiles." [54] A more limited typology of delinquent subcultures has been made by Cloward and Ohlin: the criminal, the conflict, and the retreatist or drug-culture gang.[55] They will be discussed shortly.

THEORIES OF GANG DELINQUENCY

Although the delinquent subculture of the gang has generally been explained as a product of neighborhood values of certain areas and the process of gang behavior itself, several recent theories have been advanced to explain gang delinquency in a larger context. The theories are that gang delinquency arises from (1) the characteristics of lower-class culture, (2) hostility and rejection of middle-class values, (3) anomie and differential opportunity, or (4) conflict in the transition from adolescence to adult status.

1. Gang delinquency, according to Miller, is concentrated in the male lower class and is a product of lower-class culture.[56] The chief concerns of lower-class culture are trouble, toughness, smartness, excitement, fate, and autonomy. "Getting into trouble" and "staying out of trouble" are chief concerns of lower-class individuals. "Toughness" is highly valued in the form of "masculinity," physical prowess, strength, and athletics. The gangster, the boxer, the tough guy, or the "hard" teacher become models. "Smartness" is represented by duping and outsmarting the other guy. Such models are seldom the teacher but the "con" man or the "fast-man-with-a-buck." "Excitement" relieves the dullness of hanging around drab areas. Taking a risk appeals a great deal and is evident in goading teachers and policemen, picking up girls, destroying public property, participating

---

[54] *Ibid.*   [55] Cloward and Ohlin, *op. cit.*
[56] Walter B. Miller, "Lower Class Culture as a Generating Milieu of Gang Delinquency," *Journal of Social Issues*, 14:9, No. 3 (1958). Also see Miller's remarks in W. C. Kvaraceus and W. B. Miller, *Delinquent Behavior: Culture and the Individual* (Washington, D.C.: National Education Association, 1959).

in a rumble, stealing a car, and joy-riding. "Fate" is represented by the idea of being caught because of bad luck. "Autonomy" is the desire to be bossed around by others even when the members say they want to be their own bosses. There is a testing of authority to see if it is strict enough.

The lower-class boy, therefore, wishing to belong and to achieve status, often participates in delinquent groups which express these values. Delinquent acts not only provide status but are means for satisfying those factors which dominate the way of life of the lower class.

Although the values of the lower class, such as toughness, have meaning and significance for the lower-class teen-agers, this behavior among the middle class assumes the characteristics of an adolescent fad, although it may have repercussions in real delinquent behavior.

> In the United States every generation of youngsters espouses a current fad which will distinguish it from the adult population. One function of such fads is to provide a vehicle of rebellion against parents; the fad is effective to the degree that it succeeds in shocking and dismaying the older generation. Today's middle-class youngster finds that he cannot get much of a rise out of his parents by "free" sexual references; Freud is too well known and accepted. Nor can he shock them by political radicalism; this is currently too dangerous. But he has discovered that one *really* effective way to appall his parents is to assume behavior patterns characteristic of lower-class culture. The black leather jacket, tight dungarees, a D.A. haircut, a Marlon Brando intonation pattern, or a James Dean stance—as concrete symbols of lower-class culture—or truanting, failing grades, threatening to quit school, or belittling the worth of college—as indications of a general lower-class set—are sure-fire methods for producing maximum parental agitation.[57]

2. Another explanation has suggested that the behavior of such delinquent gangs is a consequence of hostility toward middle-class values.[58] Such pertinent middle-class values include ambition, self-reliance, the postponement of immediate satisfactions, good manners and courtesy, wholesome recreation, opposition to physical violence, and respect for property. Lower-class boys, according to this theory, resent such dominant values because they have not been part of their world. Consequently, they also resent middle-class people, such as their schoolteachers, who consider them to have low status because they do not exhibit middle-class values. Lower-class delinquent gangs are a natural consequence of certain boys of this class coming together because of common hostilities. The subculture which they form is the opposite of middle-class values and is characterized by malice toward things that are virtuous, a versatility in types of delin-

---

[57] Kvaraceus and Miller, *op. cit.*, p. 82.

[58] Albert K. Cohen, *Delinquent Boys: The Culture of the Gang* (New York: The Free Press of Glencoe, 1955). This provocative approach to delinquent gang behavior will have to be affirmed or rejected by subsequent research, as Cohen does little more than suggest it as a hypothesis.

quent behavior, short-run hedonism involving nonutilitarian types of "fun" rather than long-range goals, and, finally, group automony or opposition to social control other than control by the group itself.

3. Somewhat related is the theory of anomie and differential opportunity of Cloward and Ohlin, who believe that delinquent subcultures arise where legitimate means to the attainment of the success goals of the dominant society, such as economic and higher educational opportunities, are blocked.[59] "The disparity between what lower-class youth are led to want and what is actually available to them is the source of a major problem of adjustment. Adolescents who form delinquent subcultures, we suggest, have internalized an emphasis upon conventional goals. Faced with limitations on legitimate avenues of access to these goals, and unable to revise their aspirations downward, they experience intense frustrations; the exploration of non-conformist alternatives may be the result." [60] Whether this deprivation will result in delinquency as well as the three types of gang delinquency which may arise depends, however, on the opportunity or availability of illegitimate means to obtain their goals and consequent status. In integrated slum areas where adult criminal patterns serve as models and opportunity structures are available, the subcultures will be *criminal* gangs engaged in thefts, extortion, and similar activities to achieve an illegal income and status. In unintegrated areas, characterized by mobility, transiency, and instability, such as new urban housing developments, where criminal patterns and opportunity structures are unavailable, models for delinquent behavior to achieve status come from other adolescents and tend to take the form of a *conflict* gang engaging in violence and vandalism. Another type, the "retreatist" gang or subculture, although its members live in the slum, use drugs and engage in other sensual experiences because its members find both legitimate and other illegitimate means to success closed to them and refuse to accept the moral validity of illegitimate means to status and success exemplified by stealing and vandalism.

4. Finally, a fourth explanation by Bloch and Niederhoffer is that gangs arise out of the conflict arising from the transition from adolescence to adult status.[61] In urban society there is no equivalent of the ceremonies

---

[59] Cloward and Ohlin, *op. cit.* According to their definition of delinquent subcultures, certain forms of delinquent activity are essential requirements for the performance of dominant social roles provided and supported by the subcultures. Such delinquent subcultures are characterized by a great frequency of criminal acts, stability, and resistance to change, and the recognition by members of a system of rules as binding upon their behavior. Legitimacy has been withdrawn from certain norms of law whose violations are regarded as illegitimate by official agency representatives. To these authors the acts of delinquent subcultures are much more deliberate and rational than Cohen, for example, has contended.

[60] *Ibid.*, p. 86.

[61] Herbert Bloch and Arthur Niederhoffer, *The Gang: A Study in Adolescent Behavior* (New York: Philosophical Library, Inc., 1958).

and other "rites of passage," such as puberty ceremonies, found among preliterate societies which symbolized transition to adult status. Despite his aspirations and his physical readiness for adult status the adolescent is kept in a condition of social and economic and legal dependency by the withholding of adult symbols, such as money, personal automony, and sexual relations, thus creating pressure to engage in deviant behavior to secure what adolescents regard as symbols of this adult status. One method is to form gangs whereby the adolescent may gain among his peers the equivalent of adult status through demonstrating that he is independent, tough, and capable of flaunting adult authority. In delinquent gangs this is expressed to the full. As an illustration, possession of an automobile becomes among adolescents a symbol of adulthood, and may often be used for sexual experiences as well. Some may steal automobiles for this purpose and to demonstrate their toughness.

The aspirations satisfied by the gang are supported more by the lower-class culture, but it is difficult to distinguish lower- from middle-class delinquency on this basis alone. In this connection some have suggested that one solution to gang delinquency might be to find some really constructive work for adolescents to perform for themselves and for the community, so that they would be able more adequately and quickly to achieve adult status.[62]

EVALUATION

These four theories of gang behavior have all attempted to provide a central framework for explaining delinquency in terms of basic concepts such as class, role, and status aspirations. But they are recent, and thus far little research has been done to prove or disprove them. Each seems to make a contribution, but each, as an all-inclusive explanation, is deficient. Most of them are actually attempts to explain the reasons for gang delinquency in lower-class areas in large urban communities of the United States. Whether such explanations would apply to middle-class or rural areas in the United States, or to the delinquency of other countries with different values and class structures, is open to some question. Certainly delinquency, primarily gang delinquency, is a world-wide phenomenon today and not confined to the United States. "The most important new type of juvenile delinquency found in nearly all parts of the world is the formation of juvenile gangs which commit delinquent acts." [63]

[62] Erik Erikson, *Childhood and Society* (New York: W. W. Norton & Company, Inc., 1950).
[63] *New Forms of Juvenile Delinquency: Their Origin, Prevention and Treatment*, General Report by Wolf Middendorff, Judge, Federal Republic of Germany, Second United Nations Congress on the Prevention of Crime and the Treatment of Offenders, London, August 8–20, 1960 (New York: United Nations Department of Economic and

They are reported to be extensive in places far apart, for example, England, South Africa, Sweden, Australia, the Federal Republic of Germany, France, Japan, and the Philippines. Group delinquency of a non-gang type, largely involving mass rioting and other forms of antisocial behavior, is widespread in many countries where they are known as "halb-starke" (the half-matured) in Germany, "blousons noir" in France, "teddy boys" in England, "vitelloni" in Italy, "hooligans" in Poland and Russia, "bodgies" and "widgies" (girls) in Australia and New Zealand, "tsotsio" in South Africa, and "mambo" boys and girls in Japan.[64] The problems of youth gangs are not confined to the Western world, but have been reported in the Soviet Union and its satellite countries. "East Germany's Communist rulers acknowledged today their deep concern over widespread juvenile delinquency and 'hooliganism' in the country. . . . Gangs of youthful trouble-makers have been arrested in recent months in Leipzig, Dresden and other East German industrial centers. In some cases the youths, armed with clubs, knives or pistols, battled the police, attacked passers-by or committed robberies." [65]

Subcultural gang delinquency may be more accurately explained by the lack of communication among age peer groups which has arisen with pronounced urbanism and by the lack of well-defined national goals than as being a product of class deprivation. This explanation probably accounts, in part, for the increasing juvenile delinquency among the middle class.

A number of specific criticisms have been raised about each theory of delinquency.[66] Sykes and Matza, for example, question whether a gang member actually rejects middle-class standards as Cohen claims, but, instead, rationalizes his deviant behavior by five techniques of neutralization or rationalization.[67] These are "denial of responsibility" by blaming parents, and so on; "denial of injury," by claiming, for example, that the act was a prank or the stolen car was "borrowed"; "denial of the victim," namely, that the delinquency was justified under the circumstances; "condemnation of the condemners," such as cruel police methods; and, finally, the "appeal to higher loyalties," association in gangs being more important than the larger society. In Cloward and Ohlin's theory the success-goal

---

Social Affairs, 1960), p. 43. See, for example, a study of French gangs in Philippe Parrot and Monique Gueneau, *Les Gangs d' Adolescents* (Paris: Presses Universitaires de France, 1959). A study has also been made of adolescent delinquents in Sweden. See Dick Blomberg, *Den Svenska Ungdomsbrottsligheten* (Stockholm: Falu Nya Boktryckeri AB, 1960).

[64] *New Forms of Juvenile Delinquency*, pp. 35-36.

[65] *The New York Times*, February 12, 1961.

[66] For a detailed criticism of the theories of Miller, Cohen, and Bloch and Niederhoffer, see Cloward and Ohlin, *op. cit.*, pp. 47-76. For a specific critique of Cohen's theory, see J. I. Kitsuse and D. C. Dietrick, "Delinquent Boys: A Critique," *American Sociological Review*, 24:211-212 (April, 1959).

[67] Gresham M. Sykes and David Matza, "Techniques of Neutralization," *American Sociological Review*, 22:664-670 (December, 1957).

aspirations of slum boys are not clearly stated, except the economic and educational goals, and they assume that these goals are more uniformly appreciated by subcultures in a society than is warranted. Bloch and Niederhoffer fail to show how the status deprivation of adolescence leads some but not others to delinquency.

After studying street corner gangs in Chicago, Short has proposed that gang delinquency is not so much a failure to achieve membership in the middle class, or because certain adult goals in society are denied them, as it is a failure to achieve status within the context of adult, middle-class-dominated institutions such as the school, the church, and economic and political institutions.[68] The formation of the delinquent subculture involves the establishment of new groups with new rules by which they may compete successfully to obtain status. "Participants in delinquent subcultures appear to be oriented primarily toward members of their own gangs and/or toward other individuals and gangs who share their respective subcultures rather than toward adults as status reference objects." [69] The solutions for lower-class boys provided by delinquent subcultures are primarily status-rewarding rather than economically rewarding, as suggested by Ohlin and Cloward. Money acquired by gang boys tends to be spent for status rewards within the group (e.g., $20 hats) and for "kicks" (alcoholic beverages and drugs).

The Family

Some people believe that the chief source of delinquent behavior lies in unhealthy family influences. This idea has become so strong that judges in several cities have been punishing the parents of delinquents, although they seldom specifically indicate the nature of the family influences that might be related to illegal behavior other than sometimes "lack of parental supervision." It is difficult for a number of reasons to indicate specifically what influence the family may have on delinquency and crime.

In the first place, families are not all the same; among some there are strong personal ties, but others are hardly integrated. Second, the family is an institution which has been undergoing great social change, as will be indicated later. The result of this change has been a decline in the importance of the family's role in general social life. Because many of the traditional functions of the family have declined, the socialization of young children is increasingly being done by other groups, such as the school and the street gang. As the strength of kinship ties becomes weaker and as the mother is increasingly employed outside the home, the urban child may

[68] James F. Short, Jr., "Street Corner Groups and Patterns of Delinquency," A Progress Report from the National Institute of Mental Health Research Grant M-3301 (Mimeographed; March 1, 1961).
[69] Ibid., p. 13.

spend less time with members of his immediate family. Among large sections of the urban population today the family no longer plays the dominant idealized role that certainly is in the minds of those who think of it as the primary factor in encouraging or preventing delinquency and crime.

There are, however, a number of specific family influences which may possibly be related to delinquent and criminal behavior. These influences are the family as a source of delinquent patterns, the broken-home situation, and emotional insecurity within the family.

THE FAMILY AS A SOURCE OF DELINQUENT PATTERNS

There is the possibility that delinquent patterns of behavior may be derived directly from the family. Although there may be some direct tutelage in criminal acts by father, mother, or brother, current evidence indicates that this is of minor importance. The influence of siblings on one another is not common, however, for in many families only one or two children may be delinquent. One study, in fact, has compared a delinquent group with their nondelinquent siblings on this basis.[70]

It is more likely that the family may furnish other influences, such as sexual immorality, drunkenness, and other socially unacceptable patterns of behavior which may or may not be conducive to specific acts of delinquency or crime. Certainly studies have revealed some families with different standards in regard to stealing, gambling, or sex relations, particularly a mother-daughter situation where the former is sexually promiscuous.

Nevertheless, it is probably the contemporaries of persons who engage in crime and delinquency who are the important influences. Even a higher incidence of delinquent patterns in a home does not mean that deviant standards could not have been acquired from the outside. The family can enhance the effect of deviant patterns or it can help to inhibit them, but those who regard the family as the exclusive source of social norms and therefore put the blame on the family fail to see that the family is simply a part of the larger culture and tends to reflect the norms of its neighborhood. The difficulty which any family encounters in trying to keep a child away from delinquent influences in a neighborhood well illustrates this point.

It has also been said that families of delinquents have been either too lax or too strict in their punishment. In two studies the Gluecks discovered that discipline was either insufficient or too severe for seven in ten male prisoners and for nearly two in three women prisoners.[71]

Parental discipline is, of course, not the only factor in the dynamics

---

[70] Healy and Bronner, *op. cit.*
[71] Glueck and Glueck, *Five Hundred Criminal Careers,* and their *500 Delinquent Women.*

of family interaction. Nye has attempted to study this and other factors, such as value agreement, mutual recreation, parental interaction, and rejection by parents in the lives of a group of delinquents and non-delinquents.[72] The study was not conclusive but direct control techniques were found to have a greater influence for girls than for boys, and the father's behavior was more significantly related to delinquent behavior than was that of the mother.

THE BROKEN HOME

Persistent efforts have been made to link delinquency to homes broken by separation, desertion, divorce, or death, on the assumption that such a break in the family ties would lead the child to commit delinquent acts. The United States Children's Bureau, in a report covering cases for 1936, for example, found that about one third of the delinquent boys and one half of the delinquent girls came from broken homes.[73] The Gluecks, in a study of 1000 Boston delinquents, found that 48 percent came from broken homes, and in another study of 500 inmates of the Massachusetts Reformatory found that about 60 percent came from broken homes.[74] It is quite likely, however, that there would be a higher incidence in correctional institutions of those from broken homes than in the general population because offenders with this type of background might more frequently be sent there.

A few studies have been made comparing a group of delinquents with a control group of nondelinquents. In a Chicago study the home status of 1675 delinquents was compared with that of 7278 schoolboys from the same type of residential area and of the same age and nationality background.[75] It was found that among the delinquents 42.5 percent came from broken homes, as compared with 36.1 percent of the nondelinquents. This study has been criticized because no effort was made to ascertain whether the control group actually contained no delinquents. In a later study, 300 consecutive court arraignments were matched with a control group for age, sex, and nationality, with the result that about 50 percent of the former group were found to come from broken homes as compared with one fourth of the control group.[76] Another study by Jackson Toby has shown that if the variables of sex, age, and race are considered, which was

---

[72] F. Ivan Nye, *Family Relationships and Delinquent Behavior* (New York: John Wiley & Sons, Inc., 1958).

[73] U.S. Department of Labor, Children's Bureau, *Juvenile Court Statistics* (Publication 245; Washington, D.C.: 1939), p. 49.

[74] Glueck and Glueck, *One Thousand Juvenile Delinquents*, p. 75, and *500 Criminal Careers*, p. 117.

[75] Shaw and McKay, "Social Factors in Juvenile Delinquency," *loc. cit.*, pp. 262–285.

[76] Merrill, *op. cit.*, p. 77.

not done in the Shaw and McKay study, a relationship can be shown between family control over young children and girls.[77]

The effort to link delinquency with broken homes is probably a blind alley, since the concept of a broken home is by no means a constant factor, and the relationship of broken homes to delinquency has never been conclusively demonstrated: "It is, however, clear that the broken home does not always cause delinquency. It makes a great difference how and when the home was broken and what was the effect upon family relationships and the attitudes of the children." [78] There are certainly millions of families which are broken in one form or another but whose members are not delinquent. No one knows what this exact proportion is, but some idea can be gained by the fact that there are annually about 400,000 divorces. Some homes where there is friction between the parents may, as will be indicated later, be improved by separation. How closely identified a child is with a particular parent is another question, for the effect of a broken home on one child may be quite different from its effect on another.

EMOTIONAL SECURITY AND THE FAMILY

Several studies have suggested that the family's failure to provide the child with a proper degree of security and affection produces delinquency and crime. Healy and Bronner compared 105 delinquents with 105 nondelinquent siblings from the same families,[79] and concluded that the major differences accounting for delinquency were the delinquents' experiences and attitudes. These differences were attributed to the differential treatment of the children by their parents. This study has also been criticized in a number of ways, particularly for its relative disregard of influences outside the home. The fact that 70 percent of the delinquents had delinquent companions is mentioned, for example, but not amplified.

A more recent and comprehensive study with similar conclusions about the importance of satisfactory family relationships has been made by the Gluecks.[80] They selected two groups, one of 500 Boston delinquents in a boys' training school and 500 Boston nondelinquents whom they matched with the delinquents according to the areas of the city, age, ethnic or racial derivation, and general intelligence. They then compared the differences between the two groups in family and personal background, body types, health, intelligence, temperament, and character.

As a result of this study the Gluecks recommended a prognostic in-

---

[77] Jackson Toby, "The Differential Impact of Family Disorganization," *American Sociological Review*, 22:505–512 (October, 1957).

[78] Taft, *Criminology*, p. 192.

[79] Healy and Bronner, *New Light on Delinquency and Its Treatment*.

[80] Glueck and Glueck, *Unraveling Juvenile Delinquency;* also the abridged version of this study, *Delinquents in the Making*.

strument to predict delinquency at about six years of age. It emphasized the role of the family and consisted of prediction tables which involved the following as the more important items: adequacy of discipline of boy by father, supervision of boy by mother, affection of father and mother for boy, and family cohesiveness. To this they added five personality traits from the Rorschach tests and five from psychiatric interviews. It seems unlikely that delinquency, which involves social definitions, could be predicted at an age when the child has not participated much in the wider community. This study can be criticized for its lack of an integrated theory of human behavior, its disregard of cultural factors, and the overemphasis on family and personality factors.

Such studies as those by the Gluecks, which emphasize the family, assume that a neighborhood is necessarily experienced socially in the same way by all boys simply because they live in it. This is a false idea of the impact of attitudes, motivations, and social contacts on personality. Four fifths of the delinquents had moved five times or more, as compared with two fifths for the nondelinquents, and their mobility may well have exposed them to more deviant patterns. Other equally startling differences between the groups were sneaking into motion-picture theaters (62%: 4%), running away from home (59%:1%), gambling (53%:9%), hanging around street corners (95%:58%), truancy (95%:11%). Whereas 42 percent of the delinquents spent some of their leisure time at home and 29 percent on playgrounds, the corresponding figures for the nondelinquents were 93 percent and 61 percent. Although the authors state that these "were maladjusted and delinquent children long before they were gang members," [81] no convincing evidence was given for this statement. Half of the five hundred delinquents belonged to gangs, as compared with only three of the nondelinquents. Delinquents likewise tended to be attracted to older boys and to have had more heterosexual experiences. In the light of this one wonders whether the emotional setting of the family was really of such great importance.

Alcohol and Delinquency or Crime

Some people believe that most delinquency or crime is committed under the influence of alcohol. On numerous occasions offenders have even excused their behavior as due to "one or two beers" or "drinking."

There is evidence that large numbers of arrests are for common drunkenness. Such drunkenness does have an important relation to misdemeanors and the police problem. When all offenses are examined, it is found that of all arrests, including misdemeanors as well as crimes, some one half to two thirds are for drunkenness, or for some related offense, such as

---

[81] Glueck and Glueck, *Delinquents in the Making*, pp. 88–89.

disorderly conduct or vagrancy. An alcoholic may be arrested and imprisoned as many as twenty to thirty times a year.

In some serious crimes of murder, aggravated assault, and forcible rape, drunkenness is undoubtedly of some significance.[82] After studying 588 criminal homicides in Philadelphia, Wolfgang concluded that there is a significant association between violent homicide and the presence of alcohol in the offender of either sex. "Approximately 60 per cent of all offenders who committed homicide violently had been drinking prior to the crime, while 40 per cent had not been drinking. On the other hand, among those who killed nonviolently, half had been drinking and half had not been drinking before the crime." [83]

Likewise, drunken driving is particularly serious as far as criminality is concerned. In 1959, in cities in the United States of over 2500 population, there were slightly over 104,000 arrests for drunken driving. Some of these cases involved the injury or possible injury to persons, and, where death resulted, the drivers could be charged with negligent homicide.

The very volume of drinking by offenders and nonoffenders in the United States would suggest that there are other variables involved in the problems of crime and delinquency besides alcohol. There are about 200,000 taverns in the country, and about one in five adults drinks regularly, more than one in two drinks occasionally.

It is probable that in most cases where alcohol was associated with criminal behavior, it acted as a depressant and made the person temporarily less cognizant of the probable consequences of deviant behavior, or else less able to respond in terms of his ordinary system of values and norms. In a sense it simply "released" behavior patterns already there instead of "causing" them. Although alcohol may "release" an individual's criminal attitudes, such criminal activities, involving either property or personal crimes, might have taken place sooner or later irrespective of his alcohol intake. When murders and assaults are committed under the influence of alcohol, they usually represent long-standing quarrels or difficulties in relationships with others which may culminate in violence depending upon the definition of the situation and the response of the persons involved. Forcible rape may represent the enactment of definitions of sexual behavior already present.

Summary

The chief sources of delinquent and criminal behavior appear to be the general culture, the neighborhood, and associates. Of particular im-

---

[82] See, for example, Julian Roebuck and Ronald Johnson, "The Negro Drinker and Assaulter as a Criminal Type," *Crime and Delinquency*, 3:21–33 (January, 1962).

[83] Marvin E. Wolfgang, *Patterns in Criminal Homicide* (Philadelphia: University of Pennsylvania Press, 1958), p. 166.

portance in the culture as a whole are the general and selective disobedience to law and the behavior of law-enforcement officers and agencies. Newspapers may also contribute toward the increase of criminal behavior in a society, and motion pictures, radio, television, and comic books play similar roles. It is unlikely, however, that any person, without previous deviant patterns, would engage in delinquency or crime only because of crime stories and influences arising from these sources. Delinquents who have already had association with deviant norms through other influences may be further stimulated by certain types of motion pictures, radio and television programs, or comic books.

Present evidence seems to indicate that social norms, both deviant and conventional, are primarily acquired through personal experiences of a face-to-face nature. Neighborhood influences and certain occupational situations may furnish a setting favorable to the development of delinquent and criminal behavior.

Delinquent companions are extremely important, as are delinquent gangs. Such gangs disseminate techniques of committing offenses, help the individual delinquent to progress in crime, encourage mutual excitation and common activities in connection with delinquency and crime, give social status to the delinquent, and develop in him opposition to authority.

The role of the family in delinquency and crime does not appear to be as important as many think. There is considerable variation in family integration, and there are now other institutions and influences which are also sources of deviant norms. There is little evidence to indicate that the family is the source of delinquent patterns, or that broken homes are significantly related to delinquency. Similarly, there is no conclusive evidence that the lack of emotional security in family relationships leads to delinquency and crime. There is little evidence, furthermore, to indicate that the use of alcohol plays an important part in delinquent or criminal behavior.

Selected Readings

BLOCH, HERBERT A., and ARTHUR NIEDERHOFFER. *The Gang: A Study in Adolescent Behavior*. New York: Philosophical Library, Inc., 1958. An analysis of the behavior of adolescents in a variety of cultures. Gang delinquency in American society, they maintain, results from the difficulty of adolescents in achieving adult status.

CLINARD, MARSHALL B. "Secondary Community Influences and Juvenile Delinquency," *The Annals*, 261:42–55 (January, 1949). Other influences in the general culture besides the family and neighborhood must be considered in explaining juvenile delinquency.

CLOWARD, RICHARD A., and LLOYD E. OHLIN. *Delinquency and Opportunity: A Theory of Delinquent Gangs*. New York: The Free Press of Glencoe, 1960. An explanation of how delinquent gangs arise, recruit their members, develop law-violating ways of life, and persist or change. Basically the explanation follows anomie with the addition of the concept of differential opportunity.

COHEN, ALBERT K. *Delinquent Boys: The Culture of the Gang.* New York: The Free Press of Glencoe, Inc., 1955. An analysis of delinquent gangs in terms of social class differences.

DOUGLAS, PAUL H. *Ethics in Government.* Cambridge, Mass.: Harvard University Press, 1952. Lectures given at Harvard University by a leading economist and United States senator who headed a series of investigations of unethical practices in government. He makes several proposals to improve ethics in government.

GLUECK, SHELDON and ELEANOR. *Unraveling Juvenile Delinquency.* Cambridge, Mass.: Harvard University Press, 1950. A comparison of 500 delinquents and nondelinquents on a large number of factors. Probably the best-known study of delinquency chiefly in terms of the family and certain personality traits.

KOBRIN, SOLOMON. "The Conflict of Values in Delinquency Areas," *American Sociological Review,* 16:653–661 (October, 1951). A discussion of the social norms and values of areas of high delinquency.

MILLER, WALTER B. "Lower Class Culture as a Generating Milieu of Gang Delinquency," *Journal of Social Issues,* 14:5–19, No. 3 (1958). Juvenile delinquency is explained as a product of the way of life of lower-class subculture.

ROBISON, SOPHIA M. *Juvenile Delinquency: Its Nature and Control.* New York: Holt, Rinehart and Winston, Inc., 1960. An analysis of theories seeking to explain juvenile delinquency and the research data used to support them. Includes a discussion of social class, family, the gang, the school, and mass media in relation to juvenile delinquency.

SCHRAMM, WILBUR, JACK LYLE, and EDWIN B. PARKER. *Television in the Lives of Our Children.* Stanford, Calif.: Stanford University Press, 1961. An analysis of the effects of television in the lives of over 6000 children.

SUTHERLAND, EDWIN H. *White Collar Crime.* New York: Holt, Rinehart and Winston, Inc., 1949, reissued 1961. This study of the illegal behavior of seventy large American corporations indicates that there is extensive disobedience to law among the upper classes in our society.

THRASHER, FREDERIC M. *The Gang.* Chicago: The University of Chicago Press, 1936. This study of 1313 gangs in Chicago is one of the most widely known books on criminology.

Chapter

8

Types of Delinquent and Criminal Offenders

The terms "delinquent" and "criminal" do not refer to a homogeneous group and have little meaning except as they refer to lawbreakers. There are various types and kinds of delinquent and criminal offenders, depending upon whether the offenders are classified by types of crime committed, by characteristics such as sex and age, or in terms of behavior systems. Classification by offense is useful in studying the legal definitions of offenses. Sex, age, and other characteristics of offenders are necessary in enumerations for statistical purposes. From a scientific or sociological point of view, however, offenders are best grouped according to their behavior patterns and the processes through which they develop. An adequate explanation of delinquent and criminal behavior should show how it applies to all delinquent and criminal behavior, and how it should be modified to explain various types.

> For the purposes of understanding and controlling criminal behavior, definitive generalizations are needed regarding criminal behavior as a whole, with specifications of the general theory applied to particular criminal behaviors. The relation between the general theory and the particular criminal behaviors is analogous to the relation between a germ theory of disease and the particular germs which cause particular diseases. . . . Continued efforts should be made to state valid generalizations regarding criminal behavior as a whole, and continued efforts should be made to explain particular criminal behaviors. . . . Just as the germ theory of disease does not explain all diseases, so it is possible that no one theory of criminal behavior will explain all criminal behavior. In that case, it will be desirable to define the areas to which any theory applies, so that the several theories are co-ordinate and, when taken together, explain all criminal behavior.[1]

Type of Crime

As noted above, criminal offenders are often classified, from a legal point of view, by the type of crime, such as murder, burglary, and arson.

---

[1] Edwin H. Sutherland and Donald R. Cressey, *Principles of Criminology* (6th ed.; New York: J. B. Lippincott Company, 1960), p. 71.

Such a classification enables us, presumably, to group offenders neatly according to what they did, and to show something of these tolerance limits of crimes as reflected in the different penalties of the criminal law. This classification may be quite misleading, inasmuch as persons of extremely diverse types may commit the same crime; moreover, the seriousness of a criminal act is not always correlated with criminal behavior patterns in offenders. And, as has been indicated in a previous chapter, distinctions based on misdemeanants and felons are also unsatisfactory.

There are three main categories of crimes: crimes against the person, — crimes against property, and crimes against public order. Crimes against persons involve such acts as murder, manslaughter, assault, and rape. Property crimes include burglary, larceny, forgery, automobile theft, and robbery. Crimes against public order consist of such behavior as prostitution, gambling, the use of narcotics, and drunkenness.

Of the three groups, crimes against the person receive the most publicity in newspapers, on radio and television programs, and in motion pictures. It is not surprising that most people believe, therefore, that the greatest amount of crime, as well as our most serious offenses, involve personal crimes. When murder and rape cases increase or are widely publicized in the newspapers and it is intimated that crime has materially increased, the public erroneously concludes that a "crime wave" is occurring. A single case involving the killing of one juvenile by another, or a particularly vicious sex killing of a child by an adult, immediately becomes news from coast to coast in the United States among 180 million people.

Personal crimes actually constitute a small proportion of all reported crime, less than 5 percent in 1960, with murders and nonnegligent manslaughter but a tiny fraction of all crime. During 1960 an estimated 1,767,389 major property crimes were reported to the police, but only some 82,909 personal crimes. (See Table 8.1). There were 1,104,048 reported larcenies and 432,906 burglaries, as compared with 3371 murders and cases of nonnegligent manslaughter. The distribution of types of crimes varies somewhat between different countries and between developed and underdevelopd countries.[2]

If one were trying to gauge the increase or decrease of crime it would be incorrect to cite personal crimes. Some states, for example, have so few murders that an increase of only two or three may change the proportion profoundly. Wisconsin, for example, had 45 homicides (murder and nonnegligent manslaughter) in the year 1959–1960, with a population of

[2] *Prevention of Types of Criminality Resulting from Social Changes and Accompanying Economic Development in Less Developed Countries,* General Reports to the Second United Nations Congress on the Prevention of Crime and the Treatment of Offenders (London, 8–20 August, 1960) by J. J. Panakal and A. M. Khalifa (New York: United Nations Department of Economic and Social Affairs, 1960).

Table 8.1. Major Crimes Reported to the Police in the United States During 1960

Crime index classification	Estimated number of offenses [a]	Percentage of total
Murder and nonnegligent manslaughter	9,140	0.5
Forcible rape	15,560	0.8
Robbery	88,970	4.7
Aggravated assault	130,230	7.0
Burglary	821,100	44.0
Larceny $50 and over	474,900	26.0
Auto theft	321,400	17.0
Total	1,861,300	100.0

[a] Based on reports to law enforcement agencies in 1960.

SOURCE: Federal Bureau of Investigation, *Uniform Crime Reports* (Annual Bulletin, 1960; Washington, D.C.: Government Printing Office, 1961), p. 2.

almost 4 million. Thus a difference of a few cases would alter the percentage either way.

Sex of Offenders

Delinquents and criminals may be classified according to sex. This distinction had more significance when nearly all offenses committed by women were prostitution and drunkenness, but women now engage in as wide a variety of offenses as do men, although not as frequently. Women are increasingly becoming involved in cases of embezzlement and forgery. They are also involved as associates of men in many cases of property crime, although they are rarely charged. During 1952 women committed about 9 percent of a selected group of major offenses in cities with 25,000 population and over. (See Table 8.2.) In cases of embezzlement and fraud, larceny and theft, and homicide their proportion was considerably greater. The ratio of arrests for embezzlement and fraud, larceny and theft, and murder is approximately 7 men to every 1 woman; assault, 10 to 1; robbery, 25 to 1; and burglary, 40 to 1.

Although it is increasingly difficult to distinguish clearly among offenses in terms of the sex of the offender, the apparently low ratio of crimes committed by women raises a number of questions. Some people have attributed this low ratio to factors other than the low criminality rate of women.[3] Some have suggested that women offenders often play a part in crimes committed by men offenders but that they are not as easily detected

[3] See, for example, Otto Pollak, *The Criminality of Women* (Philadelphia: University of Pennsylvania Press, 1950).

Table 8.2. Number and Percentage of Crimes for Which Women Were Arrested in Cities with 25,000 Population and Over, 1952

	Number	Percent of all arrests
Embezzlement and fraud	951	14.6
Larceny and theft	5,541	14.0
Criminal homicide	297	13.2
Assault	6,050	10.5
Driving while intoxicated	1,724	4.2
Robbery	277	4.2
Burglary—breaking and entering	548	2.4

SOURCE: Federal Bureau of Investigation, *Uniform Crime Reports* (Annual Bulletin, 1952; Washington, D.C.: Government Printing Office, 1953), Vol. 23, No. 2, p. 116.

in crime as men. Others have suggested that since women can engage in prostitution they need not turn to burglary or larceny.

Criminologists, on the other hand, have felt that, even with these allowances, the low incidence of crime among women is indicative of the importance of social rather than personality factors in crime. Certainly there must be the same range of personality traits among women as among men and the former now participate sufficiently in the general society to be able to steal a car or burglarize a home. More significant is the fact that women do not as frequently belong to gangs and are more isolated from criminal norms. And it has been suggested that women more often develop a conception of themselves in terms of future parental responsibilities, making their participation in serious crimes less likely.

Age of Offenders

Another distinction often made is the classification of offenders by age, with younger and older offenders supposedly denoting different degrees of criminal development. Cartoons usually picture the confirmed criminal as a man in his late thirties or forties, heavy set with jutting jaw and large ears, and in general a rather hardened, forbidding creature. The question is how close this stereotype of age and criminal hardness fits reality. Offenders committing serious crimes are most frequently under twenty-five years of age, and a considerable proportion are under twenty-one, according to nation-wide arrest figures collected by the FBI.

Although all types of crimes are committed by persons of all ages, there is a much greater probability of young persons being arrested for the most serious felonies. (See Table 8.3.) During 1960, in cities over 2500 population, approximately one in every two burglars and thieves ar-

*Table 8.3. Number and Percentage of Arrests of Persons under 18,
under 21, and under 25 Years of Age, 1960, in 2460 Cities
over 2500 in Population*

Offense charged	Number of persons arrested				Percentage		
	Total	Under 18	Under 21	Under 25	Under 18	Under 21	Under 25
Criminal homicide:							
a. Murder and nonnegligent manslaughter	4,507	346	827	1,393	7.7	18.3	30.9
b. Manslaughter by negligence	1,766	131	336	618	7.4	19.0	35.0
Robbery	29,326	8,154	13,892	19,333	27.8	47.4	65.9
Aggravated assault	52,277	6,074	10,715	17,463	11.6	20.5	33.4
Burglary—breaking and entering	110,047	56,221	72,867	85,554	51.1	66.2	77.7
Larceny—theft	207,548	102,093	127,284	145,334	49.2	61.3	70.0
Auto theft	54,024	33,558	42,472	47,082	62.1	78.6	87.2
Forcible rape	6,068	1,242	2,556	3,684	20.5	42.1	60.7
Prostitution and commercialized vice	25,851	424	2,523	8,447	1.6	9.8	32.7
Narcotic drug laws	23,430	956	3,965	9,190	4.1	16.9	39.2
Weapons: carrying, possessing, etc.	34,520	6,567	11,146	16,419	19.0	32.3	47.6
Driving while intoxicated	146,381	1,128	6,852	21,985	0.8	4.7	15.0

SOURCE: *Uniform Crime Reports,* Annual Bulletin, 1960, p. 93. Total population 81,660,735, based on 1960 U.S. decennial census.

rested was under eighteen. Two thirds of all those arrested for auto theft were under eighteen, and one fourth of all those arrested for robbery. Almost half of the persons arrested in 1960 for robbery and two thirds of those arrested for larceny were under twenty-one, as well as approximately four fifths of the automobile thieves and two thirds of the burglars. If the age is moved up to those under twenty-five years of age, two out of every three persons arrested for robbery and two in three arrested for larceny are included, as well as about three in four burglars, and nearly nine tenths of the automobile thieves. Younger offenders do not constitute as large a percentage of arrests for criminal homicide and aggravated assault, but one fifth of all forcible rapes are committed by those under eighteen and nearly one half by those under twenty-one.

In all probability the age at which ordinary crimes are committed is even lower than has been indicated. In the first place, many of those in the age group from fourteen through sixteen are not included, for the figures cited above are computed from fingerprint cards, and often either juvenile offenders are not fingerprinted or their fingerprints are not always reported to the FBI. In the second place, arrests tabulated in a given year do not indicate the age at first arrest. If it were possible to know when offenses first started, a greater frequency might be found even below fourteen years of age. For example, one research study of five brothers who had a long career in crime revealed that all had started their delinquency before the age of ten.[4]

In this connection, however, a somewhat different picture is revealed for other offenses, particularly those involving alcohol and gambling violations, murder, and white-collar and professional crime. About 90 percent of all persons arrested for drunkenness or for gambling are twenty-five years of age or older. Nearly two thirds of the persons arrested in 1960 for murder or for nonnegligent manslaughter, in cities over 2500 population, were twenty-five or over. Nine in ten white-collar offenders are over thirty, and one fourth over fifty, as indicated by a study of World War II black-market offenses involving price violations.[5] Four fifths of those arrested for embezzlement and fraud during 1960 were twenty-five years of age or over. About two thirds of all arrests for forgery and counterfeiting were in the older age categories. Most professional criminals are well over twenty-five.

Classification of offenders by age has little merit, for the "hardness" of an offender has little relation to his age. An offender is "hardened" if he has definite antisocial attitudes toward laws, property, and the police, professional knowledge of techniques to commit crimes and avoid prosecution, and a framework of rationalizations to support his conduct. These attitudes may be well developed in a boy of seventeen and yet be absent in a "criminal" of forty. For example, 65.9 percent of all robberies are committed by persons under twenty-five, an offense which is almost always preceded by other crimes, involves the use of a gun, and indicates definite antisocial attitudes.

There are several reasons for the decline of felonies with age. The Gluecks have referred to this as "maturation," and although they have stressed the possibility of biological factors, it seems possible to find in the social frame of reference an explanation for the differences in offenses of the various age groups.[6] Younger men are more daring and possess more physical ability, two qualities necessary for burglary and robbery. Probably the chief reason for the age differential is that the group association of those with deviant norms is greatest among younger people. Except for certain types of crime, as a person grows older he tends to lose touch with deviant associates because of marriage and family responsibilities, and there is a change in his conception of himself.

---

[4] Clifford R. Shaw, *Brothers in Crime* (Chicago: The University of Chicago Press, 1938).

[5] Marshall B. Clinard, *The Black Market* (New York: Holt, Rinehart and Winston, Inc., 1952), p. 287.

[6] Sheldon and Eleanor T. Glueck, *500 Criminal Careers* (New York: Alfred A. Knopf, Inc., 1930).

Delinquent and Criminal Behavior Systems

A more useful method of distinguishing the various types of delinquent and criminal offenders is based on social processes and behavior systems: how delinquent and criminal norms were incorporated in the individual to produce the delinquent or criminal act and what this criminal behavior means to him. The distinguishing characteristics of types of delinquent and criminal offenders are the degree of development of criminal social roles and life organization, identification with others, and progression in crime.

Noncareer offenders are, for example, represented by occasional offenders, such as most of those who commit assault or murder, statutory rape, and a rare theft, embezzlement, or forgery. Likewise, many sex offenses, such as exhibitionism, fall into this type. The most highly developed career criminals are professional and organized criminals.

A criminal career as distinguished from a noncriminal career involves a life organization of roles built about criminal activities, such as identification with crime, a conception of self as a criminal, extensive association with criminal activities, including other criminals, and, finally, progression in crime. Progression in crime means the acquisition of more complex techniques, more frequent offenses, and, ultimately, dependence on crime as a frequent or sole means of livelihood. Among career offenders group and subcultural factors are extremely important.

Career criminals make crime a definite part of their life organization. They maintain association not only with other criminals but with those persons, such as shady politicians, who may be helpful in the continuation of their way of life. They develop techniques, "a level of operation," and a philosophy of life to go with it. Frequently it is a full-time occupation and their sole means of livelihood. These offenders often concentrate in certain fields of crime. In fact, the police often proceed on this assumption and develop a *modus operandi* file which frequently enables them to pick up burglars, forgers, counterfeiters, safe-crackers, or armed robbers. Professional criminal careers are developed almost entirely within the field of property crimes.[7] For example, in American society, murderers do not ordinarily make a career out of killing, although this practice exists in the Middle East, where one may hire a professional killer for a price. Likewise, rape and aggravated assault are seldom thought of as career crimes. Even persons who participate in a long series of criminal activities may not have a real criminal career.

---

[7] Walter C. Reckless, *The Crime Problem* (3d ed.; New York: Appleton-Century-Crofts, Inc., 1961), p. 153.

Offenders can thus be classified according to the degree to which they make a long-term career out of crime, with the criminally insane at one end and the professional criminal at the other. (See Figure 3.) In between may be ranged extreme sex deviates, occasional offenders, homosexuals and prostitutes, habitual petty criminals, white-collar criminals, those with ordinary criminal careers, and organized criminals.[8]

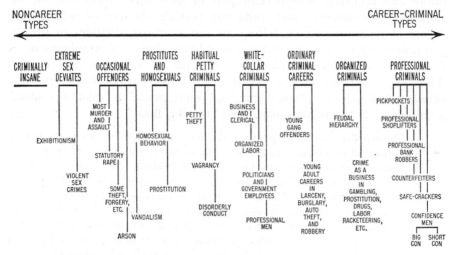

FIGURE 3.—Selected Types of Delinquent and Criminal Behavior

Most personal offenders are of the noncareer type, whereas property offenders are more likely to be of the career type.[9] Some personal offenses are the result of gang or organized groups and are of a career type. Although murder is generally regarded as an individual noncareer type of offense, it may grow out of a career situation. In fact, in New York City there was an unusual organized group, called Murder, Inc., which hired out men to kill other persons for a fee. They approached murder as though it were any property offense, and it has been claimed that during the 1930's this group committed some 1000 murders from coast to coast.[10]

---

[8] Other types have been devised for classification of prison inmates. Hayner, for example, divides them into types such as the "con forger," "the alcoholic forger," "the rapo," the "heavy," and the "graduate."—Norman S. Hayner, "Characteristics of Five Offender Types," *American Sociological Review*, 26:96–102 (February, 1961). Also see Don C. Gibbons and Donald L. Garrity, "Some Suggestions for the Development of Etiological and Treatment Theory in Criminology," *Social Forces*, 38:51–58 (October, 1959).

[9] See, for example, Alfred R. Lindesmith and H. Warren Dunham, "Some Principles of Criminal Typology," *Social Forces*, 19:307–314 (March, 1941). They use the terms "individual" and "social," which are somewhat misleading.

[10] Burton B. Turkus and Sid Feder, *Murder, Inc.* (New York: Farrar, Straus and Cudahy, Inc., 1952).

SOCIAL ROLES

Although individuals may commit offenses which are legally similar, this behavior actually has a different significance for each. In some individuals their delinquent and criminal activity may represent only a minor and relatively unimportant part of their social roles and life organization. Delinquency and crime may pervade the lives of others. This degree of incorporation of delinquent and criminal attitudes in life organization reflects, for one thing, the relative degree of development of criminal social roles and identification with an antisocial way of life. Thus offenders may play roles varying all the way from an amateur, occasional offender to a "tough guy," a "young punk," a "smart operator," a "big shot," a "strong-arm man," and "the Big Boss."

> In many respects delinquency and criminal experience does to the person just about what athletic, theatrical, sales, military, and many other semiprofessional and professional experiences do to individuals. The experience inures and steeps. It becomes integrated into the life organization of the person, establishing habits and attitudes, determining consciousness of kind and conception of self, and fixing the development of a successful role or justification of a less successful one. The behavior trend line of a life organization built out of delinquency, crime, and allied experience is more delinquency, crime, and allied behavior. The problem is for the person to revise his scheme of life and reorganize himself on a different basis. This would be true if the person took a desk job in an office and left the road as a salesman or if a newspaper reporter became an undertaker or a university professor became a barker in a circus.[11]

Similarly the social role of a "delinquent" is often different from the legal category in which he is placed by the courts. The labeling of delinquent may bring with it the playing of a definite social role, as Cohen and Short have indicated.

> But the category "delinquent" as a social "role" of everyday life is not identical with "delinquent" as a legal category. That is, the criteria by which the man in the street defines somebody as delinquent and the images, feelings and dispositions that the word arouses are not identical with the criteria and consequences in the world of the courts. The social role of delinquent entails consequences over and above those provided by law. If a boy is defined as delinquent in the world of everyday life, his whole social world may be transformed: the ways in which other people see him, how they feel toward him, their willingness to associate with him, the activities and opportunities that are open to him. In consequence of these changes, the way in which the boy sees, labels and evaluates himself, his estimate of his chances and prospects

---

[11] Walter C. Reckless, *The Crime Problem* (New York: Appleton-Century-Crofts, Inc., 1950), p. 35.

in the world of nondelinquent and conventional people, his notion of whether trying to avoid delinquency is worth the trouble, may be profoundly affected. It is quite possible, indeed, that being invested with the social role may so narrow a person's opportunities for the rewards and gratifications of nondelinquent society that it may strengthen his tendency to behavior that is delinquent in the legal sense.[12]

IDENTIFICATION WITH CRIME

The individual may gain considerable satisfaction from the acceptance of group norms and orient his life around them. Thus if a boy identifies himself with the activities of a group of "young punks," this relationship may become as satisfying as if he identified his activities with a group of Boy Scouts. Yet mere membership in a group or contact with deviant norms does not tell us what such behavior means to the individual. Criminality is the result of a person's identification with others from whose perspective his criminal behavior seems acceptable.[13] For example, for rural offenders their lack of identification with delinquent groups is almost as important in explaining their behavior as their membership in such a group.[14] The sophisticated criminal, likewise, may secure a certain status from his identification with other offenders. His knowledge of criminal techniques becomes part of his life organization and as a result he wishes constantly to add to it.

CONCEPTION OF SELF

Closely associated with identification with delinquency or crime is the conception of himself and of his social role which a delinquent or criminal offender develops. He may feel that he is essentially a "good boy" who has really done nothing more than make a technical mistake from the legal point of view, or he may regard his activities as isolated transgressions. On the other hand, he may regard himself as tough, antisocial, or even criminal. In one study farm boys were found to have conceptions of themselves as "wild" and "reckless," whereas city offenders with more pronounced activities in crime spoke of themselves as "hard," "tough," "criminal," "mean," or "no good." [15]

[12] Albert K. Cohen and James F. Short, Jr., "Juvenile Delinquency," in Robert K. Merton and Robert A. Nisbet eds., Contemporary Social Problems (New York: Harcourt, Brace & World, Inc., 1961), pp. 80–81.

[13] Daniel Glaser, "Criminality Theories and Behavioral Images," American Journal of Sociology, 61:433–445 (March, 1956).

[14] Marshall B. Clinard, "Rural Criminal Offenders," American Journal of Sociology, 50:38–45 (July, 1944).

[15] Marshall B. Clinard, "The Process of Urbanization and Criminal Behavior," American Journal of Sociology, 48:202–213 (September, 1942). Also see Walter C. Reckless, Simon Dinitz, and Ellen Murray, "Self Concept as an Insulator against Delinquency," American Sociological Review, 21:744–746 (December, 1956).

A conception of oneself as a delinquent or a criminal may become so well developed that the individual believes he is at war with society and that he is constantly being mistreated and persecuted by the police. In fact, the relation of law-enforcement agencies to the acquisition of one's conception of self often makes the first arrest or incarceration of prime importance in an offender's life organization. Tarde, the early French sociologist and judge, was one of the first to state that a criminal is created, first, by the offense and, second, by the way society treats the act. About delinquency a recent article has stated:

> Although being a "delinquent child" and having the social role of delinquent are not the same thing, if one has been legally declared a "delinquent child" and the fact is known, he is likely to be invested with the social role. Indeed, if he has merely been processed by the courts without having been found delinquent, this may suffice to endow him with the social role. This by-product of legal processing may have more far-reaching consequences in the life of the child than what happens to him in court. For this reason, it is not possible to appraise the law and the judicial institutions without considering the extrajudicial social role of delinquency and its meaning for the child.[16]

Once an offender has developed the conception of himself as a delinquent, prostitute, confidence man, robber, or forger, it is often hard to change it. The following comments show how a group of reformatory inmates looked upon themselves.

> The gang I went with was some older boys than me and some were younger than I was, and all of us thought we were very tough.

> I had the reputation of being a tough guy. I am afraid that if there was anybody that had anything that I wanted I would find some way to get it if I had to steal it.

> I got in so many fights that some people started calling me a roughneck.

> My two brothers next to my age are staying to home and taking care of the folks. They both are older than twenty-one but do not seem to care for women or dances or care for liquor. I am the only one that seems to be getting into trouble. . . . I guess it is that I am carefree and seem to try anything that comes along. I like to go out on parties. I seem to be like a clown, I guess, when I am on parties, and it seems that I have the gang in an uproar most of the time. . . . I seem to have quite a few friends. Some, of course, think that if I would leave the liquor alone and quit my stealing I would be a good boy. Some think that I just ain't no good and never will be any good.[17]

Recent sociological studies have suggested differences in self-conception as the reason that certain children residing in a delinquency area

---

[16] Cohen and Short, "Juvenile Delinquency," *loc. cit.*, p. 81.
[17] From personal documents.

do not become delinquents.[18] In a study of 125 "good boys" and 108 potential delinquents in this area, the authors concluded: "Conception of self and others is the differential response component that helps to explain why some succumb and others do not, why some gravitate toward socially unacceptable patterns of behavior and others veer away from them."[19] Additional research in this direction may furnish valuable insights into why so many middle- and upper-class boys do not engage in delinquency and may help to explain the differential response patterns of adults, including white-collar workers, to criminal norms.

DIFFERENTIAL ASSOCIATION

In addition to identification and conception of self as an important part of an offender's social role is the extent to which a lawbreaker acquires the techniques and philosophy of a criminal type. There is differential association with the pushes and pulls of conventional and criminal norms. Some tend to push the individual away from criminal behavior while others pull him toward it.

Intimate and personal associations undoubtedly have the greatest influence in the acquisition of delinquent and criminal norms. Although one may not entirely agree with Sutherland's arbitrary statement that a person who becomes delinquent does so because of an excess of definitions favorable to violations of law over definitions unfavorable to violation of law, much of crime is a product of differential association with criminal norms.[20] The effect of such association depends on the frequency, duration, priority, and intensity of exposure to conventional and criminal norms. The frequency of such association and the length of their duration have much to do with the development of a delinquent or criminal career. The priority of such association with criminal norms means that the exposure to delinquent norms early in life may have a profound subsequent effect in determining the development of a criminal career. The intensity of such association is related to the prestige of persons with criminal norms with whom an individual associates and with his reactions to such persons.

PROGRESSION IN CRIME

The history of a criminal career type is a progressive series of steps in the acquisition of criminal techniques and knowledge. This progression

---

[18] Reckless, Dinitz, and Murray, "Self Concept . . . ," *loc. cit.*; Walter C. Reckless, Simon Dinitz, and Ellen Murray, "The 'Good Boy' in a High Delinquency Area," *Journal of Criminal Law, Criminology, and Police Science*, 48:18–25 (1957); and Walter C. Reckless, Simon Dinitz, and Barbara Kay, "Self-Component in Potential Delinquency and Non-Delinquency," *American Sociological Review*, 22:566–570 (1957).

[19] Reckless, Dinitz, and Kay, "Self-component . . . ," *loc. cit.*, p. 570.

[20] Edwin H. Sutherland and Donald R. Cressey, *Principles of Criminology* (6th ed.; Philadelphia: J. B. Lippincott Company, 1960), pp. 74–81.

varies with different types of crimes. Burglars and robbers, for example, show a progression from petty theft to more serious larcenies, to crimes such as ordinary burglary or automobile theft, and then on to highly skilled burglary or armed robbery. Criminality may proceed from trivial to more serious crimes, from being a sport to being a business, and from occasional crime to more frequent crime. Along with progression in crime the offender develops a philosophy of life which justifies his criminal actions.

Personality Traits and Criminal Behavior

Many psychologists and psychiatrists have sought to explain nearly all forms of delinquent and criminal behavior as due primarily to abnormalities in the psychological structure of the individual. They believe that inadequacies in the individual's personality traits interfere with his adjustment to the demands of society. The assumption of this approach to criminal behavior is that if it were possible to ascertain the nature of trait structures which are related to criminal behavior, and if formation of these structures could be prevented or if they could be treated successfully, most crime could be eliminated. To them, delinquent or criminal behavior, even of a group nature, consists mainly of the actions of separate individuals.

There are several major difficulties in distinguishing between the personality traits of offenders and those of nonoffenders. Samples of institutionalized offenders are customarily used, which are probably unrepresentative; moreover, the test performances may be unreliable. It is also possible that experiences, such as arrests, court appearances, or imprisonment, may so affect the personality traits of offenders that it is impossible to determine what they were like prior to such experiences. Comparisons of delinquents, who are of a certain age and often of a particular cultural background, with a general test norm may be misleading. Finally, very few studies of personality traits have distinguished among types of offenders.

Some evidence that there is no necessary relationship, however, between personality traits and criminal behavior has been shown in a survey by Schuessler and Cressey. They took all 113 known studies (up to 1950) which had compared the personality characteristics of delinquents and nondelinquents, criminals and noncriminals. Although 42 percent of the studies showed differences in favor of the nondelinquents and noncriminals, in 58 percent of the studies the results, for various reasons, were indefinite: "The doubtful validity of many of the obtained differences, as well as the lack of consistency in the combined results, makes it impossible to conclude from these data that criminality and personality elements are associated." [21]

---

[21] Karl F. Schuessler and Donald R. Cressey, "Personality Characteristics of Criminals," *American Journal of Sociology*, 55:476 (March, 1950). For attempts to show the relationship of personality traits to delinquency, see Starke Hathaway and Elio D. Monachesi, *Analyzing and Predicting Juvenile Delinquency with the MMPI* (Minneapolis: University

One theory of the relation of personality traits and certain criminal behavior needs more detailed analysis. The literature of many phases of deviant behavior has had references to the existence of a deviant personality type termed a "criminal psychopath" or "psychopathic personality," a habitual antisocial deviant.[22] It has been suggested that nearly all sexual offenders are psychopaths, or that the prison population is composed partly of psychopaths. Numerous popular articles have contained such statements as "Most of the sex killers are psychopathic personalities. No one knows or can even closely estimate how many such creatures there are, but at least tens of thousands of them are loose in the country today."[23]

Since 1937, at least twenty states, acting in response to a rather hysterical belief in the wholesale existence of dangerous "psychopaths," have passed specific laws dealing with the treatment of sexual psychopaths. Although there are some variations, for the most part they provide for the indefinite incarceration of such diagnosed persons in state mental hospitals. As Sutherland has pointed out, most of these laws have had their origin in emotional and nonrational processes.[24] Generally they have been enacted after a state of fear has been aroused in a community from a small number of sex crimes occurring over a short period of time.

Although there has been considerable dispute over the meaning of the term "psychopath," some of the characteristics of a so-called psychopath are said to be that he is free from the signs or symptoms generally associated with psychoses, neuroses, or mental deficiency, and that he demonstrates poor judgment and an inability to learn by experience, which is seen in "pathological lying," repeated crime, delinquencies, and other antisocial acts.[25] "Patients repeat apparently purposeless thefts, forgeries, bigamies, swindlings, distasteful or indecent acts in public, scores of times."[26]

of Minnesota Press, 1953); Elio D. Monachesi, "Personality Characteristics and Socio-Economic Status of Delinquents and Non-Delinquents," *Journal of Criminal Law and Criminology*, 40:570–583 (January–February, 1950); Elio D. Monachesi, "Personality Characteristics of Institutionalized and Non-Institutionalized Male Delinquents," *Journal of Criminal Law and Criminology*, 41:167–179 (July–August, 1950).

[22] Harrison Gough, "A Sociological Theory of Psychopathy," *American Journal of Sociology*, 53:365 (March, 1948). There are few more unprecise psychiatric terms, or with a longer history, than the term "psychopath." Originally the terms "moral insanity" and "moral imbecility" were used. In the trial of Charles Guiteau in 1881 for the assassination of President Garfield, the issue of "moral" insanity was raised by the defense. Koch is credited with originating the term "psychopathic personality" in 1888 when he referred to a group of patients having no proper class of mental disorder but who could not be considered as entirely sane.

[23] David G. Wittels, "What Can We Do about Sex Crime?" *Saturday Evening Post*, 221:31 (December 11, 1948).

[24] Edwin H. Sutherland, "The Sexual Psychopath Laws," *Journal of Criminal Law and Criminology*, 40:543–554 (January–February, 1950).

[25] Hervey Cleckley, *The Mask of Sanity* (St. Louis: C. V. Mosby Co., 1950), and "The Psychopath, a Problem for Society," *Federal Probation*, 12:3–8 (June, 1948). Also see his "Psychopathic Personality," in the *Encyclopedia of Criminology* (W. C. Branham and E. B. Kutash, eds.; New York: Philosophical Library, Inc., 1949), pp. 413–416.

[26] Cleckley, "Psychopathic Personality," *loc. cit.*, p. 415.

Although many believe that the concept of a psychopath is real and that such a personality type sufficiently explains numerous antisocial acts, the term is used so imprecisely and with such a variety of meanings by people who are not clear as to the developmental processes of a psychopath that its entire usefulness can be seriously questioned. In fact, the authors of one study have reported that they found some 202 different terms applied in one form or another to the psychopath.[27] After a study of several years the Committee on Forensic Psychiatry of the Group for the Advancement of Psychiatry issued a warning against the use of a term in statutes with such a wide variety of meanings as the word "psychopath." [28]

The lack of precision in describing psychopathic traits has been shown by the wide differences in the diagnoses of "psychopathic" criminal offenders in various institutions and by research on the traits. Cason and Pescor isolated fifty-four traits commonly held to be characteristic of psychopaths. They selected 101 persons diagnosed as psychopathic by the Psychopathic Unit of the Federal Medical Unit at Springfield, Missouri, and from them took two groups, the 23 least psychopathic and the 29 most psychopathic.[29] This distinction was made on the basis of the number of characteristics described as psychopathic. Their findings were that forty-six of the fifty-four traits were not statistically significant in distinguishing between those least and those most psychopathic. Of the remaining eight traits, six were only slightly significant, and the two significant characteristics were being intolerant and making threats.

The view that a person is a psychopath merely because he is a repeater or is persistent in his behavior is circular reasoning.[30] Writing on the characteristic of persistent antisocial behavior as a criterion of a psychopath, Sutherland stated: "This identification of an habitual sexual offender as a sexual psychopath has no more justification than the identification of any other habitual offender as a psychopath, such as one who repeatedly steals, violates the antitrust law, or lies about his golf scores." [31]

---

[27] Halsey Cason and M. J. Pescor, "A Statistical Study of 500 Psychopathic Prisoners," *Public Health Reports*, 61:557-574 (April 19, 1946). Also see their "A Comparative Study of Recidivists and Non-Recidivists among Psychopathic Federal Offenders," *Journal of Criminal Law and Criminology*, 36:236-238 (September, 1946).

[28] Group for the Advancement of Psychiatry, Report No. 9. Also see *The Habitual Sex Offender*, Report and Recommendations of the Commission on the Habitual Sex Offender as formulated by Paul W. Tappan, Technical Consultant (Trenton: State of New Jersey, 1950), p. 38.

[29] Cason and Pescor, "A Statistical Study of 500 Psychopathic Prisoners," *loc. cit.*

[30] The question of the point at which persistent lying and evasiveness become psychopathic was an important issue in the Alger Hiss case when his defense attorneys sought to prove, by testimony of a psychiatrist, that the chief prosecution witness, Whittaker Chambers, was a psychopath. In relentless cross-examination, which at times became humorous, the prosecutor showed conclusively that the term "psychopath" lacked preciseness.—James Bell, "Your Witness, Mr. Murphy," *Life*, 28:41-42 (January 23, 1950). Also see Alistair Cooke, *A Generation on Trial* (New York: Alfred A. Knopf, Inc., 1952).

[31] Sutherland, "The Sexual Psychopath Laws," *loc. cit.*, p. 549.

Types of Delinquents

Among the many problems confronting the student of juvenile delinquency there is probably none more perplexing or elusive than the designation "juvenile delinquency." The many definitions of this term as found in recent textbooks and monographs attest to the lack of agreement as to what juvenile delinquency is. Not only has the concept been subject to a variety of definitions; it has also been utilized as an omnibus designation. Thus, as currently employed, the term "juvenile delinquency" has the doubtful function of being an inclusive category, applied without too much foresight to much juvenile behavior in general.[32]

A typological approach to delinquency permits concentration upon problems of limited scope and enables one to deal with manageable groups characterized by relatively homogeneous behavior.[33] Some of the difficulties in the prediction and control of delinquency are probably due to limited typological research on juveniles.[34] To understand delinquency more fully the various career patterns and types of offenses of delinquents must be studied. A fundamental question still to be answered is why a given delinquent engages in a particular act, such as vandalism or sex offenses, rather than in some other form of delinquency, although, to be sure, some delinquents are involved in several forms of delinquent behavior.[35] Two types of delinquency will be discussed here, vandalism and auto theft.[36]

Vandalism

Vandalism is an example of the typological approach to juvenile delinquency.[37] By vandalism is meant the deliberate defacement, mutilation,

---

[32] This confusing situation has affected the type of research done in this area, especially the prevailing emphasis on the early discovery and prediction of the potential delinquent. The usual procedure is to take a random and representative sample of delinquents, match it with an equally random and representative sample of nondelinquents, subject the samples to a variety of diagnostic tests, and thus arrive at a "scientific" formula which supposedly aids the investigator to predict with some degree of accuracy the potential delinquent, regardless of type.

[33] Marshall B. Clinard and Andrew L. Wade, "Toward the Delineation of Vandalism as a Sub-Type in Juvenile Delinquency," *Journal of Criminal Law, Criminology, and Police Science*, 48:493–499 (January–February, 1958).

[34] Steps in the right direction are the following: William W. Wattenberg and James Balistrieri, "Automobile Theft: A 'Favored-Group' Delinquency," *American Journal of Sociology*, 57:575–579 (May, 1952), and William W. Wattenberg and John B. Moir, "A Study of Teen-Agers Arrested for Drunkenness," *Quarterly Journal of Studies on Alcohol*, 17:426–436 (September, 1956).

[35] See William W. Wattenberg and David Faigenbaum, "Patterns in Delinquency," *Journal of Clinical Psychology*, 9:78–81 (January, 1953).

[36] For a discussion of types of delinquency, such as auto theft, traffic violations, vandalism, sex delinquency, drunkenness, and drug addiction in various countries, see *New Forms of Juvenile Delinquency: Their Origin, Prevention and Treatment*, General Report by Wolf Middendorff, Judge, Federal Republic of Germany (New York: United Nations Department of Economic and Social Affairs, 1960).

[37] Much of the material in this section is derived from Clinard and Wade, "Toward

or destruction of private or public property by a juvenile or group of juveniles not having immediate or direct ownership of the property so abused. Although a common type of property offense among adolescent boys, the term itself is a relatively recent one, having come into official use as applied to delinquency only since the late thirties. What is here defined as vandalism is often included in such designations of delinquent activity as "malicious mischief," "acts of carelessness or mischief," "willful and wanton misconduct," "destructiveness," "disorderly conduct," "incorrigibility," or even "assault."

Vandalism includes many acts of destruction which have been described as follows:

> Studies of the complaints made by citizens and public officials reveal that hardly any property is safe from this form of aggression. Schools are often the object of attack by vandals. Windows are broken; records, books, desks, typewriters, supplies, and other equipment are stolen or destroyed. Public property of all types appears to offer peculiar allurement to children bent on destruction. Parks, playgrounds, highway signs, and markers are frequently defaced or destroyed. Trees, shrubs, flowers, benches, and other equipment suffer in like manner. Autoists are constantly reporting the slashing or releasing of air from tires, broken windows, stolen accessories. Golf clubs complain that benches, markers, flags, even expensive and difficult-to-replace putting greens are defaced, broken or uprooted. Libraries report the theft and destruction of books and other equipment. Railroads complain of and demand protection from the destruction of freight car seals, theft of property, wilful and deliberate throwing of stones at passenger car windows, tampering with rails and switches. Vacant houses are always the particular delight of children seeking outlets for destructive instincts; windows are broken, plumbing and hardware stolen, destroyed, or rendered unusable. Gasoline operators report pumps and other service equipment stolen, broken, or destroyed. Theater managers, frequently in the "better" neighborhoods, complain of the slashing of seats, wilful damaging of toilet facilities, even the burning of rugs, carpets, etc.[38]

The available statistics on juvenile court referrals reported annually to the United States Children's Bureau indicate that property destruction is a common offense among adolescent boys. The cost to the American public of this deliberate damage is probably greater than the combined costs of other forms of juvenile property offenses. Vandalism is not confined to the United States; in Sweden, for example, the increases in willful damage committed by those aged fifteen to seventeen increased nearly 200 percent between 1950 and 1953.

The cost of an offense is not the only way to measure seriousness. Re-

---

the Delineation of Vandalism . . . ," *loc. cit.* By special permission of the *Journal of Law, Criminology and Police Science* (Northwestern University School of Law).

[38] J. P. Murphy, "The Answer to Vandalism May Be Found At Home," *Federal Pro-*

search has shown that attitudes toward respect for property are not always the same and that any concept of property rights is to a considerable extent fluid and conditional.[39] Actually a violation of property rights is not, of itself, necessarily serious. Its seriousness is dependent on such factors as the relationship of the owner to the offender, the danger of punishment for the offender, the likelihood of real injury to the owner, the kind of property involved, and the value of the property. Studies attempting to measure the relative seriousness of this offense have shown that vandalism ranks low in order of seriousness when compared with other typical juvenile offenses and that within the general designation of "vandalism" there are different types of property destruction, each with its relative degree of seriousness.[40]

Comparing a group of vandals in the Bronx of New York City with other delinquents reported during 1955, Martin found that while both vandals and other delinquents live largely in deteriorated neighborhoods there were differences. The vandal is more likely to be a male, is younger than most delinquents, more likely to be white, from less mobile families, and more likely to commit vandalism in company with others.[41]

SEX AND AGE

Statistics from the Children's Bureau, over the years it has published such figures, show that, as might be expected, far more boys than girls are involved in vandalism. Studies in such diverse localities as Denver, Detroit, Connecticut, and Great Britain also bear out this relationship.[42] There is, on the other hand, considerable disagreement as to whether the typical age group involved in this offense is preadolescent or adolescent.[43] Some of this disagreement may be due to the type of vandalism engaged in by juveniles. Some kinds of destruction of property are probably associated with certain age groups since these acts may call for the ingenuity which comes with

---

bation, 18:8–10 (March, 1954). This issue of Federal Probation contains a symposium on vandalism.

[39] See John C. Eberhart, "Attitudes toward Property: A Genetic Study by the Paired-Comparisons Rating of Offenses," Journal of Genetic Psychology, 60:3–25 (March, 1942).

[40] See Mervin A. Durea, "An Experimental Study of Attitudes toward Juvenile Delinquency," Journal of Applied Psychology, 17:522–534 (1933), and Edwin Powers and Helen Witmer, An Experiment in the Prevention of Delinquency (New York: Columbia University Press, 1951), pp. 329–332.

[41] John M. Martin, Juvenile Vandalism (Springfield, Ill.: Charles C Thomas, Publishers, 1961).

[42] A Study of Vandalism (Denver: Denver Area Welfare Council, Inc., April, 1954), p. 5; William W. Wattenberg and Frank Saunders, "Sex Differences among Juvenile Offenders," Sociology and Social Research, 39:26 (September–October, 1954); Needs of Neglected and Delinquent Children (Hartford, Conn.: Public Welfare Council, 1946), p. 14; and Hermann Mannheim, "The Problem of Vandalism in Great Britain," Federal Probation, 18:14 (March, 1954).

[43] See Ben Solomon, "Vandalism," Youth Leaders Digest, 17:162 (February, 1955);

more age and experience. There is some evidence that vandalism among children diminishes during the summer months. Most vandalism seems to occur when juveniles are en route to school or have just left school.[44]

SOCIAL CLASS

Evidence concerning the relationship of vandalism to social class position is conflicting and fragmentary. Shulman has speculated that while offenses among lower-class boys consist largely of various types of theft, malicious mischief occurring under group stimulus is more characteristic of middle-class juveniles.[45] The evidence is contradictory, however. Gingery's survey of vandalism in twenty-five cities revealed that this offense is just as high in the poorer sections as in the higher socioeconomic districts of the city.[46] On the other hand, a recent Denver study of vandalism showed that the majority of offenders lived in low-income sections, whereas Mannheim's study of juvenile delinquency in Kansas City disclosed that the highest incidence was among youth from areas composed of middle-class families.[47] A few studies have indicated that acts committed by vandals tend to be nearer the homes of their perpetrators than are any other offenses typical of juveniles.[48]

Cohen suggests that vandalism, for the middle-class boy, constitutes a protest against identification with his mother. Because of the small family, the boy's isolation from socially significant adults other than his parents, and the curtailment of his movement outside the neighborhood, the boy's mother becomes the principal agent of socialization and indoctrination of "good" behavior. Thus goodness comes to symbolize femininity for the middle-class boy. Feeling this a threat to his status as a male, he reacts negatively to those social conduct norms associated with "mother" by engaging in behavior which functions as a denial of his femininity and an assertion of his masculinity. Because property has great symbolic value for the middle-class adult as an attribute of status, a destructive attack on this

---

and Henry S. Dewhurst, *The Railroad Police* (Springfield, Ill.: Charles C Thomas, Publisher, 1955), p. 114.

[44] William W. Wattenberg, "Delinquency During Summer Months," *Journal of Educational Research*, 42:262 (December, 1948). Burt has concluded that acts of property destruction showed irregular fluctuations, revealing small correlation with the weather. See Cyril Burt, *The Young Delinquent* (New York: Appleton-Century-Crofts, Inc., 1925), p. 162.

[45] Harry M. Shulman, "The Family and Juvenile Delinquency," *The Annals*, 261: 30 (January, 1949).

[46] S. L. Gingery, "Vandalism in Schools," *School Business Affairs*, 12:5 (September, 1946).

[47] *A Study of Vandalism*, p. 7, and Ernest Mannheim, *Youth in Trouble* (Kansas City, Mo.: The Community Service Division, Department of Welfare, 1945).

[48] *A Study of Vandalism*, p. 7, and Mannheim, *Youth in Trouble*, pp. 88 f.

symbol becomes especially meaningful to the middle-class boy who has been reared to believe that property should be treated carefully, not carelessly abused or destroyed.[49]

Vandalism for the lower-class boy, on the other hand, has the same protest function but a different basis. Whereas the adult world defines the middle-class boy as a "good" boy, the definition of the lower-class boy indicates suspicion, contempt, and hostility. This negative definition is transmitted to him through the attitudes of middle-class adults with whom he has categoric contacts. His participation in property destruction constitutes an attack on the symbols of middle-class respectability and serves as a protest of this imputation of inferiority and devaluation of personal worth by the middle-class group. Destructive behavior emphasizes the difference between himself and middle-class conventionality and demonstrates a contempt for its way of life.[50]

RELATION OF VANDALISM TO OTHER DELINQUENCY

One study found that 61.8 percent of the delinquent boys and only 3.8 percent of the nondelinquent controls had previously indulged in various acts of destructiveness.[51] On this evidence the statement was made that destructive mischief is one of the first clear signs of the delinquent's social maladaptation.[52] However, this idea of vandalism as a first or eventual step in a career of crime is yet to be empirically confirmed by others. Furthermore, little is known about the amount and kind of recidivism in vandalism. Merrill's delinquency study found that only 4 percent of the delinquents had "malicious mischief" as a first offense, whereas theft was the first offense in 57 percent of the cases studied.[53]

GROUP NATURE OF VANDALISM

Studies have shown that in nearly all cases of destruction the acts are performed with companions.[54] In certain communities an additional ele-

---

[49] Albert K. Cohen, *Delinquent Boys* (New York: The Free Press of Glencoe, 1955). pp. 91 ff. and 164 f.

[50] Solomon Kobrin, "The Conflict of Values in Delinquency Areas," *American Sociological Review*, 16:656 and 659 f. (October, 1951).

[51] Sheldon and Eleanor Glueck, *Unraveling Juvenile Delinquency* (New York: The Commonwealth Fund, 1950), p. 162.

[52] *Ibid.*, p. 28.

[53] Maud A. Merrill, *Problems of Child Delinquency* (Boston: Houghton Mifflin Company, 1947), Appendix B, Table 2, p. 346.

[54] Walter Houston Clark, "Sex Differences and Motivation in the Urge to Destroy," *Journal of Social Psychology*, 36:170 (November, 1952). Also see Clifford R. Shaw and Henry D. McKay, *Social Factors in Juvenile Delinquency*, Report on the Causes of Crime, National Commission on Law Observance and Enforcement, No. 13; (Washington D.C.: Government Printing Office, 1931). II, 122 f.

ment of gang rivalry is apparent: sometimes rival gangs will compete in destructive acts.[55] There is also some evidence that such vandalism is related to racial, ethnic, or religious prejudice.[56] It is unlikely, however, that such behavior is more typical of certain racial or ethnic groups than of others. Data from the Children's Bureau indicate that there is little difference between Negro and white groups in the amount of vandalism committed.

DIMENSIONS IN A TYPOLOGY OF VANDALISM

Provided there is not serious injury to property, the American public tends to view pranks with a kind of careless tolerance, probably because most American males were once participants in this kind of activity. However, certain implied limits exist to juvenile vandalism growing out of ambiguous definitions of the roles and status of children in contemporary society. The destructiveness of very young children is often excused with the rationalization that they have not yet matured to a responsible understanding of property rights and values. Much of the damage by this group is probably accidental, hence more readily excusable. Furthermore, most of this vandalism seems to grow out of random play-group activity. In its beginning stages this activity is inherently neither recreational nor delinquent. Later it may be defined as one or the other, depending upon whether the culmination of the activity is acceptable or unacceptable to the community. With younger children vandalism is not, therefore, necessarily malicious; rather, it is more often destructive play motivated largely by curiosity.[57]

The adolescent, on the other hand, is generally held morally culpable for his destructiveness. More often than not, his vandalism is considered deliberate and malicious even by the juvenile, as a fourteen-year-old boy has stated:

> Well, my parents came over to Gene's. I told my father we'd go over to the [drugstore] . . . . Went over to the apartment house where cars were parked . . . wanted to "split tires" and did . . . meanness, I guess,—get an urge to do it—start with one and keep on doing it. . . . Well, it didn't matter, any car would do. . . . Teen-agers are different from adults, feel urge to do something ornery. . . . I didn't know the people, of course, just something mean to do . . . everybody does something mean.[58]

---

[55] Lloyd T. Delaney, "Establishing Relations with Anti-Social Groups and an Analysis of Their Structure," *British Journal of Delinquency*, 5:43 (July, 1954) and Barbara Bellow *et al.*, "Prejudice in 'Seaside,'" *Human Relations*, 1:112 (June, 1947).

[56] Raymond Gordon, "Vandalism," *Federal Probation*, 18:50 (September, 1954). See also Shaw and McKay, *op. cit.*, p. 117.

[57] A. H. Maslow, "A Comparative Approach to the Problem of Destructiveness," *Psychiatry*, 5:520 (November, 1942).

[58] This and subsequent undesignated interviews are from a study in Kansas City of teen-age vandalism, financed by Community Studies, Inc., Kansas City, Mo., and also from Clinard and Wade, "Toward the Delineation of Vandalism . . . ," *loc. cit.*

How severely the teen-ager is censured is often dependent on the nature of the damage and the property vandalized. Community tolerance limits of various types of property destruction also appear to be affected by whether it occurs in a rural or an urban area. As Ellingston has suggested, to overturn a truck in the urban community is labeled destruction of property.[59]

These normative aspects are important in the assessment of the meaning of vandalism to the community. It is commonplace for the community to overlook certain forms of vandalism on Halloween. But even within this institutionalized setting the norms are undergoing change and less destructive behavior is approved than formerly.[60] The social situation in which the offense takes place is another important dimension. Although the society may not have a well-structured and consistent set of norms relative to property destruction, within the society certain groups, or members of particular social classes, may be accorded a well-defined field in which to indulge in vandalism. One British writer has stated:

> . . . the party of public schoolboys who damage property during the course of a "rag" are behaving very differently from the street corner gang who smash street lamps or shop windows "just for the fun of it," or to work off their aggression. The mores of the Public School community allow and even encourage such explosively expressive behaviour and the scholars' participation in rowdyism has the sanction of authority in its restricted setting, whereas the casual destructiveness of promiscuous gangs has no such social approval to sustain it.[61]

Often there is a certain flavor of spontaneity present indicating the type of criminal behavior characterized by Reckless as "a striking back against authority figures" in response to certain situations.[62] Much teen-age vandalism appears to be of this kind; it is extemporaneous behavior, adventitious and fortuitous in character, an outgrowth of the restless and exuberant nature of the adolescent boy.

> In the evening, between five or six, we was out to _____ Center (this center had been burned) messin' around. We was gonna play some ball. It was gettin' too dark for that, so one of us suggested to go in; so we went in. . . . Climbed up on the rest room roof. See, it used to be a school, that's where the exits outside from the rest rooms were. We climbed up on there and went in through the window. . . . Well, first we went up and we thought

---

[59] John Ellingston, *Protecting Our Children from Criminal Careers* (Englewood Cliffs, N.J.: Prentice-Hall, Inc., 1948), pp. 197 f.

[60] See Ralph and Adelin Linton, *Halloween: Through Twenty Centuries* (New York: Abelard-Schuman, Ltd., 1950). In Great Britain, the Guy Fawkes Day Celebration (November 5) is an institutionalized occasion for college-boy pranks; students let off "steam" mainly by setting bonfires.

[61] John Barron Mays, *Growing Up in the City* (Liverpool: University of Liverpool Press, 1954), pp. 18–19.

[62] Reckless, *op. cit.*, 3d ed., p. 5.

we'd see what the Teen Town room looked like. Went up there, it wasn't bothered or burnt too much—floor was a little weak, dirty. Then we come back downstairs—we was gonna go in the art room but we couldn't get in there, the floor, it was burnt through. There was, oh, about an eighth of an inch of wood left. So we couldn't get in there. Uh—we just went messin' around. Started throwin' rocks. . . . From what we heard they was gonna tear the building down, build one the full length of the lot down there. . . . In there about an hour; just went around—throw one or two (rocks) . . . pretty soon we were going like mad. . . . While we were doing it we didn't think nothing about doing it because, like I said, what we heard they was going to tear the whole building down and I didn't think they would save them (windows)—big percentage of them were cracked and discolored, any-way. . . . What we was doing there would be about three of us outside and three of us inside and we would have wars, throwing rocks back and forth at each other. . . . I guess anybody likes to get in trouble once in a while . . . not actually go out to look for trouble, but I mean at the time we thought it was fun until the police came; that was all.

On the other hand, the differential social expectations as to the roles of boys and girls are important in the inhibition of destructive behavior by girls. Since American culture does not place the same inhibitions on the boy's outward expression of his feelings, positive or negative, as it does on that of girls, the male youth, as one author has suggested, often appears to feel it essential to be self-directive in order to be considered masculine and acceptable to his peers.[63] Participation in vandalism is one way of meeting these needs for autonomy and peer-group acceptance.

Fundamentally related is the frustration felt by the adolescent in a culture in which his role and status lack a well-defined normative structure. Moreover, there is little consensus on values and no consistency in adult behavior which might serve as guideposts. This absence of dominant and clearly defined norms, coupled with the factor of peer-group loyalty, with its attendant norms and values, results in conflict between the adolescent and authority figures, usually his parents and teachers. The consequence is behavior often termed delinquent by the adult world, while the adolescent defines it in terms of conformity to peer-group expectations.[64]

This difference in the definition of behavior is true of vandalism. Whereas the adult world thinks of the teen-age vandal as a delinquent, the vandal may often have an entirely different self-conception. His self-image is frequently that of a prankster:

We did all kinds of dirty tricks for fun. We'd see a sign, "Please keep the street clean," but we'd tear it down and say, "We don't feel like keeping

---

[63] See Aileen Schoeppe, "Sex Differences in Adolescent Socialization," *Journal of Social Psychology*, 38:175–185 (November, 1953).

[64] For a criticism of the view that adolescent culture is in conflict with its adult counterpart, see Frederick Elkin and William A. Westley, "The Myth of Adolescent Culture," *American Sociological Review*, 20:680–684 (December, 1955).

it clean." One day we put a can of glue in the engine of a man's car. We would always tear things down. That would make us laugh and feel good, to have so many jokes.[65]

One time . . . four or five of us boys went to an apartment just being built, took a whole wall of cement down. We took a chisel and knocked down hundreds of cinder blocks, just mischievous. We went to old houses, broke windows. . . . In one house we found a big Victrola. We threw it down the stairs, we pushed down the bannister, we broke the chandelier. We didn't steal anything, just broke things. . . . I had to do it so they wouldn't call me chicken.[66]

The fact that often nothing is stolen during such acts of vandalism tends to reinforce the vandal's conception of himself as merely a prankster and not a delinquent. Some writers have pointed this out as a distinguishing characteristic of the vandal when compared with other property offenders, assuming that since nothing is taken vandalism has a nonutilitarian function. However, these acts often do have a real meaning and utility for the participants, even though the reasons for participation are not expressed. Property destruction appears to function for the adolescent as a protest against his ill-defined role and ambiguous status in the social structure. Although role frustration is basic to this protest, the nature of the frustration differs as to the position of the vandal in the social structure, as implied in this statement by a sixteen-year-old delinquent.

Well, he accused us of stealing some stuff out of his joint. He didn't come right out and say it was us, but the way he talked he made it sound like it—particularly us. . . . Yeah, we was kidding him about an old rifle he had in there, about ninety years old, and he wanted fifteen dollars for it and the stock on it was all cracked up and everything. And we kept kidding his mother—she's in there (the store) with him—and we kept kidding her, and old Gay (the store owner), himself, come over there and started raising the devil, blowing off steam and everything. We didn't like it too well. We left and came back later. . . . I told him (his companion) let's go down and break those windows. He said OK and we went down there and picked up some rocks along the way. We got down there and stood in front of the place till there weren't any cars very close to it and we threw the rocks and ran. . . . I guess you gotta get into something once in a while or you don't live right out there. It didn't seem like then that it would amount to this much.

SUBTYPES OF VANDALISM

Acts of vandalism may be divided into three types: predatory, vindictive, and wanton vandalism.[67] The first type involves acts which, although

---

[65] Frederick M. Thrasher, *The Gang* (2d ed.; Chicago: The University of Chicago Press, 1936), pp. 94 f.

[66] Benjamin Fine, *1,000,000 Delinquents* (Cleveland: World Publishing Company, 1955), pp. 36–37.

[67] Martin, *op. cit.*, pp. 72–103.

destructive, end in some financial reward to the vandals. For example, metal pipes may be ripped out of a building and later sold. In vindictive vandalism the chief motivation is antagonism and hatred for individuals or groups. A Negro's home may be stoned or a Jewish synagogue desecrated with a swastika. School property may be destroyed by a boy who hates his teacher or the school in general. In the third type—wanton vandalism— we have "at one extreme, destruction of this type [occurring] as simply part of the play activity of children, particularly relatively young children. At the other it appears to be a spontaneous and wild destruction by individuals who are 'mad at the world' or by groups of marauding youths who are in open conflict with the community." [68]

A special study of vandalism in all the junior and senior high schools of Syracuse found important differences between those schools with a high rating of damage and those with a low rating:

> Low socio-economic status and high instability or transiency in the community in which the school was located, and change and instability in the school situation were found related to the . . . amount of school damage. A low level of personal identification with the school and its goals among students, teachers, and parents was found positively associated with a high rate of vandalic behavior among students. High-damage schools, also, were found characterized by inadequate administration and leadership, with poor communication among the various members of the school. In such schools, furthermore, relatively poor interpersonal relations were found between principal and teacher, teacher and teacher, student and teacher, parent and teacher, and custodian and student. The feeling that the school administration was not sufficiently concerned with the welfare of staff and students was found associated with a low level of school morale.[69]

Automobile Theft by Juveniles

In many parts of the world there has been an increase in auto thefts and in the proportion of those committed by juveniles. Such a situation has been observed in Great Britain, France, West Germany, and Sweden. The larceny of motor vehicles has been steadily increasing in metropolitan London, where 20,557 motor vehicles were stolen or driven away during 1958. Two thirds (62.6 percent) of those arrested for the larceny of motor vehicles were under twenty-one, and one in five (21.7 percent) was under seventeen.[70] The percentage of offenders arrested in West Germany for car theft who were under twenty-one increased from 46.2 in 1954 to 61.8

---

[68] *Ibid.*, p. 90.

[69] Nathan Goldman, "A Socio-Psychological Study of School Vandalism," Final report on Office of Education Contract No. SAE 181 (8453) (Mimeographed; Syracuse: University Research Institute, 1959), p. 109.

[70] In *New Forms of Juvenile Delinquency: Their Origin, Prevention and Treatment,* p. 6.

in 1958. Juveniles arrested in Sweden for the unauthorized borrowing and theft of motor vehicles (including autos, motorcycles, and power bicycles) increased from 7065 per month to 32,902, or 463.4 percent, from 1950 to 1957. About the Swedish situation Torsten Eriksson has written: "In comparison with what we know about other countries, the most striking development in Sweden is the emphasis on crimes involving automotive vehicles. Car thefts (unlawfully stolen and borrowed cars) are the main cause for concern in the case of youthful offenders. They have increased enormously and, compared with the pre–World War II era, they represent a new form of criminality." [71]

In 1960 nearly two thirds of all persons arrested for automobile theft in 2460 cities in the United States were under eighteen. Even the number of arrests for automobile theft by those under sixteen is large. In New York City in 1959 there were 1011 such arrests, or 17.3 percent of all arrests of persons under sixteen.

Two samples of eighty-one New York boys between twelve and seventeen who stole cars and a similar number who did not, have shown some statistically significant differences.[72] Boys who stole cars were more often white rather than Negro or Puerto Rican, their homes were in better economic circumstances, and fewer came from broken homes. Their delinquency generally started at an earlier age, and they were more intelligent.

Almost all the boys in the New York study stole cars more frequently from areas with a homogeneous population, lived in single-family dwellings, and had only one parent employed. Similar findings were reported in a Detroit study.[73] Such boys are well socialized as far as primary group relations are concerned, commit their offenses with companions, and are not isolated, peculiar individuals. The Detroit study reported that such boys, however, easily accept the values of companions but respond weakly to the prohibitions of the larger society. "Thus, if a boy's friends got pleasure from riding in automobiles, he would oblige in carefree fashion by borrowing a car." [74]

Summary

The term "criminal" has little real meaning, for actually there are many types of criminals. Classifications of criminals based on the type of crime, age, or sex of the offender are useful for legal or statistical purposes. From a scientific approach, behavior systems represent a more satisfactory classification, for offenders may be grouped along a continuum of noncareer and career types, with the criminally insane at one end and the professional

---

[71] *Ibid.*, p. 26.
[72] Erwin Schepses, "Boys Who Steal Cars," *Federal Probation*, 25:56–62 (March, 1961).
[73] Wattenberg and Balistrieri, "Automobile Theft . . . ," *loc. cit.*
[74] *Ibid.*, p. 578.

criminal at the other. Career types of offenders largely represent deviant attitudes which are the result of group association. Noncareer offenders generally commit personal offenses; career types, property offenses.

A behavior system considers social roles, identification with crime, conception of self, pattern of differential association with others, progression in crime, and the degree to which criminal behavior has become a part of the life organization. Persons have associations which are criminal and noncriminal, and the effect of these seems to depend in part on the frequency, duration, priority, and intensity of these associations. It has not been possible to demonstrate that certain personality traits are related to all delinquent and criminal behavior. The concept of "psychopath" or "sexual psychopath" does not appear to be a useful one in the study of criminal careers.

Delinquency should be analyzed by types rather than considered as an entity. Two types of delinquencies are vandalism and auto theft.

Selected Readings

CLINARD, MARSHALL B. and ANDREW L. WADE, "Toward the Delineation of Vandalism as a Sub-Type in Juvenile Delinquency," *Journal of Criminal Law, Criminology, and Police Science,* 48:493–499 (January–February, 1948). A discussion of the need for typological studies of delinquency as a detailed illustration of a type.

GIBBONS, DON C. and DONALD L. GARRITY, "Some Suggestions for the Development of Etiological and Treatment Theory in Criminology," *Social Forces,* 38:51–58 (October, 1959). Types of criminal behavior and the need for relating treatment programs to types rather than general programs for treating criminal offenders.

LINDESMITH, ALFRED R., and H. WARREN DUNHAM. "Some Principles of Criminal Typology," *Social Forces,* 19:307–314 (March, 1941). In this article a distinction is made between individual and social types of offenders. Psychiatrists who study primarily the individual type of offender tend to generalize about all offenders, and sociologists who study primarily social types do the same.

MARTIN, JOHN M. *Juvenile Vandalism.* Springfield, Ill.: Charles C Thomas, Publisher, 1961. One of the few studies of vandalism. Discusses the extent of vandalism. Several case histories are included.

RECKLESS, WALTER C. *The Crime Problem.* 3d ed. New York: Appleton-Century-Crofts, Inc., 1961. The concept of a criminal career is discussed, and in particular, ordinary types of criminal careers.

SUTHERLAND, EDWARD H., and DONALD R. CRESSEY. *Principles of Criminology.* 6th ed. Philadelphia: J. B. Lippincott Company, 1960, Chap. 13. A discussion of behavior systems in crime from a somewhat different viewpoint.

Chapter

9

Types of Offenders: Murderers and Sex Offenders

In the following discussion two types of offenders will be analyzed—murderers and sex offenders. Very few persons have ever made a career out of murder or become what might be called career sex offenders. Although this is less true of prostitution, many prostitutes are so engaged only temporarily and do not make a career out of such sex activities. All murder and sex offenses, however, must be viewed in the perspective of social behavior and social norms. In the case of murder we shall refer to it as arising within the general framework of a "subculture of violence." Most homosexuality and prostitution will be seen in a group and subcultural context.

Murderers

The type of criminal homicide which we shall discuss here as murder consists of both murder and nonnegligent manslaughter, but does not include justifiable homicide or attempts or assaults to kill, or accidental deaths. Another type of criminal homicide also not included is negligent manslaughter, in which a death is attributable to the negligence of some other person than the victim. Technically "murder" is determined by the police and the court through a legal process.

Criminal homicide, or what is generally referred to as murder or nonnegligent manslaughter, is one of the most socially visible crimes; yet it comprises a small proportion of the total crime. The general trend in urban murder rates in the United States has been downward. The rate in 1933 per 100,000 population was 7.1. This rate continued to move downward, with slight upward changes in 1945 and 1946, until 1954, when it was 4.8.[1] The 1960 rate was 5.1. A Philadelphia study has indicated that the decline in criminal homicide may be misleading.[2] Since rates for aggravated

---

[1] *Uniform Crime Reports*, Annual Bulletins of the Federal Bureau of Investigation, Washington, D.C.

[2] Marvin E. Wolfgang, *Patterns in Criminal Homicide* (Philadelphia: University of Pennsylvania Press, 1958), pp. 332–333.

assault and assault with intent to kill have increased, the decline in criminal homicide appears to be the result of better communication with the police to prevent homicides, more rapid transportation to a hospital, and advances in medical technology.

Popular interest has always centered on murder. In spite of this widespread public interest, however, scientific knowledge about murder and murderers is limited. It is known that murderers only occasionally have criminal careers, and that they are seldom repeaters. Most studies show that they are one of the best risks for successes on parole. It is commonly said that wardens frequently use murderers as chauffeurs and as household servants on the assumption that they are the least criminal. Warden Lawes of Sing Sing used to remark that the barber who shaved him for years had been convicted of a particularly brutal murder. Further evidence of this fact is that about half (46.7 percent) of ninety-six Wisconsin prisoners serving time for murder had never been arrested before, whereas only one in three of the sex offenders and only one in eleven of the property offenders could make this claim.[3]

TYPES OF MURDER

Murders can be classified on the basis of the situation in which they occurred. There are murders which result from a long period of hostility, those which occur in sudden anger, and, finally, those committed in connection with another crime.[4]

Prolonged Personal Disputes. The first type generally takes place after a long period of interpersonal difficulties for which murder represented a possible solution. Most murders of this cumulative type arise out of these long-standing personal frictions. They may involve disputes between neighbors and work associates, between husbands and wives or other close relatives, or between former lovers. In the case of the following murder, the difficulties extended over a long period of years and involved increasing hostility.

> The inner conflict engendered by his childhood and adolescent upbringing was not mitigated by his marriage. He and his wife had had sexual relations before their marriage, and F claims that this was part of a plot to force him to marry her. However that may be, their first child was born two months after their marriage. Shortly thereafter a friend of his wife's teasingly asked F how he could be sure that the child was his own, unnerving him so much that he fled to another room and wept. His wife induced her friend to tell him that she was merely joking, but the suspicion thus implanted continued to linger and impair the conjugal relationship.

[3] John L. Gillin, *The Wisconsin Prisoner* (Madison: The University of Wisconsin Press, 1946).

[4] Ralph S. Banay, "Study in Murder," *The Annals*, 284:26–35 (November, 1952).

After three years of married life F was in a very disturbed emotional state. He was afflicted with dizziness, which sometimes caused him to topple over, and with impairment of memory. Obviously he was suffering from a typical neurosis, an escape from thoughts about the unpleasant situation at home. His wife was totally lacking in sympathy; she mocked, tantalized, and ridiculed him for innocence and lack of virility. She neglected her home to visit at her mother's or sister's, where she sought the companionship of a male boarder. When F learned of this situation, he warned her to stay away, and she promised to do so. One day shortly thereafter, however, finding his wife absent when he returned home early, he found her again in her mother's house, joking and fooling with the man she had promised to avoid. She introduced F to him as "nothing but a fool of mine." She tortured her husband by telling him that she was trying to drive him insane, by comparing his sexual potency with that of other men she had known, and by reminding him that there was nothing to prevent her from entertaining other men without his knowledge. The check he gave her each week she turned over to her sister and sister-in-law, stoutly denying that she did so. He not only decided that his wife was an inveterate liar but became convinced, after learning that her mother had once been hospitalized for insanity, that she was also insane. He says she made grimaces at him and called him names, neglected the child and the house, and was disgustingly dirty in her personal habits. He was told by a number of persons that she was unfaithful to him.

All these disturbing factors—his wife's general attitude toward him, her nagging and mocking, her criticism of his sexual weakness, the evidence that she cared nothing for him, the current gossip about her, and his long-standing feeling of inferiority, which her superior air intensified—led to terrific emotional upheavals, heavy drinking, neglect of his work, and frequent changes of occupation. Eventually the situation reached such a pass that he no longer could face it, and he shot and killed his wife.[5]

Hostility in these cases has often accumulated over a long period of time. In one case Banay has traced this long developmental process in the life history of a murderer, a war veteran in this case. The history included frustrations in preschool and school life, the first marriage, army life, a second marriage, and, finally the climax, a mass murder which occurred after the second wife left him with the children.

Suddenly on this day, as he paced the floor or sat brooding on his bed, an upsurge of hostility and frustration told him to take matters into his own hands. If he could not see his children he would at least frighten his in-laws. He put three revolvers in his pockets, threw an army carbine into his car, and drove to the house where his family lived. There was a short conversation with his father-in-law. "No," he could not see the children. "Throw him out," urged the mother-in-law. Then his wife appeared and he pleaded "Do you love me?" "You are crazy," she answered. That was the fatal moment. He pulled his guns and shot several people in the house; chased his mother-in-law

---

[5] From John L. Gillin, *The Wisconsin Prisoner* (Madison: The University of Wisconsin Press, 1946), pp. 40–42.

to another house, shooting at anyone who came between them, and shot her. Then he drove to other relatives of his wife and shot them.[6]

Crisis Situation. In the second type of murder there has not been any building up of hostility; rather, it results from a crisis which demands an immediate solution, but for which the only immediate solution is seen as some form of violent action. Berg and Fox concluded that a violent argument plays an important role in the perpetration of certain types of homicide.[7] In such arguments verbalization tends to decline and emotionality to increase until, finally, a sudden assault with fist or weapons results in the death of the victim. Banay cites the case of a fifty-three-year-old president of a large industrial firm who shot his long-time friend and partner during an argument over the way in which the partner had represented the company at a hearing on a compensation award for an employee.

> Shortly after the death of his wife, on whom he had been very dependent, the commitment of his son to a state hospital further shook his confidence and outlook. His sexual life had been at a standstill for a number of years, and he began to feel a physical decline. His generous and open-hearted attitude began to change to a more scrupulous one, and he became overconcerned with finances. His shrinking income symbolized the waning of his power, influence, and potency. He began to transfer his dependence from his wife to his friend and partner. The feeling of impoverishment and infidelity, which so often is part of the involutional state, began to be projected on his partner. Therefore a relatively small incident acted as a fuse for the underground explosion.[8]

In Connection with a Crime. Some murders are committed in connection with a robbery or burglary, or in some sex offense, such as rape. In these cases the murder is usually an indirect result of resistance on the part of the victim or in order to forestall detection of the crime. Actually such murders are a minor part of the total crime picture. Gang murders of various types, although rare, represent efforts to remove certain opposition or hostile witnesses.

MURDER AS A BEHAVIOR SYSTEM

In the etiology of murder, the general cultural pattern seems to determine its frequency. The acceptance of murder as a method of solving interpersonal conflicts varies a great deal from country to country, region to region, and state to state. Finland, for example, has one of the highest

---

[6] Banay, "Study in Murder," *loc. cit.,* pp. 31–32.
[7] Irvin A. Berg and Vernon Fox, "Factors in Homicides Committed by 200 Males," *Journal of Social Psychology,* 26:109–119 (August, 1947).
[8] Banay, "Study in Murder," *loc. cit.,* p. 33.

homicide rates in the world, whereas the rate is quite low in Great Britain and Canada.[9] Ceylon also has a high rate in Asia.[10] A study of personal offenses in Puerto Rico indicated that the high rates of these crimes in such Latin cultures are related to personal insult or honor. In situations of personal vilification or marital triangles the culture may require the individual to attack the offender.[11] Two thirds of the offenders were found to have had some personal association with persons who had also resorted to violence under somewhat similar circumstances.

Most African homicides among tribal peoples today occur within an institutional setting which defines the social relationship between killer and victim.[12] These relationships tend to be different from Western societies, such as a woman killing her children rather than her husband in a domestic quarrel. Likewise altercations over money are rare, but fear of witches or land disputes may be more common reasons for the homicide.

Brearley's study of *Homicide in the United States* revealed that cultural definitions play an important role in murder.[13] In fact, the regional differences in the United States are so wide that "a general murder rate for the United States as a whole has no very close relation to the actual rate of any specific area or section." [14] The homicide rates of the South are considerably higher than those in other regions, and Brearley suggests that this difference is due to the fact that cultural definitions call for personal violence in certain situations and that weapons are carried more frequently in some areas than in others. The 1959 rate for murder and nonnegligent manslaughter for the New England area was 1.3; for the East North Central states 3.6; on the other hand, the South Atlantic area rate was 9.2, and the East South Central area, 9.0, or about twice the national average. In 1959, Vermont had a murder and nonnegligent manslaughter rate of 0.3 and Minnesota 1.0, in contrast with Georgia's rate of 13.4 and Alabama's 12.9.

Murder rates vary a great deal according to ethnic, racial, and class lines: "Murder would seem culturally to be somewhat more acceptable as a

---

[9] Veli Verkko, *Homicides and Suicides in Finland and Their Dependence on National Character* (Copenhagen: G. E. C. Gads Forlag, 1951).

[10] See Jacqueline and Murray Straus, "Suicide, Homicide, and Social Structure in Ceylon," *American Journal of Sociology*, 58:461–469 (March, 1953), and Arthur Wood, "Murder, Suicide, and Economic Crime in Ceylon," *American Sociological Review*, 26:744–753 (October, 1961).

[11] Jaime Toro-Calder, "Personal Crimes in Puerto Rico." Unpublished master's thesis, University of Wisconsin, Madison, 1950.

[12] Paul Bohannan, *African Homicide and Suicide* (Princeton, N.J.: Princeton University Press, 1960).

[13] H. C. Brearley, *Homicide in the United States* (Chapel Hill: University of North Carolina Press, 1932).

[14] George B. Vold, "Extent and Trend of Capital Crimes in the United States," *The Annals*, 284:3 (November, 1952).

way of expressing resentment directly among certain social classes than others." [15] Although the high rate of the southern regions reflects in part the high proportion of Negro population among which homicide is quite prevalent, the 1951 rates for southern whites is from three to seven times as great as for New England whites. Taking the years 1920 and 1925 together, Brearley found that the homicide rate for Negroes in Florida was 62.9 as compared with 12.8 for Massachusetts Negroes.[16]

Some indication of subcultural components in criminal homicide is the fact that of 489 cases in Houston, Texas, over 87 percent occurred in four areas, not far apart, located near the center of the city.[17] For the most part, outlying areas within the city had no homicides at all. Nearly all the homicides occurred in areas populated chiefly by Negroes and Spanish-Americans. In more than 70 percent of the cases victim and murderer lived less than two miles apart, and in 32.8 percent lived in the same house or the same block. The conflicts which gave rise to the disputes were chiefly between members of the same social group and in 87 percent of the cases the murderer and his victim had known each other before. The conflict patterns grew out of arguments, love triangles, and marital discord. The arguments arose from gambling disputes or in private parties in which there were drinking and boisterous conduct, all made more violent by the social concepts and the relaxed social control of the areas.

In a tabulation of the murders of 324 females, Sutherland found that nearly 60 percent were committed by relatives or other close associates. He reported that 102 of the murders were committed by husbands, 37 by fathers or other relatives closely associated with the victim, and 49 by lovers or suitors.[18]

A study of Wisconsin prisoners charged with murder disclosed in many cases a previous history of difficulties with the victim. Some were farmers who committed murder after a dispute with a neighbor over a cow or some similar matter. Two thirds of the Wisconsin murders grew out of a long-standing or an immediate quarrel, the remainder being connected with some crime. Many murders involved situations in which the marital situation was primarily important.[19]

Wolfgang's study of 588 victims and 621 slayers in Philadelphia, between 1948 and 1952, has given us many insights into what he terms the "subculture of violence." [20] Murder was found to be highest among Ne-

---

[15] Austin L. Porterfield and Robert H. Talbert, *Crime, Suicide and Social Well Being* (Fort Worth, Tex.: Leo Potishman Foundation, 1948), pp. 102–103.

[16] Brearley, *op. cit.*

[17] Henry Allen Bullock, "Urban Homicide in Theory and Fact," *Journal of Criminal Law, Criminology, and Police Science*, 45:565–575 (January–February, 1955).

[18] Edwin H. Sutherland, "The Sexual Psychopath Laws," *Journal of Criminal Law and Criminology*, 40:543–554 (January–February, 1950).

[19] Gillin, *op. cit.*, p. 60.

[20] Wolfgang, *op. cit.* Also see, for a summary, "A Sociological Analysis of Criminal Homicide," *Federal Probation*, 25:48–55 (March, 1961).

groes, males, those in the age group 20–24 and 30–34, from the lower social classes, and related to certain occupations. The rate among Negroes was four times that of whites, indicating the role of subculture and the isolating effects of segregation from the general norms of society. In fact, the rate was greatest among recent Negro migrants. The role of subcultural factors is that

> the significance of a jostle, a slightly derogatory remark, or the appearance of a weapon in the hands of an adversary are stimuli differentially perceived and interpreted by Negroes and whites, males and females. Social expectations of response in particular types of social interaction result in differential "definitions of the situation." A male is usually expected to defend the name and honor of his mother, the virtue of womanhood (even though his female companion for the evening may be an entirely new acquaintance and/or a prostitute), and to accept no derogation about his race (even from a member of his own race), his age, or his masculinity. Quick resort to physical combat as a measure of daring, courage, or defense of status appears to be a cultural expectation, especially for lower socio-economic class males of both races. When such a culture norm response is elicited from an individual engaged in social interplay with others who harbor the same response mechanism, physical assaults, altercations, and violent domestic quarrels that result in homicide are likely to be relatively common. The upper-middle and upper social class value system defines and codifies behavioral norms into legal rules that often transcend sub-cultural mores, and considers many of the social and personal stimuli that evoke a combative reaction in the lower classes as "trivial." Thus, there exists a cultural antipathy between many folk rationalizations of the lower class, and of males of both races, on the one hand, and the middle-class legal norms under which they live, on the other. The fate of 206 victims and the 227 offenders responsible for their death, whose motive has been classified as "altercation," can be partially interpreted in terms of the foregoing remarks.[21]

Nine out of ten murderers were in lower-class occupations, laborers, for example, committing more homicides than did clerks. Nearly one half of the offenders who had a previous arrest record of some type had been arrested for some form of assault more characteristic of lower-class behavior, such as wife beating and fighting.[22] Some indication of the relation of homicide to the pattern of life in certain areas of the city is suggested by the fact that 65 percent of all homicides occur during week ends, particularly on Saturday night.

---

[21] Marvin E. Wolfgang, *Patterns in Criminal Homicide* (Philadelphia: University of Pennsylvania Press, 1958), pp. 188–189. Reprinted by permission of the publishers.

[22] Wolfgang, *op. cit.*, p. 178. His study of urban offenders, largely Negro, indicated a large previous arrest record: 68 percent of the males and 48 percent of the females. Of them, 66 percent had been arrested for offenses against the person (48 percent for aggravated assault which is also included in this figure) and 34 percent for property and other offenses.

THE MURDERER AND HIS VICTIM

In a tabulation of the murders of 324 females, Sutherland found that nearly 60 percent were committed by relatives or other close associates.

A study of 713 New Jersey murderers classified according to victims and the situations in which the murders took place found that less than one fourth committed murder in connection with another crime. The largest group, about two thirds, of the murders grew out of some altercation with male acquaintances, relatives, mistresses, or sex rivals (see Table 9.1). Ap-

Table 9.1. Motivation of Murderers [a]

	Numbers	Totals	Percent
Premeditated murder	79	79	11.1
Of relatives		37	5.2
Wives	24		
In-laws	4		
Immediate blood-relatives	4		
Distant blood-relatives	5		
Of non-relatives		42	5.9
Mistresses	15		
Sex rivals	4		
Male acquaintances	23		
In connection with other crimes		134	18.8
During robbery, burglary, etc.	129		
During rape	2		
During kidnaping	3		
Resisting arrest		22	3.1
Resisting police officer	20		
Resisting jail keeper	2		
Result of altercation		478	67.0
With relatives		110	15.4
Wives	78		
In-laws	19		
Immediate blood-relatives	8		
Distant blood-relatives	5		
With non-relatives		368	51.6
Mistresses	45		
Sex-rivals	25		
Male acquaintances	298		

a New Jersey State Prison; total murders, 713.

SOURCE: E. Frankel, "One Thousand Murderers," *Journal of Criminal Law and Criminology*, 29:687–688 (1938–1939). Reprinted by special permission of the *Journal of Criminal Law and Criminology* (Northwestern University School of Law), Vol. 29, No. 5 (1939).

proximately one third (35 percent) of 588 male and female criminal homicides in Philadelphia were the result of general altercations, family and domestic quarrels accounted for 14 percent, jealousy 12 percent, altercation over money 11 percent, and, contrary to popular impression, robbery only 7 percent.[23] Close friends and relatives accounted for over half (59 percent) of all the homicides and four fifths of the women. In 28 percent of the cases the victim was a close friend of the murderer, in 25 percent a family relative, in 14 percent an acquaintance. In only one out of eight murders was the victim a stranger. Women, as contrasted with men, generally kill someone in their own family or one in two of those murders committed by women in Philadelphia as compared with one in six committed by men. In all, one in five homicides represented husband or wife killings. Since the number of wives killed by their husbands constituted 41 percent of all women killed, and husbands only 11 percent of the men killed, it can be concluded that "when a woman committed homicide she was more likely to kill her mate; and when a man was killed by a woman he was most likely to be killed by his wife." [24]

Personal contacts have been found to play a significant role in murders in Denmark and India.[25] In a Danish study it was found that the murderer's victim was a relative or an acquaintance in nine out of ten cases. Strangers were seldom the victims. Most murders in India occur within the same caste and also frequently involve husband and wife.

Where there are racial aspects in homicide, as shown in a study of 500 Alabama homicides, the circumstances of the murder differ according to whether a Negro male killed a Negro male, a Negro male killed a Negro female, a Negro female killed a Negro male, a Negro female killed another Negro female, a white man killed another white man, and a white man killed a white female.[26] In the Philadelphia study reported above, 94 percent of all homicides were within the same race.

In one study over one in four criminal homicides were precipitated by the victim in that the victim was the first to show or use a deadly weapon, or to strike a blow in an altercation.[27] Victim-precipitated homicides were found to be significantly associated with Negroes, victim offender relationships involving male victims of female offenders, mate slayings, alcohol in the homicide situation, or in the victim, and victims with a previous record of assault or arrest. Other homicides, not included in this figure, involved the infidelity of a mate or a lover, failure of the victim to pay a debt, use

[23] Wolfgang, *op. cit.*, p. 191.   [24] *Ibid.*, p. 325.

[25] Kaare Svalastoga, "Homicide and Social Contact in Denmark," *American Journal of Sociology*, 62:37–41 (July, 1956), and Edwin D. Driver, "Interaction and Criminal Homicide in India," *Social Forces*, 40:153–158 (December, 1961).

[26] Howard Harlan, "Five Hundred Homicides," *Journal of Criminal Law and Criminology*, 40:736–752 (March–April, 1950).

[27] Wolfgang, *op. cit.*, p. 252. Also see Hans von Hentig, *The Criminal and His Victim* (New Haven, Conn.: Yale University Press, 1948).

of vile names by the victim in such a way that the victim had a great deal to do with the homicide. Even in robbery the behavior of the victim may incite the robber to kill.

Sex Offenders

Many people today believe that all sex offenders are "beasts" and should be put away for life either in a prison or in a mental hospital. Such a belief is based on many misconceptions about sex offenders, the principal one being a rather general confusion in definition of the term "sex offender." Some people have the erroneous idea that all sex offenders are sexual degenerates who have, or try to have, sex relations with young children or who engage in sexual delinquencies accompanied by acts of violence.

Actually, sex crimes involve many different acts, most of which are unaccompanied by violence. Sex offenses which are considered deviations and punishable by law consist, mainly, of rape, homosexual behavior (sodomy), adultery, fornication, indecent exposure, incest (intercourse with a relative, as prohibited by law), and prostitution. The following is a classification of sex offenses by the nature of the deviant behavior.[28]

    Sexual assault
        Mild sexual assault
        Serious sexual assault
    Forcible rape
    Statutory rape
    Incestuous relations
    Noncoital sex relations with a minor
    Exhibitory acts
    Disseminating "obscene" material
    Homosexual relations
        Homosexual relations with adults
        Homosexual relations with minors
    Bestiality

Forcible rape should be distinguished from statutory rape—sexual intercourse, with or without force, with a female below the age of consent, which is usually set at sixteen or eighteen years of age. Although we do not know what percentage of all rapes are statutory, it appears likely that they are in the majority. Only about one in six convictions for rapes in New York City during 1930–1939 involved force, and these cases represented only 12 percent of all serious sex offenses.[29] In a group of Wisconsin sex offenders in the state prison, only 14 had been convicted of forcible rape,

---

[28] Albert Ellis and Ralph Brancale, *The Psychology of Sex Offenders* (Springfield, Ill.: Charles C Thomas, Publisher, 1956), p. 31.

[29] Sutherland, "The Sexual Psychopath Laws," *loc. cit.*, p. 545.

as compared with 89 who had been convicted of statutory rape.[30] Many statutory, as well as some forcible rapes, are legally so called, but they may have been committed with passive consent, or they may have involved blackmail or prostitution on the part of the woman.

What is sexually normal or deviant behavior can be looked at from a number of ways, all involving cultural norms. One is a statistical definition of normality which might, for example, follow the most prevalent sex practices disclosed by the Kinsey report. Still another would be whether the sex practices lead to procreation, thus excluding acts of homosexuality and exhibitionism. Finally, the most likely definition would be acts which are prescribed by law. While there are variations in different cultures, most sex laws in American society govern four relationships: the degree of consent, such as forcible rape; the nature of the object, restricting legitimate sex objects to human beings of the opposite sex, of a certain age, of a defined distance in kinship, and to the spouse; the nature of the sexual act to certain behavior in heterosexual intercourse; and, finally, the setting in which the sex act occurs.[31]

Some persons who have studied the operation of sex laws have maintained that the regulations of law are too wide and that those sex acts which should be punishable are those which involve (1) the use of force or duress, (2) adults who take advantage of a minor, and (3) public sex acts which are distasteful to the majority of those in whose presence they are committed.[32] They maintain that it is questionable whether sex acts, other than those in which adults engage publicly, should be punished. Such a view would affect the legality of many present-day sex acts, including much of unmarried adult heterosexual relations and adult homosexuality, as is the case in many European countries such as Sweden and Denmark.[33] It has also been suggested that the age of statutory rape, or age of consent, be lowered from eighteen to fifteen, as is generally the case in Europe. Originally, in common law, the age of consent was under ten, but this age has been moved upward to what one leading legal writer claims is entirely unrealistic because of the voluntary nature of much of such sex relations in middle and late adolescence and the knowledge of sex relationships on the part of the girl. In the United States "each such sexual contact may

---

[30] Gillin, *op. cit.,* p. 120.

[31] Stanton Wheeler, "Sex Offenses: A Sociological Critique," in *Law and Contemporary Problems,* 25:258–259 (Spring, 1960). Also see Morris Ploscowe, "Sex Offenses: The American Legal Context," in the same issue, which is a symposium on sex offenses, pp. 217–225, and Morris Ploscowe, *Sex and the Law* (Englewood Cliffs, N.J.: Prentice-Hall, Inc., 1951).

[32] Ellis and Brancale, *op. cit.,* pp. 88–89.

[33] Even in Britain the well-known Wolfenden Parliamentary Committee on Homosexual Offenses and Prostitution of 1957 recommended the legalizing of homosexual acts between consenting adults in private. For a discussion see J. E. Hall Williams, "Sex Offenses: The British Experience," *Law and Contemporary Problems,* 25:334–360 (Spring, 1960).

technically be rape under some law and may subject the male to ferocious penalties." [34]

MISCONCEPTIONS ABOUT SEX OFFENDERS

In many ways the term "sex offender" is misleading. Sex is but one, and often a minor, aspect of a person's total life; it is not independent, but rather is often an expression of other aspects of personality, so that to speak of a person as a "rapist" or a "homosexual," or to use the general term "sex offender," tends to make an aspect of a person's life cover his entire personality. The same comment might also be made of many other types of criminal offenders, including particularly the murderer and the occasional property offender. One writer has objected to the title of sex offender being applied to juveniles.

> One technically violates the sexual conduct norm through behavior and thereby commits a *delinquent* offense. The term sex offender should perhaps signify no more nor less than this. Certainly, it should not imply that this is the only major kind of delinquent activity the person has committed. To classify a person as a sex offender may only serve to develop self and public definitions of the person as a sex offender.[35]

Many other misconceptions exist about sex offenders. Contrary to popular belief, a study of the first 300 sex offenders committed to a state diagnostic center revealed that the majority of sex offenders were rather harmless "minor" deviates rather than dangerous "sex fiends." [36] Of the sex offenders, 58 percent had committed relatively minor sex offenses. Only 10 in the entire group of 300 were considered to be dangerous in the sense that they had used force or duress. Moreover, aside from those convicted of statutory rape and incestuous relations, most sex offenders tend to be "sexually inhibited" rather than oversexed persons.

Another report on sex offenders has summarized a number of facts about them.

1. There are not tens of thousands of homicidal sex fiends abroad in the land.
2. Sex offenders are usually not recidivists (repeaters), at least in police and other official records.
3. Sex offenders do not progress to more serious types of sex crimes.
4. It is impossible at the present time to predict the danger of serious crimes being committed by sex deviates.

---

[34] Ploscowe, "Sex Offenses: The American Legal Context," *loc. cit.*, p. 222. The age of consent is generally sixteen in England and Norway, fifteen in Sweden, Denmark, and France, and fourteen in Belgium and Germany.

[35] Albert J. Reiss, Jr., "Sex Offenses: The Marginal Status of the Adolescent," *Law and Contemporary Problems*, 25:311 (Spring, 1960).

[36] Ellis and Brancale, *op. cit.*, p. 32.

5. "Sex psychopathy" is not a clinical entity.
6. Sex offenders are not oversexed.[37]

After the elimination of statutory rape, incest, and the majority of homosexual cases, which as a general rule do not constitute a serious menace to females, there remains a relatively small number of violent sex cases in most countries. Sutherland estimated that in the United States there are annually about 5.7 sex killings of women and 4 of children.[38] He suggested that if these figures seem to be too low they could be multiplied fivefold or twentyfold and still not be large. He made a tabulation of all murders of women and of children as reported in *The New York Times* during the years 1930, 1935, and 1940, on the assumption that it would carry nearly all offenses of this type reported in the United States. He found that of the 324 murders of women reported, only 17 involved rape or suspicion of rape. Since the latter type of case would be more completely reported nationally, the ratio of such cases may be actually smaller. During these three years only 39 murders of children were reported and only 12 were indicated to be rape-murders.

There is considerable doubt about sex offenders being psychopathic, not only because this term is vague but because the percentage of them diagnosed as such varies tremendously. The Psychiatric Clinic of the Court of General Sessions in New York City diagnosed 15.8 percent of its sex offenders as psychopathic, but the psychiatrists in Bellevue Hospital in the same city diagnosed 52.9 percent as psychopathic.[39] A more recent study has shown that the term "sexual psychopath" is applicable to only a small minority (about 3 percent) of convicted sex offenders.[40] Sutherland has concluded that "the concept 'sexual psychopath' is too vague for judicial or administrative use either as to commitment to institutions or as to release as 'completely or permanently cured.' "[41] He states, moreover, that there is no indication that such laws are extensively used or that their enactment in such states as California, Illinois, Michigan, and Minnesota has resulted in any different trend in rape rates of adjoining states which do not have the law. Morris Ploscowe, a well-known legal authority has written:

---

[37] Derived from *The Habitual Sex Offender*, Report and Recommendations of the Commission on the Habitual Sex Offender as formulated by Paul W. Tappan, Technical Consultant (Trenton: State of New Jersey, 1950), pp. 13–16.

[38] Sutherland, "The Sexual Psychopath Laws," *loc. cit.*, pp. 545–546.

[39] Jack Frosch and Walter Bromberg, "The Sex Offender—A Psychiatric Study," *American Journal of Orthopsychiatry*, 9:761–776 (October, 1939); and Benjamin Apfelberg, Carl Sugar, and Arnold Z. Pfeffer, "A Psychiatric Study of 250 Sex Offenders," *American Journal of Psychiatry*, 100:762–770 (May, 1944).

[40] Ellis and Brancale, *op. cit.*, p. 37.

[41] Sutherland, "The Sexual Psychopath Laws," *loc. cit.*, p. 551.

Any revision of sex offender laws must also repeal much of the sexual psychopath legislation that is presently in force. These laws were passed to provide a means for dealing with dangerous, repetitive, mentally abnormal sex offenders. Unfortunately, the vagueness of the definition of sexual psychopaths contained in these statutes has obscured this basic underlying purpose. There are large numbers of sex offenders who engage in compulsive, repetitive sexual acts, which may be crimes, who may be mentally abnormal, but who are not dangerous. The transvestite, the exhibitionist, the frotteur, the homosexual who masturbates another either in the privacy of his bedroom or in a public toilet, the "peeping tom"—are typical of large numbers of sex offenders who are threatened with long-term incarceration by present sexual psychopath legislation. And what is even worse is that such legislation has not usually been implemented by facilities for treatment. The result is that many nuisance-type, nondangerous sex offenders have been imprisoned for long periods of time, without treatment, in those jurisdictions where such laws have been enforced. This is not to say that the compulsive nondangerous types of sex offenders should be immune from prosecution and punishment; but short sentences or probation are more than adequate to deal with these derelictions, unless better treatment facilities are provided.[42]

Evidence indicates that sex offenders, contrary to common beliefs, have a low rate of recidivism in comparison with other types of offenders. Out of a total of twenty-five kinds of crime reported in the FBI's *Uniform Crime Reports* for 1937, rapists ranked nineteenth as repeaters and the category "Other sex offenses" was seventeenth. Only 1 in 20 of 1447 males arrested in 1937 for rape had previously been convicted of rape. A special study of New York City juvenile delinquents revealed that only 3 boys in 108 brought in for sex delinquencies had subsequent appearances, none of which were sex offenses.[43] Between two thirds and three fourths of the sex offenders referred to the New Jersey Diagnostic Center were first offenders.[44] Of 1985 convicted English sex offenders over four out of five (83 percent) had no previous conviction for a sex offense.[45]

A California study covering sex offenders committed to correctional institutions during the five years 1945–1949 reported that one half of all sex offenders had a prior commitment record and one fifth a previous record. Recidivism was greater among the homosexuals than among any other group. On the other hand, sex offenders who had been committed to prison were found to be fairly good risks on parole. Only 31.8 percent of 568 California sex offenders committed another offense while on parole, as

[42] Reprinted from a symposium, *Sex Offenses*, by permission from *Law and Contemporary Problems*. Vol. 25, No. 2, Spring 1960. Published by the Duke University School of Law, Durham, North Carolina. Copyright, 1960, by Duke University.

[43] Lewis I. Doshay, *The Boy Sex Offender and His Later Career* (New York: Grune & Stratton, Inc., 1943).

[44] *The Habitual Sex Offender*, p. 24.

[45] Leon Radzinowicz ed., *Sexual Offenses: A Report of the Cambridge Department of Criminal Science* (London: Macmillan & Co., Ltd., 1957), p. 137.

compared with 50.3 percent of all offenders.[46] Of these violators, less than 10 percent committed a serious offense.

Of 206 patients committed under the New Jersey sex offender law between June, 1949, and April, 1953, 57 were released on parole or discharged by this latter date, but no offender had violated his parole even though half had been out more than six months.[47] In Illinois, sex offenders have the lowest parole violation rate of any group of offenders, being about one third that of those committed for property offenses.[48] In England, of a group of 1985 convicted sex offenders who had been released for four years, 85 percent had no subsequent convictions.[49]

SUBCULTURAL FACTORS AND SEX OFFENDERS

The most feasible distinction which can be made of sex offenders is between aggressive and passive offenders. The aggressive are those who attempt rapes and sexual assaults on persons of the opposite sex beyond the age of puberty. Passive offenses include exhibitionism and noncoital sex play with children. Offenders of the aggressive type, in comparison with the passive type, appear to exhibit less clear-cut psychological symptoms and have more in common with nonsexual offenders. They are more likely to be judged normal on psychiatric diagnosis and to be regarded as less inhibited sexually, and to have fewer symptoms of emotional disturbances. Their prior arrest records show fewer sex and more nonsexual offenses. Finally, they show the attitudes that one finds among those from delinquent subcultures. Frequently their offenses are committed in gangs. Consequently, instead of thinking of their behavior as sexually motivated in nature or that they are "sick offenders," it would be better to view their "offenses as part of a broader system in which force may be used to attain their goals. It is the use of force, rather than any specifically deviant sexual motivation that distinguishes these offenders from those who fall within the law." [50] The victim may also play a part in an act of rape where the offense may be a product of an evening of drinking or sexual arousal. "Consideration of the victim's role means that the offense can be viewed as a product of a social situation; its explanation cannot easily be reduced

---

[46] *California Sexual Deviation Research,* January, 1953 (Sacramento: State Printing Office, 1953), pp. 21–22.

[47] *A Follow-Up Study of 206 Sex Offenders Committed to State Mental Hospitals in New Jersey* (Trenton: New Jersey Department of Institutions and Agencies, June, 1953), pp. 1–2.

[48] *Report of the Illinois Commission on Sex Offenders,* To the 68th General Assembly of the State of Illinois (Springfield: State Printing Office, March 15, 1953), p. 25.

[49] Radzinowicz, *op. cit.,* p. 268.

[50] Wheeler, "Sex Offenses . . . ," *loc. cit.,* p. 277. Also see Eugene J. Kanin, "Male Aggression in Dating-Courtship Relations," *American Journal of Sociology,* 63:197 (September, 1957).

to a search for the childhood emotional disorders of the party who becomes labeled the offender." [51]

Some striking variations exist in the norms of sex conduct, reported by Kinsey and various public opinion surveys, according to education, social class, race, religion, and region.[52] Sexual offenses may be the result of the influence of different subcultural definitions of sexual behavior. Commenting on sexual offenses in Michigan, one report stated that when some southern rural families move north into more urban, middle-class areas, certain types of sexual behavior which previously received little attention in the old permissive environment are looked upon as sex offenses.[53]

The Illinois report likewise referred to cultural factors in sex offenses. This report further indicated that the stability of sexual patterns is related to the stability of the social structure. "For example, the sex conduct of soldiers exposed to disorganized social conditions overseas varied widely from their sex conduct at home. Modern, industrialized, mobile, impersonal living has also affected traditional standards of sex behavior." [54] Sutherland has referred to cultural influences in the etiology of sex offenses:

> The absurdity of this theory [sexual psychopathy] should be evident to anyone who has an acquaintance with the variations in sexual behavior and sexual codes throughout the history of mankind; practically all of the present sex crimes have been approved behavior for adults in some society or other. Similarly within our society deviant cultures with references to sex behavior prevail in sub-groups. The manner in which juveniles are inducted into the cultures of these sub-groups in the toilets of schools, playgrounds, and dormitories, as well as in other places, has been shown in many research reports on juvenile sex behavior.[55]

Sex violations, both heterosexual and homosexual, occurring among juveniles appear largely to take place with other juveniles rather than with adults and are the result of definitions of sexual behavior by the peer group.[56] The sexual behavior of adolescents is primarily peer-organized and peer-controlled.

> Adolescents themselves set standards for what is a violation of their sexual codes. The standards in these adolescent codes vary considerably according to the social status position of the adolescent and his family in the larger society. A comparison of the prescribed heterosexual coition patterns

---

[51] Wheeler, "Sex offenses . . . ," *loc. cit.*, p. 278. Also see von Hentig, *op. cit.*

[52] Alfred C. Kinsey, Wardell B. Pomeroy, Clyde E. Martin, and Paul H. Gebhard, *Sexual Behavior in the Human Female* (Philadelphia: W. B. Saunders Company, 1953) and Alfred C. Kinsey, Wardell B. Pomeroy, and Clyde E. Martin, *Sexual Behavior in the Human Male* (Philadelphia: W. B. Saunders Company, 1948).

[53] *Report of the Governor's Study Commission on the Deviated Criminal Sex Offender* (Lansing: State of Michigan Printing Office, 1951), p. 31.

[54] *Report of the Illinois Commission on Sex Offenders*, p. 10.

[55] Sutherland, "The Sexual Psychopath Laws," *loc. cit.*, p. 549.

[56] Reiss, "Sex Offenses . . . ," *loc. cit.*

of middle- and lower-status boys and girls may illustrate this variability. Among the lower-status white adolescent boys in our society, premarital heterosexual intercourse is prescribed to secure status within the group, while it is not necessary to secure status within most middle-peer status groups, even though it does confer some status.[57]

HOMOSEXUALITY

There is ample evidence that cultural attitudes toward homosexual or one-sex behavior have differed from one period in history to another. In Greek and Roman times this behavior was prevalent, and in some societies homosexual practices were related to certain religious rites. Ford and Beach studied 76 folk societies and found that among 49 of them, or 64 percent, "homosexual activities of one sort or another are considered normal and socially acceptable for certain members of the community." [58] Some of the attitude in parts of Western society that homosexuality is deviant behavior can be explained by certain aspects of the Christian tradition.[59]

There are indications that overt homosexuality, that is, sex relations with one's own sex, is much more prevalent now than many assume. A great deal of this behavior is unknown to the public and to the law authorities. Kinsey reports that about 37 percent of the white male population has had some homosexual experience and to the point of orgasm somewhere between adolescence and old age. Only half as many females as males have had homosexual experiences, and males have more frequent relations, continue their activities for more years, and are more promiscuous.[60] There is ample evidence that homosexual relationships exist to a considerable extent in our prisons and other one-sex communities. Most homosexual relationships are of a transitory nature, occurring perhaps only once or twice over a number of years, or as a result of a unique social situation. Kinsey reports that 4 percent of his sample of males were career homosexuals.

Some studies have shown that homosexuals are generally above average in intelligence and education and that, except for their sex behavior, they are generally law-abiding and hard working.[61] Most of them are unmar-

---

[57] *Ibid.*, p. 312.

[58] Clellan S. Ford and Frank A. Beach, *Patterns of Sexual Behavior* (New York: Harper & Row, Publishers, 1951), p. 130. Also see Ruth Benedict, *Patterns of Culture* (Boston: Houghton Mifflin Company, 1934).

[59] David S. Bailey, *Homosexuality and the Western Christian Tradition* (New York: David McKay Company, Inc., 1955).

[60] Kinsey *et al., Sexual Behavior in the Human Female,* and Kinsey, *et al., Sexual Behavior in the Human Male.*

[61] L. H. Loeser, "Sexual Psychopaths in the Military Service," *American Journal of Psychiatry,* 102:92–101 (July, 1945). Also see Kinsey *et al., Sexual Behavior in the Human Male.*

ried, separated, or divorced, and they come primarily from cities rather than from the country.

Homosexual behavior appears to be a product of the adoption of certain homosexual cultural norms and a conception of self. The channeling of sexual expressions into homosexual patterns must come through some cultural or subcultural definitions, just as do heterosexual relations. The very first homosexual experience among 127 homosexuals studied in Great Britain was usually with a school boy of the same age and generally constituted sex play, often in a school situation.[62] These experiences, however, did not necessarily lead to homosexuality as a pattern of sex behavior. The first "significant homosexual experience" can be defined as one carried out with an adult or repeated acts carried out with the same boy over a year or so. Over two thirds of such experiences were with another boy. Only 18 percent were first introduced to homosexuality as boys by adults and a further 11 percent had no experience of any sort until they were adults, and in all such cases their partner was an adult. Contrary to the popular view, seduction is not a very important factor. With most homosexuals there was a long period during which they fought against their homosexual activity before recognizing it as permanent behavior and assuming a conception of themselves as homosexuals.

Although our culture as a whole does not approve of this type of sex behavior, there exists a subcultural world of homosexuals who indoctrinate new individuals into it. This subcultural world consists of a special language which serves to keep its members secret from the out-group. There are special words for this sex behavior, such as "gay," "straight," and "queen," which are "similar in some respects to that of the underworld; in others to that of the theater." [63] Recognition by other homosexuals appears to involve particularly gestures, walk, clothes, and a special vocabulary.[64] There are subculturally defined ways in which homosexual relations are established. Many communities have special meeting places where homosexuals gather, usually at certain street corners, parks, taverns, clubs, or lavatories.[65] After an intensive study of 60 homosexuals in a large Canadian city the following conclusions were reached about the homosexual community.

The homosexual community thus consists of a large number of distinctive groups within which friendship binds the members together in a strong and

---

[62] Gordon Westwood, *A Minority: A Report on the Life of the Male Homosexual in Great Britain* (London: Longmans, Green & Co., Ltd., 1960), pp. 24–39.

[63] Donald W. Cory, *The Homosexual in America* (New York: Greenberg: Publisher, Inc., 1951), p. 90. Also see J. D. Mercer, *They Walk in the Shadow* (New York: Comet Press, 1959).

[64] Westwood, *op. cit.*, pp. 83–86.

[65] For discussion see Gordon Westwood, *Society and the Homosexual* (New York: E. P. Dutton & Co., Inc., 1953), Chaps. 19–21, and Cory, *op. cit.* Also see Westood, *A Minority*, pp. 68–77.

relatively enduring bond and between which the members are linked by tenuous but repeated sexual contacts. The result is that homosexuals within the city tend to know or know of each other, to recognize a number of common interests and common moral norms. . . . This community is in turn linked with other homosexual communities in Canada and the United States chiefly through the geographic mobility of its members.[66]

PROSTITUTION

While the extent of prostitution and the reaction of society to it has fluctuated over many years, the definition has remained the same. Prostitution is sexual intercourse on a promiscuous and mercenary basis, with emotional indifference.[67] The patron pays for this intimacy, but the method of payment often serves to cloud the definition of a true prostitute. For example, when a customer "dates" a shopgirl for an evening dinner and show and later has sex relations with her, the relationship is often on a mercenary, emotionally indifferent basis; yet the girl may not be considered, or consider herself, a real prostitute. Such a girl has a job, may have a family and other group attachments, and may not make a practice of exchanging sexual favors for an evening's entertainment.

Many women are promiscuous but are not prostitutes, for their sex relations have an element of affection, even if transitory. The prostitute "sells" her sex relations with an element of indifference. While some prostitutes may be selective of their customers on the basis of race, age, economic status, or physical attractiveness, generally an act of intercourse may be carried out with almost anyone. So indifferent are most prostitutes to the emotional aspect of sex relations that they rarely experience an orgasm with a customer, although they frequently do with their "pimp" or male consort.

Extent. The true prostitute might be considered as one who primarily makes her living from selling, for money, her sexual favors, but there is no way of ascertaining the number of these women.[68] Some of them have part- or full-time legitimate jobs which serve to cover up their real occupation. Usually statistical reports of prostitution are gathered from arrest figures, which themselves are not always reliable. Estimates have ranged from around 100,000 for the United States to as high as Reitman's estimate of 100,000 in 1931 for the city of Chicago alone.[69] It is likely that a much

[66] Maurice Leznoff and William A. Westley, "The Homosexual Community," *Social Problems,* 3:263 (Spring, 1956).

[67] In some countries, as well as in many of our states, it is not prostitution which is legally a criminal offense; rather, soliciting is the offense for which the prostitute is punished. See Williams, "Sex Offenses: The British Experience," *loc. cit.*

[68] There are also male prostitutes in homosexuality, and Kinsey estimates their number to be as high in large cities as the number of female prostitutes.

[69] Ben L. Reitman, *The Second Oldest Profession: A Study of the Prostitutes' "Business Manager"* (New York: Vanguard Press, Inc., 1931).

more conservative estimate than Reitman's figure is more nearly correct—possibly 275,000 live, in America, by prostitution alone.[70] About 69 percent of the total male population has some experience with prostitutes, but a large part have had only one or two experiences and some 15 to 20 percent have relations more than a few times a year.[71] Prostitution accounts for less than 10 percent of the total nonmarital sexual outlet for males. Not more than 1 percent of extramarital sexual intercourse is with prostitutes.

There appears to have been a steady decline in prostitution throughout the past two decades, except for periodic increases in wartime. During World War II it was estimated that in America there were about 600,000 regular prostitutes and about an equal number who were engaged in prostitution but had other means of livelihood.[72] Kinsey states that the frequency with which American males go to prostitutes has been reduced by about one half of what it was prior to World War I.[73] Kingsley Davis has explained the decrease in prostitution as a result of increased sexual freedom for women. As young women have less restraint in their sexual relations, it is easier for men to have sex relations without recourse to prostitutes.[74] Even if prostitution continues to decrease there will probably always be a certain amount of it, because there will continue to be a group of men who are able to secure sexual satisfactions only through payment for such services.

Patrons. Kinsey has indicated a number of reasons for the existence of prostitution, which has often been referred to as the oldest profession.[75] Men go to prostitutes because they do not have sufficient other sexual outlets. It is simpler and often cheaper to secure extramarital intercourse through a prostitute than by dating. Likewise, there are no responsibilities for a resulting pregnancy. Married men also go to prostitutes for the sake of variety in sexual intercourse, a variety often not otherwise available even to married persons. Others go if they are ineffective in securing sexual relations with women because they are timid, deformed, deaf, blind, or otherwise physically handicapped. Kingsley Davis has summarized the appeals of prostitution.

> In short, the attempt of society to control sexual expression, to tie it to social requirements, especially the attempt to tie it to the durable relation of marriage and the rearing of children, or to attach men to a celibate order, or to base sexual expression on love, creates the opportunity for prostitution.

[70] Edwin M. Lemert, *Social Pathology* (New York: McGraw-Hill Book Company, Inc., 1951), p. 231.

[71] Kinsey *et al.*, *Sexual Behavior in the Human Male,* p. 597.

[72] "Regulations of Vice," *Encyclopedia Americana* (1945 ed.; New York: Encyclopedia Americana), XXVIII, 58.

[73] Kinsey *et al.*, *Sexual Behavior in the Human Female,* p. 300.

[74] Kingsley Davis, "The Sociology of Prostitution," *American Sociological Review,* 2:744–755 (October, 1937).

[75] Kinsey *et al.*, *Sexual Behavior in the Human Male,* pp. 606–609.

It is analogous to the black market, which is the illegal but inevitable response to an attempt fully to control the economy. The craving for sexual variety, for perverse gratification, for novel and provocative surroundings, for ready and cheap release, for intercourse free from entangling cares and civilized pretense—all can be demanded from the woman whose interest lies solely in the price. The sole limitation on the man's satisfactions is in this instance not morality or convention, but his ability to pay.[76]

Societal Reactions. Attitudes toward prostitution have varied historically, and today vary in different countries. The attitude toward, and the social status of, the prostitute, as Davis has suggested, vary according to three conditions: (1) if the prostitute practices a certain discrimination in her customers, (2) if the earnings are used for some socially desirable goal, and (3) if the prostitute combines with her sexual role others which are more acceptable.[77] In ancient Greece, for example, brothel prostitutes were given a different status from the hetaerae who, educated in the arts, often were wealthy, powerful personages who had great influence on many important leaders. Although prostitutes, they generally were highly respected. The devadasis, or dancing girls, were connected with the temples of India for centuries and, besides singing and dancing, they engaged in temple prostitution. In general, these girls were the only Indian women who learned to read. Because the devadasi was one of a social group of religious prostitutes attached to the temple, the money was given to the temple and the act of intercourse was, to some extent, a religious ritual. Finally, the famous Japanese geishas can be cited as another example of women who could often engage in prostitution but still have high status in their society. They were trained in the arts, such as music, in conversation, and in social entertaining.

In France prostitution is illegal but condoned, and in many other parts of the world, particularly in Latin American, it is countenanced. Prostitution, particularly soliciting, is strongly disapproved under Anglo-American law, but there are persons who would tolerate it as necessary and even have certain areas of a city set aside for prostitutes who could, they naïvely believe, be regularly inspected for venereal disease. Prostitution is opposed on many grounds: (1) the degradation of the women who engage in it; (2) the threat to public health because of the transmission of venereal disease; (3) the effect on general law enforcement through police protection; (4) the effect on marital relations where recourse is had to prostitutes; and (5) the patronage of prostitutes by young persons, soldiers in particular, and its effect on national values.

Types of Prostitutes. Prostitutes can generally be classified according

---

[76] Kingsley Davis, "Prostitution," in Robert K. Merton and Robert A. Nisbet, eds., *Contemporary Social Problems* (New York: Harcourt, Brace & World, Inc., 1961), pp. 275-276.

[77] *Ibid.*, p. 267.

to their methods of operation. There are individual common prostitutes, organized houses of prostitution, call-girl and similar arrangements, and the high-class independent prostitute.[78] The individual common prostitute operates alone, procuring her trade as she can, on the streets or in such places as bars and hotel lobbies. She takes her customers to a prearranged cheap rooming house or hotel. Generally she has no connection with organized crime, but often she must pay for her own protection.

Similar to this kind of prostitute is the girl who works in an organized house or brothel. Such houses, which flourished in the red-light districts, were probably more predominant a few decades ago than they are today. They vary a great deal as to size, type of customers, and degree of respectability. New girls are "broken in" to the rules and regulations of the house, and each new prostitute soon learns various sex techniques. She learns how to handle a large number of customers without running the risk of losing them as patrons, how to deal with rough and uncouth men, and how to protect herself against venereal disease. These girls are often exploited by the madame or the manager of the house, for they have small chance to protect themselves, and a high percentage of their earnings, from 50 to 60 percent, is deducted for the "house," for linens, medical examinations, police protection, and the like. Usually these houses are operated in conjunction with some type of organized crime, through which police "protection" is usually secured. They are also usually associated with panderers who solicit for the girls, taxicab drivers who receive commissions, and pimps who live off the girls' earnings.

Another type of organized prostitution has become more and more prominent as police and health authorities have become more effective in doing away with street soliciting and red-light houses. This is the so-called call girl, who depends upon some organization for recruiting her patrons, although she may operate independently and have her own list of patrons who call upon her services. More frequently these patrons are secured through the intermediary services of a bellhop, a hotel desk clerk, a taxi driver or other type of agent who, for a fee, will give her telephone number to the patron or arrange for a room in a hotel where the girl is known. Usually call girls work in lower-class hotels, but even some of the best-known expensive hotels allow this type of prostitute to operate on their premises. During the past few years the call girl has become widely known, and her methods of operating have been thoroughly publicized. In some New York City cases patrons are reported to have paid large sums of money, reputedly as high as $500, for an evening's entertainment. Since this type of prostitution is less visible than the "parlor house" type, it gives more concealment to the prostitute and more anonymity to the patron.

---

[78] For a discussion of prostitutes see Walter C. Reckless, *Vice in Chicago* (Chicago: The University of Chicago Press, 1933). Also see Sheldon and Eleanor T. Glueck, *500 Delinquent Women* (New York: Alfred A. Knopf, Inc., 1934).

Some prostitution is not strictly organized as such, but is knowingly permitted and often even encouraged, through legitimate, but often shady, businesses, especially those in the commercial recreation industry, such as burlesque shows, night clubs, amusement parks, and the like. Taxi-dance halls particularly afford opportunities for the dancers to make engagements with their patrons, either in a room hired for the occasion or in the dancer's own room or apartment.[79] Through a variety of techniques performers in cabarets or burlesque shows recruit patrons for later dates.

There is, finally, the independent professional prostitute who lives in her own apartment house or flat, often in a more expensive part of town, and encourages middle- and upper-class patrons. Most of her clientele is secured on an individual basis through referrals from taxicab drivers or other persons.

Backgrounds of Prostitutes. Inasmuch as physical attractiveness and youth are a necessity for the prostitute, she is usually between seventeen and twenty-four years old, the peak ages being twenty and twenty-one years. Some prostitutes are older, but most of these have taken up the profession for special reasons, such as drug addiction, where their need for a continued supply of drugs has brought about increased financial demands. Single girls constitute the largest proportion of prostitutes, although many prostitutes are divorced or separated. Many of those who give their marital status as married are either living with or are married to pimps. On the whole, the professional common prostitute has less opportunity for marriage than the "high-class" type of prostitute.

Prostitutes are highly mobile persons, being often recruited from those classes and groups in society which are the most mobile. In the past the most recent migrant groups have swelled the ranks of prostitution, and at one time there was probably a disproportionate number of prostitutes from various foreign-born groups. Contemporary studies, however, seem to refute the idea that the foreign-born are overrepresented among prostitutes, although there is a disproportionate percentage of racial minorities.[80] The high mobility among Negroes, together with their lower socioeconomic conditions and their cultural standards of less rigid sex mores, has no doubt accounted for the higher proportion of Negro prostitutes. Other than the fact that prostitutes may primarily come from the lower socioeconomic groups, from which many women come, there is no evidence that they enter this profession because of poverty even though they may desire to better their economic status.

Although the modern prostitute differs a great deal from her flamboyantly dressed and heavily made-up predecessor, they still have characteristics in common. They have often been indoctrinated into the profession

---

[79] Paul Cressey, *Taxi-Dance Hall* (Chicago: The University of Chicago Press, 1932).
[80] Lemert, *op. cit.*, pp. 240–241.

by those who have been closely associated with prostitution, they have usually been poorly integrated into socially acceptable groups, and they seldom develop a high degree of organization within their profession. The very nature of the profession is competitive, each prostitute attempting to build up and keep her own clientele; hence there is little group solidarity except for cases where they must band together for protection from the police or from others who threaten their profession. Prostitutes have a limited argot or special language of their own, which is a mark of a degree of association and group cohesiveness.[81]

The Process of Prostitution. At one time it was rather widely believed that the prostitute was often the victim of a "white slaver" who had induced a sexually unexperienced girl to go into prostitution. The White-Slave-Traffic Act (the Mann Act) was aimed at eliminating what was called white slavery. Movies and sermons were used to portray graphically the evils which might befall an unsuspecting young girl, and it was believed that once a girl had thus been seduced her only alternative was to continue a life of prostitution. Another theory with very little substance to it is that women enter prostitution because of economic necessity. Actually, the earnings of most prostitutes, even allowing for deductions in payments to a madame, to a pimp, or for "protection" from the police, are higher than the earnings of most working women. The prostitute is paid for her loss of esteem through the societal reaction. In fact, Davis concludes that "since the occupation is lucrative, the interesting question is not why so many women become prostitutes, but why so few of them do." [82]

Present-day studies of girls who make their living in this way indicate that the process of becoming a prostitute is quite different. Generally there is agreement that most girls of this type have lived in local communities where the moral standards about sex have not been high. Although most have had considerable sexual experience, either with or without marriage, this fact in itself does not account for the prostitution. Generally the important other factor is association with persons on the fringe of prostitution:

> In the United States, these contacts with persons in or on the fringe of prostitution are largely with women, practitioners of prostitution themselves. Although some prostitutes are exploited by pimps, this parasitism is not usually the mode. One should expect that those girls who acquire pimps do so after they have entered the trade. It is very rare to find a case in American prostitution in which a girl who has never been a prostitute was persuaded or forced into the business by a pimp.[83]

---

[81] David Maurer, "Prostitutes and Criminal Argots," *American Journal of Sociology,* 44:546–550 (January, 1939).

[82] Davis, "Prostitution," *loc. cit.,* p. 277.

[83] Walter C. Reckless, *The Crime Problem* (2d ed.; New York: Appleton-Century-Crofts, Inc., 1955), p. 275. Reprinted by permission of the publisher.

Mere sexual experiences do not make the prostitute, for prostitution is largely a product of playing a social role.[84] Quasi-prostituting experiences, such as those of a waitress who after hours accepts favors from customers in return for sexual intercourse, may lead to prostitution. Arrest or treatment for venereal disease may strengthen this concept of self, as will the attitude of other prostitutes and persons associated with them.

After going into prostitution the girls tend to develop attitudes and behavior patterns which are a part of the social role they play. In this connection they develop an argot or special language for their work, special acts and services, patterns of bartering with their customers and an impersonal relationship with them, as well as a large number of rationalizations for their activities.[85]

Many prostitutes are able to leave this occupation for marriage or for employment as waitresses, domestic servants, or salesgirls. A few others are able to achieve a high standard of living and maintain it. But for many of them, eventually ravaged by venereal disease, alcoholism, and drug addiction, the end result is a derelict life, punctuated more or less regularly by arrests and jail sentences. From there it is an easy step to petty stealing and shoplifting.

Summary

Murderers and sex offenders generally are not of the career type. They should be looked at, however, from the perspective of social behavior and social norms. Murder can be thought of as arising primarily from a subculture of violence. Most homosexuality and prostitution can also be explained within a group and subcultural context.

Selected Readings

DAVIS, KINGSLEY. "Prostitution," in Robert K. Merton and Robert A. Nisbet eds., *Contemporary Social Problems*. New York: Harcourt, Brace & World, Inc., 1961. A sociological explanation of prostitution in terms of its relation to the general society.

LEMERT, EDWIN M. *Social Pathology*. New York: McGraw-Hill Book Company, Inc., 1951, Chap. 8. A comprehensive discussion of prostitution, including an analysis of the social visibility, societal reaction, and tolerance of prostitution.

RECKLESS, WALTER C. *Vice in Chicago*. Chicago: The University of Chicago Press, 1933. Although an older study, this is one of the best on prostitution. Includes case material.

"Sex Offenses." Volume 25 (Spring, 1960) of *Law and Contemporary Problems*. A symposium on the legal, anthropological, ethical, sociological, clinical, and

---

[84] Lemert, *op. cit.*, p. 270.   [85] Reckless, *The Crime Problem*, 2d ed., pp. 276–277.

medical-legal aspects of sex offenses. Includes also a study of British and Scandinavian experiences with sex offenders.

SUTHERLAND, EDWIN H. "The Sexual Psychopath Laws," *Journal of Criminal Law and Criminology*, 40:543–554 (January–February, 1950). A criticism of the concept of a psychopath and of the sexual psychopath laws.

WESTWOOD, GORDON. *A Minority: A Report on the Life of the Male Homosexual in Great Britain*. London: Longmans, Green & Co., Ltd., 1960. A study of 127 homosexuals primarily from a sociological approach.

WOLFGANG, MARVIN E. *Patterns in Criminal Homicide*. Philadelphia: University of Pennsylvania Press, 1958. Surveys the literature on homicide and studies nearly 600 cases of criminal homicide in Philadelphia, including both the offender and the victim. Presents the legal aspects of homicide, an analysis of race, sex, and age differences; methods and weapons used to inflict death; spatial patterns; relation to the use of alcohol; the degree of violence in homicide; and victim-precipitated homicide.

Chapter

10

Career Criminals

The characteristics of a fully developed criminal career have been previously indicated. This is a life organization built about criminal activities which include identification with crime, a conception of the self as a criminal, extensive association with criminal activities including other criminals, and, finally, progression in crime. The last represents progression toward more complex techniques and more frequent offenses, and, ultimately, making crime a frequent or a sole means of livelihood.

Obviously, persons who commit personal offenses such as murder and sex offenses can rarely be thought of as having criminal careers. It is true that professional murderers can be hired in other parts of the world, but seldom in the Western world. Those who have criminal careers generally commit theft or a crime involving some other form of gain. In this chapter three main types of criminal careers will be discussed, the ordinary criminal career, the organized criminal, and the most highly developed of all criminal careers, the professional. To serve as a contrast to them, three types of offenders who generally do not represent fully developed careers in crime will first be discussed—the occasional property offender, the habitual petty offender, and the white-collar offender.

Occasional Property Offenders

There are many offenders whose entire criminal records rarely consist of more than an occasional theft of some kind. Such offenses are incidental to their way of life and are so rare that these offenders in no way make a living from crime and they do not play a criminal role. This type of criminal behavior is often of a fortuitous nature, embarked upon at a particular moment, perhaps for a thrill or for suddenly needed funds. Often the offense is committed alone, and without prior criminal contacts; at other times there may be one companion, or at most two.

The occasional offender does not conceive of himself as a criminal. His offenses show little sophistication in the techniques of crime; he has small knowledge about crime and no vocabulary of criminal argot. To him stealing an automobile is more like "borrowing" the car and does not involve any of the techniques commonly associated with career types of offenders—selecting a special type of car, knowing how to open car locks, strip cars, find "fences," and so on. The occasional criminal makes no effort to progress to types of crimes requiring greater knowledge and skill.

It has been estimated that some 75 percent of all check forgeries are committed by persons who have no previous pattern of such behavior. Analyzing a small sample of twenty-nine cases, Lemert concluded that such persons generally do not come from a delinquency area, have no previous criminal record, or have had no previous contact with delinquents and criminals. He suggests that the novice check forger, who generally comes from the higher socioeconomic groups, is a product of certain difficult social situations in which he finds himself, a certain degree of social isolation, and a process of "closure" or "constriction of behavior alternatives subjectively held as available to the forger." [1]

Rural persons who commit theft usually have these characteristics of an occasional property offender. Many white-collar offenders also have them but these will be discussed in a separate section. A rural offender has described his offense in this way:

> The crime I done was a few miles from home. Perhaps I would of done it anywhere, as I had to be at a certain place at a certain time. I wanted to go to a dance, and my folks would not give me any money, so I really didn't care what I done. I had a car, but it was getting fixed and I didn't have the money to pay for it, so I stole my neighbor's car, just to show my folks I was not scared. I told them I was going to do it, but they didn't think I would. I have never thought about any crime as far as that goes. Like breaking into a place is way out of my line. I always was honest. My father is one of the best citizens. I consider him one of the best in that county. The boys I went with never stole anything. I never had any experience stealing cars. Guess it don't take any practice. When a boy I would use dad's car without asking him, but he didn't care. Sometimes he didn't like it very well, but he always got over it somehow. [2]

The Habitual Petty Offender

Habitual petty offenders [3] are one of the largest criminal groups. They constitute a large proportion of arrests, but since they do not often commit serious felonies they are commonly confined in city and county jails. Generally they begin their criminal activities while young, and they continue in petty crime, vagrancy, and disorderly conduct for a long period of time. These offenders have long criminal records, maintain extensive connections with a criminal underworld, and conceive of themselves as criminals. Habitual petty offenders do not, however, possess much sophistication about

[1] Edwin M. Lemert, "An Isolation Closure Theory of Naïve Check Forgery," *Journal of Criminal Law and Criminology,* 44:298 (September–October, 1953).

[2] From Marshall B. Clinard, "Rural Criminal Offenders," *American Journal of Sociology,* 50:44 (July, 1944).

[3] Here this term is being used to describe a behavior system and is not the legal term discussed on page 159.

crime, do not employ elaborate techniques, and are not particularly effective at "fixing" their cases in court.

The criminal pattern of habitual offenders is complicated by their conception of themselves as failures in social adjustment. This self-conception has considerable basis in fact in their tendency to be lazy, shiftless, and irresponsible; moreover, they are likely to have been arrested not only for petty stealing but also for alcoholism, for the sale of or addiction to drugs, for vagrancy, or for other similar offenses: "Consequently they are easily caught, and, since they have no means of protection such as the professional criminal has established, are easily convicted. They do not steal consistently at first, but as their reputation becomes known they find it more and more difficult to find employment and live without criminal activity." [4] The following is a good example of a habitual criminal career.

Doe was born in S. County, Washington, June 10, 1908, the second child in a family of 3 girls and 2 boys. Father was a blacksmith in a rural community, who provided very poorly for family. Mother divorced him when subject was 15 years old. Since 1928, defendant has traveled about the country, supporting himself chiefly by gambling. He has a delinquency record going back to the age of 15. He was married in 1931, separated six years later, divorced in 1941. No children. Wife had 8th grade education and a good reputation. Father was a heavy drinker, a cruel personality, and a poor provider for the family. The mother had an 8th grade education. Married again. Stepfather was a naturalized Austrian, mill worker and logger, 3 years of schooling, has police record for drunkenness in A. Was once on relief and certified for W.P.A. Has had no effective ties with defendant and no interest in him. Records on sisters and brothers are clear.

The defendant lived mainly in cheap hotels, although he considers his mother's address as his permanent address. Mother says John "just comes and goes, where, we don't know." Doe completed the 8th grade. According to mother he made a good record in school, leaving school when he was 13. As a child he attended the Church of God but does not now attend any church. He was never a member of any character building organization. He bowls and "does some drinking." He admitted that he often associated with prostitutes, gamblers, and "because of the need for narcotics," with addicts and peddlers. His mother said he "chased around with just no good people."

He weighs 185 pounds and is 5' 11" in height. His health history discloses the usual childhood diseases. He denied he was a narcotic addict. He admitted he had syphilis, and also "social drinking of whiskey." At the Veterans' Hospital he was given malarial fever treatment for tertiary syphilis. He was also diagnosed here as "psychopathic personality with asocial trends." His employment history is as follows, verified only in case of the shipyard job and Army service: 6–9–43 to 9–29–43, U.S. Army, private, discharged because of syphilis, 3–3–42 to 12–10–42 the Q.R. Shipyard, S. as shipfitter's helper, 95 cents per hour, left to enter army; 1937 to 1942, "several" employers as a gambler; 1928, salesman for used cars. The subject has also worked as a cigar salesman, traveled about the country as a gambler and salesman of electric razors. References consulted expressed the opinion that many of the defendant's activities were illegal "rackets," and that he had the reputation of being connected with prostitution as a pimp.[5]

The following is the report of [his] FBI fingerprint clearance, with explanatory comments given by the defendant.

Date	Place	Charge	Disposition	Defendant's Comment
4–26–26	PD A., Wn.	Dis. Con.	Dismissed	None
1–16–29	SO M., Wn.	Assault & Bat.	30 days: $22.80	"Drunk, hotel fight."
12–27–34	PD P. A., Wn.	Opera. auto with revoked driver's lic.	$75 fine and costs	"Served 5 days, paid fine."
12–20–34	PD S., Wn.	Manslaughter, reduced to accessory after fact	6 months jail, 5 months suspended	"Loaned friend car, who killed person getting off bus."
7– 5–38	PD B., Ida.	Investigation	None	"Gambling, picked up, told to get out of town."
7–31–39	SO L., Ida.	Susp. Vag.	None	"Just gambling, released."
7– 1–40	PD M., Wis.	Inv. Vag.	Susp. Sent. on vag. charge	"Served 10 days, released."
12–19–40	SO S., Calif.	Vio. Sec. 502 CVC	None	"Lost license, paid $75 fine, got 60 days on drunken driving."
4– 8–41	PD L., Neb.	Susp. white slavery	Released	"Roe and I were arrested, just asked taxi driver to get us a girl."
11–13–41	PD W.W., Wn.	Drunk	None	"Got $10 fine."
2– 4–42	SO T., Wn.	Burglary 2nd degree	0–15 yrs., deferred on condition join Army	"Could not get into Army, reported to parole officer until case dismissed 5–19–43" (verified)
6– 6–42	USM S., Wn.	O.P.A. (gas without coupons)	65 days jail	None
2–22–44	Bur. Narc., Wash.	Conceal. transp. poss. of opium	Current case	
2–22–44	PD S., Ore.	Burglary	Pending, warrant with USM	"Not guilty of charge"

[5] Walter C. Reckless, *The Crime Problem* (New York: Appleton-Century-Crofts, Inc., 1950), p. 104. Reprinted by permission of the publisher.

The following additional information, which does not duplicate the above, was obtained from the records of the sheriff's office in A., H., and M., Washington. (Offenses were committed in A.)

Date	Charge	Disposition	Explanation
9–11–23	Vagrancy	Dismissed	Police dismissed, subject only 15 yrs old
11–29–25	Drunk	Forfeited $25	Subject then only 17
7–18–27	Vagrancy	No disposition	Defendant not consulted for comment
6– 2–27	No driver's license	$5 fine	Defendant not consulted for comment
4–16–29	Vagrancy	None	Defendant not consulted for comment
1– 1–34	Drunken driving	$50 fine, license suspended	Defendant not consulted for comment
10–10–40	Drunk	$10 fine	Defendant not consulted for comment

SOURCE: Walter C. Reckless, *The Crime Problem* (New York: Appleton-Century-Crofts, Inc., 1950), pp. 103–104. Reprinted by permission of the publisher.

White-Collar Offenders

White-collar crime is committed by persons of high occupational status in connection with their occupations: it includes crimes by businessmen, politicians, doctors, and lawyers. Offenses by labor union officials are also included, since these leaders increasingly enjoy reasonably high status and are in important positions of trust where both power and influence can be exercised. White-collar crime does not include such crimes as murder or robbery, which could be committed by persons of any occupation. As has been pointed out in the discussions of crime, no act committed by white-collar groups, however unethical, should be considered as crime unless it is punishable by the state in some way. For example, the deliberate sale of a pair of odd-lot shoes which are too small for a customer is unethical but it is not a crime. This is also true of advertising which is unethical but not necessarily illegal.

One of the most significant recent cases of white-collar crime involved conspiracy in price-fixing and price-rigging violations of the federal antitrust laws by many of the leading electrical concerns of the United States. Twenty-nine leading electrical companies, including General Electric and Westinghouse and forty-five executives of the companies involved, were convicted in 1960 of illegalities in sales of heavy electrical equipment amounting to $1,750,000,000 a year. Such violations meant that government and private purchasers of equipment had been deceived about the open competitive nature of bids and had to pay sums far in excess of a regular bid. In the end, such illegal behavior, when perpetrated against a government agency, costs the taxpayers. Consequently, the convictions were later followed by civil suits amounting to millions of dollars filed by various federal, state, and local agencies to recover damages from the illegal price fixing and price rigging.

Fines amounting to $1,924,000 were imposed by the federal court, including a fine of $437,000 against General Electric and $372,000 against Westinghouse. Seven executives who were high enough in their companies to make policy were sentenced to thirty days in jail and twenty-four other executives received suspended jail sentences. Those sentenced to jail included three officials from General Electric and two from Westinghouse. Among the seven receiving sentences of thirty days in prison was a vice-president of General Electric, who also received a $12,500 fine, and a vice-president of Westinghouse, who was fined $2000. General Electric was fined $437,000, and Westinghouse $372,500. The salaries of the convicted executives ranged from $25,000 to $135,000 a year.

The jail sentences imposed on these business executives of this high status, and the severity of the fines, were unique punishments for white-collar crime. In pronouncing sentence, Judge Ganey said: "This is a shocking indictment of a vast section of our economy, for what is really at stake here is the survival of a kind of economy under which this country has grown great, the free enterprise system." The judge then noted that the court did not yet have enough evidence to convict the highest echelons in the electrical firms, but he went on to state the following: "One would be most naïve . . . to believe . . . these violations . . . so long persisted in and affecting so large a segment of the industry and involving so many millions upon millions of dollars were facts unknown to those responsible for the corporation and its conduct." [6]

Secret meetings had been arranged by representatives of the companies in hotel rooms. Participants were cautioned to conceal their bids in expense-account reports. At the secret meetings pricing schedules were arranged and arrangements were made for each company to submit the lowest bid for each of various contracts.

As an example of how the conspiracies worked, one of the most involved conspiracies, and also of longest duration, was in the switchgear division, which handles the sale of electric circuit breakers and the like.[7] This conspiracy operated for a number of years and was well organized. Conspirators had their own lingo and operating procedures. Attendance lists at secret meetings of the companies were called "Christmas card

---

[6] Quoted in Richard A. Smith, "The Incredible Electrical Conspiracy: I," *Fortune*, April, 1961, p. 133. Also see John Herling, *The Great Price Conspiracy: The Story of the Antitrust Violations in the Electrical Industry* (Washington: Robert B. Luce, Inc., 1962.)

[7] Herling, *op. cit.*, pp. 106–114.

lists"; meetings were known as "choir practices." The companies involved in this conspiracy—General Electric, Westinghouse, Allis-Chalmers, Federal Pacific, and I.T.E.—were given a code number which was used in the book price listings, and in communications between executives. The job of initiating memos on the subjects of jobs coming up, and on book price listings by each company, was rotated among executives, each performing this task for thirty days. Several times over a period of about eight years the conspiracy was given up because participants from the different firms tended to cheat on the "rules" of the conspiracy itself and attempted to "chisel" one another. However, slumps in profits and sales, combined with productive overcapacity, would generally force the executives to do something to remedy this situation. Since price fixing had succeeded before in solving the low-profit versus overcapacity dilemma, it was easily resorted to again. During slumps in profits and sales the division executives would be pressured from the central echelons to "do something" to raise profits and sales. This appeared to contribute to the decisions of lower-echelon executives to resume conspiracies. Through searching investigations during which extensive records, including minutes, of the conspiracy meetings were obtained, the government was able to secure sufficient evidence to indict the forty-five executives. Also, executives of one company decided to go along with the government and submitted documents and other supporting evidence to the investigators.

One writer has suggested that in these cases a factor of major importance was the separation of business and personal ethics.[8] In the minds of the executives there was a cleavage between ordinary morals and business morals; what applied in one area did not in another. Following these cases Henry Ford II, President of the Ford Motor Company, delivered a major address calling for strong condemnation by businessmen of violations of law.

CONCEPTION OF SELF

The major difference between white-collar crime and other forms of crime lies in the offender's conception of himself.[9] A white-collar offender does not play as consistent a criminal role as do many other types of offenders. He may play a variety of other roles, such as that of a respected citizen; hence the degree of recognition of the conflict between this role and that of a criminal offender may vary with different individuals. Since he is likely to regard himself as a respectable citizen, at most he regards himself as a "lawbreaker" and not as a "criminal." In this sense he has the attitude

---

[8] Smith, "The Incredible Electrical Conspiracy: II," *Fortune*, May, 1961, pp. 161–164 and 210–224.

[9] Edwin H. Sutherland, *White Collar Crime* (New York: Holt, Rinehart and Winston, Inc., 1949, reissued 1960), pp. 223–224.

of some offenders convicted of such crimes as statutory rape, nonsupport, or drunken driving.

Most career offenders, such as the ordinary, professional, or organized, think of themselves primarily as "criminals," and do not ordinarily put white-collar offenders in the same category with themselves. The higher social status of white-collar criminals makes it difficult for the general public, while not condoning their activities, to conceive of them as being associated with real criminal behavior, which is largely stereotyped as the more overt offenses. This attitude is, in turn, reflected in the conception that white-collar offenders have of themselves.[10]

DIFFERENTIAL ASSOCIATION

A new man in some white-collar occupations may learn the techniques by which the law can be violated, and he may build up a series of rationalizations such as "Business is business," or "One cannot conduct a profitable business or profession in any other way." This diffusion of illegal practices is spread from a person already in the occupation to new persons entering it, and from one business establishment, political machine, or other white-collar group to another. Sometimes the diffusion may be the result of an effort to meet illegal competitive activities of another business or political machine. How this diffusion of unethical and illegal behavior works is described by a person in the used-car business.

When I graduated from college I had plenty of ideals of honesty, fair play, and cooperation which I had acquired at home, in school, and from literature. My first job after graduation was selling typewriters. During the first day I learned that these machines were not sold at a uniform price but that a person who haggled and waited could get a machine at about half the list price. I felt that this was unfair to the customer who paid the list price. The other salesmen laughed at me and could not understand my silly attitude.

---

[10] Some people would, therefore, define behavior as really "criminal" only when it is considered so by general public opinion. According to such a definition neither violations of Prohibition laws, many types of gambling, nor similar kinds of illegal behavior should be considered as crimes. The same reasoning would be offered by those who feel that a crime has been committed only when an individual conceives of his offense as being criminal. According to this position, if persons do not think of their acts as violations of law either because of personal, situational, or occupational reasons, their acts would not be crimes no matter what the law or public opinion felt. Thus a person who refuses to register for the draft because of religious reasons, as did thousands of Jehovah's Witnesses during World War II, would not be considered a criminal even though many were sentenced to prison. Nor would a person necessarily be a criminal if he held certain political beliefs that were opposed by the majority. Many feel that statutory rape is often not criminal, since these cases, which involve sexual intercourse with girls under the age of eighteen, usually are with consent and seldom are the result of coercion. The same argument might apply to persons sentenced to prison for nonsupport of their families or for injuring someone through their negligent or drunken driving.

They told me to forget the things I had learned in school, and that you couldn't earn a pile of money by being strictly honest. When I replied that money wasn't everything they mocked at me: "Oh, no? Well, it helps." I had ideals and I resigned.

My next job was selling sewing machines. I was informed that one machine, which cost the company $18, was to be sold for $40 and another machine, which cost the company $19, was to be sold for $70, and that I was to sell the de luxe model whenever possible in preference to the cheaper model, and was given a list of the reasons why it was a better buy. When I told the sales manager that the business was dishonest and that I was quitting right then, he looked at me as if he thought I was crazy and said angrily: "There's not a cleaner business in the country."

It was quite a time before I could find another job. During this time I occasionally met some of my classmates and they related experiences similar to mine. They said they would starve if they were rigidly honest. All of them had girls and were looking forward to marriage and a comfortable standard of living, and they said they did not see how they could afford to be rigidly honest. My own feelings became less determined than they had been when I quit my first job.

Then I got an opportunity in the used-car business. I learned that this business had more tricks for fleecing customers than either of those I had tried previously. Cars with cracked cylinders, with half the teeth missing from the fly wheel, with everything wrong, were sold as "guaranteed." When the customer returned and demanded his guarantee, he had to sue to get it and very few went to that trouble and expense: the boss said you could depend on human nature. If hot cars could be taken in and sold safely, the boss did not hesitate. When I learned these things I did not quit as I had previously. I sometimes felt disgusted and wanted to quit, but I argued that I did not have much chance to find a legitimate firm. I knew that the game was rotten but it had to be played—the law of the jungle and that sort of thing. I knew that I was dishonest and to that extent felt that I was more honest than my fellows. The thing that struck me as strange was that all these people were proud of their ability to fleece customers. They boasted of their crookedness and were admired by their friends and enemies in proportion to their ability to get away with a crooked deal: it was called shrewdness. Another thing was that these people were unanimous in their denunciation of gangsters, robbers, burglars, and petty thieves. They never regarded themselves as in the same class and were bitterly indignant if accused of dishonesty; it was just good business.

Once in a while, as the years have passed, I have thought of myself as I was in college—idealistic, honest, and thoughtful of others—and have been momentarily ashamed of myself. Before long such memories became less and less frequent and it became difficult to distinguish me from my fellows. If you had accused me of dishonesty I would have denied the charge, but with slightly less vehemence than my fellow businessmen, for after all I had learned a different code of behavior.[11]

---

[11] Personal document in Sutherland, *White Collar Crime*, pp. 235–236. Copyright 1949 by Holt, Rinehart and Winston, Inc. Reissued 1961. Reprinted by special permission.

Most World War II black-market violations, involving violations of price and rationing regulations, appear to have had their origin in behavior learned in association with others.[12] Unethical and illegal practices were circulated in the trade as part of a definition of the situation, and rationalizations to support these violations of law were transmitted by this differential association. Many types of violations were picked up from conversations with businessmen and from descriptions of violations in trade newspapers and the general press. The following case illustrates, at least in part, the explanation of the violations through differential association:

During 1942 two eastern tire salesmen were instrumental in organizing a state-wide ring which purchased, received, and transferred new rubber tires and tubes without exchanging rationing certificates. In this case the two principal defendants arranged a meeting with retail tire dealers, who later became involved also, and explained the method that they were using to transfer tires without surrendering rationing or replenishment certificates and advised them that they could get any tires they needed. The plan was to have signed blank billheads on printed stationary to be used as "sign-offs," giving the impression that the principals were bona fide agents when acquiring tires in large metropolitan centers. The tires were then sold to the retailers at a cash profit and then resold to the latter mostly in bulk sales. No certificates were to be used in transferring these tires, and no accurate records were to be kept of the transactions, since it was suggested that the retailers bill these tires to "phony" individuals or to defunct garages which had been out of business for many years. The eventual tire ring involved a large number of dealers in scattered cities and towns who disposed of thousands of tires through this illegal device.[13]

When one considers that the social background of persons engaging in white-collar crime is different from that of such types as the ordinary, habitual, or organized criminal, one might ask why such exposure to illegal norms has any effect. Sutherland has listed a number of factors which tend to isolate businessmen from unfavorable definitions of illegal activity.[14] Agencies of mass communication play up conventional crime as abhorrent but treat white-collar crime much more leniently. Also, businessmen are often shielded from severe criticism by government officials, many of whom either were formerly in business or accepted contributions from business sources. Finally, businessmen chiefly associate with other businessmen, both at work and in their social life, so that the implications of white-collar crime are shielded from objective scrutiny.

---

[12] Marshall B. Clinard, *The Black Market* (New York: Holt, Rinehart and Winston, Inc., 1952), pp. 298–313.

[13] *Ibid.*, pp. 301–302.   [14] Sutherland, *op. cit.*, pp. 247–253.

ORGANIZATION AND WHITE-COLLAR CRIME

In many areas of white-collar crime there is often considerable organization. In fee splitting, for example, there must be a reciprocal relationship between the doctors. In political corruption there is an organized tie-up with businessmen or criminal syndicates. After studying the criminal behavior of seventy large corporations, Sutherland has pointed out a number of ways in which crimes among this type of business are organized: [15]

1. The criminality of corporations is persistent. In fact, in his study he found that 97.1 percent of the corporations were repeaters.[16]

2. The illegal behavior is far more extensive than the prosecutions would indicate; in many violations they are industry-wide. The fact that there are few prosecutions is due to the differential implementation of the criminal law.

3. There is generally no loss of status by an offender among his business associates.[17] In fact, while some members of his group may look down upon his behavior, others may even admire him for it. The shrewdness of the illegal transacation in which he was involved may give him added status.

4. In those areas which immediately affect white-collar offenders there is apt to be fairly general contempt for the law, the government as a whole, and for the personnel who administer the law.

5. Most white-collar business crimes are organized in the sense that the violation is a corporation affair or may extend to several corporations or subsidiaries. The organization may be more informal, as in false advertising. The organization of white-collar crime is indicated by the selection of certain types of illegal behavior. The selection of a particular form of illegal behavior, as Sutherland points out, may be either on the basis of the smallest danger of detection and difficulty in obtaining proof, or on the basis of the firm's capacity to "fix" the case, have the law not properly enforced, or change the law itself.[18]

ROLE ORIENTATIONS

Although many cases of white-collar crime can be satisfactorily explained by a theory of differential association, particularly if there had been

---

[15] *Ibid.*, pp. 217–220.

[16] Lane, in another study of business violations, did not reach such a conclusion and states that "unlike the crime records, the records of business violation show that recidivism is infrequent."—Robert E. Lane, "Why Business Men Violate the Law," *Journal of Criminal Law and Criminology*, 44:162 (July–August, 1953).

[17] In 1961 several high executives of the leading American electric companies referred to above were sentenced to jail for serious violations of law and some also received large fines. A number who resigned from their companies within a short time were appointed to positions of nearly equal executive responsibility in other companies—*The New York Times*, June 23, 1961, p. 37.

[18] Sutherland, *op. cit.*, pp. 230–233.

continuous and intimate association with unethical and illegal differential norms and at the same time some isolation from other norms, such a general theory as an explanation for *all* cases has several limitations. Some individuals do not engage in such practices, even though they are familiar with the techniques and the rationalizations of violations and frequently associate with persons similarly familiar. It is doubtful if any businessman could be in a given line of business for any length of time, either in peacetime or in wartime, without acquiring a rather complete knowledge of the illegalities practiced in it.

Persons tend, in part, to accept or reject opportunities for whitecollar crime according to their orientations toward their roles and their attitudes toward general social values. Some of these factors are negative attitudes toward other persons in general, the relative importance attached to status symbols of money as compared with law obedience, and the relative importance attached to personal, family, or business reputation.[19]

EMBEZZLEMENT AND OTHER VIOLATIONS OF TRUST

Embezzlement, a form of white-collar crime, is more common than most people assume. During 1951, for example, there were 608 reports of defalcations among banks insured by the Federal Deposit Insurance Corporation. These defalcations involved 759 persons, including 217 bank officials, 412 employees, and 130 other persons. An analysis of the irregularities showed currency manipulation, deposit manipulation, and loan manipulation as the chief violations. Some examples of such violations included mislabeling money bags of $50 in pennies as $500 in dimes, withholding deposits or making unauthorized charges to deposit accounts, extending credit to certain customers by means of unauthorized and unrecorded overdrafts, withholding interest or principal payments, forging or fabricating notes, and diverting income from service charges.[20]

Contrary to popular views and some scientific writers, white-collar crimes involving violations of trust, such as embezzlement, cannot be ex-

---

[19] Clinard, *The Black Market*. See also Lane, "Why Business Men Violate the Law," *loc. cit.*, pp. 161–163. Sutherland has stated, however, that he believes the variation in crimes of a group of corporations which he studied was not the result of personality factors.—Sutherland, *op. cit.*, p. 265. For example, corporations which have violated the antitrust laws have been doing so for over forty years. The presence of philanthropists and public-spirited citizens on boards of directors at various times has made little difference in the extent of violations. Moreover, the composition of boards of directors may vary from one concern to another and yet there are similar violations, indicating that personalities have little bearing on violation. These conclusions, however, have been reached with only preliminary research and, while true in some cases, cannot be taken as evidence that individuals have little to do with the violations.

[20] For a general account of the extent of embezzlement as well as many case histories, see Norman Jaspan with Hillel Black, *The Thief in White Collar* (Philadelphia: J. B. Lippincott Company, 1960).

plained simply by gambling, extravagant living standards, unusual family expenses, undesirable associates, inadequate income, or personality.[21] There have been a number of different classifications of embezzlers. Redden, after studying 7629 cases of embezzlement,[22] classified them into the more or less self-explanatory types of the little-fellow embezzler, the grab-and-run embezzler, the little-fellow-who-becomes-a-big-fellow embezzler, the one-hundred-thousand-dollar embezzler, the clever-account embezzler, the untrained bookkeeper embezzler who pockets errors he makes, the prevaricator embezzler who denies he receives goods or reports them as lost, damaged, or the like. Probably a more meaningful type was developed by Cressey, who used 65 cases and divided them on the basis of the systems of trust violation and on the basis of their rationalizations.[23] Thus he divided embezzlers into "independent businessmen," violators who were in business for themselves and who converted "deposits" which were entrusted to them for a specific purpose while at the same time maintaining their regular business. The second group was composed of the "long-term" violators or those individuals who as employed persons converted their employers' funds, or funds belonging to their employers' clients, by taking relatively small amounts over a period of time. "Absconders" were those who converted funds or property at hand and absconded with it, regardless of whether or not they were employed by the person or institution in whose trust the funds or property had been placed.

After studying 133 persons imprisoned for violations of trust as well as cases collected by others, Cressey has developed what he claims to be a universal explanation of trust violation. According to him, there are three elements which are necessary in a trust violation and all must be present: (1) opportunity and a nonsharable financial problem, (2) knowledge of how to violate, and (3) rationalizations about the violations.

First are the opportunity to commit a trust violation and the presence of what Cressey terms a nonsharable problem which, if revealed, would have lost the individual group approval: "Trusted persons become trust violators when they conceive of themselves as having a financial problem which is nonsharable." [24] These difficulties include important obligations where the status of the individual might be interfered with, a feeling of personal responsibility, or a business reversal. Others involve situations where the individual is isolated from others who might help him in his financial

---

[21] For some beliefs along this line see Virgil W. Peterson, *Why Honest People Steal* (Chicago: Chicago Crime Commission, 1947), p. 4, and *1000 Embezzlers* (Baltimore: United States Fidelity and Guaranty Co., 1937).

[22] Elizabeth Redden, "Embezzlement: A Study of One Kind of Criminal Behavior, with Prediction Tables Based on Fidelity Insurance Records." Unpublished doctoral dissertation, University of Chicago, 1939.

[23] Donald R. Cressey, *Other People's Money* (New York: The Free Press of Glencoe, 1953).

[24] *Ibid.*, p. 30.

difficulties, situations where the person's general behavior is not approved by others, and problems arising from employer-employee relations where the individual feels underpaid or overworked, or has a "grudge."

The second aspect of a violation is the knowledge of how to violate. Trust violators are aware "that this problem can be secretly resolved by a violation of the position of financial trust." Finally, the third necessary part of a violation is the presence of acceptable explanations "which enable them to adjust their conception of themselves as users of the entrusted funds or property." The potential trust violator defines the situation through rationalizations in terms which enable him to look upon his criminality as essentially noncriminal, such as merely "borrowing," as justified, as part of the "general irresponsibility" for which he is not completely accountable, or as due to unusual circumstances which are different in his case. Both the rationalizations and the techniques for violating are acquired through differential association. Indirectly the acceptance of a position of trust carries with it some idea of possible violation through the mere fact of being bonded; moreover, there are conversations with others about violations of trust, and observance of others who are dishonest.

Unfortunately, Cressey's study describes only the process of violation and not the characteristics of a person who violates a trust obligation. Moreover, it does not tell us what specific situations are likely to be more productive of violations. Perhaps future studies will enable us to predict with some accuracy who will violate, and what situations are more likely than others to lead to violations of trust.[25]

Ordinary Criminal Careers

A criminal career more typical than any previously described is the one which moves from juvenile gang associations to adult criminal behavior of a more serious type, primarily in burglary, automobile theft, or robbery. Such a career involves early group experience with delinquent behavior patterns. These experiences are intense in the sense that effective delinquent models have been furnished to the individual. There is a continuous acquisition of techniques and rationalizations about crime, and the delinquent acts move from petty to more serious offenses. During this progression there are usually a considerable number of experiences with official agencies including the police courts, juvenile authorities, juvenile institutions, reformatories and, finally, prison. Institutional experience adds to the offender's status and sophistication and helps mold his conception of himself as a criminal. The degree of development and sophistication

---

[25] Some suggestions for the prevention of embezzlement have been given by Cressey, *ibid.*, pp. 153–157, and by Jaspan and Black, *op. cit.*, pp. 233–254.

in crime of an ordinary career, however, is much less than among professional criminals. It is for these reasons that they are termed "ordinary" criminal careers.[26] These careers, as noted in an earlier chapter, usually terminate somewhere between the early twenties and the late twenties or early thirties. This type has been referred to by Cohen and Short as those gang subcultures which carry out semiprofessional theft with a utilitarian emphasis and represent the later stages of a long history of frequent stealing which began at an early age.[27] It is likely that boys going in for these activities represent small cliques in larger gangs who are "serious minded" about their delinquency rather than being nonutilitarian and malicious. They are characterized by

a. the use of strong-arm methods (robbery) of obtaining money.
b. the sale of stolen articles, versus using for oneself, giving or throwing away, or returning stolen articles.
c. stating, as a reason for continued stealing, "want things" or "need money" versus stealing for excitement, because others do it, because they like to, or for spite.[28]

A comparison of 32 Negro armed robbers with 368 other Negro offenders revealed a pattern which can be designated as an ordinary criminal career.[29] Their arrest histories showed a mean of 18.2 arrests.

> An early patterning of stealing from their parents, from school, and on the street; truancy, and suspension or expulsion from school; street fighting, association with older delinquents, and juvenile delinquent gang memberships, all were usually evident in their social backgrounds. When compared with the men in the other criminal categories it was found that there was more destruction of property in their delinquent activities, and there were more frequent fights with schoolmates, male teachers, and delinquent companions. There was a higher incidence of "mugging" and purse snatching. They had more often been the leaders of delinquent gangs, and, they claimed they were leaders because of their superior size and physical strength. . . . Criminal progression appeared to occur at a more rapid rate with an early trend toward crimes of violence—from petty thefts and playground fights, to the rolling of drunks and homosexuals, and on to holdups with such weapons as pistols and knives.[30]

As juvenile delinquents they frequently carried and used weapons of violence.

---

[26] Much the same distinction is made by Walter C. Reckless. See his chapter, "Ordinary and Professional Criminal Careers," in *The Crime Problem* (3d ed.; New York: Appleton-Century-Crofts, Inc., 1961), Chap. 9.

[27] Albert K. Cohen and James F. Short, Jr., "Research in Delinquent Subcultures," *Journal of Social Issues*, 14:20–37, No. 3 (1958).

[28] *Ibid.*, p. 13.

[29] Julian B. Roebuck and Mervyn L. Cadwallader, "The Negro Armed Robber as a Criminal Type: The Construction and Application of a Typology," *Pacific Sociological Review*, 4:21–26 (Spring, 1961).

[30] *Ibid.*, p. 24.

"Sometimes you gotta carry some heat to put the pressure on. Some people won't get up off that money less they see you are ready. The studs I ran with, Jack, had to have some kind of heat . . . knife, gun, blackjack or something." [31]

One study has described five brothers whose criminal careers cost the state of Illinois $25,000 for board alone during the total of fifty-five years they spent in institutions.[32] All five brothers started begging at around five years of age. John and Elwood, the oldest brothers, began their delinquency in company with a gang of twelve boys ranging in age from five to twelve. "Their playgrounds were the alleys, streets, and railroad yards; their activities were largely spontaneous, random, and unsupervised; simple forms of stealing were interspersed with nondelinquent activities with little realization of their moral implications." They stole all varieties of objects, most of them for fun. The more experienced and older delinquents furnished the models and encouraged the younger and less experienced to engage in more serious thefts.

The three younger brothers became involved in this network chiefly through the indoctrination of their older brothers and other boys. All moved from begging to truancy and petty stealing, then to stealing more valuable objects. All of them were arrested by the police many times from the age of five on, for wandering the streets late at night, begging and stealing. They all appeared frequently in courts on dependency and delinquency complaints and all served at least ten periods of confinement in correctional and penal institutions besides being placed on probation and parole several times.

The delinquent and criminal acts of the five brothers were not isolated acts but were rather part of the organized life of the community. Their contacts with conventional society were limited. They had intimate association with at least 250 known delinquents and criminals. "They lived in a social world in which delinquency served a dual purpose—on the one hand, it was a means by which they secured the friendly regard, approval, and approbation of their fellows, while on the other hand, it served as a source of economic gain." Their associations gave them the moral sanction to commit crime and sell their stolen articles. Edward was arrested at twenty-one for stealing a car and at twenty-four for carrying a concealed weapon, James at seventeen was arrested four times for attempted or actual theft of autos; Michael at fifteen for robbery with a gun, burglary and larceny of cars, and Carl at thirteen for the theft of two cars. Nearly all their crimes were committed in company with either a brother or a brother and other persons. All except one had terminated their criminal careers by the time they were twenty-five years of age.

---

[31] *Ibid.*

[32] Clifford R. Shaw, Henry D. McKay, and James F. McDonald, *Brothers in Crime* (Chicago: The University of Chicago Press, 1938). Quotations are from pages 109 and 119.

Organized Crime

Organized crime is represented by criminal syndicates or rings which engage in criminal activities as a career. The public bestows the epithet "mobster" or "gangster" upon those active in organized crime, even though these terms technically should be reserved for those few individuals of this group who use force and violence. Criminal syndicates are usually well organized, with a boss, lieutenants, and subaffiliates, and their operations often are of an intracity, intercity, or interstate character. The characteristic features of organized crime are these:

1. Hierarchy involving a system of specifically defined relationships with mutual obligations and privileges.
2. Not confined by political or geographic boundaries. Intracity or intercity; intra- or interstate.
3. Dependence upon
   a. the use of force and violence to maintain internal discipline and restrain competition;
   b. the securing and maintaining of permanent immunity from interference from law enforcement and other agencies of government.
4. Criminals operating for large financial gains and specializing in one or more combinations of enterprises which fall in the area of moral problems where public opinion is divided.
5. Striving for either monopolistic control or establishment of spheres of influence between or among different organizations.

FEUDAL STRUCTURE

The most important characteristic of organized crime is its feudal pattern. All-powerful "lords of the underworld" or leaders of particular syndicates have the allegiance of several underlords who, in turn, have coteries of henchmen varying from lieutenants to what might be termed "serfs." Burgess has stated that an organized crime syndicate is "held together by powerful leaders, by intense personal loyalties, by the gangsters' code of morals, by alliances and agreements with rival gangster chiefs, and by their common warfare against the forces of organized society." [33]

There are interlocking relations between one syndicate and another and between one individual leader and another so that a given syndicate or leader may be engaged in several areas of crime. These syndicates may use strong-arm techniques to enforce their rules among their own members, to eliminate other syndicates when peaceful methods have failed, and to secure the cooperation of intended victims among the general public. Al-

---

[33] Ernest W. Burgess, "Summary and Recommendations," *Illinois Crime Survey* (Chicago: Illinois Association for Criminal Justice, 1929), Pt. 3, p. 1092.

though this use of force is becoming much less a feature of organized crime than it was in the Capone era of Prohibition days, it still is a characteristic of organized as compared with professional crime.

WIDESPREAD OPERATIONS

Organized criminal operations involve branches of the syndicate as well as tie-ups with legitimate enterprises which give them public respectability and power in the community. The Senate Special Committee to Investigate Organized Crime found that organized criminals were engaged in about fifty areas of legitimate business enterprises, in particular the liquor industry, automobile and trucking business, steel, oil, banking and finance, the garment industry, juke boxes, cigarette-vending and slot machines, real estate, hotels, restaurants, night clubs, food products, and unions.[34]

In 1951 the two major crime syndicates in this country were the Accardo-Guzik-Fischetti syndicate, whose headquarters were in Chicago but whose influence was felt in Kansas City, Dallas, Miami, Las Vegas, and the West Coast, and the Costello-Adonis-Lansky syndicate, emanating from New York City, with operations in Saratoga, New Jersey, New Orleans, Miami, Las Vegas, and the West Coast.[35] Both groups had close relationships, and their leaders appeared to know one another personally.

ORGANIZED CRIME AND POLITICS

Organized crime is more than a feudal hierarchy built to carry on particular criminal activities; it is also organized to keep its members out of legal entanglements. Connections with political machines or with branches of the legal system, such as the police or courts, bring almost permanent immunity from arrest or, if there should be an arrest, enable the "fix" to be applied.

The Kefauver Committee reported in 1951 that in New York City the Gross bookmaking empire had paid over $1,000,000 a year for police protection; in Philadelphia approximately $152,000 was paid each month in thirty-eight police districts.[36] The fix is not worked out individually by each criminal when a need arises; instead, organized criminal syndicates maintain such close political connections that local immunity for their members is almost assured, especially for the top men in the syndicate.

---

[34] Third Interim Report of the Special Committee to Investigate Organized Crime in Interstate Commerce, United States Senate, 82d Cong., 1st Sess., S.R. 307 (Washington, D.C.: 1951), pp. 171–181. Also see Estes Kefauver, *Crime in America* (New York: Doubleday & Company, Inc., 1951).

[35] Third Interim Report of the Special Committee to Investigate Organized Crime in Interstate Commerce, pp. 1–2.

[36] *Ibid.*, p. 184.

The same pattern of organized crime found in large metropolitan areas exists in the medium-sized cities with similar evidence of official sanction or protection. In some cases the protection is obtained by the payment of bribes to public officials, often on a regular basis pursuant to a carefully conceived system. In other cases, the racketeering elements make substantial contributions to political campaigns of officials who can be relied upon to tolerate their activities. Sometimes these contributions will support a whole slate of officers in more than one political party, giving the racketeers virtual control of the governing body.[37]

Organized criminal syndicates maintain their close association with political machines either through direct payoffs or through delivery of votes, honest or fraudulent. The payoffs are used by politicians, police commissioners, or police captains or lieutenants either as personal assets or as contributions for the political machine. Both the contributions and the aid in delivering votes, which usually requires only the endorsement of the party by the syndicate leader in local community areas, bring immunity, either direct or indirect. Immunity also comes through the appointment of councilmen, police officers, prosecutors, judges, and other government officials who will cooperate with the leaders of organized crime and who will pass the word along that the syndicate is to be let alone. The head of the Department of Justice's Special Group on Organized Crime declared in 1960: "The underworld gets about $9 billion of the estimated $47 billion spent annually on illegal gambling. . . . Fully half of the syndicates' income from gambling is earmarked for protection money paid to police and politicians." [38]

The relation of political machines to organized crime has been repeatedly demonstrated in the past by the close relationship of Chicago Democratic and Republican organizations to various gang leaders such as Al Capone.[39] The bosses of the Chicago underworld were, first, Big Jim Colosimo, then John Torrio, Mont Tennes, Scarface Al Capone, and a host of others. Even the funerals of underworld leaders have revealed the closeness of the relation between politicians and organized criminals. In the 1920's two congressmen and seven aldermen were honorary pallbearers at Big Jim Colosimo's funeral; at Anthony D'Andrea's funeral twenty-one judges were honorary pallbearers.[40]

The Seabury investigation in New York City in 1930 and 1931 showed

[37] Final Report of the Special Committee to Investigate Organized Crime in Interstate Commerce, United States Senate, 82d Cong., 1st Sess., S.R. 725 (Washington, D.C.: 1951), p. 5.

[38] Quoted in Daniel P. Moynihan, "The Private Government of Crime," The Reporter, July 6, 1961, p. 14.

[39] Virgil W. Peterson, Barbarians in Our Midst (Boston: Little, Brown & Company, 1952).

[40] John Landesco, "Organized Crime," Illinois Crime Survey, Pt. 3, pp. 1033–1034.

that Tammany Hall controlled the judges and at the same time performed services for organized crime. James J. Hines, leader of Tammany Hall in New York City in the 1930's, had close relations with New York underworld leaders, for which he finally was sent to Sing Sing. Frank Costello, leader of an organized criminal syndicate who was later sent to prison, was found in 1950 to have been friendly with many of the district leaders of the Democratic party and with many judges in New York City. Some political appointments were Costello's friends. Asked about them, Costello replied, "I know them, know them well and maybe they got a little confidence in me." [41]

AREAS OF ORGANIZED CRIME

Organized crime largely operates in those areas which are "moral problems," areas where public sentiment is divided over the actual immorality of such behavior.[42] As a result, organized crime finds less coordinated opposition from the general public and law-enforcement agencies in these areas. Furthermore, since so many people want some of these services, the illegal revenues from them are large. It is thus possible for organized racketeers to make a substantial income and at the same time pay off properly those political officials without whose connivance no organized criminal activity could operate. Some of the more important areas in which organized crime has operated include the following: liquor, prostitution, narcotics, gambling, union shakedowns, and industrial and business shakedowns.

During Prohibition organized crime operated most extensively in prostitution and in alcohol, which largely went out with the repeal of the Prohibition Amendment, except for running liquor into some dry states. Prostitution is still a large area for racketeering but not as large or as profitable as it was formerly. It now usually involves a syndicate of many prostitutes who are chiefly "call girls" and for whom the organized syndicate helps arrange the necessary "fix" or other over-all business arrangements. Another area of organized crime has been, and still is, the drug traffic.

GAMBLING

Organized crime today finds that gambling and various forms of labor and industry racketeering bring the highest returns; hence it dominates these activities. To wager money or other objects upon an outcome which

---

[41] Third Interim Report of the Special Committee to Investigate Organized Crime in Interstate Commerce, p. 121.

[42] Richard Fuller and Richard R. Myers, "Some Aspects of a Theory of Social Problems," *American Sociological Review*, 6:24–32 (February, 1941).

largely depends on chance is gambling.[43] Gambling is illegal in nearly all parts of the United States, although most forms of gambling are legal in Nevada.

There are wide variations in the attitudes of people toward private and public gambling. Gambling among friends for small stakes in such card games as poker, blackjack, and bridge is generally not regarded as gambling which is essentially bad. When gambling becomes public and commercialized so that its operation requires bets from a great many persons in an impersonal urban situation over which the individual has practically no control, public attitudes are divided over its social usefulness; moreover, it is an inviting situation for organized racketeers.

Generally, wherever opportunities are presented for gambling, large numbers of persons are interested in participating, even though they may be publicly against it. There appear to be a number of reasons for this.[44] Gambling appeals because of the chance factor for success, regardless of the type of skill involved in it. In some societies, generally those where social status is achieved by, and depends upon, successful competition for money and material goods, the chance element is more important than in others. In Western European society it is very difficult to distinguish between situations in which there is a chance element called gambling and those situations like stock market or commodity speculations or, indeed, many other financial transactions which also contain a chance element and yet are not officially classified as forms of gambling.

Gambling also represents relief from the routine and boredom of contemporary urban life. Betting on something is often fascinating both to the participant and to the spectator. Whether one wins or not, for a while there is excitement over the possible result. The appeal of different forms of gambling varies according to social class, sex, and other differences.

In some parts of Western society opposition to commercialized gambling seems to be based on the fact that gambling does not perform any socially productive economic functions, for in a sense it is securing money without earning it through work. Moreover, the fact that some people have lost all their money through excessive gambling has stirred up much opposition to it. The odds in some forms of gambling, particularly organized gambling, are so great that the chances of winning are actually very small. Finally, because commercialized gambling must bribe law-enforcement officers and other public officials in order to secure the necessary "protection," it is opposed by many because of the effect of its methods.

---

[43] For a full discussion, see the series of articles on "Gambling," *The Annals*, Vol. 269 (May, 1950). This issue dealt with the legal status, various forms of gambling, the gambler, and gambling in foreign countries.

[44] Herbert A. Bloch, "The Sociology of Gambling," *American Journal of Sociology*, 57:215–221 (November, 1951), and David D. Allen, *The Nature of Gambling* (New York: Coward-McCann, Inc., 1952).

Commercialized gambling is of two types. In one, the person gambles in an establishment with such devices as roulette wheels, dice, or slot machines. In the other, bets are placed on larger events, such as illegal lotteries and "policy," the "numbers racket," horse or dog races, or various sports events. Policy is a variation of the lottery in that bets are placed on the drawing of numbers. The numbers racket involves a bet placed on the three digits of certain events such as, for example, the daily United States Treasury balance of clearinghouse totals or racing pari-mutuels. In both policy and the numbers racket the amount of the wager, as well as the chance of winning, is small, but the odds paid are large.

The lucrative returns from gambling enterprises make them most attractive to organized crime. A considerable organization is required to distribute forms and collect bets. In the Detroit numbers racket, which has been studied by Carlson, there were some thirty-five separate organizations, some of which were grouped into syndicates. These organizations had "cover banks" which underwrote the bets placed by the local gambling place as a protection against a run on a particular number. For efficient operation the gambling syndicate employed writers or runners, pick-up men or collectors of bets, cashiers, clerks, checkers, and operators. Tickets with winning numbers were redeemed by cashiers on the spot; if the holders were not present, the money was delivered by a runner.[45] There is also the "fix," as one New York bookmaker has stated:

> "The whole business is pretty damn complicated, let me tell you. I gotta worry about my runners so I gotta pay off beat cops, squad cars, detectives, everybody. In the last ten years I paid off $1 million to cops. It cuts into the profits, but, what the hell, a business is a business." [46]

The present-day bookmaker with whom the public deals is often nothing more than a runner or contact man who tells his customers what unlisted telephone number to use to place their bets. He gives the bettor a code, such as the cryptic words: "This is Doc for Hollywood." The bettor then simply phones his bets directly to headquarters, and the runner later settles with the bettor for his wins or losses.

Gambling interests are protected through collusion between politicians and organized criminal syndicates. In 1951 the Special Senate Committee to Investigate Organized Crime reported that the most shocking thing about organized criminal activities in gambling was "the extent of official corruption and connivance in facilitating and promoting organized crime." Top mobsters were found to be immune from prosecution, policemen and

---

[45] Gustav G. Carlson, "Number Gambling: A Study of a Culture Complex." Unpublished doctoral dissertation, University of Michigan, Ann Arbor, 1940.

[46] Roger Kahn and Richard Schaap "The Mania to Bet on Sports," *Newsweek*, June 6, 1960, p. 41. Reprinted by permission.

sheriffs were bribed, and political leaders were bought off. The committee gathered evidence of corruption of law-enforcement officers in practically all the numerous cities in which it held hearings. In New York City a threat of testimony by a bookmaker brought about the resignation of many police officials. The sheriff of the county in which Miami is located was reported to have had $2500 in assets when elected, and six years later $75,000; one deputy testified that another deputy had delivered a $36,000 pay-off from gamblers to the sheriff's wife.

Betting on horse races began as a personal type of gambling, later shifted to clubs and county fairs, and now operates almost exclusively in a complex urban environment, largely indulged in by millions of urban persons who seldom see horses, let alone horse races. Although several states permit pari-mutuel betting at race tracks, almost every state prohibits absentee betting through bookmakers. In many states, regardless of whether pari-mutuel betting is legal or not, absentee betting through organized criminal syndicates constitutes a large-scale violation of law.

In many large cities, as well as elsewhere, some bookmakers special-ize in bets on other events—professional boxing matches, baseball, hockey, and professional or amateur football and basketball games. Formerly the betting was concentrated on professional events, but college football and basketball games have drawn more and more of it. In fact, one reason given for canceling the Army–Notre Dame football game series in 1948 was the extremely heavy betting, one estimate on the gamblers' pay-off wires being as high as $15,000,000 to $20,000,000. Investigations have also revealed extensive syndicated betting on college basketball games in Madison Square Garden in New York. In 1951 a series of gambling cases involved a large number of star basketball players of four New York colleges, a midwestern, and a southern university, who were bribed either to throw important games or to keep the point score within a range designated by gambling syndicates. The usual price received by these college athletes was $500 to $1500 a game. A similar series of cases occurred in 1961. (See page 171.)

In 1951 the Special Senate Committee to Investigate Crime found that organized criminals derive enormous profits from gambling. The "take" on a slot machine is about $50 a week; thus a mere two hundred machines would bring in $10,000 weekly. A single one of the eight large policy wheels in Chicago made an annual net profit of over $1,000,000. One New Jersey gambling casino made over $250,000 a year; another, in Florida, $205,000; and a Kansas City newsstand handbook, $100,000. According to a 1960 survey, week-end bets alone on football, baseball, basketball, horse racing, and boxing were as follows:

> *Football:* On a typical fall week end, with 30 to 35 college and professional football games on the bookmakers' boards, the illegal betting (the "handle") fluctuates between $50 million and $60 million.

Baseball: Throughout the summer, with sixteen or more major-league games scheduled each week end, the handle runs between $40 million and $50 million.

Basketball: On a Friday–Saturday week end, with a full schedule of 40 college and professional games, the basketball handle approaches $15 million, but is gradually slipping. The reason: suspected fixes.

Horse Racing: Except for special races (off-track betting on the Kentucky Derby may exceed $30 million), the racing handle is roughly $25 million on any week end. As a twelve-month, daily enterprise, racing has the largest illegal handle of any sport.

Boxing: Except for a heavyweight championship fight, two-day action rarely exceeds $2 million. Boxing has lost much of its betting appeal in the sport's general decline.[47]

Some people believe that the solution to illegal gambling in the United States is to legalize it as it is in Nevada. Most countries have state lotteries, sweepstakes, or other forms of betting which bring in much revenue for the state after the winners are paid off. Sweden, for example, legalized betting on sports pools in 1934, the betting being supervised by a corporation consisting of members of several sports organizations. Some of the revenue is used for such organizations and for expenses, but the largest share goes to the government.

There is some question as to whether commercialized gambling could be legalized throughout the United States. Most but not all students of the problem believe that legalization is not the solution.[48] They argue that it would be too large an enterprise for the government and, in the long run, would add nothing to the economy even if it did produce revenue. In other countries gambling has not been associated with organized crime; in fact, most European countries do not have this type of crime. Legalized gambling in the United States might tend to become infiltrated by the same criminal elements that now control illegal gambling, as has happened to a considerable extent in Nevada.[49] Moreover, politicians and public officials would be even more vulnerable to corruption. Finally, the American people, on the whole, do not participate in commercialized forms of gambling, according to a Gallup poll taken in 1951.[50] Should gambling be legalized they might engage in it more extensively than they do now, or than is done in countries where gambling is legal.

Probably the most effective way to deal with gambling in the United States is to develop in the public a realization not only of the effects of

---

[47] Kahn and Schaap, *loc. cit.,* p. 39.

[48] See, for example, Virgil W. Peterson, "Gambling: Should It Be Legalized?" *Journal of Criminal Law and Criminology,* 40:259–329 (September, 1949), and Allen, *op. cit.*

[49] See Kefauver, *op. cit.,* pp. 229–237.

[50] Public Opinion News Service, June 11, 1951, American Institute of Public Opinion, Princeton, N.J. Cited in Herbert L. Marx ed., *Gambling in America* (New York: The H. W. Wilson Company, 1952), p. 26.

commercialized gambling on law-enforcement personnel and other public officials but of the need for stronger enforcement of the laws against gambling. The states will need help from the federal government, which can give it because commercialized gambling is interstate. Since 1951, for example, there has been a federal tax on bookmakers amounting to 10 percent of the gross bets each month and a $50 tax on those who accept bets. Finally, federal lotteries might succeed in diverting some illegal betting, but their use would present many difficulties. In 1961 three new federal laws were passed making it a federal crime to

1. cross state lines or use the mails to distribute the proceeds of gambling, prostitution, narcotics, or illegal liquor sales. The law was aimed at "absentee" organized criminals who operate outside the jurisdiction of state officials. Violators face a maximum sentence of five years in jail and a $10,000 fine.
2. carry or send across state lines records, ticket slips or other data used in bookmaking, the numbers racket, or sports wagering pools. Exempted were betting slips sent to Nevada, a state where gambling is legal, and pari-mutuel tickets used at tracks where betting is legal.
3. use such communication facilities as cables, telephones, or the telegraph to transmit across state lines any information useful to gamblers. Common carriers under the jurisdiction of the Federal Communications Commission must withdraw service from subscribers known to be using the facility for gambling.

RACKETEERING IN LABOR UNIONS AND BUSINESS

Second only to gambling in its attractiveness to organized crime is racketeering in labor unions and business. The term "racketeering" is often loosely used to refer to almost any criminal activity. In a strict sense, however, it refers to the use of organized force to maintain control over some organization, to extort money from it, or to force some services upon it. Racketeering has been used to maintain control of the members of a union or to defeat another union which is competing with it for members. In business racketeering, efforts are made to force concerns to pay tribute to "protect" themselves from violence, such as damaging clothes in a cleaning and dyeing establishment, or to maintain price fixing. Tribute may also be demanded to avoid a wildcat strike. Although racketeering activities have affected many industries, they have been particularly prevalent in the movies, building trades, liquor, laundry and cleaning establishments, and the waterfront, trucking, and loading businesses.[51] Senate investigations of the relation of certain union officials with organized criminals have in recent years brought this area of organized crime particularly to the

[51] Malcolm Johnson, *Crime on the Labor Front* (New York: McGraw-Hill Book Company, Inc., 1950).

public's attention.[52] The New York water front, for example, has a long history of domination by labor racketeers, and repeated attempts on the part of local and state officials to control this situation in the past have proved unsuccessful. Investigations in 1953 indicated that the average pier boss is largely "responsible for the crime and corruption on the waterfront." [53] The pier boss usually operates from his position within the union, and his "ultimate power rests in his control of some number of the locals that supply the dock-wallopers to the stevedoring concerns." He has close connections with the underworld, and "in some instances his rise to power has been sponsored by unscrupulous management officials. Connivance with such individuals has also been necessary, at times, to insure the retention of his position. More than one industry spokesman has openly boasted that such men are good for the waterfront because they 'keep the dock-walloper in his place and maintain order.'"

Racketeers in unions and businesses may use overt force in the form of property damage or physical violence to intimidate; or they may be more subtle and simply threaten a strike. Hostetter has distinguished two types of rackets, the simon-pure collusive and the collusive agreement.[54] The former is usually a one-man operation in which an individual coerces a business firm into cooperating. For example, the notorious racketeer Bioff, a high official of a motion-picture union, shook down certain Hollywood producers on threat of a strike. The collusive agreement is a much more complex operation and generally involves a criminal syndicate. Here a hierarchy of henchmen may maintain a certain leadership in control of a union, or may force certain retail outlets to pay a money tribute or to purchase a designated commodity, on the threat of destroying their merchandise or equipment. In return for acquiescence in its demands the syndicate may offer to "protect" members of a given trade association not only from outside forces but even from unfair competition in their own field, thus providing something in return for its exactions.

There are two types of rackets in business, monopoly and association.[55] The monopoly, with the aid of politicians, coerces businessmen to buy through an unnecessary middleman. An association type of racketeering denotes just that, businessmen being forced to join an association and pay dues to it in order to be protected from violence. In its more extreme form "the association" may also control and fix prices in order to avoid price cutting. The Special Senate Committee to Investigate Organized

[52] See Robert Kennedy, *The Enemy Within* (New York: Harper & Row, Publishers, 1960).

[53] George C. Wright, "The Boss on the Pier: Waterfront Portraits," *The New York Times,* January 25, 1953, sec. 4.

[54] Gordon L. Hostetter and Thomas Q. Beesley, *It's a Racket!* (Chicago: Les Quin Books, Inc., 1929), p. 4.

[55] Murray L. Gurfein, "Racketeering," *Encyclopedia of the Social Sciences* (New York: The Macmillan Company, 1934), VII, 45–46.

Crime reported that in "some instances legitimate businessmen had aided the interests of the underworld by awarding lucrative contracts to gangsters and mobsters in return for help in handling employees, defeating attempts at organization, and in breaking strikes. And the committee has had testimony showing that unions are used in the aid of racketeers and gangsters, particularly on the New York water front." [56]

It is extremely difficult for law-enforcement officers to control such activities. Seldom has prosecution been as successful as that of District Attorney Thomas E. Dewey in the convictions of many racketeers in New York City in the 1930's. Intimidation through fear of violence, the tie-ups among politicians, police, and organized criminals, the "fix," the difficulty of securing legal evidence, and inadequate laws interfere with the successful prosecution of racketeering. Occasionally businessmen have banded together to form a crime commission, as in the case of Chicago, and to resist racketeering pressure more effectively through the threat of publicity.

ORGANIZED CRIME AS A CAREER

The feudal organization of a crime syndicate makes generalization about the backgrounds of its members difficult. Many have histories similar to the ordinary criminal career, in which there is progression in a long series of delinquencies and crime and of association with a tough gang of young offenders. Instead of ending their careers in their twenties, however, they have continued their criminal activities in association with some syndicate. One significant factor in this continuance is their habituation to crime, which means that they may attach themselves to criminal groups as conditions seem suitable. "Organized crime, manifesting itself in gangs and in the larger structures within which gangs function, may be regarded as the result of a process of sifting and selection whose final product is a criminal residue." [57]

The delinquent gang of the slum produces the adult "gangster" who uses strong-arm methods and is employed for this very purpose by the organized criminal groups. Gangsters usually come from our large cities, frequently have long criminal records of armed robberies, and have a conception of themselves as "tough." Those who are successful in the syndicate sometimes take it over.

In many instances organized criminal machines have called upon the services of gangsters for protective or offensive operations only to have the

---

[56] Third Interim Report of the Special Committee to Investigate Organized Crime in Interstate Commerce, p. 5. Also see Wright, "The Boss on the Pier," *loc. cit.*

[57] Alfred R. Lindesmith, "Organized Crime," *The Annals,* 217:123 (September, 1941). Also see life history of a gangster in John Landesco's "The Gangster's Apologia Pro Vita Sua," in *Illinois Crime Survey,* Pt. 3, pp. 1043–1057.

gangsters take over the operations themselves. In other instances gangsters have been content to be on the payroll of a prosperous organization and to get a considerable cut of the profits without assuming full control. Gangsters are usually recruited from the slums of American cities. They have come up through the sand lots of crime and have made crime their career. Most of them have been members of small boys' gangs and have graduated to larger boys' gangs and later to affiliation with organized crime and political machines. They have made themselves useful to both political machines and organized crime. The gangster is the toughest of American criminals and invariably his is a blatant career of criminal activity.[58]

The Professional Offender

Of all criminal offenders the "professionals" have the most highly developed criminal career, social status, and skill. The use of the respected term "professional" to apply to criminal activities requires some explanation. The characteristics of any professional man, whether a doctor, an accountant, a lawyer, a professor, or a professional criminal, involve differential association, technical skill, consensus, organization, and status.[59] Since the professional criminal has all these attributes, the designation "professional" can be challenged only on the basis that a term carrying with it such high status is applied to an activity whose ends are hardly legitimate.

Professional criminals as a group engage in a variety of highly specialized crimes. They develop a great deal of skill in a particular type of offense. Their activities include pickpocketing (cannon), shoplifting (the boost), sneak-thieving from stores, banks, and offices (the heel), stealing from jewelry stores by substituting inferior jewelry for valuable ones (penny-weighting), stealing from hotel rooms (hotel prowling), and a variety of miscellaneous rackets such as passing illegal checks (hanging paper), and extorting money from others engaged in illegal activities (the shake). These professional criminals seldom use force in connection with their activities, as is done in the "heavy rackets," although occasionally certain of them, particularly bank robbers and safe-crackers, are professionals.

Confidence games are divided into the "short con" and the "big con." In the former, money is secured illegally from an individual directly and in a brief time, through the sale, for example, of false jewelry. The "big con" usually requires a longer period of time and involves a larger sum of money, which is secured, for example, through the operation of a

---

[58] Reckless, *op. cit.*, 3d ed., p. 203. Reprinted by permission of Appleton-Century-Crofts, Inc.

[59] Edwin H. Sutherland, *The Professional Thief* (Chicago: The University of Chicago Press, 1937), p. 197. Written by a professional thief and annotated and interpreted by Sutherland.

"money-making machine" or the sale of fraudulent securities. These professionals, particularly those operating in the "big con," must be highly intelligent, well organized, and able to "fix" law-enforcement agencies. These abilities account, in part, for the fact that few confidence men ever go to prison or are even brought to trial. A great asset of the "con" man is the fact that his victim is often also out to violate the law, either in accepting the illegal proposition of the confidence man or engaging in illegal activity to raise money for the confidence game. Probably 90 percent of the victims, therefore, never complain to the police.

One of the most famous of all confidence men was "Yellow Kid" Weil, who is estimated to have made some $8,000,000 in a variety of swindles over a lifetime.[60] Weil, who was always well dressed, wore yellow gloves. He specialized in the sale of stolen and fraudulent securities, as well as in "money-making" machines and other devices. Because of his ability to fix his cases, the "Yellow Kid" was rarely arrested and served only one prison term, five years in Leavenworth, in a lifetime of criminal activities. Maurer has sketched the steps in rackets such as the "Yellow Kid" used:

1. Locating and investigating a well-to-do-victim. (Putting the mark up.)
2. Gaining the victim's confidence. (Playing the con for him.)
3. Steering him to meet the inside man. (Roping the mark.)
4. Permitting the inside man to show him how he can make a large amount of money dishonestly. (Telling him the tale.)
5. Allowing the victim to make a substantial profit. (Giving him the convincer.)
6. Determining exactly how much he will invest. (Giving him the breakdown.)
7. Sending him home for this amount of money. (Putting him on the send.)
8. Playing him against a "big store" (a false permanent setup with props and assistants, often in a store, to convince the victim) and fleecing him. (Taking off the touch.)
9. Getting him out of the way as quietly as possible. (Blowing him off.)
10. Forestalling action by the law. (Putting in the fix.) [61]

SOCIAL ROLE

Highly skilled criminal activities, however, do not alone make a criminal a professional, for even more important are other characteristics of his social role. In terms of social role, according to Sutherland, "a person who is received in the group and recognized as a professional thief is a professional thief." This role is the result of extensive contacts with others. Professional thieves have in common "acquaintances, congeniality, sym-

[60] Joseph R. Weil, *"Yellow Kid" Weil* (as told to W. T. Brannon; New York: A. S. Barnes and Company, 1948).
[61] David W. Maurer, *The Big Con* (New York: Pocket Books, Inc., 1949), pp. 3-4.

pathy, understandings, agreements, rules, codes of behavior, and language." [62]

In comparison with other offenders, an extremely high degree of consensus exists among professional criminals. Professional criminals develop common attitudes toward themselves, toward their crimes, and toward their common enemy, the police. These common attitudes include the support of other thieves in order to overcome the ostracism of conventional society. Other thieves help the individual to find solace and rationalizations for his behavior. The group gives him a cultural situation in which to carry on his social existence and a group of values held in common by all thieves. More specifically, the relationships among professional criminals are characterized by a "code of honor." In a sense this corresponds to the code of ethics and standards governing conduct in the more respectable professions. A professional thief, for example, is always punctual about his obligations and appointments. He must never "squeal" on another member of the profession. In fact, a professional thief will endure severe punishment rather than inform on another. There is considerable agreement on this rule, for it is supported by loyalty and identification with other thieves. It is also supported by certain motives of self-interest, including loss of prestige, danger of reprisal, and the difficulty of finding other thieves with whom to work if one fails to live up to the code of honor among them.

Probably the best example of consensus in any profession, including professional crime, is the special language or argot by which members communicate with one another in a separate set of symbols. Various academic departments—sociology is one example—have separate symbols for conversation, as do the medical and legal professions.

This language is not employed to hide anything, for its use in public would attract considerable attention among laymen. It is handed down from one generation to another; hence many of the terms used by professional criminals, like the terms used by doctors, can be traced back several hundred years.[63] Hundreds of terms are used and understood by professional criminals, but rarely by other criminals. Their argot refers to other criminals, the rackets, the public, law-enforcement officers, and many other aspects of their lives.

Bandhouse (n): House of correction or workhouse.
Big-time (adj): Theft in which preparations are elaborate and prospective gains large.
Boost (n): The racket of shoplifting.
Cannon (n): The pickpocket racket; a member of a mob engaged in the racket of picking pockets.
Clip (v): Steal from, beat.

[62] Sutherland, *op. cit.*, pp. 207, 4.
[63] Sutherland, *op. cit.* Also see Eric Partridge, *A Dictionary of Slang and Unconventional English* (New York: The Macmillan Company, 1950).

Fix (v): Arrange immunity for a thief on a criminal charge.

Fix (n): The act of arranging immunity; one who arranges immunity.

Hang paper (v): Write fradulent checks.

Hook (n): A member of a pickpocket mob who extracts the pocketbook from the pocket of the victim.

Inside man (n): A member of a confidence mob to whom a victim is brought.

Moll-buzzer (n): One who steals from pockets of women.

Poke (n): Pocketbook.

Push grift (n): Theft in a crowd by pickpockets.

Score (n): Successful theft, referring to the value of the stolen property.

Slave (n): A workingman, wage earner.

Sucker (n): Victim; anyone who is not a thief.[64]

ROLE SKILLS OF A PROFESSIONAL CRIMINAL

In addition to tutelage, however, the new recruit for professional crime must develop certain abilities. He must demonstrate such role attributes as "front," wits, talking ability, honesty, nerves, determination, and reliability, for without these qualities he could never be a successful thief. Sutherland writes the following about a professional thief:

> Chic Conwell was an attractive person. A friend made the comment: "Chic was a confidence man and a good one. A good confidence man must have something lovable about him." He could have passed readily as a lawyer, a banker, or a merchant so far as personal appearance and casual conversation were concerned. He had the initiative, ingenuity, and abilities that are characteristic of leaders. He was near the top of his profession.[65]

Without association and tutelage with other professional thieves, the mere possession of certain abilities would be insufficient, for specific knowledge of professional crime must be transmitted to the individual. As in all professions, a certain amount of withdrawal from association with others occurs, as well as a maximum of participation with those of one's own group.

HIGH STATUS OF PROFESSIONAL CRIME

The high status of professional criminals is reflected by the attitudes of other criminals and by the special treatment usually accorded them by the police, court officials, and others. This social status of the professional criminal is the result of several factors including "technical skill, financial standing, connections, power, dress, manners, and wide knowledge acquired in his migratory life." [66] Offenders of lower status groups tend to

---

[64] Edwin H. Sutherland, *The Professional Thief* (Chicago: The University of Chicago Press, 1937), pp. 235–243. Copyright 1937 by the University of Chicago.

[65] *Ibid.*, p. ix.   [66] *Ibid.*, p. 200.

look up to the professional, whereas professional thieves are contemptuous of amateurs and have many epithets for them, such as "snatch-and-grab thief," "boot-and-shoe thief," and "best-hold cannon." A professional thief has nothing in common with those who commit sexual or other emotional crimes, and he would not even be courteous to them if he chanced to meet them in jail. He also has little in common with an occasional or ordinary offender, other than sympathy for a fellow lawbreaker, for they would seldom have common acquaintances or similar techniques of stealing.

Evidence of social gradations within the profession appears to be contradictory. Some professional thieves state that there are no gradations, but others make a division within professional theft into "big-time" and "small-time" thieves, according to the size of the theft involved, the complexity of the preparations, and the status of the connections. One professional criminal has written:

> While he is undoubtedly a professional thief, I should a few years ago (before he was committed to prison) have been ashamed to be seen on the street with him. I say this not out of a spirit of snobbishness but simply because for business reasons I feel that my reputation would have suffered in the eyes of my friends to be seen in the company of a booster (shoplifter).[67]

A COMPLEX OF TECHNIQUES

The professional's time is spent in planning and carrying out crimes, disposing of stolen goods, "fixing" cases in the event of arrest, and, finally, developing other useful skills and techniques to add to those he possesses. He has been highly trained by other professionals and frequently the techniques he uses have a long history.[68]

The newcomer in the profession is first given preliminary instruction about the crime. His first efforts are made in a minor capacity, and he is given the kind of assistance he would later resent. If he does these minor assignments well, he is promoted to more important ones. During this probationary period he is taught the morality and etiquette of his profession. He acquires "larceny sense," learns how to dispose of stolen goods, and how to "fix" cases. He builds up associations with other criminals and the appropriate public officials. If successful, he is admitted to full status with other thieves.

How to arrange the "fix" is one of the more skilled techniques which the professional criminal learns: how to keep out of prison by knowing

---

[67] *Ibid.*, p. 201.
[68] Arthur V. Judges, *The Elizabethan Underworld* (London: Routledge & Kegan Paul, Ltd., 1930).

how to have the case dismissed or have no disposition entered; how to se-cure the unwilling assistance of the victim, witnesses, police, court clerks, jury, prosecutor, judge, and others in order to escape a conviction. Some work through a "fixer" with connections, whereas others use direct bribery, restore the stolen property, jump a small bail bond, or buy off the victim. Often subtle legal procedures are resorted to, such as the use of a writ of habeas corpus.

ORGANIZATION OF PROFESSIONAL CRIME

Although professional crime is not characterized by the same degree of formal organization as is organized crime, there is a system of extensive informal unity and reciprocal relations among thieves. In fact, the system consists of the whole complex of techniques, status, consensus, and differ-ential association among thieves. Each professional thief, because of his ex-tensive mobility, is known personally by a large number of professional thieves. He not only knows thieves in other cities but usually knows them by a nickname—Yellow Kid, Curly, or Chic. Information regarding meth-ods and situations becomes known and shared by all professionals, as is illustrated by phrases such as "Toledo is a good town," "The lunch hour is the best time to work that spot," "Look out for the red-haired saleslady —she's double smart," and "See Skid if you should get a tumble in Chi-cago." Likewise, any thief will assist another if he is in difficulty. A pro-fessional thief may warn another, or he may take up a collection to help a thief who is in jail or to assist the man's family. Although these services may be reciprocal, they are not performed with this purpose in mind.

Summary

Career criminals identify themselves with crime, have a conception of themselves as criminals, have extensive association with criminal activities, and have progressed in criminal techniques and in the frequency of offenses. Crime is a chief source of income. Career criminals, who are largely of the group type of offender, are the ordinary, the organized, and the professional.

Habitual petty offenders have had long criminal careers, but their criminal pattern is complicated by certain life organizations and concep-tions of themselves. White-collar offenders are largely products of differen-tial association, but in some instances it is important to take into account their role organization. There is considerable organization in white-collar crime. A white-collar offender does not generally conceive of himself as a criminal. Violations of trust appear to be products of opportunity and the existence of a nonsharable problem, along with the knowledge of how to violate and rationalizations about the violation.

In ordinary criminal careers the offender moves from juvenile gang associations to adult criminal behavior of a more serious type. There is a continuous acquisition of techniques and rationalizations about crime.

Organized crime is a feudal structure involving widespread criminal operations, often of an interstate nature. There is a close relation between organized crime and political corruption. Areas of organized crime are largely those in which public sentiments are divided over the actual immorality of the behavior. Gambling today is one of the chief areas of organized crime. Professional criminals are characterized by a high degree of differential association, technical skill, consensus, organization, and status.

Selected Readings

BLOCH, HERBERT A. "The Sociology of Gambling," *American Journal of Sociology,* 57:215–221 (November, 1951). An analysis of the function of gambling in a society and the reasons for opposition to gambling in Western European society.

CLINARD, MARSHALL B. *The Black Market.* New York: Holt, Rinehart and Winston, Inc., 1952. A study of price and rationing violations during World War II and an explanation of this white-collar crime.

CLINARD, MARSHALL B. "Rural Criminal Offenders," *American Journal of Sociology,* 50:38–45 (July, 1944). One of the few studies made of rural property offenders. They were found to be chiefly occasional offenders.

CRESSEY, DONALD R. *Other People's Money.* New York: The Free Press of Glencoe, 1953. A study of 133 violators of trust, primarily embezzlers, in which a universal explanation was suggested for this kind of criminal behavior.

GIBNEY, FRANK. *The Operators.* New York: Harper & Row, Publishers, 1960. A highly readable account of white-collar crime which originally appeared as a series in *Life* magazine.

HERLING, JOHN. *The Great Price Conspiracy: The Story of the Antitrust Violations in the Electrical Industry.* Washington: Robert B. Luce, Inc., 1962. A detailed and comprehensive analysis of probably the most important case of white collar crime. In this study of antitrust violations in the electrical industry use was made of Senate committee investigations, court records, and interviews.

KEFAUVER, ESTES. *Crime in America.* New York: Doubleday & Company, Inc., 1951. A nation-wide investigation of organized crime was conducted by a United States Senate committee during 1951, many of the hearings being televised. Senator Kefauver, who was chairman of the committee, writes of the findings of this investigation.

KENNEDY, ROBERT. *The Enemy Within.* New York: Harper & Row, Publishers, 1960. Describes the findings of the Senate investigations of the connections of certain labor unions with organized criminals.

MAURER, DAVID W. *The Big Con.* New York: Pocket Books, Inc., 1949. Originally published in 1940 by Bobbs-Merrill Company. An excellent description of the activities of confidence men by a professor of English who had a particular interest in their special vocabulary.

PETERSON, VIRGIL W. *Barbarians in Our Midst*. Boston: Little, Brown & Company, 1952. An account by the Operating Director, Chicago Crime Commission, of organized crime in Chicago and its relation to politics.

RECKLESS, WALTER C. *The Crime Problem*. 3d ed. New York: Appleton-Century-Crofts, Inc., 1961. See Chaps. 10 and 11 for a comprehensive discussion of white-collar, organized, and professional crime. In the chapter dealing with white-collar crime the author discusses the issue of considering white-collar violations as crimes.

SHAW, CLIFFORD R. *The Jack Roller*. Chicago: The University of Chicago Press, 1930. A life history and analysis of a delinquent.

SHAW, CLIFFORD R. *The Natural History of a Delinquent Career*. Chicago: The University of Chicago Press, 1931. A life history and analysis of a delinquent career.

SHAW, CLIFFORD R., HENRY D. MC KAY, and JAMES F. MC DONALD. *Brothers in Crime*. Chicago: The University of Chicago Press, 1938. In these well-known life histories the process of development of the ordinary criminal career is outlined. Each life history is analyzed.

SUTHERLAND, EDWIN H. *The Professional Thief*. Chicago: The University of Chicago Press, 1937. This account of stealing as a profession was written by a professional thief and analyzed by Sutherland.

SUTHERLAND, EDWIN H. *White Collar Crime*. New York: Holt, Rinehart and Winston, Inc., 1949, reissued 1960. Chapters 13 and 14 deal with white-collar crime as organized crime and present a general theory of white-collar crime.

Drug Addiction

Men have used drugs for centuries. Opium, which is easily grown from a poppy, was and is, in its various forms, the most widely used drug, not only in Europe and America but particularly in the Orient.[1] Its early use in medical treatment helped to spread it. Two important drugs were derived from opium: morphine, a potent drug, in 1804; and heroin, about three times as powerful as morphine, in 1898. These drugs, as well as opium, which could be smoked or drunk, became widely used in America in the nineteenth century, when many of them could be easily purchased.

According to Lindesmith, the public's attitude toward drug users was different then from that of today.[2] Although the use of drugs was not approved, there was considerable tolerance about it, drug addiction was regarded as a personal problem, and in general drug addicts were pitied. It was later that they came to be regarded as derelict characters, most people associating addiction with criminal behavior. This change in the public attitude was partly due to the prevalence of opium smoking among the criminal underworld in the nineteenth century.

The Harrison Act, passed in 1914, strictly regulated opiates and cocaine. This legislation, and subsequent statutes, made the sale and use of such drugs and marihuana illegal without a doctor's prescription.[3] Actually, it made drug users "criminals," and drugs something mysterious and evil, further influencing public attitudes against their use and making it difficult for persons to secure or use them without associating with other drug users. Within recent years the use of drugs by juveniles has created even greater public concern. In fact, the Federal Narcotics Control Act of 1956 imposes a severe penalty for selling, bartering, or transferring any

---

[1] According to a British government report in 1960, Hong Kong had an estimated 250,000 drug addicts, or one in every twelve of that British colony's population. A bill has been introduced into the Legislative Council to establish treatment centers where an addict would be able voluntarily to obtain treatment. Under present legislation an addict would have to commit a crime and be arrested before being sent to a hospital.

[2] Alfred R. Lindesmith, *Opiate Addiction* (Bloomington: University of Indiana Press, 1947), p. 183.

[3] See Donald J. Cantor, "The Criminal Law and the Narcotics Problem," *Journal of Criminal Law, Criminology and Police Science*, 51:512–527 (January–February, 1961).

narcotic drug or marihuana to a person under eighteen. If the offender is himself over eighteen a sentence of from ten to forty years' imprisonment is mandatory in addition to a possible fine of $20,000.

The Effect of Drugs

According to the federal statutes, a drug addict is any person who "habitually uses any habit-forming narcotic drug as defined . . . so as to endanger the public morals, health, safety, or welfare, or who is or has been so far addicted to the use of such habit-forming narcotic drugs as to have lost the power of self-control with reference to his addiction." [4]

Although habit-forming narcotic drugs include many compounds, addiction is generally from morphine and heroin, which are derived from opium, and cocaine and marihuana.[5] From the standpoint of physiological effect, these drugs fall roughly into two categories, the depressants and the stimulants. As their names imply, depressants decrease mental and physical activity in varying degrees, depending upon the dosage, whereas the stimulants excite and sustain activity and diminish symptoms of fatigue.

The most important depressant drugs are marihuana, morphine, and heroin. Marihuana (or marijuana), which is derived from the hemp plant and often known as "Indian hemp," is usually inhaled by smoking specially prepared cigarettes called "reefers." Although there is some controversy about the effects of marihuana, it is not usually considered by investigators in this country as a real form of narcotic addiction. The usual effect is giggling and laughter, accompanied by a distorted sense of time and space, but there are no unpleasant aftereffects and little physical dependence upon the drug. It has been said that it is easier to quit smoking marihuana than to quit smoking cigarettes. Although the prolonged use of marihuana in this country is an exception rather than the rule, it often serves as a preliminary to heroin or morphine addiction, particularly for juveniles.

The other depressant drugs most commonly used—morphine and heroin—account for the greatest proportion of drug addiction in the United States. A study of 1036 addicts, patients at the United States Public Health Service Hospital at Lexington, Kentucky, showed that morphine was the drug most often used first, most preferred, and also the last used. Other drugs used are also listed in Table 11.1.

Morphine, a white powder derived from opium, ranks highest in usage, and heroin is next. They are most frequently taken by injections either subcutaneously or directly into the vein. Almost immediately after the injection of either drug the person becomes flushed and he experiences a mild itching and tingling. Gradually he becomes drowsy and relaxed and

---

[4] *Code of Laws of the United States of America*, sec. 221, Title 21.
[5] See Nathan B. Eddy, "The History of the Development of Narcotics," *Law and Contemporary Problems*, 22:3–9 (Winter, 1957).

enters a state of reverie. Soon this state of euphoria is reached only with
larger injections of the drug. Thus the addict builds up his tolerance for
the drug as well as his dependence upon it. As this tolerance builds up, the
addict becomes comparatively immune to the toxic manifestations of the
drug. With morphine, for example, the tolerance may be as high as seventy-
eight grains in sixteen hours, a dosage strong enough to kill twelve
or more unaddicted persons. The safe therapeutic dosage of morphine given
in hospitals is usually considered to be about one grain in the same period
of time.

*Table 11.1. Drugs Used First and Last, and Drug Preferred
by 1036 Patients at the United States Public Health
Service Hospital at Lexington*

Drugs	First used	Preferred	Last used
Morphine	63.1%	67.3%	50.7%
Opium smoking	14.7	6.9	3.0
Heroin	12.3	23.2	43.3
Cocaine	4.8	0.7	0.2
Opium, orally	2.5	0.5	1.3
Others	2.0	0.7	0.8
No record, or no drug used	0.6	0.7	0.7
Total	100.0%	100.0%	100.0%

SOURCE: Michael J. Pescor, "A Statistical Analysis of the Clinical Records of Hospitalized Drug Addicts," *Public Health Reports,* Supplement 143 (1938), Appendix, p. 24.

The heroin or morphine addict becomes dependent upon his injections
over a varying length of time, usually quite short, the addiction increasing
slowly in intensity thereafter. Authorities are generally agreed that this
dependence is favored more by the regularity of administration than by the
amount of the drug or the method of administration. The addict becomes
as dependent on drugs as he is on food, and if he is receiving his usual daily
supply he is not readily recognized as an addict. Even intimate friends and
family may not know of the addiction. If the individual does not receive
this daily supply, however, clearly characteristic symptoms, referred to as
withdrawal distress or the abstinence syndrome, will appear within approximately ten to twelve hours. He may become nervous and restless, he
may develop acute stomach cramps, and his eyes may water and his nose
run. Later he stops eating and he may vomit frequently, develop diarrhea,
lose weight, and suffer muscular pains in the back and legs. During this
period the "shakes" may develop, and if the addict cannot get relief by
obtaining drugs he is in for harrowing mental and physical tortures. Consequently, an addict will go to almost any lengths to obtain a supply of

drugs to relieve the suffering of withdrawal distress. Once the drugs are obtained, he appears normal again within about thirty minutes.

Cocaine is the best-known stimulant drug, but it is not as popular now as it once was. Taken intravenously, this drug produces pleasurable sensations, described by addicts as similar to sexual orgasm. The pleasurable sensations, however, are so fleeting that repeated doses must be taken to recapture them. These cumulative dosages often result in such disagreeable symptoms as heavy perspiration, trembling hands, and even, occasionally, convulsions. Hallucinations may occur, and those who become addicted to this drug may develop delusions of persecution; hence the cocaine addict is potentially dangerous.

This physiological and psychological dependence on drugs, with the stage being set for the withdrawal syndrome, makes the drug addict a serious problem, both for himself and for society. As tolerance for the drug is developed and more and more must be taken to relieve the physiological and psychological symptoms of withdrawal distress, the habit is well established. It is difficult, if not impossible, to break the habit. A Bureau of Naroctics agent once said, "When you're hooked your chances are 10,000 to 1 of ever snapping out of it." It is generally said that only a negligible number of addicts have been known to break their habit "cold," "riding out" the tortures of the withdrawal syndrome.

Extent of Addiction

It is impossible to know how many drug addicts there are in the United States today. Since the taking of drugs for nonmedical purposes is illegal, in all probability many of them are neither reported officially as such nor arrested. Most users carefully protect those who supply them so that to detect both users and suppliers requires great skill. Therefore the number of persons arrested for narcotic violation is probably representative of only a small proportion of actual violators.

According to estimates of the Federal Bureau of Narcotics, there were, on January 1, 1960, in the United States, 45,391 active drug addicts, which is 5000 to 15,000 less than were reported in 1951. Some estimates are much higher than this. Using the number of arrests of narcotic peddlers by the New York City Police Department, one study estimated that there were 90,000 addicts in that city alone.[6]

According to reports of various governmental committees investigating the problem, drug addiction has been increasing among younger persons, although arrests for the use of drugs constitute but a small proportion of all arrests for persons in this age group. It has been estimated that about

[6] New York City Mayor's Committee on Drug Addiction, *Report of Study of Drug Addiction among Teen-Agers* (New York: 1951).

60 percent of these young addicts use marihuana and the rest use heroin. According to FBI records of arrests for violation of the narcotic drug laws, there has been an increase in the percentage of those under twenty-five years of age, 31.4 percent being under twenty-five in the period January–June, 1941, as contrasted with 48.8 percent in the same period in 1951. Most of those arrested for federal narcotic law violations during 1955 were thirty years of age or under. Those under twenty-one constituted 9 percent, and those between twenty-one and thirty made up 54.2 percent of the total.[7] It has been estimated that of the reported 7500 addicts in the city of Chicago in 1952 approximately 60 percent were in the age group seventeen to twenty-five.[8] The changing pattern of rates of drug addiction arrests in Chicago between 1934–1938 and 1951 is shown in Table 11.2. By 1951 the rates for younger age groups had become much higher.

Table 11.2. Rates of Arrest for Narcotic Drug Law Violations (Chicago) per 10,000 Population for Different Age Groups

Age group	1934–1938	1951
16–20	0.43	13.64
21–30	2.10	10.08
31 and over	1.09	1.48

SOURCE: Table from Harold Finestone, "Narcotics and Criminality," *Law and Contemporary Problems,* 22:70 (Winter, 1957).

Approximately the same sex ratio, nine men to every one woman, exists for arrested addicts as for general crimes. Whereas about a fourth of those arrested for crimes in general are Negroes, this ratio is even higher for drug violations. According to the Federal Bureau of Narcotics in 1960 over half (57.6 percent) of the active addicts in the United States were Negroes. This greater ratio does not necessarily mean, however, that Negroes actually constitute this proportion of drug addicts, for it is known that they are less likely than others to be protected for this specific crime and more likely to be arrested.[9]

Drug addiction in the United States appears to be much more prevalent in large urban centers, particularly New York, Philadelphia, Washing-

[7] Report of the United States Treasury Department, Bureau of Narcotics, *Traffic in Opium and Other Dangerous Drugs* (Washington, D.C.: Government Printing Office, 1956).

[8] "Children and Drugs" (Madison, Wisc.: State Department of Public Welfare, Division for Children and Youth, March, 1952). Also see *Drug Addiction among Young Persons in Chicago* (Chicago: The Illinois Institute for Juvenile Research and The Chicago Area Project, October, 1953).

[9] The Narcotics Bureau figures of 1960 also reveal that 9 percent of the active addicts are Puerto Ricans and 6 percent are Mexicans.

ton, Baltimore, Chicago, Cleveland, Detroit, and Los Angeles.[10] In these cities drug addicts seem to come largely from the transitional areas, although addiction is by no means restricted to the lower socioeconomic classes. Faris and Dunham report the highest rates of addiction in the hobo and rooming-house districts, although some high rates appeared in the apartment and apartment-hotel districts. They concluded that drug addicts tend to select areas of the city where they can associate with other addicts and be more easily supplied by peddlers, and where, because of the mobility of the areas, their habits and activities are much less likely to be carefully scrutinized.[11]

Age and Length of Addiction

The United States Public Health Service maintains hospitals for the treatment of committed and voluntary narcotic drug addicts at Lexington, Kentucky, and Fort Worth, Texas. The age at addiction of 1036 of the patients at the Lexington hospital indicated that two thirds of those persons who became addicted did so before they were thirty. (See Table 11.3.) About two fifths were below the age of twenty-five. According to the Federal Narcotics Bureau, in 1960 over half the addicts in this country were between the ages of twenty-one and thirty.

Table 11.3. Age at Beginning of Addiction of 1036 Patients at the United States Public Health Service Hospital at Lexington

Age at onset of addiction	Percent
19 or less	16.5
20–24	28.1
25–29	25.1
30–34	14.2
35–39	6.9
40–44	5.4
45–49	1.7
50–54	0.8
55–59	0.5
60 or over	0.5
No record	0.3
Total	100.0

SOURCE: Michael J. Pescor, "A Statistical Analysis of the Clinical Records of Hospitalized Drug Addicts," *Public Health Reports,* Supplement 143 (1938), Appendix, p. 24.

[10] H. J. Anslinger and William F. Tompkins, *The Traffic in Narcotics* (New York: Funk & Wagnalls Company, 1953), p. 281.
[11] Robert E. L. Faris and H. Warren Dunham, *Mental Disorders in Urban Areas* (Chicago: The University of Chicago Press, 1939).

According to a study of these same 1036 patients, the length of addiction had generally been considerably more than five years; in fact, over 10 percent had been addicted more than twenty-five years. (See Table 11.4.)

Table 11.4. Length of Addiction among 1036 Patients at the
United States Public Health Service Hospital at Lexington

Duration of addiction	Percent
1 year or less	4.1
Over 1 year, under 2	4.5
Over 2 years, under 3	6.4
Over 3 years, under 4	5.3
Over 4 years, under 5	5.3
Over 5 years, under 10	24.7
Over 10 years, under 15	15.3 (Average: 12.5 yrs)
Over 15 years, under 20	13.7
Over 20 years, under 25	9.9
Over 25 years	10.4
No record or no drugs used	0.4
Total	100.0

SOURCE: Michael J. Pescor, "A Statistical Analysis of the Clinical Records of Hospitalized Drug Addicts," *Public Health Reports,* Supplement 143 (1938), Appendix, p. 24.

These patients, of course, were more likely to be adults, and the length of addiction should be somewhat less for adolescents.

A New York City study of 115 adolescent users reported that 61 had used narcotics less than six months, and 24 had used them more than a year.[12] In another study the range was from one to eighteen months, with an average of five to six months.[13]

Education and Occupation of Drug Addicts

About one third of the drug addicts who undergo treatment at the United States Public Health Service Hospital at Lexington have high school educations or more. The distribution for educational attainment was comparable to that of the general population. One can assume that most patients in private hospitals have an even higher average level of education.

Although there is a wide divergence in the occupations of narcotic addicts, certain occupations are known to offer more hazards. The medical

[12] Welfare Council of New York City, *The Menace of Narcotics to the Children of New York: A Plan to Eradicate the Evil* (New York: The Council, 1951).

[13] Paul Zimmering, James Toolan, Ranate Safrin, and S. P. Wortis, "Heroin Addiction in Adolescent Boys," *Journal of Nervous and Mental Diseases,* 114:19–34 (July, 1951).

profession, for example, has an excessive share of addicts.[14] The United States Commissioner of Narcotics has estimated the incidence of opiate addiction among physicians as being about 1 addict among every 100 physicians, as contrasted to a rate of about 1 in 3000 in the general population.[15] The Federal Bureau of Narcotics reported that 1012 physicians were addicts, while 659 were found guilty of illegal narcotics sales or prescription activities from 1942 through 1956. Other countries have reported a substantial incidence of addiction among physicians. In England physicians are reported as being the occupational group most heavily represented among addicts, accounting for 17 percent of the addicts there. One report, summarizing United Nations data on the subject, has stated that 1 physician in every 550 in England, and 1 in every 95 in Germany, was an addict.[16] A study of 457 consecutive admissions to the United States Public Health Service Hospital at Lexington, for meperidine ("Demerol," an opiate derivative) addiction, revealed that 32.7 percent of the cases of primary addiction were physicians and osteopaths.[17] Doctors can obtain drugs easily and rather inexpensively. Moreover, physicians have knowledge of what drugs can do for someone who is tense or tired, which is an important factor in their becoming addicted. Many of these physicians do not come to the attention of authorities because they can often maintain their addiction without detection.

In a study of 98 physicians who either were or had been opiate addicts, pronounced differences were found between them and the typical addict who buys drugs from a "pusher."

The most obvious difference is that the age at which the physicians began to use drugs is just about the age that the typical addict stops using drugs, whether by "maturing out" or for other reasons. The "street" addict typically begins drug use in adolescence, while the physician begins when he is an established community and professional figure. The "street" addict takes heroin, while the typical physician addict took meperidine. The physician can get a pure quality of his drug, although it is not as strong as heroin. The "street" addict gets a diluted drug. He often starts with marijuana, although none of the physicians ever smoked marijuana.

The physician is usually discovered by the indirect evidence of a check of prescription records, while the "street" addict is usually arrested either because he has narcotics in his possession or has been observed making an illegal purchase. The physician is usually not arrested, while the typical "street" addict is arrested. Money to obtain drugs was not a problem for the

[14] Charles Winick, "Physician Narcotic Addicts," Social Problems, 9:174–186 (Fall, 1961).

[15] "Interview with Hon. Harry J. Anslinger," Modern Medicine, 25:170–191 (October 15, 1957).

[16] Lawrence Kolb, "The Drug Addiction Muddle," Police, 1:57–62 (January–February, 1957).

[17] Robert W. Rasor and H. James Crecraft, "Addiction to Meperidine," Journal of the American Medical Association, 157:654–657 (February 19, 1955).

physicians, as it usually is for the typical addict who must steal in order to obtain money to buy drugs illegally. The physicians could use their professional access to narcotics to obtain drugs without much money. Even if they paid, the legal prices of narcotic drugs are very low.

Most non-physician addicts associate with other addicts. In contrast, the physicians interviewed almost never associated with other physician addicts, or did not do so knowingly. They did not have any occasion for doing so, either for the purpose of getting drugs or for passing time, or for emotional support. They were solitary about their addiction. The "street" addict usually talks in a special jargon and often has a kind of wry insight into drug use, which stems from his extended discussions with his peers. The physicians did not talk in jargon and manifested very little insight into their drug use.[18]

Performers in the entertainment world, such as jazz musicians, sometimes become marihuana users, largely because such deviant behavior appears to be much less disapproved by their associates. The use of drugs has been studied among 357 jazz band musicians in New York City, 73 percent of whom were white. It was reported that 82 percent had tried marihuana at least once, 54 percent were occasional users, and one in four, or 23 percent, were regular users.[19] Heroin was used less than marihuana, but still by a large proportion: 53 percent at least once, 24 percent occasionally, and by one in six, or 16 percent, regularly. Only 3 percent expressed any moral objections to the use of either marihuana or heroin by their musical colleagues, and while two thirds of the nonusers felt sorry for the drug users, the common reaction was, "It's their business if they want to do it."

Over a third of the sample believed that most jazz musicians think they play better when using marihuana, even if they actually are playing worse. Nearly one in five believed that it actually helps a musician to play better, and 31 percent felt that the musicians played worse. More specifically, marihuana seems to establish "contact high," a special kind of emotional group contagion, among those taking marihuana, resulting in "musical whimsy or humor," and can permit the musician to perceive new space-time relationships by altering his perception of time. In general the comments were much more negative in relation to heroin. No significant relation, however, could be found between the use of heroin or marihuana and the degree of professional success attributed to the musician by his peers.

A number of group factors are related to the musician's drug use. One was the extent of use by the band itself. About half (53 percent) felt that the use of drugs was related to upward or downward mobility. For ex-

---

[18] Winick, "Physician Narcotic Addicts," *loc. cit.*, pp. 178–179.
[19] Charles Winick, "The Use of Drugs by Jazz Musicians," *Social Problems*, 7:240–254 (Winter, 1959–1960).

ample, a young musician may take a drug to accelerate his progress to the top. Drugs may be used to help tide a musician over when he is out of work. About one in five, especially those over thirty, felt that drug usage was related to "one nighters" as this type of traveling is tiring for musicians. As one heroin user described it:

> "I was traveling on the road in 1952. We had terrible travel arrangements and traveled by special bus. We were so tried and beat that we didn't even have time to brush our teeth when we arrived in a town. We'd get up on the bandstand looking awful. The audience would say, 'why don't they smile? They look like they can't smile.' I found I could pep myself up more quickly with heroin than with liquor. If you drank feeling that tired, you'd fall on your face." [20]

The Process of Opiate Addiction

To be an addict, a person must use the drug consciously. He must be aware of the drug, know how to administer it, and recognize its effects.

> Beyond this, one must have some motivation for trying the drug—whether to relieve pain, to produce euphoria, to please a loved person, to achieve acceptance in a group, or to achieve some other goal. The goal need have little to do with the specific effects of the narcotic. Moreover, the motivation or goal of initial drug use must be sharply distinguished from the motivation to maintain a drug habit. The latter is a product of learning which seems to depend on the interaction between drug effects, especially in the first experience of withdrawal, and the self-conception of the drug user.[21]

Generally addicts have personality disturbances, but it is not sound reasoning to assume that such personality traits necessarily existed before addiction.[22] In only a few cases are comparisons made with the traits of the population as a whole, and there is some doubt as to whether the addicts studied are always representative of the entire population.

The most significant sociological work in this field has challenged the general view that differences in personality traits or need for an escape mechanism accounts for addiction to opiates. Lindesmith explains addiction on the basis of the addict's association of the drug with the distress which accompanies the sudden cessation of its use. "If he fails to realize the connection between the distress and the opiate he escapes addiction, whereas if he attributes it to the opiate and thereafter uses the opiate to

---

[20] *Ibid.,* p. 246.

[21] John A. Clausen, "Social and Psychological Factors in Narcotics Addiction," *Law and Contemporary Problems,* 22:38–39 (Winter, 1957).

[22] Donald Gerard and Conan Kornetsky, "Adolescent Opiate Addiction: A Study of Control and Addict Subjects," *Psychiatric Quarterly,* 29:457–487 (1955).

alleviate it he invariably becomes addicted. Addiction is generated in the process of using the drug consciously to alleviate withdrawal distress." [23]

Addiction is impossible without recognizing the withdrawal distress which may come several hours after a "shot" and in some cases may be difficult to detect. In support of his argument Lindesmith claims that there are no persons who have not become addicts after experimenting with withdrawal symptoms. Doctors may successfully prevent addiction by keeping patients unaware of the effects of the drug upon them. Patients who have experienced withdrawal distress without understanding the connection between it and the drug have therefore escaped addiction.

Lindesmith cites several crucial cases of persons who were receiving drugs without becoming addicted, but when they later took drugs and began to associate the taking of drugs with the fear of withdrawal symptoms they became addicted. This interpretation is supported by the fact that an addict seldom experiences the uplift or buoyancy attributed to the drugs unless he has been "taught" to expect it. Even the argot of addicts themselves in the word "hooked" indicates the process of addiction. The following case shows how a person begins to realize that he is addicted.

> Mr. G. was severely lacerated and internally injured in an accident. He spent thirteen weeks in a hospital, in the course of which he received opiates frequently both by mouth and hypodermically. He was unconscious part of the time and suffered considerable pain during convalescence despite the intake of opiates. He did not know what he was getting and noticed no effects except that his pain was relieved by the shots. He was discharged from the hospital but in several hours he began to feel restless and uncomfortable, without recognizing his condition. That night he became nauseated and vomited blood. Fearing that he was going to die, he summoned his family doctor. The physician did not realize what was the matter and administered a mild sedative. During the next day Mr. G.'s condition became steadily worse, and by the second night he was in such misery that, as he said, he began to wish that he would die. He again summoned his family doctor. This time the doctor began to suspect that Mr. G. was suffering from opiate withdrawal and prepared an injection of morphine. Mr. G. remembers nothing after the injection except that the doctor sat down by his bed and asked him how he felt. He replied that he noticed no effect, but the doctor said, "You will in a few minutes." Soon the patient fell asleep and continued in perfect comfort for many hours. When he awoke, he was informed of the true nature of the relieving dose by his wife and by the physician's comment: "Now we're going to have a hell of a time getting you off." The patient remained free of the drug for a few days and then purchased a syringe and began to use it himself.[24]

[23] Alfred R. Lindesmith, "A Sociological Theory of Drug Addiction," *American Journal of Sociology*, 43:599 (January, 1938).
[24] Alfred R. Lindesmith, *Opiate Addiction* (Bloomington: University of Indiana Press, 1947), p. 72. This extract and others reprinted from this work are used with the permission of the author and the publisher.

In becoming an opiate addict the individual changes his conception of himself and of the behavior he must play as a "drug addict." These new conceptions have both social psychological and sociological implications. The more he associates with others who are "hooked" and finds that he cannot free himself from dependence on drugs, the more he comes to play the new role of the addict.

> It is evident that the drug addict assumes the group's viewpoint with respect to his experience of withdrawal distress by virtue of the fact that, prior to addiction, he has been a non-addict and a participating member of society. In view of the very use of language symbols, in terms of which the processes of re-evaluation which constitute addiction proceed, the addict necessarily shares the traditional heritage which includes knowledge of, and attitudes toward, the drug habit. Prior to addiction addicts acquire the attitudes of non-addicts, and when they become addicted they must adjust themselves to these attitudes. In other words, as our theory emphasizes, addiction pre-supposes life in organized society. Children and animals can not become addicts because they lack the ability to use and respond to the complex linguistic structures which have grown up in human society.[25]

Drug addiction is learned just as other behavior is learned, primarily from association with others who are addicts. The usual pattern is that of association for other means, rather than the person seeking another simply because the other person is a drug addict. Dai found that some were introduced to drugs at "pleasure parties," through co-workers, at dance halls and pool rooms, by prostitutes or in homosexual experiences, and, in some cases, by peddlers.[26] Similarly, younger persons learn addiction from the group, as has been previously discussed. Dai has thus summarized the role of association in drug addiction:

> The process in which this pattern of opium addiction is taken over by an individual is not very much different from that in which other cultural patterns are transmitted. In a number of cases we found that the drug habit was started less for the effect of the drug than as a sign of identification with the group they happened to be in. . . . This process of identification is found to take place when a young person associates with an older one who uses drugs and who, because of the habit or otherwise, commands the former's admiration and respect, or when two persons are in some form of love relationship . . . when one of them is a drug user.[27]

The Process of Using Marihuana

There are two objections to the claim that the use of marihuana, which actually does not cause addiction, is associated with personality

---

[25] *Ibid.*, p. 168.
[26] Bingham Dai, *Opium Addiction in Chicago* (Shanghai: The Commercial Press, 1937).
[27] *Ibid.*, p. 173.

traits.[28] First, marihuana users do not exhibit any uniform personality traits; second, there is great variation in the use of the drug by a given person. At one time the individual may be unable to use the drug for pleasure, on a later occasion he may use it, and still later not do so.

To use marihuana for pleasure a person must learn to conceive of the drug as something which can produce pleasurable sensations.[29] The user of marihuana drugs must learn three things: (1) to smoke the drug in a way which will produce certain effects; (2) to learn to recognize the effects and connect the drug with them; and (3) finally, to enjoy the sensations he feels. These three steps occurred in the case of fifty marihuana users whom Becker studied. He claims that when a person first uses the drug he does not ordinarily "get high" because he does not know the proper technique of drawing on the cigarette and holding the smoke. Even after learning the technique he does not form a conception of the smoking as being related to pleasure. Even though there are pleasurable sensations, the new marihuana user may not feel that they are enough, or he may not be sufficiently aware of their specific nature to become a regular user. He learns to feel the sensations of "being high" as defined by others. With greater use he learns to appreciate more of the sensations of the drug.

Finally, one more step is necessary to continue the use of marihuana. The person must learn to enjoy the sensations he has experienced. Feeling dizzy, being thirsty, misjudging distances, or a tingling scalp may not of themselves be pleasurable experiences. He must learn to define them in this way. Association with other marihuana users helps to define sensations that were frightening into something pleasurable and to be looked forward to. An experienced marihuana user has described how newcomers are helped to define the use of the drugs as giving pleasurable sensations:

> "Well, they get pretty high sometimes. The average person isn't ready for that, and it is a little frightening to them sometimes. I mean, they've been high on lush (alcohol), and they get higher that way than they've ever been before, and they don't know what's happening to them. Because they think they're going to keep going up, up, up till they lose their minds or begin doing weird things or something. You have to like reassure them, explain to them that they're not really flipping or anything, that they're gonna be all right. You have to just talk them out of being afraid. Keep talking to them, reassuring, telling them it's all right. And come on with your own story, you know: 'The same thing happened to me. You'll get to like that after awhile.' Keep coming on like that; pretty soon you talk them out of being scared. And besides they see you doing it and nothing horrible is happening to you, so that gives them more confidence." [30]

---

[28] Howard S. Becker, "Becoming a Marihuana User," *American Journal of Sociology.* 59:235–243 (November, 1953).
[29] *Ibid.,* pp. 235–242.   [30] *Ibid.,* p. 240.

The Culture of Drug Addiction

Much of drug addiction involves an elaborate subculture. The drugs must be imported illegally into the country and then distributed through suppliers or peddlers. There are "pushers" who help to indoctrinate new persons into addiction. Those who use the drugs are, to a large extent, also part of this subculture, since drug addicts must generally associate with peddlers and other addicts in order to secure their supply.

To understand why this illegal trade in narcotics flourishes and why it is so difficult to wipe out, one must realize the potential large profit in the handling of illegal drugs. The price for a shot of heroin varies considerably, and is often what the traffic will bear. Although police often have little difficulty in apprehending the common addict who is searching restlessly for his next shot, it is much more difficult to track down the supplier or successive line of suppliers to the source. Many addicts would rather sweat out the "shakes" than disclose the name of their supplier, and often there is a high degree of organization among those who manage to get supplies of drugs illegally into the country.

The extremely high profits involved in the sale of illegal drugs can be seen from the return which is likely on one kilogram (approximately thirty-five ounces) of heroin. This amount of 86 percent pure heroin in Italy costs about $1000, and it might cost as much as $5000 more to smuggle it into the United States. However, this kilogram of heroin, which will be diluted as much as 90 percent with milk sugar, will eventually be made into about 20,000 capsules (at $437\frac{1}{2}$ grains to an ounce and $1\frac{1}{2}$ grains to a capsule of the cut product) which will sell for about $2 to $3 apiece. Thus the return on the original investment is up to $40,000 to $60,000. Where profits as high as this exist it is inevitable that well-organized techniques will be developed to protect them. It is also inevitable that such an enterprise should become a fertile field for organized crime.

Most drug addicts are introduced to the habit knowingly. Only rarely does the use of drugs during illness lead to addiction; probably not more than 5 percent of the cases have this origin. As for the large numbers who take them because of curiosity, there has usually been some association with addicts. There is a desire to "try something once," especially if it happens to be something as frowned upon by society in general as is drug addiction. The chain-reaction process of addiction has often been called a "sordid and tragic pyramid game" in which the average addict can be counted on to lure several friends into the habit, often as a means of solving his own supply problem. Persons are often initiated at parties where the first several marihuana cigarettes or "shots" are "on the house" in order to initiate the beginner.

Teen-age addiction is more group in nature. In their attempts to acquire status, adolescents in certain areas often appear to be willing to explore socially unacceptable areas of behavior. Drug use among juveniles, consisting primarily of heroin and marihuana, flourishes in the interstitial areas of cities. In New York, for example, almost 90 percent of the cases are concentrated in only 13 percent of the census tracts.[31] In fact, in some of the tracts as many as 10 percent of the young men, aged sixteen to twenty, were known, during a three-year period, to be involved with drugs. In such areas the desire to enjoy life by having new experiences and taking chances means that there is a readiness to try the drug, as it, they are told, will give them an immediate "kick" or a "high" feeling. In some groups, namely delinquent gangs, this idea is even more widespread than among others. Great determination is required to escape the pull or, rather, push of delinquent subcultures which are associated with the use of drugs. "The pressure to fall in with the fast, noisy, aggressive 'cats' is great. The derisive taunts of 'chicken,' 'yellow,' 'punk,' and 'square' are powerful weapons to use against an adolescent boy." [32]

In spreading to young persons, as it did, narcotics use made its inroads within a distinctive and uniquely vulnerable social milieu, the world of the adolescent in the most disadvantaged areas of the city. Like their age-mates everywhere, these adolescents spontaneously form peer groups, which exert a significant influence upon their conduct. In other types of communities, however, particularly those of higher socioeconomic status, the control over behavior exerted by the peer group is subject to restraint by the obligations and loyalties binding the individual adolescent members to other conventional groups, such as the family and the school. By way of contrast, such competing obligations and loyalties fail to exert their limiting and moderating influences in the most disadvantaged areas, and the peer group assumes a virtually sovereign control over the behavior of the individual adolescent. Under such conditions, the introduction of a novel practice may lead to its rapid diffusion, and, because it is unchecked by pressures counter to those exerted by the peer group itself, go to extremes that are not possible among adolescents elsewhere. In this milieu, narcotics use could spread more selectively and with somewhat greater difficulty, perhaps, but in a manner analogous to a new fashion in language, dress, or music. . . .

It is evident from this description that there are significant influences originating in street-corner society itself that would be hospitable to experimentation with narcotics. An orientation to life which gives zestful sanction to many forms of unconventional activity appears to have spread the welcome mat for narcotics use. Much of the behavior reported by these young addicts clearly indicates that they had actively sought out narcotics—and not only heroin, but every other substance of which they had heard which yielded a "kick" such as marijuana, cocaine, benzedrine, and the barbiturates. The

[31] Isidor Chein and Eva Rosenfeld, "Juvenile Narcotics Use," *Law and Contemporary Problems*, 22:52–69 (Winter, 1957).
[32] *Ibid.*, p. 56.

activity centering around these narcotics had many of the characteristics of a
fad—that is, the restless searching, the uncertainty and excitement and exclusive preoccupation with a novel experience, the pressures to "go along,"
and the final capitulation on the part of many, despite the existence of strong
initial doubts and inhibitions.[33]

Teen-agers in high delinquency areas, which are also high drug use
areas, can be divided into four groups: (1) delinquents who also use drugs,
(2) delinquents who do not use drugs, (3) drug users who were not drug
users prior to involvement with heroin, and, finally (4) nondelinquent
nondrug users. Not all delinquent groups engage in the use of drugs, a fact
which appears to be related to the area where they are located. Finestone
has suggested that the use of narcotics spreads to adolescents in those
communities deficient in two essential types of social control: "first, controls originating in conventional institutions which define the limits of
permissible behavior for adolescents; and secondly, the controls by means
of which the community is enabled to resist encroachments by those
espousing values to which it is strongly antagonistic." [34] In regard to lack
of the first type of social control he writes:

> In the localities frequented by adult criminals, the notoriety, glamour,
> and symbols of material success that are sometimes associated with them en-
> hance their attractiveness as role-models to members of street-corner society,
> who, as adolescents, may find it easier to identify with them than with con-
> ventional role-models. In a similar vein, interviews with young narcotic ad-
> dicts in 1952 suggested the observation that in at least certain social circles
> where these youngsters sought status and recognition, adult addicts or
> "junkies" enjoyed a certain prestige. Many of these young addicts reported
> that they and others had tried to simulate the mannerisms and philosophy of
> life of addicts before they themselves had become addicted.[35]

Most juvenile gangs that use drugs, however, often try to set the limits
of drug usage by their members. In a study of eighteen gangs by Chein
and Rosenfeld it was found that 65 percent of the members were opposed
to the use of heroin, or felt ambivalent about it, but very few gang members had strong feeling about the use of marihuana.[36] Any leader who became a drug addict was demoted. Delinquent gangs are more tolerant of
occasional use, but resist immoderate usage, on the grounds that it interferes with their stealing or that it will get the gang into trouble. Some
writers, such as Ohlin and Cloward, have referred to a type of delinquent
gang which, in its inability to achieve the conventional goals of society,

[33] Harold Finestone, "Narcotics and Criminality," *Law and Contemporary Problems,*
22:73–74 (Winter, 1957).

[34] *Ibid.,* p. 74.

[35] *Ibid.,* p. 75. For discussion of some group factors in younger drug addicts also see
Alexander H. Leighton, John A. Clausen, and Robert N. Wilson, *Explorations in Social
Psychiatry* (New York: Basic Books, Inc., 1957), pp. 230–277.

[36] Chein and Rosenfeld, "Juvenile Narcotics Use," *loc. cit.*

becomes preoccupied with the use of drugs rather than stealing except to get money for drugs.[37]

There is a widespread assumption that juvenile addicts are introduced to the drug habit by drug peddlers. One study has shown that the first shot of heroin came through some adult in only 10 percent of the cases.[38] Nearly all were introduced to the drug in the company of a boy their own age or in a group of boys. The first trial use of drugs was free to most. Only 10 percent had to pay for the first "shot" or "snort." The first dose was often taken in the home of one of the boys, although a large number tried it on the street, in a cellar, or even on a roof top. Frequently, it was taken before a party as a bracer to give poise and courage. Clausen reports: "There is general agreement that the great majority of these [marihuana and heroin] users were not tricked into addiction by drug peddlers." [39]

Once the adolescent becomes involved in a group which is using drugs and becomes addicted, it is difficult for him to withdraw from the group. Later his whole life may revolve around maintaining a regular supply of "shots," and there is consequently less and less opportunity for him to have any contacts with acceptable groups. In these groups of youthful addicts loyalties become intensified because of the constant fear of being arrested and cut off from sources of supply. And the constant search for sources of supply compels them to seek the company of known adult addicts.

Suppliers and most addicts live in a world that often has its own meeting places and its own argot. Possibly nothing more clearly demonstrates the fact that addiction has cultural components than the argot which is used. It includes special names for the drugs, for those who supply the drugs, and for addiction. It also includes special descriptive terms for those who use drugs.

Selected Glossary of Terms Used by Addicts
Bang: The thrill in drug taking.
Being on the nod: Peculiar semisomnolent condition after taking injection.
Belong: After habit is formed, individual "belongs" to pusher.

---

[37] Richard A. Cloward and Lloyd E. Ohlin, *Delinquency and Opportunity* (New York: The Free Press of Glencoe, 1960). Also see Harold Finestone, "Cats, Kicks, and Color," *Social Problems,* 5:3–13 (July, 1957). In this study some fifty Negro male users of heroin in their late teens and early twenties were selected from areas of highest incidence of drug usage in Chicago. Through intensive interviews between 1951 and 1953, these drug users served as subjects to elicit expression of many common values, schemes of behavior and general social orientation, suggesting the existence of a social type, "the cat." It was concluded that "the cat" is a product of social change, representing a reaction to a feeling of exclusion from adequate access to the goals of our society. Therefore, measures, such as improved educational opportunities which put these means within his grasp, will hasten the extinction of this type.
[38] Chein and Rosenfeld, "Juvenile Narcotics Use," *loc. cit.,* p. 58.
[39] Clausen, "Social and Psychological Factors in Narcotics Addiction," *loc. cit.,* p. 40.

Boy: Another name for heroin.

Burned out: A vein no longer useful for injection because of numerous puncture wounds.

Chicken: One who declines to take drugs because he is fearful.

Cold turkey: Complete and sudden withdrawal from drugs in jail.

Den: Place where several gather to use narcotics.

Drive: Addict's description of feeling good.

Fad party: Group of cats gathered.

Good ball: A pill or capsule of barbiturate used by addicts when they cannot get their supply of narcotics.

Girl: Slang for cocaine.

Hard stuff: Heroin, when compared to marihuana.

High: When an individual is under the effect of marihuana or other drugs.

Hooked: One who no longer can resist taking drugs.

Hophead: One who has become addicted to use of drugs.

Horse: Another name for heroin.

Hot shot: An overdose of drugs, sometimes fatal.

Joy popper: One who takes drugs only occasionally.

Junk: Any illegal drug.

Junkie: A drug addict.

Kick: Feeling of satisfaction after taking drugs (also lift).

Kicking the habit: Constant twitching of arms, legs and feet, some twenty-four hours after last dose of morphine, during withdrawal.

Main-liner: Any addict who uses intravenous injections.

Muggles: Marihuana cigarettes.

Pusher: Makes first contact for recruits. May give first few samples free.

Reefer: Marihuana cigarette.

Shakes: Uncontrolled physical tremors of addict when withdrawn from drugs.

Skin-popping: Injection of drugs, but not intravenous.

Sniffer: Inhalation of cocaine from thumbnail or match cover.

Snorting: Inhaling cocaine.

Snow: Slang for cocaine.

Speedball artist: One who mixes cocaine and heroin.

Stick: A marihuana cigarette.

Stuff: Any drug used illegally.

Wigged: An addict who can no longer think clearly.

Yen sleep: Restless, tossing sleep, eight to fourteen hours after last dose of morphine, during withdrawal.[40]

The argot of professional musicians makes use of many expressions which are widely used by addicts. They use terms and phrases to describe the music they like, such as "frantic," "it kills me," "wild," "crazy," "the end," "hip." [41]

[40] Derived from Lindesmith, *Opiate Addiction*, pp. 211–221; Anslinger and Tompkins, *op. cit.*, pp. 305–316; and "Children and Drugs," pp. 23–25. Also see J. E. Schmidt, *Narcotics Lingo and Lore* (Springfield, Ill.: Charles C Thomas, Publisher, 1959).

[41] Winick, "The Use of Drugs by Jazz Musicians," *loc. cit.*, pp. 249–250. "Drug users probably developed most of the key phrases in this jargon as outgrowths of various aspects

Since the 1920's, one popular procedure for combining musical expression with interest in drugs was to make records or perform pieces with thinly veiled references to narcotics in their titles: Hophead, Muggles, Reefer Song, Viper's Drag, Sweet Marijuana Brown, Weed Smoker's Dream, Chant of the Weed, Pipe Dream Blues, Kicking the Gong Around, You're a Viper, Reefer Man, Doctor Freeze, and Vonce, are among many such titles, some of which achieved considerable success. The lyrics as well as the title of many jazz pieces have dealt with narcotics, at least up to fairly recently.[42]

Delinquency, Crime, and Drug Addiction

Two factors are involved in the relationship between delinquency, crime, and drug addiction. First of all, the use of narcotics is so expensive that an addict must often engage in various illegal activities to maintain his supply. Second, the influence of drugs upon human behavior varies, and it is difficult to determine how much effect narcotics have on criminal behavior generally.

Once an individual becomes addicted to a narcotic drug, such as morphine or heroin, his dependence upon a continuous supply usually becomes the most important single aspect of his daily life. Although they took the drug earlier for pleasure or for an effect, most addicts soon take it to ward off withdrawal symptoms. The addict knows that conventional society is extremely hostile to his use of drugs, so he resorts to devious ways in his attempt to secure them. As his tolerance is built up and he requires more and larger dosages, it may cost as much as from fifteen to forty dollars a day to support the habit. This daily expenditure is generally much more than the addict earns, and thus he or she is literally compelled to engage in theft or prostitution in order to maintain an adequate supply.

Most crimes associated with drug addiction involve direct or indirect violations of narcotic laws. Drug addicts may engage in petty stealing, and occasionally robbery, to get enough money to buy their drugs, break into hospitals and doctors' offices to steal drugs, turn to prostitution, or sell drugs and become drug peddlers or "pushers." Drug addicts may also purchase a small supply of a drug from a peddler and then "water" down the powder with the addition of milk sugar before selling it to the next in line. By the time the last packet is bought by an addict it is mostly milk sugar. Doctors sometimes illegally prescribe drugs for an extra fee; indeed, some addicts have paid thousands of dollars to doctors for illegal prescriptions. One writer has thus described the young addict or "junky" and the need to commit crimes in order to secure drugs.

---

of drug-taking activity. For example, the key concept of being 'hip' (a member of the in-group) derives from the slight atrophy of the hip which resulted from lying on one preferred hip and balancing opium on the other hip. A 'hip' person was thus originally an opium smoker."—*Ibid.*, p. 250.

[42] *Ibid.*, p. 251.

At the time when many of these young addicts were interviewed in 1952, most were still in the early stages of their addiction. They were "snatch-and-grab" junkies, supporting their habits through petty thievery, breaking into cars, shoplifting, and a variety of "scheming," such as "laying a story" on "a sucker" in the hope of gaining sympathy and some cash. Some enterprising ones actually had girls out "hustling" for them through "boosting" (shop-lifting) and "turning tricks" (prostitution). Despite the ragged state of their clothing and the harried nature of their existence, they regarded themselves as the members of an elite, the true "down cats" on the best "kick" of them all, "Horse" (heroin). Many of them were still living at home, although they had long since exhausted the last reserves of patience of their families and "fenced" much of their movable property. Few, if any, of them had finished high school, and, on the average, they had little or no employment experience. Their attitudes towards work and the daily routine that steady employment presupposed were entirely negative. Their number-one hazard was the "man" (the police). Once they became "known junkies"—that is, known to the police—they were frequently picked up and sometimes sentenced—mostly for misdemeanors and, consequently, for short sentences. . . . The impression gained from interviewing them was that these addicts were petty thieves and petty "operators" who, status-wise, were at the bottom of the criminal popu-lation or underworld. It is difficult to see how they could be otherwise. The typical young junkie spent so much of his time in a harried quest for nar-cotics, dodging the police, and in lockups, that he was hardly in a position to plan major crimes.[43]

The second factor is the relationship of drug addiction to crime in general and to crimes of violence in particular. In a study of the criminal records of 1036 patients at the United States Public Health Service Hos-pital in Lexington it was found that 75.3 percent had no official record of delinquency prior to addiction.[44] Generally they were not involved in offenses other than drug violations and where they were involved the of-fenses were not serious. Most younger drug users appear to have en-gaged in prolonged delinquent activities either prior to their first arrest or prior to their first regular use of drugs. A report of a Chicago study states:

With few exceptions known drug users engage in delinquency in more or less systematic form. Contrary to the widely held view that the delinquency of the young addict is a consequence principally of addiction, it was found that delinquency both preceded and followed addiction to heroin. Persons who became heroin users were found to have engaged in delinquency in a group-supported and habitual form either prior to their use of drugs or simultaneously with their developing interest in drugs. There was little evi-dence of a consistent sequence from drug use without delinquency to drug

---

[43] Finestone, "Narcotics and Criminality," *loc. cit.*, pp. 76–77.
[44] Michael J. Pescor, "A Statistical Analysis of Clinical Records of Drug Addicts," *Public Health Reports,* Supplement 143 (1938), p. 26.

use with delinquency. Three observations may be made about the effect of addiction upon the delinquent behavior of the person: (1) The pressure of need for money to support his addiction impels the user to commit violations with greater frequency and with less caution than formerly. (2) Delinquents after becoming addicted to heroin do not engage in types of delinquency in which they are not already skilled. The post-addict delinquent, in other words, does not generally engage in more serious crimes than those he committed prior to his addiction. (3) Delinquents who as pre-addicts tended to engage in riotous behavior such as street fighting and gang attacks tend after addiction to abandon this kind of activity. Three elements are probably responsible for the change: (a) the sedative effect of the opiate; (b) the desire to avoid attracting the attention of public and police; and (c) the tendency for adolescents to become quieter in their conduct as they approach maturity.[45]

According to 1951 Chicago data, arrests for nonviolent property offenses is proportionately higher among addicts, whereas arrests of addicts for violent offenses against the person, such as rape and aggravated assault, are only a fraction of the proportion among the population at large. (See Table 11.5.) A group of young addicts was found seldom to have

Table 11.5 The Percentage Distribution of Arrests for the Most Serious Types of Offenses in the Narcotic Bureau and the Chicago Police Department, 1951

	Narcotic Bureau	Chicago Police Department
Larceny—theft (except automobile theft)	58.8	31.0
Robbery	16.2	7.3
Burglary—breaking and entering	9.9	9.4
Stolen property: buying, receiving, possessing	5.1	3.2
Forgery and counterfeiting: embezzlement and fraud	4.2	4.9
Sex offenses: Rape	1.6	11.0
Automobile theft	1.5	9.1
Weapons: carrying, possessing, etc.	1.4	4.4
Aggravated assault: other assault	1.3	19.7
	100.0	100.0

SOURCE: Chicago Police Department, Annual Report (1951), p. 13.

committed serious offenses against either persons or property, and those who did generally had committed similar offenses before becoming ad-

[45] The Illinois Institute for Juvenile Research and Chicago Area Project, "Drug Addiction among Young Persons in Chicago," Summary Report of a Study Made by the Staff of the Chicago Area Project for the National Institute of Mental Health (Mimeographed; October, 1953).

dicted, so that violence was only a part of the total picture. The conclusion was: "Addiction, thus, appears to reduce both the inclination to violent crime and the capacity to engage in sophisticated types of crime requiring much planning." [46] Reckless concludes that there is little evidence to support the idea that addicts commit violent crimes: "One notices that sex crimes and crimes against the person are not the sorts of crime committed by the drug addict, in spite of the marihuana mythology. The most commonly used drugs, morphine and its derivatives, decrease an individual's aggressive tendencies." [47]

Treatment

All studies of the results of treatment indicate that drug addiction is one of the most difficult forms of deviant behavior to treat effectively. The rate of relapse is high. A follow-up study of 4776 addicts was made six months after their discharge from the United States Public Health Service Hospital at Lexington. Although the status of 39.6 percent of the patients could not be ascertained, it was revealed that 39.9 percent had relapsed, 7.0 percent had died after release, and only 13.5 percent were abstinent.[48]

Lindesmith attributes the high recidivism rate of the opiate addict to social psychological, rather than merely physiological, reasons. Recidivism in drug addiction is the result of long experience with the drugs and a conception of oneself as an addict, association with other addicts, and recognition of the importance of the drug in relation to withdrawal symptoms. It is often difficult to quit the use of drugs, or to abstain from beginning to use them again, because many friends and acquaintances are addicts. This feeling of boredom at being a nonaddict is also a factor in relapse. After the addict has been taken off drugs the old attitudes persist.

> The former user still believes in the efficacy of the drug. He still interprets the vicissitudes of life to some degree in terms of opiates and never again exhibits a feeling of disgust or moral indignation toward drug usage such as he may have had before addiction. These changes are produced by the influence of withdrawal distress, as has been demonstrated, but once formed, they are independent of the withdrawal symptoms.[49]

Addicts generally cannot be treated properly in their own homes or in general hospitals, for it is essential that they be under constant specialized observation.[50] Most treatment of this type is given in only a few private

---

[46] Finestone, "Narcotics and Criminality," *loc. cit.,* p. 77.

[47] Walter C. Reckless, *The Crime Problem* (2d ed.; New York: Appleton-Century-Crofts, Inc., 1950), p. 356.

[48] Michael J. Pescor, "Follow-Up Study of Treated Narcotic Addicts," *Public Health Reports,* Supplement 170 (1943), pp. 1–18.

[49] Lindesmith, *Opiate Addiction,* p. 139.

[50] For a description of specific methods of treatment, see Marie Nyswander, *The Drug Addict as a Patient* (New York: Grune & Stratton, Inc., 1956).

sanatoria, to a limited extent in some state hospitals, and in two federal hospitals, at Lexington, Kentucky, and at Fort Worth, Texas. The latter two institutions were established by Congressional action in 1929 for the confinement and treatment of narcotic addicts. They are now under the Mental Hygiene Division of the Public Health Service under the Department of Health, Education, and Welfare. Voluntary commitments are accepted at these institutions, but the majority of patients are those who have failed on probation and have been committed by federal courts.

The optimum treatment period is from four to six months. The longer a patient stays at a hospital the less likely he is to return, for there is little opportunity for him to continue treatment outside. A newly admitted drug addict is, first of all, given a thoroughgoing medical examination and treatment, which includes building up his general physical condition along with removal of drugs. The use of drugs is reduced gradually to minimize the severity of the symptoms. Currently the most frequently used drug is methadon, for it has much milder abstinence symptoms than either heroin or morphine. The next step—removal of the patient's psychological dependence on drugs—is a much more difficult process. It usually involves psychiatric treatment, recreational and occupational therapy, and vocational training. It is also important that the addict receives follow-up supervision, as most relapses among addicts occur within the first two years after their release from the hospital. If cure is to be permanent, any problems in the home which have directly or indirectly led to the addiction must be corrected. Through an organization called Narcotics Anonymous some use has been made of group therapy after release. See pages 653–655 for a description.

The Control of Drug Addiction

The best approach to the entire difficult problem of drug addiction is, of course, prevention. This means efforts to prevent the individual from coming into illegitimate contact with the drug. Prevention is largely a function for law-enforcement agencies through international agreements, federal agencies, and local authorities. Two United Nations groups, the Permanent Central Opium Board and the Narcotic Drugs Supervisory Body, control the lawful traffic in drugs.[51] In 1961, thirty-eight members of the United Nations agreed to a new, more rigid international regulation and control of drugs, subject to ratification by their home countries. A third group, the United States Commission on Narcotic Drugs, watches over lawful opium traffic in the United States, and suggests measures for controlling all illegal trade. The task of preventing unlawful trade in nar-

---

[51] See Bertil A. Renborg, "International Control of Narcotics," in *Law and Contemporary Problems*, 22:86–112 (Winter, 1957).

cotics within the United States is assigned to the Bureau of Narcotics, a branch of the Treasury Department, which administers the Harrison Narcotic Act. This act requires the registration and payment of a graduated occupational tax by all persons who import, manufacture, produce, compound, sell, deal in, dispense, or give away narcotic drugs. In addition, it provides for a commodity tax imposed on the drug. The Bureau of Narcotics also administers the Marihuana Tax Act, which has regulatory features similar to those used in the control of narcotics. There are about two hundred federal Bureau of Narcotics agents for the entire country, but they are aided by state and local enforcement officers.

Uniform state laws are now in operation in forty-two states, and there is increased cooperation among various enforcement agencies. Although greater penalties are being demanded for violators of narcotic laws and for some drug users, it is being urged that the penalties imposed on young novices be less severe than those given the organized dope peddler. One reason advanced is that long sentences for peddlers keep them out of circulation and thus make it harder for them to re-establish connections later.

In the United Kingdom, where a much different procedure from that used in the United States is in effect, there were only 335 heroin and morphine addicts known to the authorities in 1955, as compared with the estimated minimum of about 60,000 in the United States, a country three and a half times larger. Even if the official figure is inaccurate, the actual number is said to be probably not large.[52] The black market in drugs there is not great, nor are there many addicts who are "pushers" (peddlers of drugs). There drug addiction is considered as a medical problem, a matter to be treated by the physician with prescription of drugs at low cost, often not as high as the price of cigarettes.[53] Doctors are supposed to prescribe a minimum dosage and to make prolonged attempts to cure the addict. British officials, as well as the public, do not regard the addict as a criminal. The addict does not have to steal, become a prostitute, or peddle drugs in order to secure drugs, and addicts are therefore relatively noncriminal. The system does not appear to have brought about an increase in drug addiction. Lindesmith states that since the present British system seems to work, in that the problem is small and is not growing larger, there is an understandable reluctance to change it in any important way.[54]

Based on British and other experience, a different approach to this

---

[52] Alfred R. Lindesmith, "The British System of Narcotics Control," *Law and Contemporary Problems*, 22:141–142 (Winter, 1957).

[53] Marihuana is not prescribed, as it is regarded as an illicit drug and is dealt with by the police. It does not appear to lead often to heroin addiction, as it appears to do in the United States.

[54] Lindesmith, "The British System of Narcotics Control," *loc. cit.*, p. 147.

problem in the United States has been suggested by several authorities.[55] They believe that suppression has actually increased the difficulties of controlling the drug traffic because it has made necessary the development of an elaborate organization for illicit supply which seeks to extend itself by inducing nonaddicts to become users of narcotics. They also believe that crime has been increased because of addicts' efforts to obtain enough money to buy illicitly the high-priced drugs which could be obtained legally for a fraction of the cost charged by peddlers. After a two-year study Schur suggested that the British policy might well be applied to the American drug situation, even allowing for differences in the public image of the addict and in the detection and prevention of drug smuggling.[56] He feels that drug addiction should not be treated as a crime: "One also becomes aware that current American policies cannot help but fail. The policy of withholding legal satisfaction of the demand for narcotics inevitably leads to a profit-motivated and socially-dangerous illicit market in drugs." [57] Finally, the Joint Committee on Narcotic Drugs (of the American Bar Association and the American Medical Association) has recommended that drug addiction be viewed as a disease rather than a police problem. They have recommended a review of laws to abolish prison terms for addicts, to allow qualified doctors to dispense narcotics, and to establish an experimental outpatient clinic for the care of addicts.

Summary

At one time drug users were tolerated, even in the United States, but later the use of drugs was made illegal. Men use drugs much more than do women, and the use of drugs appears to be increasing among younger persons.

In order to become an addict a person must be aware of the drug, know how to administer it, and recognize its effects. Drug addiction has a culture associated with it. This includes a system of sale and distribution of the drugs and the indoctrination of many persons into the use of drugs by others who are already addicted. Drug addicts have an elaborate argot.

The use of drugs does not appear to be an important factor in crime.

---

[55] Lindesmith, *Opiate Addiction*, pp. 204–210, and August Vollmer, *The Police and Modern Society* (Berkeley: University of California Press, 1936), pp. 117–118. Also see *Drug Addiction: Crime or Disease*, Interim and Final Reports of the Joint Committee of the American Bar Association and the American Medical Association on Narcotic Drugs (Bloomington: Indiana University Press, 1960), and Edwin M. Schur, "British Narcotics Policies," *Journal of Criminal Law, Criminology and Police Science*, 51:619–630 (March–April, 1961). Also see Edwin M. Schur, "Drug Addiction under British Policy," *Social Problems*, 9:156–157 (Fall, 1961).

[56] Schur, "British Narcotics Policies," *loc. cit.*   [57] *Ibid.*, pp. 628–629.

Most criminals do not appear to use drugs. Addicts, however, may commit offenses in order to secure drugs or the money with which to purchase them.

There are two different approaches to the control of drug addiction. Some believe in rigid suppression, whereas others feel that this procedure has increased the deviant behavior by causing the development of an organization for illicit supply. They feel that drugs should be supplied to addicts through governmental and medical agencies.

Selected Readings

ANSLINGER, H. J., and WILLIAM F. TOMPKINS. *The Traffic in Narcotics*. New York: Funk & Wagnalls Company, 1953. A general description of drugs, the methods of their use, and the laws controlling them. Anslinger, for many years United States Commissioner of Narcotics, resigned in 1962.

BECKER, HOWARD S. "Becoming a Marihuana User," *American Journal of Sociology*, 59:235–243 (November, 1953). This study of a group of marihuana users describes the process of becoming a user. A good deal of case material is included.

Drug Addiction: Crime or Disease? Interim and Final Reports of the Joint Committee of the American Bar Association and the American Medical Association on Narcotic Drugs. Bloomington: Indiana University Press, 1960. Contains a comprehensive analysis of the drug problem in the United States by Morris Ploscowe, as well as a survey of drug control programs in Britain and other European countries. The reports reveal widespread dissatisfaction with existing legislation and law enforcement among medical and legal authorities in this country.

Law and Contemporary Problems. "Narcotics" Vol. 22, No. 1 (Winter, 1957). Contains a series of articles on many phases of drug addiction including the history of the development of narcotics, addiction and its treatment, social and psychological factors in narcotics addiction, juvenile narcotics use, narcotics and criminality, international control of narcotics, narcotic drug laws and enforcement policies, alternative solution to the problem, and the British system of narcotics control.

LINDESMITH, ALFRED R. *Opiate Addiction*. Bloomington: University of Indiana Press, 1947. A social psychological study of the process of opiate addiction containing many cases.

SCHUR, EDWIN M., "British Narcotics Policies," *Journal of Criminal Law, Criminology and Police Science*, 51:619–630 (March–April, 1961).

Alcohol Drinking
and Alcoholism

Problems related to the consumption of alcohol, the role of the tavern in a society, and the alcoholic are far from being unique to any culture or age. Researches on the contents of the tombs of ancient Egypt and in the buried cities of Babylon reveal that as early in history as three thousand years ago the use of wine and beer was a subject of moral concern.

Socrates, Aristotle, Plato, Cicero, and others inveighed against intoxication as debasing the dignity of man. The Spartans and Carthaginians limited drinking among soldiers on active duty for reasons of efficiency. The Ethiopians, who were water drinkers, boasted of their long life and vigor in contrast to the shorter life span of their wine-using neighbors, the Persians.

The barbarian Gauls invading Roman territories reacted violently when they discovered the effects of wine. This was noticed by Roman leaders and by the Greeks, who avoided giving battle until the invaders were stuporous from drinking, then slaughtered them easily. But it should be noted that although Egyptian civilization attained a remarkably high level, both men and women gorged themselves with wine to the point of deep intoxication. The Spanish and Portuguese people, on the other hand, appear to have been remarkably abstemious.

Various attempts at regulatory controls of drinking appear in the ancient literature. In China during the Chou Dynasty (1134–256 B.C.) and the reign of the fourth emperor of the Yuan Dynasty, about 1312 A.D., laws against the manufacture, sale, and consumption of wine were established and repealed no less than forty-one times. Penalties for violation of the decrees were extremely severe.[1]

Today the use of alcohol represents a conflict of values, while excessive drinking and alcoholism may be considered as deviant behavior. The value conflicts over the use of alcohol actually represent a struggle between a Calvinistic tradition that it is the community's responsibility to

---

[1] Raymond G. McCarthy ed., *Drinking and Intoxication* (New York: The Free Press of Glencoe, 1959), pp. 39–40.

supervise the individual's drinking and an individualistic tradition that regards drinking as a matter of free choice.

In 1959, 85.3 percent of the population of the United States resided in areas where alcoholic beverages were sold.[2] Local option is provided in many states so that the percentage of population living in "wet" areas was less than two thirds in many states: in Tennessee, 33.1; Georgia, 38.1; Kentucky, 42.5; Alabama, 51.1; Texas, 54.1; Kansas, 50.1; Arkansas, 57.0; and North Carolina, 57.1. Mississippi is the only completely dry state, Oklahoma having repealed its dry law in 1959. Moreover, some counties in many states do not permit alcoholic beverages to be drunk where it is sold; that is, liquor is sold only in the bottle in privately or publicly owned liquor stores. In nineteen states, in 1960, the sale of distilled spirits by the bottle was controlled by a state board selling through state stores.

As a result of their continually conflicting claims and propaganda, temperance organizations and concerns manufacturing and distributing alcoholic beverages have done much to crystallize value judgments surrounding the use and misuse of alcoholic beverages. Frederick Lewis Allen in *Only Yesterday* wrote about the conflict during the Prohibition era:

> Whatever the contributions of the Prohibition regime to temperance, at least it produced intemperate propaganda and counter-propaganda. Almost any dry could tell you that Prohibition was the basis of American prosperity as attested by the mounting volume of savings-bank deposits . . . or that Prohibition had reduced the deaths from alcoholism, emptied the jails, diverted the workman's dollars to the purchase of automobiles, radios, and homes. Almost any wet could tell you that Prohibition had nothing to do with prosperity but it caused the crime wave, the increase of immorality and of the divorce rate, and a disrespect for all law which imperiled the very foundations of free government. The wets said the drys fostered Bolshevism by their fanatical zeal for laws which were inevitably flouted; the drys said the wets fostered Bolshevism by their cynical lawbreaking. Even in matters of supposed fact, you could find, if you only read and listened, any sort of ammunition that you wanted. One never saw drunkards on the streets any more; one saw more drunkards than ever. Drinking in the colleges was hardly a problem now; drinking in the colleges was at its worst. There was a still in every other home in the mining districts of Pennsylvania; drinking in the mining districts of Pennsylvania was a thing of the past. Cases of poverty as a result of drunkenness were only a fraction of what they used to be; the menace of drinking in the slums was three times as great as in Pre-Volstead days.[3]

---

[2] The Joint Committee of the States to Study Alcoholic Beverage Laws, *Alcoholic Beverage Control* (Washington, D.C.: 1960). The data for the states presented here were furnished to the Joint Committee by the Distilled Spirits Institute.

[3] Frederick Lewis Allen, *Only Yesterday* (New York: Harper & Row, Publishers, 1931), pp. 254-255. For a discussion of the issues and organizations involved in Repeal, see Raymond G. McCarthy and Edgar M. Douglass, *Alcohol and Social Responsibility* (New York: Thomas Y. Crowell Company and the Yale Plan Clinic, 1949), pp. 25-41, also reprinted in McCarthy, *Drinking and Intoxication*, pp. 368-435. Sweden has tried

The Drys have concentrated their attack by upholding the home, family, children, religion, and morality, which they claim are endangered by the use of alcohol and the existence of taverns. Newspaper headlines assist them in their attempts to show the deleterious consequences of the use of alcohol: "Stampede for Holiday Liquor"; "Drink Turns Patrolman into Murderer"; "Paralytic Struck by Drunk Driver"; "Liquor and Bad Company Lead to Jail"; "Drunken Boys Led to Jail"; "Man Killed in Tavern Brawl"; "Drunken Father Beats Family"; "Drunken Driver Kills Three." A speaker at a convention of the National Temperance Movement stated:

> At the close of the first ten years of repeal a committee of fifty, after extensive research, reported that the use of liquor is responsible for 20 per cent of divorces, 20 per cent of fatal accidents, 25 per cent of insanity, 37 per cent of poverty, 50 per cent of crime, 75 to 90 per cent of venereal infection. My guess is that every one of these percentages is now greater after five additional years of repeal—with the possible exception of the one of poverty.[4]

Although many of these claims cannot be supported, there is no question that the excessive use of alcoholic beverages is costing industry huge sums of money in the form of absenteeism, inefficiency on the job, and accidents. Landis, in 1945, for example, estimated the total monetary cost of excessive drinking as nearly $800 million; it is, of course, impossible to estimate the indirect social cost.[5]

A comparison between a group of industrial workers who were problem drinkers and two control groups revealed that the problem drinkers had 2.9 times as many days absent and 2.5 times as many cases of illness or injury-caused absences of eight days or more as the control groups.[6] The cost of sickness payments was 3.3 times as great and, in the case of women problem drinkers, twice as great.

There are conflicts not only about the use of alcohol but also about the tavern as a public institution. An investigation in Wisconsin revealed that both patrons and nonpatrons of taverns differ within each group in their attitudes toward the tavern and drinking in general.[7] Some non-

---

modified prohibition, and Finland, prohibition, but both countries have changed their laws. For a discussion of some of the results see McCarthy, *op. cit.*, pp. 347–367.

[4] Paul S. Rees, "Forward to Victory," a synopsis of his closing address at the Biennial Convention of the Convention of the National Temperance Movement in *The National Temperance Digest*, 3:5 (February, 1949).

[5] Benson Y. Landis, "Some Economic Aspects of Alcohol Problems," *Memoirs of the Section on Alcohol Studies* (No. 4; New Haven, Conn.: Quarterly Journal of Studies on Alcohol, 1945), pp. 28–29.

[6] Observer (a pseud.) and Milton A. Maxwell, "A Study of Absenteeism, Accidents and Sickness Payments in Problem Drinkers in One Industry," *Quarterly Journal of Studies on Alcohol*, 20:302–312 (June, 1959). Also see Harrison M. Trice, "Work Accidents and the Problem Drinker: A Case Study," *ILR Research*, 3:2–6, No. 2 (1957).

[7] Boyd E. Macrory, "The Tavern and the Community," *Quarterly Journal of Studies on Alcohol*, 13:609–637 (December, 1952).

patrons, for example, believe that the contemporary tavern is a lesser evil than the speakeasy of bootleg days and that there is no harm in an occasional drink with friends in a tavern; other nonpatrons think of the tavern as a place to relax and meet friends; but other nonpatrons view the tavern as an unmitigated evil related to drunkenness, unhappy home life, marital difficulties, and neglect of children. Regular tavern patrons were similarly divided in their opinions. Some believed that the tavern is useful because it provides a place for relaxation, a meeting place, and an orderly place for drinking as opposed to Prohibition days. Other regular patrons, however, believed that the tavern contributed to various types of crime, loss of jobs, domestic difficulties, highway accidents, and alcoholism.

The attitudes of certain groups in the population toward drinking and public drinking houses are also reflected in the rigid regulation of alcohol distribution through taverns.[8] These regulations imply that the tavern is the source of immorality, delinquency, and drunkenness and that a man of high moral character must be in charge if the community is to be protected. Regulations generally limit the number of taverns to a certain ratio of the population and specify high license fees, generally between $200 and $900 a year, regardless of the size of the establishment. Some states closely scrutinize prospective tavernkeepers' past histories for records of criminal or other immoral behavior. In some communities, the license of a tavern owner who knowingly employs a bartender with a criminal background is subject to revocation. Taverns must observe strict closing hours, they must generally remain closed on election days, on Christmas Eve, and on certain other holidays. They must not permit minors on the premises, are not allowed to obscure a full view of the interior from the outside, may not give "credit," and may not serve visibly intoxicated persons. Women, except relatives, are generally prohibited from working in taverns, although the employment of women is customary in Great Britain. In several states so-called dram acts make the tavern owner responsible for injuries incurred by a patron after leaving the tavern.

Physiological Effects of Alcohol

Alcohol is a chemical substance which is derived through a process of fermentation or by distillation. Although the process of distillation of alcoholic beverages from barley, corn, wheat, and other grains is fairly recent in human history, nearly all societies have made fermented beverages, such as wine, beer, and similar products, for thousands of years.[9]

[8] See Marshall B. Clinard, "The Public Drinking House and Society," in David J. Pittman and Charles R. Snyder eds., *Alcohol, Culture and Drinking Patterns* (New York: John Wiley & Sons, Inc., 1962), pp. 270–292.

[9] Clarence H. Patrick, *Alcohol, Culture and Society* (Durham, N.C.: Duke University Press, 1952), pp. 12–39.

Following the intake of alcoholic beverages, a certain amount of alcohol is absorbed into the blood stream from the stomach, but most of it is absorbed in the small intestine. It is carried in the blood to the liver and then disseminated in diluted form to every part of the body. Because there can never be more than 1 percent of alcohol in the blood stream, it cannot directly cause organic brain damage, neither "corroding," "dissolving," nor in any way directly harming the brain cells.[10] In fact, all substances classed as volatile anesthetics, such as ether, can produce precisely the same reactions upon the brain.[11] Alcohol is not physiologically habit-forming in the sense that certain narcotics are. One does not become a chronic drinker as the result of the first, twentieth, or even one hundredth drink. Moreover, it has never been demonstrated that the craving for alcohol is inherited.[12]

Actually the effect of alcohol is determined by the rate at which it is absorbed into the body, which depends upon the kind of alcoholic beverage consumed, the proportion of alcohol it contains, the speed with which it is drunk, and the amount and type of food in the stomach, as well as on certain minor physiological differences among individuals.[13] In moderate quantities alcohol has relatively little effect on a person, but large quantities disturb the activity in the organs controlled by the brain and cause the phenomenon known as "drunkenness." The effect on behavior of different kinds and quantities of alcoholic beverages on the human system of a 150-pound person is shown in Table 12.1.

As alcohol is consumed, it acts increasingly as a depressant and as an anesthetic.

The prime action of alcohol in the body is its depressant action on the function of the central nervous system, the brain. This is an anesthetic action no different from that of ether or chloroform. The part of the brain affected and the degree of impairment depend on the concentration of alcohol in the blood and therefore acting on the brain. Although this action is entirely on the brain, disturbance in behavior is manifested in the organs controlled by the particular brain areas affected. Speech is thick, hands clumsy, knees sag, the person appears drunk—not because of the presence of alcohol in his tongue, hands or knees, but because it has depressed those parts of his brain controlling these organs.

In a person of average size, 2 or 3 ounces of whisky present in the body will produce 0.05 per cent of alcohol in the blood. With this amount the uppermost levels of brain functioning are depressed, diminishing inhibi-

---

[10] McCarthy and Douglass, *op. cit.,* pp. 89–93.

[11] See Howard W. Haggard, "The Physiological Effects of Large and Small Amounts of Alcohol," in *Alcohol, Science and Society* (New Brunswick, N.J.: Quarterly Journal of Studies on Alcohol, 1945), pp. 59–72.

[12] Anne Roe, "Children of Alcoholic Parents Raised in Foster Homes," in *Alcohol, Science and Society,* p. 124.

[13] McCarthy and Douglass, *op. cit.,* p. 89.

Table 12.1. The Effect of Alcoholic Beverages

Amount of beverage consumed	Concentration of alcohol attained in blood	Effect		Time required for all alcohol to leave the body
1 highball (1½ oz. whisky) or 1 cocktail (1½ oz. whisky) or 3½ oz. fortified wine or 5½ oz. ordinary wine or 2 bottles beer (24 oz.)	0.03%	No noticeable effects on behavior		2 hrs.
2 highballs or 2 cocktails or 7 oz. fortified wine or 11 oz. ordinary wine or 4 bottles beer	0.06%	Increasing effects with variation among individuals and in the same individuals at different times	Feeling of warmth—mental relaxation—slight decrease of fine skills—less concern with minor irritations and restraints	4 hrs.
3 highballs or 3 cocktails or 10½ oz. fortified wine or 16½ oz. (1 pt.) ordinary wine or 6 bottles beer	0.09%		Buoyancy—exaggerated emotion and behavior—talkative, noisy, or morose	6 hrs.
4 highballs or 4 cocktails or 14 oz. fortified wine or 22 oz. ordinary wine or 8 bottles (3 qts.) beer	0.12%		Impairment of fine coordination—clumsiness—slight to moderate unsteadiness in standing or walking	8 hrs.
5 highballs or 5 cocktails or (½ pt. whisky)	0.15%	Intoxication—unmistakable abnormality of gross bodily functions and mental faculties		10 hrs.

For those weighing considerably more or less than 150 pounds the amounts of beverage indicated above will be correspondingly greater or less. The effects indicated at each stage will diminish as the concentration of alcohol in the blood diminishes.

SOURCE: Leon A. Greenberg, "Intoxication and Alcoholism: Physiological Factors," *The Annals*, 315:28 (January, 1958). Reprinted by permission of the American Academy of Political and Social Science.

tion, restraint, and judgment. The drinker feels that he is "sitting on top of the world," many of his normal inhibitions have vanished; he takes many personal and social liberties as the impulse prompts; he is long-winded and has an obvious blunting of self-criticism. At a concentration of 0.10 per cent of alcohol in the blood, resulting from 5 or 6 ounces of whisky in the body, function of the lower motor area of the brain is dulled. The person sways perceptibly; he has difficulty putting on his coat; he fumbles with the key at the door; words stumble over a clumsy tongue.

The states so far described are popularly designated as mild intoxication or "feeling high." The significant feature of these states is depression and dulling of sensory and motor function and, contrary to popular belief, not stimulation. The illusion of stimulation is given by the increased tempo and altered quality of behavior occurring when the normally prevailing inhibitions and restraints are removed by alcohol. The effect may be compared to releasing the brakes rather than stepping on the accelerator. Notwithstanding this illusion there is actually measurable reduction in sensitivity, impaired discrimination, and diminished speed of motor responses. The drinker, however, often denies that this occurs; often asserts, on the contrary, that after a few drinks his reactions, perception, and discrimination are better. This is an important effect of alcohol; his judgment about himself and his own activities is blunted, allowing for an inflated feeling of competence and self-confidence.

With increasing concentrations of alcohol in the blood there is a corresponding progression of impairment of functions. At 0.20 per cent, resulting from about 10 ounces of whisky, the entire motor area of the brain is profoundly affected. The individual tends to assume a horizontal position; he needs help to walk or undress. At 0.30 per cent, from the presence of a pint of whisky in the body, sensory perception is so dulled that the drinker has little comprehension of what he sees, hears, or feels; he is stuporous. At 0.40 per cent, perception is obliterated; the person is in coma, he is anesthetized. At 0.60 or 0.70 per cent, the lowest, most primitive levels of the brain controlling breathing and heartbeat cease to function and death ensues. Throughout this entire progression the concentrations of alcohol in the body are far too low to cause any direct organic damage to the tissues. The disturbance is entirely one of nerve function and is reversible; short of death, when the alcohol disappears the effect goes with it.[14]

If taken in moderate amounts, alcohol can lessen tensions and worry, and in general it may ease the fatigue associated with anxiety.[15] It presents an illusion of being a stimulant because it reduces or alters the cortical control over action. Under the influence of alcohol a person may become active, boisterous, aggressive, silent, or even fall into a stupor, all as a result of this reduction in cortical control and not from stimulation.

Much has been made of the so-called alcoholic diseases, such as beriberi, pellagra, and cirrhosis of the liver. Although these diseases are found among nonalcoholics as well as among alcoholics, the continuous drinking of alcohol brings about an almost complete loss of appetite, and, if this drinking is not curbed, disease may follow, not from the alcohol consumed but rather because of the nutritional deficiencies resulting from prolonged drinking. These deficiencies may produce an organic ailment called polyneuritis, or, less technically, beriberi, caused by a lack

[14] Leon A. Greenberg, "Intoxication and Alcoholism: Physiological Factors," *The Annals*, 315:26–27 (January, 1958). Reprinted by permission of the American Academy of Political and Social Science.
[15] Haggard, "The Physiological Effects . . . of Alcohol," *loc. cit.*, p. 63.

of vitamin B_1; or pellagra, caused by a deficiency of niacin. The fact that these deficiencies are present has caused some researchers to believe that alcoholism can be prevented or controlled by proper nutrition.[16] The disease which the man in the street most often associates with chronic alcoholism is cirrhosis of the liver. Although this disease occurs proportionately more often among inebriates than among nondrinkers, medical men state that it is not caused directly by alcohol but instead is due to some nutritional deficiency which has not as yet been conclusively demonstrated.[17]

Drinking as a Social Phenomenon

Alcoholic beverages of one type or another have been widely used for centuries by most ancient and modern peoples.[18] The people of Western Europe, and those who first colonized America, were no exception.

> In New England and the Middle and Southern colonies along the eastern seaboard, beer and ale were part of the daily diet and believed necessary to maintain health. However, from the earliest days, drunkenness was frowned upon and punishments were imposed on those who consumed more than was considered seemly. During the late eighteenth century, rum, which has a far higher alcohol content than ale or beer, became an integral part of the economic and social life of the colonies. Numerous distilleries were established in all the population centers.[19]

Drinking patterns today appear to vary in terms of the beverage used, the circumstances under which drinking takes place, the time, the amount, and the individual's own attitude and that of others toward his drinking. All drinking patterns are learned, just as other behavior is learned. As one writer on alcohol has stated, there are no universal drinking patterns for John, the average citizen: "In any event, John will not drink like a Zulu or an Austrian or a Japanese; in fact, he will not drink like a New Yorker or a Californian or a ditch digger or a Yale man or a Kentucky mountaineer, unless he is or has been in socially significant contact with such a group." [20] Patterns of drinking come down to us from

---

[16] Roger J. Williams, *Alcoholism: The Nutritional Approach* (Austin: University of Texas Press, 1959).

[17] Norman Jolliffe, "Alcohol and Nutrition: The Diseases of Chronic Alcoholism," in *Alcohol, Science and Society*, pp. 76–77.

[18] For a discussion of drinking practices of ancient Greece and Rome, the Far East, Central and South America, as well as France, England, Canada, and Russia, see McCarthy, *op. cit.*, pp. 39–179.

[19] Raymond G. McCarthy, "Alcoholism: Attitudes and Attacks, 1775–1935," *The Annals*, 315:13 (January, 1958).

[20] Selden D. Bacon, "Sociology and the Problems of Alcohol," *Memoirs of the Section of Studies on Alcohol* (No. 1; New Brunswick, N.J.: Quarterly Journal of Studies on Alcohol, 1946), pp. 17–18.

a long past in which alcohol has been used. The knowledge, ideas, norms, and values involved in the use of alcoholic beverages which have passed from generation to generation have thus maintained the continuity of an alcohol culture.

Drinking plays a significant role in everyday interpersonal affairs. Alcohol is used by many people to celebrate national holidays, such as Christmas and New Year's, and to rejoice in victories, whether those of war, the football field, or the ballot box. The bride and groom are often toasted, and the father may celebrate the birth of a child with a drink "all around." Promotions, anniversaries, and important special events of achievement by the family and close friends often call for a drink. Businessmen may negotiate contracts over a few glasses, and meeting an old friend is often the occasion for a drink. In some homes guests are welcomed with a drink or cocktails before dinner to help get the guests acquainted.

Even some church ceremonials and, on occasion, the bereavement of death are accompanied by alcoholic beverages. On a more inclusive level, it has been said: "The custom of drinking together to symbolize common feeling and unity is almost universal in present-day culture. . . . Thus imbedded in the culture pattern is the notion that in alcohol is magic which, in sorrow and in joy, in elation and in depression, in rebellion against the misery of travail and the restraints which hem one in, frees the human spirit and permits it to soar into the heavens unhampered by the ills of the flesh." [21]

Drinking by teen-agers is almost entirely a group activity and represents culturally patterned and socially controlled behavior. The drinking of teen-agers is almost entirely "partying action." [22] Drinking, for at least some teen-agers, is related to the passage from youth into young male adult roles in our society. Teen-age groups are important reference groups to the members.

There are also drinking patterns among college students. Dating often includes having a drink before or after a dance, show, or party. In some places college men have a tradition of drinking to celebrate the conclusion of examinations. "Bull sessions" often involve beer drinking, and some fraternities and other social organizations have drinking traditions. In European universities there were, and still are, "drinking fraternities" for which members qualified by their ability to consume a large quantity of wine, beer, ale, or other liquor. College drinking songs, expressing friendship and other deep feelings, have at times attained great popularity. A detailed study of college drinking habits found that motivations for

---

[21] Ernest R. Mowrer, *Disorganization: Personal and Social* (Phildelphia: J. B. Lippincott Company, 1942), pp. 263–264. Reprinted by permission of the publisher.

[22] Christopher Sower, "Teen-Age Drinking as Group Behavior," *Quarterly Journal of Studies on Alcohol*, 20:656 (September, 1959).

drinking, as given by men and women who drink, were approximately the same.[23] However, women more frequently felt that they drank in order to get along better on dates and they drank more often than men did to relieve illness and physical discomfort.

Despite the widespread use of alcohol in connection with many social functions, one writer has contrasted the value systems implicit in American drinking patterns with those on the Continent.

> Traditionally, in European cultures, aside from past dietetic necessity, drinking has been a phase of a deeply rooted, stable and integrated social and recreational pattern. Among Europeans, drinking may remain a satisfying social practice rather than a vice or social problem, largely because it remains an element within otherwise integrated and participating recreational practices. . . . With Europeans, for example, drinking has traditionally been a phase of the occasion of the group's coming together; with Americans, conversely, coming together has all too frequently provided the occasion for drinking. In this distinction, and its historical evolution, appears to lie one of the salient factors in the more disturbing features of our drinking habits.[24]

Public Drinking Houses and Society

A large proportion of drinking is done in groups, much of it in public drinking houses, which are found in most of the world today under a variety of names: American taverns and bars, British pubs, French bistros, German beer halls, Italian wine houses, and Japanese bars. In the United States alone there are over 200,000 bars and taverns.

A tavern, as we shall refer to a public drinking house, is more than a place where alcoholic beverages are sold for consumption on the premises. There are several important characteristics of a contemporary tavern: (1) A tavern involves group drinking. (2) This drinking is commercial in the sense that the ability to buy a drink is available to all as opposed to the bars of private clubs. (3) A tavern serves alcohol, however, and can thus be distinguished from the modern soda fountains, the coffeehouses of the Middle East, or the teahouses of the Orient. (4) It has a tavernkeeper or bartender who serves as a functionary of the institution and around whom, in part, the drinking gravitates. (5) There are many customs connected with a tavern, including the physical surroundings, types of drinks, and hours of sale.[25]

---

[23] Robert Straus and Selden D. Bacon, *Drinking in College* (New Haven, Conn.: Yale University Press, 1953), p. 71. Also see C. A. Hecht, R. J. Grine, and S. E. Rothrock, "Drinking and Dating among College Women," *Quarterly Journal of Studies on Alcohol,* 9:252–259 (September, 1948); and F. C. Berezin and N. R. Roth, "Drinking Practices of College Women," *Quarterly Journal of Studies on Alcohol,* 11:212–221 (June, 1950).

[24] Herbert A. Bloch, "Alcohol and American Recreational Life," *American Scholar,* 18:56–57 (January, 1949).

[25] Clinard, "The Public Drinking House and Society," *loc. cit.*

Taverns can be traced to Babylon, where the Code of Hammurabi provided for their regulation. In ancient Greece there were many taverns, although they had quite an unsavory reputation.[26] In Roman times there was a great variety of public drinking houses, ten different types being distinguished according to location, type of patron, and type of tavern operator. Some Roman taverns were regarded unfavorably and some were well accepted. One writer has flatly stated that more harm to Roman society would have resulted from their abolition than actually resulted from their continued existence.[27]

The inns of seventeenth- and eighteenth-century England, however, are more generally regarded as the forerunners of the modern tavern. In the earliest of these inns alcoholic beverages were served in the kitchen to travelers and persons of the local community. Eventually a special room was set apart for serving alcoholic beverages to persons who were of the upper classes and who did not care to associate with others in the kitchen. There were two classes of public houses in England, the ale and the wine taverns. The latter were considered more "respectable than the ale taverns and catered to a wealthier clientele." [28] Although some people regarded taverns as dens of iniquity, others considered them as necessary public institutions. One writer has stated that many of the public drinking houses in London were the meeting places of politicians and traders and were "the only places of convenient sojourn and pleasant sociality." [29]

Taverns played a significant role not only in England, where they came from, but in colonial America. In part because they believed that drinking not done in public was likely to be excessive and that the sale of liquor in a tavern could be regulated, the Puritan authorities in Massachusetts in 1656 even enacted a law making towns liable to a fine for not maintaining an ordinary (tavern).[30] During Puritan times tavernkeepers enjoyed a rather high status, and attempts were made to attract the right kind of person into this occupation. Tavernkeepers were granted land or pasturage and were often exempted from school taxes and church rates.[31]

In colonial America taverns served as coach stations or wayside stops and as places of lodging for strangers in the community. They were used as schools, courthouses, public meeting houses, post offices, job markets, and

---

[26] W. C. Firebaugh, *Inns of Greece and Rome* (Chicago: F. M. Morris, 1928).

[27] *Ibid.*, p. 65.

[28] J. D. Rolleston, "Alcoholism in Medieval England," *British Journal of Inebriety*, 31:46 (October, 1933).

[29] Frederick W. Hackwood, *Inns, Ales and Drinking Customs of Old England* (New York: Sturgis and Walton Co., 1911), p. 172.

[30] Eugene Field, *The Colonial Tavern* (Providence: Preston and Rounds, 1897), pp. 11–12.

[31] Herbert Asbury, *The Great Illusion* (New York: Doubleday & Company, Inc., 1950), p. 8.

as places for celebrations of weddings and national holidays.[32] One writer asserts that in colonial America the people found that "the tavern was their club, their board of trade, their 'exchanges,' and indeed, to most of the colonists it served as their newspapers." [33]

In both England and the United States the coming of the railroads gradually eliminated the necessity for taverns as coach stations, and their number declined. The Industrial Revolution, in turn, brought thousands of migrants, particularly single men, to work in the factories. A new type of public drinking house, the saloon, replaced the wayside taverns. The saloon became the urban standard characterized by strictly male patronage, drinking at an elaborate bar with free meals, and a special "family entrance." The overelaborate *décor* was in dramatic contrast to the squalid everyday environment of the workingman.[34] Most saloons performed an important function by helping to relieve the poverty, loneliness, and monotony of city life, although some were centers of deviant behavior such as drunkenness, gambling, and prostitution. A sociological study of saloons in the nineteenth ward of Chicago between 1896 and 1897 found that most saloons in this area were not centers of intemperance or vice.[35] In fact, the saloon was found to have many other functions:

> It [the saloon] is the workingman's club. Many of his leisure hours are spent here. In it he finds more of the things which approximate to luxury than he finds at home, almost more than he finds in any other public place in the ward. . . . But his demand for even these things is not fundamental, they are but the means to his social expression. It is the society of his fellows that he seeks and must have.[36]

After enactment of the Eighteenth Amendment in this country the saloon as a type became legally extinct. It was replaced by the illicit "speakeasy" with its select clientele, often adulterated alcoholic beverages, and an urban sophisticated setting. After the repeal of Prohibition the modern tavern made its appearance; more correctly, at least five different varieties of public places emerged, these types being largely associated with certain areas of the city. They were different from the saloon in that women in general were permitted, the surroundings were more attractive, and patrons more frequently drank while seated at tables rather than while standing at a bar. Contemporary taverns may be classified as Skid Row, the downtown

---

[32] Simon Dinitz, "The Relation of the Tavern to the Drinking Phases of Alcoholics." Unpublished doctoral dissertation, University of Wisconsin, Madison, 1951.

[33] Field, *op. cit.,* pp. 232–233.

[34] Maurice Gorham and M. McDunnett, *Inside the Pub* (London: The Architectural Press, 1950), p. 68.

[35] Ernest C. Moore, "The Social Value of the Saloon," *American Journal of Sociology,* 3:1–12 (July, 1897). Also see Raymond Calkins, *Substitutes for the Saloon: An Investigation Made for the Committee of Fifty* (Boston: Houghton Mifflin Company, 1901).

[36] Moore, *loc. cit.,* pp. 4–5.

bar, the dine and dance establishment, the night club, and the neighborhood tavern, which is divided primarily by location, and secondarily by patronage, into four subtypes: the rural, village, suburban, and city neighborhood types.

1. The Skid Row tavern is located close to the business district of urban centers. It offers little more than drinking and the blaring juke box. The bulk of its patrons are drifters, transients, and alcoholics. Drunkenness, prostitution, gambling, and violations of other state laws and ordinances are frequent.

2. The downtown bar is located in the business district, has long bars, few tables, and a predominantly male patronage. There are few recreational facilities but much drinking over business agreements or prior to going home from work.

3. The drink and dine establishment is located in the business district or close to the city limits, where it competes with night clubs which not only often serve fine food but afford an opportunity to dance as well. It has well-kept and often spacious dining rooms where fine food is served; yet much of its income and most of its profit are derived from the sale of alcoholic beverages.

4. The night club is usually located near the city limits along main highways. This type of tavern offers drink, food, and dancing, and the seating arrangement usually centers about the stage and dance floor. A larger proportion of women patronize both this type of tavern and the drink and dine establishment than the downtown bar. It is patronized by the business and professional classes, as well as by draftsmen and laborers.

5. The neighborhood tavern is the most numerous, constituting probably three fourths of all taverns. Most drinking is done seated around tables. It is patronized by people, largely couples, in the neighborhood. There are several subtypes, the city, suburban, village, and rural. It has many functions as a meeting place for regular patrons, offering them amusement, recreation, a chance to talk and to enjoy music, and general relaxation.[37]

Public drinking houses, as well as package liquor stores, are disproportionately concentrated in lower-class areas and constitute a highly visible symbol of the lower-class way of life.[38] There tends to be little distance between the place of residence and public facilities for alcohol consumption. This suggests that "people in the upper reaches of the social hierarchy might do most of their drinking at home or in downtown lounges and hotels, public places for imbibing being separated by some distance from place of residence." [39]

---

[37] Condensed from Macrory, "The Tavern and the Community," loc. cit.
[38] Harold W. Pfautz and Robert W. Hyde, "The Ecology of Alcohol in the Local Community," Quarterly Journal of Studies on Alcohol, 21:447–456 (September, 1960).
[39] Ibid., p. 455.

It appears that the functions of a tavern reflect the type of tavern and the conditions of its neighborhood. Examples are the Skid Row taverns, where drunkenness and other deviant behavior may flourish, and respectable neighborhood taverns, each of which reflects the norms of the local community. Drinking does not appear to be the actual reason for patronizing most neighborhood taverns.[40] Rather, such taverns function primarily as a place for people to meet for the sake of establishing and maintaining social relationships.[41] People also go to taverns to avoid loneliness and to relax from the cares and problems of the home and the factory, office, or farm. The neighborhood tavern also serves as a place for recreation, which includes such entertainments as card games, shuffleboard, pinball machines, juke boxes, or television. Finally, sympathetic tavernkeepers, bartenders, and others give the patron an opportunity to talk over his personal problems. Much the same reasons appear to account for the extensive participation in British pubs (public drinking houses) and French bistros.[42] According to one study, British pubs are patronized not only for the sake of drinking but for the opportunities for sociability and recreation they provide.[43]

> No pub can simply be regarded as a drinking shop. It may be lacking in facilities for games and music, present no organized forms of social activity and its actual accommodation be of the crudest, but none the less the activities of the drinkers are not confined to drinking. . . . The pub is a centre of social activities—for the ordinary pub goer the main scene of social life. Worktown working people rarely meet in each other's homes for social activities in the way middle classes do. For some there is the social activity of politics, football, or cricket clubs. But participators in these activities are a small minority. The place where most Worktowners meet their friends and acquaintances is the pub. Men can meet and talk [out] of the way of their womenfolk.[44]

Finally, the neighborhood tavern exercises a degree of control over the drinking behavior of those who patronize it. As one writer who studied

---

[40] Clinard, "The Public Drinking House and Society," loc. cit. and Margaret K. Chandler, "The Social Organization of Workers in a Rooming House Area." Unpublished doctoral dissertation, University of Chicago, 1948.

[41] Macrory, "The Tavern and the Community," loc. cit., pp. 630–636.

[42] Joseph Wechsberg, "They Debate L'Alcoholisme—Over Their Drinks," The New York Times Magazine, March 26, 1961. Wechsberg remarks that the French bistros are the hub of French democracy and where the average Frenchman spends most of his leisure time. Also see Gabriel Mouchot, "France: Drinking and Its Control," in McCarthy, Drinking and Intoxication, pp. 149–158.

[43] Mass-Observation, The Pub and the People (London: Victor Gollancz, Ltd., 1943), pp. 82–83. Authorities on British labor history, such as the Webbs, have shown that a significant portion of the old union budgets went to supply the members with ale and other drinks at meetings and social gatherings. Also see B. Seebohm Rowntree and G. R. Lavers, English Life and Leisure (New York: David McKay Company, Inc., 1951), pp. 159–198.

[44] Mass-Observation, The Pub and the People, p. 311.

a number of them stated, "Each tavern seems to set its own norms as to what degree of inebriation it will tolerate. The old timers are allowed a certain freedom. In others, drunkenness and boisterousness are generally not acceptable. . . . The sense of participation is rewarding; loss of it hurts him." [45]

Attitudes toward the tavern are influenced by a person's position in the social structure as well as by his tavern patronage.[46] While a large proportion of the general population in all social strata drink alcoholic beverages, not all go to taverns. Many consumers of alcohol, particularly those of the middle and upper classes, drink at home, at cocktail parties, or at the bars of private clubs, such as golf clubs. While they may go to cocktail lounges or night clubs, they seldom visit neighborhood taverns. Taverns are often not even located in the immediate vicinity of their homes.

Extent of Drinking in the United States

In the United States the drinking of alcohol, in order of amount consumed and cost, consists chiefly of beer, followed by distilled spirits, and wine fermented from grapes. Over the past eighty years there has been a downward trend in the drinking of distilled spirits and an increase in the consumption of beer. From the period 1860–1870 to 1960 the consumption of distilled spirits declined well over a third, while the consumption of beer almost doubled. (See Table 12.2.) In the year 1850 almost 90 percent of the absolute alcohol consumed, that is, the alcohol content of a beverage, in the United States was in the form of distilled spirits, and nearly 7 percent was beer. A century later only 38 percent was in the form of spirits; 51 percent was beer. In 1948, $8.8 billion were spent on alcoholic beverages of all types, and in 1959, $9.6 billion. In the fiscal year 1960 the United States Treasury Department reported excise tax collections of $3,193,714,000 on alcoholic beverages, or one fourth of all excise taxes, and exceeding by far those collected on tobacco, automobiles, or gasoline.[47]

Approximately two thirds of the adult population over twenty-one years of age drink some type of alcoholic beverage during the year. (See Table 12.3). A larger proportion of men drink than women, three in four men as compared with one in two women. There is considerable evidence, however, that with the increasing trend toward equality in the behavior of the sexes drinking patterns may eventually become nearly the same.[48]

---

[45] David Gottlieb, "The Neighborhood Tavern and the Cocktail Lounge: A Study of Class Differences," *American Journal of Sociology*, 62:561 (May, 1957).

[46] Clinard, "The Public Drinking House and Society," *loc. cit.*

[47] The federal excise tax rate on distilled spirits is $10.50 per proof gallon.

[48] John W. Riley and Charles F. Marden, "The Social Pattern of Alcoholic Drinking," *Quarterly Journal of Studies on Alcohol*, 8:265–273 (September, 1947).

Table 12.2. Apparent Consumption of Alcoholic Beverages, per Capita (Aged 15 and Over), United States, 1850–1960, in United States Gallons

Year	Spirits Beverage	Spirits Absolute alcohol	Wine Beverage	Wine Absolute alcohol	Beer Beverage	Beer Absolute alcohol	Total absolute alcohol
1850	4.17	1.88	0.46	0.08	2.70	0.14	2.10
1860	4.79	2.16	0.57	0.10	5.39	0.27	2.53
1870	3.40	1.53	0.53	0.10	8.73	0.44	2.07
1881–90	2.12	0.95	0.76	0.14	17.94	0.90	1.99
1906–10	2.14	0.96	0.92	0.17	29.27	1.47	2.60
1916–19	1.68	0.76	0.69	0.12	21.63	1.08	1.96
1940	1.48	0.67	0.91	0.16	16.29	0.73	1.56
1950	1.72	0.77	1.27	0.23	23.21	1.04	2.04
1960	1.90	0.86	1.32	0.22	21.95	0.99	2.07

SOURCE: Mark Keller and Vera Efron, *Selected Statistical Tables on Alcoholic Beverages, 1850–1960, and on Alcoholism, 1930–1960* (New Brunswick, N.J.: Quarterly Journal of Studies on Alcohol, Inc., 1961), p. 3. Used by permission of the publisher.

The number of taverns in the United States gives an additional indication of the extent of drinking, even though only about one third of all liquor sales are made in taverns. In spite of the enormous value conflicts raging over the tavern, there are over 200,000 in the United States. Chicago has more than 9000; New York City alone has 12,000. Wisconsin has 14,000 taverns which sell beer, four in every five of them also serving

Table 12.3. Proportion of United States Population Twenty-one Years and Over Who Drink Alcoholic Beverages

Study	Total population %	Men %	Women %
Ley (1940)	57	60	34
Riley and Marden (1946)	65	75	56
Gallup (1947)	63	72	54
Maxwell (1951)	63	76	51
Mulford and Miller (1960)	60	69	51

SOURCES: H. A. Ley, "Incidence of Smoking and Drinking Among 10,000 Examinees," *Proceedings of the Life Extension Examiners,* 2:57–63 (May–June, 1940); John W. Riley and Charles F. Marden, "The Social Patterns of Alcoholic Drinking," *Quarterly Journal of Studies on Alcohol,* 8:265–273 (September, 1947); News Release, American Institute of Public Opinion (Princeton, N.J.: December 18, 1948); Milton A. Maxwell, "Drinking Behavior in the State of Washington," *Quarterly Journal of Studies on Alcohol,* 13:221 (June, 1952); Harold A. Mulford and Donald E. Miller, "Drinking in Iowa: II. The Extent of Drinking and Selected Socio-cultural Categories," *Quarterly Journal of Studies on Alcohol,* 21:28 (March, 1960).

distilled spirits. A Chicago study found that the tavern has more buildings, accommodates more people, and takes more of the money and time of people in that city than do all the motion-picture houses, sporting events, and other forms of commercial recreation put together.[49]

FREQUENCY OF DRINKING

Statements about the proportion of the general population that drinks are often misleading, however, because they give no indication of the frequency of drinking. In one national survey some 17 percent of the total group (27 percent of the men and 8 percent of the women) were regular drinkers defined as those who drank three or more times a week.[50] In a sample of the state of Washington only one in ten persons was found to drink this frequently, one in five men and only three in a hundred women. (See Table 12.4.)

Table 12.4. Drinking Frequency by Percentage of Drinkers, Washington, 1951

	Total	Men	Women
Each day	3.6	7.5	0.0
4–6 times a week	2.5	4.0	1.2
3 times a week	4.9	7.9	2.0
1–2 times a week	8.0	10.1	6.1
2–3 times a month	14.2	15.9	12.7
Once a month	11.9	14.5	9.4
1–5 times a year	18.2	16.3	20.0
Total drinkers	63.3	76.2	51.4

SOURCE: Milton A. Maxwell, "Drinking Behavior in the State of Washington," *Quarterly Journal of Studies on Alcohol,* 13:221 (June, 1952). Reprinted by permission of the Journal.

Using both an index of drinking frequency and the amount of alcohol consumed, a more recent Iowa study found that 40 percent of the population are abstainers, 22 percent drink infrequently (not more than once a month) and consume small amounts of alcohol at a single sitting (not more than 1.6 ounces of absolute alcohol). Using three various similar indices, the same study classified 27 percent as light drinkers, 20 percent as moderate drinkers, and, at the extreme, the 9 percent who drank more than

[49] Walter O. Cromwell, "The Tavern in Community Life" (Chicago: Juvenile Protective Association, 1940), p. 11. Similar statements have been made about the English pub, to which it is estimated about one in twelve adults go on a Saturday night.— *The Pub and the People.*
[50] Riley and Marden, "The Social Pattern of Alcoholic Drinking," *loc. cit.*

once a week and consumed medium (1.6 to 2.88 ounces) or large (more than 2.88 ounces) at one sitting.[51]

There is little information on the proportion of drinking done in taverns. The Washington survey found that most drinking is done either at home or in the homes of friends.[52] About 70 percent of the men and 83 percent of the women did their drinking at home, which meant that a relatively small proportion drank in taverns, cocktail lounges, clubs, or other places. Only 2.4 percent of the women patronized taverns as compared with 14.1 percent of the men.[53] In a sample of Wisconsin replies from 872 men and 569 women, it was found that three fourths of the men patronized taverns, about half of them regularly, that is, once a month or more, whereas only about two fifths of the women went to taverns, only one in seven women being a regular patron.[54]

A larger proportion of the population drink in New England, the Middle Atlantic states, and the Pacific Coast than in the Middle West or the South.

DRINKING AND AGE

One of the most striking differences in drinking is that between various age groups. A large proportion of the younger age groups drink. A survey of high school drinking studies has concluded: "A considerable proportion of young people 14–18 years of age have had some experience with drinking. This has frequently been done with parental consent. However, drinking practices of young people can only be understood in terms of their social class, economic status, religious affiliation and drinking customs of their parents." [55]

In a study of a highly urbanized and industrialized county in Wisconsin, two in three high school students reported that they used alcoholic drinks, almost entirely beer, on social and other nonreligious occasions.[56] There was a steady increase in age until the proportion who drank at the age of eighteen was four in five. Girls drank slightly less in most age

---

[51] Harold A. Mulford and Donald E. Miller, "Drinking in Iowa. II. The Extent of Drinking and Selected Socio-cultural Categories," *Quarterly Journal of Studies on Alcohol*, 21:26–39 (March, 1960).

[52] Milton A. Maxwell, "Drinking Behavior in the State of Washington," *Quarterly Journal of Studies on Alcohol*, 13:224 (June, 1952).

[53] This figure should be slightly larger because the study combined drinking in "clubs or cocktail lounges," which accounted for 7.9 percent of the women and 9.1 percent of the men.

[54] Macrory, "The Tavern and the Community," *loc. cit.*, pp. 611–612.

[55] Raymond G. McCarthy, "High School Drinking Studies," in McCarthy, *Drinking and Intoxication*, p. 205.

[56] John L. Miller and J. Richard Wahl, *Attitudes of High School Students toward Alcoholic Beverages* (New York: The Mrs. John S. Sheppard Foundation, 1956). This was a study of Racine County, Wisconsin.

groups, but there was little difference by the age of seventeen or eighteen. Some 17 percent of the Kansas high school students in the urban Wichita area had one or more drinks of alcoholic beverages, generally beer or wine, in the week before a survey was made, compared with 11 percent in Kansas rural counties.[57] The amount of drinking was small, 9 percent of the urban students and less than half of that number in the rural areas having had four or more drinks during the previous week. Although drinking among teen-agers was positively associated with the frequency of drinking by the parents and with the fact that alcoholic beverages were kept in the home, the drinking patterns generally followed were those considered appropriate to the member of the group. A Michigan study of 2000 persons, junior and senior students in six high schools, showed even more drinking. One in every ten students considered himself a person who drinks and about one third drank with some regularity.[58]

In a national sample, approximately three fourths of those between twenty-one and twenty-nine years of age drink, two thirds between thirty and forty-nine, and only one half of those fifty years and older.[59] Those adults with a higher education drink more than those with less education. In a Washington study, similar age differences in drinking were found.[60] One survey revealed that 70 percent of those with more than a high school education drank as compared with 62 percent of the less educated group.[61] The proportion among city residents of light drinkers declines and that of heavy drinkers increases as education increases, but among farm and town dwellers the reverse is true.[62]

A large proportion of college students, some 74 percent, drink alcoholic beverages, according to Straus and Bacon's survey of 15,747 students in twenty-seven American colleges.[63] Of the total group, 80 percent of the men and 61 percent of the women belong in this category. Actually these figures are misleading, for the drinking of college students varies a great deal by the type of institution, income, family drinking, religion, and ethnic background.[64] In addition, the extent of drinking increases with each year in college. More students drink at private, nonsectarian colleges attended only by men or by women than at any other type. The least amount of drinking is done at private, coeducational, "dry" colleges. (See Table 12.5.)

The frequency of drinking among college students who drink, how-

---

[57] E. Jackson Baur and Marston M. McCluggage, "Drinking Patterns of Kansas High School Students," *Social Problems*, 5:317–326 (Spring, 1958).

[58] Christopher Sower, "Teen-Age Drinking as Group Behavior," *Quarterly Journal of Studies on Alcohol*, 20:655—668 (September, 1959).

[59] Riley and Marden, "The Social Pattern of Alcoholic Drinking," *loc. cit.*

[60] Maxwell, "Drinking Behavior in the State of Washington," *loc. cit.*, p. 229.

[61] News Release, Institute of Public Opinion (Princeton, N.J.: December 18, 1948).

[62] Mulford and Miller, "Drinking in Iowa," *loc. cit.*, p. 33.

[63] Straus and Bacon, *op. cit.*, p. 46.   [64] *Ibid.*

Table 12.5. Incidence of Drinking, by Type of College

	Users of Alcoholic Beverages Men (%)	Women (%)
Private, men or women only, nonsectarian	92	89
Private, coeducational, nonsectarian	92	84
Private, coeducational, "dry"	65	39
Public, coeducational, general	83	74
Public, coeducational, teachers	79	44
Public, coeducational, southern Negro	81	40

SOURCE: Robert Straus and Selden D. Bacon, *Drinking in College* (New Haven, Conn.: Yale University Press, 1953), p. 47. Reprinted by permission of the publisher.

ever, is not great. Only 21 percent of the men and 10 percent of the women are reported to drink more than once a week, and two fifths of the men and more than half of the women drink no more than once a month. (See Table 12.6.)

Table 12.6. Frequency of Drinking During Past Year

Frequency	Users of Alcoholic Beverages Men	Women
1 to 5 times	19%	26%
6 to 12 times	24	27
Twice a month to once a week	36	37
2 or 3 days a week	18	9
4 or more days a week	3	1
Total	100%	100%

SOURCE: Robert Straus and Selden D. Bacon, *Drinking in College* (New Haven, Conn.: Yale University Press, 1953), p. 101. Reprinted by permission of Yale University Press.

Types of Drinkers

Drinkers can be classified in terms of the deviation from norms of drinking behavior within a culture and dependence on alcohol in the life organization of the individual. Persons learn in interaction with others to think and converse about alcohol in terms of what should be done with alcohol and what it will do to and for them. This includes the amount of alcohol consumed, the purpose and meaning of drinking as an aspect of role playing, the degree to which such drinking handicaps the individual in his interpersonal relations, and his ability to refrain from taking a drink. More specifically, the classification of types of drinkers involves the analysis of behavioral phenomena involving (1) the amount of consumption of beverage alcohol (2) in an excessive manner indicating preoccupation with alcohol which (3) interferes with the drinker's interpersonal relations.[65] One study has devised a scale to measure preoccupation with drinking so that the differences between types of responses to the use of alcohol may be measured with Group I, representing the most highly preoccupied, and with IV, the least preoccupied, with alcohol. (See Table 12.7.)

There are several types of drinkers: the social or controlled drinkers, the heavy drinkers, the alcoholics, and the chronic alcoholics.

A *social or controlled drinker* drinks for reasons of sociability, conviviality, and conventionality. He may or may not like the taste and effects produced by alcohol. Above all else, he is able to desist from the use of intoxicating beverages when he chooses to do so. He drinks in a take-it-or-leave-it manner. There are two types of social drinkers, the occasional and the regular drinker. The former drinks sporadically and may have only a few drinks a year, whereas the regular social drinker may drink three or more times a week.

Not only does the *heavy drinker* make more frequent use of alcohol than the regular social drinker; in addition and occasionally, he may consume such quantities that intoxication results. Some studies have defined a heavy drinker as one who takes three or more drinks of liquor at a "sitting" more than once a week. He is sometimes, but not always, given to week-end binges or, at a party, may be drinking too heavily or just having a few more than anyone else in the place. Whatever else may be said about the excessive drinker, this type, in common with social drinkers, but with greater difficulty, may be able to curtail or completely cease drinking on his own volition. Depending upon circumstances, he may continue drinking in this manner for the rest of his life, he may later reduce the frequency and quantity of his alcohol consumption, or he may become an alcoholic.

Alcoholics are those whose frequent and repeated drinking of alcoholic beverages is in excess of the dietary and social usages of the community and is to such an extent that it interferes with health or social or economic functioning. The alcoholic is unable to control consistently, or to stop at will, either the start of drinking or its termination once started.[66] Some of the elements in this definition are (1) reliance on al-

---

[65] Harold A. Mulford and Donald E. Miller, "Drinking in Iowa. IV. Preoccupation with Alcohol and Definitions of Alcohol, Heavy Drinking and Trouble Due to Drinking," *Quarterly Journal of Studies on Alcohol*, 21:279–291 (June, 1960).

[66] See Mark Keller, "Alcoholism: Nature and Extent of the Problem," *The Annals*, 315:1–11 (January, 1958) and Mark Keller, "Definition of Alcoholism," *Quarterly Journal of Studies on Alcohol*, 21:125–134 (March, 1960). Some authorities feel that such definitions make it difficult for scientists to replicate research. Consequently, an operational definition of alcoholism in terms of community standards and societal re-

coholic beverages, (2) repetitiveness or chronicity of the drinking in the sense that the drinking does not take place on rare occasions, (3) ill effects which derive from the drinking and not from other causes. The drinking must affect the drinker's life and not just society. These ill effects may be either definite ill-health, social or interpersonal ill effects, such as disruption of the family or ostracism which would not occur if the drinking were stopped, or economic effects, such as inability to keep a job, work efficiently, or take care of one's property as well as one could without the drinking.

Alcoholism is drinking behavior which is conceived of by others as an extreme deviation. While the drinking of alcoholic beverages and heavy drinking are the necessary prerequisites, it should be regarded as behavioral phenomena and not as a biological or psychological entity. On a scale of preoccupation with alcohol it would probably fit in as responses to Groups I and II. (See Table 12.7.)

Chronic alcoholics characteristically have a "compulsion" to drink continually. Of particular importance are such other characteristics as solitary drinking, morning drinking, and general physical deterioration.

In the United States an estimated 3,760,000 men and 710,000 women, or a total of 4,470,000 were alcoholics in 1960.[67] This is equivalent to a rate of 4000 alcoholics per 100,000 adults aged twenty years and over.[68] Chronic alcoholics (alcoholics with complications) were estimated to be 1,147,000 in 1953, or one fourth of the alcoholics. Of this total, 971,000 were men and 176,000 were women. California and New Jersey had the highest rates, and South Carolina and Wyoming the lowest.

Although it is difficult to compare the alcoholism rates of various countries, the most accurate figures indicate that in terms of total population the United States has the highest rate, or 4390, followed by France and Sweden. (See Table 12.8.) Rates for chronic alcoholism are highest in Switzerland, with the United States being fourth.

During the past several decades there has been a great increase in the number of American women who drink, and while the rate of alcoholism has tended to increase there are indications that this increase has

---

action has been used involving frequent arrests for drunkenness, contact with social agencies, clinics, mental hospitals, or Alcoholics Anonymous. See William and Joan McCord, *Origins of Alcoholism* (Stanford, Calif.: Stanford University Press, 1960), pp. 10–11.

[67] Mark Keller, "The Definition of Alcoholism and the Estimation of Its Prevalence," in *Society, Culture and Drinking Patterns*. Estimates of the number of alcoholics with complications (chronic alcoholism) are derived by multiplying the reported number of deaths from cirrhosis of the liver by a certain ratio, usually by three in the United States. To arrive at the estimated number of alcholics in the United States, this figure is then usually multiplied by four.

[68] Mark Keller and Vera Efron, *Selected Statistical Tables on Alcoholic Beverages, 1859–1960, and on Alcoholism 1930–1960* (New Brunswick, N.J.: Quarterly Journal of Studies on Alcohol, 1961).

Table 12.7. The Iowa Scale of Preoccupation with Alcohol

Item	Content of Statement	Method of scoring
I	I stay intoxicated for several days at a time. I worry about not being able to get a drink when I need one. I sneak drinks when no one is looking.	Agree on any two.
II	Once I start drinking it is difficult for me to stop before I become completely intoxicated. I get intoxicated on work days. I take a drink the first thing when I get up in the morning.	Agree on any two.
III	I awaken next day not being able to remember some of the things I had done while I was was drinking. I take a few quick ones before going to a party to make sure I have enough. I neglect my regular meals when I am drinking.	Agree on any two.
IV	I don't nurse my drinks; I toss them down pretty fast. I drink for the effect of alcohol with little attention to type of beverage or brand name. Liquor has less effect on me than it used to.	Agree on any two.

SOURCE: Adapted from Harold A. Mulford and Donald E. Miller, "Drinking in Iowa. IV. Preoccupation with Alcohol and Definitions of Alcohol, Heavy Drinking and Trouble Due to Drinking," *Quarterly Journal of Studies on Alcohol,* 21:281 (June, 1960). The scale is cumulative in that with few exceptions respondents beginning with the bottom item agree to each item up to a point and then reject the remaining items.

been small.[69] Several reasons appear to account for the differences between the rates of alcoholism among men and women. First, proportionately fewer women than men drink. Second, greater social stigma is attached to excessive drinking by women than by men. Third, a housewife does not face the same occupational drinking hazards that men face. Fourth, women are generally not as directly involved in the competitive economic struggle, and, since they have the responsibility for the care and upbringing of the children, are not as "free" to drink regularly as are men, especially in the lower classes. Fifth, a woman's self-image is not as seriously threatened. Because her role is more restricted, primarily to that of a wife and mother, failure in this role is less likely to be known to outsiders. "A man, on the other hand, can fail not only in his familial

[69] Edith S. Lisansky, "The Woman Alcoholic," *The Annals,* 315:73–82 (January, 1958).

Table 12.8. Estimated Rates of Alcoholism in Various Countries

Country	Year	With complications (chronic alcoholism)	With and without complications (alcoholism)
Switzerland	1947	1590	2385
Chile	1946	1497	1500
France	1945	1420	2850
United States	1953	1098	4390
Australia	1947	671	1340
Sweden	1946	646	2580
Denmark	1948	487	1950
Italy	1942	476	500
Canada	1952	407	1630
Norway	1947	389	1560
Finland	1947	357	1430
England and Wales	1948	278	1100

SOURCE: Mark Keller and Vera Efron, "The Prevalence of Alcoholism," *Quarterly Journal of Studies on Alcohol,* 16:634 (December, 1955). Reprinted by permission of the Journal.

but also in his occupational role; the possibility that a man's self-image will be *publicly* deflated is greater." [70]

The Alcoholic Process

Shifts from the excessive drinking to the alcoholic stage with its social and often physical deterioration, and to the chronic alcoholic state are imperceptible transitions. One is never a full-blown alcoholic after a few experiences with the effects of liquor, for alcoholism means more than sporadic intoxication. It implies changes in the nature of interpersonal relations with others, in attitudes toward drinking, in social roles, and in conceptions of the self, including increasing dependence on drinking, attitudes which are at variance with those held by others and which were developed through a marginal social existence, numerous rebuffs, social isolation, and physical deterioration.

The alcoholic process usually extends over a period of ten to twenty years of drinking, and can be sketched by the drinking symptoms of alcoholism in a group of 252 alcoholics.[71] These alcoholics became in-

[70] McCord and McCord, *op. cit.,* p. 163.
[71] Harrison M. Trice and J. Richard Wahl, "A Rank Order Analysis of the Symptoms of Alcoholism," *Quarterly Journal of Studies on Alcohol,* 19:636–648 (December, 1958). Also see E. M. Jellinek, "Phases in the Drinking History of Alcoholics," *Memoirs of the Section of Studies on Alcohol* (No. 5; New Brunswick, N.J.: Quarterly Journal of Studies on Alcohol, 1946).

toxicated for the first time at a mean age of 18.3 years, and within 11 years, or at age 29.5 they had already experienced "blackouts," or amnesia during intoxication. By 35.6 years they were engaging in morning drinking, and at 36.1 they began to drink alone on a regular basis. At 37.8 they were first protecting their supply of alcohol, and by 38.6 years were first experiencing tremors. (See Table 12.9.)

Table 12.9. Symptoms and Mean Onset Ages (Years) of 13 Selected Symptoms in a Wisconsin Study Group of 252 Alcoholics, 1955

Symptoms	Mean age
First drink for self	17.6
First intoxication	18.3
First blackout	29.5
First frequent blackouts	33.6
First morning drinking	35.6
First "benders"	36.0
First daytime bouts	35.7
First loss of control	36.0
First drinking alone	36.1
First convulsions	37.6
First protecting of supply	37.8
First tremors	38.6
First drunk on less liquor	38.4

SOURCE: Derived from Harrison M. Trice and J. Richard Wahl, "A Rank Order Analysis of the Symptoms of Alcoholism," *Quarterly Journal of Studies on Alcohol,* 19:637 (December, 1958).

Alcoholics, on the average, reach their lowest point and conceive of themselves as having reached this lowest point in their late thirties, and after one or two decades of drinking. In the interim they have tried to change their drinking patterns; have "gone on the water wagon"; have experienced daytime drunks, "benders," or prolonged drinking sprees; have begun taking drinks in the morning; have sought to escape their environment; and have begun losing working time, jobs, and friends. They also have irrational fears, resentments, and "remorse," the latter being particularly characteristic. Alcoholics then often drink alone, "protect their supply," and experience tremors.

A more detailed description of the alcoholic process can be sketched in terms of early, middle, and late stages of alcoholism.[72] Many persons, of

[72] Derived from Jellinek, "Phases in The Drinking History of Alcoholics," *loc. cit.*; Marty Mann, *A Primer on Alcoholism* (New York: Holt, Rinehart and Winston, Inc., 1950), pp. 18–57; and Simon Dinitz, "The Relation of the Tavern to the Drinking Phases of Alcoholics," cited above.

course, do not inevitably go on to the next stage. Each stage can be divided into physical symptoms and drinking roles.

EXCESSIVE DRINKING STAGE

In the excessive drinking stage the drinker begins to lose control over his drinking, finding it difficult to stop at one or two drinks or from going on occasional week-end drunks. Blackouts frequently begin at this stage, although generally not until the end of a hard-drinking evening. He begins to gulp drinks, and he may take a drink *before* going to a party where there undoubtedly will be drinking, or *before* an appointment at which drinking would be quite in order. He feels the necessity of having drinks at certain regular times and the need for a certain amount of time spent in drinking before dinner, regardless of the inconvenience to others. He also needs to drink before special events, and he must have a drink for "that tired feeling," or for his "nerves," or to forget his worries or troubles for a while, or to avoid depression.

MIDDLE OR ALCOHOLIC DRINKING STAGE

The prealcoholic at this stage begins to have ugly hangovers, which include physical near collapse, mental remorse and self-disgust, and a terrifying self-doubt because his schemes for control of his drinking no longer work. Nausea is still rare during drinking, but it now has become a frequent morning-after experience. Blackouts are increasing, and the time of their onset grows steadily earlier. He now passes out frequently, sometimes early in the course of an event to which he had genuinely looked forward.

His growing dependence on alcohol is indicated by the fact that he no longer seems able to function well without drinks, and apparently makes little effort to do so. He is less willing to talk about drinking especially his own. The increasing use of alcohol often masks his real feelings toward himself and his role aspirations, as it also does toward increasing feelings of isolation and of "not belonging."

At this middle stage the alcoholic promises over and over again to stop drinking, but his drinking by now is so obviously different from other people's drinking that he lies about it to prevent discovery of this difference. He gulps drinks, makes sure of having enough "under his belt" before going anywhere, even to a scheduled drinking party, and to avoid any risks he carries his own supply. At this stage the alcoholic prefers to spend the allotted span of drinking time before meals at a tavern rather than at home, and he often arrives home late. He must be "well away" for any special event, he is always "dog-tired and cannot go on without something to drink." He is generally "nervous," plagued with worries and troubles, and life seems unbearable without drinks. His almost constant depression, often about his drinking, cannot be dealt with except by drinking.

The alcoholic at this stage now adds to the accepted drinking time, he may no longer care whether friends go with him, and he may prefer to sneak off-hour drinks. He keeps a bottle in his desk or hidden at home for purely private consumption, and signs of his drinking, even actual intoxication, begin to show up at the wrong time, such as at work or at gatherings where everyone else is sober. He no longer admits to having been drunk; he says he "wasn't up to par," "had eaten something," or was "under the weather." He does not usually admit having hangovers, an admission which might lead to inquiries about how much he has been drinking, a fact which he wishes to conceal carefully.

Episodes of drunkenness occur more and more often during this middle phase of alcoholism. Week ends are often real drinking bouts, with Sundays still reserved for "straightening out," but often matching Saturday in drinking intensity. Extravagance in buying drinks and other things for people and excessive tipping are characteristic of his drinking behavior. Some persons also commit various antisocial acts, such as fighting with others, vandalism in the form of malicious destruction, and practical jokes. Then the morning drink to "get going" increases rapidly in frequency as its efficacy becomes appreciated. As drinking behavior changes and the drinker's situation becomes more difficult, he starts "going on the wagon," something he is able to do at this stage for extended periods of time. He has a false sense of power over his alcoholism during these periods of nondrinking, but he is noticeably irritable, his family, friends, and business colleagues label him as a "difficult" person.

LATER OR CHRONIC ALCOHOLIC STAGE

At the chronic alcoholic stage it is no longer a question of merely gulping drinks, either publicly or privately; there is now a pressing physical need to get and keep a certain amount of alcohol in the system at all times. Although hangovers are not now the usual morning-after discomfort known to social drinkers, they do make themselves felt in the peculiarly horrible form known to the chronic alcoholic. If at all possible they are immediately wiped out by drinks. An added problem, however, is nausea, and the morning drinks often do not stay down. Blackouts set in, and disappear, at any time, leaving unaccountable memory blanks possibly lasting for several days. Passing out also occurs at any time, and much of the alcoholic's sleep is actually no more than this.

The major psychological symptom is now an overwhelming compulsion to drink, and the greatest difficulty of all is the inability to control drinking. Drinking is apparently completely accepted as natural and inevitable. When sober, he does not admit or discuss his drinking, drunkenness, or behavior, although there are rare outbursts, usually when half-drunk, of horror and self-disgust, as well as the expression of a tragically real desire to "be like other people." His ordinary morning hang-over is not allowed to occur, for round-the-clock drinking generally prevents it. A feeling of inferiority because of his drinking now frequently appears in an extreme form, contrasting sharply with equally extreme swings toward grandiosity.

The alcoholic now drinks to live and lives to drink. The full-fledged alcoholic's eating behavior is phenomenal: he seems to many people not to eat at all, a fact which is often quite true. He now maintains an adequate supply of liquor at all times in order to be able to "sneak drinks" because of the psychological need and desire for liquor during various parts of the day and night. It is almost impossible to describe adequately the terror that getting "caught short" holds for the addict, and the lengths to which he will go to prevent what to him would be a catastrophe of the most major proportions. Ingenious methods of safeguarding an ever-present supply indicate more clearly than almost anything else the compulsive need to drink experienced by the chronic alcoholic.[73]

Drunken behavior now usually, almost inevitably, takes place at the wrong time, drinking bouts occur regardless of the time of week, month, or year, their duration depending upon the financial and physical condition of the alcoholic, from a day or so to a week or longer. Even at this late stage, however, there may be times when the alcoholic manages his drinking well. Morning drinks and solitary drinking are indices of the chronic inebriate. He needs a few sips on awakening because he feels unsteady, has a headache, or has the "shakes" or tremors. This morning drink makes him "normal," if only psychologically so, and he feels he can meet his obligations for the day. In one novel the alcoholic is described as waiting for the corner tavern to open so that he can get his morning "shot." [74] This effect, unfortunately for the alcoholic, may wear off, and he is forced to resort to his hidden stock repeatedly during the day. "He may start utilizing techniques for the ingestion of alcohol which are beyond the pale of any conceivable development in the drinking usages of his

---

[73] To keep a supply of alcohol available alcoholics devise many original schemes for hiding their bottles from the family. Some hang bottles just outside the window below the ledge on strings, others under their pillows, under porches, in stockings, and in every other conceivable place. One informant stated that he would return in the evening with a large supply of alcohol and since his wife anticipated this, he would hide one or two bottles in a conspicuous place so that his wife would find them. The remainder he hid more securely. When his wife located the decoys she would feel relieved and he would put on a most pitiable mien. Of course, what she did not know was that several times during the course of a night, when alcoholic tremors would awaken him, he would repair to his supply and after a few drinks would be quieted down enough to go back to sleep.

[74] Charles Jackson, *The Lost Weekend* (New York: Holt, Rinehart and Winston, Inc., 1948).

group: starting off the day with 7 or 8 ounces of gin or whiskey; spending 4 or 5 days of the ordinary work-a-day week doing nothing but ingesting alcohol; taking alcohol in such forms as mouth-wash, canned heat preparations, vanilla extract, and so on; in addition, he may omit such practices (if they were the norm in his group) as using ice, glasses, chasers, mixes." [75]

Periods of being "on the wagon" still occur, although less often unless the patient is under treatment. Complete drunkenness is his condition most of the time, although this is not always evident, and he has great difficulty on the job. This produces another unpleasant situation, the necessity for getting money to pay for drinks; this is often difficult, and ordinary borrowing soon deteriorates into the "touch." He often watches his family sink into destitution, or leave him, without showing any feeling about it. His behavior at this time shows an almost complete loss of time sense.

In areas other than drinking there develop socially unacceptable changes in his relations with others. Their strong societal reaction to him in turn causes further drinking. "Dishonesty, excessive rationalization, avoidance, and the other deviations, once perhaps even rare in his behavior, then noticeable where alcohol was concerned, now begin to appear in the family situation or perhaps in friendship groups or on the job. Accidents, job losses, family quarrels, broken friendship, even trouble with the law may take place, not just when he is under the influence of alcohol, but even when he is not. And such occasions quite usually set off further drinking." [76]

Personality Traits and Excessive Drinking

Why some social drinkers become excessive drinkers and some excessive drinkers develop into alcoholics is not entirely clear at the present time. Most psychiatrists believe that alcoholism is a consequence of personality maladjustment. According to this view, certain childhood experiences produce feelings of insecurity which, together with difficulties in interpersonal relationships of adult life, produce tensions and anxieties. Because the use of alcohol reduces anxiety some persons may come to depend upon it. Over a period of years this dependence on alcohol as a way of escaping hidden or obvious difficulties with which the individual cannot deal increases.

The psychiatric explanation, although widely held, has several limitations. In the first place, such a theory is largely dependent for evidence on the personality traits of alcoholics and the differences between them and

---

[75] Selden D. Bacon, "Alcoholics Do Not Drink," *The Annals,* 315:62 (January, 1958).
[76] *Ibid.,* p. 63.

nonalcoholics. The personality traits of an alcoholic are measured after some ten to fifteen years of drinking in which the individual has usually had many problems due to his drinking, problems not only with his family but with his employer and others, and experiences which the nonalcoholic has probably not had.

Although efforts have been made to sketch an "alcoholic personality," presumably applicable to all alcoholics, more recent surveys have concluded that scientific reports to date do not permit us to define such an alcoholic personality, or even to come to any substantial agreement as to what it might be like. For example, two reviews of all personality studies of alcoholics and nonalcoholics up to 1956, using projective and nonprojective tests, found that there was no reason for concluding that persons of one type are more likely to become alcoholics than persons of another type.[77] Moreover, it cannot be assumed that the personality traits displayed by the alcoholic were there *before* excessive drinking began. It is possible that a number of types, such as the person who takes pride in his ability to consume large quantities of alcohol without becoming drunk, have a susceptibility for alcoholism, but more research is needed before any definite conclusions of this type can be reached.

Group and Subcultural Factors in Alcoholism

Rather than seek any universal explanation of alcoholism, either in the biological constitution or the personality trait structures, one should look for a variety of social and group situations under which alcoholism develops. Excessive drinking, for example, does not itself make the alcoholic. If it is continued over a long enough time he may increasingly become involved in difficulties which arise from the drinking itself. He may lose his job, his friends, and his wife because of his drinking, and he may even be arrested and placed in jail. Drinking may become a way of getting away from problems caused by drinking. He "is involved in a circular process whereby his excessive drinking creates additional problems for him which he can only face with the aid of further excessive drinking. The condition of true alcoholism has been established." [78] The Protestant ethic appears to play a role in this, since drunkenness is regarded as a lack of moral strength, will power, and devotion to the goals of personal discipline and work. The societal reaction to excessive drunk-

---

[77] Edwin H. Sutherland, H. C. Schroeder, and C. L. Tordella, "Personality Traits and the Alcoholic: A Critique of Existing Studies," *Quarterly Journal of Studies on Alcohol,* 11:547–561 (December, 1950) and Leonard Symes, "Personality Characteristics and the Alcoholic: A Critique of Current Studies," *Quarterly Journal of Studies on Alcohol,* 18:288–302 (June, 1957).

[78] Expert Committee on Mental Health, "Second Report of the Alcoholism Sub-Committee" (Technical Report No. 48; Geneva, Switzerland: World Health Organization, 1952).

enness may be expressed through the husband or wife, employer, work associates, parents, in-laws, neighbors, church members, and the police representing the larger community. The comparatively low rate of alcoholism in Japan may be due, in part, to the fact that drunkenness does not seem to provoke quite the same reaction. It is largely regarded as a personal matter, often with good humor by other members of society.

Group associations and cultural factors, therefore, play an important part in determining who becomes an excessive drinker and who does not. There are differences not only in the drinking customs of societies but in those of subgroups within a modern society. Subgroups differ in the way in which alcohol is used, the extent of drinking, and attitudes toward drunkenness. The correlation of diverse drinking patterns with alcoholism can help us to test a number of hypotheses. Some believe that frequent drinking will lead to alcoholism; yet those groups with relatively high frequency of drinking, such as the American Jews, particularly the Orthodox, and the Italian-Americans, have low rates of alcoholism.[79] Still others say that frequency of drunkenness leads to alcoholism, and yet the Aleuts, the Andean Indians, and those of the northwest coast of America, among whom drunkenness is common, appear to have little alcoholism.[80] In an isolated Peruvian mestizo community drinking and drunkenness among adult males over fifteen years of age is virtually universal.[81] The few who abstain plead health reasons, but since liquor is regarded as "healthful," their lot is hard. Alcoholism is rare, however.

Ullman has stressed the role of the integration of drinking behavior patterns in low rates of alcoholism.[82] If conformity to drinking standards is supported by the entire culture or subculture, there will be low rates. If the individual drinker does not know what is expected or if the expected situation varies, he is in a position of ambivalence. Therefore, "in any group or society in which the drinking customs, values and sanctions —together with the attitudes of all segments of the group or society—

[79] See Charles R. Snyder, *Alcohol and the Jews* (New York: The Free Press of Glencoe, 1958) and Giorgio Lolli, Emilio Serianni, Grace M. Golder, and Pierpaolo Luzzatto-Fegis, *Alcohol in Italian Culture* (New York: The Free Press of Glencoe, 1958).

[80] See Gerald D. Berreman, "Drinking Patterns of the Aleuts," *Quarterly Journal of Studies on Alcohol*, 17:503–514 (September, 1956), William Mangin, "Drinking among Andean Indians," *Quarterly Journal of Studies on Alcohol*, 18:55–66 (March, 1957), and Edwin M. Lemert, *Alcohol and the Northwest Coast Indians* (University of California Publications in Culture and Society, Vol. 2, No. 6; Berkeley: University of California Press, 1954).

[81] Ozzie G. Simmons, "Drinking Patterns and Interpersonal Performance in a Peruvian Mestizo Community," *Quarterly Journal of Studies on Alcohol*, 20:103–111 (March, 1959).

[82] Albert D. Ullman, "Sociocultural Backgrounds of Alcoholism," *The Annals*, 315: 48–55 (January, 1958).

are well established, known to and agreed upon by all, and are consistent with the rest of the culture, the rate of alcoholism will be low." [83]

COMPANIONS AND EXCESSIVE DRINKING

In modern society, group patterns of excessive drinking, of companions, of social class, and of religious and ethnic groups are important.

> There seems to be a good deal of evidence to the effect that many problem drinkers are "processed" into it, that is, they are encouraged by informal drinking groups to use alcohol as a way to adjust to anxiety and difficulty. Having once been conditioned by such experiences to use alcohol as a way to manage the ever-present problems of living, it is a simple step to increase its use when these problems become larger, as they do at one time or another for all of us. To this group encouragement there is frequently added the reward of group recognition. Often the early symptoms of problem drinking are given prestige in such groups. For example, the ability to "drink 'em under the table" may provide the person so characterized with the esteem of a drinking group. At the same time, it may well signal a dangerous increase in the tolerance to alcohol. Furthermore, drinking groups have a subtle "limit" beyond which they believe a drinker gets "sloppy" and disgusting. At this point the rewards and recognition previously accorded tend to become rejection. This constitutes a further anxiety that must be met by a technique already well known: more alcohol. . . .[84]

Drinking generally takes place in small groups, and within these groups drinking norms tend to develop. More than two thirds of the drinking occasions among men, for example, in rural Finland involve groups of two to four persons.[85] Moreover, while conformity between drinking habits and drinking norms is the rule in small groups, identification with a group is a variable on the basis of which it is possible to explain an individual's norms and his behavior.[86]

---

[83] *Ibid.*, p. 50. Also see Harrison M. Trice and David J. Pittman, "Social Organization and Alcoholism: A Review of Significant Research Since 1940," *Social Problems*, 5:294–308 (Spring, 1958). Among folk societies prior to contact with Western Europeans, alcoholism appears to have been infrequent. The ceremonial use of alcohol to produce mass intoxication among male adults was permitted in many folk societies but drinking for individualistic reasons was rare and alcoholism virtually unknown.—Donald Horton, "The Functions of Alcohol in Primitive Societies," in *Alcohol, Science and Society*, p. 157. For a general discussion of group association and cultural factors, also see Edwin M. Lemert, "Alcoholism and the Sociocultural Situation," *Quarterly Journal of Studies on Alcohol*, 17:306–317 (June, 1956).

[84] Harrison M. Trice, "The Problem Drinker in Industry," *ILR Research* (Ithaca: New York State School of Industrial and Labor Relations, Cornell University, June, 1956), II, 11. Reprinted by permission of the New York State School of Industrial and Labor Relations.

[85] P. Kuusi, *Alcohol Sales Experiment in Rural Finland* (Helsinki: Finnish Foundation for Alcohol Studies, 1957).

[86] Eric Allardt, "Drinking Norms and Drinking Habits," in *Drinking and Drinkers* (Helsinki: Finnish Foundation for Alcohol Studies, 1957).

The drinking norms of an individual appear to conform closely to those of age contemporaries, and particularly of friends or the marital partner.[87] These individuals appear to be more influential than the drinking partners of the parental generation in determining how people drink. In fact, wives of alcoholics have been found to have encouraged their husbands' alcoholism.[88] Another study has reported a close relation between the development of alcoholism and the type of companion with whom the individual associates and drinks.[89] Of twenty-eight excessive drinkers under thirty-five, nearly all belonged to social groups in which regular drinking and drunkenness were accepted and approved. Becoming drunk became a pattern of behavior from about nineteen years. Before they began drinking about half felt that they had been isolated and ridiculed for not drinking. It has been suggested, in one study, that the first drinking experience of potential alcoholics may have a particular meaning.[90] Excessive drinkers, as compared with nonexcessive drinkers, had their first drink in a place other than a private home or tavern but with friends or older persons who were not members of the family. Moreover, the prealcoholic more often became intoxicated in his first drinking and was ridiculed by his drinking companions. Later he seemed to take pride in having learned how to "drink like a man."

Studying the work experiences in industry of problem drinkers, Trice found that their drinking was influenced by the fellow employees with whom they drank after work. In fact, fellow workers were first to notice the problem drinker's developing loss of control. With their drinking problem becoming greater they tended to stop drinking with their work companions and to look for those whose drinking norms were more in line with their own.[91]

After studying two hundred homeless men, Straus found that only seven abstained entirely, and seventeen were moderate drinkers.[92] Suther-

[87] John L. Haer, "Drinking Patterns and the Influence of Friends and Family," *Quarterly Journal of Studies on Alcohol*, 16:178–185 (March, 1955).

[88] Samuel Futterman, "Personality Trends in Wives of Alcoholics," *Journal of Psychiatric Social Work*, 23:37–41 (October, 1953); Thelma Whalen, "Wives of Alcoholics: Four Types Observed in a Family Service Agency," *Quarterly Journal of Studies on Alcohol*, 14:632–641 (December, 1953); and G. M. Price, "A Study of the Wives of 70 Alcoholics," *Quarterly Journal of Studies on Alcohol*, 5:620–627 (March, 1945).

[89] Marvin Wellman, "Towards an Etiology of Alcoholism: Why Young Men Drink Too Much," *Canadian Medical Association Journal*, 73:717–719 (November 1, 1955).

[90] Albert D. Ullman, "The First Drinking Experience of Addictive and 'Normal' Drinkers," *Quarterly Journal of Studies on Alcohol*, 14:181–191 (June, 1953). Unfortunately, the addictive drinkers were prison inmates and the normal drinkers college students; thus they may represent samples which are not completely comparable.

[91] Harrison M. Trice, "Identifying the Problem Drinker on the Job," *Personnel Magazine*, 33:527–533 (May, 1957).

[92] Robert Straus, "Alcohol and the Homeless Man," *Quarterly Journal of Studies on Alcohol*, 7:360–404 (December, 1946). See also Robert Straus, "Some Sociological Concomitants of Excessive Drinking in the Life History of the Itinerant Inebriate," *Quarterly Journal of Studies on Alcohol*, 9:1–52 (June, 1948).

land and Locke, who studied several thousand shelter-house men in Chicago, wrote of them:

> Drinking is one of the most pervasive elements of shelter life. The men fall into four classes with reference to drinking. There is a comparatively small number of teetotalers. The majority partake of intoxicating drinks occasionally but rarely become drunk. A number go on periodic sprees and become completely drunk. Possibly 10 per cent of the men are chronic alcoholics. The chronic alcoholics are called "booze hounds" and are divided into yaki dockers, or those who make every effort to secure palatable liquor, and derailers, or those who drink denatured alcohol, sterno or anything "that will give them a bang." [93]

Many homeless persons become excessive drinkers but by no means all become alcoholics. In a study of 444 homeless men, 10.6 percent were found to be nondrinkers, 16.9 percent moderate drinkers, 28.0 percent "heavy controlled" drinkers, 43.2 percent heavy "uncontrolled" drinkers or alcoholics, while 1.3 percent were not classified.[94]

Skid Row excessive drinkers can be classified into six types: "older alcoholics," "bums," "characters," "winos," "ruby-dubs," and "lushes," the last referring to the prestige group of alcoholics.[95] Among those alcoholics with the most prestige on Skid Row, few are solitary drinkers. There are group definitions of behavior in the sharing of alcohol and, when drunk, in protecting each other from the police. Such alcoholics share in the financing of a bottle, and in drinking from a bottle to which an alcoholic has contributed: "he should drink in turn, his turn being dictated by the size of his donation, and he should take only one gulp with each round." [96] So great are the group influences on Skid Row that if an individual is to deal effectively with his alcoholism he must leave.

Group life and cultural factors play a role among "winos" studied in Seattle's Skid Row (or Road). Winos are those who habitually get drunk on wine, with a consequent unpleasant characteristic odor, and who exhibit an extremely rundown appearance. They drink wine not only because it is the cheapest but because the subculture believes it to have the longest and the most deadening effect, to kill the appetite, and to be the easiest drink to keep down. The wino has association with small groups of men with whom he does almost all of his drinking. Among the most imperative mores is the obligation to share: "Winos are not

[93] Edwin H. Sutherland and Harvey Locke, *Twenty Thousand Homeless Men* (Philadelphia: J. B. Lippincott Company, 1936), p. 113.

[94] Robert Straus and Raymond G. McCarthy, "Nonaddictive Pathological Drinking Patterns of Homeless Men," *Quarterly Journal of Studies on Alcohol*, 12:601–611 (December, 1951).

[95] W. Jack Peterson and Milton A. Maxwell, "The Skid Road 'Wino,'" *Social Problems*, 5:308–316 (Spring, 1958).

[96] Joan K. Jackson and Ralph Connor, "The Skid Road Alcoholic," *Quarterly Journal of Studies on Alcohol*, 14:475 (September, 1953).

isolates. Instead, they are found to live as social beings within a society of their fellows. It is a society which prescribes and provides mutual aid in meeting the problems of survival: food, drink, shelter, illness and protection. But more than that it is a society which also provides the emotional support found in the acceptance by, and the companionship of, fellow human beings." [97]

A study of a random sample of 187 chronic police case inebriates, most of them from a predominantly lower-class background, showed that their drinking occurred in small intimate groups, less than 8 percent being usually solitary drinkers.[98] "The major function of these drinking groups . . . is in providing the context, social and psychological, for drinking behavior. In reality we have subcommunities of inebriates organized around one cardinal principle: drinking. The fantasies concerning the rewards of the drinking experiences are reinforced in the interaction of the members, who mutually support each other in obtaining alcohol and mutually share it." [99]

CLASS DIFFERENCES IN EXCESSIVE DRINKING

Drinking customs and attitudes toward drinking vary in terms of the class structure. Dollard has shown, for example, that in the upper classes both sexes drink a good deal, and their drinking generally does not involve a moral issue, provided it is done "properly." "One is condemned in the Upper classes, not for drinking, nor for drunkenness, but for anti-social acts while drunk. Fighting is taboo; aggressive behavior is heavily penalized even when expressed only in verbal assaults." [100]

The lower-upper class is said to be distinguished from the other members of the upper class by the "cocktail set." In this particular group there is more alcoholic drinking in general and some excessive drinking which may result from the fact that the persons in the lower-upper class, in striving to reach the top of the social ladder, feel more insecure. The role of the host varies with the structure of the cocktail party, the composition of the guests, and the objectives of the party.[101] Cocktail parties

---

[97] Peterson and Maxwell, "The Skid Road 'Wino,'" loc. cit., p. 316. "For a wino to survive as a wino he needs someone to get him something to drink when he is sick and broke. Where it would be difficult for an individual to keep enough money for liquor coming in, two or three men bumming together can usually manage to keep enough money coming in for wine."—Ibid., p. 312.

[98] David J. Pittman and C. Wayne Gordon, Revolving Door (New York: The Free Press of Glencoe, 1958). Also see Earl Rubington, "Relapse and the Chronic Drunkenness Offender," Connecticut Review on Alcoholism, 12:9–12 (November, 1960).

[99] Pittman and Gordon, op. cit., p. 71.

[100] John Dollard, "Drinking Mores of the Social Classes," in Alcoholic, Science and Society, p. 99.

[101] David Riesman, Robert J. Potter, and Jeanne Watson, "The Vanishing Host," Human Organization, 19:17–28 (Spring, 1960).

vary in the degree to which persons "responsible" for them can influence course. At the large urban cocktail party, for example, the host tends to be relatively powerless, for such parties most often lack formal structure. The array of guests is heterogeneous, consisting of a wide cross section of persons of varying social statuses. Lack of space forces persons into little clusters where they may offer bits of polite small talk. Other persons, whose isolation is concealed by the unstructured nature of the group, may find solace in the food and drink. Such parties as these cannot be described as purely "sociable" occasions; rather, they are often "coming-out" parties for men, products, or ideas. Thus, the socially mobile couple who would not ordinarily give such a party, because of their lack of money and experience, may find themselves in a position which demands that they preside over such an affair.

On the upper-middle rungs of the success ladder, men drink at social gatherings and for business reasons. Women generally refrain from much drinking, however, and on the whole there seems to be a neutral attitude toward the consumption of liquor. Drinking parties seem to be increasing among middle-class groups who find escape, relaxation, and release through alcohol. A study of drinkng parties, as compared with nondrinking parties, revealed that they were attended by white-collar groups who, among the men, found increasing tensions in the insecurity of their status in an era of high-speed industrial and commercial activity and high-pressure salesmanship.[102] Members of the lower-middle class, striving desperately for recognition and status, and, in fact, for anything which would widen the gap between them and those whom they consider lower than themselves, have strong taboos against drinking, particularly among the women, because excessive drinking is associated in their minds with the behavior of the lower classes.

According to Dollard, the lower classes, in contrast to the lower-middle class, often do not exert restraints on drinking.[103] Both men and women may consume alcoholic beverages, and many, including primarily workers for whom drinking is in the norms, come, with few exceptions, to think of the tavern as the "poor man's club." The rates for military rejections during World War II for alcoholism were greater in the lower social strata of the population.[104]A study of a working class area in Santiago, Chile, found that 30 percent of the adult males have an episode of drunkenness every week end, twice a month, or once a month.[105]

[102] Duane Robinson, "Social Disorganization Reflected in Middle-Class Drinking and Dancing Recreational Patterns," *Social Forces*, 20:455–459 (May, 1942).

[103] Dollard, *loc. cit.*, pp. 99–101.

[104] R. W. Hyde and L. V. Kingsley, "Studies in Medical Sociology: The Relation of Mental Disorders to the Community Socioeconomic Level," *New England Journal of Medicine*, 231:543–548 (October, 1944).

[105] McCarthy, *Drinking and Intoxication*, pp. 99–105.

OCCUPATION AND EXCESSIVE DRINKING

Social patterns call for more immoderate drinking in certain occupational categories than in others. This view has been supported by the finding that a heavy disproportion of alcoholic psychoses are found in jobs with relatively low income and prestige, a result of the acceptance of heavy drinking as a norm in certain lower-class occupational groups.[106] On the other hand, McCord and McCord, after studying a group of 254 persons, found that middle-class Americans were significantly more prone to alcoholism than were members of the lower-lower class.[107]

Business is an occupation with which is often associated frequent and heavy drinking. Salesmen away from home for varying lengths of time stop overnight in towns where they have few acquaintances. They find people in taverns to talk to and with a few drinks the long hours pass quickly. Drinking is also a common practice among salesmen who travel in groups, drinking parties in hotel rooms being a particularly relaxing way to break monotony. Taking prospective customers out to dinner and having a few cocktails before the meal is often regarded as a traditional way of doing business and is provided for in the expense account.

A business executive in New York City has described how his daily luncheons are usually preceded by Martinis, followed by the leisurely drinking of highballs after the luncheon. In addition, important negotiations are often conducted over a drink in a bar. The executives who commute generally leave the office early enough to have two or three "for the road" before boarding the train. When they arrive home they usually find that their wives have cocktails ready, or that they have been invited out for cocktails at the home of some acquaintance. One alcoholic, in giving the reasons which led to his heavy drinking, has written:

> After finishing college and at the age of 27 I married and also picked up a job as an insurance salesman. Both my social life and my business life called for a good bit of social drinking and this was particularly true for the latter. To make a long story short, my drinking became progressively worse for fifteen years and it wasn't long before I was drinking almost daily.[108]

Seamen are an excellent illustration of occupational heavy drinkers. Life at sea for many becomes monotonous, frustrating, and socially isolating. Seamen have limited social outlets aboard ship, and often gain the satisfactions they need by looking forward to docking at the various ports of call in order to "have a good time." Enjoying oneself in port involves a

---

[106] Robert E. Clark, "The Relationship of Alcoholic Psychoses Commitment Rates to Occupational Income and Occupational Prestige," *American Sociological Review*, 14:539–543 (August, 1949).

[107] McCord and McCord, *op. cit.*, p. 41.   [108] From a personal document.

good many things, and almost invariably excessive drinking. It is no wonder, then, that the percentage of seamen who eventually become alcoholics is high. In the traditions of the trade, some form "bottle gangs," and tend to lose their individuality in these gangs. Often men in these gangs know little about each other, sometimes nothing more than their nicknames; yet in reference to norms such as excessive drinking and sexual promiscuity they may act as one.[109] Sailors often share their pay, for example, in order to continue drinking. During World War II an Alcoholic Seaman's Club was set up along the pattern of Alcoholics Anonymous. Treatment was directed toward breaking down the social isolation of the men and redirecting their desire for importance and recognition by letting them participate in more conventional social groups.[110]

It is not surprising that drinking is almost universal among migratory workers, "hoboes," and "tramps," and that drunkenness is frequent. In his classic study of this group Anderson stated:

> The only sober moments for many hobos and tramps are when they are without funds. The majority, however, are periodic drinkers who have sober periods of a week, a month or two, or even a year. These are the men who often work all summer with the avowed purpose of going to some lodging-house and living quietly during the winter, but usually they find themselves in the midst of a drunken debauch before they have been in town more than a day or two. Rarely does one meet a man among migratory workers who does not indulge in an occasional "spree"; the teetotalers are few indeed.[111]

A large percentage of chronic police-case inebriates studied by Pittman and Gordon had experience with all-male institutional living, and this experience appears to have affected their heavy drinking patterns.

> The Army, the Navy, the work camp, the railroad gang, and the lake steamer, all are rich in drinking culture. In these groups the harsh, the monotonous and the protective but controlled routines are broken by the nights, weekends and lay-offs which offer opportunities to drink. Drinking is a preoccupation and conversations at work are filled with talk of drink. The imagery and love of drinking are built up through these talks and stories. Fantasy around future drinking episodes serves the function of reducing the impact of heavy jobs in heat and cold, and of alleviating dull routines, sexual deprivation, and the loneliness of the all-male group. Drinking becomes a symbol of manliness and group integration.[112]

On the other hand, drinking does not appear to constitute a major problem among domestic servants. The close supervision exercised in this

---

[109] Anonymous, "Alcoholism—An Occupational Disease of Seamen," *Quarterly Journal of Studies on Alcohol,* 8:498–505 (December, 1947).

[110] R. G. Heath, "Group Psychotherapy of Alcohol Addiction," *Quarterly Journal of Studies on Alcohol,* 5:555–562 (March, 1945).

[111] Nels Anderson, *The Hobo: The Sociology of the Homeless Man* (Chicago: The University of Chicago Press, 1923, reissued by Phoenix, 1961), pp. 134–135.

[112] Pittman and Gordon, *op. cit.*, p. 67.

occupation means that a developing alcoholic is quickly noticed and dismissed from his position as a domestic servant.[113]

RELIGIOUS DIFFERENCES IN EXCESSIVE DRINKING

Differences in drinking patterns also exist among religious groups. One study, for example, revealed that 41 percent of the Protestants, 21 percent of the Catholics, and only 13 percent of the Jews abstained from drinking.[114] Studies have indicated that in spite of the fact that drinking is quite pervasive among the Jewish people, their rates for alcoholism fall far below what one would expect.[115] Only 4 percent of Jewish students in one study experienced social complications on account of their drinking; Episcopalians, 39 percent; Methodists, 50 percent; and nonaffiliates, 57 percent.[116]

In a comparative study Orthodox Jews have been found to have less drunkenness than more secular Jews, and, in general, to use alcohol differently.[117] A number of subcultural factors seem to explain the low alcoholism rates among Orthodox Jews. Among Orthodox Jews wine drinking is almost universal, since nearly all occasions, such as births, deaths, confirmations, and religious holidays, require it both by prescription and by tradition. Thus the Orthodox Jew becomes used to alcohol in moderation. He starts to use alcohol in childhood, later drinks with great frequency, but largely in a ritualistic context. Early socialization in the use of alcohol and ceremonial drinking is not as common among non-Orthodox Jews, and therefore they use alcohol in less moderation. Patterns of Orthodox drinking and their ritualistic associations are further supported by a normative structure of ideas of drunkenness as a gentile vice. The strength of the taboo among Orthodox Jews against conspicuous or excessive drinking can be seen from an old folk saying sometimes heard: "Drunk he is, drink he must, because he is a gentile."

Through the internalization of ideas and sentiments associated with Jewishness and the Jewish situation, and ideas of sobriety as a Jewish virtue,

[113] Robert Straus and Miriam Winterbottom, "Drinking Patterns of an Occupational Group: Domestic Servants," *Quarterly Journal of Studies on Alcohol,* 10:441–460 (December, 1949).

[114] Riley and Marden, *loc. cit.*

[115] Charles R. Snyder, *Alcohol and the Jews* (New York: The Free Press of Glencoe, 1958) and Robert F. Bales, "Cultural Differences in Rates of Alcoholism," *Quarterly Journal of Studies on Alcohol,* 6:480–500 (March, 1946).

[116] Jerome H. Skolnick, "Religious Affiliation and Drinking Behavior," *Quarterly Journal of Studies on Alcohol,* 19:452–470 (September, 1958). "The interpretation given to this finding is that abstinence teachings, by associating drinking with intemperance, inadvertently encourage intemperance in those students of abstinence background who disregard the injunction not to drink. However, frequent religious participation, even among students who drink, seems to diminish social complications."—*Ibid.,* p. 470.

[117] Snyder, *Alcohol and the Jews,* Chap. 6.

drunkenness as a Gentile vice, Jews bring to the drinking situation powerful moral sentiments and anxieties counter to intoxication. That these factors do not derive from the specific experience of drinking does not preclude their being a part of the normative orientation toward the act of drinking itself. We might say, then, that through the ceremonial use of beverage alcohol religious Jews learn how to drink in a controlled manner; but through constant reference to the hedonism of outsiders, in association with a broader pattern of religious and ethnocentric ideas and sentiments, Jews also learn how not to drink.[118]

The implications of these findings are great, as Snyder has suggested.

More generally, the findings of this study indicate that the problems of alcohol which beset American society cannot be understood apart from a consideration of the broader sociocultural matrix in which drinking occurs. Drinking itself is obviously not the exclusive cause of these problems since Orthodox Jews clearly demonstrate that virtually every member of a group can be exposed to drinking alcoholic beverages with negligible departure from a norm of sobriety and without the emergence of drinking pathologies such as alcoholism. Still more important, these findings suggest that the emergence of drinking pathologies where drinking is prevalent cannot be explained by exclusive reference to individual psychology or to a mysterious "craving" for alcohol presumed to be physiologically determined. The possible role of psychophysical processes is not denied but social and cultural phenomena, especially those related to normative or cultural traditions regarding drinking, appear to be essential for the emergence of these pathologies. Where drinking is an integral part of the socialization process, where it is interrelated with the central moral symbolism and is repeatedly practiced in the rites of a group, the phenomenon of alcoholism is conspicuous by its absence. Norms of sobriety can be effectively sustained under these circumstances even though the drinking is extensive. Where institutional conflicts disrupt traditional patterns in which drinking is integrated, where drinking is dissociated from the normal process of socialization, where drinking is relegated to social contexts which are disconnected from or in opposition to the core moral values and where it is used for individual purposes, pathologies such as alcoholism may be expected to increase.[119]

ETHNIC DIFFERENCES IN EXCESSIVE DRINKING

The extent and differences in drinking patterns of various ethnic groups are so pronounced that some people believe they have a biological rather than a cultural origin. The Irish, for example, have long been associated with traditions of excessive drinking. Studies indicate that their rates of chronic inebriety probably exceed those of any other single ethnic

---

[118] *Ibid.*, p. 182.   [119] *Ibid.*, p. 202. Reprinted by permission.

group.[120] It appears that the prevalence of the drinking habits in this group cannot be attributed, however, to any biological basis. Irish men drink because their culture permits drinking, particularly whiskey, probably more than many other ethnic groups permit it, although alcohol is not used in this group extensively for ceremonial purposes. After an examination of differences in Irish and Jewish rates of public drinking, one writer has suggested this as one of the chief reasons for the differences in the two groups.[121]

Bales has suggested that the explanation for the high rate of alcoholism among the Irish can be traced to a number of other factors.[122] In the 1840's the Irish farmer lived a marginal existence, the sexes were strictly separated, and at the same time there was difficulty in getting married because of economic conditions. The "older" young men were expected to spend their spare time with others drinking in the tavern. When relatives met in the tavern it was a matter of obligation to "stand" a drink for the others, who then had to reciprocate. The teetotaler was a suspicious character because he was not one of the "boys" in his drinking. Some of these drinking patterns have been carried on by immigrants who have left Ireland.

Italians in Italy have always had a tradition of using wine with the meals. Despite their extensive use of alcohol, the Italians have a low incidence of alcoholism. In fact, the United States rate is eight times as great. While the rate of alcoholism is also low among Italian-Americans, it appears to be higher than in Italy, even though the consumption of total alcoholic beverages was higher among the Italians. This was the problem of a unique joint research project on the use of alcohol in Italian culture among Italians and first-, second-, and third-generation Italian-Americans, conducted by the University of Rome and Yale University. In Italy milk is regarded primarily as a drink for children, whereas wine is for adults. Italians regard wine as healthful and a part of their tradition. Of 1459 adults interviewed in Italy, 79 percent said it was healthful to drink wine with the meals, 1 percent claimed it was not, and only one person expressed the fear that wine would lead to alcoholism.[123] Such an attitude appears, in part, to prevent alcoholic excesses and addiction. Most Italians first drink wine early in life, both men and women drink wine, and there

---

[120] William and Joan McCord, with Jon Gudeman, "Some Current Theories of Alcoholism: A Longitudinal Evaluation," *Quarterly Journal of Studies on Alcohol*, 20:746 (December, 1959).

[121] D. D. Glad, "Attitudes and Experiences of American-Jewish and American-Irish Male Youth as Related to Differences in Adult Rates of Inebriety," *Quarterly Journal of Studies on Alcohol*, 8:452 (December, 1947).

[122] Robert F. Bales, "Cultural Differences in Rates of Alcoholism," *Quarterly Journal of Studies on Alcohol*, 6:480–500 (March, 1946).

[123] Lolli *et al.*, *Alcohol in Italian Culture*. Also see Pierpaolo Luzzatto-Fegis and Giorgio Lolli, "The Use of Milk and Wine in Italy," *Quarterly Journal of Studies on Alcohol*, 18:355–381 (September, 1957).

is little opposition to the drinking of wine by young persons. Drinking is generally done in connection with meals. An interesting fact is that single persons appear to drink less wine, and "it would appear, therefore, that the use of wine—linked as it is with food events—loses much of its appeal for the unattached individual in the Italian culture, where alcoholic beverages are seldom used for 'escape' purposes." [124]

These drinking patterns were, in general, found to be present among Italian-Americans, although they are undergoing change. For example, 70 percent of Italian men, and 94 percent of the women, did all of their drinking at mealtimes, in comparison with 7 percent of the first-generation Italian-American men and 16 percent of the women, and 4 percent of the men and 11 percent of the women in the second generation. All of these factors, particularly drinking with the meals, tend to "inoculate" the Italian and Italian-Americans from alcoholism, and as they decline in importance alcoholism increases. Neither the cocktail hour, nor drinking after meals is a feature of Italian drinking; moreover, drinking with meals constitutes a safety factor for intoxication, as pointed out by Lolli:

> The relationship between the beverage used and the frequency of episodes of intoxication is outstanding. The occurrence of such episodes is lowest among the Italians, who drink almost exclusively table wine. The frequency increases among the first-generation Italian-Americans, who begin to drink more of other beverages. It is highest in the succeeding generations, who move still further away from the ancestral drinking customs and, presumably, the associated behaviors, attitudes and controls.[125]

Alcoholic beverages are widely used among the Chinese of New York City, but the incidence of excessive drinking or alcoholism is low.[126] The social control exercised by the Cantonese or Chinese subcultural pattern is such that alcohol is largely consumed as a part of social functions, public drunkenness is disapproved, and children are educated to observe these patterns. Unlike the Jews, frequent mild intoxication may occur, but statistics show low prevalence of alcoholism among Chinese-Americans.

Summary

The problems related to the consumption of alcohol, the role of the tavern, and the alcoholic in modern society are far from unique to any culture and age. Today there are extensive value conflicts over the use of alcohol as well as over taverns.

---

[124] Lolli *et al., op. cit.,* p. 79.   [125] *Ibid.,* p. 85.

[126] Milton L. Barnett, "Alcoholism in the Cantonese of New York City: An Anthropological Study," in Oskar Diethelm ed., *Etiology of Chronic Alcoholism* (Springfield, Ill.; Charles C Thomas, Publisher, 1955), pp. 179–227. Also see Merrill Moore, "Chinese Wine: Some Notes on Its Social Use," *Quarterly Journal of Studies on Alcohol,* 9:270–279 (September, 1948).

Alcohol acts physiologically as a depressant. The effect of alcohol depends on the rate at which it is absorbed, the kind of beverage consumed and the proportion of alcohol it contains, the amount and type of food eaten, and certain individual physiological differences. In moderate quantities alcohol does not appear to be harmful, but larger quantities can produce drunkenness.

Drinking is a social phenomenon. Group associations determine the kind of beverage and the amount used, the circumstances under which drinking takes place, the time of drinking, and the individual's, as well as others', attitudes toward drinking. Most taverns are of the neighborhood type, and their chief functions appear to be to provide social relationships, recreation, and a place to talk over common problems.

Approximately two thirds of the adult population of the United States drink alcoholic beverages. The proportion who drink varies by sex, religion, age, and education.

Those who drink can be classified in terms of deviations from norms of drinking behavior within a culture or subculture, and their dependence on alcohol in their life organization. This dependence includes the purpose and meaning of drinking, the degree to which such drinking handicaps the individual in his interpersonal relations, and his ability to refrain from taking a drink. On this basis drinkers can be classified as social or controlled drinkers, heavy drinkers, alcoholics, and chronic alcoholics.

The excessive use of alcohol seems to be learned from others. Group associations and cultural factors are important in determining who will become excessive drinkers and who will not. The drinking norms of the individual appear to be associated with those of his associates. They learn to drink excessively because of the type of drinking behavior of their companions, social class, occupation, or ethnic status. Involvement in difficulties because of their excessive drinking leads some into a circular process of further excessive drinking.

Selected Readings

Alcohol, Science and Society. New Brunswick, N.J.: Quarterly Journal of Studies on Alcohol, 1945. The first comprehensive discussion of alcoholism, and still one of the best. Many topics are discussed by different writers.

CLINARD, MARSHALL B. "The Public Drinking House and Society," in David J. Pittman and Charles R. Snyder eds., *Alcohol, Culture and Drinking Patterns.* New York: John Wiley & Sons, Inc., 1962. A comprehensive discussion of the tavern or public drinking house from the standpoint of the value conflicts involved, types of taverns, functions of taverns, and the relation of the tavern to alcoholism and delinquency.

JELLINEK, E. M. "Phases in the Drinking History of Alcoholics," *Memoirs of the Section of Studies on Alcohol.* No. 5. New Brunswick, N.J.: Quarterly Journal of Studies on Alcohol, 1946. An analysis of the symptoms of the various stages in the development of alcoholism, with a number of cases.

LOLLI, GIORGIO, EMILIO SERIANNI, GRACE M. GOLDER, and PIERPAOLO LUZZATTO-FEGIS, *Alcohol in Italian Culture.* New York: The Free Press of Glencoe, 1958. A comparative study of drinking patterns and attitudes of Italians in Italy and Americans of Italian extraction, based on interviews and dietary diaries. An analysis of the place of alcoholic beverages in the total pattern of eating and drinking behavior in Italian culture.

MC CARTHY, RAYMOND G. ed. *Drinking and Intoxication.* New York: The Free Press of Glencoe, 1959. A comprehensive selection of materials on historical and contemporary drinking customs, attitudes toward drinking, and methods of control of drunkenness from earliest times to the present.

MC CARTHY, RAYMOND G., and EDGAR M. DOUGLASS. *Alcohol and Social Responsibility.* New York: Thomas Y. Crowell Company, 1949. A general survey of the literature dealing with the use of alcohol in our society. Various issues are discussed, in particular education about the use of alcohol.

PATRICK, CLARENCE H. *Alcohol, Culture and Society.* Durham, N.C.: Duke University Press, 1952. A study of alcohol in a cultural context, including the influence of society on the use of alcohol and its effects on society.

PITTMAN, DAVID J., and C. WAYNE GORDON. *Revolving Door.* New York: The Free Press of Glencoe, 1958. An intensive, systematic study of the men who are repeatedly jailed for drunkenness. Analyzes and interprets the family backgrounds, childhood and adolescent experiences, and criminal careers of men caught up in the circular process of arrest, imprisonment and rearrest on charges related to public intoxication. Illustrated with cases.

PITTMAN, DAVID J. and CHARLES R. SNYDER eds. *Alcohol, Culture and Drinking Patterns.* New York: John Wiley & Sons, Inc., 1962. A collection of articles, many of them original, by sociologists on various aspects of the use of alcohol, including drinking patterns and the public drinking house and society.

SNYDER, CHARLES R. *Alcohol and the Jews.* New York: The Free Press of Glencoe, 1958. A study of the influence of cultural norms on patterns of drinking behavior. Based on interviews with a random sample of adult Jewish men and on the results of a questionnaire study of the drinking practices of college students of various religious denominations.

SYMES, LEONARD. "Personality Characteristics and the Alcoholic: A Critique of Current Studies," *Quarterly Journal of Studies on Alcohol,* 18:288–302 (June, 1957). A follow-up of an earlier survey by Sutherland and Tordella covering all studies from 1949 to 1956 which tried to differentiate the personality traits of alcoholics from nonalcoholics. Reaches a largely negative conclusion about the relationship.

"Understanding Alcoholism." *The Annals,* Vol. 315 (January, 1958). Contains chapters by specialists on every phase of the problem of alcoholism: the alcoholic personality, sociocultural backgrounds, the chronic drunken offender, the woman alcoholic, the family, psychiatric treatment, Alcoholics Anonymous, physiological factors, role of the physician, social work, nature and extent of the problem of alcoholism, current therapy, education, and research.

The Functional Mental Disorders

Mental disorders have long constituted a vast, mysterious, and challenging frontier in contemporary society. The basis of mental illness and the appropriate methods of preventing it are still frequently elusive. Only within recent times has society come to regard the mentally disturbed person as a "sick person." Yet this recognition has not completely eliminated the societal attitude of rejection of the mentally ill. Indeed, rejection is manifested in many ways, including often the disposal of society's "insane" to the "human dumping grounds" found in many state mental hospitals.[1] That state mental hospitals should function as dumping grounds was not, of course, the manifest intent of their founders. This situation has arisen largely from the divergent attitudes which society holds toward physical as opposed to mental disorder. Toward the physically disordered there is generally a societal attitude of sympathy, perhaps because of the fact that the features of physical disorders can be seen, felt, and objectively observed. On the other hand, mental disorders, which involve intangibles, such as feelings and ideas which are often incomprehensible to other persons, are ordinarily reacted to with fear, revulsion, and ridicule. Despite this societal pattern of rejection toward the mentally ill, frank recognition of the problem of mental illness constitutes the first step in its control.[2]

There are increasing scientific interest and research on mental disorders on the part of sociologists and anthropologists as well as psychiatrists and psychologists. The role which social and cultural factors play in the development of such disorders is of particular interest. Of concern also have been the effects on society of mental disorder, including the concepts of mental disorder held by society, the status and role of the mentally ill, and the changing nature of treatment.

---

[1] *Action for Mental Health,* The Final Report of the Joint Commission on Mental Illness and Health (New York: Basic Books, Inc., 1961), pp. 56–63.

[2] *Ibid.* Also see Ernest M. Gruenberg and Seymour S. Bellin, "The Impact of Mental Disease on Society," in Alexander H. Leighton, John A. Clausen, and Robert N. Wilson eds., *Explorations in Social Psychiatry* (New York: Basic Books, Inc., 1957), pp. 341–364.

Problems of Definition

It is difficult to define adequately such terms as "mental health" and, consequently, to define "mental illness" or "mental disorder." It is not easy to say who is mentally ill and who is not.[3] Mental health or mental disorder can be defined in several ways—statistically, clinically, operationally, and in terms of value judgments and middle-class standards.

Mental health is not the same as the statistically normal in terms of averages. According to this view, the mental health of the person in the "middle" would represent what might be termed "normality." It is difficult to measure the mental health of the average citizen either in terms of averages, such as the mean, median, or mode, because there is no satisfactory frequency curve of mental health as in the case of intelligence curves. A norm of this type would also mean one which changed with the state of mental health of a given population.

In clinical medicine the terms "normal" and "health" are used in the same sense. The problem of definition of normality in organic medicine, while difficult enough, cannot quite compare with the complexities in behavioral disorders. From a clinical point of view, mental disorder is often regarded as behavior which does not "function according to design." [4] Thus a catatonic stupor would be clinically regarded as maladjusted behavior. It is difficult for the clinician to measure the signs of the beginning of mental disorder as distinguished from mental health. Hallucinations, for example, which are often considered to be signs of mental disorder, may be found in normal people. Catatonic stupor may be thought to be maladjustive in our society, but in Asia it might be associated with religious mysticism. As Redlich has written, there are three ideas which must be met before behavior can be labeled clinically as normal or abnormal.[5] (1) The motivation of the behavior must be taken into account, such as "normal" washing of the hands and a neurotic washing compulsion. (2) The context or situation in which the behavior occurs must also be considered. Wearing swimming trunks on a New England street in winter is one thing; on a summer bathing beach, another. (3) By whom is the judgment made that the behavior is clinically abnormal—the experts, such as the psychiatrist, or the general public? "As we do not possess a universal, rigorous science of man, many propositions on normality of behavior have a palpably low degree of validity and reliability and are apt to be chal-

---

[3] See Thomas S. Szasz, *The Myth of Mental Illness* (New York: Paul B. Hoeber, Inc., 1961).

[4] Psychoanalysts would regard mental health as freedom from anxiety and where the rational replaces the irrational.

[5] Frederick C. Redlich, "The Concept of Health in Psychiatry," in *Explorations in Social Psychiatry*, pp. 145–146.

lenged by a startled public, especially if scientific evidence for them is not particularly strong or runs counter to prevalent public opinion." [6]

The clinical definition of mental health gets us into the area of value judgments. Mental health is thus defined by listing certain traits, capacities and relationships which are considered to be "normal." All kinds of criteria exist. Among the definitions which have been used by leading psychiatric writers are strivings for happiness and effectiveness and sensitive social relationships, freedom from symptoms, being unhampered by conflict and having the capacity to love other than himself; successful integration of personality and the balance of instinctual and ego force. Karl Menninger, in a widely quoted definition, has stated: "Let us define mental health as the adjustment of human beings to the world and to each other with a maximum of effectiveness and happiness. Not just efficiency, or just contentment, or the grace of obeying the rules of the game cheerfully. It is all of these together. It is the ability to maintain an even temper, an alert intelligence, socially considerate behavior, and a happy disposition. This, I think, is a healthy mind." [7]

With such criteria it is often difficult to see how anyone could be regarded as normal. A state of emotional health is thus regarded as par (to use the golf term) for the upper levels of health attainment.[8] They are ideals and are often contradictory. Actually behavior contrary to such ideal values may often be considered normal in another society. Hysterical reactions, for example, are common and normal in many societies.

So-called mental disorders have been studied in a number of preliterate societies, and the findings have a bearing on our understanding of the definition of mental disorders in more complex urban societies. The Berens River Ojibwa in northern Canada, for example, have various fears about encounters with animals, as well as phobias about snakes and huge imaginary animals, such as toads.[9] The belief also exists that personal transgressions are related to disease. Finally, their most pronounced fear concerns beliefs about Windigo, or cannibals. Human beings can be transformed into cannibals, and this fact may be perceived by certain phenomena exhibited by individuals. To an outsider these fears appear to be

[6] *Ibid.*, p. 146. Also see Jurgen Ruesch and Gregory Bateson, *Communication: The Social Matrix of Psychiatry* (New York: W. W. Norton & Company, Inc., 1951). See also H. Warren Dunham, *Sociological Theory and Mental Disorder* (Detroit: Wayne State University Press, 1959); Joseph W. Eaton, "The Assessment of Mental Health," *American Journal of Psychiatry*, 108:81–89 (August, 1951); and Marie Jahoda, *Current Concepts of Positive Mental Health* (New York: Basic Books, Inc., 1958).

[7] Karl Menninger, *The Human Mind* (New York: Alfred A. Knopf, Inc., 1946), p. 1.

[8] Leslie A. Osborn, *Psychiatry and Medicine* (New York: McGraw-Hill Book Company, Inc., 1952), p. 211. See Jahoda, *op. cit.*, for a critique of ideal definitions of mental health, pp. 5–9 and 65–80.

[9] A. Irving Hallowell, "Fear and Anxiety as Cultural and Individual Variables in a Primitive Society: Ojibwa," in Marvin K. Opler ed., *Culture and Mental Health* (New York: The Macmillan Company, 1959), pp. 41–62.

"neurotic" in the sense that there is no real danger and they arise from fantasies. Hallowell believes we should distinguish between individual fears and such culturally induced fears. This is a prevalent problem in the diagnosis of mental disorder in more complex societies with various subcultures and social classes.

> In the first place, the Berens River Indian *is* responding to a *real* danger when he flees from a cannibal monster or murders a human being who is turning into a *windigo,* or when he becomes apprehensive in a certain disease situation. To act or feel otherwise would stamp an individual either as a fool or as a phenomenal example of intellectual emancipation. For, psychologically, the actual order of reality in which human beings live is constituted in a large measure by the traditional concepts and beliefs that are held. Furthermore, the Indians themselves are able to point out plenty of tangible empirical evidence that supports the interpretation of the realities that their culture imposes upon their minds. They are naïve empiricists but not naïvely irrational.[10]

Value judgments about mental health, moreover, often merely represent certain middle-class criteria, thus implying lower-class behavior to be the reverse. Frequently mental health is defined in middle-class terms, and an attempt is made to associate the definition with the Protestant ethic.[11] An analysis of the content of pamphlets attempting to improve the mental health of the general population has revealed these middle-class themes in the definition of the mentally healthy person: [12] adjustment to group and prevailing norms by getting along with others, facing up to problems and then doing something about them, the value of work through enjoying it and getting satisfaction out of one's job, control of emotions, planning ahead without fear of the future, striving to achieve goals and community participation.

An operational definition of mental normality has been proposed by Redlich as "normal for what" and "normal for whom." [13] This definition seems to be helpful for our purposes. The extent to which mental problems, for example, can be tolerated by others may be different for a business executive or a person employed in a minor capacity in an industrial plant, both in terms of what is presumed to be "normal" and what is the societal reaction of others. "The self-perception of the person with the problem and the role assignment of all actors involved will determine subsequent labeling (normal or abnormal with reference to certain tasks) and subsequent action." [14]

---

[10] *Ibid.,* p. 53.

[11] Kingsley Davis, "Mental Hygiene and the Class Structure," *Psychiatry,* 1:55–64 (February, 1938).

[12] Orville R. Gursslin, Raymond G. Hunt, and Jack L. Roach, "Social Class and the Mental Health Movement," *Social Problems,* 7:210–218 (Winter, 1959–1960).

[13] Redlich, "The Concept of Health in Psychiatry," *loc. cit.*   [14] *Ibid.,* p. 155.

Operationally it is difficult, therefore, to draw a sharp line between mental health and mental disorder. What we really have is the problem of the social limits of "eccentricity," as an English writer has concluded: "It appears in fact that there is *no* clear-cut criterion of what constitutes a psychiatric case. Whether a person is regarded as in need of medical treatment is always a function of his behavior *and* the attitude of his fellows in society." [15] The person may be slightly, moderately, or severely impaired, depending upon the way his behavior is evaluated by others.[16] An operational definition depends also upon the societal reaction, including urgency of treatment as this is defined by society, and disorders may be divided into two groups.[17] One category is the severely mentally ill or psychotic, those cases in which the societal reaction to the behavior is strong and treatment is often urgent. Their behavior is regarded as social or antisocial in terms of the prevailing cultural norms and their level of social performance is not in conformity with norms current for persons of their particular age and status.[18] Such deviations are more easily recognized by the expert and the lay public with whom the persons are in contact, and they may even be treated without the consent of the patient. The second category represents those mild and transitory mental disturbances where there is little urgency and the problem is felt more by the individual than by others. The more moderately disturbed group includes those persons whose behavior deviates less markedly from the norms (of perception, belief, and feeling) and who may or may not be reacted to by most lay persons as "odd" or "peculiar." Professional persons would probably describe these persons with technical terms, such as the neuroses.[19]

In evaluating the criteria by which visible symptoms might be judged, one practical basis is the extent to which the person failed to fulfill adequately expectations in performing his primary social roles (especially his familial and occupational roles), and the extent to which he violated legal and moral norms and highly important values of the group. Whether a definition of deviancy is made and acted upon will depend, largely, on how serious the consequences of this deviation are for the social group. Some deviant behaviors are rewarded and tolerated, others have some idiosyncratic function for the group as is often the case with the "comic," or the deviant may be thought of as "eccentric," "queer," or "strange" but not sufficiently so to merit a definition of illness. On the other hand, should the deviancy begin to

---

[15] G. M. Carstairs, "The Social Limits of Eccentricity: An English Study," in Opler, *op. cit.,* p. 377.

[16] See A. Hollingshead and F. Redlich, *Social Class and Mental Illness* (New York: John Wiley & Sons, Inc., 1958), Chaps. 1, 2, 6.

[17] Redlich, "The Concept of Health in Psychiatry," *loc. cit.,* pp. 154–158.

[18] Norman Cameron, *The Psychology of Behavior Disorders* (Boston: Houghton Mifflin Company, 1947), p. 8.

[19] See Hollingshead and Redlich, *op. cit.,* Chap. 6, and *Action for Mental Health,* Chap. 3.

have serious consequences, either in that it is damaging or harmful to the individual, a group, or both, or becomes so visible to external groups that the family suffers status loss, it might be redefined as "mental illness" and the person sent for treatment. In some groups, of course, the stigma attached to a definition of mental illness is sufficiently great to bring about group resistance to such a definition.[20]

Traditionally, mental ill-health has been classified as the neuroses and the psychoses. Neuroses are the mildest and the most common type. Among psychotics, thoughts, feelings, expressions, beliefs, and acting deviate more markedly from approved norms. Psychotic behavior, as contrasted with neurotic, is often characterized by a loss of contact with reality. Furthermore, the psychotic's ability to communicate intelligently with others may be partially or completely interrupted, a factor which is not generally characteristic of the neurotic. The essential feature of the neuroses is that they involve behaviors which deviate less markedly from societal norms than is true of the psychoses. They are therefore regarded as "less serious," and generally there is greater societal tolerance for them.[21]

Actually, it is much easier to recognize the behavior which is labeled psychotic because the deviation from norms is often more pronounced and visible. The so-called neuroses are much harder to designate and label. Role distortions or role inadequacies are not generally apparent. Consequently, among psychiatrists and others there is little agreement on the definition of a neurosis. This fact is shown by estimates of the neurotics in the general population. Some estimate as high as 40 percent, others about 5 percent. Some have gone so far as to suggest that nearly everyone in a modern urban society is neurotic. Obviously, the concept becomes almost meaningless when used in this way.

Extent of Mental Disorders in the United States

It is impossible to know the extent of mental illness in the United States today. Even if one knew how many are so incapacitated mentally that they require hospitalization, are being treated by psychiatrists, or are being counseled by their clergymen or by others, this total might well exclude many others who are mentally ill. The sources of knowledge about the extent of mental illness have been chiefly from (1) data on patients in mental hospitals, (2) data from Selective Service examinations and the records of the armed forces, and (3) community surveys of the prevalence of mental disorders.[22]

---

[20] David Mechanic, "Some Factors in Identifying and Defining Mental Illness," *Mental Hygiene,* 46:66–74 (January, 1962).

[21] *Action for Mental Health,* Chap. 3.

[22] These data have several limitations. They have largely not been made on random samples of the population, and they have not used "standardized methods of case finding,

In 1959 there were 616,964 mental patients in long-term mental hospitals, about 88 percent of them in public mental hospitals—state, county, or city. The movement of patients in and out of these hospitals during a given year is so extensive that the total is actually much higher, and on any one day of the year, patients in mental hospitals make up almost half of all the patients in all the hospitals of the United States. From 1955 to 1960 there had been a slight decline in the resident population of mental hospitals, which has been thought to be due to the increased use of tranquilizers as well as to a spreading conviction that patients should, if possible, be treated without hospitalization.[23]

These figures are not an actual index of mental disorder because the proportion with mental disorders not hospitalized is not known. Also, there are considerable variations throughout the country: "Hospitalization rates are a resultant not only of the true incidence of mental disorder but of a number of factors such as availability of mental hospital beds, public attitudes toward hospitalization, and availability and use of other community resources for diagnosis and treatment."[24] These other resources include such facilities as general hospitals with psychiatric treatment services, psychiatric clinics, and private psychiatrists.

More Selective Service registrants were rejected during World War II for personality defects other than mental deficiency than for any other cause. Up to August 1, 1945, 900,000 men between the ages of eighteen and thirty-seven were rejected for military service and classed as neuro-psychiatric casualties, a figure which represented 18 percent of all men rejected in the armed forces.[25] In a study of the prevalence of defects among those between the ages of eighteen and forty-four who were examined during the period 1940–1943, mental illness ranked sixth in prevalence, with a rate of 55.8 per 1000 men. During World War II the armed services gave a medical discharge to about 460,000 men for neuropsychiatric reasons, or about 36 percent of all medical discharges. Such figures, high as they are, should not be taken as representative of the general male population of military age. Persons were deferred for a large number of reasons, others volunteered, and some of those with certain physical defects or low educational standards were not examined at all. Furthermore, the standards for military acceptance changed, and draft boards did not use

---

diagnosis, and classification, as well as comparable definitions of case and prevalence."— R. H. Felix and Morton Kramer, "Extent of the Problem of Mental Disorders," *The Annals*, 286:13 (March, 1953).

[23] For a discussion of mental hospital populations see Chapter 21.

[24] Felix and Kramer, "Extent of the Problem of Mental Disorders," *loc. cit.*, p. 12.

[25] United States Selective Service System, *Physical Examination of Selective Service Registrants* (Special Monograph No. 15; Washington, D.C.: Government Printing Office, 1948). This figure did not include those rejected because they were mentally deficient (feeble-minded) or those who were in mental hospitals.

identical methods in screening.[26] Moreover, the figures should be regarded with extreme caution because of inefficiencies in the general screening process for military service.

Estimates of the incidence of mental disorder in the general population have been made, but it is difficult to know the true rate. Most of the estimates appear to be highly exaggerated. To give some estimate they will be presented with this reservation. A community survey was made in the Eastern Health District, Baltimore, Maryland, in 1936, and another in Williamson County, Tennessee, in 1938.[27] The Baltimore study found 3337 "active" cases of mental illness during the year in a population of 55,129, or 60.5 per 1000 population. The Williamson County survey found that there were 1721 cases of mental illness in a population of 24,804. The two studies cannot be compared, however, because of demographic differences and the methods they used.[28]

One of the most intensive metropolitan surveys ever made in the field of mental health involved a cross-section of a heterogeneous midtown Manhattan residential population of 110,000 persons.[29] From interviews with 1660 residents the conclusion was reached that only 18.5 percent were free enough of emotional symptoms to be considered "well." A total of 58.1 percent were found to have mild to moderate symptoms, such as tensions, nervousness, and other indications of emotional disturbances, although not to the extent of impairing life functioning. Marked, severe, and incapacitating symptoms were found in 23.4 percent of the cases.

---

[26] William A. Hunt and Cecil L. Wittson, "Some Sources of Error in the Neuropsychiatric Statistics of World War II," *Journal of Clinical Psychology*, 5:350–358 (October, 1949). Also see Eleanor Leacock, "Three Social Variables and the Occurrence of Mental Disorder," in Leighton, Clausen, and Wilson, *op. cit.*, pp. 308–340. Leacock points out that a good proportion of those rejected as "neuropsychiatric casualties" were actually mentally deficient and/or illiterate.

[27] Paul Lemkau, Christopher Tietze, and Marcia Cooper, "Mental Hygiene Problems in an Urban District," *Mental Hygiene*, 25:624–646 (October, 1941), 26:100–119, 257–288 (January, 1942), and 27:279–295 (April, 1943). Also see William F. Roth and Frank Luton, "The Mental Health Program in Tennessee, I: Description of the Original Study Program; II: Statistical Report of a Psychiatric Survey in a Rural County," *American Journal of Psychiatry*, 99:662–675 (January, 1943). It is unfortunate that the studies were not confined to mental illness, for the Baltimore study also included about 6.8 percent cases of mental deficiency, and the Tennessee study 8.2 percent. Feeble-mindedness, which represents a lack of intellectual development for organic or other reasons, is not considered here as a mental disorder. The distinction is often made between *amentia*, or the absence of mental faculties, and *dementia*, which is the disorder of such faculties. Occasionally feeble-minded persons develop disorders, but these generally have no connection with the feeble-mindedness. Feeble-minded persons probably have no more, and possibly even less, personality disorders than those with higher intelligence.

[28] In the former study, for example, "active" meant being a client of certain social agencies, whereas in the other "active" meant cases presenting both serious and mild personal problems.

[29] Leo Srole *et al., Mental Health in the Metropolis: The Midtown Manhattan Study,* (New York: McGraw-Hill Book Company, Inc., 1962). The validity of this study depends, of course, upon the criteria used to determine degrees of mental health.

A study of Texas has used a different measure, namely, of incidence of first cases of psychoses who came under diagnosis and treatment during the two-year period 1951 through 1952, whether private or public and whether in or outside a hospital, rather than merely hospitalization.[30] Jaco found the average number of Texans considered to be psychotic for the first time in their lives was 5649, or a crude annual incidence rate of 73.3 per 100,000. The age-adjusted rate was 68 for males and a higher rate of 78 for females. The median age was 44 for males and 40 for females. The incidence increased with each advancing age-group category in the total group and among males, although there were some slight exceptions among the female groups. As other studies have shown, highest standardized rates for psychoses were found among the divorced, followed in order by those who were single, separated, widowed, or married.

Trends in Mental Illness

There is some question as to whether there has been a real increase in the rate of resident patients in mental hospitals in the United States. Actually, the rate has about doubled, from nearly 200 per 100,000 population in 1903 to nearly 400 in 1950.[31] It may actually represent a real increase in mental disorders, or it may reflect an increase in the age of the general population, a greater awareness of mental illness on the part of laymen and professional men, more hospital space, or increased difficulties encountered by mentally ill persons who remain outside hospitals in urban areas where living conditions are crowded. One study suggests that the apparently greater flow to mental hospitals may be also a function of our highly complex, industrial society.[32] Thus some elderly persons who have simply outlived their function and who have difficulties in interpersonal relations may be placed in mental hospitals because there is no place for them outside.

A study of first-admission rates to Massachusetts and New York institutions for the mentally ill for the periods 1840–1885 and 1917–1940, a detailed comparison of 1885 and 1939–1941 being made, concluded that "there has been no long-term increase during the last century in the incidence of the psychoses of early and middle life." [33] More specifically, it was claimed that when comparisons are made which take into account the class of patients received, and the conditions affecting hospitalization, that the

[30] E. Gartly Jaco, *The Social Epidemiology of Mental Disorders* (New York: Russell Sage Foundation, 1960).

[31] Felix and Kramer, "Extent of the Problem of Mental Disorders," *loc. cit.,* p. 9.

[32] *Action for Mental Health,* Chap. 3.

[33] Herbert Goldhamer and Andrew W. Marshall, *Psychoses and Civilization* (New York: The Free Press of Glencoe, 1953), p. 92.

rates by age for first admissions under fifty "are revealed to be just as high during the last half of the 19th century as they are today." [34] A marked increase in the older groups was attributed to the increased tendency today to hospitalize older persons suffering from mental disorders.

A number of major objections to this study can be raised, however, some of which the authors recognize. First of all, Massachusetts has been highly urban for a long time: 75 percent in 1880 as compared with 90 percent in 1940; therefore conclusions drawn from this sample do not measure the possible increase in mental disorders in larger areas of the country where urbanization has been more recent and more rapid. There has been a decline in the relative incidence of organic psychoses, such as paresis, which is caused by syphilis, a disease more common a century ago. Moreover, the study did not include most neurotic cases, since they are only infrequently hospitalized; but, as will be indicated, these cases constitute a large proportion of contemporary mental illness. In addition, there are today a large number of persons with mental illness who are treated by outpatient clinics and private practitioners who could not have been so treated to any large extent a hundred years ago because there were few such facilities.

Organic Mental Disorders

According to conventional classification, there are two types of mental illness: those having an organic basis, and those having a nonorganic, or functional, basis. Organic types of mental disorders are usually linked to some germ, to a brain injury, or to other physiological disorder, and, in certain rare types of mental disorders, possibly to some hereditary factors. The three most important organic mental disorders are the arteriosclerotic senile psychoses, paresis, and the alcoholic psychoses, none of which is really hereditary.

The senile or old-age psychoses, which are generally classified as organic on the assumption that they are produced by certain physiological processes of aging, accounted for about a fourth of all admissions to state hospitals in 1957. Some of these cases are arteriosclerotic and result from changes in the circulatory system, but others are not. Senile psychoses are characterized by a loss of memory, particularly for recent events, inability to concentrate, or certain delusional thoughts. There is increasing evidence that many of the psychoses due to aging are the product of nonorganic conditions arising from interpersonal relations, such as social isolation and loss of status.[35]

Paresis, or dementia paralytica, is caused by syphilis, and accounts for

---

[34] *Ibid.*, p. 91.   [35] See Chapter 16.

about 4 percent of all state hospital admissions. This illness begins at least ten years after the initial syphilitic infection, and there is often progressive degeneration in the brain of untreated patients. Although the symptoms of a paretic may not be different from those of many functional psychoses, the paretic may be relatively easy to diagnose through positive Wassermann and Kahn reactions. There may also be tremors, convulsive seizures, and a lack of coordination in bodily movements. The mental symptoms are often a complete alteration in the personality traits: "The neat well-dressed individual becomes careless and slovenly; the efficient businessman shows poor judgment in the office; the moral, upright man suddenly becomes degraded." [36] Eventually memory about time and places may become defective and in some cases there is depression. As a rule, paretics do not live long. The elimination of syphilis would end paresis, and great advances have been made toward this goal. Today a number of factors have reduced not only the incidence of syphilis but, particularly, that of paresis. Widespread public health methods, including education, have reduced the incidence of syphilis; and drugs, including formerly arsenic and now the more effective antibiotics, which work on the nervous system, have helped to cure syphilis and thus prevent paresis. Some evidence exists, moreover, that present-day syphilis is of a milder form than that of a half century or so ago.

The psychoses resulting from alcoholism are not as definitely organic as paresis, although they are usually classified as the same type. Only relatively few alcoholics develop psychoses. In 1949 there were only 5381 new admissions to state mental hospitals for this illness as a result of alcoholism, or 5.2 percent of all admissions. In 1957 17,286 persons were admitted to public, prolonged-care hospitals, with mental disorders associated with alcoholic intoxication or alcohol addiction. Of this total, 10,527 were classified under "personality disorders" with "alcoholism addiction." There is some doubt as to how much mental illness is organically produced by the alcohol and what proportion is the result of certain sociopsychological conditions.[37] The prolonged existence of chronic alcoholism, with its vitamin and nutritional deficiencies, may in some cases produce such deterioration in physical and psychological behavior that alcoholic psychoses may result. Some patients become rigid and develop terrifying hallucinations, others have tremors which are often referred to as delirium tremens or "D.T.'s," and still others show general progressive deterioration. Not all cases of D.T.'s indicate a psychosis, however, for many of these symptoms may be short-lived and without marked personality changes.

---

[36] Roy M. Dorcus and G. W. Shaffer, *Textbook of Abnormal Psychology* (3d ed.; Baltimore: Williams & Wilkins Company, 1945), p. 278.

[37] See Chapter 12.

Functional or Nonorganic Mental Disorders

Previously we have indicated that mental disorder should be regarded as a deviation from norms and can be understood only in terms of the societal reaction to certain behavior. What may be regarded as mental disorder—that is, beyond the tolerance limit of eccentricity—is therefore not necessarily the same from one culture to another.

Such a view conflicts with the general psychiatric tendency which regards such behavior as clinical entities, as constituting a type of "sickness" which would, presumably, be the same in all cultures. Because of their medical training, psychiatrists obviously look for disease entities and think in terms of a medical diagnosis.[38] In the case of mental disorder these diagnoses have come to be known as neuroses and psychoses, and the latter in turn have been divided into schizophrenia, manic-depressive disorders, paranoia, and other entities. They have come to be regarded as real disease entities which are important to the psychiatrist who, being a physician, assumes that this enables him to deal with the "causes" and therefore to suggest treatment of the mental disorders. Rather than being disease entities they are actually *descriptions* of certain behavior.

The diagnostic categories themselves, and the adequacy of the diagnosis by psychiatrists, have been severely criticized by many writers. As Hollingshead has written: "Currently, psychiatry does not have a standard test which researchers may use to diagnose any of the functional mental illnesses. A standardized, valid, diagnostic test would enable a researcher to determine the presence or absence of functional mental illness in individuals. Until this problem is solved, research into mental illness will continue to be hampered." [39]

The lack of reliability and validity of psychiatric diagnosis has been shown in several studies. For example, it was recently reported by Hoch that the ratio of first admissions, with a diagnosis of manic depressive in comparison with schizophrenia, reversed itself over a five-year period in one state hospital system. He attributed this reversal to a change in personnel and policy in the hospital system, not to a shift in the distribution of disease in the population of the state.[40] This report was supplemented by Pasamanick, with findings from another hospital where from one ward to another significant differences were found in the diagnostic classifications

---

[38] For a critical discussion of the implications of medical training for psychiatric treatment, see Erving Goffman, *Asylums* (New York: Doubleday Anchor Books, 1961), pp. 320–386.
[39] August B. Hollingshead, "The Epidemiology of Schizophrenia," *American Sociological Review*, 26:10 (February, 1961).
[40] Paul H. Hoch, in "Work Conference in the Mental Disorders" (Mimeographed; New York: February 15–19, 1959), pp. 145–146.

of patients with functional psychoses.[41] For example, on one ward the diagnosis changed with the change in the ward administrator. The diagnoses had been made by residents, as well as by the ward administrator, who was a trained psychiatrist. Whereas these data were based on reports of hospitalized patients, Leighton did research in which he attempted to assess the mental status of a nonpatient group. In his study six psychiatrists were asked to read the field protocols on fifty adult white males, and were instructed to assess whether each man was mentally "ill" or "well." Fifteen were placed in an equivocal category, and five were thought to be "well," although these five men diagnosed as "well" differed for each of the six psychiatrists. In fact, one psychiatrist's five "wells" had been placed in another's "sickest" group.[42]

Having stated such criticisms, one might well question the relevance of including in the following section a description of various types of mental disorder. In the first place, they are terms widely used by psychiatrists, who are the persons mainly responsible for the treatment of mental disorders. Second, they are terms used by laymen. It is therefore necessary to become familiar with such terms and their use. Again, however, it should be understood that actually these are not clear-cut entities in the sense, for example, of tuberculosis. In fact, many persons exhibit the behavior described in each type, although in all probability to a lesser degree and in a manner which does not provoke much societal reaction. Probably all persons have, to some degree, exhibited such behavior as hallucinations, phobias, persecution complexes, and emotional extremes of elation and depression. For example, everyone will remember how many times during his lifetime he has had irrational fears, daydreams, flights of idea, and disorders of memory:

> . . . sense of inferiority, sublimation, imperception, illusion, hallucinations, delusions, disorders of judgment, disturbance of the train of thought, flight of ideas, nonessential ideas and thoughts, incoherence, retardation or inhibition of thought, disorders of orientation, disturbance of consciousness, clouding of consciousness, confusion, dream states, negativism, inaccessibility, obsession, fears, phobias, disorders of attention, disorders of memory, conflict, complexes, compensation, symbolization, etc.—all of these are found operating in varying degrees in minds that are considered normal, as well as in minds that are disordered to such an extent that the case is diagnosed as insanity.[43]

According to many psychiatrists, the functional or nonorganic mental disorders "function" to adjust the individual to his particular difficulties;

---

[41] Benjamin Pasamanick, in "Work Conference in the Mental Disorders," pp. 143–145.

[42] Alexander H. Leighton, in "Work Conference in the Mental Disorders," pp. 147–148.

[43] Lawrence Guy Brown, *Social Pathology* (New York: Appleton-Century-Crofts, Inc., 1946), p. 62. This quotation and others from this work have been used by permission of the publisher.

hence the term "functional." The idea that such mental disorders are necessarily an adaptation to stress is difficult to prove, although in many cases this adaptation may play an important part. As yet no one has been able to demonstrate conclusively that functional disorders result from heredity, physiological disorders, or other organic deficiency. Although there have been reports of organic deficiencies in some cases, most leading authorities in psychiatry today agree that nothing of a universal nature has so far been established. The neuroses and the psychoses are the two types of these disorders.

THE NEUROSES

Some neurotic symptoms can be classified as dissociated behavior and others as compulsive disorders. In all of them the societal reaction to the behavior is not as great as with the psychoses. Hysteria, amnesia, and disturbances of speech, hearing, and sight are examples of dissociated behavior. It was once thought that hysteria, which was quite common, was a peculiarly feminine disease, since women were frequently given to "swooning." In addition to hysterical fainting, there may often be facial tics or uncontrolled movements. Ingenious tests have been devised, for example, to separate the person who is hysterically blind in one eye from the truly blind.[44]

Compulsive behavior is a form of neurosis where there are "irrepressible tendencies to do, say or think something in a particular way which persist in spite of strong contrary tendencies. In this situation anxiety reactions develop and their periodically rising intensity leads to indulgence, followed by temporary relief."[45] This behavior includes stepping on cracks in the sidewalk, excessive washing of the hands or bathing, counting telephone poles, dressing in a certain set manner, and requiring everything to be in a certain meticulous order, such as all drawers carefully closed or shoes or other objects lined up in order.

Often the compulsive behavior is not physical in nature but consists of obsessions or persistent ideas, emotional fears of objects, acts, or a situation. Some obsessions may be a more or less constant fear of death, of losing one's mind, or of losing one's friends, prestige, or job. A fairly common neurotic fear is anxiety about one's health, hypochondria, which may involve fears about the general state of health or about nonexistent heart conditions, cancer or tuberculosis. Sometimes neurotic obsessions are di-

---

[44] Red and green letters are put on a card so that the letters are alternately colored. On one there may be the red letters JHSOKN and the green letters ONHPIS. The subject is given glasses, through one lens of which he can see only the red letters, the other only green. If he reads "Johns Hopkins" it is apparent that he is using both eyes even if he reports he has vision in only one eye.

[45] Cameron, *op. cit.*, p. 12.

rected at destructive notions of injuring someone. Neurotic phobias are often of a general nature such as fear of confinement (claustrophobia) or its opposite, fear of open places, and fear of high places. Persons suffering from these fears are generally not only ashamed of this behavior but become perplexed and resentful of it as absurd and burdensome.[46]

Studies have shown that members of the upper class are more likely to be given the polite label of "neurotic," whereas those in the lower class are labeled as psychotic or, more specifically, schizophrenic.[47] In this connection Clausen has stated:

> Every community has some members who are regarded by their fellow citizens as "queer," "mean," "shy," "offensive," and the like. Many of these persons would be diagnosed by a psychiatrist as neurotic and some as psychotic, even though other community members may not regard them as mentally ill. It is not unlikely that many persons whose social background is grossly divergent from that of the psychiatrist (e.g., lower-class persons) will be seen as sicker than those whose attitudes and behaviors are closer to the psychiatrist's own outlook.[48]

THE FUNCTIONAL PSYCHOSES

The functional psychoses are generally divided into three main types: schizophrenia, the manic-depressive psychoses, and paranoia. In all of these the societal reaction tends to be greater than it is toward the neuroses. About 21 percent of all new admissions to state mental hospitals each year are diagnosed as schizophrenic. This illness is sometimes referred to as dementia praecox, because it develops primarily between the ages of fifteen and thirty. Few persons develop schizophrenia after the age of fifty. The manic-depressive psychotics constitute about 15 percent of all institutionalized patients, women making up roughly three quarters of all these cases. Only about 1 percent of all new admissions to state mental hospitals each year have a diagnosis of true paranoia.

Schizophrenic Behavior. The most characteristic symptom of a schizophrenic is his withdrawal from contact with the world around him and his inability to play the roles expected of him. Even before institutionalization becomes necessary, the schizophrenic may show a great deal of emotional indifference and inattention. He does not share the expectations and interest of the group, and there is a great indifference to things previously considered important. In addition, the emotional tone is passive, often even negative, so that the patient has little interest in activities.

---

[46] *Ibid.*, p. 281.   [47] See, for example, Hollingshead and Redlich, *op. cit.*
[48] John A. Clausen, "The Sociology of Mental Illness," in Robert K. Merton, Leonard Broom, Leonard S. Cottrell, Jr., *Sociology Today* (New York: Basic Books, Inc., 1959), p. 494.

Finally, his thought processes are so disturbed that he builds a world of his own imagination, including false perceptions and hallucinations of various kinds, such as ideas, voices, and forces which enter his daily living and which he cannot control. Schizophrenics have undergone a collapse in their personalities which involves a detachment of their emotional selves from their intellectual selves. It is for this reason that the term "schizophrenia," or "split personality," as it is often called, is used to refer to this illness.

Several subtypes of schizophrenia have been identified. A conventional distinction has been a fourfold classification of simple, hebephrenic, paranoiac, and catatonic schizophrenia. The symptoms of severe hebephrenics and catatonics are not seen as frequently today in institutions because of the use of tranquilizers. In simple schizophrenia patients begin from early life to show increasing tendencies to withdraw, to daydream, and to be unable to concentrate. They become exceedingly careless of their personal appearance, manners, and speech, are listless and apathetic, and lose their interests and ambitions. There is little loss of memory and no serious mental deterioration, if any. Many of these cases are never institutionalized because they are not harmful to themselves or to others and because they may make some sort of adjustment to the world, inadequate as that adjustment may be.

Hebephrenic symptoms include a pronounced silliness of behavior with a great deal of situationally unwarranted smiling, giggling, odd mannerisms, gesturing, and incoherent speech and thought. There is pronounced mental deterioration with bizarre delusions and auditory and visual hallucinations.

Unlike those of the true paranoid, to be discussed shortly, the delusions of persecution of the schizophrenic paranoid are transitory and are based on his own social reality. Moreover, the schizophrenic with a paranoid reaction hears and sees varying images and noises and exhibits the characteristic emotional indifference of the schizophrenic. The following case illustrates a typical paranoid schizophrenic patient.

A 46-year-old laborer admitted to the state hospital with complaint of feeling weak, mixed up, unable to work. Following admission to hospital he appeared shy, mixed poorly, and complained that someone was following him and wanted to get rid of him. He improved spontaneously, was discharged to his family, then readmitted seven years later. On readmission he had a crutch and cane, claimed he had not been working for several years because of a spinal injury. He offered various ideas of persecution and strange expressions, i.e., that he was surrounded by detectives who were trying to "run a secret world." He was being bothered by "radio tones." After a course of 23 electric shock treatments he discarded his cane and crutch and gave up his ideas about not being able to walk. He has remained chronic with persistent delusions, some persecutory and others grandiose, e.g., identifying himself with Roosevelt and Truman, thinks he has done important "government work" in the past and that he is entitled to a large pension. He was well adjusted in the hospital.[49]

Catatonic schizophrenics have episodes of excitement and stupor. Since they live in a private world of their own, their behavior is characterized by apathy and impulsiveness. They display the most complete withdrawal from the social world of any mental patients. Many catatonics' withdrawal may be so complete that the muscular or waxy rigidity of the limbs and the stuporous appearance of the catatonic reminds an observer of a dummy. Such catatonics may sit for hours and days in the same position without movement or speech, and some have to be fed. One is able to lift the arm of many catatonics in such a stupor or place them in an uncomfortable position and for an indefinite time they will make no effort to alter their position. They seem to take no interest in things going on around them; yet they are often conscious of the most minute details in their surroundings. The catatonic syndrome also includes a manic state, with increased speech, muscular movements, and action. Gesturing and frenzy are also common. Probably most catatonics, but not all, alternate between these periods of severe depression, frenzied excitement, and stupor.

Some have suggested that some of the more bizarre reactions of hospitalized patients may, in fact, be reactions to their institutionalization and complete deprivation of civil rights. This might apply not only to the catatonic but to other types of patients as well.[50]

Manic-Depressive Behavior. As the name implies, manic-depressive behavior may be extremely elated, in the manic stage, or depressed, although manic-depressives do not necessarily pass through cyclical stages of mania and depression.[51] In the manic stage the patient is agitated and excited, elated and aggressive. He rapidly shifts from one topic, object, or activity, and there is a constant flow of manic talk, which, although continuous, is socially understandable. This method of talking is often filled with quips, rhymes, poems, and other witticisms, much with a personal reference. The manic patient sings or whistles, shouts, dances, walks, teases or clowns. He may dress himself lavishly or prefer to go unclothed. Since he often disregards such bodily needs as food, rest, and elimination, he may be in need of immediate physical attention.[52]

---

[49] From a case record collected by the author.

[50] *Action for Mental Health.* See also M. Greenblatt, D. Levinson, and R. Williams, *The Patient and the Mental Hospital* (New York: The Free Press of Glencoe, 1957), pp. 438–471, 517–526.

[51] Thomas Rennie, "Prognosis in Manic-Depressive Psychoses," *American Journal of Psychiatry*, 98:801–814 (May, 1942). In this study of 208 manic-depressive cases Rennie found that about one fourth had both manic and depressive attacks, although not as often in cycles.

[52] Cameron, *op. cit.*, p. 513.

In the depressed phase there is much brooding and unpleasantness, but little serious mental deterioration. Agitated depression involves restless overactivity and despair, whereas activity is minimized and stupor is not uncommon in retarded depression. This disturbance is generally characterized by feelings of dejection, sadness, and self-deprecation. The patient seems to have lost friends, home, family, and all purpose in life. He feels guilty about acts committed or omitted, and he believes he has grievously wronged and been wronged. Contact with reality is nonetheless maintained, as are memory and place-time orientation.

Not all depressed behavior is symptomatic of a manic-depressive psychosis. Neurotics may display secondary depression. Involutional melancholia is another fairly common mental disorder characterized largely by depression. This condition may occur among women during the menopause period and among men at a slightly older age. For example, it is difficult to distinguish schizophrenia from the extreme or manic phases of the manic-depressive disorders. In fact, today schizophrenia is apt to be a more popular diagnosis than formerly, and the manic-depressives are likely to be largely the depressive cases.

Paranoia and Paranoid Behavior. At one time a large proportion of mentally ill persons were diagnosed as suffering from paranoia, but today paranoia is not widely used as a diagnostic category. Most of those suffering from paranoid disorders are now considered to exhibit a form of schizophrenic behavior. Paranoids are thought to be extremely suspicious and have ideas of persecution with an intellectual defense which often appears to have plausible reasons for it. Their delusions are usually limited to a few areas and may even be centered on a single person. The behavior of most people who are paranoid, however, does not seriously interfere with most of their life activities; their personalities do not deteriorate nor do they have hallucinations.

Mental Disorder as a Process

Although a description of the symptoms of neurotic and psychotic behavior has been presented, it gives little insight into the developmental process in mental disorders. The mere description of mental disorders has, in fact, become an increasingly sterile approach in their understanding, prevention, or treatment. Although there are various biological, psychoanalytic, sociocultural and other explanations of mental disorder, none as yet offer an adequate explanation of mental disorder. We shall emphasize the sociocultural explanation, with the full realization that it is recent and requires much more research before it can be fully accepted. As explained in a sociocultural framework, the functional mental disorders are primarily the product of a breakdown of effective communication between persons and defective role playing.[53] Although the psychoses may sometimes be more severe disorders than the neuroses, both arise from, and are perpetuated by, the use of the same unskilled and inappropriate adjustive techniques in dealing with other persons and social situations in general.[54] Not everyone, of course, who has difficulties in dealing with other people has a mental disorder, for many people, regardless of occasional erratic behavior, are progressively effectual as social persons.

Mental disorders appear to be continuous, dynamic processes, and not a series of separate stages. There are periods of childhood, adolescent, and adult influences, but actually all the experiences which affect the person have a profound effect on his relationships with others and his self-reactions. A mother, for example, may be overprotective and thus produce in a child techniques of dealing with people or situations which may continue throughout life. If the child is pampered and spoiled he may develop and use techniques of getting his own way through bullying, fighting, and temper tantrums. On the other hand, the child who is dominated by his mother may become withdrawn, timid, and submissive. The child who does not know how to deal effectively with other people may become shy, and this shyness, in turn, may make him excessively obedient and submissive. It is out of such childhood training and later influences that the "shut-in," seclusive characteristics of many mental disorders develop, including the neurotically withdrawn person and the schizophrenic. The relation of family dynamics to schizophrenia has been described thus:

> The mothers of schizophrenics have been characterized as cold, perfectionistic, anxious, over-controlling, and unable to give spontaneous love and acceptance to the child. They often seem unwilling to accord the child any privacy, attempting to intrude even into its thoughts. . . . The family network appears to be characterized by great stress and conflict, though often this is covered over by a desire to conceal the existence of differences. The net effect of most of the patterns noted is that they would make it difficult for a child to achieve an identity of his own, to be able to confront life situations with self-reliance and confidence.[55]

---

[53] A well-known psychiatrist stated that the objectives of psychiatry should be the study of processes that involve or go on between people: "The field of psychiatry is the field of interpersonal relations, under any and all circumstances in which these relations exist."—Harry Stack Sullivan, "Conceptions of Modern Psychiatry—The First William Alanson White Memorial Lectures," *Psychiatry*, 3:5 (February, 1940). Also see Osborn, *Psychiatry and Medicine*.

[54] Cameron, *op. cit.*, p. 11.

[55] John A. Clausen, "Mental Disorders," in Robert K. Merton and Robert A. Nisbet eds., *Contemporary Social Problems* (New York: Harcourt, Brace & World, Inc., 1961), p. 164. Also see J. A. Clausen and M. L. Kohn, "Social Relations and Schizophrenia," in Don Jackson ed., *Etiology of Schizophrenia* (New York: Basic Books, Inc., 1960), pp. 295–320.

Such patterns may be carried over into social situations outside the home where such techniques, not being replaced by new ones, are used on others. As a result, these children may not be accepted into normal play groups and the development of more adequate role taking on their part is hindered. They are often ostracized by their peers or tend to avoid playing with those of a similar age. Not every child who is overprotected or reared in an unhappy family situation, however, will necessarily develop a pronounced mental illness. Childhood patterns can be altered at any time if the strategy of dealing with people can be reversed. Other influences may help this change: the social relations of the wider community, the reaction of the child himself, and adjustments to other children in the family. In fact, efforts to predict the personalities of children from early rearing experiences have not been successful.[56]

The patterns of childhood strategy in dealing with others may be carried on indefinitely and, by recurring at each successive phase of growth, may result in a feeling of successful interpersonal relations or one of personal failure. In fact, the difficulties in adolescence, when serious, are often simply a reflection of past situations. The child who reaches this stage, not liking people and having personal difficulties, will probably continue to have these difficulties. Adjustment difficulties become important when there are excessive conflicts in social roles, habitual anxieties over other persons' attitudes, or little real satisfactions in other aspects of life organization.[57]

Mental disorders thus generally have a long history and are cumulative rather than products of a single circumstance or a few situations. Childhood experiences and those of early and later adult life have their influence. Difficulties in interpersonal relations and social roles, as well as faulty conception of self, may continue for years before there is the full-fledged development of a mental disorder. The more a person becomes mentally ill the more sensitive he becomes to events that probably would not affect him at all if he were well. A depressed person, for example, may increasingly find more and more types of situations to depress him. This cumulative nature of mental illness often makes its treatment a long and laborious process.

One study of schizophrenia, for example, has emphasized the distinctive effects of social relationships in many areas of life.[58] The reactions of the schizophrenic, his withdrawal, his attitudes of low self-worth, his anx-

---

[56] William H. Sewell, "Infant Training and the Personality of the Child," *American Journal of Sociology*, 58:150–159 (September, 1952).

[57] Cameron, *op. cit.*, pp. 48, 52, and 499.

[58] S. Kirson Weinberg, "Social Psychological Aspects of Schizophrenia," in Lawrence Appleby, Jordan M. Scher, and John Cumming, *Chronic Schizophrenia* (New York: The Free Press of Glencoe, 1960).

iety concerning further social rejection, and his distorted meanings of reality all emerge from a series of social relationships. The weakening of the self-system is a product of social isolation and difficulties in interpersonal relations in the family, in peer relations, and with the opposite sex, as well as in work associations. In the following case the patient was unable to deal with a series of frustrations and conflicts in interpersonal relations and finally developed schizophrenia.

The subject, when last seen, was 28 years old and married. She had been committed in the hospital as schizophrenia undetermined, remained four months and then was discharged outright. After her discharge her general personality condition was perhaps better than it was before the schizophrenic onset.

The youngest of three siblings, she was always an obedient and "model" child. Though she claims never to have wanted for affection from her parents, she felt certain subtle attitudes of rejection because the parents had hoped for a boy and were disappointed with a girl. Though the center of attention, and considered the baby of the family, she felt lonely because of the age discrepancy between herself and her sisters. As a child she often played alone but made friendships which were cut short by the family movements. Her predominant feeling, even as a child, was that of being "different" and "inferior" because her playmates dressed better than she did; she felt that she was poorer than other girls, notions which her parents laughingly dispelled. During early adolescence the initial rejection which she formerly felt in a vague way became more manifest. This feeling was aggravated because she could not compete successfully with her older sisters. In addition, her parents set such high standards for the children that she often felt that she was a "failure" in anything she attempted. Because the father was so intent upon his daughters getting married, she made every effort to know boys. With this outlook she was seduced when she was 16 by a man 25, who promised to marry her.

At 17 she left home to attend college; had a difficult time in her studies and was unable to foster friendships with other students. After one year she transferred to another college. Apart from her studies her main preoccupation was in getting dates. Since this was during the war years, male students were fewer and dates harder to get. In a trial and error process she finally met, became enamored of and engaged to a soldier. Having been sexually intimate with him, she became struck with periodic guilt, but became very dependent upon him because, as she stated, he proved she "was worthy enough to be loved." She made friends at her dormitory, was pledged to a sorority and became an accepted member of the group. After getting to know them well she quarrelled with these dormitory friends. By siding with one group who promised to get her into a sorority she so antagonized her other friends that they would not speak to her. Very lonely and dejected, she felt that her chief self-support and fulfillment of her father's desire were concentrated in sustaining her engagement and the hope of eventually getting married. When her fiancé broke the engagement because he preferred another girl, she became despondent and confused, had a spree of crying, feared she would never get married, and considered herself a failure. But she had no one to whom to turn for consolation or advice. She dared not tell her parents, whom she felt were nicer to her during her engagement. She could not go to her friends who were not on speaking terms with her. Perplexed, distracted and depressed, she was unable to study, would stare about her until finally a glass caught her eye. She kept thinking "how easy it would be" to eat some glass and get out of her misery. The next day, while attempting to study, she abruptly got up, broke the glass, ate some splinters, became frightened at what she had done, ran to the psychiatrist who also became upset, but who said she could not stay in school and advised her to become a volunteer patient at a mental hospital.

When she entered the hospital she was uncommunicative, disoriented and intermittently agitated. She received seven shock treatments and improved continually until her release.[59]

Notwithstanding the cumulative nature of mental disorders, immediate situations occasionally do have a bearing. They act as precipitants and bring the process to a climax. The effect of an immediate situation is particularly important in the manic-depressive disorders, where the anxiety builds up and tends to be set off by it. Although the underlying process would still be there, more study of precipitating situations might reduce the incidence or at least the recurrence of these disorders. A study of a group of manic-depressive cases, for example, revealed that nearly four fifths of them were precipitated by some particularly disturbing life situation, a marital disagreement, the death of someone, a crisis situation in a career, or a feeling of personal failure induced by harsh criticism.[60] These conditions cause particularly severe anxiety and tension. In most cases there had been a period of from one to six months in which anxiety and conflict had been built up.

STRESS AND MENTAL DISORDER

In social living all persons frequently encounter circumstances in which their personal desires are not achieved. These conflicts bring about a situation of stress. An interference of one kind or another may prevent the adequate development or achievement of a person's desires. In fact, one theory of schizophrenia is that it arises from a situation called the "double bind," a situation in which no matter what a person does he cannot win.[61] Davis has classified the conflicts which may be involved in mental disorder thus: (1) ends may be incompatible because they are opposite in character, (2) different ends many compete for scarce means, and

[59] S. Kirson Weinberg, "Sociological Analysis of a Schizophrenic Type," *American Sociological Review*, 15:605–606 (October, 1950).

[60] Rennie, "Prognosis in Manic-Depressive Psychoses," *loc. cit.*

[61] Gregory Bateson, Don D. Jackson, Jay Haley, and John Weakland, "Toward a Theory of Schizophrenia," *Behavioral Science*, 1:251–264 (October, 1956).

(3) conflict may arise from too great a disparity between ends and means.[62]

A certain amount of conflict is a part of the normal process of social living. Life is not all clear and precise; there is always an unknown quantity. The individual is faced throughout life with conflicts, hazards, and overwhelming demands and perplexities. These tend to produce a certain amount of anxiety which many claim plays an important part in mental illness. In many ways anxiety resembles fear. Like fear, it is an emotional reaction produced by stimulation with which one is unable to deal, leaving the person with a feeling of possible loss of security and support. Unlike fear reactions, however, which call forth avoidance and even flight from a real danger when this is possible, in anxiety the emotional reaction does not go on to completion. Fear is overt but anxiety is covert, and leaves the person in an undefined emotional state with which he would like to cope but cannot. He is afraid, but since he is unable to identify what he fears he cannot eliminate it. As contrasted with overt fear reactions which can be identified, anxiety reactions are less visible and are often inaccessible both to the individual and to others.

With most people conflicts tend to solve themselves or become reformulated. Many people find that other activities and interests help the tensions of anxiety to disappear or to be absorbed. And there are some people who, through adequate role playing in their interpersonal relations and an adequate estimate of themselves, are able to continue to have anxieties, even of a cumulative nature, for a long period of time without developing a mental disorder.

In a nation-wide survey, anxiety, expressed through physical symptoms, has been found to be more prevalent in the lower-income groups where "low income" suggests current unhappiness and worries, no confidence in the future, and anxiety expressed through physical symptoms. On the other hand, psychological anxiety is more common at both extremes, the high and low income, with middle-income groups expressing the least.

> It may be that psychological anxiety symptoms reflect blocking and consequent indirect expression of energy. In both high- and low-income groups, this blocking of energy and inability to find direct outlets may derive from an inability to give it direct expression in one's interaction with the world, specifically, in this instance, in efforts directed toward bringing about concrete environmental changes that have visible effects on one's status. For the economically deprived groups, this inability would spring from overwhelming environmental blocks; for the economically privileged group it would spring from the fact that many concrete aspirations were already

---

[62] Kingsley Davis, *Human Society* (New York: The Macmillan Company, 1949), pp. 260–262.

fulfilled. Thus, under highly dissimilar conditions, these two groups may experience similar problems.[63]

Some persons cannot endure the tensions of anxiety. This difference in the tolerance for anxiety and in the extent of its stress may explain why some persons develop mental disorders while others do not. The inability to deal with frustrations and conflicts producing anxiety appears to be the result of previous inadequate interpersonal relations over perhaps many years which have left the individual without the adequate supports with which to face anxiety-producing situations. If the anxiety-producing situation is one of difficult interpersonal relations, as it frequently is, anxiety reactions may be even further increased because the individual can neither deal with the situation nor face the fact that he cannot meet it.

If the tensions develop beyond the limits of the individual, there may be chronic anxiety reactions and even acute anxiety attacks. Not only do the symptoms of anxiety continue for a long time; a person may be subject to very pronounced anxiety attacks and even panic reactions. With mounting anxiety the individual may reach the end of his tolerance limit and be subject to great fright. Such persons may become agitated, there may be nausea and salivation, dizziness, weakness in the knees, and hot flushes. He may feel that impending disaster is at hand—that he is going insane, is about to die, is on the verge of a heart attack, and so on. One patient described her anxiety attack after a hot, tiring day in which she had to deal with a domineering superior: "My heart suddenly stopped. Then it came up in my throat and turned over and quivered so fast you couldn't count it. I had a pain in my chest and down my arm. I was like in a tight vice, I couldn't breathe. It seemed like I was going to die." [64]

Likewise, neurotic compulsive behavior, such as orderliness and obsessional ideas, helps to relieve the anxiety. The acts, words, and thoughts involved in the relief of the anxiety may include tapping, counting, saying a set word, recalling or imagining a certain scene, and even snapping the fingers. In hypochondria, for example, the individual's constant preoccupation with his health simply constitutes solutions in which this preoccupation diverts and releases anxiety. In fact, "the fruit of resistance to the compulsion is mounting anxiety, while the reward of indulgence is a temporary respite." [65] Although tendencies to compulsive neurotic behavior are an irritation and are opposed, the momentary feelings of anxiety lead to the behavior and the subsequent relief. The relief is always temporary, for eventually the anxiety begins to mount again and the pa-

[63] Gerald Gurin, Joseph Veroff, Sheila Feld, *Americans View Their Mental Health*, Joint Commission on Mental Illness and Health (Monograph Series No. 4; New York: Basic Books, Inc., 1960), p. 218.

[64] Cameron, *op. cit.*, p. 255.   [65] *Ibid.*, p. 277.

tient has to give in to the compulsive behavior in order to reduce it. More-over, the societal reaction of others to the bizarre behavior, whether neu-rotic or psychotic, may tend to increase anxiety.

In the schizophrenic disorders and depression, the individual may withdraw and find anxiety fended off as he retreats from threat and con-flict to what Cameron calls a "protective shell of incapacity." The para-noid may relieve the prolonged excessive anxiety by focusing it on some individual or situation to which he can attribute his uncomfortable feel-ings. Manic behavior may constitute "an escape from insupportable anx-iety into overt action," or, as often stated, constitute "an escape into re-ality." [66] Like depressions, this excitement begins after prolonged stress. There is a period of greatly increased anxiety of from a few hours to several weeks. In his excited behavior, shifting as he does from one thing to another, the patient is able to find some avoidance of his anxiety feel-ings. There is an increase in initiative and through what appears to be boundless energy he seeks to avoid his anxiety and, therefore, his prob-lems.

SELF-REACTIONS AND COMMUNICATION

All persons have a self-reaction to their appearance, status, and con-duct. They come to conceive of themselves not only as physical objects but as social objects as well. Likewise, human beings learn to express ap-proval of themselves and they are able to reproach themselves. This ca-pacity of self-conception which all persons have plays an important part in mental illness.[67]

Mentally disordered persons develop distorted self-conceptions or self-images which are reflections of difficulties in interpersonal relations and continuing anxiety. Other persons may come to think of them as "odd," "crazy," or "difficult." Some may become less confident and more preoccupied with themselves. Without logical reasons they may adopt egocentric ideas of being either a great success or a great failure. Where interpersonal relations have been difficult, the mentally ill person may learn to use his self-reactions in fantasy. He may dream of himself as someone he is not in order to overcome conflicts. A seventeen-year-old dishwasher who became mentally disordered built up a strongly organized role of fantasy so that she considered herself a "beautiful duchess, walked on her tiptoes, her mien proud and sweet, her gestures graceful and com-manding" [68]

---

[66] *Ibid.*, p. 276.

[67] See, for example, William R. Rosengren, "The Self in the Emotionally Disturbed," *American Journal of Sociology*, 66:454–463 (March, 1961).

[68] Cameron, *op. cit.*, p. 101.

The schizophrenic has a self-feeling of social isolation and does not strive for social relationships any more, as Weinberg has indicated:

> The process of schizophrenic breakdown involves the recasting of self-hood on several levels. . . . First, when the schizophrenic feels that he is losing hold of himself or even anticipates a disordered reaction in a projected intolerable situation, he frequently reaches for some means to regain control of his capacities, or at least to regain his self-esteem on an acceptable level. This bid for regaining an acceptable self-esteem, without having the defensive techniques for doing so, intensifies his panic reactions. The intensity of this bid for regaining self-acceptance is measured by the degree of explosiveness and conflict during the breakdown. With a gradual, insidious lapse into a disorder, the conflict to regain a former self-esteem is minimal. On the other hand, the schizophrenic with few settled defenses, in a state of panic, may resort to random aggression and abusive declamation as a futile means of self-reclamation.
>
> Second, the normal individual's range of identity is circumscribed subjectively by reactions which he can consciously control or intentionally will. The schizophrenic, however, is beset by uncontrollable impulses, somatic reactions, and inner experiences which challenge the range of his identity. Since he cannot control his inner experiences, he attributes them to forces or agents external to his identity and disrupts his ability to differentiate the self from the outer environs.[69]

Third, as Weinberg has indicated, the schizophrenic's continued preoccupation with self and his lessened ability to share his experiences with others intensifies self-centeredness. His self-centered reactions obstruct his capacity to relate, and this consequently magnifies his own concern about his symptoms and his conflicts, so that he is less able to act with emotional feeling. The reactions and interpretations of a schizophrenic to his hallucinatory behavior are illustrated by the following statement of a patient.

> When I first commenced hearing these voices I am hearing and having them unusual feelings in the arms I could tell by them feelings that I was having was caused by electric flashing and drawing through my body and head and them voices I was hearing about everything that I thought and I knew at the time that it was someone communicating with me in the way of having a short wave connected to me; and I knew that the short wave was working on my heart for every time I heard a voice my heart fluttered and pounded; and at night when I went to bed in the army barracks that electric would make me shake all over and I knew it was someone broadcasting to me in the way of having a short wave connected to me, but I could not figure out what they could have to do me them ways or who they was and when they first commenced talking to me.[70]

---

[69] S. Kirson Weinberg, "Social Psychological Aspects of Schizophrenia," *loc. cit.*, pp. 81–82.

[70] As quoted in Weinberg, *ibid.*, p. 82.

The paranoid self-reaction is one of conceit and suspicion which affects his relations with others. The overprotected child may develop an idea of his abilities which is entirely divergent from the opinions of those outside his closed family circle. The self-delusions of grandeur that develop out of this glorified self-conception are seen in extreme form in the paranoids who claim that they "own the entire world."

What a person does can result in self-approval or self-reproach. He can praise himself for what he has said or done, or he may be disturbed by what he has done and rebuke himself, producing frustration and conflict. For adults with a depressive psychosis, this self-punishment, representing an internalization of difficulties with their outside social situations, can become a "tragic melodrama, where the depressed self-accused lashes himself so mercilessly in talk and fantasy that death seems the one promise of penance and relief." [71] If the depressed person feels guilty, self-hostility may result in such a loss of self-respect and so much self-reproach that suicide may even result. In such mental disorders the self may become so detached from the individual that it becomes not a social object but a physical object to be mutilated and punished for sin.

In certain forms of neurotic behavior involving dissociation the person may even be able to forget his own identity. In some cases of hysteria and amnesia the person may even identify with a past role or with another self. In these cases there is an attempt to get away from one's conflicts by changing oneself. The new selves may be alternating or coexisting and one self may not be aware of the other.

Disturbances in language, which are often a part of the symptoms in mental illness, indicate rather clearly its connection with interpersonal relations.[72] Although verbal imagination is perfectly normal, for without it books, poems, or great music could not be written, a person with a mental disorder, being socially isolated, verbalizes his thoughts and then becomes afraid of what he has created. The mentally disordered person is able to invent a world of his own through his thought processes. With language the neurotic is able to conjure up all types of evil thoughts of which he is afraid. The depressed person is able to talk himself into self-depreciation; the manic, into a frenzy. The schizophrenic is able to invent a world of private fantasy which lifts him in his own estimation. This expansion of fantasy, growing out of inadequate responses to shared social situations, continues until it no longer responds to the role taking of others in the culture. The disorders in thought processes are eventually expressed through his language and are a result of retreat from reality.

---

[71] Cameron, *op. cit.*, p. 101.

[72] A recent study has indicated that part of what is called disturbances in language or meaningful conversation of the mentally ill is actually a reflection of social class. See Lloyd H. Rogler and August B. Hollingshead, "Class and Disordered Speech in the Mentally Ill," *Journal of Health and Human Behavior*, 2:178–185 (Fall, 1961).

The fact that the schizophrenic lives in a world of his own making, through verbal imagery, not only reflects and influences his thought processes but distorts his verbal reactions until they swing completely away from socially adequate responses. Language becomes private and not social; whether the other person understands it is immaterial.

The schizophrenic patient, living in his private world, invents his own common words and links them in such a fashion as to make his speech seem incoherent to others. In response to the question, "Why are you in the hospital?" one patient replied:

> I'm a cut donator, donated by double sacrifice. I get two days for every one. That's known as double sacrifice; in other words, standard cut donator. You know, we considered it. He couldn't have anything for the cut, or for these patients. All of them are double sacrifice because it's unlawful for it to be donated any more. (Well, what do you do here?) I do what is known as the double criminal treatment.
>
> Something that he badly wanted, he gets that, and seven days criminal protection. That's all he gets, and the rest I do for my friend. (Who is the other person who gets all this?) That's the way the asylum cut is donated. (But who is the other person?) He's a criminal. He gets so much. He gets twenty years' criminal treatment, would make forty years; and he gets seven days' criminal protection and that makes fourteen days. That's all he gets.[73]

MENTAL DISORDER AND INAPPROPRIATE ROLE PLAYING

As has been indicated, we do not yet have, despite many claims, any final, definitive answers as to the causes of mental disorders. Role-playing difficulties seem to offer, however, a profitable clue. More specifically, difficulties in interpersonal relations found among persons with functional mental disorders appear to arise from inappropriate role playing. As has been indicated, social roles are organizations of attitudes and responses to certain social situations. Roles must be played so that the points of view and expectations of others in society are shared. In mental disorder the individual in varying degrees either never acquired this ability, or, having acquired it, later lost it. The social roles of a person with a mental disorder, for example, may appear rigid and unalterable, or they may be unstable and confused. His responses to social stimuli may be extremely inappropriate, contradictory, exaggerated, ineffectual, or apathetic.

Paranoid behavior, according to Cameron,[74] appears to be a product of inappropriate role playing and role taking. There is an inflexible way of looking at things, they cannot shift roles or see alternative explanations for the behavior of others. Gradually a private world is built up in which the

---

[73] Cameron, *op. cit.*, pp. 466–467.
[74] Norman Cameron, "The Paranoid Pseudo-Community," *American Journal of Sociology*, 49:32–38 (July, 1943.)

self as a social object becomes central and in which slights and discriminations, some real and some imagined, from the outside world are interpreted to fit their preconceptions. The paranoid develops a "pseudo community" which is a product of his unique interpretation of "persecution" in the ordinary behavior of others toward him. He is unable to interpret adequately the roles of others and is therefore not socially competent to interpret their motives and intentions. His systematized paranoid or paranoiac delusions of discrimination and persecution develop out of his attempt to account for situations and happenings which are the products of his own lack of socialization and his fantasies. "His socially inadequate interchange of attitudes and interpretations with others not only throws him upon his own limited resources for explanations and hypotheses but allows these also to be elaborated without the checks and modifications that the contrary opinions of others, if entertained seriously, would inevitably induce. Such preoccupation, with its collection and noting of incidents, becomes more and more engrossing; it narrows down the interests and activities of the person and further isolates him from the affairs of others." [75]

The pseudo community in which the paranoid lives is a private world which is real but not shared with others. Often his public world in the earlier stages of paranoid behavior gives little overt indication of his thoughts. He may be quite adequate in his manners, in courtesy, in impersonal conversation, and in community activities. As his delusions grow in intensity the paranoid becomes, however, more and more suspicious. On those rare occasions when he comes later to share his suspicions with others their ridicule makes him even more convinced that he is right. As a result he may suddenly decide that an extensive plot is being directed against him. The reactions of the real community in the form of restraint or retaliation to any of his vengeful or defensive overt behaviors make him convinced that the interpretations of his paranoid pseudo community are correct.

Recently, Lemert, a sociologist, has challenged this interpretation of a "pseudocommunity." He maintains, after studying a number of cases of paranoia, that the community to which the paranoid reacts is real and not a pseudo or symbolic fabrication.[76] Lemert states that "while the paranoid person reacts differentially to his social environment, it is also true that 'others' react differentially to him and this reaction commonly if not typically involves covertly organized action and conspiratorial behavior in a very real sense." Moreover, the reaction of the future paranoid with others is reciprocal and results in exclusion. The delusions and associated

---

[75] *Ibid.*, p. 35.
[76] Edwin M. Lemert, "Paranoia and the Dynamics of Exclusion," *Sociometry*, 25:2–20 (March, 1962). Quotations are from pages 2 and 7.

behavior which develop must be understood in the context of a process of exclusion which disrupts his social communication with others.

> The paranoid process begins with persistent interpersonal difficulties between the individual and his family, or his work associates and superiors, or neighbors, or other persons in the community. These frequently or even typically arise out of bonafide or recognizable issues centering upon some actual or threatened loss of status for the individual. This is related to such things as the death of relatives, loss of position, loss of professional certification, failure to be promoted, age and physiological life cycle changes, mutilations, and changes in family and marital relationships. The status changes are distinguished by the fact that they leave no alternative acceptable to the individual, from whence comes their "intolerable" or "unendurable" quality.

Inappropriate role playing takes several forms: (1) Some persons are unable to play certain roles. (2) There may be contradictions in role playing to which persons cannot adjust. (3) Some individuals are unable to make the necessary shifts from one role to another as required in normal social relationships.

Incapacity for Certain Roles. Some neurotic difficulties appear to develop when a person who is much more suited to one role tries to play another that is beyond his capabilities, leaving him in a state of chronic anxiety. This results partly from the contradictions between sheltered successful role playing in the family and the often brutal competitive adjustments required in the outside world. These contradictions are largely a product of segmentalized urban living: "Thus, the individual who emerges from the family as a dependent person may acquire the hard-driving, indirectly aggressive way of life from his secondary groups. The contradiction between these two sets of relationships is perhaps the basis of many of our disorders." [77]

Many neurotic persons have tried to achieve success beyond their ability. Because of their conception of themselves or the driving impetus of their parents, wives, or friends, they cannot retreat to a lesser goal. Ambitious parents or ambitious wives undoubtedly have much to do with the formation of a neurosis.

Contradictory Roles. The necessity for persons to play many and contradictory roles is perfectly normal. With normal activity an individual can meet this contradiction in roles. A woman, for example, can give solicitous affection to all members of her immediate family and at the same time be an aggressive leader in her relations outside it. A person may have to play one role with the marital partner and another with his parents. Individuals who cannot adjust to these changes often develop anxiety and mental disorder.

---

[77] Weinberg, *Society and Personality Disorders,* p. 156.

It has been suggested that the causal agent in the manic-depressive psychoses may be such intense group relationships and so many conflicting and contradictory roles that the resulting strain is enough to cause a breakdown. The individual who is all things to all people in his desire to please and to gain attention and prestige and who is continually participating in group activities may lose his basic and characteristic orientation. The demands and values of too many groups and too fervent participation leave him in a position in which he is unable to incorporate them coherently into his life organization.

The hypothesis has been advanced by some writers that the intense striving for material goods and the enormous competitive emphasis lead many persons to irreconcilable conflicts. The sacrifice of mental health to the ever-continuing struggle for goods, possessions, power, and status appears to be more characteristic of men than of women and of urbanites than of rural persons. Group contacts are maintained not for the social and personal gratifications to be derived from them, but because they might serve as steppingstones to getting ahead. Should prestige, status, class position, or material goods be threatened, the individual's world may collapse, leaving him with no supports. Economic competition, for example, operated in five hundred psychiatric cases as a factor in their mental illness.[78] The struggle for achievement liberated in some patients feelings of hostility. In other cases the culturally prescribed standards of success and prestige presented goals impossible of achievement, which augmented already existing conflicts. In still others, economic life offered a new arena for the enactment of competitive struggles which had been going on in one guise or another since early childhood.

Inability to Shift Roles. The main characteristic of many persons who develop mental illness is their inability to shift from one social role to another. They have not had the kind of social experiences to develop such skill. As has been indicated, everyone normally plays many roles, even in a single day, depending upon the situation and the expectations of others. An inflexible personality that cannot adapt to social situations will develop anxiety. Muncie has referred to the "rigid personality" pattern of an individual who develops a psychosis.[79] He is unable to abandon one role in a situation that calls for different behavior; his activity seems incongruous. Likewise, such a person cannot satisfactorily predict the behavior of others.

An individual's inability to shift roles means that when "insurmountable personal difficulties arise [he] cannot abandon the non-adaptive

---

[78] Stanley A. Leavy and Lawrence Z. Freedman, "Psychoneurosis and Economic Life," *Social Problems*, 4:55–67 (July, 1956). Also see Karen Horney, *The Neurotic Personality of Our Time* (New York: W. W. Norton & Company, Inc., 1937).

[79] Wendell Muncie, "The Rigid Personality as a Factor in Psychoses," *Archives of Neurology and Psychiatry*, 26:359–370 (August, 1931).

perspective by shifting through roles to one that might offer a different solution. This fixity of perspective, so characteristic of nearly all delusions, is what psychiatrists mean when they say that a patient lacks insight. He sees things only from a single standpoint for which he seems unable to substitute any other, even for the purposes of the moment." [80]

The schizophrenic person, for example, often does not play the roles expected of him in normal social relations. He has never developed the necessary skill, when under stress, to be able to change his role in social situations. He is so closely identified with his parents and an older generation that he does not know how to work and play with others of his own age. This social incompetence means that situations which require social adjustment, and are easily handled by the average person, take on enormous proportions for the preschizophrenic. Shy and retiring as a child, he may not only be misunderstood by his more active playmates but be the subject of their abuse as well. The so-called period of strain and stress of adolescence, during which time schizophrenic disorders begin to make their appearance, carries some of the elements of isolation. In a detailed study of forty-two catatonic schizophrenics in Chicago, Dunham has shown that their solitary social roles prior to the onset of the illness was different from those of other boys in the community. These future patients could not establish intimate and informal relationships with others their age and as a result were unable to gain an adequate social conception of themselves.[81] In a study of fifty-three transitory schizophrenics, Weinberg found that their isolation resulted from the fact that they were unable to communicate their conflicts to others and assumed their characteristic role taking as a matter of self-protection. By withdrawing they avoided the evaluation of others, building, in turn, a world which they did not share. After a study of schizophrenics from upper and lower social classes, the patterns of withdrawal were described as follows:

> Briefly, schizophrenics in both classes displayed patterns of submissive and withdrawn behavior. They complied with parental and community authority and were inhibited socially and sexually. At the same time, certain pressures bore more heavily upon the schizophrenics than upon the neurotics in both classes. Specifically, most schizophrenic patients had few positive or rewarding contacts with family members. The home was disorganized and full of tension and antagonism. . . . Their mothers showed little genuine interest or affection for the schizophrenic patients. Their fathers were inadequate both at home and in the community, so that their mothers had to assume responsibility for family affairs.
>
> Whatever the factors responsible for the schizophrenics' shy personalities, be they constitutional, social, interpersonal, or other, it was clear that the

---

[80] Cameron, *op. cit.*, p. 94.

[81] H. Warren Dunham, "The Social Personality of the Catatonic-Schizophrenic," *American Journal of Sociology*, 49:508–518 (May, 1944).

above presses supported the further development of their deviant adjustments. Feeling neglected and overwhelmed by the chaos of the home, it was easy for the schizophrenics to avoid unpleasantness and seek the affection and guidance they lacked in autistic withdrawal. It was also clear that these presses gave rise to certain common stresses among schizophrenics. They felt isolated from warm intrafamilial relationships and neglected and rejected by their parents.[82]

In fact, Robert Faris has concluded that there is limited evidence to support the hypothesis that "in primitive culture the nature of social life is such that a 'shut-in' personality type, and consequently [the psychotic state] schizophrenia, could not occur." [83] Deveraux contends that this relative lack of schizophrenia among folk cultures is due to their "one-answer" universe, that is, the consistent set of norms and values in their societies.[84] Others, however, have reported evidence of schizophrenia among folk societies.[85] Some believe that much of the research on this problem to date has been unscientific and not based on a really intensive survey, so that no worthwhile conclusions can be drawn.[86]

Cultural Factors in Mental Disorders

Sociocultural factors have been shown in a variety of studies to play a significant role in the development of the functional mental disorders. These have included studies of mental disorders in comparative cultures and subcultures, social stratification and occupation, and ecological studies of distributions within cities.[87] Finally, another aspect has been the effects of mental hospital environment on the treatment of mental disorders.

---

[82] Reprinted with permission from Jerome K. Myers and Bertram H. Roberts, *Family and Class Dynamics in Mental Illness*, copyright 1959, John Wiley & Sons, Inc. Contrary to most previous findings, one study of schizophrenic children found that only one third had been isolated from their peers prior to the development of the disorder.—M. L. Kohn and J. A. Clausen, "Social Isolation and Schizophrenia," *American Sociological Review*, 20:265–273 (June, 1955).

[83] Robert E. L. Faris, "Some Observations on the Incidence of Schizophrenia in Primitive Societies," *Journal of Abnormal and Social Psychology*, 29:30 (April–June, 1934).

[84] George Deveraux, "A Sociological Theory of Schizophrenia," *Psychoanalytic Review*, 26:315–342 (June, 1939).

[85] Berend J. F. Laubscher, *Sex, Custom and Psychopathology* (London: Routledge & Kegan Paul, Ltd., 1938). James C. Carrothers, "A Study of the Mental Derangement in Africans and an Attempt to Explain Its Peculiarities More Especially in Relation to the African Attitude to Life," *Psychiatry*, 1:47–86 (February, 1948). Margaret Mead found schizoid personalities among the wives of the Manus who live in the Admiralty Islands in the South Pacific. See Margaret Mead, "Adolescence in Primitive and Modern Society," in V. F. Calverton and S. D. Schmalhausen eds., *The New Generation* (New York: The Citadel Press, 1930). Also see Opler, *Culture and Mental Health*.

[86] N. J. Demareth, "Schizophrenia among Primitives," *American Journal of Psychiatry*, 98:703–707 (March, 1942); and John Gillin, "Personality in Preliterate Societies," *American Sociological Review*, 4:681–702 (October, 1939).

[87] For a discussion of the ecological aspects of mental disorders, see Chapter 3.

(See Chapter 21.) Our knowledge is, as yet, only suggestive as to clues to the origins of the functional mental disorders. Most studies are recent, and much more research needs to be done.

Cultural factors play an important role in mental disorders. The incidence of mental illness, for example, varies widely in different cultures. Eaton and Weil's comparison of ten intensive studies of the incidence of mental disorder in different societies has shown considerable variation in the total incidence of the psychoses.[88] These authors suggest that this variation is a product of the amount of stability and integrated cultural traits, consistent role expectation, and close interpersonal, family, and community ties. Hindus, Chinese, and Malayans in Singapore, for example, have differing amounts and types of disorders depending upon their cultural experiences.[89] In our own society differences in the nature of schizophrenic symptoms have been found between persons from Irish and Italian subcultures, the former favoring fantasy and withdrawal to the extent of paranoid reactions, while the Italian patients suffered from poor emotional and impulse control.[90] Jaco has found pronounced differences in the extent and nature of mental disorders among Spanish-Americans and Anglo-Americans in Texas.[91]

The relation of community social structure and culture has been studied among the Hutterites, members of a religious sect of European origin who have lived in South Dakota, North Dakota, Montana, Manitoba, and Alberta for over sixty years.[92] This group of 8542 persons was studied for any incidence of mental illness, since commitment to a mental hospital had been reported as rare among the group. When studied, their incidence of diagnosed mental disorder was not too different from that of other populations, but they tended to deal with it by unofficial means. Moreover, there were few cases of schizophrenia and little free-floating anxiety or physical aggression. Diagnosed manic-depressive behavior, nearly all of it depressive, was much more common than schizophrenia, or the reverse of data in most urban studies. Very few persons diagnosed as mentally disordered had ever been admitted to mental hospitals for treatment. In fact, only five persons had been admitted, and these five for a short time, ranging from a day to several months. The recovery rate among the Hutterites was also found to be very high—far in excess of that found for the general United States population of mentally ill. The

[88] Joseph W. Eaton and Robert J. Weil, *Culture and Mental Disorders* (New York: The Free Press of Glencoe, 1955).

[89] H. B. M. Murphy, "Culture and Mental Disorder in Singapore," in Opler, *op. cit.,* pp. 291–316.

[90] Marvin K. Opler, "Cultural Differences in Mental Disorders: An Italian and Irish Contrast in the Schizophrenias—U.S.A.," in Opler, *op. cit.,* pp. 425–442.

[91] E. Gartly Jaco, "Mental Health of the Spanish-American in Texas," in Opler, *op. cit.,* pp. 467–489.

[92] Eaton and Weil, *op. cit.*

explanation of the low incidence of hospitalized mental illness, both the neuroses and the psychoses, may be in the homogeneous and highly integrated social system of the Hutterites. Instead of rejecting and segregating their mentally ill by having them committed to public hospitals, the Hutterites attempt to keep these persons within their own group. Arrangements are made for necessary care, and the mentally ill person is given affection and understanding and offered a situation which is favorable to recovery.

Other cultural situations furnish illustrations of conflict. Many Andean Indians who migrate to coastal urban centers of Peru have pronounced psychiatric problems, in part because of the migrations but also because of "the extreme differences between the cultures of the Sierran Indians and the coastal urban populations which magnify the dimensions of change required of the Indian." [93] Mental disorders were increased among the Ifaluk of Micronesia as a result of culture conflict arising from the Japanese occupation during World War II.[94]

Social Stratification and Mental Disorders

There is evidence that diagnosed mental disorders are related to differences in occupation and social class. Mental illness is not distributed either as a whole or by type randomly in the population. Schizophrenic behavior appears to be most common among unskilled laborers, farmers, urban residents in rooming-house areas, as well as others who are isolated.[95] On the other hand, manic-depressive behavior seems to be more prevalent among professional and socially prominent persons. Most studies have found a higher incidence rate of first admissions to mental hospitals of those from the lower occupational categories.[96]

In a Texas study adjusted incidence rates for persons who became psychotic for the first time showed the highest rates among the unemployed,[97] which might, in fact, reflect the fact that psychotic persons are often less likely to be employed. Among those who were employed at the time of the psychosis, the highest standardized rates of diagnosed illness were found among the professionals and semiprofessionals, followed by

---

[93] Jacob Fried, "Acculturation and Mental Health Among Indian Migrants in Peru," in Opler, op. cit., p. 136.

[94] Melford E. Spiro, "Cultural Heritage, Personal Tensions, and Mental Illness in a South Sea Culture," in Opler, op. cit., pp. 141–171.

[95] See Johns Hopkins University research referred to by Eaton and Weil in Arnold M. Rose ed., Mental Health and Mental Disorder (New York: W. W. Norton & Company, Inc., 1955), p. 233.

[96] See, for example, Robert E. Clark, "Psychoses, Income and Occupational Prestige," American Journal of Sociology, 54:433–440 (March, 1949) and "The Relationship of Schizophrenia to Occupational Income and Occupational Prestige," American Sociological Review, 13:325–330 (June, 1948).

[97] Jaco, The Social Epidemiology of Mental Disorders, pp. 125–148.

managerial, official, and proprietary occupations, clerical and sales workers, service workers, agricultural workers, and manual workers of all levels
of skill. Jaco included public and private cases but maintains that this
occupational difference does not reflect any bias in ability to pay.

A study of all persons in New Haven, Connecticut, who were patients of a psychiatrist or a psychiatric clinic, or were in psychiatric institutions on December 1, 1950, revealed rather decided class differences.[98]
The total group of 1891 patients was compared with a 5 percent random
sample of the normal population, or 11,522. When both groups were divided into five classes and compared, with Class I at the top and Class
V at the bottom, it was found that the lower the socioeconomic class the
more prevalent the diagnosis of disorder. Class I contained 3.1 percent
of the population and only 1.0 percent of the mental patients, whereas
the lowest group, with 17.8 percent of the population, had almost twice
as many mental patients. When sex, age, race, religion, and marital status
were analyzed, social class was still found to be the important factor.

The diagnosis of neuroses was found to be more prevalent at the
upper-class levels, whereas the psychoses were more frequent in the lower
groups. Neurotics constituted nearly two thirds of all patients in the two
upper-class levels, but among the lowest level, neurotics were less than
10 percent of the patients. A further analysis of the 847 diagnosed schizophrenic cases showed that in comparison with the normal population,
the diagnosis of this disorder is disproportionately high among the lower
classes. In Class I this disorder was found to be only one fifth as great as
it would be if proportionately distributed, whereas among those in Class
V it was two and a half times as great.

Some comparison of the dynamic factors in the relation of social
class and family dynamics to mental disorders has been made of a small
sample of schizophrenics and psychoneurotics in Class III and Class V.[99]
Those in Class III were believed to supervise their families more closely,
but threats to economic, social and physical security were judged stronger
in Class V than in Class III. The schizophrenic patients, who were largely
concentrated in Class V, were found to be withdrawn and submissive personalities, to have unstable parental relationships and home situations,
and to lack parental interest and affection. On the other hand, the neurotics,
mainly from Class II, were thought to have more stable home environments, to have the presence of more affection and positive emotional
attachment between parents and the family members, and to be characterized by greater rebellion than were the schizophrenics.

Two values appeared to permeate all aspects of Class III—respectability and success; throughout life they reported being taught to focus

---

[98] Hollingshead and Redlich, *Social Class and Mental Illness.* Some of this difference
was undoubtedly due to differential diagnosis on the part of the psychiatrist.

[99] Myers and Roberts, *op. cit.*

their energies on social acceptance and upward mobility. Both of these objectives were difficult for many Class III persons who later developed mental disorders. First, they had difficulty in enjoying the more sensual aspects of life. Second, they expressed frustration in living up to respectability and success values, and "when their behavior did not measure up to these standards they were likely to develop serious inner conflicts, manifested in feelings of shame and guilt." [100] Third, they appeared to be under constant tension because of pressures toward upward social mobility. As they moved upward in social status, they felt a need to modify continually their behavior to conform to new roles, and were under constant tension. Furthermore, in upward mobility they tended to alienate their families and former friends and were never fully accepted by the new groups. Fourth, they apparently were taught to curb aggressive behavior. Fifth, their relations to their mothers were described as very close and the patients had difficulty in emancipating themselves. Warner and Green have tried to show that class structure affects the production of mental disorders.[101]

Heredity and Schizophrenia

Geneticists have attempted to demonstrate that heredity plays a leading part in schizophrenic disorders. For example, in Sweden there have been a number of studies which have indicated the possibility of genetic family patterns. While the incidence of the disorder may be 1 percent in the general population, the incidence in those persons with schizophrenic parents is 10 to 12 percent. In the case of brothers and sisters it was found to be 10 to 15 percent.[102] This finding obviously does not refute the fact that social situations in a schizophrenic family may be the cause rather than heredity.

Kallman has been a leading proponent of the theory that the functional mental disorders are inherited. He studied 1087 Berlin schizophrenic cases selected from 15,000 cases between the years 1893 and 1902; later, in New York, he made a study of pairs of twins of which one or both were diagnosed as schizophrenic.[103] He diagnosed the Berlin cases

[100] *Ibid.*, p. 251. Reprinted with permission of the publisher.

[101] W. Lloyd Warner, "American Caste and Class," *American Journal of Sociology*, 42:234–237 (September, 1936), and "The Society, the Individual, and His Mental Disorders," *American Journal of Psychiatry*, 94:275–284 (September, 1937); and A. W. Green, "The Middle-Class Male Child and Neurosis," *American Sociological Review*, 11:31–41 (February, 1946).

[102] J. A. Böök, "A Genetic and Neuropsychiatric Investigation of a North Swedish Population," *Acta Genetica et Statistica Medica*, 4:1–100, 133–139, 345–414 (1953).

[103] Franz J. Kallman, *The Genetics of Schizophrenia* (Locust Valley, N.Y.: J. J. Augustin, Inc., 1938). Also Franz J. Kallman, "The Genetic Theory of Schizophrenia," *American Journal of Psychiatry*, 103:309–322 (November, 1946); reprinted in Clyde Kluckhohn, Henry A. Murray, and David M. Schneider, *Personality in Nature, Society, and Culture* (rev. ed.; New York: Alfred A. Knopf, Inc., 1959), pp. 80–100.

from information which he secured and then compared them with the case histories of relatives. He found that 68.1 percent of the children whose parents were both schizophrenic developed the disease. Where there was one schizophrenic parent the chances were about one in six; with brothers and sisters, one in ten; nephews and nieces, one in twenty-five; and grandchildren, one in twenty. In the later study Kallman used 794 twin index cases, obtained over a nine-year period from New York mental hospitals, and compared them with the case histories of relatives. He also concluded that the more distant the relationship the less likelihood of schizophrenia. Among his findings were the following:

(1) The morbidity rate [of schizophrenics] obtained with the "Abridged Weinberg Method" are in line with the genetic theory of schizophrenia. They amount to 1.8 per cent for the step-siblings; 2.1 per cent for the marriage partners; 7.0 per cent for the half-siblings; 9.2 per cent for the parents; 14.3 per cent for the full-siblings; 14.7 per cent for the dizygotic cotwins; and 85.8 per cent for the monozygotic cotwins. This morbidity distribution indicates that the chance of developing schizophrenia in comparable environments increases in proportion to the degree of blood relationship to a schizophrenic index case.

(2) The differences in morbidity among the various sibship groups of the index families cannot be explained by a simple correlation between closeness of blood relationship and increasing similarity in environment. The morbidity rates for opposite-sexed and same-sexed two-egg twin partners vary only from 10.3 to 17.6 per cent, and those for non-separated and separated one-egg twin partners from 77.6 to 91.5 per cent. The difference in morbidity between dizygotic and monozygotic cotwins approximates the ratio of 1:6. An analysis of common environmental factors before and after birth excludes the possibility of explaining this difference on non-genetic grounds.

(3) The difference between dizygotic and monozygotic cotwins increases to a ratio of 1:55, if the similarities in the course and outcome of schizophrenia are taken as additional criteria of comparison. This finding indicates that constitutional inability to resist the progression of a schizophrenic psychosis is determined by a genetic mechanism which seems to be non-specific and multifactorial.

(4) The predisposition to schizophrenia—that is, the ability to respond to certain stimuli with a schizophrenic type of reaction—depends on the presence of a specific genetic factor which is probably recessive and autosomal.[104]

Although Kallman's is the leading study, others have tried to show that schizophrenia is hereditary. All of these efforts have been subject to severe criticism.[105]

---

[104] Franz J. Kallman, "The Genetic Theory of Schizophrenia," *American Journal of Psychiatry*, 103:321 (November, 1946). By permission of the author and the Journal.

[105] Don D. Jackson, "A Critique of the Literature on the Genetics of Schizophrenia," in Jackson, *The Etiology of Schizophrenia*, pp. 37–87.

1. Kallman's study has been accepted by many writers as demonstrating the link between schizophrenia and heredity. Today his work is the single major source referred to by most authors writing on schizophrenia. In spite of this, Jackson made an exhaustive search of American and European literature of the past forty years and uncovered only two cases of twins who developed schizophrenia after having been allegedly reared apart. These two cases of twins who developed schizophrenia could have occurred on a chance basis, considering the incidence of schizophrenia. "Evidently the rumor that there are many such cases stems from . . . the fact that Kallman in his 1946 paper designated a category among identical twins of 'separated' and 'nonseparated.' However, his terms refer only to *separation five years prior to the psychosis.*" [106] The average age of Kallman's twins was 33; thus they had, in most instances, remained together well into adult life.

2. A Yale sociologist and psychiatrist who made a comprehensive study of schizophrenic cases in the Greater New Haven area failed to show a significant number of relatives with schizophrenia.[107] Their cases consisted of all private and public mental hospital cases, as well as cases treated privately outside the hospital by psychiatrists. Of the 847 schizophrenic cases studied, only 25 percent of the cases studied had schizophrenic relatives.[108]

3. A truly Mendelian approach to the inheritance of schizophrenia cannot be carried out with human beings in the same manner as with plants and animals because human environments do not remain constant as is required in Mendelian studies.[109]

4. The problem of diagnosis is the greatest obstacle in the genetic study of schizophrenia. Often the diagnosis of schizophrenia is made on the basis of family history, a person being diagnosed as schizophrenic if someone in his family has been so diagnosed. There is a tendency even among clinicians to see twins as similar, whether they actually are or not.

5. Diseases may run in families, even physical ones, without having a genetic basis. For example, beriberi does so, but "what is 'inherited' is the pattern of preference for vitamin-poor foods which children pick up from their parents." [110] The fact that mental disorder may appear in a family line does not prove that it is inherited. These studies need to take into account the effects on children of being reared in a family where one or both parents are mentally disturbed and the effect of the total environment.

6. Jackson notes that the genetic mode of transmission has not been determined, and until this is done the genetic nature of schizophrenia will remain questionable. Also there has been no relationship established

---

[106] *Ibid.,* p. 40.   [107] Hollingshead and Redlich, *op. cit.*
[108] From a private communication from A. B. Hollingshead.
[109] Jackson, *op. cit.*   [110] Jackson, *op. cit.,* p. 44.

between hereditary taint, type of schizophrenia, age of onset, and outcome. Such studies do not tell us how the symptoms of mental disorder are related to hereditary transmission. In schizophrenia, for example, the person does not share reality with others, he has blunted emotional behavior, and he has disrupted role playing. Just how social behavior of this type is carried in the genes is not only not clarified; this crucial question is rarely raised. As Hollingshead has concluded about the inheritance of schizophrenia, "This theoretical approach has not been explored adequately; its validity remains in doubt." [111]

Summary

Mental disorders involve behavior which deviates from approved norms of perceiving, feeling, and interpreting. The psychoses encounter stronger societal reaction than do the neuroses. Regardless of type, the so-called functional mental disorders appear to arise from fundamentally the same processes, namely, difficulties in interpersonal relations expressed through inappropriate role playing. Inappropriate role playing includes the incapacity for certain roles, contradictions in role playing, and an inability to shift from one role to another.

Selected Readings

CAMERON, NORMAN. *The Psychology of Behavior Disorders.* Boston: Houghton Mifflin Company, 1947, Chap. 4. One of the best discussions of role playing, language, and self-conception in relation to personality disorders. The author is both a psychiatrist and a psychologist.

CLAUSEN, JOHN A. "Mental Disorders," in Robert K. Merton and Robert A. Nisbet eds., *Contemporary Social Problems.* New York: Harcourt, Brace & World, Inc., 1961. A critical discussion of the sociological aspects of mental disorder.

DUNHAM, H. WARREN. *Sociological Theory and Mental Disorder.* Detroit: Wayne State University Press, 1958. A collection of both new and previously published papers on mental disorder. The author adds a new section on epidemiology and details the underlying assumptions of two current alternative conceptions of mental illness and health.

EATON, JOSEPH W., and ROBERT J. WEIL. *Culture and Mental Disorders.* New York: The Free Press of Glencoe, 1955. This is primarily a study of the limited extent of mental disorders among a religious sect, the Hutterites. In this joint study by a sociologist and a psychiatrist there is also a detailed comparison of ten other studies of mental disorder in various cultures.

HOLLINGSHEAD, AUGUST B., and FREDERICK C. REDLICH. *Social Class and Mental Illness.* New York: John Wiley & Sons, Inc., 1958. An analysis of the incidence and types of mental disorders in terms of social class.

HORNEY, KAREN. *Our Inner Conflicts.* New York: W. W. Norton & Company, Inc.,

---

[111] Hollingshead, "Epidemiology of Schizophrenia," *loc. cit.*

1945. A study of neuroses primarily in terms of reactions of going away from, against, and toward other people.

JAHODA, MARIE. *Current Concepts of Positive Mental Health*. New York: Basic Books, Inc., 1958. Monograph Series: Joint Commission on Mental Illness and Health. A discussion of the problems involved in attempting to define mental illness. The author does not resolve any of the issues which her discussion raises, but she specifies the necessary considerations involved.

LEIGHTON, ALEXANDER H., JOHN A. CLAUSEN, and ROBERT N. WILSON. *Explorations in Social Psychiatry*. New York: Basic Books, Inc., 1957. A collection of papers by representatives of several disciplines dealing with the issues, approach, and specific problems studied in social psychiatry.

ROSE, ARNOLD ed. *Mental Health and Mental Disorder*. New York: W. W. Norton & Company, Inc., 1955. This is a collection of articles having a sociological approach to mental disorder. Nearly all important articles written by sociologists about mental disorders to this date are in this book.

WEINBERG, S. KIRSON. *Society and Personality Disorders*. Englewood Cliffs, N.J.: Prentice-Hall, Inc., 1952. A study of mental disorder by a sociologist in which there is a more complete discussion of several topics presented here.

Chapter

14

Suicide

Generally, suicide refers to the destruction of one's self, self-killing, or, in a legalistic sense, self-murder. In one widely quoted definition, suicide is either "the intentional taking of one's life or the failure when possible to save one's self when death threatens." [1] Durkheim, the leading authority on suicide, defined it in a way as to include such acts of altruism as religious martyrs, "all cases of death resulting directly or indirectly from a positive or negative act of the victim himself, which he knows will produce the result." [2]

Two main forms of suicide may be distinguished. [3] One form is the definite desire on the part of a person to take his own life largely for this reason only. In the second form there is the additional desire to attract attention, to secure sympathy, or to revenge oneself on someone. Sometimes the same objective is then accomplished by a mere attempt at suicide.

Many persons commit suicide each year, although in comparison with such forms of deviant behavior as crime or mental disorders the number is small. During 1949 in the United States, 18,330 persons took their lives, a rate of 10.4 per 100,000 population. Probably at least another 100,000 made unsuccessful attempts to kill themselves. [4] Since 1950 the suicide rate in this country, per 100,000 population, has fluctuated from a high in 1950, of 11.4, to a low of 10.0 in 1952, (See Table 14.1.) Over a long period of time the fluctuation in suicide rates is more marked. The rate in 1900 in the United States was 10.2, 15.3 in 1910, 10.2 in 1920, and 15.6 in 1930. As has been previously indicated, suicide rates are responsive to

---

[1] Ruth S. Cavan, *Suicide* (Chicago: The University of Chicago Press, 1928), p. 3.

[2] Emile Durkheim, *Suicide,* tr. by John A. Spaulding and George Simpson (New York: The Free Press of Glencoe, 1951), p. 44.

[3] Ernest R. Mowrer, *Disorganization, Personal and Social* (Philadelphia: J. B. Lippincott Company, 1942), p. 332.

[4] Harry Alpert, "Suicides and Homicides," *American Sociological Review,* 15:673 (October, 1950). The statistical department of the Metropolitan Life Insurance Company estimates that the number of attempted suicides is six to seven for each actual suicide. Quoted in G. L. Williams, *The Sanctity of Life and the Criminal Law* (New York: Alfred A. Knopf, Inc., 1957), p. 272. For an interesting, semipopular analysis of the problem of suicide, see Edward R. Ellis and George N. Allen, *Traitor Within: Our Suicide Problem* (New York: Doubleday & Company, Inc., 1961).

Table 14.1. Number and Rate of Suicides per 100,000 Population,
United States, 1950–1960

Year	Number	Rate per 100,000
1950	17,145	11.4
1951	15,909	10.4
1952	15,567	10.0
1953	15,947	10.1
1959	18,633	10.6
1960	19,450	10.8

SOURCES: *Statistical Abstracts of the United States,* 1950–1961. Rate of 1953 computed from data in *Vital Statistics of the United States, 1953* (National Office of Vital Statistics, Public Health Service, U.S. Department of Health, Education, and Welfare; Washington, D.C.: Government Printing Office, 1955). Population estimates July 1 each year. Data for 1959, 1960 obtained from *Monthly Vital Statistics Report,* Provisional Statistics, Annual Summary for 1960, Part II, U.S. Department of Health, Education and Welfare, Vol. 9, No. 13 (July 28, 1961). Data for 1959 includes Alaska; data for 1960 includes both Alaska and Hawaii.

marked economic changes, being generally higher during periods of depression and lower during periods of prosperity.[5] Wars are usually characterized by a marked decline in suicide rates.[6]

Suicide and Cultural Norms

So strongly is suicide condemned by Western European peoples that one might assume this attitude to be universal. Both today and in the past, however, attitudes toward self-destruction have varied widely. Mohammedan countries strongly condemn suicide, and in actuality it rarely occurs there. The people of the Orient, however, do not disapprove of suicide. In fact, suttee, or the suicide of a widow on her husband's death, was common in India until well into the last century. Priests taught that such a voluntary death would be a passport to heaven, atone for the sins of the husband, and give social distinction to the relatives and children. Other aspects of the Hindu religious philosophy encouraged suicide, particularly the tendency to disregard the physical body. Suicide has been regarded as acceptable in China; when committed for revenge it was considered a particularly useful device against an enemy because it not only embarrassed him but enabled the dead man to haunt him from the spirit world. Voluntary death has been given an honorable place in Buddhist countries, but for devout Buddhists there is neither birth nor death, the individual being

[5] See pp. 427–428.   [6] See p. 586.

expected to prepare himself to meet all types of fate with stoical indifference.

For many centuries suicide has been favorably regarded in Japan. Among all classes, but particularly among the nobility and the military, it was traditionally taught that one must surrender to the demands of duty and honor. Hara-kiri, originally a ceremonial form of suicide to avoid capture after military defeat and later to avoid disgrace or other punishment, was practiced even during and after World War II. The suicide compact of lovers who wish to terminate their existence in this world and to go to another is not unusual in Japan, nor is suicide for revenge or as a protest against the actions of an enemy.

The attitude of contemporary Western European peoples toward suicide originated mainly in the philosophies of the Jewish and later the Christian religions. The Talmudic law of the Jewish religion takes a strong position against suicide: respect should not be paid the memory of the suicide although comfort should be given to his family. Suicide and infanticide had been prevalent in ancient Rome, but with the spread and acceptance of Christianity came a change in the attitude toward human life. Basic to the Christian condemnation of suicide were the concepts that human life is sacred, that the individual is subordinate to God, and that death should be considered an entrance to a new life to which one's behavior in the old is important. Moreover, death was followed by Purgatory, in which an individual suffered in order to expiate some types of sins, but those who had committed sins such as suicide were banished eternally to the torments of Hell. Death, to the Christians, unlike the pagans of Rome, was not something to look forward to without some misgivings. This concept of life after death strengthened the position of the Church.[7] In addition, Christian doctrine looked upon life as an opportunity for moral discipline and resignation in the presence of pain and suffering endured in the hope of another and happier world.

Although at first Christians sanctioned suicide connected with martyrdom or the protection of virginity, eventually they disapproved of it for any reason and it became not only a sin in Christian countries but a crime against the state. The property of a suicide might, for example, be confiscated and the corpse subjected to various mutilations. The laws of some European countries provided that the body of a suicide could be removed from a house only through a special hole in the wall, should be dragged through the streets, might be hung on the gallows, thrown into a sewer, burned, or even transfixed by a stake on a public highway as a sign of disrespect.

In the medieval ages church leaders denounced suicide, particularly Augustine, who stated, in the *City of God,* that suicide is never justifiable.

---

[7] William E. H. Lecky, *A History of European Morals* (3d ed.; New York: Appleton-Century-Crofts, Inc., 1906), pp. 209–211.

He maintained that suicide precludes the possibility of repentance, that it is a form of murder prohibited by the Sixth Commandment, and that a person who kills himself has done nothing worthy of death. Similarly, Thomas Aquinas opposed it on the grounds that it was unnatural and an offense against the community. Above all, he considered it a usurpation of God's power to grant life and death. Generally, in both England and Scotland, as well as on the Continent, laws provided for special treatment of the bodies of suicides, often outside regular graveyards. Throughout the medieval ages and well into modern times the strong religious opposition, the force of condemnatory public opinion, and the severe legal penalties were so effective that few had the temerity to take their lives, despite infrequent sporadic outbreaks of mass suicide on certain occasions such as epidemics, religious fanaticism to gain martyrdom, or crises.[8]

These views did not go unopposed by later philosophers, particularly those of the Age of Enlightenment, who challenged many existing institutions and discussed the importance of individual choice, even of life and death. David Hume, in his *Essay on Suicide,* argued that man has the right to dispose of his life without its being sinful. Other writers, such as Montesquieu, Voltaire, and Rousseau in France, challenged the laws on suicide and the denial of individual choice about life and death. In Germany, however, Kant opposed such views and said that suicide was contrary to reason. Today both Catholics and Protestants are opposed to suicide, although the Catholic position is a stronger one and the rates in such Catholic countries as Italy, Spain, and Ireland are generally lower. (See Table 14.2.)

Variations by Country

In 1958 Japan had the highest suicide rate in the world, followed by Hungary and Austria (see Table 14.2). The United States ranked fifteenth. Comparisons of the suicide rates of different countries indicate such great variations, however, that it is difficult to establish many uniformities. For example, among the Scandinavian countries Denmark, Finland and Sweden were high, but Norway was quite low. While the six highest countries are industrialized and urbanized, the United States, England and Wales, and Canada were not as high as some countries which are less developed in this respect. Predominantly Catholic countries were generally lower in the scale, but Austria, also a Catholic country, had the third highest rate. Asiatic countries had the lowest rates generally. Next to Japan, Ceylon had the highest rate of suicide in Asia, but it ranks nineteenth in the world.

---

[8] Louis I. Dublin and Bessie Bunzel, *To Be or Not to Be: A Study of Suicide* (New York: Harrison Smith and Robert Haas, 1933), p. 210.

Table 14.2. Suicide Rates for Selected Countries, 1958

Country	Rate per 100,000 population	Country	Rate per 100,000 population
Japan	25.9	Portugal	8.8
Hungary	23.5	Scotland	8.5
Austria	23.3	Ceylon	8.3
Finland	21.3	Canada	7.5
Denmark	21.2	Norway	7.3
Switzerland *a*	20.9	Israel	7.0
West Germany	18.9	Netherlands	6.8
Sweden	17.3	Italy	6.3
France	16.6	Poland	6.1
Belgium	14.9	Venezuela	6.0
Union of South		Spain *a*	5.8
Africa		Mauritius	5.5
white	12.4	Iceland	5.4
colored	3.1	Trinidad and Tobago	3.7
Asiatic	8.5	Greece	3.2
Australia	12.3	Guatemala	3.2
England and Wales	11.5	Ireland	2.7
El Salvador	11.5	Costa Rica	2.7
United States	10.7	Dominican Republic	2.1
New Zealand	9.9		

ª Rates are for 1957.
SOURCE: World Health Organization, *Epidemiological and Vital Statistics Report,* Vol. 13, No. 10 (1960), p. 466. The accuracy of official reports has been questioned because of the possibility of relatives and others concealing the actual facts in some cases. It is generally concluded that, while the figures are not accurate, the amount of error may not be great. See Jack P. Gibbs, "Suicide," in Robert K. Merton and Robert A. Nisbet eds., *Contemporary Social Problems* (New York: Harcourt, Brace & World, Inc., 1961), pp. 227–229.

Suicide and the Law

Suicide was punished as a felony or crime in England for centuries, and the suicide's property was forfeited to the Crown. In fact, these provisions were not abolished until 1870, although they had been largely in disuse since the eighteenth century. In his famous *Commentaries* on the law Blackstone had given these reasons for forfeiture: "The suicide is guilty of a double offense: one spiritual, in evading the prerogative of the Almighty and rushing into his immediate presence uncalled for; the temporal, against the King, who hath an interest in the preservation of all his subjects." [9] To a certain extent, this concept, but without the law of

[9] William Blackstone, *Commentaries on the Laws of England* (1765–1769), IV, 188.

forfeiture, was carried to America. In 1660 the Massachusetts law forbade burial of a suicide in the common burying place of Christians. Instead, burial was in some common highway, with a cartload of stones laid upon the grave, as a brand of infamy, and as a warning to others to beware of similar "damnable practices." This law was repealed in 1823, but it helped shape the attitude toward attempted suicide in America.

In England, in some states in the United States, and in a number of other countries it is against the law to attempt suicide. It is not against the law in any other European country, including the Soviet Union, nor is it against the law in Scotland. This is a fairly recent development, having been applied in England in 1854.

Prior to World War II in England, most attempted suicides were punished by a short period of imprisonment and for a second attempt up to six months. Since then it has largely been used only in those cases where there have been repeated attempts, where the would-be suicide threatens to try it again, refuses treatment, or becomes an unnecessary nuisance.[10] Actually, in 1955, out of 5220 attempted suicides (a large number are not reported), only 535, or about 1 in 10, were brought before the courts. Of these cases, only 43 were sentenced to prison. Nearly all, however, are found guilty, and, as a result, have a criminal record.[11]

Attempted suicide is also a crime in New Jersey and in North and South Dakota. As in England, there is a general rule in the United States, under common law, that in the case of a suicide the life insurance policy is not recoverable. Several states, however, have statutes providing that a suicide does not affect the policy if it occurs after a certain period of time, unless it can be proved that the insured intended to take his life when he took out the policy.

Attempted suicides raise an interesting legal problem, since by definition "a suicidal act is not punishable as an attempt unless it was intended to result in suicide." [12] Some cases are genuine attempts; others are suicidal demonstrations where what is done is not really a serious attempt; and, finally, there are probably cases which fall in between. Many attempts, whether real or not, may endanger the lives of other persons or rescuers, as do those who resort to carbon monoxide gas in rooms or garages, who try to drown themselves, or who use firearms.

Suicide and the Type of Society

Self-destruction is reported as not occurring among some folk societies. One observer who asked Australian natives about suicide stated that whenever he interrogated them on this point they invariably laughed at him

---

[10] Williams, *op. cit.*, p. 280.
[11] Kenneth Robinson, "Suicide and the Law," *The Spectator*, March 14, 1958, p. 317.
[12] Williams, *op. cit.*, p. 283.

and treated the question as a joke.[13] A similar response was reported from natives of the Caroline Islands. A survey of some twenty sources dealing with the Bushmen and Hottentots of South Africa revealed no references to suicide among these people.[14] The Andaman Islanders in the Indian Ocean appear to have had no knowledge of suicide prior to their association with people from India and Europe. Nor has suicide been reported among such folk societies as the Indians of Tierra del Fuego and the Zuñi of southwestern United States.

It would be simple to analyze the problem of suicide in folk societies if other data were as consistent as those just cited. Suicide occurs among some folk societies, however, some having a much higher rate than others. Suicides have been reported among the natives of Borneo, the Eskimos, and many African tribes. It is also said to have been fairly common among the Dakota, Creek, Cherokee, Mohave, Ojibwa, and Kwakiutl Indians, and the Fiji Islanders, the Chuckchee, and the Dobu Islanders.

Since folk societies are generally well integrated, the problem of any suicide among them particularly interested the French sociologist Durkheim. As a result of his studies he classified suicides by type, and examined the different motives underlying suicide.[15] On the whole, according to Durkheim, suicide occurring among a folk people is considerably different from that in modern society. To him suicide was a measure of the degree of social integration in a society. Suicide occurring in Western European countries is generally either *egoistic* or *anomic,* whereas nearly all suicide among folk peoples is of an *altruistic* nature.

Among folk societies suicides tend to be altruistic in that a person takes his life with the idea that by doing so he will benefit others. The individual in such societies thinks primarily of the group welfare. When his actions or his continued living hurts the group he may turn to suicide so that the group will have one less mouth to feed or so that he may protect it from the gods. Suicides among folk peoples which may be classified as altruistic are those arising from physical infirmities, or connected with religious rites or with warfare, or in expiation for the violation of certain mores, such as tabus. Under such conditions suicide does not constitute a deviation; in fact, it would be considered a transgression to refrain from the act.

1. Suicides occur in certain primitive societies where limited food supplies make an old or infirm person a burden to the tribe. Among the

---

[13] Edward Westermarck, *Origin and Development of the Moral Ideas* (London: Macmillan & Co., Ltd., 1908), II, 220.

[14] Robert E. L. Faris, *Social Disorganization* (New York: The Ronald Press Company, 1948), p. 198.

[15] Durkheim, *op. cit.* Gibbs feels that while Durkheim's theory is important, he did not really test his data in terms of a set of rigorous criteria of social integration. See Gibbs, "Suicide," in Robert K. Merton and Robert A. Nisbet eds. *Contemporary Social Problems* (New York: Harcourt, Brace & World, Inc., 1961), pp. 255–256.

Eskimos and the Chuckchee, for example, old people who can no longer hunt or work kill themselves so that they will not consume food needed by other adults in the community who produce it.

2. On the death of certain persons in some folk societies it is customary to commit suicide as part of a religious observance. Women, for example, commit suicide on the death of their husbands, and relatives may kill themselves in order to propitiate the souls of the dead. In some societies when a chieftain dies his retainers kill themselves. At one time it was the custom among certain Indian tribes of the Pacific Northwest for slaves to commit suicide on the death of their masters. It has been reported that some Central American Indian tribes required the wives, servants, and friends to kill themselves following a chieftain's death. Certain warriors among some Brazilian tribes commit suicide on the death of the tribal leader.

3. Some suicide occurs in warfare when persons kill themselves to avoid capture and slavery or because of the disgrace of their failure as warriors.

4. Probably the most common form of altruistic suicides among folk societies is the suicide committed as expiation for a violation of the mores, such as a tabu. In these cases the society itself feels that since it has been made unclean, the only recourse for the offender is death by execution or by his own hand to avoid public disgrace. This type of suicide may occur, as among the Dobu, in connection with marital infidelity. Unmarried pregnant girls may kill themselves, as happens occasionally among the Kwakiutl Indians. Among the Indians of British Columbia a forbidden marriage between two persons closely related is reported to have ended in a double suicide as a result of public ostracism. Individuals who fail to commit suicide in atonement for these wrongs risk the imposition of other sanctions, such as perpetual public disgrace. Malinowski thus describes the motives of Trobriand Islanders, who generally commit suicide by climbing a palm tree, from which they give a speech before jumping to their deaths:

> Two motives must be registered in the psychology of suicide: first, there is always some sin, crime or passionate outburst to expiate, whether a breach of exogamous rules, or adultery, or an unjust injury done, or an attempt to escape one's obligations; secondly, there is a protest against those who have brought this trespass to light, insulted the culprit in public, forced him into an unbearable situation. One of these two motives may be at times more prominent than the other, but as a rule there is a mixture of both in equal proportions. The person publicly accused admits his or her guilt, takes all the consequences, carries out the punishment upon his own person, but at the same time declares that he has been badly treated, appeals to the sentiment of those who have driven him to the extreme if they are his friends or rela-

tions, or if they are his enemies appeals to the solidarity of his kinsmen, asking them to carry on a vendetta (lugwa).[16]

The types of suicide found in modern Western European society, egoistic and anomic, must be clearly distinguished from the group-oriented, altruistic type which is common among folk societies. Egoistic suicides are not the products of a tightly integrated society but of one in which interpersonal relations are neither close nor group-oriented. These suicides, which are the most common in modern societies, are a measure of a lack of close personal identity with others. In such societies, individual-istic motives for suicide are not unusual and are associated with such personal problems as financial difficulties, loss of a desired goal, or ill-health.

The anomic type of suicide occurs when the individual "feels lost" in the face of situations where the values of a society or group are con-fused or break down. In such instances the equilibrium of society has been severely disturbed. There exists a social void in which the social order cannot adequately satisfy the desires of the person, and he does not know which way to turn. Commonly such anomic suicides occur in modern society as an aftermath of severe economic "crashes" or depressions, such as the stock market crash of 1929, which was followed by a large number of suicides. A similar situation has confronted persons after a severe political crisis or a defeat in war. In Hong Kong the suicide rate for post–World War II immigrants, who were mainly refugees, was five times greater than the combined rate for prewar immigrants and those born in Hong Kong.[17]

It would be a mistake to assume that all suicides among folk societies are altruistic. For example, although a recent study of suicide found little or no egoistic suicide among African tribes, they did find a moderate amount of anomic suicide: suicides committed by Africans who are not integrated satisfactorily into operating institutions.[18] Conversely, in modern societies, occasionally in peacetime but more frequently during war, individuals may give their lives in order to accomplish some goal in-volving group values. Sometimes this behavior is approved as being heroic. These suicides in modern society resemble the altruistic type found among folk people. In peacetime people will give their lives to save others. Soldiers volunteer for dangerous missions knowing that there is no chance of returning alive. The Japanese on many occasions during World War II engaged in what was termed suicidal behavior. Faced with certain

---

[16] Bronislaw Malinowski, *Crime and Custom in Savage Society* (London: Routledge and Kegan Paul, Ltd., 1926), p. 97.

[17] P. M. Yap, *Suicide in Hong Kong* (Hong Kong: Cathay Press, 1958), p. 76.

[18] Paul Bohannan, "Patterns of Murder and Suicide," in Paul Bohannan ed., *African Homicide and Suicide* (Princeton, N.J.: Princeton University Press, 1960), pp. 262–264.

death, large numbers of Japanese troops died to a man in suicidal banzai charges. In the latter days of that war the Kamikaze pilots became legendary for their disregard for their own lives. Loading their planes with explosives, they dived into Allied warships in order to make sure of destroying them completely.

Because of the peculiar settings in which the altruistic type of suicide takes place in modern society, however, much of it cannot be classed with typical altruistic suicides in folk societies. Group attitudes and pressures in a military unit under battle conditions and the emotional nature of a peacetime crisis situation involving the saving of a human life are not found in most ordinary modern situations giving rise to suicide. Elderly or incurably sick persons may sometimes end their lives so as not to become a burden on others, but this type of altruistic suicide is generally not approved.

Social Differentials in Suicide

Few forms of deviant behavior exhibit such pronounced differences in rates among various segments of the population as does suicide. Great differences can be found by sex, race, age, marital status, and religion. These differences in social factors have, in general, been found not only in Western societies but in most societies, as has been shown in studies of suicide in the Philippines, Ceylon, Singapore, and Hong Kong.[19] Many of these factors operated in the same fashion in these cultures.

Sex. Suicide is much more common among men than among women in Western European civilization, generally three to four times higher. In Norway, South Africa, Finland, and Ireland four times as many men as women commit suicide. (See Table 14.3.) In France, for example, three times as many men as women commit suicide.[20] In 1958 in the United States nearly four times as many men as women committed suicide. In the older age group the ratio of male to female suicides is even greater. In one American study of insurance policyholders the rate rose steadily with each age group: twice as many men as women committed suicide between twenty to twenty-four years of age; three and a half as many between thirty-five to forty-four; five and a half as many between fifty-five and sixty-four; and seven times as many in the age group over seventy-five.[21] On the other hand, the difference in adolescence is generally not nearly as great. One study found the rate for boys and girls to be the same among those fifteen to nineteen years of age.[22]

[19] See references in Yap, *op. cit.*
[20] Jean Daric, *L'Évolution de la Mortalité par Suicide en France et à l'Étranger* (Trends in Deaths from Suicide in France and Abroad), *Population*, II, No. 4, 673–700, October–December, 1956.
[21] Dublin and Bunzel, *op. cit.*, pp. 44–45.   [22] *Ibid.*, p. 43.

Table 14.3. Suicides by Sex by Country, 1958, 1959

Country	Male		Female	
	Number	Rate per 100,000 population, male	Number	Rate per 100,000 population, female
Norway (1959)	208	11.7	71	4.0
Union of South Africa (1958)	283	18.9	91	6.0
Finland (1959)	677	31.9	204	9.0
Ireland (1959)	55	3.8	17	1.2
United States (1959)	14,250	16.4	4,080	4.6
France (1959)	5,496	25.1	2,075	8.9
Canada (1959)	1,017	11.5	270	3.1
Spain (1958)	1,077	7.5	417	2.7
Sweden (1959)	1,012	27.2	338	9.0
New Zealand (1959)	154	14.1	48	4.4
Portugal (1959)	659	15.1	170	3.6
Belgium (1959)	843	18.8	351	7.5
Switzerland (1958)	794	31.6	299	11.2
Australia (1959)	827	16.3	288	5.8
Hungary	1,808	37.6	572	14.6
Italy (1958)	2,151	8.8	928	3.6
Austria (1959)	1,176	35.8	573	15.2
Denmark (1959)	647	28.7	309	13.5
West Germany (1959)	6,377	25.7	3,514	12.6
Ceylon (1958)	580	11.7	197	4.4
Netherlands (1959)	488	8.6	306	5.4
England and Wales (1959)	3,116	14.2	2,091	8.9
Japan (1958)	13,895	30.7	9,746	20.8

SOURCE: World Health Organization, *Epidemiological and Vital Statistics Report*, Vol. 14, No. 5 (1961), pp. 144–151.

With few exceptions, the same ratio of suicides seems to apply regardless of the type of situation.[23] Whether it be a love affair, an economic situation, or an illness, for example, approximately three to four men kill themselves to every woman. One cannot be sure if this is the result of men's being involved in more critical situations, or if they are less able to adjust to them. In Asia, however, women commit suicide much more frequently than they do in Western Europe and America. Hence, there the difference in the ratios is much less. In Japan the rate for males in 1958 was 30.7 and for females 20.8.

In some areas of India the suicide rate for women is greater than

[23] Cavan, *op. cit.*, pp. 309–310.

that for men, as shown in a study of 1129 cases of suicide between 1952 and 1955 in Sarashtra, in the state of Gujarat, where the rate was twice as great.[24] The reasons appear to lie in the conflicting roles and subordinate status of women in the Indian family. The realization of their often difficult family role has become greater with increasing freedom for women. Some of the factors given for the high suicide rate among Indian women follow.

1. Inferior social status of the women, discrimination shown against girls since birth and childhood.
2. Desire on the part of parents to marry off the daughter as soon as she reaches puberty.
3. Caste system and endogamy which restrict a wide choice for the bridegroom.
4. Child marriages, marriages against the will of the boy or the girl, and incompatibility in marriage.
5. Dowry and related customs. Girls from poor homes have to suffer taunts, humiliation, and persecution for not bringing a handsome dowry.
6. Oppression of the daughter-in-law in the joint family at the hands of the in-laws.
7. Unhelpful attitude of the parents of the woman. Even when they come to know that the daughter is unhappy in her family they are hesitant to give her shelter for long for the sake of social prestige.
8. Dual standard of morality for man and woman. While all actions of men are condoned, young widows or unmarried mothers are ostracized for any moral lapse.
9. Lack of education, confidence, and courage among women. Lack of knowledge regarding alternative arrangements should she decide to leave home.
10. Economic dependence of women, inability to stand on their own and make a living, due to lack of educational and vocational opportunities.

From American studies more women *attempt* suicide than do men. Many of these attempts by women, however, do not appear to be entirely sincere, for the suicidal arrangements are too often such that rescue is not only a possibility but even a probability.[25] In a study of 1000 attempted suicides in Detroit, the rate per 100,000 population was nearly twice as great for females as that for males: 35.5 as compared with 18.4.[26] This fact invited at least two interpretations: women were less successful in committing suicide, or, more likely, women more frequently use the

---

[24] Jyatsna H. Shah, "Causes and Prevention of Suicides." Paper read at the Indian Conference of Social Work, Hyderabad, India, December 29, 1959.

[25] Dublin and Bunzel, *op. cit.*, p. 55.

[26] F. C. Lendrum, "A Thousand Cases of Attempted Suicide," *American Journal of Psychiatry*, 13:479–500 (November, 1933). Also see Calvin F. Schmid and Maurice D. Van Arsdol, Jr., "Correlated and Attempted Suicides: A Comparative Analysis," *American Sociological Review*, 20:273–283 (June, 1955).

threat of suicide to accomplish a certain goal.[27] Threats or attempts at suicide must, however, be taken seriously, at least among men. Three fourths of a group of Los Angeles County male suicides had previously threatened or attempted to take their own lives.[28]

Race. White persons in the United States generally have a much higher suicide rate than do nonwhite persons. In 1953, 15,307 white persons committed suicide, a rate of 10.7 per 100,000 population, or approximately three times as great as the nonwhite rate of 3.8, or 640 nonwhite suicides in the entire country. In 1959, of the total of 18,633 suicides in the United States, 17,719 were committed by white persons and 914 by nonwhites. This ratio increases in the older age groups. In a Chicago study Negroes had a rate of 7.7 as contrasted with 28.8 for native whites.[29] The rate for white females was 4.6 with only 1.3 for nonwhite females. There is some evidence, however, that suicide attempts are approximately twice as great among Negroes as among whites.[30]

The probable explanation for the differences between white and Negro suicide rates is the more rural background of the Negroes, even where they have moved to a city. This factor tends to inhibit suicide. Furthermore, Negroes, because of racial discrimination, are more accustomed to restrictions on their participation in the general society, so that crises are less likely to produce disastrous results. Higher status opportunities for Negroes have developed only recently; as a consequence there have been, in the past, few competitive status pressures at a high level. That the Negro rate may be expected to increase as Negroes experience greater equality and urbanization is indicated by the fact that the northern Negro suicide rate is much higher than that of the southern Negro.

Age. The older a person is, in the United States and generally in Western European countries, the more likely he is to take his own life. This likelihood progresses steadily with each age category. (See Table 14.4.) The rates in 1959 for those between forty-five and sixty-four were nearly three times as great as for those between fifteen and forty-four. The rates for those over sixty-five in the United States was approximately twice as high as for those between thirty-five and forty-four. Suicide is largely a product of the weariness and disillusionment of the older years. Youthful optimism offers some protection against the temptation to commit suicide. Conversely, in Japan in 1956 the age group with the highest suicide was fifteen through forty-four, with a rate of 34.6, as compared with a rate of 31.0 for those forty-five through sixty-four.

---

[27] Mowrer, *op. cit.*, p. 339.

[28] Edwin S. Schneidman and Norman L. Farberow, "Clues to Suicide," in Edwin S. Schneidman and Norman L. Farberow, eds. *Clues to Suicide* (New York: McGraw-Hill Book Company, Inc., 1957), p. 9.

[29] Cavan, *op. cit.*, p. 78.

[30] Lendrum, "A Thousand Cases of Attempted Suicide," *loc. cit.*

Other variations can be seen in suicides by age and sex when one compares the rate in the United States with that of Japan, which has the highest suicide rate in the world. The rates for both sexes in the United States show a steady rise, although much less for females. The suicide rate for Japanese males rises sharply through adolescence up to twenty-four, when it reached 60 per 100,000 in 1952–1954. It then fell to a rate of about 25 between thirty to fifty, and then rose steadily until at seventy it was 95. The rate for females follows a similar but lower pattern.

Table 14.4. Suicide Rates in the United States, by Age, 1959

Age	Number	Rate
Below 1 year	—	0
1–14	70	0.1
15–24	1,230	5.2
25–34	2,250	9.9
35–44	3,240	13.7
45–54	4,060	19.8
55–64	3,640	23.7
65–74	2,460	24.5
75–84	1,160	25.8
85 and over	20	23.3

SOURCE: *Monthly Vital Statistics Report*, Annual Summary for 1959, Part II; U.S. Department of Health, Education, and Welfare.

Adolescent suicides receive so much publicity that their number has been exaggerated in the popular mind. Actually, the rate for those fifteen to twenty is exceedingly low, being less than a fifth the rate for all age groups and amounted, as reported in one study, to about 3 percent of all suicides.[31] In 1959 there were 1230 suicides, or a rate of 5.2, for the ages fifteen through twenty-four. The rate for those aged twenty-five through thirty-four was twice as great, and for every age group thereafter the rate increased, as shown in Table 14.4.

Children under ten practically never commit suicide, and only occasionally are there suicides between the ages of ten and fifteen. No suicides were reported, for example, of children under ten years of age during 1953. During this same year only 58 children, aged ten to fourteen, in the entire United States, committed suicide. In 1959 there were only 70 suicides, or a rate of 0.1, among those aged one through fourteen. These figures do not mean that many children, as they grow up, do not on occasion, when encountering frustrating situations, "wish they were dead," as studies have shown. This is particularly the case following certain

---

[31] Dublin and Bunzel, *op. cit.*, p. 39.

punishment situations. That these do not end in suicide seems partly the result of an incomplete formation of a definite conception of self, status, and social roles which are endangered by certain situations. Also, childhood crises are usually temporary, and there is seldom the long-term "brooding" which often occurs among adults.

Marital Status. In general, marriage, with its personal relationships, seems to be one of the best guarantees against the desire to commit suicide, although some situations produced by an unsatisfactory or a broken marriage may be conducive to it. The rate for married persons is considerably lower than that for widowed or divorced persons. In 1940 the rate per 100,000 married persons was 18.0, as compared with rates of 30.9 for the widowed and 64.3 for divorced persons.[32] Regardless of the age grouping over twenty years of age, the pattern is the same, although there is a much greater difference in the older age categories. Single persons had a lower rate in 1940 than married, or 6.8. The probable explanation is that single persons are largely in the younger age groups and younger persons generally have a lower suicide rate. Further evidence for this is the fact that in each age grouping over age twenty the suicide rate is lower for married persons than for single persons of the same age group. On this basis it would be correct to say that married persons have a lower rate than the single, the divorced, or the widowed. Yet these comparisons should not minimize the fact that many married persons take their lives. About half (50.3 percent) of the 50,047 suicides in the United States from 1949 to 1951 were married persons, between fifteen and sixty-four years of age.[33]

Another indication that the family has an important relationship to suicide is the fact that suicide appears to be greater among couples without children than among couples with children, who naturally have greater personal ties and feelings of responsibility that act as inhibiting factors.

Religion. Suicide rates among the main religious groups in Western European civilization vary greatly. In general, both in Europe and in America, Catholic rates are much lower than Protestant. Formerly the Jewish rate appears to have been lower than the Catholic, except that, on occasions when persecution made their situation particularly difficult or hopeless, waves of suicides occurred. Within recent years the Jewish suicide rate has risen considerably, perhaps reflecting changes in religious influence and greater participation in the general society. Both Catholic and Protestant rates have increased during the past century.

Religious differences in suicide rates have been interpreted as meaning in part the degree of integration of the various religious groups. Protestant religious groups tend to be more individualistic than Catholic.

[32] Andrew F. Henry and James F. Short, Jr., *Suicide and Homicide* (New York: The Free Press of Glencoe, 1954), p. 73.

[33] National Office of Vital Statistics, *Vital Statistics—Special Reports, Selected Studies,* 39:370 (May, 1956).

The Catholic position on suicide is more specific than that of most Protestant groups, at least in regard to the effect of suicide on the individual's afterlife and on the right to burial in consecrated ground.

Analysis of data from countries with large Catholic and Protestant populations, such as Germany and Switzerland, shows that even when all other factors are similar, fewer Catholics commit suicide. Catholic countries, such as Spain and Portugal, Ireland, and Italy, have low suicide rates, and predominantly Protestant countries, such as Denmark and Sweden, have high rates. (See Table 14.2.) Even this general rule does not explain the relatively low rate of Norway and Scotland.

It is difficult, however, to place too much emphasis on the factor of religious affiliation alone. The rate of Italian suicides for the period 1947–1951 in northern Italy is almost exactly twice as great as in the south, where economic conditions are poorer, there is less education, and adherence to Catholicism seems greater.[34] Most of the conclusions about the relation of religion, moreover, are based on large statistical categories and not on the effect of Catholicism at the individual level. Ferracuti has emphasized the possible role which the Catholic confession may play in furnishing a mechanism which might reduce the number of suicides.[35]

Occupation. In his classic study of suicide, Durkheim found that occupational status is linked to suicide, occurring more frequently in the upper ranks of various occupations as well as in positions of higher status. Suicides, for example, were found to be more frequent among army officers in proportion to population than among enlisted men, a fact which he attributed to the officers' feeling of status responsibility.[36] In later studies in America it has been found that United States Army officers are more likely to kill themselves than do enlisted men of the same race.[37] In a study of 955 persons who committed suicide in New Zealand between 1946 and 1951 the suicide rates were significantly greater among persons of high prestige, upper-class fathers producing more than their proportion of suicidal sons.[38] Moreover, suicide occurred more often when there was pronounced climbing and descending on the prestige scale. In Hong Kong attempted and actual suicide rates are highest at the two ends of the economic scale—businessmen and the unemployed—with high rates also among entertainers and prostitutes. Lowest rates were among the police, farmers, and fishermen. The explanation given was that rates tend to be higher among groups subject to great economic insecurity and uncer-

---

[34] Franco Ferracuti, "Suicide in a Catholic Country," in Schneidman and Farberow, *op. cit.*, p. 74.

[35] *Ibid.*, pp. 76–77.   [36] Durkheim, *op. cit.*

[37] Dublin and Bunzel, *op. cit.*, pp. 112–113.

[38] Austin L. Porterfield and Jack P. Gibbs, "Occupational Prestige and Social Mobility of Suicides in New Zealand," *American Journal of Sociology*, 66:147–153 (September, 1960).

tainty, and lower among those groups with security of employment or from well-integrated groups.[39]

In America suicide is more common among those with high social status. Although suicides occur disproportionately among those at both extremes of socioeconomic status, they are higher among those who are more wealthy.[40] Studies have shown that Londoners from the higher occupational status groups are more given to suicide, a fact attributed by those making the study that such groups are more subject to changes and social isolation.[41] Gibbs has summarized the relation of occupation, social status, and suicide as follows:

> Extremely high suicide rates generally prevail in occupations at the extremes: those with either very high income and prestige or very low income and prestige. For example, high rates are often found in both the professional-managerial category and the category of unskilled laborers, with occupations ranking midway between these two in status having lower rates. The high rate that typically prevails among the unemployed and retired appears to fit the low income-low prestige pattern.[42]

The Suicide Process

Although only a relatively few persons commit suicide, one writer claims that over half the people of the United States have contemplated it.[43] Death wishes are expressed in a variety of ways. One is the vague wish "never to have been born." Others occur in daydreams of death in which the person is likely to imagine himself dead and to speculate on the reaction of others to his death. By doing so the person lives out an experience which he desires but which he probably wishes will not occur. Similar death wishes are felt by those who wish for it but have no particular suicidal plans. Some persons may express a contingent wish for suicide about which they feel fairly safe, such as "If this thing happens, I will kill myself." Still others may make specific threats of suicide. In such cases if the threat is not effective, or the crisis is of long duration, suicide may result.

Suicides may be definitely planned without being carried to completion. Some persons may even have planned to kill themselves on a number of occasions, the final act being prevented by the removal of the original cause, an alternative solution, or the reinforcement of some attitude, particularly a strong religious one, opposed to self-destruction. A clinical investigation of material, obtained from the psychiatric inter-

[39] Yap, *op. cit.*, pp. 33–36.   [40] Dublin and Bunzel, *op. cit.*

[41] Peter Sainsbury, *Suicide in London: An Ecological Study* (London: Chapman & Hall, Ltd., 1955), p. 91.

[42] Gibbs, "Suicide," in Merton and Nisbet, *op. cit.*, p. 244.

[43] Cavan, *op. cit.*, p. 178.

views of 100 attempted suicides, confirmed the social isolation hypothesis in that it was found that suicides have had some difficulty in forming friendships. In addition, the study found that "the human being . . . wants to exist for somebody and for something . . . [he] wants his achievements to be accepted and acknowledged. . . . he wants his place to be defined clearly by love and work." [44] The individual wants an accepted, useful role in a community which provides him with the means of satisfying his needs and desires. When such things are lacking he becomes demoralized and confused, life loses its meaning, and he resorts to suicide.

Various types and stages of the suicidal process have been identified. A distinction can be made between those suicides which are situational in pattern and those which represent an escape.[45] Situational suicides may range from those in which the act is impulsive and unpremeditated to those in which the individual deliberately plans to end his life. The former may be illustrated by adolescent suicides, which are usually impulsive actions after a broken infatuation, the denial of some privilege, or a severe rebuke. These situations may be of minor importance to an adult, but to the adolescent, suicide seems the only solution. Such adolescent suicides may be inspired by revenge or the desire for attention. Conversely, some persons, such as old people, may shrewdly calculate the balance between the difficulties of continued living and death. Situations such as ill-health and the loss of loved ones and friends may lead to suicide. Between the extremes of impulsive and planned suicides are others in which each of these patterns may play an important or a minor part. Most suicides among Africans, for example, appear to take place around domestic situations involving the husband and wife, or in status-linked situations.

> These additional, non-domestic situations in which men commit suicide in Africa are for the most part seen by Africans in terms of over-all status or rank in the society. The high suicide rates for Gisu, for example, come at an age when a man's total status is in some doubt—in the years immediately following initiation, and in the years when a man should be settling down to assume the status of elder. The Luo, to take another example, phrase their loss or uncertainty of total social status in terms of shame. The loss of status or "face" may occur in institutional contexts of the traditional tribal system or of the modern system of Kenya, but can nonetheless be recognized as status problems.[46]

Other suicides represent escape patterns from the responsibilities of continued life. The individual does not wish to face reality and instead seeks a way out of a dilemma which may seem impossible of fulfillment or

---

[44] Margarethe von Andics, *Suicide and the Meaning of Life* (London: William Hodge & Co., Ltd., 1947), p. 173.

[45] Mowrer, *op. cit.,* pp. 357–365.

[46] Bohannan, *op. cit.,* p. 262.

change. Such suicides may have a long history of continuous struggle against various circumstances.

Another type of escape pattern is exemplified by those suicides who take a calculated risk to achieve a goal. For example, after killing another person some commit suicide. In a Philadelphia study about 4 percent of those who committed homicide took their own lives. Other studies in America have shown an incidence of from 2 to 9 percent in such suicides.[47] In England and Wales the proportion is much larger; in 1950, for example, it was 35 percent [48] and between 1900 and 1949, 31 percent in cases of the murder of a person one year or older.[49] Likewise, when a law violator escapes the consequences of his acts by committing suicide when caught, he does so in the same calculated manner in which he planned his illegal activities. Many swindlers, such as Ivar Kreuger, the Swedish match king, or embezzlers may take this way out of their predicaments.

Suicides have also been classified into other types: those which result from an unidentified craving for a goal, from a recognized wish, from a specific wish, from mental conflicts, or from a broken life organization.[50] These types of suicidal processes represent interruptions or blocked desires which occur at different stages in some ongoing enterprise. Such suicidal processes are somewhat similar to any other behavior involving a social act which is blocked.

One type of suicidal process may simply be a general dissatisfaction with life or some unsatisfied need, or what might be termed an undefined craving. The idea of suicide is often vague and there is a high degree of restlessness, although the nature of this dissatisfaction is often not specified. The person feels "disgusted with life," or "useless." Emotional tone is low, but there is "no sharp crisis, no mourning for something lost, no resentment toward anyone, no impassioned emotions, no self-judgment, but a strong desire to stop living, since life is flavorless." [51] A divorced man of fifty left this suicide note.

> To the Police—
>   This is a very simple case of suicide. I owe nothing to anyone, including the World; and I ask nothing from anyone. I'm fifty years old, have lived violently but never committed a crime.
>   I've just had enough. Since no one depends upon me, I don't see why I shouldn't do as I please. I've done my duty to my Country in both World

---

[47] Marvin E. Wolfgang, *Patterns in Criminal Homicide* (Philadelphia: University of Pennsylvania Press, 1958), p. 274.

[48] *Criminal Statistics for England and Wales, 1950* (London: 1951, p. xxiv) as cited by Max Grünhut, "Murder and the Death Penalty in England," *The Annals*, 284:158 (November, 1952).

[49] Based on *Royal Commission on Capital Punishment, 1949–53 Report*, Appendix 3, Table 1, pp. 298–301.

[50] Cavan, *op. cit.*, pp. 148–177.   [51] *Ibid.*, p. 149.

Wars, and also I've served well in industry. My papers are in the brown leather wallet in my gray bag.

If you would be so good as to send these papers to my brother, his address is: John Smith, 100 Main Street.

I enclose five dollars to cover cost of mailing. Perhaps some of you who belong to the American Legion will honor my request.

I haven't a thing against anybody. But, I've been in three major wars and another little insurrection, and I'm pretty tired.

This note is in the same large envelope with several other letters—all stamped. Will you please mail them for me? There are no secrets in them. However, if you open them, please seal them up again and send them on. They are to the people I love and who love me. Thanks.

George Smith [52]

Another case of this type was a wealthy, middle-aged businessman who had devoted his life to building up his company to achieve something he had always wanted, namely, a merger with a larger company. In this merger he retained the presidency of his own concern and became the vice-president of the larger company. After the agreement was concluded he immediately went into a depression. As the coroner commented, "The action was the reaction of a man who had built his business, makes the deal he wanted to make and then realizes he is no longer the direct owner of the business he spent his life building." He had no financial troubles, health problems, or marital difficulties to cause suicidal despondency.

Like the person with the unidentified craving, the individual with the specific need has not focused on a particular object or person. He is aware of how he feels and what he wants, but he is unaware of how this general need can be satisfied. The feeling may be one of loneliness, a wish for a better job, or something equally vague. Various situations are available for the potential suicide. A married woman, aged twenty-four, left this note.

I've proved to be a miserable wife, mother and homemaker—not even a decent companion. Johnny and Jane deserve much more than I can ever offer. I can't take it any longer. . . . This is a terrible thing for me to do, but perhaps in the end it will be all for the best. I hope so.

Mary [53]

The specific wish is at a more advanced level of needs, namely, a specific object or person. A person who is lonely may find other ways of overcoming his loneliness besides suicide. If he centers his interests on a specific goal or a love object which cannot be achieved, the situation be-

---

[52] From *Clues to Suicide,* Farberow and Schneidman eds., p. 44. Copyright, 1957. McGraw-Hill Book Co., Inc. Used by permission.
[53] *Ibid.,* pp. 43–44.

comes less one to which alternative solutions besides suicide can be applied. As attention is centered in a certain definite direction for a particular girl, man, or job, frustrated emotion tends to build up, until the suicidal process has moved decidedly from a condition of general dissatisfaction to a recognized wish. Any thwarted wish may take on the character of a "fixed idea" and become a predominant part of the person's life organization. Sometimes such suicides take the form of hate for the person who had been desired; suicide then becomes a form of revenge. In one case a husband wrote his reactions while taking gas because his wife had fallen in love with his brother.

A young clerk twenty-two years old killed himself because his bride of four months was not in love with him but with his elder brother and wanted a divorce so that she could marry the brother. The letters he left showed plainly the suicide's desire to bring unpleasant notoriety upon his brother and his wife, and to attract attention to himself. In them he described his shattered romance and advised reporters to see a friend to whom he had forwarded diaries for further details. The first sentence in a special message to his wife read: "I used to love you; but I die hating you and my brother, too." This was written in a firm hand; but as his suicide diary progressed, the handwriting became erratic and then almost unintelligible as he lapsed into unconsciousness. Some time after turning on the gas he wrote: "Took my 'panacea' for all human ills. It won't be long now. I'll bet Florence and Ed are having uneasy dreams now." An hour later he continues: "Still the same, hope I pass out by 2 A.M. Gee, I love you so much, Florence. I feel very tired and a bit dizzy. My brain is very clear. I can see that my hand is shaking—it is hard to die when one is young. Now I wish oblivion would hurry"—the note ended there.

Another note regretted the inconvenience to the landlady for using her premises as a death-house. Still another read: "To whom it may interest: The cause of it all: I loved and trusted my wife and trusted my brother. Now I hate my wife, despise my brother and sentence myself to die for having been fool enough to have ever loved any one as contemptible as my wife has proven to be. Both she and her lover (my brother) knew this afternoon that I intended to die tonight. They were quite pleased at the prospect and did not trouble to conceal their elation. They had good reason to know that I was not jesting."

The brother who is twenty-three years old spoke frankly to the police about his friendship with his brother's wife. Though separated in childhood when the parents had drifted apart, the two brothers had later on become inseparable companions until shortly before the tragedy, when both fell in love with the same girl. The younger man attempted suicide when his love was not returned and upon his recovery, the girl agreed to marry him out of pity—but later on she found she could not live up to her bargain. After a few weeks of married life, the husband discovered the relationship existing between his wife and his brother. He became much depressed and threatened suicide. The day before his death, there was a scene and when assured that the two were really deeply in love with each other, the clerk retorted: "All right, I can do you more harm dead than alive." [54]

Instead of a specific wish involving a person or object, another type represents a conflict between two social roles which the individual holds and which he cannot reconcile. On the one hand, he may wish to be married, for example, but at the same time he has responsibilities to his family which make it necessary to postpone marriage. Conflicts growing out of participation in two different sets of cultural groups or sets of ethical norms are also examples of a situation which has potentialities for suicide.

Suicides as the result of a broken life organization represent those cases where individuals, whose lives had previously been satisfactory, encounter some crisis. If this crisis is associated with great emotional disturbance and no alternative action seems available they may feel they can no longer continue to face life. This type of suicide, in a broad way, resembles the anomic type of Durkheim, and includes crises like blindness, incurable illness, arrests, breaking up of a home, death of a marital partner, or sudden loss of a business. The individual is unable to reconcile his previous conception of himself with the change required by a new situation. The individual's life organization has collapsed through no fault of his own. In the following case the crisis situation in the death of the wife led to the suicide.

> The entire life-organization of Dr. A. B. was centered about his one object of interest and affection. The death of Mrs. A. B. was a vital turning-point in his personality, for it necessitated either a thoroughgoing reorganization of his fundamental interests and attitudes, or else an indefinite period of unadjustment and later personal demoralization. What actually happened is well attested to by the ensuing events. In order to regain a state of healthy equilibrium, it would have been necessary for Dr. A. B. to find an interest, or interests, . . . as absorbing as the one he lost, something that he could reaccommodate himself to and continue his role in society. However, this tremendous disturbance to his personality resulted in a feeling of loneliness, hopelessness, futility, and inadequacy. He was unable to cope with such a radically new situation born of this change; nothing could satisfy this one dominant interest. He just literally "went to pieces." [55]

Prolonged frustrations and crises by no means always result in suicide, and it is not clear as yet just why some do. People face innumerable unpleasant crises in different ways. Some people may become drunk, others may seek religion, some will make light of the situation, and others will evade the issue or even consciously try to avoid it. The person who commits suicide is unable to find a satisfactory alternative solution.

---

[54] Dublin and Bunzel, *op. cit.*, pp. 294–295.
[55] Calvin F. Schmid, "Suicides in Seattle, 1914 to 1925: An Ecological and Behavioristic Study," *University of Washington Publications in the Social Sciences*, 5:71 (October, 1928).

Several factors probably play a significant role in a suicide. First, the desired goal may become so *dominant* that in many cases it becomes almost an obsession. A girl, for example, whose engagement has been broken may feel that nothing else—parents, career, or other interests—is of any consequence. Second, there is a *fixity* in the interest so that nothing else can satisfy it: "In the suicide, this non-adaptability seems unusually prominent. If he has determined upon a certain way to satisfy it he can consider no alternative way. If a system of relationships once found satisfactory is for any reason broken, he can conceive of no system doing the work of the old." [56] Third, a particular *lack of objectivity* on the part of those who commit suicide makes them see the difficulty only from their own point of view. A fourth factor is the *interpretation of the difficulty* by the person. Circumstances such as economic losses or other difficulties which may seriously disturb one person may have little effect on another. The need for the object desired or his loss of status may be interpreted by a suicide as destroying all future hope. A prosperous businessman who has lost his fortune and commits suicide may have felt that because of the loss of money his previous social status is irrevocably ended. Satisfaction and material comforts, the future of his family, and the plans for his old age have all come tumbling down at once and he has no desire to try to rebuild his life. Sometimes persons commit suicide for some provocation which might seem unimportant or even trivial to others but which to the suicide has assumed tremendous proportions. The situation is defined as irremediable, intolerable, or even hopeless:

> The man who kills himself is through with life; he has literally died psychologically before he kills his body. Over and over again in the notes left by suicides appears the phrase, "I can't stand it any longer." It is a crisis which cannot be adjusted to—which ends in defeat. Externally, there may be little or even no evidence of the difficulty, but in his subjective life the person is enduring doubts, unsatisfied longings and finally hopelessness and inability to struggle longer. [57]

Suicide and Mental Disorder

Persons who commit suicide are not generally "mentally deranged," or suffering from "temporary insanity." Such an idea has developed from the assumption that "no one in his right mind" would take his own life. To be considered a suicide resulting from a psychosis the patient generally must have been under treatment or there must exist some other demonstrable evidence of psychosis. Hearsay evidence from relatives cannot be accepted. Reliable studies indicate that only approximately 15 to 30 percent of suicides are suffering from a psychosis. In a study of 291 Chicago

---

[56] Cavan, *op. cit.*, p. 173.   [57] *Ibid.*, p. 177.

suicides, only 58 were presumed to have had a psychosis.[58] Approximately 20 percent of 22,000 suicides among industrial policyholders of a large life insurance company were found to have had a recognized mental illness.[59]

From a study of suicides in New York mental hospitals, severe depression, either involutional melancholia or manic-depressive psychosis, seems to be the most common form of psychosis associated with suicide, although paranoia, senile dementia, and dementia praecox are also found.[60] The percentage of psychotic disturbances, although not large, is great enough to account for concern, in most cases of attempted suicide, lest there be present some severe mental disorder which will lead to a repetition of the attempt unless the disturbance is discovered and treated. Likewise, psychiatrists must be on guard for such possibilities in patients suffering from severe depression.[61]

On the other hand, a much larger percentage of suicides, at the time of the suicide, are in some way emotionally disturbed, although not to the point where their disturbance explains their action. In many instances they may have been agitated over a period of several days prior to the suicide. Some of these undoubtedly have acted "strange" or "queer." This is a different conception from that of suicide being basically a result of prolonged mental disturbance. Actually many suicides are rationally planned and carried out with no more evidence of mental disorder than would be found in the so-called normal person. The goals sought by most suicides, no matter how exaggerated, generally are real goals, the personal losses suffered are real losses, and are usually not the product of psychotic hallucinations or delusions having little or no basis in reality.

Suicide and Status

An explanation of suicide and homicide within the framework of different adjustments to status frustrations which produce aggression has been offered by two sociologists, Henry and Short.[62] Suicide and homicide, they claim, can be differentiated in terms of the target of the aggression; in suicide the aggression is directed at the self, whereas in homicide it is directed at others.

> The sociological evidence suggests that suicide is a form of aggression against the self aroused by some frustration, the cause of which is perceived by the person as lying within the self. Failure to maintain a constant or ris-

---

[58] *Ibid.*, p. 569.   [59] Dublin and Bunzel, *op. cit.*, p. 300.
[60] Study by H. M. Pollock of 200 suicides among patients with mental illness in New York mental hospitals, 1919–1929, quoted in Dublin and Bunzel, *op. cit.*, p. 11.
[61] Dublin and Bunzel, *op. cit.*
[62] Henry and Short, *op. cit.* Suicide and homicide are related in that both respond to the business cycle and are, they claim, therefore simply common responses to frustration.

ing position in the status hierarchy relative to others in the same status reference system is one—but by no means the only—important frustration arousing aggression. When this frustration is perceived as being the fault of the self, the aroused aggression may flow against the self. This is most likely when the person is relatively freed from the requirement that his behavior conform to the demands and expectations of others. Persons of high status and those isolated from meaningful relationships are most likely to blame themselves and commit suicide when frustration occurs, since their behavior is relatively independent of the demands and expectations of others.[63]

Suicide is related to three things: (1) the strength of the relational systems of a given population, (2) this strength of relational system varies with the external restraints on the behavior of the population, and, finally, (3) the external restraints placed on the behavior of the members of a population varies inversely with their status position.

As evidence of this relation they explain the lower suicide rate of married persons as compared with those who are single, divorced, or widowed as due to the fact that married persons are involved in a stronger relational system in which they must conform more to the demands and expectations of others. The degree of involvement with other persons also explains the lower rates of rural areas, the high rates in the central parts of the city, and the general tendency for suicide rates to increase as the person grows older and has fewer close relations with others.

For some time it has been well established that suicide rates fluctuate with the business cycle. Henry and Short offer the explanation that status frustrations caused by the business cycle, such as depressions, result in different degrees of aggressive behavior in the form of suicide according to the status position of persons. Groups in higher status positions react more violently to fluctuations in the business cycle, they claim, than do those in lower status positions. The rate of male suicides reacts more to economic fluctuations than that of women. Similarly, white suicide rates change more than Negro, and those in higher-income groups more than those in lower-income groups. The likelihood of suicide is thus related not only to the degree of interpersonal relations but also to position in the status hierarchy. Here external restraint, demands, and expectations by those in higher status categories operate to control the behavior of those in lower status and prevent suicide. Thus the lower suicide rate of the Negro and those in lower status occupational categories, such as an employee, can be partly explained in this way. The higher the status category the less restraint imposed on a person if he desires to commit suicide. This general explanation of suicide in terms of status frustration is intriguing

---

[63] Andrew F. Henry and James F. Short, Jr., "The Sociology of Suicide," in *Clues to Suicide*, p. 68.

but does not seem to be proved by the evidence presented and is largely a theory read into certain broad statistical findings.

Another recent sociological theory has attempted to link suicide to a particular pattern of status occupancy or the degree of status integration in a society.[64] There is less suicide in populations where one status position is closely associated with other status positions and, consequently, the members are likely to experience less role conflict, are more capable of conforming to the demands and expectations of others, and are more capable of maintaining stable and durable social relationships. As an illustration, of the males in 1950 from sixty to sixty-four, 79.3 percent were married, 9.6 widowed, 8.6 single, and 2.5 percent divorced. The corresponding suicide rates for each of the four marital status groups was 36.2, 64.7, 76.4, and, finally, for the divorced, 111.1. This presumably indicates that, although an older age group, the infrequently occupied status clusters, e.g., the divorced, are assumed to be characterized by role conflict and consequently weak social relationships.

Summary

Suicide is strongly condemned among Western European peoples and in Mohammedan countries. The negative attitude in Western European civilization can be traced primarily to the attitude of the Christian and Jewish religious teachings toward self-destruction.

Suicides appear to differ in their nature according to the type of society. Among folk societies most suicides are altruistic, whereas in modern societies they tend to be predominantly egoistic or anomic.

Rates of suicide fluctuate with the business cycle, being higher during periods of depression and lower at times of prosperity. Suicide rates for males are much higher than those for females. White persons in the United States have a higher rate than nonwhites.

The likelihood of suicide increases with age. In general, married persons have a lower suicide rate than do single, divorced, or widowed persons. Rates for Catholics are, in general, lower than those for Protestants.

Suicides can be distinguished according to whether they are situational or escape patterns. They can be classified into those arising from an unidentified craving for a goal, a recognized wish, a specific wish, mental conflicts, and a broken life organization. Whether a person commits suicide appears to be dependent upon the dominance of the goal, the fixity, the lack of objectivity, and the interpretation of the difficulty. Various theories have attempted to associate social status with suicide.

---

[64] See Jack P. Gibbs and Walter T. Martin, "A Theory of Status Integration and Its Relationship to Suicide," *American Sociological Review*, 23:140–147 (April, 1958). Also see Gibbs, "Suicide," in Merton and Nisbet, *op. cit.*, pp. 257–259.

Selected Readings

BOHANNAN, PAUL, ed. *African Homicide and Suicide*. Princeton, N.J.: Princeton University Press, 1960. A study of homicide and suicide among seven African tribes. Contains case materials and statistical comparisons with Western society.

CAVAN, RUTH S. *Suicide*. Chicago: The University of Chicago Press, 1928. This is one of the leading reference materials on suicide. Has considerable case material and statistical data from Chicago.

DUBLIN, LOUIS I., and BESSIE BUNZEL. *To Be or Not to Be: A Study of Suicide*. New York: Harrison Smith and Robert Haas, 1933. A comprehensive study of suicide, using in particular Metropolitan Life Insurance Company data on suicides.

DURKHEIM, ÉMILE. *Suicide*. John A. Spaulding and George Simpson, trans. New York: The Free Press of Glencoe, 1951. This is one of the most important books by the famous French sociologist. Originally published in 1897, it has been translated into English for the first time. Contains a detailed discussion of egoistic, altruistic, and anomic types of suicide.

HENRY, ANDREW F., and JAMES F. SHORT, JR. *Suicide and Homicide*. New York: The Free Press of Glencoe, 1954. An explanation of suicide and homicide primarily in terms of a theory of frustration and aggression. Contains considerable recent statistical data on suicides analyzed by race, sex, age, and income.

SAINSBURY, PETER, *Suicide in London: An Ecological Study*. London: Chapman & Hall, Ltd., 1955. An ecological study of 409 suicides occurring in North London analyzed according to residence, occupation, and other factors.

Conflicts in Marital
and Family Roles

At present one divorce is granted in the United States for every four marriages performed. Although this represents a marked decline from the immediate postwar peak, when the ratio was one to two and a half, there has been in general an increase over the past sixty years in the proportion of divorces to marriages. These statistics, however, do not give the full account of contemporary marital unhappiness. Many more applications for divorce are filed than are finally granted, and none of these figures includes separations and desertions.

Various studies have shown that a legally intact marriage is not necessarily a "happy" one, indicating that marital unhappiness is far more pervasive than divorce statistics alone show. In general, marital unhappiness is taken as evidence of marital and family conflict. Conflict specifically refers to a situation where there is a discrepancy between the role expectations and role behaviors of family members in relation to one another. A conflict may thus be temporary or permanent. In its temporary aspects, it may hasten or assist the ability of marital partners to develop role skills or to deal with problems which arise.

Concept of Marital and Family Conflict

A marriage or family operates as a group in much the same manner as other social groups. Certain characteristics of such groups, however, make for a greater degree of interdependence, and hence interaction, than is true of most groups. The interlocking of the roles comprising the family group means that many of the actions of a family member deeply affects the other members. There are parallel intimate relations between many members, such as the parents' relations between themselves and with their children. Each of these conditions interacts with others and tends to intensify them.[1]

---

[1] Kurt Lewin, *Resolving Social Conflicts* (New York: Harpers & Row, Publishers, 1948). See also Talcott Parsons, "The Social Structure of the Family," in Ruth Nanda Anshen ed. *The Family: Its Function and Destiny* (rev. ed.; New York: Harper & Row, Publishers, 1959), p. 241.

When the beliefs and expectancies about the bonds in a family remain fairly constant over a period of time and from situation to situation, the family is able to perform its functions, the individuals within the marital group are comparatively free of tension, and the interacting individuals form a "unity." [2] Thus when all these conditions exist, the family is organized; that is, there is cooperation in the "process of building up organized attitudes in which all concur." [3] This set of mutually shared attitudes or expectations comprises what we call the organization or structure of the family, or the network of statuses and roles, common aims, and values, which make up the system of relationships. When family members share the same expectations and aims, and are able to act in accordance with them, the day-to-day needs of family members are generally met. Sometimes, however, obstructions to understanding or to role enactment may arise—either from within the family group or outside it. When this occurs, there may be a temporary conflict between the expectations of different family members. This conflict may, if it is permanent, affect the family unit as a whole.[4] In the same manner, social changes occurring in the society of which the family is a part can impinge upon the family structure. For example, an economic depression may leave a father unemployed. Not only will this alter the father's breadwinning role; it will affect the attitudes and expectations of family members in relation to one another, and so affect, in varying degrees, the total network of relationships.[5]

Interpersonal relations in marriage and family relations have many facets. Some involve intimacy of association, others influence the development of such an association, and still others affect the ability to meet these demands after association is developed.[6] The intimate relations of companionship can give great strength to the marriage relationship. Some of these intimate relationships involve the development and expression of sentiment, such as love and affection, physical contact, such as sexual relations, and sharing of valued experiences and hopes.[7] Generally, it is supposed that marital happiness and stability are greater in marriage relationships characterized by affection, mutual dependence and compati-

---

[2] Ernest W. Burgess, "The Family as a Unity of Interacting Personalities," *Family*, 7:3-9 (March, 1926). Some writers have suggested that the family, rather than a "unity" is more of an "arena" of interacting personalities.—Willard Waller, *The Family* (revised by Reuben Hill; New York: Holt, Rinehart and Winston, Inc., 1951), pp. 25-37.

[3] Annabelle Bender Motz, "Conceptions of Marital Roles by Status Groups," *Marriage and Family Living*, 12:136 (Winter, 1950).

[4] Elizabeth Bott, *Family and Social Network* (London: Tavistock Publications Ltd., 1957), p. 59.

[5] J. Cohen, R. Robson, A. Bates, *Parental Authority: The Community and the Law* (New Brunswick, N.J.: Rutgers University Press, 1958), p. 197.

[6] Ernest W. Burgess and Paul Wallin, *Engagement and Marriage* (Philadelphia: J. B. Lippincott Company, 1953), p. 418.

[7] Parsons "The Social Structure of the Family," in Anshen, *op. cit.*

bility, and shared satisfactions. On the other hand, it is believed that marital unhappiness and instability are more common where there is indifference, hostility, dissatisfaction, mutual independence, and incompatibility. Marital role relationships may be predominantly "joint": that is, they may involve many shared or similar activities carried out by husband and wife together. Or they may be "segregated": that is, they may involve many independent activities carried out by husband and wife separately. But marital stability and happiness seem to occur with about equal frequency among "joint" and "segregated" marital role relationships. Happiness and stability appear to be influenced more by the total social system of which the husband-wife relationship is a part, than by the marital relationship alone.[8]

In the marriage situation a number of factors may operate to produce marital stability or success. In each instance, however, they may operate in reverse and contribute, instead, to lack of success or instability in marriage. The similarities or differences in cultural backgrounds which each partner contributes to the marriage can make for harmony or for conflict. The development of interests and values likewise can strengthen the association through mutual stimulation and complementary interests or it can take a course which may produce boredom and conflict. Domestic activities, including household tasks, the rearing of children, family activities, illness, friends, may be mutually shared or, as in some marriages, one partner may escape to activities outside the family circle. One study has even shown the importance of social approval from others in the adjustment of a married couple, particularly to new situations.[9]

The dynamics of a marriage are more, however, than the development of intimacy and association. Marriage also means decision making and adaptability. In such activities the marriage means not individuals making separate decisions but a couple deciding together. If mutual decisions are made about such things as expenditures and the children, they serve to integrate the marriage; if they are made in an authoritarian way or unilaterally they weaken it.

If the partners in a marriage adapt to one another, a marriage can be greatly strengthened. Adaptability represents a process of change. "In marriage, adaptability enables husband and wife to adjust successfully despite the conflicting facets of their personalities which reveal themselves in the exigencies of marriage, and to cope with changes in the social situation which impinge upon and affect their roles as husband and wife." [10] Although there are other facets, one of the most important is the determination that the marriage will succeed.

---

[8] Bott, *op. cit.*, pp. 53-58, p. 219; and Carle C. Zimmerman and Lucius F. Cervantes, *Successful American Families* (New York: Pageant Books, Inc., 1960), pp. 35-55.

[9] Motz, "Conceptions of Marital Roles by Status Groups," *loc. cit.*

[10] Ernest W. Burgess and Paul Wallin, *Engagement and Marriage* (Philadelphia: J. B. Lippincott Company, 1953), p. 623. Excerpts from this work are used with the permission of the publisher.

Burgess and Wallin have constructed an index of marital adjustment which stresses the need for consensus or common agreement, common interests and activities, demonstration of affection, satisfaction with marriage, and absence of feelings of unhappiness and loneliness. Their list of the developmental and integrative, as opposed to the frustrative and disruptive, forces in interpersonal relations in marriage appears in Table 15.1.

Table 15.1. Interpersonal Relations in Modern Marriage

	Developmental and integrative	Frustrative and disruptive
I. Intimacy of Association:		
Love and affection	Mutual love, affection	Indifference, hostility
Sexual relations	Enjoyment and satisfaction	Dissatisfaction
Emotional interdependence	Mutual dependence	Emotional independence
Temperamental interaction	Compatibility	Incompatibility
II. Development of the Association:		
Cultural interaction	Assimilation and creativity	Accommodation and conflict
Interests and values	Stimulation and complementation	Boredom and conflict
Domesticity	Mutual enjoyment of home activities	Escape into outside activities
III. The Association in Operation:		
Decision making	Interdependent	Authoritarian and unilateral
Adaptability	Mutual adaptability	Unadaptability of one or both

SOURCE: Ernest W. Burgess and Paul Wallin, *Engagement and Marriage* (Philadelphia: J. B. Lippincott Company, 1953), pp. 418–419. They also include a factor "Expectations of Continuity," which is not discussed in this section.

The Process of Family Disintegration

Every family has its breaking point, and it is possible to sketch the process through which marital and family conflicts may pass to their culmination in crisis. After the first aura of passion and erotic newness of marriage has worn off, a monotonous pattern of day-to-day living may begin. Many withstand ripples of discontent and difficulties, finding more in the marital relationship than any contemplated escape from it would provide. For others, however, small difficulties mount in frequency and intensity until one of the partners feels that there are more satisfactions to be gained outside marriage than within it. The series of steps in this process as it leads finally to divorce have been listed by Locke as follows:

1. Developing tensions and difficulties between family members
2. Debating the issues of the conflict within oneself
3. Overtly expressing the conflicts
4. Intermittently attempting to solve marital difficulties
5. Sleeping in different beds or in different rooms
6. Mentioning divorce as a possibility to the mate
7. Separating into different domiciles
8. Making a temporary reconciliation
9. Making application for a divorce
10. Getting the application discussed
11. Reapplying for a divorce
12. Getting the application dismissed
13. Reapplying for a divorce
14. Securing the divorce
15. Trying to achieve emancipation from the mate
16. Adjusting to the crisis of the divorce.[11]

In the following case is a sequence of some of these steps. The woman, who was quite dominant, had worked in her husband's business and after it failed he was no longer important to her. There was a separation after which she applied for a divorce, only to have it dismissed.

> We were happy as could be for the first twenty years of our marriage. Then two things occurred which changed our marriage into unhappiness. I lost most of my business; second, my wife had the change of life. I would come home and would be worried about my business, and then she would argue and fuss and make me nervous, and I would have indigestion. So I got to staying down town and eating out.
>
> Then she became cold. We were very active sexually in our earlier life. Now she wouldn't have anything to do with me. I moved into another bed and then into another room. I told her that I would give her time to adjust to her change—four or five years. At the end of that time things were no better, so I packed up and left.
>
> Since I went away, I have been back occasionally. But when I go back for Christmas or Thanksgiving, she does not pay any attention to me. She talks and laughs with the others, but not with me. I may go out to the kitchen and try to wipe the dishes like I used to, but she says that she can get along all right by herself.
>
> A few weeks ago she suggested that I come back; we would live as man

---

[11] Derived from Harvey Locke, *Predicting Adjustment in Marriage* (New York: Holt, Rinehart and Winston, Inc., 1951), p. 71.

and wife; and I went over and talked with her. I found that the old trouble would still be there.[12]

Marital unhappiness may find a number of outlets short of annulment, separation, desertion, or divorce. Some persons resort to a world of fantasy and daydreams to escape a difficult marital situation. Through their emphasis on romantic love, motion pictures, romantic stories, and particularly the soap operas of radio and television furnish escapes. Chronic "illness" may also provide escape from an unpleasant marital situation. If either person feels neglected, dissatisfied, or unloved, he may resort to "illness" to obtain care and attention or to inflict discomfort on the other. Being constantly "tired" without a physical basis may be indicative of dissatisfaction with marriage. Studies have also shown that alcohol and other substitute satisfactions offer escapes from unsatisfactory marital situations. Some may take a more conventional outlet for such frustrations by minimizing interaction in the family and instead devote all their spare time to housework, their hobbies, their jobs, or to golf, music, art, or club activities. Finally, many parents who are not happy in their marital situation may project their frustrations through displaying excessive affection for their children and excessive interest in their children's goals.

Desertion

Some couples separate without a divorce, maintaining the fiction of marriage but with two households. Some separations are temporary, but others may be permanent. The law may even recognize this fact by providing for a "legal separation." Separations may meet religious objections to divorce or one partner's refusal to grant a divorce. Some partners simply desert by leaving home without making provisions for financial or other responsibilities. It is usually the husband who deserts. This does not always mean that he is the more dissatisfied partner; rather, he is more mobile.

The number of separations and desertions can be but an estimate. However, some idea of the total may be obtained from the number of divorces granted for desertion, from the census enumeration which shows the number of husbands or wives absent from the household, and from child-support cases. The number of divorces granted for desertion in the United States has increased during the past several decades. A peak of 112,000 was reached in 1946. By 1950 there was a decline to 68,000 divorces granted for desertion. Estimates of the extent of separation and desertion may be found in census data which show that, in 1957, 791,000 men and 1,146,000 women were listed as "separated." These figures include

---

[12] Locke, *op. cit.*, pp. 72–73. Reprinted by permission of Holt, Rinehart and Winston, Inc., publishers.

only those legally separated, those expecting to obtain a divorce, and those temporarily or permanently estranged. These data showed 1.9 percent of all married women to be separated from their husbands. Of nonwhite women only, chiefly Negro, 8 percent were separated from their husbands.[13] Desertions accounted for 33 percent, and divorce 5 percent, of all cases of children receiving aid in Philadelphia.[14] Over the past thirty years new desertion and nonsupport cases in Philadelphia were twice the number of divorce cases. In 1955, of the 2,600,000 children receiving aid-to-dependent children grants in the United States, the fathers of 1,400,000 were separated from their families.[15]

Desertion appears to be more frequent among groups where social controls are weaker, and where family groups may be presented with conflicting norms. Thus, it is observed that desertion occurs more frequently in "newer cities" which are presumably undergoing more rapid change, and in which associations may occur more frequently among heterogeneous groups.[16] Desertion is also more frequent among those religious groups for whom divorce is not acceptable. Among Catholics, for example, desertion is much more common than among Protestants. According to estimates, the desertion rate for Catholics in the United States exceeds that for the general population by about 40 percent.[17]

Divorce

Although many persons regard divorce as the only index of family disintegration, it is but one of many signs. Since it represents the legal dissolution of the marriage, it certainly is the final one. Two major types of legal divorce can be distinguished: absolute divorce, which restores marital partners to the status of single persons, completely absolving marital rights; and partial divorce, or legal separation, which gives legal status to separate maintenance without dissolving marital rights.[18]

EXTENT OF DIVORCE

About 400,000 divorces and annulments are granted annually in the United States. The ratio of divorces to marriages is about one in four,

[13] Bureau of the Census, *Population Characteristics, Marital Status, Economic Status, and Family Status:* March, 1957, *Current Population Reports*, Series P-20, No. 81 (March 19, 1958), Table 1.

[14] William M. Kephart and Thomas P. Monahan, "Desertion and Divorce in Philadelphia," *American Sociological Review*, 17:719 (December, 1952).

[15] Jessie Bernard, *Social Problems at Midcentury* (New York: Holt, Rinehart and Winston, Inc., 1957), p. 383, from a report from the Commissioner of Social Security.

[16] Zimmerman and Cervantes, *op. cit.*, pp. 51–55.

[17] Thomas P. Monahan and William M. Kephart, "Divorce and Desertion by Religious and Mixed Religious Groups," *American Journal of Sociology*, 59:454–465 (March, 1954).

[18] Mabel Elliott and Francis E. Merrill, *Social Disorganization* (New York: Harper & Row, Publishers, 1961), p. 390; and Paul H. Jacobson, *American Marriage and Divorce* (New York: Holt, Rinehart and Winston, Inc., 1959).

and about 4 percent of the children in the population who are under eighteen have been affected by divorce. In 1956 there were 2,418,000 divorced persons, 60 percent of whom were women. These figures do not include all persons who had been divorced, for about two thirds of divorced women and three fourths of divorced men eventually remarry.[19]

Divorce rates per 1000 marriages have increased in general since 1890, in the United States and in some Western European countries and Australia.[20] "It is therefore not merely an 'American' phenomenon, but is somehow related to the evolution of the family in Western society in general." [21]

The number of divorces increased during and after World War II. In the United States an all-time high of approximately 610,000 divorces were granted in 1946. (See Table 15.2.) The annual number of divorces

Table 15.2. Divorces and Divorce Rates in Relation to Population, United States, 1890–1957 (Rates per 1000 of mid-year Population)

Year	Population in millions	Divorces Number	Rate
1890	63.1	33,461	0.5
1900	76.1	55,751	0.7
1910	92.4	83,045	0.9
1920	106.4	170,505	1.6
1930	123.1	195,961	1.6
1940	131.97	264,000	2.0
1946 [a]	141.2	610,000	4.3
1950	150.7	385,144	2.6
1956	167.2	382,000	2.3
1957	170.3	381,000	2.2

[a] Peak year.

SOURCE: Table, "Marriages and Divorces, United States and Each State and Alaska, Hawaii, Puerto Rico and the Virgin Islands," 1957, Vital Statistics: Special Reports, Vol. 50, No. 7 (June, 1959), p. 187; and Table IX, "Provisional Marriage and Divorce Statistics," United States, 1948, Vital Statistics: Special Reports, Vol. 31, No. 16 (November 4, 1949), p. 229; and Paul H. Jacobson, American Marriage and Divorce (New York: Holt, Rinehart and Winston, Inc., 1959), p. 90.

has gradually decreased. In 1957 there were approximately 381,000 divorces, a fact which suggests that the increase in divorces during and after World War II may have been due, in part, to the increase in marriages.[22]

[19] Elliott and Merrill, op. cit., p. 391.
[20] William J. Goode, "Family Disorganization," in Robert K. Merton and Robert R. Nisbet eds., Contemporary Social Problems (New York: Harcourt, Brace & World, Inc., 1961), Table 3, p. 406.
[21] Kingsley Davis, "Statistical Perspective on Marriage and Divorce," The Annals, 272:17 (November, 1950).
[22] Goode, "Family Disorganization," in Merton and Nisbet, op. cit., p. 411.

Although the total number of divorces in the United States, as well as the rate of divorce in relation to the population and divorces per 1000 married females fifteen years and over, has decreased in the past few years, the number of divorces relative to the number of 1000 yearly marriages has, in general, increased. In 1890 the number of divorces was 55.6; in 1910, 87.4; in 1930, 173.9; in 1950, 231.7; and in 1956 it was 259.[23] The increase in divorce rates in the past sixty years is no evidence that marital unhappiness has increased to the same extent, for there are other variables. Divorce laws have become increasingly liberal during this time, and the grounds for divorce have been broadened. South Carolina, for example, did not permit divorce for any reason until 1949. Moreover, there has been a decided change in public opinion about divorce. Many persons who formerly continued unsatisfactory marriages, or separated, or were deserted, now secure a divorce. Formerly a divorce was often a matter of family disgrace, but now public attitudes are more tolerant. These changes in public opinion seem to reflect more fundamental transformations in values and norms relating to the nature of marriage and divorce.[24]

FACTORS IN DIVORCE RATES

Monahan lists three categories of factors which influence the divorce rate. First, there is the historical trend. People who marry this year are more likely to become divorced than those who married twenty or thirty years ago because the attitudes and expectations of married couples, as well as the change in values, make divorce more acceptable. Second, situational factors, such as depression, affect the divorce rate at particular times. During the last depression the divorce rate dropped over 20 percent in three years. Finally, the last category concerns biographical aspects, or the time at which the marriage was contracted, as during wars, when there are many hasty marriages.[25]

In the United States considerable differences in divorce rates depend largely on area, religion, education, occupation, and number of children. In urban areas there is a much higher divorce rate than in rural areas, and Cannon has concluded that the rural-urban differential is the greatest single factor affecting divorce rates.[26] The rural divorce rate is not markedly below the urban rate in all states, however, and some suggest that since

[23] Ibid., Table 3, p. 406.

[24] See Elliott and Merrill, op. cit., Chap. 17; S. Kirson Weinberg, Social Problems in Our Time (Englewood Cliffs, N.J.: Prentice-Hall, Inc., 1960), p. 442; and Goode, "Family Disorganization," loc. cit., pp. 412–413.

[25] Thomas P. Monahan, "The Changing Probability of Divorce," American Sociological Review, 5:536–545 (August, 1940).

[26] Kenneth Cannon, "Marriage and Divorce in Iowa, 1940–47," Marriage and Family Living, 9:81–83 (February, 1947).

1940 the rural rates have shown a tendency to catch up with the urban rates. In Wisconsin, for example, the rural divorce rates have been about as high as the urban rates since World War II.[27]

Divorce rates are also higher in western than in eastern states. The higher divorce rates for western states may be due in part to differences in religious concentration and in legislation concerning divorce, as well as to the greater mobility of the population. In the northern and eastern states which have large Catholic populations, although divorce rates tend to be low (as an average of 1.3), the number of desertions contributed by these states appears to be markedly in excess of the national average.[28] Divorces and desertions are lowest for Jewish groups from 1937 to 1950; divorces were more frequent among Protestants but desertion was highest among Catholics, exceeding the Protestant rate by about 100 percent and the Jewish rate by about 500 percent.[29]

Differences in divorce rates exist between occupational groups. One author has indicated, for example, that available evidence demonstrates an inverse relationship between divorce rate and socioeconomic rank; thus, professional groups which are highest in socioeconomic rank, have the lowest divorce rate, whereas service workers and laborers which occupy the lowest socioeconomic ranks, have the highest divorce rates.[30] However, Monahan found that farm laborers in Iowa had the lowest divorce rates. Whatever the precise relation between divorce and occupation, data relating to these variables must be interpreted with caution. In the first place, before assessing the divorce rate, it is necessary to know how many persons within a given occupational category *marry*. In the second place, if we are examining the relative degree of family disintegration in various occupational groups, then it is necessary to know how many families in given occupational groups are broken by means other than divorce.

Divorces are most likely to occur early in marriage, the majority before the fifth year, and most frequently in the third.[31] Although slightly over half of the couples who are divorced in the United States have no children, many children are affected by divorce. In 1955, about 343,000

---

[27] E. E. LeMasters, *Modern Courtship and Marriage* (New York: The Macmillan Company, 1957), p. 571. See also Jessie Bernard, *Remarriage* (New York: Holt, Rinehart and Winston, Inc., 1956) for a review of urban and rural trends in divorce.

[28] See Monahan and Kephart, "Divorce and Desertion by Religious and Mixed Religious Groups," *loc. cit.*

[29] *Ibid.* Also see Paul Glick, *American Families* (New York: John Wiley & Sons, Inc., 1957).

[30] William J. Goode, *After Divorce* (New York: The Free Press of Glencoe, 1956), p. 46 and Chaps. 4 and 5. For contrasting views, see also Thomas P. Monahan, "Divorce by Occupational Level," *Marriage and Family Living*, 17:322–324 (November, 1955); and William M. Kephart, "Occupational Level and Marital Disruption," *American Sociological Review*, 20:456–465 (August, 1955).

[31] Harold T. Christensen, *Marriage Analysis* (New York: The Ronald Press Company, 1950), p. 13. See also Jacobson, *op. cit.*, pp. 144–147.

children were involved in divorce and annulment cases, or an average of slightly less than two children per couple.[32] The proportion of children involved in divorces has continued to increase during the past twenty or thirty years. Between 1922 and 1932 the average number of children affected by a divorce was 0.68; in 1955 the number was 0.87. This suggests that children are no longer as great a deterrent to divorce as they once were. The woman usually files for the divorce, either for reasons of chivalry on the part of the husband, or because he may be unwilling to sever relationships with his children, whose custody the wife usually retains.

Likewise, the legal grounds used in the divorce proceedings are seldom the real grounds for the proposed separation; the law permits divorce only for certain reasons and these reasons often do not fit the circumstances of a particular couple who wants a divorce. Usually the couple agrees on one of the generally "fictitious" legal grounds permitted by the state in which the pair resides. The grounds agreed upon are generally those least socially injurious to the other partner, and yet the most effective, legally. Divorce is not regulated by a national law, and there are consequently great differences in state divorce laws. Some states require a minimum residence (six weeks in Nevada and Idaho) and allow a wide variety of grounds. This leads to migratory divorce from those states which have exceptionally severe grounds, such as, for example, South Carolina, where no divorce was permitted until 1949, and New York, where at present divorce is permitted only on grounds of adultery. Consequently, many persons in some states who desire a divorce and have sufficient money to finance it, migrate to states with shorter residence requirements and less stringent grounds.[33]

A large proportion of divorced persons remarry, and there is evidence that this remarriage rate is increasing. In general, about one out of every five marriages in the United States is a remarriage. About two thirds of divorced women remarry, and about three fourths of divorced men remarry. The median length of time between the divorce and subsequent remarriage is 2.7 years, for both men and women. About one half of all brides aged thirty-five to forty-four are divorcees, and about one half of all grooms aged forty to forty-nine are previously divorced men. Of brides aged twenty-five to twenty-nine about one fourth have been divorced as compared to about one eighth for grooms aged twenty-five to twenty-nine.[34] About two thirds of the total remarriages are between persons who

---

[32] Bernard, *Remarriage*, pp. 301–303. See also Goode, "Family Disorganization," in Merton and Nisbet, *op. cit.*, p. 454.

[33] For a discussion of some of the legal and social problems which this presents for those seeking a divorce, see Herbert F. Goodrich, "Migratory Divorce," in *Conference on Divorce* (Chicago: The University of Chicago Law School, February, 1952), pp. 82–87.

[34] Elliott and Merrill, *op. cit.*, p. 437.

have previously been divorced. One study found that divorced women generally have a more successful remarriage than those who have never been divorced.[35]

Conflicting Roles and Role Expectations in the Family

Marriage and family relations, like all group relations, involve role playing, and deficiencies and conflicts over role playing in the family situation play a leading part in breaking down relationships.[36] Marital partners and other members of the family may each have different aspirations and evaluations of the roles which they play and expect of others in marriage and family relationships.[37] Conflicts in marriage and family roles may occur between marital partners over their duties and obligations.[38] There are also conflicts between family roles and roles outside the family: conflicts, particularly with parents, in the roles of children, and conflicts in marital roles and those of other relatives.

Difficulties in role playing on the part of husband, wife, and children have been accentuated by the changes which have taken place in the family and in urban living over the past century. This is due to the fact that the roles of family members, but particularly of the wife, are ambiguously defined in contemporary American society. In the American rural family of the past, roles were well defined, with the father being largely a patriarchal figure. Women played a subordinate role and were largely concerned with household duties. Families were large, and children were expected to perform household duties and to be obedient to parents and to family traditions.

ROLE CONFLICTS BETWEEN MARITAL PARTNERS

Until quite recently a woman was dependent upon her family prior to her marriage; thereafter she relied upon her husband for support. Today about three fourths of all women work before marriage. In 1890 only 4.6 percent of married women were gainfully employed. In 1940 this

---

[35] Locke, *op. cit.*, p. 301.

[36] If conflicts do result in marital unhappiness they may not always precipitate divorce or other forms of marital breakup. It is probable that many marriages do endure, despite conflict and unhappiness. There is little knowledge of the extent of unhappy but enduring marriages.

[37] One study has measured differences between role performances and role expectations of husbands and wives and constructed an index of marital strain. See Nathan Hurvitz, "The Measurement of Marital Strain," *American Journal of Sociology*, 65:610–615 (May, 1960).

[38] See, for example, a study of husbands' and wives' expectations regarding their roles in the sexual relationship: Paul Wallin and Alexander Clark, "Cultural Norms and Husbands' and Wives' Reports of Their Marital Partners' Preferred Frequency of Coitus Relative to Their Own," *Sociometry*, 21:247–254 (September, 1958).

percentage was 15.2, and by 1951 it was 26.7 percent, or one in four married women. Women's ability to work has made marriage for the sake of economic "security" less frequent; yet today a woman's lifetime chances for social status are still associated with marriage.[39] Divorce may not present the same difficulties that it once did, because more women today have had employment experience prior to marriage. Yet divorce does introduce problems, usually of both an economic and a social-psychological sort. In the first place, the great majority of men and women in our society have different expectations about their future and their roles. For men, work or a job becomes the focus of self-identity and emotional investment, as well as of social status. On the other hand, women's socialization experiences are such that self-identity and emotional investment are intimately linked to successful wifehood. Thus, employment prior to marriage is regarded by most women as only temporary; after marriage it may serve other purposes.[40] The different societal attitudes which men and women incorporate in their own work roles are today reflected in societal practices which allocate differential salaries and statuses to male and female workers performing the same duties.[41]

The larger number of women employed today, which is in part a reflection of the "emancipation" of women occurring largely in this century, does not mean that women are no longer socialized differently from men. But the so-called emancipation of women has introduced additional roles for women. This does not mean that the old role of wife-mother is obsolete, but rather that today the wife-mother is subtly forced by social pressures to play additional roles. Some women may resist these pressures; others may regard them as a signal to abdicate the "drudgery" of wife-motherhood and become a full-fledged "careerist." Women today may feel ambivalent concerning their marital roles.[42]

Moreover, contrasted with the relatively limited education given women formerly, women today frequently go beyond high school, either to college or to business or secretarial school. This greater amount of education makes the wife a different kind of mate: she will tend to define her role in such a relationship differently; she does not respect her husband's position to the same extent; and she is more able to discuss things on an equal basis with her husband. The college-trained girl sets higher standards for her mate, and is less likely to accept a man with an education inferior to hers. As a result of both work experience and education,

[39] See Parsons, "The Social Structure of the Family," in Anshen, op. cit.; and David Riesman, "Permissiveness and Sex Roles," Marriage and Family Living, 21:1–11 (August, 1959).
[40] Riesman, "Permissiveness and Sex Roles," loc. cit.
[41] See Eli Ginsberg, Woman Power (New York: Columbia University Press, 1957).
[42] See Nora Johnson, "The Captivity of Marriage," Atlantic Monthly, 207:38–42 (June, 1961).

a woman is less likely than formerly to leave all decisions to her husband; more probably she will demand an equal share in this activity.

Some role conflicts involve the pattern played by the marriage partner in his marital and familial responsibilities. In some families, members may play their roles in a way which deviates markedly from that generally prescribed, so that any organization of roles becomes difficult. Sometimes, deviation in role playing in marriage is due to role expectations, as in the case of many adolescents, which are not even the same as those normally required for the marriage role.[43] The popular explanation that "neither was prepared to assume marriage and family responsibilities" probably best applies to these cases.

In other situations the role of one marital partner may be derived from a patriarchal or a matriarchal tradition, whereas the other partner may come from a more equalitarian or democratic background. One of the partners may then wish to assume entirely the major decision-making functions, such as the expenditure of money and the disciplining of the children. For example, a husband who was raised in a patriarchal family, and has expectations of playing a similar role in his own marriage, may marry a girl who has been supporting herself and making her own decisions. The husband can refer to families where the husband makes decisions, and the wife can refer to other families in which decisions are made on a democratic basis. In general, it has been shown that marital happiness and stability are more probable if the marital partners are from similar social backgrounds.[44]

A reverse situation may occur where "the woman plays the authoritative roles, ruling over her husband and children despotically. A man who has grown up in such a family will perhaps expect his wife to dominate him, but she may have had a family experience which prepared her for a submissive and dependent role. If such a man married such a woman, a struggle arises which is won by the person who forces the other to make decisions for the pair." [45]

It appears that in general the roles played by the marital partners largely reflect the marital roles played by the parents or other persons with whom each of the partners was intimately associated in childhood. The reason is that the parents or other "significant persons" are merely the "instruments" through which societal attitudes, norms, and values regarding sex-associated roles are communicated to children. "Married adjustment may be regarded as a process in which marriage partners attempt to re-enact certain relational systems or situations which obtained

---

[43] See Marie S. Dunn, "Marriage Role Expectations of Adolescents," *Marriage and Family Living,* 22:99–111 (May, 1960); and Alvin Moser, "Marriage Role Expectations of High School Students," *Marriage and Family Living,* 23:42–43 (February, 1961).

[44] See Robert F. Winch, *Mate Selection* (New York: Harper & Row, Publishers, 1958).

[45] Waller, *op. cit.,* p. 285.

in their own earlier family groups." [46] The reaction to such role playing may cause tensions in the family. One husband said:

> "I'm naturally a 'Little Caesar.' I want my way all the time. Mother has the 'old' idea of a husband's role in the house. She thinks the husband should be the lord and master of the household. I usually get my way by insisting strongly." [47]

A wife said this about her husband, who was critical of her housekeeping role:

> "His mother was a perfectionist as a housekeeper. I do the best I can. When he comes home he will rub his white handkerchief over the top of the piano. He will not believe me when I tell him that I dusted the room only that morning, and that the city is notorious for its smoke and dirt." [48]

ROLE CONFLICTS BETWEEN MARRIAGE AND OTHER ACTIVITIES

Role-playing difficulties may represent a conflict among family roles and those required in various outside activities. There may be a degree of incompatibility between the role of a man as a husband and father and the demands of his occupation, or between the role of a wife and mother and outside interests, whether connected with a job or social activities. These difficulties which the family faces in meeting other role demands have been accentuated in American society by an urban way of life. In some instances these numerous demands may not represent conflict so much as the necessity for playing too many different roles; that is, the behaviors required of different roles may not actually be incompatible, yet the necessity of shifting to several roles during each twenty-four-hour period may seriously impede a person's skill in the playing of a single role.

Even when certain goals and conceptions of roles to be played are decided upon, society may make them difficult to carry out. The goal of becoming a professional man is highly rewarded by society; yet it makes early marriage difficult. A community may feel that having two or three children is desirable; and yet in housing and participation in social life it often rewards those without children. Parents may feel that their children have too much freedom; yet they offer them little "controlled" recreational facilities and permit commercial establishments to fulfill their recreational needs. A wife and husband may agree on the roles each is to play—for instance, companionship roles—but for economic reasons

---

[46] Leonard S. Cottrell, Jr., "Roles and Marital Adjustment," *Publication of the American Sociological Society*, 27:107 (May, 1933). Also see Ernest W. Burgess and Leonard S. Cottrell, Jr., *Predicting Success or Failure in Marriage* (Englewood Cliffs, N.J.: Prentice-Hall, Inc., 1939).

[47] Burgess and Wallin, *op. cit.*, p. 628.   [48] *Ibid.*, p. 630.

move to a small rural town which does not approve such roles. Thus, even if there is agreement as to the roles to be played in marriage, societal frustrations may prevent their being performed. If in the marital situation there is a failure to accept alternative conceptions of roles and goals, the potential unity is not realized.

Society has established, for example, no definite status for the working wife. It is undecided whether to reward or punish her for her emancipated form of living, especially the working wife in the middle classes.[49] As a result of his reaction to the uncertainty of others and the internal uncertainty he has learned, the husband is often ambivalent about his wife's working, particularly when it is not necessary. When the woman works from necessity there may be other difficulties in her role in the marriage.[50] This situation may be especially acute when the family lives in a community where many of the wives do not work. One study of married veterans on a college campus found that the employment status of wives was the most significant difference in the roles of husband and wife. The women who worked full time tended to have authoritarian conceptions of marriage, whereas those who worked only part time leaned toward the companionate conception of marriage.[51]

Differences about the need for children are reflections of conflict in the role playing of husband and wife. The husband may be influenced by his image of the traditional family, with the satisfactions derived from having many children around the house. If the woman has an occupation in which she is interested she may not want to give up her position in order to raise children. The man, on the other hand, may not want the obligation and expense which children bring.

ROLE CONFLICTS BETWEEN PARENTS AND CHILDREN

There may be conflicts between the roles of children and parents. Such conflicts have been intensified by the democratic and individualistic training now given children in an urban world, training which increases the adolescent conflict with a generation having different values and a different conception of the family roles. It has become increasingly difficult to impose authoritarian traditions of the last century on children of the present generation:

---

[49] See Riesman, "Permissiveness and Sex Roles," *loc. cit.*, for a discussion of how younger persons incorporate these societal attitudes toward their own working roles. See also Ginsberg, *op. cit.*, for a discussion of how, in salaries and status, society reflects a differential attitude toward male and female workers.

[50] See *Work in the Lives of Married Women* (National Manpower Council Conference; New York: Columbia University Press, 1958); and Lee Rainwater, Richard Coleman, and Gerald Handel, *Workingman's Wife: Her Personality, World, and Life Style* (New York: Oceana Publications, Inc., 1959).

[51] Motz, "Conceptions of Marital Roles by Status Groups," *loc. cit.*

"My mother is always picking on me or nagging at me constantly. I'm sure getting sick and tired of it all, but I realize that, if I ran away from home, I would never be able to live, dress, and eat as I do now. Besides, if I did go away, it would break my mother's heart, so I guess I will stick it out as long as possible. They never let me do what I want to do, so I do it anyway and tell them afterwards. Then it's too late to deprive me of my fun, and I can stand my punishment easily enough." [52]

Parents' expectations for their children frequently conflict with the children's desires. In an urban society children are often presented, through peers and others, with conflicting norms and values. As a result, younger persons may acquire attitudes which conflict with those of the parents, for the former have closer contacts with these emerging patterns and are more adaptable in learning them.[53]

ROLE CONFLICTS BETWEEN MARITAL PARTNERS
AND OTHER RELATIVES

Relations of members of a family to other relatives may be still another source of difficulty arising from role playing. In particular, the adjustment of satisfactory relationships with the "in-laws" of both families presents a difficulty in many marriages.[54] Patterns of respect for parents may conflict with the desire for freedom from them, and feelings of affection and obligation toward them may place the partner whose parent is in the home or living nearby in a peculiarly difficult position.

Family difficulties may start between parents and their son or daughter as the former attempt to continue or to reassume the familiar protective role. The presence of in-laws may magnify difficulties which would normally be temporary. Koos cites a case in which a wife's mother was taken into the husband's home. Trouble resulted because the mother immediately began to "side" with her daughter against the son-in-law in small matters which would have been resolved under other circumstances.[55] There is, consequently, an increasing tendency in America to escape involvement with parents and in-laws, as indicated by the plots of many of our motion pictures: "American films tend to picture both hero and heroine unbound by family ties. Homeless, in the main jauntily self-sufficient, they make their way through city streets, night clubs, lunch wagons, and hotel rooms until they find each other. . . . More than half of the heroes and half of

---

[52] Case document in Ernest W. Burgess and Harvey J. Locke, *The Family: From Institution to Companionship* (2d ed.; New York: American Book Company, 1960), p. 531.

[53] Kingsley Davis, "The Sociology of Parent-Youth Conflict," *American Sociological Review*, 5:523–535 (August, 1940).

[54] See Burgess and Wallin, *op. cit.*, pp. 603–608.

[55] Earl L. Koos, *Families in Trouble* (New York: King's Crown Press, 1946), p. 76.

the heroines have no relations. If they do have any, they are not likely to have more than one." [56]

Conflicts Involving Cultural Background and Interests

When members of a marriage or a family have backgrounds and social norms which are drastically different, this difference can be a source of a great deal of conflict and tension. In former rural societies in America, where the population within an area was quite homogeneous, an individual generally married someone who had grown up in the area and accepted the ideas and norms of the community. The marital situation offered little opportunity for a conflict of fundamental norms and values.

Conflicting definitions of the marital situation, and especially of the relation of the marital group to outside group activities, have developed within modern urban society. One study has shown that residence in rural areas during childhood is a favorable factor in marital adjustment, whereas residence in a city is unfavorable.[57] Moreover, spatial and vertical class mobility have increased the possibilities of the marriage of persons with diverse backgrounds and interests. Cultural differentiation appears to occur when a family or an individual goes up or down in the scale of occupation or of social class.

In a comparative study of happily married and divorced couples, Locke has pointed out the importance of agreement between marital partners on certain fundamental activities. He cites in particular the importance of always, or almost always, agreeing on "handling finances, recreation, religion, demonstration of affection, sexual relations, ways of dealing with in-laws, amount of time spent together, table manners, conventionality, and aims or objectives of the family." [58] These factors conform to common sense, for they refer to the general areas of interaction in marriage.

Similarity of family and cultural background is an important favorable factor in marital adjustment; a pronounced difference is unfavorable: "One may safely predict conflicts in a union where a rural person dominated by orthodox religious values and attitudes marries a cosmopolitan person characterized by unorthodox religious views and by Bohemian or other radical ideas and practices." [59] It has been suggested that marital adjustment is easier for persons who have similar social backgrounds, and that marriage stability and success is more probable if both partners are

---

[56] Martha Wolfenstein and Nathan Leites, *Movies: A Psychological Study* (New York: The Free Press of Glencoe, 1950), p. 101.

[57] Burgess and Cottrell, *op. cit.*, pp. 253–254.   [58] Locke, *op. cit.*, p. 85.

[59] Ernest W. Burgess and Harvey Locke, *The Family: From Institution to Companionship* (New York: American Book Company, 1945), p. 566.

from backgrounds with a strong set of values against divorce or other forms of disruption. Actually, the process of mate selection serves to bring together persons with similar backgrounds, for persons do tend in general to associate with, and to marry, others of similar social class, status, education, or religion.[60]

Some interests bind a marriage together, but others appear to have less effect. One study found that sports and games have little or no binding effect; friends, reading, and dancing have some effect; music, theater, and the church have considerable; and professional interests, active community service, and a common cause have great binding effect.[61] It is probable that agreement on a single factor or area of marriage interaction would not be of great significance in contributing to marriage success unless it were the outward expression of some more fundamental agreement —such as that concerning life values and goals.

Psychological Characteristics and Marital Interaction

The bulk of evidence on marital selection strongly suggests that similarity (or homogamy) of social characteristics is conducive to marital happiness and stability. Some have suggested, however, that whereas homogamous social characteristics may contribute to marriage stability, perhaps persons are happier if certain of their psychological characteristics are *not* alike, but "complementary."[62] Some feel that successfully married persons generally are those who have chosen partners whose traits tend to complement, at least emotionally, their needs. For example, as Winch has stated, aggressive persons sometimes appear to marry shy and retiring individuals:

> There is no evidence that persons with similar need patterns tend to marry. In the absence of evidence an explanation must depend upon theories of personality and of social psychology, and upon the implications of these theories. As we shall point out, there are strong theoretical reasons for believing that within the field of eligibles people tend to mate with those whose need patterns generally *complement* their own, rather than with those whose need patterns are *similar* to their own.[63]

In a test of this theory, Winch studied twenty-five married couples, all college undergraduates. The "needs" included dominance, submissiveness, receptiveness, and nurturance. "Nurturant" is the tendency or need to give support, aid, or care to a supposedly weak or helpless person. A

---

[60] Goode, *op. cit.*, pp. 525–526. For a partial bibliography of studies on "social homogamy" or common characteristics of marital partners, see Winch, *Mate Selection*, pp. 5–7.

[61] Burgess and Wallin, *op. cit.*, p. 442.   [62] Winch, *op. cit.*

[63] Robert F. Winch, *The Modern Family* (New York: Holt, Rinehart and Winston, Inc., 1952), p. 463. Italics added.

woman who behaves maternally toward her husband, whom she regards as a "little boy" needing to be looked after, would be nurturant. The following are Winch's complementary need types: Ibsenian (husband dominant and nurturant; wife receptive and submissive), Thurberian (husband nurturant and submissive; wife receptive and dominant), Master–Servant Girl (husband receptive and dominant; wife nurturant and submissive), and Mother-Son (husband receptive and submissive; wife nurturant and dominant).[64] Sixteen of the twenty-five couples could be classified satisfactorily in one of these types, with nine couples being exceptions.

At present the evidence on psychological characteristics does not definitely support the notion of either complementariness or of homogamy in mate selection. It is possible, of course, that there are general psychological characteristics and that some persons will be happier with mates who have dissimilar characteristics, whereas others would prefer mates with similar characteristics. The kind of mate a person seeks may depend upon his social background, which would tend to orient him toward one type of mate or another. It might be more appropriate to use the terms "expectations" or "role orientations," which clearly involve situational referents, rather than such static concepts as "trait" or "need." [65]

Terman has made one of the most complete and extensive studies of psychological factors in marital happiness.[66] It was based chiefly on the examination of the differences between 300 couples scoring high on the happiness index he used, and 150 who scored relatively low. More specifically, Terman found that one of the marital partners in an unhappy marriage is characterized by such symptoms as being grouchy, irritable, critical of others, dominative in relation to members of the opposite sex, and resentful of discipline. In general Terman found that happiness and emotional stability are closely related, though it is difficult to say which is the cause and which the effect.

There are a few studies which have attempted to "test" the consistency of psychological characteristics by obtaining couples' responses in many different situations. One study examined the characteristics "sympathy" (or empathy) and "adaptability," since previous researchers had suggested that positive marital adjustment was highly related to these factors. It was found that no general traits conforming to these factors could be observed. Instead, marital partners seemed to behave "sympathetically" or "adaptably," according to situational role demands. In some instances, it was found that the situation prescribed "sympathetic" role behavior

---

[64] Winch, *Mate Selection*, pp. 212–233.

[65] See Nelson N. Foote and Leonard S. Cottrell, *Identity and Interpersonal Competence* (Chicago: The University of Chicago Press, 1956).

[66] L. M. Terman, *Psychological Factors in Marital Happiness* (New York: McGraw-Hill Book Company, Inc., 1938).

for the wife, but not for the husband. In other situations, the role demands were reversed. These researchers concluded that the characteristics examined were not general factors, but that they must be interpreted in terms of situational norms governing sex roles.[67] Other studies have found no relation between marital happiness and personality characteristics, as measured on personality tests, such as the Minnesota Multiphasic Personality Inventory and the Edwards Personal Preference Scale.[68]

Social Participation and Marital Happiness

Since the family is a social group, one might well expect that the extent of social participation prior to marriage is related to marital happiness. According to some evidence, the number of friends, including those of the opposite sex, and the frequency of participating in social organizations are related to marital happiness.[69] The possession of many friends need not, of course, be related to marital happiness, but the presence of some satisfying relationships with other persons is probably a reflection of the manner in which an individual interacts with others. To the extent that a mode of interaction results in satisfying relationships prior to marriage it should also be conducive to later marital happiness.

Both American and British researchers have shown that the character of family friendship systems may contribute to marital stability or instability. In this case, it has been shown that it is not the number of friends which is significant so much as their similarity (in terms of values, goals, and so forth) to the particular family involved. Where friends of a family are similar, family disruption is much less frequent than when they are dissimilar.[70]

---

[67] Jack V. Buerkle, Theodore R. Anderson, Robin F. Badgley, "Altruism, Role-Conflict, and Marital Adjustment," *Marriage and Family Living*, 26:20–26 (February, 1961). For other studies relating to this, see Jack V. Buerkle and Robin F. Badgley, "Couple Role-Taking: The Yale Marital Interaction Battery," *Marriage and Family Living*, 21:53–58 (February, 1959).

[68] See Dorothy T. Dyer and Eleanor B. Luckey, "Religious Affiliation and Selected Personality Scores as They Relate to Marital Happiness in a Minnesota College Sample," *Marriage and Family Living*, 26:46–47 (February, 1961). See also Charles F. Bowerman and Barbara R. Day, "A Test of the Theory of Complementary Needs as Applied to Couples During Courtship," *American Sociological Review*, 21:602–605 (October, 1956).

[69] Burgess and Cottrell, *op. cit.*, and Locke, *op. cit.*

[70] See Bott, *op. cit.*, and Zimmerman and Cervantes, *op. cit.* The social characteristics referred to here included the proportion of kindred among the friend-families, the social backgrounds, as evidenced in region of origin, religion (ethical and moral views), income, and tastes. For further discussion of how the friend matrix of the family may operate as a means of social control, see Eugene Litwak, "Occupational Mobility and Extended Family Cohesion," *American Sociological Review*, 25:9–21 (February, 1960), and his "Primary Group Instruments for Social Control in Industrial Society: The Extended Family and the Neighborhood." Unpublished doctoral dissertation, Columbia University, New York, 1958.

Marital Happiness, Companionship, and the Sexual Relation

Some older studies have suggested that marital happiness and the degree of companionship in marriage were positively associated. One study reported marital happiness to be related to close association as demonstrated by always or nearly always talking things over, by joint participation in all or almost all outside activities, equality in accepting the judgments of the other, shared cultural activities, democratic relationships in making family decisions, and frequent kissing.[71] This shift in emphasis from a marriage based on status to one based on companionship is not easy, and the new emphasis has undoubtedly had a great deal to do with contemporary marital difficulties and divorce:

> First the right selection of a partner is much less easily accomplished for marriage as a companionship relation. Furthermore, the companionship marriage is sustained primarily by the happiness and satisfaction which husband and wife secure from it. If either partner concludes that the marriage is not offering these returns, divorce may be considered with the hope that another marriage may prove to be more rewarding.[72]

More recent investigations by both British and American sociologists have not supported the assertion that the degree of companionship in marital role relationships and happiness are necessarily correlated.[73] Instead, marital happiness occurs with about equal frequency in both the traditional and companionship types of marital role relationships. There was a tendency toward greater stability in the traditional type, and for expression of somewhat greater happiness.

Sexual incompatibility may in some cases create tensions in the marital relationship and may even contribute to the possibility of extramarital relationships. Burgess and Wallin conclude that "the problem of sexual maladjustment appears to spring most often from a divergence between husbands and wives in their attitudes to sexual intercourse and the frequency of their desire for it," with women more likely to have a negative attitude and to desire sexual relations less frequently.[74] Terman's findings indicate that such incompatibility is mainly expressed through the orgasm capacity of the wife and lack of similarities in sexual drive. He found that the orgasm capacity and similarities in sexual drive are correlated highly with marital happiness, whereas little or no correlation is reported for frequency of coitus, reported duration of coitus, or use of contraceptive techniques.[75]

An Indiana study found the following attitudes favorably related

---

[71] Locke, *op. cit.*, pp. 266–267.
[73] See, for example, Bott, *op. cit.*
[75] Terman, *op. cit.*, pp. 372–373.

[72] Burgess and Wallin, *op. cit.*, p. 30.
[74] Burgess and Wallin, *op. cit.*, p. 695.

to satisfying sexual relations: [76] the same degree of interest in sex; the rating of sex relations as enjoyable by men and enjoyable by women; rare or infrequent refusal of intercourse when mate desired it; no desire for intercourse with others during the marriage; no belief, knowledge, or suspicion that mate has had intercourse with others during marriage; no fear of pregnancy; and no jealousy on the part of mate if the other danced, talked, or associated with members of the opposite sex.

The relation of sexual enjoyment to marital difficulties is sometimes close and at other times remote. Sexual factors in marriage appear to affect men and women differently. An unsatisfying sexual relationship is more likely to affect the views of men about the success of the marriage, whereas with women there may be a low or a high degree of marital success regardless of the quality of the sexual relationship. Burgess and Wallin found that women enter marriage with a low sexual expectation, or that their sexual response may be a more general, rather than specific, expression of affection for the husband. Among men there are high sexual expectations, with the sexual factor being dependent on the wives' sexual expression. It is likely, of course, that marital happiness is the "cause" of sexual compatibility, rather than the reverse, as many have supposed.[77]

Sexual factors probably never operate in isolation and rarely of themselves break down a marriage. Burgess and Cottrell, as well as Terman, found that sexual difficulties were secondary expressions of conflicts arising from personality and cultural factors. Terman concludes that "sex factors combined are far from being the one major determinant in marriage." [78] Burgess and Locke concluded that "the sex factor was secondary to personality and cultural factors in influencing marital adjustment." [79] When sexual difficulties do seem to be a primary cause they may be an expression of tensions diffused from other conflicts or unresolved differences concerning the way each believes other conflicts should be settled. Burgess and Wallin found that "sexual adjustment can . . . be treated as being, to a large extent, an effect or a reflection of success in other areas of the marriage relationship." [80]

Economic Problems and Marital Stability

Contrary to many statements of married couples, economic factors do not appear to be the real reasons for disturbances in family unity. The

---

[76] Locke, *op. cit.*, pp. 156-157.

[77] Goode, "Family Disorganization," in Merton and Nisbet, *op. cit.*, pp. 433-434. Goode suggests that sexual expectations of persons entering marriage are probably not as great as they were following the decline of Victorianism and the emancipation of women. He suggests that young people today are better prepared for sex in marriage, and that their expectations are likely to be more realistic.

[78] Terman, *op. cit.*, p. 373.   [79] Burgess and Locke, 2d ed., *op. cit.*, p. 437.

[80] Burgess and Wallin, *op. cit.*, p. 696.

economic relationship, like the sexual relationship, is secondary in comparison with other factors, such as social roles, cultural backgrounds, social participation, and affection. The attitude of the marital partner toward economic factors appears to be dependent upon other factors.

Burgess and Cottrell found these economic factors related to marriage stability: (1) those occupations which tended to require more stable personalities and little mobility, (2) employment of the wife before marriage, (3) moderate income, (4) regular employment of the husband before marriage, and (5) some savings.[81] The last two items, as has been indicated, are probably more expressions of certain social roles rather than merely economic factors. Burgess and Wallin state that a number of economic circumstances constitute a major adjustment difficulty in marriage including "the unemployment of husband, living within a small income, disposal of income, to save or not to save, and the wife working after marriage." [82]

As was previously stated, members of a family play more than one role. Often tensions engendered in other roles express themselves in the family relationship. The family is often a vehicle for tensions arising in other parts of the society. Business and industry, for example, may encourage "supervisor anxiety." [83] This anxiety is often carried home from the plant or office, and the marital partner may be used as a scapegoat.

Loss of earning power may also serve to create family tensions. Often a man's salary is part of the image a woman marries, and with a loss in earning power due to illness or depression, a part of this image disappears, weakening the affectional bond between the two members. Numerous studies have shown that both depressions and unemployment sometimes tend to increase family problems.[84]

Marital Stability and Social Structure

Throughout this chapter, it has been emphasized that the family unit is part of a larger social matrix. There are great differences in family structure by class, occupation, and ethnic and religious groups. There may also be marked differences in the family roles played by persons of different ethnic groups, religions, or occupations. A marriage counselor who is helping with any crisis situation in the family must be aware of them.

Catholics, Jews, Mormons, and Quakers, to cite but a very few, have different expectations and must be understood in terms of them. The concepts

---

[81] Burgess and Cottrell, *op. cit.*, pp. 136–138.

[82] Burgess and Wallin, *op. cit.*, p. 609.

[83] John J. Honigmann, "Culture Patterns and Human Stress: A Study in Social Psychiatry," *Psychiatry*, 13:25–34 (February, 1950).

[84] Ruth S. Cavan and Katherine Ranck, *The Family and the Depression* (Chicago: The University of Chicago Press, 1938).

of the good husband and good wife are variously defined by these groups, and the marriage counselor needs to know these definitions when dealing with members of these groups. For example, Jews, especially Orthodox Jews, tend to define the good husband more in terms of the good provider than do, let us say, the Quakers, who lay greater store by psychological factors. The counselor might minimize the importance of the economic function and instead emphasize, say, romantic roles. It is difficult for a Protestant Anglo-Saxon counselor to appreciate the weight attached to this economic factor by an Orthodox Jewish wife. The problem of the marriage counselor is made even more difficult by the fact that there are types of Jews, Quakers, Catholics, and so on. There are Orthodox Jews, Conservative Jews, and Reform Jews; and there is considerable variation within each subculture. Religion is, moreover, only one social factor among many and has to be viewed in the light of the total constellation of causes. . . . When we turn to the influence of occupational factors on family behavior, we note that members of different professions, even those belonging to the same social class, religion, and ethnic group, may define proper family behavior differently. For example, the college professor's wife usually expects her husband to spend more time with her than does the doctor's wife. The minister's wife is expected to help her husband with his work more than the doctor's wife or the college professor's wife. The requirements of the professional lead to different expectations.[85]

As the character of American society has changed during the past century, so has the nature of family life been altered. Patterns which were once well adapted to the former type of society have become a source of marital conflict as ways of life have become more urbanized. As a result of the transfer of economic functions, the social and economic independence of women, and changes in the ideologies concerning marriage, the nature of the family has changed under urban conditions.

The modern urban family has lost many of its functions which formerly strengthened the unity of the group. The economic, religious, educational, and recreational functions of the family have diminished, and it has lost much of the protective functions with the development of various social services furnished by the state.

One of the greatest changes in family structure, brought about not only by the Industrial Revolution but by urban life, was the shift of economic functions from the family to other institutions. In contrast to the self-sufficient family of early rural America, the modern American family virtually produces nothing of its own. It now buys most of its clothes, household necessities, furniture, and various services. Most of its food is produced entirely outside the home and generally is even ready for serving. Thus the family has become primarily a consumption and distribution center, surrendering nearly all its productive functions to commercialized institutions. This function of consumption and distribution is important, however, and a failure to manage the family budget judiciously, especially

[85] Meyer F. Nimkoff, "Contributions to a Therapeutic Solution to the Divorce Problem: Sociology," in *Conference on Divorce,* p. 59.

in view of the numerous inducements to spend, may contribute to family instability.

> The family has become increasingly a unit of consumption, through which goods and services are purchased for money and within which they are consumed. Most of the making, canning, preserving, washing, clothes-making, and similar operations formerly performed by the family have been assumed by specialized agencies outside the home. Even the outside consumption of meals has increased in recent years, as evidenced by the growing number of restaurants, waiters and waitresses in proportion to the population as a whole. Bakeries and delicatessens have grown more rapidly than the population in recent decades.[86]

The religious activities of the family, which at one time included daily religious services at home, the saying of grace, and considerable religious instruction of the child, have been taken over by the Sunday school and the church. Training of the child in matters of moral conduct, hygiene, home economics, manners, and skills used to be done mainly in the family household. Beginning with five-year-old children, in most communities, these functions have increasingly been taken over by the school. The teacher has become the substitute parent in many ways. In school the young child is taught how to read and write, as well as how to get along with others, how to use a toothbrush, and how to do many other things formerly taught exclusively in the home: "The school has thus taken over those elements in the social heritage which relate to practical knowledge, in addition to those less utilitarian elements which are assumed to make life more meaningful. The relative importance of the home and the school in the broad function of education has undergone a considerable change, with the home perforce the loser." [87]

Recreation has also moved toward largely nonfamily and commercial types. The increase in leisure time in urban areas has been followed by more demands for recreational facilities and opportunities, and the marked differences in the recreational interests of the children and even of the husband and wife have resulted in more individualized recreation, often of a commercial nature. Many of the activities of family groups, such as motion pictures or television, offer little opportunity for communication and social interaction.

The family has been modified in this urban setting. This new family no longer operates as a separate economic unit, and its role as a socializing agent, including its educational, religious, and character-building functions, has diminished. In addition, the family has largely lost its ability to confer status on the individual by reason of his simply being a member of it; nor is status now as easily acquired by marriage into another family.

This change in the nature of the family has definitely represented seri-

---

[86] Andrew G. Truxal and Francis E. Merrill, *The Family in American Culture* (Englewood Cliffs, N.J.: Prentice-Hall, Inc., 1947), pp. 330–331.

[87] *Ibid.*, p. 351.

ous maladjustment to those who believe that the traditional functions of the family are its only real functions.[88] The traditionalists believe that it is necessary to reinstate many of these activities of the family so that it will be a large cohesive unit with a number of important functions, as it was in an agricultural economy.

Others regard these changes in the modern family as improvements because it is not the family as a functional unit which is important but rather the development of individual happiness.[89] If the position is taken that a new function, that of providing affection and companionship, is the chief integrative mechanism of the contemporary family, the loss of certain former functions does not constitute maladjustment but rather value conflicts over the success of the contemporary family and how it is achieving its new role.[90] Table 15.3 lists the distinctions between the former family of the rural type and the modern urban type:

Table 15.3. The Nature of Marriage

Former Rural Life Conditions	*Modern Urban Life Conditions*
1. Marriage a status of reciprocal rights and duties.	Marriage an interpersonal relation of compatibility.
2. Marriage largely arranged by parents (or by young people in accordance with parental standards of mate selection).	Freedom of young people in choosing a mate (ranging from predominance of romantic love to predominance of companionship as motives).
3. Separation of children and youth of the different sexes before marriage or only formal relations under strict chaperonage.	Increasing freedom of social relations before marriage with decline of parental supervision and control.
4. Love after marriage.	Love and companionship before marriage.
5. Emphasis upon the economic and legal aspects of marriage.	Stress upon the primacy of personal relations.
6. Evaluation of children as potential workers and economic assets.	Appreciation of children as persons and interest in their personality development.
7. Marriage relatively indissoluble.	Divorce resorted to if marriage regarded as failure.

SOURCE: Adapted from Ernest W. Burgess and Paul Wallin, *Engagement and Marriage* (Philadelphia: J. B. Lippincott Company, 1953), p. 31.

[88] Carle C. Zimmerman, *Family and Civilization* (New York: Harper & Brothers, 1947).
[89] Burgess and Locke, 2d ed., *op. cit.* and Joseph K. Folsom, *The Family and Democratic Society* (New York: John Wiley & Sons, Inc., 1947).
[90] For a discussion of the changes in the family, see Arthur W. Calhoun, *A Social History of the American Family* (New York: Barnes & Noble, Inc., 1945), and Zimmerman, *op. cit.*, pp. 610–634.

In general, the urban family has tended to become an affectional companionship and democratic unit. There is considerable evidence that the nature of interpersonal contacts of urban life results "in the urge to find love, affection, security and acceptance in a familial relationship." [91] One study of equalitarian, patriarchal or matriarchal patterns in family decisions, for example, found no significant difference in the relative dominance of husband and wife among the families of white professors, white skilled workers, Negro professors, and Negro skilled workers. Equalitarian patterns predominated in all of these groups. Nonworking wives, however, tended to be more dominant in decisions than working wives.[92] Some studies, however, have shown wide variations among social classes and occupational, educational, religious, and other groups. A British researcher, for example, found that the traditional type of marital role relationship was more frequent among working-class families, whereas the companionship type was more frequent among those of higher social status. Yet the correlation was not perfect, for the companionship type was observed in some working-class families, and the traditional type in some of higher social status.[93] "If both husband and wife are highly educated, they are likely to have a common background of shared interests and tastes, which makes a [companionship] relationship easier to conduct." [94]

Today in the United States there seems to be greater emphasis on what has been called the "romantic complex." [95] Probably the "romantic complex," which involves an emphasis on love and personal satisfaction as the sole justification for marriage, is in part a consequence of the decline of Victorianism occurring especially during the last half century.

Modern urban society has probably served to increase this romantic emphasis, because of the greater "individualism" of the family within the urban setting. As some have noted, the urban family is not necessarily "isolated," for members do retain many relationships with groups and families outside the family unit. But these groups and families are less likely, in the urban setting, to be connected or linked in some fashion with one another. Thus, although each group or family may exert control on some aspect of the family's activity, the social control of the entire family unit may be divided among many different sources. The result of this is that the urban family is often given greater freedom of individual choice and privacy in regulating its own activities. Hence, in cases such as these, marital partners are thrown more directly upon one another for emotional satisfaction and for carrying out family tasks. Yet this situation cannot be

---

[91] Winch, *Mate Selection,* p. 479.

[92] Russell Middleton and Snell Putney, "Dominance in Decisions in the Family: Race and Class Differences," *American Journal of Sociology,* 25:605–609 (May, 1960).

[93] Bott, *op. cit.*   [94] *Ibid.,* p. 112.

[95] Parsons, "The Social Structure of the Family," in Anshen, *op. cit.*

described as applying to *all* urban families. It merely appears that urban living increases the probability of its occurrence.[96]

Rather than being conceived of simply as a status relationship, the family is now coming to be regarded as a unit in which the roles of husband, wife, and children are companionship roles which emphasize the personal needs of all and are more nearly equal in the assumption of responsibilities. Moreover, the greater amount of social freedom given to each member is far different from that accorded in the traditional rural type of family. It is essentially a democratic orientation toward marriage, and involves equal participation in the privileges and obligations incurred in the family situation.

Summary

Divorce rates appear to have increased rapidly in Western society, although the rate varies greatly among different groups within a society. Most divorces occur early in marriage, the legal grounds for divorce being rarely the real reasons. A large proportion of divorced persons eventually remarry.

Role conflicts play a particularly important part in marital and family problems. They represent conflicts between marital partners over their duties and obligations; conflicts between family roles and roles outside the family; conflicts in the roles of the children, particularly with parents; and, finally, conflicts between marital roles and those of other relatives.

Conflicts of cultural background and interests are another area which may produce marital instability. Disagreements over values and goals in the marriage are the most significant. Similarities in norms are important in marital stability. The mutual expression of affection and satisfactory sexual relations are important factors in marital happiness. Sexual and economic difficulties in marriage appear, however, to be largely an expression of incompatibility in other areas of the marriage.

A new type of family which is more related to modern urban life is emerging. Although it has lost many of the economic, religious, educational, and recreational functions of the former rural family, the new urban family tends to be more democratic and puts more stress on affection and companionship.

Selected Readings

BOTT, ELIZABETH. *Family and Social Network.* London: Tavistock Publications Limited, 1957. A study of urban British families, which examines the relation-

---

[96] See Zimmerman and Cervantes, *op. cit.;* Litwak, "Occupational Mobility and Extended Family Cohesion," *loc. cit.;* and Talcott Parsons and Robert F. Bales, *Family, Socialization and Interaction Process* (New York: The Free Press of Glencoe, 1955), Chaps. 1 and 2.

ships between family roles and norms and the social matrix in which the family functions. The manner in which the social matrix acts as a medium of social control is thoroughly described.

BURGESS, ERNEST W., and LEONARD S. COTTRELL, JR. *Predicting Success or Failure in Marriage.* Englewood Cliffs, N.J.: Prentice-Hall, Inc., 1939. One of the major prediction studies in which difficulties in role playing are emphasized. A study of 526 Illinois couples primarily from Chicago. There is extensive case material.

BURGESS, ERNEST W., and HARVEY J. LOCKE. *The Family: From Institution to Companionship.* Rev. ed. New York: American Book Company, 1960. A comprehensive analysis of marriage and family relations emphasizing the shift from an authoritarian to a democratic family system.

BURGESS, ERNEST W., and PAUL WALLIN. *Engagement and Marriage.* Philadelphia: J. B. Lippincott Company, 1953. A detailed study of 1000 engaged and 600 married couples. In addition to statistical material there are numerous quotations from interviews and personal documents. The book also includes an extensive analysis of nearly all similar studies.

FOOTE, NELSON N., and LEONARD S. COTTRELL, JR. *Identity and Interpersonal Competence.* Chicago: The University of Chicago Press, 1955. An examination of family and marriage from a symbolic interactionist view. Theoretical issues in family study are discussed and a new approach to family research is suggested. Such concepts as "compatibility," "adjustment," "maladjustment," and many others are critically evaluated.

LOCKE, HARVEY J. *Predicting Adjustment in Marriage.* New York: Holt, Rinehart and Winston, Inc., 1951. A comparative study of divorced and happily married persons. In contrast to other studies which have generally studied college-educated persons, the sample is more representative of the general population.

WINCH, ROBERT F. *The Modern Family.* New York: Holt, Rinehart and Winston, Inc., 1952. An analysis of marriage and family relations with a sociopsychological emphasis. Chapter 15 deals with the theory of complementary needs.

ZIMMERMAN, CARLE C., and LUCIUS F. CERVANTES. *Successful American Families.* New York: Pageant Books, Inc., 1960. A study of over 9000 American families representing a cross section of social classes, ethnic and religious groups, and regions of the United States. The authors examine family friendship systems and find that the character of this system is one of the main determinants of family success or failure.

Chapter 16

Role and Status Conflict
in Old Age

The social roles of older people today are ambiguously defined. They have little place in our modern social structure, for there are few regular, institutionally sanctioned opportunities for full participation in an urban society. There is conflict between the role aspirations of older people and the actual role accorded them by our contemporary society. In this sense their difficulties in role adjustment are similar to those of the adolescent. Among both groups there is often a feeling of not being useful, participating members of society as well as a feeling that their desires are not fully recognized.

Age and aging have been defined in various ways by different researchers. Some have regarded aging as a period of physiological deterioration; others have viewed it as simply the advancement of years, and still others have emphasized that aging involves a restriction on cultural roles.[1] What, then, is the nature of aging, and what does it involve?

Physiological Changes

Aging is accompanied by certain physiological changes which are not necessarily the result of any disease. There is generally cellular atrophy and degeneration, as well as the more readily observable aspects of graying hair, baldness, wrinkling of the skin, stiffness, and changes in bodily form. These general progressive changes due to age can be listed as follows:

1. Gradual tissue desiccation. Recent studies of electrolyte (salt) concentrations in the tissue cells have cast some doubt as to the reliability of older experiments which formerly appeared to have established gradual tissue drying as part of the aging process.
2. Gradual retardation of cell division, capacity of cell growth, and tissue repair. This involves also a decline in capacity to produce the products of secretion, whether they be known substances such as pepsin or thyroxine or the less well identified antibodies involved in immunity.

---

[1] Leonard Z. Breen, "The Aging Individual," in Clark Tibbitts ed., *Handbook of Social Gerontology* (Chicago: The University of Chicago Press, 1960), p. 147.

3. Gradual retardation of the rate of tissue oxidation (lowering of the speed of living, or, in technical terms, the metabolic rate).

4. Cellular atrophy, degeneration, increased cell pigmentation, and fatty infiltration.

5. Gradual decrease in tissue elasticity, and degenerative changes in the elastic connective tissues of the body.

6. Decreased speed, strength, and endurance of skeletal neuromuscular reactions.

7. Progressive degeneration and atrophy of the nervous system, impairment of vision, of hearing, of attention, of memory, and of mental endurance.

8. Gradual impairment of the mechanisms which maintain a fairly constant internal environment for the cells and tissues (a process known as homeostasis). It is evident that sufficient weakening of any one of the numerous links in the complex processes of homeostasis produces deterioration.[2]

These physiological criteria, however, must be properly interpreted, for they cannot be applied to all members of a given age group, such as some chronological age like sixty-five. No longer is the concept of aging based on "an assumption of general organic, functional and psychological deterioration beginning in middle life and proceeding rather rapidly until it becomes disabling and finally incapacitating." [3] Physiological aging is a gradual process which varies tremendously among individuals. Contrary to popular opinion, for example, sexual activity does not suddenly decline among males, for the decline is so gradual that it is not until the late seventies or eighties that there is complete impotency, and exceptions occur even then. In some activities one function may decline while another increases, as in the case of physical speed as contrasted with endurance.[4] Some have expressed the view that the physiological changes associated with age are not significant unless they affect either the older person's ability to maintain relationships with others, or unless they alter his appearance in such a way as to affect society's judgment of him.[5]

The physiological deterioration of the aged is real in some cases, but it has probably been overemphasized for the total group. There is no question that certain conditions, such as heart disease and cancer, increase with age. For the year 1958, heart disease caused 747 deaths per 100,000

---

[2] Anton J. Carlson and Edward J. Stieglitz, "Physiological Changes in Aging," *The Annals*, 279:22 (January, 1952).

[3] Clark Tibbitts and Henry D. Sheldon, "Introduction: A Philosophy of Aging," *The Annals*, 279:6 (January, 1952). See also Breen, in Tibbitts, *op. cit.*, p. 146, and Hans Selye, "The Philosophy of Stress," in Clark Tibbitts and Wilma Donahue, *Aging in Today's Society* (Englewood Cliffs, N.J.: Prentice-Hall, Inc., 1960), p. 118.

[4] For example, the records for the 100-yard and 220-yard dashes are held by men from eighteen to twenty-two years of age, but the records for the long grind of the marathons are held by men between thirty-eight and forty-five.

[5] Robert W. Kleemeier, "Behavior and the Organization of the Bodily and the External Environment," in James E. Birren ed., *Handbook of Aging and the Individual* (Chicago: The University of Chicago Press, 1959), pp. 400–447.

persons between the ages fifty-five and sixty-four years; the cancer deaths for this age group were 392 for the same base population.

Chronological age is an unsatisfactory criterion for "old age" because of the great individual variation in the rate of physiological aging. Some people are relatively young at seventy or older, whereas some are quite aged physically at fifty. Some men have children in their eighties, some play golf in their eighties; Bernard McFadden, for example, made a parachute jump when he was over eighty. Many farmers past seventy can out-work a younger man in the field. As Stieglitz has pointed out, one of the more important concepts in the study of aging is that "physiologic age or biologic age is not the same as chronologic age. . . . Often biologic age is greater than chronologic age; sometimes it is less." [6] The attitude toward chronological age is well expressed by an eighty-year-old retired Army officer who had volunteered at the age of seventy for Army service and was rejected because of age.

> Comes 1942 and World War II. I still held a hold-over commission as Captain in the United States Army, inactive reserve. I wrote a letter to the powers that be at the War Department asking that I too may be ordered to active duty. Come back instructions to present myself to the regular Army examining board in session at Fort Sheridan, Illinois for complete and final examination for active duty. . . . Could not imagine why I seemed to be the main attraction there, but I later learned that it was due to my age, only 70 and that I made the various tests with flying colors. I did not feel a day older than I did when I first enlisted in the Army 48 years ago. At the conclusion of the exam the commanding officer had me call at his office to congratulate me on the almost perfect score, and asked me the question asked me several times that day. This usually was, "What do you do to keep in such perfect physical trim?"
>
> Now I waited from day to day hoping, with each mail, to receive that order directing me to report to the commanding officer at so and so for active duty. But alas a letter came OK but it simply said that my physical condition was quite perfect but that due to my age I would not be allowed to serve my country. A nice letter of appreciation was enclosed. Thus ended my military career forever. Again I had the pain of completely separating myself from the military service. I have discovered this. That as we age we do not feel our hurts, both physical or emotional pains, as keenly as we do in our younger days. This is because we are no longer as much alive. It is a melancholy fact that man begins to die the day he is born.[7]

It is clear that physiological age is not determined wholly by chronological age, but that these two variables are partially independent. Yet physiological deterioration alone does not define aging, for in addition

---

[6] Edward J. Stieglitz, *The Second Forty Years* (Philadelphia: J. B. Lippincott Company, 1946), p. 10. See also Selye, "The Philosophy of Stress," in Tibbitts and Donahue, *op. cit.*

[7] From a personal document.

there must be a societal reaction to such deterioration which defines it as symptomatic of aging. When a person's bodily functions become altered to such an extent that he begins to "look" old, the chances are great that he will increasingly withdraw from groups with which he has been formerly associated.[8] To the extent that he does withdraw, his social and psychological adjustment will be affected, and he will validate society's judgment of a relationship between chronological age and deterioration. Shock has further clarified the relationship between the behavioral and physiological aspects of aging. Although aging brings bodily changes such as a gradual "loss of cells," these changes do not account for the sudden behavioral changes or "breakdowns" noted in older persons following such events as retirement or widowhood. The latter are "imposed by society." [9]

Psychological Changes

Psychological changes in aging relate to differences in sensory and motor functions, learning ability, memory, and to changes in performance on intelligence tests.[10] Sensory and motor functions of the aged show some marked differences. Hearing difficulties, particularly for the higher tones, increase with age, and there is less visual acuity where there is speed and poor contrast or dim illumination. Motor responses requiring speed generally decline. In fact, soon after maturity there is a decline in the swiftness of dealing a blow, in simple reaction time, and in strength of grip. Older persons generally may not be as fast in a given task, but they make fewer errors than younger persons. If an older person has retained his mechanical skill, however, he may be able to keep up with the speed of younger workers. A number of studies have shown that older persons are more expert at tasks which stress accuracy rather than speed.

There is some uncertainty about changes in learning abilities with old age. It would seem that learning *speed* declines slowly past the age of thirty and more rapidly past the age of fifty. However, studies in learning *power,* i.e., grasp or comprehension, show that it declines at a much slower rate, with some persons showing no apparent decline even in their eighties.[11] It is difficult to draw definite conclusions because of the artificial nature of many of the experiments on speed of learning and age. According to Kaplan, the continuance of an occupation or interest and motivation probably affect learning ability a great deal.[12] One of the primary dif-

---

[8] Breen, "The Aging Individual," in Tibbitts, *op. cit.,* p. 152.

[9] Radio address by Nathan W. Shock, Director of the Michigan Institute of Gerontology, in a radio address on "Aging," June 20, 1961, University of Wisconsin Station WHA.

[10] Oscar J. Kaplan, "Psychological Aspects of Aging," *The Annals,* 279:32–42 (January, 1952).

[11] Irving Lorge, "Intellectual Changes during Maturity and Old Age," *Review of Educational Research,* 17:326–332 (1947).

[12] Kaplan, *loc. cit.,* pp. 35, 36.

ficulties in drawing conclusions from studies dealing with the relationship of age and learning stems from the fact that factors such as motivation, speed of performance and physiological status are intimately correlated with age, and exert a definite influence on learning task performance.[13]

Loss of memory, particularly the ability to recall present events, is often part of the popular characterization of the aged. Unfortunately, the evidence is not too clear on the extent of this loss. In Kaplan's words, these memory changes appear to "vary with the complexity of the task, loss being smallest on simple memory tests such as one dealing with visual memory for digits. There is a tendency for those of superior intelligence to sustain less memory loss than those who are mentally dull." [14] Since memory is related to personality, the role of motivation should play an important part. The decline on memory tasks may be due to perceptual speed in "grasping" the material to be recalled, rather than to an actual "loss" of memory.[15] There is no evidence that loss of memory is essentially a biological function.

At present, no definite conclusions can be drawn from studies dealing with the relationship of intelligence test performance and aging. In general, these studies have shown lowered performance with aging, yet this decline is particularly prominent on those test items which require visual acuity and motor agility.[16] This would suggest that the apparent intellectual deterioration of the older person may be partially due to sensory impairment rather than to decline of intelligence. Moreover, the lowered performance of the older person may be partially due to changes in schooling that have taken place and that may make him less able to perform at a high level on present-day intelligence tests. Also the older person may not be interested in the items on an intelligence test, and thus not be motivated to respond to them.[17] In addition, the speed factor, which is involved in all intelligence tests, creates a handicap for the older person.

Changes in Social Roles and Status

Neither the physiological nor the psychological characteristics of old age seem adequately to explain the differences in the status and role of older persons in various types of societies. Likewise, they do not sufficiently explain the difficult adjustment problems of older persons in contemporary society. Actually old age is a sociological process which is only partly de-

---

[13] Edward A. Jerome, "Age and Learning—Experimental Studies," in Birren, op. cit., p. 696.

[14] Kaplan, "Physiological Aspects of Aging," loc. cit.

[15] Harold E. Jones, "Intelligence and Problem-Solving," in Birren, op. cit., p. 732.

[16] George K. Bennett, "Relationship of Age and Mental Test Scores among Older Persons," in Clark Tibbitts and Wilma Donahue eds., The New Frontiers of Aging (Ann Arbor: University of Michigan Press, 1957), 153–157.

[17] Jones, "Intelligence and Problem-Solving," in Birren, op. cit., p. 722.

termined by age; yet it occurs in the middle years in other cases. As a sociological concept, it may be regarded as "that point in an individual's life at which he ceases to perform all those duties, and enjoy all those rights, which were his during mature adulthood, when he begins to take on a new system of rights and duties." [18] This new system of rights and duties, or the status and role of the older person, is largely determined by the societal definitions of the nature of age and of the older person. From this point of view, aging is understood and interpreted "in terms of the behavior characteristics of persons designated by the society as aged." [19] The adjustment of the older person, which is the degree to which his behavior corresponds to the societal role expectations, depends upon the clarity with which his roles are defined, the compatibility of the roles, the degree of preparation for assuming the roles, the consistency with which other persons allow them to play these roles, and the extent to which motivations of older persons can be realized.

The process of sociological aging does not arbitrarily begin at any set age. Unlike chronological and biological aging, which takes place fairly continuously throughout life, sociological aging varies with societal definitions of age and the responses of individuals to changed age status. In this sense, chronological and physiological age are independent of the societal reaction, whereas sociological age is not. Thus, the aged person may not regard himself as aged, as was indicated when 499 men and 759 women, whose median age was 73.5 and 71.7, respectively, were asked whether they considered themselves middle-aged, elderly, old, or aged.[20] Only a small proportion regarded themselves as "old" or "aged." About half the men defined themselves as middle-aged, and in the age group sixty to sixty-four, two thirds put themselves in this category. In fact, not until they reach the seventies do most men and women have a conception of themselves as elderly. One woman in her eighties remarked, "I feel old only when I look at myself in the mirror."

Several factors account for the lowered status and undefined role of the aged. In a sense it is the result of urbanism, with its rapid social change and the tendency to emphasize youth and activity. Urbanized societies seem to regard older persons as having already had their turn at living and experiencing the gratifications of life. Old people no longer have the claim on kin for role, support, and social participation that they formerly did. Rarely is their advice given consideration, even if proffered, because their experiences and values are often out of line with those of the modern urban world. Some have therefore described the fundamental problem

---

[18] B. Hutchinson, *Old People in a Modern Australian Community* (Melbourne: Melbourne University Press, 1955), p. 1.
[19] Breen, "The Aging Individual," in Tibbitts, *op. cit.*, p. 149.
[20] Robert J. Havighurst, "Social and Psychological Needs of the Aging," *The Annals*, 279:16–17 (January, 1952).

of the aged as involving role transition to a socially nonfunctional role which is only ambiguously defined.[21]

In an urban society as a whole, and in the family group as well, the aged are often marginal people. The smaller family unit no longer has a place for the aged person, for the modern democratic family is organized around the interests, wishes, and activities of its young and active members, who are more highly valued in the urban culture. The older persons may be pampered, protected, or left to their own devices, but rarely are their wishes given equal consideration with those of others.

In urban areas today "what was good enough for father is not good enough for me." Present-day vertical class mobility has meant that the son may acquire more material goods, education, and status than his father had. The older person is thought to have lost his close touch with the dynamic occurrences and changes in everyday existence and undoubtedly he has to some extent. But this depends, of course, upon the older person himself. In times of rapid social change, each generation, in a sense, becomes a sort of subculture with its own set of values and motivations. This situation creates social distance between age groups. In rural communities social change is less rapid, and there is less friction between generations. The old person has met most of the problems which his progeny face. This picture is often reversed, however, in urban areas, where the tempo of life is so accelerated that an older individual has increased difficulty adapting to the pace. New norms are constantly appearing, and what mother said ten years ago about the "correct" way to bring up children, handle money matters, and run the household is often almost as dated as last year's top tunes. At the same time, attitudes and patterns of behavior are often extremely rigid among older persons. Habits are difficult to alter at any time in life, but this statement is especially true of old age.

This general characterization of the status of older people is by no means equally applicable to all classes or to all occupations, for there are many individual exceptions. The tendency for older persons to play a reduced status role is undoubtedly greater among the lower socioeconomic groups than among the upper classes, whose position and wealth continue to give them status even into advanced age. Likewise, in certain professions, such a law and medicine, an elderly person may even have increased status.

Many immigrants to America, in particular, have experienced conflicts upon reaching later maturity. With their predominantly rural back-

---

[21] See B. S. Phillips, "A Role Theory Approach to Adjustment in Old Age," *American Sociological Review*, 22:212–217 (1957), and H. L. Orbach and D. M. Shaw, "Social Participation and the Role of the Aging," *Geriatrics*, 12:241–246 (1957). For a discussion of a general theory of role change see Arnold M. Rose, *Theory and Method in the Social Sciences* (Minneapolis: University of Minnesota Press, 1954), p. 23. Also see the section on old age in S. Kirson Weinberg, *Social Problems of Our Time* (Englewood Cliffs, N.J.: Prentice-Hall, Inc., 1960).

ground, they have a heritage of strong family ties and high status for the aged. Not receiving the status and care which their early training led them to anticipate in their old age, they feel resentful and neglected. Old age often becomes a trying existence for them, especially because of the difficult relations with their children.

The basic difficulty seems to be the conflict between the behavior patterns which older people are supposed to display in urban society and the aspirations of older persons themselves.[22] They still have the same wishes and motivations as other persons for response, recognition, security, and new experience; yet there is increasing evidence that contemporary urban society and the newer rather undefined cultural definitions of the status and role of the aged are unsatisfactory to them and their peer generation. Consequently, personal adjustment among the aged appears to be the exception.

In modern society old age has become associated with a feared loss of physical attractiveness. Strenuous efforts are made to preserve this physical attractiveness on the assumption that to most people "to look young is to be young." Some observers have remarked that styles of clothing and other apparel are geared primarily to the youthful and not to the older person. Havighurst has recognized this fear in his discussion of the social and psychological needs of the aged person.

> Most of us, men as well as women, learn to place a high value upon our beauty and our strength. At the very least, we value highly our physical and mental vigor, our ability to do a hard day's work. In addition, most of us value our manliness or womanliness—the things that make us attractive to the other sex. Against these values the advancing years wage war. They rob a woman of her ability to have children, usually before she is fifty. Many women interpret this as a sign that they have lost much of their worth as women. Men do not fare much better. Already in their forties most of them lose much of their hair, grow fat in awkward places, and have to wear bifocal glasses. Both sexes lose the smooth skin that they value highly as a sign of youth. Then as the years go on, there is a real decrease of enjoyment of the physical aspects of love between the sexes, and finally the external sense organs of hearing and sight begin to lose their acuity.
>
> These insults to the self usually strike us in vulnerable places. We express it by saying that we do not like to grow older—but what we really mean is that we have invested a great deal of emotional capital in our physical attractiveness, and this investment is going bad on us.[23]

---

[22] Ruth S. Cavan, Ernest W. Burgess, Robert J. Havighurst, and Herbert Goldhamer, *Personal Adjustment in Old Age* (Chicago: Science Research Associates, Inc., 1949), pp. 18–29.

[23] Robert J. Havighurst, "Social and Psychological Needs of the Aging," *The Annals*, 279:11 (January, 1952). Reprinted by permission of *The Annals* of the American Academy of Political and Social Science. Whereas there has been intensive study of physiological changes associated with aging which affect bodily form and appearance, the effect of

One study found that a large proportion of older persons had feelings of unhappiness which seemed, on the whole, to increase as they grew older.[24] Older people vary considerably, however, in their responses to their changing situations. Riesman has suggested three different responses.[25] There are those who have psychological resources of self-renewal, lose little of their ability to enjoy life, and are relatively independent of the attitudes of the larger society. The majority have few resources of self-renewal, but at the same time do not decay because of their previous attitudes derived from work and other activities. Their adjustment, however, can be disturbed by a considerable change in their social situation. Others have neither inner resources nor the background of adequate social experiences and simply decay with old age and its problems. Which of these responses an individual makes seems to depend upon his past experiences and the social context surrounding transition to the aged role.

EMPLOYMENT AND OLD AGE

Work has more function and meaning than simply a source of income.[26] It also represents an expenditure of time and energy devoted to doing something and thus helps to prevent boredom. Work provides identification and status through a definition of role and a way of achieving recognition or respect from others. Association with others at work means having friends and contacts with members of one's peer or age group generation. According to the nature of the work, it may provide a source of meaningful life experience through creativity, new experience, or service to others. The findings of some recent studies have shown that work in American society has lost some of its function as a central life activity, and that its value has shifted somewhat from being an end in itself to a means.[27] Yet these studies also show that work continues to be a primary focus of self-identification and role conception. These latter factors may

---

these changes on the self-concept of the aged has not been studied.—Kleemeier, "Behavior and the Organization of the Bodily and the External Environment," in Birren, *op. cit.*, pp. 413, 447. Kleemeier poses the following questions for future research: What is the relationship of body size, self-concept, and acceptance of age roles? Are small size and youth associated in the formation of "age stereotypes"? Do body form and size affect adjustment to aging? Is selection of clothing related to these variables?

[24] Cavan *et al.*, *op. cit.*, pp. 58–59.

[25] David Riesman, "Some Clinical and Cultural Aspects of Aging," *American Journal of Sociology*, 59:379–384 (January, 1954).

[26] Eugene A. Friedmann and Robert J. Havighurst, *The Meaning of Work and Retirement* (Chicago: The University of Chicago Press, 1954), pp. 1–9.

[27] See Robert Dubin, "Industrial Workers' Worlds," in E. Larrabee and R. Meyersohn eds., *Mass Leisure* (New York: The Free Press of Glencoe, 1958), pp. 215–228; David Riesman, "Leisure and Work in Post-Industrial Society," in Larrabee and Meyersohn, *op. cit.*, pp. 363–385; R. S. Weiss and R. L. Kahn, "On the Definition of Work among American Men" (Mimeographed; Ann Arbor: University of Michigan, Institute for Social Research, 1959).

explain why loss of work, as occurs at the time of retirement, is associated with problems of adjustment.

Many workers look forward to the time when, at sixty-five, there will be no more clock punching, when they can engage in activities of their choice or travel if they wish. Retirement, however, may not be a pleasant experience, even when social security or retirement payments are adequate.[28] For a person who has worked eight or more hours a day, five or six days a week, for thirty or more years, enforced idleness and the loss of opportunities to use developed skills often produce a crisis situation. Such an individual finds himself with little to do that is constructive, day in and day out; he has lost many companions, particularly those with whom he has worked; and with the additional loss of other social contacts he becomes bored and lonely. New habits must be developed, and this is difficult at any age. Just as students often soon tire of long-awaited summer vacations and wish for a return to the "grind" or routine of the college year, so the older person may at first be delighted by the "vacation," but in time fervently desires to return to some socially useful role. Riesman suggests that it is not work, but having a job, which is important to the individual.[29] Many authorities are now of the opinion that the concept of "retirement" is perhaps unfortunate and that most persons should be retained indefinitely at some work, even in an industrial society.

Older people without jobs need more than just leisure or a satisfactory income. As important, from the standpoint of personal and social adjustment, as the loss of employment or household duties is the loss of certain social roles which a person has played during the greater part of his mature life. A person's job determines many of his extrafamilial associations, and may offer opportunities for satisfaction of needs not met within the family. For men, earning a living is regarded in our society as the most appropriate mode of life. The job is the basis of status in the eyes of the family and associates. It is also a source of reference groups which come to function as an anchor of self-identity.[30] Thus, when they are unable to maintain an independent existence in an urban society, the aged tend to lose self-respect. They are often forced to relinquish authority in the family because they no longer contribute to its economy. If they live with their children, the latter often become head of the households, and the older persons no longer, as they once did, have the status of head of an economic unit. Since the aged person seldom owns a farm or other property of consequence he cannot maintain status through the possibility of transmitting it. Thus, for a man or woman who has always been a self-

[28] Clark Tibbitts, "Retirement Problems in American Society," *American Journal of Sociology,* 59:301–309 (January, 1954).

[29] Riesman, "Leisure and Work in Post-Industrial Society," in Larrabee and Meyersohn, *op. cit.*

[30] Wilma Donahue, Harold L. Orbach, and Otto Pollak, "Retirement: The Emerging Social Pattern," in Tibbitts, *Handbook of Social Gerontology,* p. 377.

supporting, solid citizen, old age may become a fate often to be feared rather than anticipated.

The role of the retired old person is especially difficult where no other roles carrying equal status are available. The loss of the social function, through loss of jobs and forced or voluntary retirement, usually brings with it lowered social status and a diminution of self-esteem. Where the individual has been prepared to accept the new status, however, and has developed hobbies, interests, and a new and self-embracing image to fit the new roles and status, the situation may be different.

One of the most striking differences between rural society and an urban industrial economy is the fact that many of the urban aged are not gainfully employed. Although the proportion of those sixty-five years and over has increased greatly since 1890, by 1954 there was a marked reduction in the proportion employed. (See Table 16.1.) In 1890, 68.2 percent

Table 16.1. Percentage of Population Aged 45 Years and over in the Labor Force, 1890–1954

Age and Sex	1890 (June)	1900 (June)	1920 (June)	1930 (April)	1940 (April)	1950 (April)	1954 (Nov.)	1975 (est.)
Males								
45–54	93.9	92.8	93.5	93.8	92.7	91.7	96.7	94.6
55–64	89.0	86.1	86.3	86.5	84.6	82.9	88.8	82.3
65 and over	68.2	63.2	55.6	54.0	42.2	41.6	40.6	35.3
Females								
45–54	12.5	14.2	17.9	19.7	22.4	33.0	42.8	52.2
55–64	11.5	12.6	14.3	15.3	16.6	22.8	31.8	35.4
65 and over	7.6	8.3	7.3	7.3	6.0	7.6	9.5	11.8

SOURCE: *Trends in Gerontology* by Nathan W. Shock, with the permission of the publishers, Stanford University Press. Copyright, 1951 and 1957, by the Board of Trustees of Leland Stanford Junior University. Data from John S. Durand, *The Labor Force in the United States, 1890–1960* (New York: Social Science Research Council, 1948), Bureau of the Census, *U.S. Census of Population 1950*, Preliminary Reports, Series PC-7, No. 2; Bureau of the Census, *Current Population Reports, Labor Force*, Series P-57, No. 149 (December, 1954).

of the men in this group were employed, as compared with 42.2 percent in 1940 and 40.6 percent in 1954. In 1954, 96.7 percent of the men between the ages of forty-five and fifty-four were employed. This figure declined some 10 percent by the ages fifty-five through sixty-four, and among those over sixty-five the proportion was nearly one half as great. Although social security and other retirement benefits have had something to do with this change, the explanation is actually much more involved.

The trend in the employment of older women has differed from that of older men. As noted in Table 16.1 there has been an increase from 14.2 in 1900 to 42.8 in 1954 in the percentage of females aged forty-five to fifty-four who were employed. For females aged sixty-five and over, there has been a slight increase in the number employed from 1900 to 1954, whereas for men of this same age group, the trend has been consistently downward.[31] Considerable changes take place in the occupational distribution among persons as they grow older. In 1959, industries which hired greater proportions of workers forty-five years of age and older were agriculture, finance, insurance, and real estate. Those hiring the lowest proportions were construction, manufacturing, and trade. However, the greatest proportions of older women are employed in trade and service industries.

Increasing unemployment among older persons in an urban industrial world results from many factors, including their numbers, changes in skills, the growing emphasis on youth, and compulsory retirement at an arbitrarily chronological age. Their employment difficulties do not arise primarily from mere physical impairments due to age. The emphasis on youth and the arbitrary retirement at a certain age are partly a reflection of the impersonality of modern urban life and the categoric contacts between large numbers of persons. It is possible today to shelve people arbitrarily, irrespective of a particular individual's physical, mental, and social qualities. Rather than adjusting work speed and capacity to older persons, society asks the older person to adjust to the machine. Methods in industry change so rapidly that an older worker who has not been retrained often finds himself at a distinct disadvantage when competing with a new worker. There is increasing evidence that older persons, if given a chance, can adjust much better to industrial work than society thinks they can, and that they often have qualities, such as conscientiousness, carefulness, and precision, which younger workers do not have. This situation differs from that in many rural societies, where the young must learn from the older men the traditional ways of doing things. At no time in history have the skills of the aged been so rapidly discarded as today in urban society.

The consequences of a reduced income or of unemployment go far beyond mere figures. Between 1948 and 1957, the money incomes of older persons increased, although their incomes tended to remain below those of persons in the age groups from twenty to sixty-four. For example, the median income for men of sixty-five and over rose from $998 in 1948 to $1421 in 1957, or by 42 percent. Although this increase was substantial, it was nevertheless smaller than the 54 percent increase in the median in-

---

[31] Fred Slavick and Seymour L. Wolfbein, "The Evolving Work-Life Pattern," in Tibbitts, *Handbook of Social Gerontology*, pp. 322–323.

come of all men for this same period. Comparable figures for women of sixty-five and over for this period are $589 in 1948, and $741 in 1957.[32] Of the approximately 14.1 million persons aged sixty-five and over in July, 1957, some 3.9 million were employed, with this the chief source of their income. Approximately 6.7 million, or 47.3 percent, were supported principally by Old Age and Survivors Insurance benefits. About 10 percent, or 1,400,000, reported no income, or income only from public social insurance programs, or from other than earnings.[33]

The amount of money received from various outside sources is actually so small that it by no means makes up for the loss of regular wages.[34] Monthly payments under the 1958 amendments to the Old Age and Survivors Insurance program, for example, were between $33 and $127 for a retired worker, aged sixty-five and over, and between $49.50 and $190.50 for a retired worker and his wife. Women qualified at sixty-two rather than at sixty-five, although at a reduced benefit.[35]

OLD AGE AND THE FAMILY IN AN URBAN SOCIETY

Aged persons in the United States live under a variety of different family situations. About one third of the men sixty-five and over are married, as contrasted with only 18 percent of the women, who were generally younger when they married and who tend to outlive their husbands. Some of the others who live with their children have satisfying relationships, whereas others do not. Likewise, some who live apart from their children are happy, others unhappy.[36] The old and the young may work out a mutually satisfying relationship in the family group, but these adjustments, if any, are usually made in spite of the difficulties imposed upon the unity of the family rather than because of them. The following case illustrates some of the difficulties faced by the old person in working out satisfactory family adjustments as well as the difficulties faced by the younger members in making this adjustment.

There is the case of elderly Mrs. Snow, who had been born and brought up in the country in very humble circumstances. Always there had been enough in a way, so that she and her family had preserved their dignity by self-support, but with little or no margin. The mother always was the accepted

---

[32] Current Population Survey of the Bureau of the Census, as quoted by Margaret S. Gordon, "Aging and Income Security," in Tibbitts, *Handbook of Social Gerontology*, p. 209.

[33] John W. McConnell, "Aging and the Economy," in Tibbitts, *Handbook of Social Gerontology*, pp. 490–491, and pp. 502–503.

[34] For a discussion of this problem see John W. Corson and John W. McConnell, *Economic Needs of Older People* (New York: The Twentieth Century Fund, 1956). Also see Gordon, *loc. cit.*, Table 9, p. 224.

[35] Gordon, "Aging and Income Security," in Tibbitts, *op. cit.*, p. 233.

[36] Ernest W. Burgess, "Family Living in the Later Decades," *The Annals*, 279:110–112 (January, 1952).

head of the family, for the father and husband was not much of a manager, although he worked hard as a gardener on a large estate. After the death of her husband, Mrs. Snow had very little cash, just as all through her life. With no near relatives in the country who would or could have her with them, she came to the city to live with a married daughter. The latter did not quarrel with this plan because she accepted it as her duty, even though at the time her home was crowded, for not only did her own children live there but one son had married and brought his young wife into the home. The old lady, moreover, was handicapped by very poor eyesight as well as by unfamiliarity with the neighborhood and had to stay indoors most of the time.

Friction was inevitable, and yet Mrs. Snow's record in the country as a neighbor, a worker, and a mother was a creditable one. She was crude and simple, but sternly Puritanical in her attitude toward family life and the duty of one's children toward their own. After a fairly exhaustive study of the family needs, it was decided that the mother—or grandmother—faced what for her was a pretty hard situation, and that the family friction between generations was the direct result of very crowded living conditions and limited income. A final source of conflict was the widely divergent attitudes of the two and three generations, one from the country and one from the present-day city, toward family, moral and economic standards.

The daughter was genuinely anxious to do what could be done, but was torn between the so-called respectability of the old-age assistance grant for her mother, whose physical limitations made it hard for her to get along in the city, and residence in a home for the aged in the country where all their former friends and neighbors would know that she had "put her mother away." The mother finally decided the matter for herself by choosing the home in the country. There Mrs. Snow has found a certain measure of contentment, because she is in familiar surroundings, and there is a certain freedom of activity because of the fact that she is out of the city; but she has also proved herself to be a very stubborn old lady. Her daughter now admits reluctantly that her mother was always the one at home who "told everyone else what to do and when to do it" and the yielding habit is so strong with this daughter, herself now a grandmother, that she will make any sacrifice rather than raise an issue with her mother over anything at all.[37]

The urban housing situation often limits the inclusion of aged persons within the household. If a family living in an apartment, which usually has no more than two bedrooms, includes an old person, it has the effect of reducing the number of children or it necessitates living under crowded conditions. Under crowded conditions, widely separated generations do not make good adjustments unless there are strong ties between the individuals and a feeling of mutual responsibility. On the other hand, urban housing situations have often been used as rationalizations for not including the aged in the household when actually there are other reasons, such as the

---

[37] Ollie A. Randall, "The Older Person in the World of Today—In the Family," in George Lawton ed., *New Goals for Old Age* (New York: Columbia University Press, 1943), pp. 61–62. Reprinted by permission of the publishers.

desire to maintain an independent household. In fact, Moore maintains that there is considerable crowding in rural housing, as "not all rural families live in large, rambling dwellings where aged parents may be given a room and a corner in a spacious living room. The spacious dwelling unit is a rarity in rural as in urban communities; crowding is common in both." [38]

ROLE AND STATUS OF THE AGED IN NONURBAN SOCIETIES

The lower status of aged persons in urban society today is not dependent upon chronological or physiological age; rather, it is a reflection of the values of the culture. In many cultures older persons occupy positions of high status. In a study of a large group of folk societies, Simmons has reported that almost without exception older people have such an enviable position that, rather than fearing old age, many look forward to it. [39] Among certain groups, such as the Palaung of North Borneo, who attribute long life to a person's virtue in a previous existence, the aging years of life are regarded as the best. [40] Although this is partly a reflection of the fact that few of these people ever reach old age, even though it is chronologically defined as younger than it is in urban society, social values appear to play the leading role in the status of the old.

In folk societies the old person usually has a fixed role to play. Among folk societies he is likely to be the dominant member of the family group, controlling its property and acting as leader for the kinship group. In fact, among many groups, such as the Australian aborigines, older males have preference in the selection of younger women for wives. This, in turn, enables them more effectively to continue their hold on family ties. Even very old people have a place in the family and community life. There is seldom idleness, but rather always a feeling of being useful, no matter how small the task. The following excerpt describes how the Hopi Indians of northeastern Arizona regard their aged:

> Old men among the Hopi tend their flocks until feeble and nearly blind. When they can no longer follow the herd, they work on in their fields and orchards, frequently lying down on the ground to rest. They also make shorter and shorter trips to gather herbs, roots, and fuel. When unable to go to the fields any longer they sit in the house or kiva where they card and spin, knit, weave blankets, carve wood, or make sandals. Some continue to spin when they are blind or unable to walk, and it is a common saying that "An old man can spin to the end of his life." Corn shelling is women's work

---

[38] Wilbert Moore, "The Aged in Industrial Societies," in *The Aged and Society* (Champaign, Ill.: Industrial Relations Research Association, 1950), p. 36.

[39] Leo W. Simmons, *The Role of the Aged in Primitive Societies* (New Haven, Conn.: Yale University Press, 1945).

[40] Leo W. Simmons, "Social Participation of the Aged in Different Cultures," *The Annals*, 279:43 (January, 1952).

but men will do it, especially in their dotage. Old women will cultivate their garden patches until very feeble and "carry wood and water as long as they are able to move their legs." They prepare milling stones, weave baskets and plaques out of rabbit weed, make pots and bowls from clay, grind corn, darn old cloths, care for children, and guard the house; and when there is nothing else to do, they will sit out in the sun and watch the drying fruit. The old frequently express the desire to "keep on working" until they die.[41]

One of the most important roles that old people play in folk societies is that of being the leading person in knowledge and decision making. Where there is no writing the old become the source of knowledge about many specialized techniques, religious rites, ethics, and physical ailments. Medicine men and priests are almost always old people. In fact, aged persons who have special qualifications in knowledge, wisdom, and experience find many opportunities to use their influence in the more formalized ceremonies, magical rites, and religious practices. Often they officiate at such events as child naming, initiations, weddings, funerals, and memorial ceremonies.

Old men in folk societies also exercise great political power: "Political, judicial and civil preferments and positions are often also the normal outcome of such personal growth in the lifetime acquirements of knowledge, wisdom, and sound judgment. The titles and often the offices tend to be lifelong. Old men may serve long and well as lawmakers, judges, and administrators of justice. Moreover, as leaders in exclusive societies and in initiating rites, the aging quite generally exercise the powers of discrimination and receive considerable deference." [42]

Role and status problems connected with old age rarely exist in those areas of the world, such as India, and many parts of Asia and Africa, where the family and not the individual is the unit of social status and action. It is axiomatic that wherever a predominantly traditionalistic social system flourishes, old age and aging are largely not problematic. The reason is that the role and status of aged persons are clearly defined by the traditional values. In addition, there are generally a series of preparatory roles preceding assumption of the aged role. In this situation, the aged generally occupy positions of high status. Peasant China of some years ago, when the large-family system still predominated, was a classic example of a society where aged people were an asset rather than a problem. Because of their Confucianist philosophical and religious orientation, others in the Chinese culture were obligated to care for, obey, and revere the old. Filial piety was a chief commandment in this culture and one which was part and parcel of the larger value systems. The longer one lived, the more

---

[41] Leo W. Simmons, "Attitudes toward Aging and the Aged: Primitive Societies," *Journal of Gerontology*, 1:79 (January, 1946).
[42] Simmons, "Social Participation of the Aged in Different Cultures," *loc. cit.*, p. 49.

he had to look forward to in the way of psychic and social gratifications.[43] Social change was at a minimum, and the old, as the bearers of the traditions and enforcers of the mores, had the highest status in the society. Far from being considered senile, the old, in fact, were the persons revered and cherished. A major goal in life was to reach old age. The aged controlled the lives and destinies of the family group. The old settled with the tax collectors upon the amount of the tax which the family contributed to the public treasury, contracted marriages for their children and great-grandchildren, served on the community councils, meted out the punishments, and gave their approval to certain types of behavior. The old conceived of themselves as having the highest possible status in the society and were so regarded by others.

Most older persons have a much more satisfactory status in rural societies than in urban. In the country almost everyone has a place in the cooperative activities of producing agricultural and household goods. The aged contribute in good measure, for they possess much of the rural society's technical skill and managerial experience. Furthermore, the integrated family system of rural areas gives the older person a continuing high place in the society. The individual is part of a group and rarely is in an individualistic setting. Old people are a part of this group, "the moving, directing, and controlling agents in this old rural type of collective entity. Because of this their status in such a society is greatly enhanced over that [which] they are privileged to enjoy in societies where familism does not persist." [44] In the larger rural families an extra person or two does not constitute the burden it may in an urban society. Moreover, the larger and more diverse rural household offers opportunity for much more interesting and productive work than does a household in the cities. The status of elderly persons in rural areas is also linked to the important roles they play as heads of households and in religious activities. Thus it is not likely that the older person's opinions and ideas will be scornfully disdained.

Increase in Aged Population

The magnitude of the problems of the aged in contemporary society which have been described can be more readily seen when it is understood that for the past hundred years the older age groups have continued to be an increasingly large proportion of the population. This situation exists not only in the United States but in most Western European countries as well.

Several European countries exceed the United States in the proportions of persons sixty-five and over relative to total population. The greatest

---

[43] Max Weber, *The Religion of China* (Hans W. Gerth, trans.; New York: The Free Press of Glencoe, 1951). Also see Olga Lang, *The Chinese Family and Society* (New Haven, Conn.: Yale University Press, 1946).

[44] Lynn Smith, "The Aged in Rural Society," in *The Aged and Society*, p. 46.

proportion of older persons in 1950 was to be found in France, with Great Britain, Sweden, and Germany following, in that order. The United States is fifth in rank, followed by Italy, Canada, and the Netherlands. (See Table 16.2.) In the United States, the proportion of those sixty-five and over has

Table 16.2. Percentage of Population 65 Years of Age and Over in Eight Western Countries

Country	1950	1900	1850
France	11.8	8.2	6.5
Great Britain	10.8	4.7	4.6
Sweden	10.3	8.4	4.8
Germany	9.3	4.9	—
United States	8.2	4.1	2.1
Italy	8.1	6.2	—
Canada	7.8	5.1	—
Netherlands	7.7	6.0	4.8

SOURCE: Reprinted from "Aging in Western Culture," by Ernest W. Burgess ed., *Aging in Western Societies,* Table 29, p. 15 and Table 2, p. 35, by permission of the University of Chicago Press. Copyright 1960 by the University of Chicago.

increased from 4.1 percent of the population in 1900 to 9.2 percent in 1960. (See Table 16.3.) Since 1900 there have been increases in all groups over thirty-five years. (See Figure 4.)

In 1960 the northeastern and midwestern states had the highest proportions of older persons, with percentages ranging from 10 to 12 percent.

Table 16.3. Population of the United States, by Age, 1960, 1950, and 1900 (In millions)

Age	Number			Percent		
	1960	1950	1900	1960	1950	1900
0– 4	20.3	16.3	9.2	11.3	10.8	12.1
5–19	48.8	35.1	24.5	27.1	23.1	32.1
20–44	58.2	57.1	28.8	32.4	37.7	37.9
45–64	36.1	30.8	10.5	20.0	20.3	13.8
65 and over	16.6	12.3	3.1	9.2	8.1	4.1
Total (all ages)	180.0	177.1	76.1	100.0	100.0	100.0

SOURCE: U.S. Department of Commerce, Bureau of the Census, *Current Population Reports:* Population Estimates, Series P-25, nos. 98, 114, 170, 187, 193, and 212. Figures given in mimeographed booklet, "Health, Education, and Welfare Trends" (Office of Program Analysis, Office of the Secretary, U.S. Department of Health, Education and Welfare; Washington, D.C.: Government Printing Office, 1961).

These proportions were lowest for the western states, with the exception of Oregon, and for the southern states, with the exception of Florida.[45] Some cities have a large percentage of older persons, for example, St.

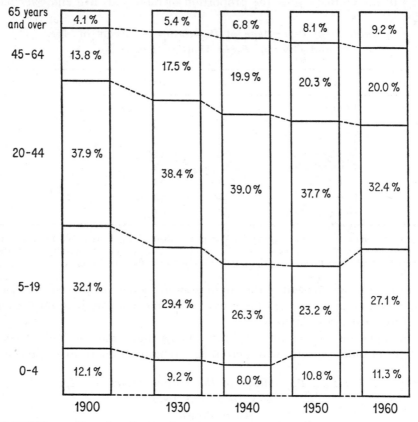

FIGURE 4.—Changing Proportion of Age Groups in the Population, 1900–1960

SOURCE: U.S. Department of Commerce, Bureau of the Census, *Current Population Reports:* Population Estimates, Series P-25, Nos. 98, 114, 170, 187, 193, and 212. Figures given in mimeographed booklet, "Health, Education, and Welfare Trends" (Office of Program Analysis, Office of the Secretary, U.S. Department of Health, Education and Welfare; Washington, D.C.: Government Printing Office, 1961).

Petersburg, Florida, where 22.2 percent of the population in 1950 was sixty-five or over.[46]

There has been a continuous increase in the life expectancy of both

---

[45] From the 1961 White House Conference on Aging, *Chart Book*, published by the Federal Council on Aging, Arthur S. Flemming, Chairman, p. 15.

[46] William H. Harlan, "Community Adaptation to the Presence of Aged Persons: St. Petersburg, Florida," *American Journal of Sociology*, 59:332–340 (January, 1954).

whites and nonwhites. Generally white and nonwhite women live longer than men and therefore their percentage of the population increases with age. Life expectancy of white males under one year of age was 50.2 years in the period 1909–1911 and by 1958 had increased to 67.2 years. The corresponding life expectancy of white females increased during this period from 53.6 to 73.7 years. Nonwhite males do not live as long as white males, the expectancy for nonwhite males under one year in 1958 being 6.8 years less and that for nonwhite women being 8.2 years less than that for white women.

This increased life expectancy, with the consequent rise in the proportion of the population in the older age groups, has been largely attributed to the industrial development of Western civilization over the past hundred years. The application of industrial techniques to agriculture has increased and improved the food supply. Industrialization has also brought, as one writer has suggested, increased emphasis on the values of health and longevity.[47]

One reason for this increased life expectancy has been the success in combating infant mortality, the dread childhood diseases, including diphtheria and scarlet fever, and such youth-killing diseases as tuberculosis. This triumph of medicine has vastly extended the life span of the population and has added millions of persons to the older age groups. Of all children born at the beginning of the century, less than 60 percent would have lived to be fifty; but by 1948 this percentage had increased to 86.[48] Until recently little progress has been made in increasing the average life expectancy by reducing the death rate from certain diseases of old age. The average life expectancy of white males forty-five years and older has only increased from 23.9 years in 1909–1911 to 27.1 years in 1952. So far there has been little improvement since 1850 in the life expectancy of persons reaching sixty or seventy years.[49] Since 1940, however, the development of the antibiotic drugs has made it possible to pull many older persons through otherwise fatal illnesses, and if similar advances are made in the effective control of such characteristic ailments of old age as cancer and heart disease a longer life span may be expected.[50]

In 1960 life expectancy was continuing to increase faster for women than for men, with the result that the excess of females to males has also increased. At approximately age forty, the number of women and men was

---

[47] Moore, "The Aged in Industrial Societies," *loc. cit.*

[48] Tibbitts and Sheldon, "Introduction: A Philosophy of Aging," *loc. cit.*, p. 5.

[49] Nathan W. Shock, *Trends in Gerontology* (rev. ed.; Stanford University, Calif.: Stanford University Press, 1957).

[50] Even so, the only animal that normally lives longer than man is the giant tortoise. The longest that an elephant is known to have lived is sixty; fifty-four is the oldest for a parrot. Dogs of fourteen are about as old as an eighty-year-old man, and rats are old at four.—Carl V. Weller, "Biologic Aspects of the Aging Process," in Clark Tibbitts ed., *Living through the Older Years* (Ann Arbor: University of Michigan Press, 1949), p. 27.

about equal, but thereafter the number of women increasingly exceeded the number of men. Thus, for the ages forty-five to fifty-four, women exceeded men by about 5 percent, whereas for the group eighty-five and over, women were in excess by about 46 percent.[51]

Another factor of importance in producing this change in age composition has been the general decline in the birth rates throughout the Western European countries over the past century.[52] In the final analysis this decline in birth rate has been an expression of the increasing urbanization of the world.

Prior to the 1924 Immigration Act the United States received millions of immigrants, and for several years around the turn of the century the number was as high as a million a year. These newcomers were largely young, able-bodied persons in their teens and twenties when they came, but they are now in the older age groups and have had a marked effect on the composition of the population.

By 1975 it is estimated that there will be about 22 million Americans aged sixty-five and over compared with 16.6 million in 1960, even without further progress in medical science.[53] As of 1960 there were 34 persons aged eighty and over for every 100 persons aged sixty to sixty-four; by the year 2000 there will be 67. By 1980 a larger proportion of the aged will be women.

Old Age and Mental Disorders

The older person may often work out ways of dealing with his unhappiness which may be inappropriate in terms of satisfactory interpersonal relationships. When faced with difficulties old people often "respond by petulance, bitterness, exaggerated efforts to secure attention, and sometimes by hysterical symptoms." [54] Havighurst calls some of these symptoms "irrational defenses." [55] In some cases the aged person may retreat into a world of neurotic behavior, fantasies, and even psychoses, wherein the self is satisfied by past beauty or success in business or on the job. Another defense is loss of hearing, sight, and memory, a loss which is not genuine and which takes them, in the eyes of others, out of situations they wish to avoid. Some develop psychotic behavior but not all such behavior actually is psychotic. Havighurst explains why some old people escape through hallucinations:

---

[51] 1961 White House Conference on Aging, *Chart Book, op. cit.*, pp. 9–14.

[52] In recent years the birth rate in the United States has increased.

[53] Harold L. Sheppard, "Relationship of an Aging Population to Employment and Occupational Structure," *Social Problems*, 8:159–163 (Fall, 1960). See also McConnell, "Aging and the Economy," in Tibbitts, *Handbook of Social Gerontology*, p. 491.

[54] Stuart A. Queen and Jeannette R. Gruener, *Social Pathology* (New York: Thomas Y. Crowell Company, 1940), pp. 100–101.

[55] Havighurst, "Social and Psychological Needs of the Aging," *loc. cit.*, pp. 15–16.

Sometimes a woman who has lost her husband or a man who has lost his wife will go on talking to the absent loved one. Why not? It is a pleasure to have someone to talk to. So why not go on talking to the people one loved? If one listens carefully, one may hear them reply; and so a person living alone may converse a great deal with absent persons. Then when some-one—a son or daughter—notices this, that person becomes disturbed and goes to a doctor and says, "My old mother (father) is having hallucinations." Yet when a child discovers what we call an imaginary playmate, which often happens with only children or first children, and carries on long conversations with that imaginary person, the parents are often quite proud, and they say, "My, what a good imagination that child has!" [56]

There are two major types of senile psychotic mental disorders. The first is probably strictly organic in origin, resulting, it is believed, from a shrinkage or "hardening" of the blood vessels in the brain, arteriosclerosis, which in extreme instances causes an almost complete destruction of brain tissue. Such physiological deterioration may not always be accompanied by a mental disorder, but where the latter does occur there is a sudden upset by convulsions or an epileptic seizure, severe headaches, emotional out-bursts, instability, and varied episodic confusion.[57] There is the usual mem-ory loss, particularly for recent occurrences. Some senile psychoses have an organic basis in that there is a shrinkage of the brain tissue, but they differ from arteriosclerosis in that there is no sudden onset. However, the evidence concerning the presence of arteriosclerosis and "shrinkage" of brain tissue is, in the majority of studies, based only upon hospitalized diagnosed cases, without an attempt to discover how frequently these same neurological changes occur in nonhospitalized and nonpsychotic cases. For this reason, the assertion that senile psychosis and arteriosclerotic degenera-tion and other brain changes are inevitably associated must be interpreted with caution.[58]

Although brain damage may produce psychotic behavior in older per-sons, there is considerable evidence that psychotic conditions in a large number of older persons are not proportional to the amount of brain deterioration. Lewis, for example, indicates that in most post-mortem examinations the pathologist can tell whether or not a brain is that of an old person, but cannot tell whether the person was normal or was mentally ill.[59] Many individuals who exhibited great mental deterioration in their

---

[56] *Ibid.*, p. 16. Reprinted by permission of *The Annals* of the American Academy of Political and Social Science.

[57] David Rothschild, "Senile Psychoses and Psychosis with Cerebral Arteriosclerosis," in Oscar Kaplan ed., *Mental Disorders in Later Life* (rev. ed.; Stanford University, Calif.: Stanford University Press, 1956).

[58] Rothschild, *loc. cit.*, p. 292. See also Eugene A. Confrey and Marcus S. Goldstein, "The Health Status of Aging People," in Tibbitts, *Handbook of Social Gerontology*, p. 183.

[59] Nolan D. C. Lewis, "Applying Mental Health Principles to Problems of the Aging," in Lawton, *op. cit.*, p. 94.

actions, which were thought to be due to biological old age, show little pathological changes of the brain at autopsy.[60] In addition, it should be pointed out that although diagnoses such as "senile psychosis" are frequently given to older persons referred for commitment to mental hospitals, such diagnoses are ordinarily given without conclusive evidence of senile neurological damage. Rather, there is a growing body of evidence which suggests that such diagnoses are given on the basis of the patient's *age* status, and not on the basis of specific organic changes associated with age.[61]

The functional disorders of paranoia, depressive behavior, and involutional melancholia appear to be common among institutionalized senile patients, although it is difficult to determine the precise extent. Functional mental disorders among the aged are probably an outgrowth of difficulties in interpersonal relations that characterize any such disorders regardless of age.[62] In this sense there are no truly "senile" functional psychoses; rather, there are functional disorders among the aged.

Manias and schizophrenic disorders are comparatively rare among senile patients, whereas depressions and paranoia are most common.[63] Perhaps the rarity can be explained by the hypothesis that the aged are too physically and socially feeble to revolt against an environment which they regard as oppressive. It is also possible and even probable that because of the wide breadth of experiences in the lifetime of the average person of later maturity he need not completely withdraw from the world of reality through schizophrenia, but merely retreats periodically to the recollection of those situations which have occurred during his lifetime and from which he has always derived satisfaction and can still do so.

Depressions among senile patients may result from excessive brooding over the lowered status, functions, and roles imposed upon them by our society, from the lack of satisfying outlets, and especially from the conflicts of the wish to quit living as against the desire to continue to live. Paranoid reactions are fairly common psychotic difficulties among older persons: "Depending on their previous modes of reaction, people may extrude the knowledge that they are growing older and their resentment of the younger generations which are making them aware of it, and attach their feelings to others about them. They become suspicious and even paranoid, feeling that they are persecuted and treated unfairly. There may be some truth in this at times, and they make the most of it." [64] Cameron has tried to show

---

[60] Robert B. McGraw, "Recoverable or Temporary Mental Disturbances in the Elderly," *Journal of Gerontology*, 4:234–245 (July, 1949).

[61] Evidence concerning the influence of sociological factors on commitment of older persons is given in the Technical Report, New York Department of Mental Hygiene, Mental Health Research Unit, 1958 (Albany: State Department of Mental Hygiene), p. 82.

[62] Moses M. Frohlich, "Mental Hygiene of Old Age," in Tibbitts, *op. cit.*

[63] Norman Cameron, *The Psychology of Behavior Disorders* (Boston: Houghton Mifflin Company, 1947), p. 572.

[64] Frohlich, "Mental Hygiene of Old Age," in Tibbitts, *Living through the Older Years*, p. 88.

that the proportionately higher commitment rates of paranoia in old age may partially stem from the fact that those close to the senile person find it easier to tolerate a sad and self-reproachful attitude than an aggressive and other-accusing one. On the other hand, the person who suffers impairment of his sense organs often tends to become suspicious and anxious. At the same time, restrictions are placed on the aged, and these, coupled with the sense organ handicaps of the old, are "optimal conditions for the development of paranoid reactions." [65]

However, there is considerable evidence that the higher rates of commitment of older persons to mental hospitals in recent years are related to structural changes in society. Among these changes are those affecting family organization, housing conditions, and concepts of family responsibility. According to some authors, children today are more willing to deal with the mental problems of older parents by placing them in mental hospitals.[66] A study in Syracuse, New York, analyzed the socioeconomic status of patients admitted to mental hospitals because of alleged senile psychosis or arteriosclerosis. It was found that the area of the city with the highest admission rate had the highest number of unemployed or disabled persons, the highest proportion of widowed and divorced, multiple-dwelling structures, tenant occupancy, and one-person households.[67] This would suggest that aside from any specific behavioral pathology, there are sociological factors which may condition or affect the societal reaction to the older person such as to result in commitment.[68]

In summary, psychic disturbances of the aged seem to be a product of cultural factors, a breakdown in customary channels of communication, and an interruption of routinized ways of living.[69] All of this is tied up with social changes in the status of the aged, their economic livelihood, and the nature of their family relations. Mental disorders of later maturity among males would appear to be at a minimum if the continuity between generations is maintained, spatial and social mobility is at a minimum, and if the person's status is not abruptly lowered.[70]

---

[65] Cameron, *op. cit.*, p. 572.

[66] R. H. Felix, "Mental Health in an Aging Population," in Wilma Donahue and Clark Tibbitts eds., *Growing in the Older Years* (Ann Arbor: University of Michigan Press, 1951), pp. 23–44.

[67] Confrey and Goldstein, "The Health Status of Aging People," *loc. cit.*

[68] See also Robert H. Kleemeier, "The Mental Health of the Aging," in Ernest W. Burgess ed., *Aging in Western Societies* (Chicago: The University of Chicago Press, 1960), pp. 265–266; and George Rosen, "Health Programs for an Aging Population," in Tibbitts, *Handbook of Social Gerontology*, pp. 530–531; L. S. Rosenfeld, F. Goldmann, and L. A. Kaprio, "Reasons for Prolonged Hospital Stay," *Journal of Chronic Diseases*, 6:141–152 (1957).

[69] See H. Warren Dunham, "Sociological Aspects of Mental Disorders in Later Life," in Oscar Kaplan ed., *Mental Disorders in Later Life* (Stanford, Calif.: Stanford University Press, 1956).

[70] Ivan Belknap and Hiram J. Friedsam, "Age and Sex Categories as Sociological Variables in the Mental Disorders of Later Maturity," *American Sociological Review*, 14: 367–376 (June, 1949).

Social Participation of the Aged

There is evidence that social participation among the aged is related to satisfactory adjustment. Yet in contemporary society, opportunities for such participation are apparently difficult. A study of 499 men and 759 women primarily from large cities found that the companionship of friends decreases with increasing years.[71] Including their spouses, only about 50 percent of the males had a high degree of companionship at age sixty to sixty-four, and this proportion declined to about 33 percent in the subsequent years. There is a curious contradiction in the fact that although old age means increased leisure it also seems to mean decreased social participation. According to one study, the age group sixty to sixty-four had a low degree of social participation (28 percent), but this low degree of participation increased to 35 percent among those sixty-five to sixty-nine years of age.[72]

Recent evidence has shown that the number of friendships an older person has will be influenced by status changes, such as retirement or widowhood which affect his location in the age, sex, and class structure of a given community. For example, a comparison of friendships of older persons in two different communities revealed that either widowhood or retirement decreased a person's friendships *if* they placed the individual in a different position with respect to his peers. Yet neither widowhood nor retirement had a detrimental effect on friendships if both of these changes were also relatively prevalent among a person's peers.[73] These data suggest that aging as such does not necessarily adversely affect social participation, but that status changes which normally occur in the later years may adversely affect participation if they place an individual in a position different from that of his peers.

A recent development, somewhat different from the isolation from the community of "Old Folks' Homes" of the past, has been community situations which increase friendships among the aged. Although it is true, as Weinberg suggests, that loss of friends through death or dispersion is more probable with advancing age,[74] the creation of "retirement villages" and apartment communities for older persons both in the United States and

---

[71] Cavan *et al., op. cit.,* p. 48.

[72] *Ibid.,* p. 49. In this study nine types of participation were included: daily informal activities, hobbies, plans for the future, listening to the radio an hour or more daily, attendance at group meetings two or more times a month, holding club office, employment, attendance at church at least once a week, and voting in last election. High degree of participation indicated seven or more activities; moderate degree, five or six activities; and low degree, four or fewer activities.

[73] Zena Smith Blau, "Structural Constraints on Friendships in Old Age," *American Sociological Review,* 26:429–439 (June, 1961). See also Zena Smith Blau, "Old Age: A Study of Change in Status." Unpublished doctoral dissertation, Columbia University, New York, 1957.

[74] Weinberg, *op. cit.,* p. 515.

abroad, would seem increasingly to provide living arrangements which would offer significant opportunities for social participation among aged peers.[75] In addition, so-called Golden Age Clubs, where older persons get together at some community center, are becoming more common.[76]

A number of studies have shown that social participation among older persons is influenced by their social class. These studies show that in the United States, persons of upper and middle social classes generally participate more in both formal and informal associations than do those of lower-class status. This trend has been observed among the rural aged as well as among those in urban areas.[77] Some have suggested that lower-class status among the aged is associated with severe economic handicaps which necessitate a restriction of social participation.[78] In general, the evidence shows that economic and retirement status are more important than age in influencing social participation or withdrawal. Others do not participate because they never did so when younger and now are so socially isolated that they do not know how to go about it.

Studies of the social participation of European aged do not uniformly support the findings of American studies, which show a marked decline of participation with age. One study conducted in Sweden, for example, found no significant differences in the extent of participation in associations between those aged eighteen to fifty-six and those fifty-seven and over.[79] Havighurst suggests that older working-class people in Sweden participate more in mixed-age associations than is the case in the United States. In addition to mixed-age groups, there are in Sweden a significant number of "old peoples' clubs" whose membership consists predominantly of working-class persons. These clubs may foster some specific project or may exist primarily to promote informal social relations. Among the Swedish middle- and upper-class elderly people, traveling and visiting resorts are popular.

Although there is a general decline in the aged person's general social and community participation, some writers report that there is an increase in favorable attitudes toward religion, in religious activities, and in a belief in an afterlife. One study stated: "Apparently, as the prospect of an earthly future fades, the belief in a future after death replaces it." [80] There

---

[75] See Ernest W. Burgess ed. *Retirement Villages* (Ann Arbor: University of Michigan, Division of Gerontology, 1961) for a discussion of such living arrangements for older persons. See also I. L. Webber, "The Organized Social Life of the Retired: Two Florida Communities," *American Sociological Review*, 59:340–346 (November, 1954), for data showing the greater participation among older persons living in retirement communities.

[76] See Chapter 22.

[77] Philip Taietz and O. F. Larson, "Social Participation and Old Age," *Rural Sociology*, 21:229–238 (1956).

[78] Blau, "Structural Constraints on Friendships in Old Age," *loc. cit.*, and Peter Steiner and Robert Dorfman, *The Economic Status of the Aged* (Berkeley: University of California Press, 1957), pp. 146–147.

[79] Cited by Robert J. Havighurst, "Life beyond Family and Work," in Burgess, *Aging in Western Societies*, pp. 305–306.

[80] Cavan *et al., Personal Adjustment in Old Age*, p. 57.

is conflicting evidence, however, on this point. More recent studies have suggested that religious feeling and religious participation do not necessarily increase with age.[81] It was found, for example, that women in all groups attended church much more often than did men, whose attendance declined with age. Among Protestants, only Negro men showed an increase in attendance with advancing age. Among Roman Catholics, attendance for men decreased with age, whereas for women it showed no change. Jews were the only group showing an increase in attendance for both men and women with increasing age. In addition to denominational and sex differences, religious participation seems definitely to be influenced by the type of community. Barron suggests that research data in general show greater religious feeling and church attendance among the aged in smaller communities but not in larger communities. This trend would probably also apply to other age groups.[82]

Social Adjustment of the Aged

The problems of adjustment which older persons in our society face stem largely from the fact that aging involves a *change of roles as well as of the statuses associated with these roles*. Adjustment, or conformity to changed role expectations, is complicated if the new role is poorly defined, or if there is inadequate preparation for it. Unfortunately, in modern urban society, in contrast to folk societies, both of these complicating factors are present in the case of older persons.

Several factors seem to be related to more adequate adjustment among older persons; yet the evidence concerning them must be interpreted with caution. For one thing, what is defined as "adequate adjustment" will vary for different subcultures, as will the factors which are taken as indices of "adjustment." [83] Some earlier studies suggested that such factors as these were conducive to adequate adjustment: new friends, new interests in civic and community affairs, new leisure-time activities and hobbies, and the avoidance of too much reminiscing over the past.[84] From adjustment scales,

[81] Harold L. Orbach, "Aging and Religion: Church Attendance in the Detroit Metropolitan Area," a paper read at the Annual Gerontological Society Meeting, Philadelphia, November, 1958. Also see H. Lee Jacobs, *Churches and Their Senior Citizens* (Grinnell, Iowa: Congregational Christian Conference of Iowa, 1957), p. 2.

[82] Milton L. Barron, *The Aging American* (New York: Thomas Y. Crowell Company, 1961), p. 177. For a further discussion on religious participation among the aged see Delton L. Scudder, *Organized Religion and the Older Person* (Gainesville: University of Florida Press, 1958).

[83] Raymond G. Kuhlen, "Aging and Life Adjustment" in Birren, *op. cit.*, p. 890.

[84] Havighurst, "Social and Psychological Needs of the Aging," *loc. cit.*, pp. 16–17. See, for example, Ethel Shanas, "The Personal Adjustment of 388 Cases of Recipients of Old Age Assistance." Unpublished doctoral thesis, University of Chicago, 1940; and John F. Schmidt, "Patterns of Poor Adjustment in Persons of Later Maturity." Unpublished doctoral thesis, University of Chicago, 1950

these studies found that good adjustment among older persons was associated with "the fields of good health, the maintenance of marital and family relations and of friendships, leisure-time and other activities, membership in at least one organization, no discrimination or unhappy period in life, conception of oneself as middle-aged rather than elderly, old, or aged, feeling of permanent economic security, no lowered social status, plans for the future, church attendance and belief in an after-life." [85]

One of the most extensive recent studies of adjustment and old age found that certain factors may be positively related to adjustment in one socioeconomic group, and negatively related to another.[86] In this study, a measure of "morale" (adjustment) was used, and persons of high, medium, or low morale were compared on a number of variables, after they had been divided into high and low socioeconomic groups. On the variable "health," the morale of those in the high socioeconomic group tended to be high whether their health was "good" or "poor." Yet surprisingly, the morale of those in the low socioeconomic group tended in the low direction for those with "good" and those with "poor" health. On self-image, the same relationship appeared, with those of high socioeconomic status tending toward high morale, whether their self-image was "positive" or "negative," and those of low socioeconomic status showing the opposite tendency. In general, similar relationships were observed for the variables "social isolation," "visiting with children," and "visiting with friends," with those of high status tending toward high morale, whether socially isolated or not, and regardless of the frequency (or absence) of visits with children and friends.[87]

These findings raise questions concerning the universality of factors previously assumed to indicate good adjustment. Although the married tended to have higher morale than the divorced, widowed, or single, this may vary by social class. In addition, greater income was associated with an increase in morale only among those who were employed. Among those retired, greater income was not associated with a rise in morale.

There is some evidence that a conception of self as "younger" is associated with more favorable adjustment.[88] Some have suggested that identification with a younger age tends to "insulate" the aged individual against

[85] Ernest W. Burgess, "Personality and Social Adjustment in Old Age," in *The Aged and Society*, p. 147.

[86] B. Kutner, D. Fanshel, Alice M. Togo, and T. S. Langner, *Five Hundred Over Sixty: A Community Survey on Aging* (New York: Russell Sage Foundation, 1956).

[87] This study, unlike previous ones, was based on an adequate sample of older persons, and the measure of morale avoided circular reasoning in the definition, as the indices employed in the measurement of morale were independent of the attributes included in its definition.

[88] Kuhlen, "Aging and Life Adjustment," in Birren, *op. cit.*, p. 890; Burgess, "Personality and Social Adjustment in Old Age," *loc. cit.*, p. 147; and Zena Smith Blau, "Changes in Status and Age Identification," *American Sociological Review*, 21:198–203 (April, 1956).

the impact of role transition.[89] There is evidence, however, that self-conception is conditioned by situational or social factors. Blau found, for example, that socially isolated aged persons tended to regard themselves as "old" more readily than did those aged persons who were not socially isolated. Aged persons who participated in friendship cliques tended to conceive of themselves as more youthful than did nonparticipants.[90]

Many studies suggest that retirement entails greater adjustment problems for men than for women.[91] However, as one writer notes, "evidence is not consistent as to which sex is generally happier and better adjusted in old age." [92] Some data show that widowhood may pose especially difficult adjustment problems for women, but not for men.

These findings concerning sex differences in the response to circumstances associated with aging raise many significant questions which bear on the problem of *role change*. It is possible that, for either sex, an event or circumstance will not complicate adjustment to aging unless it deprives the individual of his primary role: that role which serves as an anchor of self-identity, status, and is the pivot of an entire "way of life." It may be that for most men in our society, work, or making a living, constitutes a primary role, whereas for women generally, being a wife has similar value.

When we consider each sex separately, however, we find that retirement or widowhood has a different impact, depending upon social class. For example, it was shown that widowhood has more consistent *adverse* affects on friendship participation among lower-class women than among middle- and upper-class women.[93] This is due, apparently, to the fact that the latter have developed social ties independent of their husbands prior to widowhood. Thus, by drawing upon these resources, the upper- and middle-class women are more readily able to find significant substitute roles following widowhood. This again seems to emphasize that the impact of the change of roles associated with aging will be eased if there are available satisfying substitute roles for which there has been some previous preparation.

Summary

The aged are in a deviant position in contemporary American society. As a group, the aged in modern urban society are deprived of former tradi-

[89] Kuhlen, in Birren, *op. cit.*

[90] Blau, "Changes in Status and Age Identification," *loc. cit.*

[91] Kutner *et al., op. cit.;* Blau, "Social Constraints on Friendship in Old Age," *loc. cit.;* Steiner and Dorfman, *op. cit.,* pp. 148–152.

[92] Kuhlen in Birren, *op. cit.,* p. 890.

[93] Blau, "Structural Constraints on Friendships in Old Age," *loc. cit.,* p. 439. The greater tendency of middle- and upper-class women to foster associations was also pointed out in Robert L. Havighurst and Ruth Albrecht, *Older People* (New York: David McKay Company, 1953).

tional roles and statuses. They are poorly integrated into the social structure. The shift to the ambiguous role and lowered status of old age is the result of social change during the past few decades. Our society has no series of "role gradations" which precede the aged role, thus serving to prepare the aged individual to assume his new role and status. This situation differs from that of older people in folk and rural societies, where the aged have generally occupied well-defined roles associated with high statuses.

The number and proportion of old people in Western European society have greatly increased over the past hundred years. During that period the proportion of those over sixty in the United States has grown, largely because of technical advances which have increased the food supply and have improved the nation's health. Infant mortality and childhood diseases have declined, thus increasing life expectancy. There are indications that recent improvements in medicine will also be reflected in an increase in life expectancy among older persons. The decline in the birth rate has also contributed to the proportion of older persons, and in some societies a large number of immigrants has tended to age the population.

Although physiological and psychological changes occur in old age, these changes in themselves do not account for the position or the behavior of aged persons. Old age is a sociological phenomenon which reflects the manner in which the social roles of the aged are defined, the amount of compatibility in these roles, the degree of preparation for assuming the roles, and the consistency with which other persons allow these roles to be played.

Selected Readings

BIRREN, JAMES E., ed. *Handbook of Aging and The Individual: Psychological and Biological Aspects.* Chicago: The University of Chicago Press, 1959. A collection of articles dealing with physiological changes associated with age and suggestions for their possible effects on the social and psychological adjustment of the aged.

BURGESS, ERNEST W., ed. *Aging in Western Societies: A Survey of Social Gerontology.* Chicago: The University of Chicago Press, 1960. Reviews the trends in the phenomenon of aging in a number of Western European countries and Great Britain. Offers a wider perspective and basis of comparison of aging in the United States. Includes articles by leading authorities on social gerontology.

CAVAN, RUTH S., ERNEST W. BURGESS, ROBERT J. HAVIGHURST, and HERBERT GOLDHAMER. *Personal Adjustment in Old Age.* Chicago: Science Research Associates, Inc., 1949. One of the first sociological studies of the aged. There are extensive case materials.

FRIEDMANN, EUGENE A., and ROBERT J. HAVIGHURST. *The Meaning of Work and Retirement.* Chicago: The University of Chicago Press, 1954. A study of adjustment to retirement in a number of different occupations.

KAPLAN, OSCAR J., ed. *Mental Disorders in Later Life.* Revised edition. Stanford University, Calif.: Stanford University Press, 1956. A collection of articles by scholars from medical and social science fields, reviewing present research on the problems of mental illness among the aged, and suggesting important problems for future research.

POLLAK, OTTO. *Social Adjustment in Old Age.* New York: Social Science Research Council, Bulletin 59, 1948. A comprehensive analysis of the definitions of old age and of the psychological and sociological aspects of aging.

SHOCK, NATHAN W. *Trends in Gerontology.* Stanford University, Calif.: Stanford University Press, 1951, 1957. This book is a series of articles dealing with a number of aspects of aging.

SIMMONS, LEO W. *The Role of the Aged in Primitive Societies.* New Haven, Conn.: Yale University Press, 1945. A study of the social position of aged persons in a large number of folk societies. In nearly every society they were found to have an important position.

TIBBITTS, CLARK, ed. *Handbook of Social Gerontology: Societal Aspects of Aging.* Chicago: The University of Chicago Press, 1960. A series of articles dealing with research on the phenomenon of aging as it relates to the changes in roles and status occurring with age, and the effect of these on behavior and adjustment.

Chapter
17

Minority Groups

Human rights have been a matter of debate for centuries, but it was not until a historic session of the General Assembly of the United Nations in 1948 that there has been anything like a universal declaration of these rights. On December 10 of that year the General Assembly adopted thirty articles setting them forth in some detail. This declaration stated: "All human beings are born free and equal in dignity and rights" and "Everyone has rights without distinction of race, color, sex, language, religion, political or other opinions, national or social origin, property, birth or other status." Among the rights to which all persons are entitled are the following:

1. "Life, liberty and security of person"
2. Equal treatment before the law
3. Opportunity to take part in the government, directly or through freely chosen representatives who are elected by universal and equal suffrage
4. Opportunity to work, equal pay for equal work, and an adequate standard of living
5. Freedom of thought, conscience, and religion
6. Participation in the cultural life of the country [1]

Admittedly these are general statements which do not apply to all citizens in many countries today. On the other hand, they are statements which come as close as any to being universal norms of rights. For that reason they serve as a vantage point from which to examine "The American Creed."

The American Creed

A classic study of the American Negro has been aptly titled *An American Dilemma,* the dilemma being the contradiction between the American creed of democratic values and the actual treatment of the Negro.[2] The

---

[1] United Nations Department of Public Information, *These Rights and Freedoms* (New York: United Nations, 1950), pp. 170–176.

[2] Gunnar Myrdal, *An American Dilemma* (New York: Harper & Row, Publishers, 1944).

American Creed gives expression to certain humanitarian ideologies and includes these fundamental beliefs, which apply regardless of race, creed, ethnic background, or any hereditary status: (1) the right of political equality, (2) the right of due process of law and of equal justice before the law, (3) freedom of opportunity to achieve economic and political success, and (4) the right to express one's religious beliefs.

These beliefs permeate the American social scene, regardless of social class or geographic location. They are found expressed in such venerated documents as the Declaration of Independence, the Constitution, and the Bill of Rights, and, more explicitly, in countless Supreme Court decisions. The Creed is taught in schools and churches, and is regarded as a basic guiding principle by the Boy Scouts and the Girl Scouts of America, the YWCA and the YMCA, and many other similar organizations. It is symbolized in such national songs as "America," in the Statue of Liberty, and in countless stories, books, and plays dealing with the oppressed who sought freedom in America. Even those groups who experience discrimination believe in our American Creed, for, as Myrdal has written, "They, like the whites, are under the spell of the great national suggestion. With one part of themselves they actually believe, as do the whites, that the Creed is ruling America." [3]

SOURCES OF THE AMERICAN CREED

The American Creed appears to have been derived from a number of sources, including the Philosophy of the Enlightenment, Christianity, English law, capitalism, and the nature of American nationalism itself. The so-called Philosophy of the Enlightenment, with its emphasis on the sacredness of the individual, came out of the English, American, and French revolutions and the writings primarily of Locke, Rousseau, and Voltaire. These beliefs were probably best expressed by Thomas Jefferson in this country. Such philosophical and political writings from earliest times have been important factors in the development of this basic heritage. Another and somewhat similar source of the American Creed has been the tradition of justice contained in English law, upon which the law of this country is based. These traditional beliefs in statutory enactments, fair trial, due process of law, and judicial interpretations expressive of humanitarian principles have time and again met conflict in such behavior as lynchings and the third degree.

Individual opportunity for economic success, regardless of race, creed, ethnic origin, or class position, is the cardinal principle of capitalism, success being presumed to be based on individual initiative, hard work, and private savings. Nothing in the capitalist ideology implies that success

---

[3] *Ibid.*, p. 4.

shall go, largely, to American citizens of the white race. Christianity, another source of these values, emphasizes the brotherhood of man and the essential dignity of the individual. Although in practice "brotherhood" frequently means one's own religion, from a strictly Christian point of view it includes Jew and Christian, Protestant and Catholic, and all races, regardless of the color of their skin.

Finally, American nationalism probably emphasizes the diversity of its people more than do most other countries, where common cultural or religious ideals, tribal separativeness, or military history is more often stressed. Many historians have pointed out that Americans have generally stressed their racial and ethnic diversity and have been proud of their nation's being a refuge for those discriminated against in other countries. In fact, the diversity of the American people is probably their most important distinguishing characteristic. Regardless of their skin color, religious heritage, or ethnic background, all Americans believe that America is made up of people drawn from the ends of the earth and that there is true equality for all. A Negro leader has put it this way: "Every man in the street, white, black, red or yellow, knows that this is 'the land of the free,' the 'land of opportunity,' and 'cradle of liberty,' the 'home of democracy,' that the American flag symbolizes the 'equality of all men' and guarantees to us all 'the protection of life, liberty and property,' freedom of speech, freedom of religion and racial tolerance." [4]

DISCRIMINATION AND THE REINTERPRETATION OF
THE AMERICAN CREED

Along with the American Creed there has always existed another series of social norms and values which have reflected racial ideas and the superiority of certain groups over others.[5] Consequently, these two series of norms and values have existed simultaneously, the American Creed generally permitting some degree of discrimination. The basic rights of minorities have been interpreted and modified according to circumstances; even slavery was at one time reconciled by many with this creed. This struggle between the American Creed and racism is strong in certain parts of the United States where racial doctrines are supported by state laws. The simultaneous presence of contradictory norms within the same person has resulted in a situation which has been described as follows: "Although many Southerners today will agree that segregation is wrong in principle, the vast majority still fiercely defends it as right in practice. A mass of state laws and city ordinances enforce it. But Southerners seem to know in their hearts that it is not really defensible, and that the tide of events is against

[4] Ralph Bunche, as quoted, *ibid.*, p. 4.
[5] Robin M. Williams, Jr., *American Society* (New York: Alfred A. Knopf, Inc., 1954), pp. 438–440.

it. The result is a war in the South's own soul which many Northerners, who see the South only as stubborn and narrow-minded, fail to understand." [6]

The American Creed cannot, therefore, be thought of as a stable system of norms, for, like the interpretations of the Constitution by the courts, the Creed has also undergone continuous interpretations. Not only have the "rights" of minority groups changed from one generation to another; within the population at a given time and in a given place there are pronounced differences of opinion as to what behavior on the part of a given minority should be approved or disapproved and still be in line with the Creed. Some of the conflict between the older and newer generations represents an outgrowth of these systems of differential norms.

This frame of reference has been termed the "race relations cycle." [7] In this cycle successive stages of social interaction take place between subordinate and superordinate groups, and in each of them a series of temporary balances is established to avoid conflict. These levels become disturbed by new norms, and further new levels of adjustment arise among groups. More specifically, the parts of the race relations cycle are referred to as *conflict,* or the awareness of mutually exclusive ends; *accommodation,* or the establishment of a working arrangement in which reciprocal relations based on higher and lower status are accepted; and, as a final goal, *assimilation,* or the disappearance of accommodation and the establishment of an unconscious process of consensus or common norms. These processes are occurring simultaneously at various levels during the continuous process of conflict and redefinitions in a variety of areas. The following discussion will present, more or less specifically, the former conception of the American Creed at the outbreak of World War II, the new emerging definition, and possible future interpretations. [8] These statements should be regarded as only general comparisons.

Former Interpretation of the American Creed. For some time before the outbreak of World War II most Americans of the majority group, as well as many of the minorities themselves, were in fairly general agreement about the following minimum "rights" and obligations of Americans in terms of the American Creed. Many of these rights were actually not in full agreement with the American Creed. Some of these limited rights, moreover, had been achieved after a long and arduous struggle.

---

[6] "The U.S. Negro, 1953," *Time,* 61:55 (May 11, 1953).

[7] Robert E. Park, *Race and Culture* (New York: The Free Press of Glencoe, 1950), pp. 149–151. Also see Brewton Berry, *Race and Ethnic Relations* (2d ed.; Boston: Houghton Mifflin Company, 1958).

[8] Negroes, mainly from the West Indies, have come in considerable numbers to Great Britain since 1942. There have been conflict and some accommodation, processes which have been analyzed by Anthony H. Richmond in *Colour Prejudice in Britain* (London: Routledge and Kegan Paul, Ltd., 1954).

1. Approval of segregated but "equal" education and other facilities as being in line with the American way of life.
2. The right to a job, an unskilled or semiskilled one at the least, with adequate relief if no jobs are available.
3. The right to vote, except in certain areas of the South.
4. Some elementary school education for every American, including members of the lowest minority group.
5. Decent health standards for all minority groups and the reduction of their high infant mortality rate and the incidence of such diseases as tuberculosis.
6. The elimination of substandard housing, the agency not agreed upon.
7. Condemnation of lynching and the protection of minorities from such un-American practices.

Emerging "Rights." The issues involved in granting full "rights" to minorities are now on a higher status level and many are of a different character from those accepted before World War II:

1. The elimination of the concept of "separate but equal" in education and in public facilities of an interstate nature.
2. The right to vote even in most of the South; the right to full participation in public housing facilities, public recreational facilities, and professional athletics such as baseball, and in the armed forces.
3. The right to higher jobs, such as those of foremen and junior executive positions, as in personnel work.
4. Elimination of discriminatory provisions in union membership and in employment.
5. The right to membership in professional groups.
6. The right to social participation in fraternities, sororities, and general club organizations in most parts of the country.

Future "Rights." Most people today would probably say that once conflict over the foregoing rights has been resolved, minority problems will have reached a stage of permanent accommodation. On the contrary, in terms of the American Creed, other issues involving new norms and values can be expected to arise. Some of these future "rights" include the elimination of segregation in municipal facilities within a state, full political equality, attainment of important positions in business and finance, and election or appointment to positions of leadership in professional and other formal organizations:

1. The elimination of all forms of segregation including intrastate and municipal public facilities and in living areas.[9]

---

[9] The elimination of segregation presents a problem for the Negro business and professional classes whose short-term status is based on being Negro businessmen, doctors, lawyers, teachers, or ministers. Negro enterprises, separate Negro churches, and higher status among the Negro group are endangered by the elimination of segregation.— E. Franklin Frazier, "Human, All Too Human," *Survey Graphic*, 36:75, 99–100 (January, 1947).

2. Full political equality in terms of both the appointment and the election of minority group members to high positions. This far transcends merely the granting of full suffrage. It would mean the election of qualified Negroes, American Orientals, Spanish-speaking Americans, Indians, and others to municipal, state, and national offices and the possibility of minority group members becoming governors, senators, cabinet members, Supreme Court members, Vice-President, or even President.

3. Right to position of high status in business and finance either as officers or as members of boards of directors. In America such a strategic position in the economy would bring with it important power considerations.

4. Position of leadership and not merely membership in professional and other formal organizations.

These trends merely represent a reinterpretation of rights or norms, new conflicts, and new accommodations. They do not constitute the final goal of the social and cultural process, which is the elimination of superordination and subordination. In such a situation social relations, as well as political and economic activities, are conducted largely without regard to racial, ethnic, or religious status. In the earlier history of the United States certain groups, such as the Germans, and later to a large extent the Irish, were discriminated against. These groups have now largely reached a state of assimilation. In Brazil the Negro, once a slave, has now reached a stage where he is identified largely as a Brazilian and not commonly as a Negro Brazilian.[10] A great deal of assimilation has taken place in the so-called racial laboratory, Hawaii.[11] Here live over half a million persons of diverse ethnic and racial groups—203,455 Japanese, 69,070 Filipinos, 38,197 Chinese, 4943 Negroes, 472 Indians, and 114, 405 "others," including Hawaiians. There are 202,230 white persons, and 430,542 nonwhites.[12] These people of Hawaii, who are even more racially mixed than the figures would indicate, live in a situation, even if not perfect, of harmony. Schoolteachers and principals are of all races. There are no racial restrictions in accommodations or employment. Hawaii in 1961 had an

[10] Donald Pierson, *Negroes in Brazil* (Chicago: The University of Chicago Press, 1942). A later study has challenged some of Pierson's findings. See Roger Bastide and Pierre Van Den Berghe, "Stereotypes, Norms and Interracial Behavior in São Paulo, Brazil," *American Sociological Review*, 22:689–694 (December, 1957).

[11] Andrew W. Lind, *Island Community: A Study of Ecological Succession in Hawaii* (Chicago: The University of Chicago Press, 1938). These nearly harmonious race relations, almost unique under the American flag, are the result of a long history of amicable race relations going back to the days before 1898 when Hawaii was a united self-governing stopover on voyages across the Pacific. Formerly Hawaii, as an independent nation with a cultural pattern of harmonious relationships between races, was in a position to require white persons who desired to trade or live there to accede to a pattern of respect and nearly equal treatment. Subsequently, the introduction of many racial groups resulted in a blending of cultures and in racial hybrids which served to perpetuate the original situation of race contacts.

[12] United States Bureau of the Census, *General Population Characteristics* (March 30, 1961), Bulletin PC (A2)–13.

elected Caucasian governor, both a Chinese and a Caucasian senator, and a Japanese congressman.

Segregation and the American Creed. Since to a minority group, the forced segregation of one group from another is probably one of the most important discriminations, the changing definition of segregation necessitates detailed discussion. Before 1941 there was consensus among the majority groups, as expressed through the Supreme Court, that, in general, segregation, at least for the Negro and similar groups, was in line with the American Creed. In pre–Civil War days the southern churches sanctioned segregation in the form of slavery, even citing Biblical passages in support of this practice. In the famous Dred Scott decision of 1857 the Supreme Court decided that Negroes were property, not citizens, and if freed they had no rights. Although segregation has a long history dating from the Negro freedmen group, it did not appear in the form of a real separation of the races until the 1890's and in the decades to follow, when more and more laws separating the races were enacted. Many of the laws relating to segregation, such as taxis and sports, were actually enacted much later. A city ordinance requiring Jim Crow taxis, for example, was adopted by Atlanta in 1940. After surveying the laws of segregation Woodward has concluded that most laws of segregation are neither as old nor as "natural" as some think. Racism as a legislative doctrine, to secure legal white supremacy and power, distinct from the inferior social position of Negroes, is much more recent.

> In a time when the Negroes formed a much larger proportion of the population than they did later, when slavery was a live memory in the minds of both races, and when the memory of the hardships and bitterness of Reconstruction was still fresh, the race policies accepted and pursued in the South were sometimes milder than they became later. The policies of proscription, segregation, and disfranchisement that are often described as the immutable "folkways" of the South, impervious alike to legislative reform and armed intervention, are of a more recent origin. The effort to justify them as a consequence of Reconstruction and a necessity of the times is embarrassed by the fact that they did not originate in those times. And the belief that they are immutable and unchangeable is not supported by history.[13]

Segregation in schools was maintained until recent years, sometimes unofficially, in communities in many northern and border states such as Illinois, Indiana, Missouri, Delaware, and West Virginia. Kansas did not completely abolish segregation until 1952. The Supreme Court had affirmed the belief that separate facilities constituted no violation of the American Creed, and in 1896 the Court, in a case involving segregation in transportation, stated: "We think the enforced separation of the races, as applied to the internal commerce of the state, neither abridges the immu-

---

[13] C. Vann Woodward, *The Strange Career of Jim Crow* (New York: Oxford University Press, 1957), p. 47.

nities of the colored man, nor denies him the equal protection of the laws, within the meaning of the 14th amendment." [14] Segregation was not a badge of servitude nor did it mean the inequality of races. Public education and transportation were "social" rights and not rights of citizenship and, therefore, could be segregated. Such segregated facilities, however, must be "equal."

The belief of the Court in segregation as "right" and "natural" in terms of the American Creed is clearly indicated by this statement: "Legislation is powerless to eradicate racial instincts or to abolish distinctions based on physical differences." This 1896 decision did indicate, however, that there were some unreasonable limits to segregation. A city, for example, could not require white persons to walk on one side of the street and Negroes on another.

The Supreme Court redefined this interpretation in 1914, stating that these segregated facilities in interstate commerce must be "equal," as in the case of railroad coach travel. This belief in segregation but equality was approved by many, but by no means all, of the leaders of minority groups, such as Booker T. Washington. How "equality" was to be maintained in various services, living accommodations, and social interaction was not clearly stated.

An example of some of these controversial issues was the question of higher education. In 1938 the Supreme Court ordered the state of Missouri to provide Lloyd Gaines, a Negro, with an education in law which would be substantially equal to that given white students.[15] In similar cases brought before the Court the ruling had favored "segregated but equal" facilities. Since few southern states provided graduate or professional training for Negroes, this redefinition of legal rights was extremely important.

In 1948 the Supreme Court ruled that if states did not provide equal separate facilities they must admit Negro students to white schools. In a desperate effort to avoid this step, some states set up makeshift separate facilities, and other southern states attempted to set up regional graduate schools to which Negroes from various southern states would be sent under a system of joint state expense. Others decided to admit a few Negro graduate students, but with various barriers to full participation. In Oklahoma,

---

[14] Plessy v. Ferguson, Supreme Court of the United States, 1896, 163 U.S. 537, 41 L. Ed. 256, 16 S. Ct. 1138. The only dissent from this decision was that of Justice Harlan, who maintained that "our Constitution is color-blind and neither knows nor tolerates classes among citizens." He also felt that segregation would create distrust and misunderstanding between the races. For a detailed discussion of the various Supreme Court decisions on segregation as well as the actual court decisions see Herbert Hill and Jack Greenberg, *Citizens' Guide to De-Segregation* (Boston: The Beacon Press, 1955) and Benjamin Munn Ziegler editor, *Desegregation and the Supreme Court* (Boston: D. C. Heath & Company, 1958). Also see Jack Greenberg, *Race Relations and American Law* (New York: Columbia University Press, 1959).

[15] Missouri ex rel. Gaines v. Canada, Supreme Court of the United States, 1938, 305 U.S. 337, 83 L. Ed. 208, 59 S. Ct. 232.

for example, one Negro graduate student was seated in an anteroom off the main classroom, and later in the same school had a small railing erected around his desk as a way of meeting the legal requirement of segregation. This was the situation existing in 1950, when the Supreme Court made a drastic redefinition of American rights.

The elimination of the concept of "separate but equal" facilities is probably one of the most important recent developments in race relations in the United States. Not only has actual "equality" been challenged as a fiction, but the maintenance of two types of facilities is thought to indicate second-class citizenship and to be harmful to the full dignity of the individual's personality. This is well illustrated in interstate travel. Before 1941 Negroes often had to ride in chair cars on trains because it was impossible to furnish separate Pullman cars for them. In a 1941 Supreme Court decision interstate railroads were ordered to provide first-class rail travel for everyone, which meant the admittance of Negroes to Pullman cars. A 1946 decision ordered segregation eliminated on buses in interstate travel. An important symbolic barrier was removed from interstate rail travel in 1950, for then dining cars no longer could require the segregated seating of Negroes and whites at opposite ends of a dining car or utilize a curtain to screen one race from another.

The barrier of "partial equality" of higher education was also torn down by the Supreme Court in 1950. The Court unanimously agreed in the McLaurin and Sweatt cases that the universities of Oklahoma and Texas must accept graduate students on the same basis as whites.[16] In the Oklahoma case a Negro graduate student named McLaurin was segregated in seating and eating arrangements from the white students, and the Court ruled that this denied him equal protection before the law and that he must be admitted under the same conditions of participation as white students. The Supreme Court stated that the setting apart of a student impairs and inhibits "his ability to study, to engage in discussions, and to exchange views with other students."

Previously the Court had implied that a makeshift separate law facility provided by Texas in downtown Austin was suitable, but now it argued not only that this segregation was contrary to the rights of an American citizen but also that "equality" was an impossible fiction. In regard to Sweatt's petition to enter the University of Texas Law School rather than the separate Negro school the Supreme Court said:

> What is more important, the University of Texas Law School possesses to a far greater degree those qualities which are incapable of objective measurement but which make for greatness in a law school. Such qualities, to name but a few, include reputation of the faculty, experience of the administration,

[16] McLaurin v. Oklahoma State Regents, Supreme Court of the United States, 1950, 339 U.S. 637, 94 L. Ed. 1149, 70 S. Ct. 851. Also Sweatt v. Painter, Supreme Court of the United States, 1950, 339 U.S. 629, 94 L. Ed. 1114, 70 S. Ct. 848.

position and influence of the alumni, standing in the community, tradition and prestige.

The Supreme Court also felt that Sweatt, as a practicing lawyer, could not function in a setting in which most Texas lawyers were not the products of a segregated school.

> This law school to which Texas is willing to admit petitioner excludes from its student body members of the racial groups which number 85% of the population of the state and exclude most of the lawyers, witnesses, jurors, judges, and other officials with whom petitioner will inevitably be dealing when he becomes a member of the Texas Bar. With such a substantial and significant segment of society excluded, we cannot conclude that the education offered petitioner is substantially equal to that which he would receive if admitted to the University of Texas Law School.

Few Supreme Court decisions have been more drastic than that of May 17, 1954, which stated that segregation in public schools is unconstitutional. The decision affected about 48 million persons, including some 10 million Negroes. It was a culmination of the series of previous decisions on higher education, but in its philosophy and effect was far more drastic than any one of them. In a unanimous decision the Court repudiated completely the "separate but equal" doctrine. The decision took into account the changes in the importance of education and the findings of psychological studies of children made since 1896. All children, to succeed, must have opportunities for equal education, and segregated but equal physical facilities are not "equal" in actuality.

> Education is perhaps the most important function of state and local governments. . . . It is the very foundation of good citizenship. . . . In these days, it is doubtful that any child may reasonably be expected to succeed in life if he is denied the opportunity of an education.
> To separate them [Negro children] from others of similar age and qualifications solely because of their race generates a feeling of inferiority as to their status in the community that may affect their hearts and minds in a way unlikely ever to be undone. . . . Separate educational facilities are inherently unequal.[17]

In 1955 the Supreme Court included recreation as a right of all citizens, ordering the end to segregation in public parks, playgrounds, and golf courses.[18] Each year since then additional desegregation decisions by the Supreme Court and other federal agencies, such as the Interstate Commerce Commission, have affected other facilities, such as bus travel and waiting rooms. In 1962 the Supreme Court ruled that *all* racial segregation in transportation facilities was unconstitutional. In the decision the Supreme Court said: "We have settled beyond question that no state may

---

[17] 347 U.S. 483.   [18] 350 U.S. 879.

require racial segregation in inter-state or intra-state facilities. The question is no longer open: it is foreclosed as a litigable issue."

Many forces operating in our society today have brought about some basic changes in American life leading to desegregation, particularly in the field of education. These forces include the increasing urbanization and industralization of the South, which make the maintenance of many forms of segregation difficult. The cost of maintaining separate school systems, theaters, and other facilities, for example, is becoming too difficult a financial burden. Desegregation in the Armed Forces, which took place after the Korean War, has had much effect upon the South, where there are a large number of military installations on which both Negro and white military and civilian personnel work and live without segregation. The policy of the industrial type of labor union to incorporate members of both races in the South is affecting many social relationships formerly based on segregation. The integration of the schools will, in the long run, as the present-day generation grows up, affect other forms of segregation. The insularity of the Deep South has been broken by the more rapid desegregation in the border states, the mobility of Southerners and Northerners, and such media as television, on which Southerners see, for example, Negroes participating in sports and political life. Finally, the whole picture of segregation is one which increasingly has been recognized as affecting adversely the international relations of the United States. Incidents like this have hurt the appeal of American democracy, particularly in Asia, Africa, and parts of South America:

> A Hindu dance team canceled an appearance at Centenary College here [Shreveport, La.] today after a spokesman said that two nearby restaurants had refused to serve two dark-skinned members of the troupe. Tom Burrows, manager of the troupe, Indrani and her Hindu Dancers, said that the Indian embassy was studying whether the entire Southern tour should be canceled. . . . Mr. Burrows said that the group had previously been refused service in Charlotte, N.C. To avoid an incident in Bossier City, the troupe explained at two restaurants that two of the musicians were "dark-skinned." . . . The dance team appeared before President and Mrs. Kennedy earlier in its tour. The tour is supported and encouraged by the State Department.[19]

The Concept of a Minority Group

A minority group is simply a group of people who, because of their racial, ethnic, or religious origin, are discriminated against, are given lower status, and thus in a sense are "second-class citizens." Louis Wirth has defined a minority as a "group of people who, because of their physical or cultural characteristics, are singled out from the others in the society in

---

[19] *The New York Times*, November 21, 1961, p. 32 C.

which they live for differential and unequal treatment, and who therefore regard themselves as objects of collective discrimination." [20]

More specifically, a minority group situation is characterized by (1) discrimination against a certain *group* of people; (2) the clash of this discriminatory treatment of the minority group with other norms and values in the culture, such as the American Creed, which would tend to give the groups equal status; (3) the recognition of this treatment as discriminatory by both minority and majority groups; and (4) an organized effort by the minority group to remove the discrimination.

As used here, a minority group should not be confused with a colonial problem, a separate cultural minority, or simply any group which is numerically in the minority. Although the native group in a colonial society may occupy a more or less inferior status, these "natives" are usually regarded as distinctly different from the ruling citizens. A separate status system exists for each. The American Indian of fifty years ago constituted a colonial problem rather than a minority problem. Within the past twenty-five years the 6 million natives of South Africa have been rapidly becoming transformed into a group which aspires to equal treatment instead of being segregated by the 2 million European whites of the dominant group.

In other parts of the world certain cultural groups may be referred to as minority groups, because they have often been denied opportunities to maintain a separate culture, to preserve their own language, and to exercise a degree of political autonomy.[21] Minorities of this type, however, may actually not even desire to have equal status within the larger society. The Negro in the United States well illustrates the fact that a minority is not the same as a distinct cultural group. Most authorities agree that among American Negroes there are practically no vestiges of African culture,[22] and that they desire to be Western Europeans as much as do members of the white population.

A minority group cannot necessarily be regarded as smaller in number than the majority. In many counties of the South the Negro population greatly exceeds the white population. (See Figure 5.) Nearly 1 million Negroes live in Mississippi, or about one in every fifteen Negroes in the United States. Although the Negroes in Mississippi represent about 42 percent of the population of the state, most of the western counties along the Mississippi River or in the Delta country have Negro populations generally outnumbering the white populations, in some instances as much as four to one. The Spanish-speaking population of the Southwest, which for a

---

[20] Louis Wirth, "The Problems of Minority Groups," in Ralph Linton ed., *The Science of Man in the World Crisis* (New York: Columbia University Press, 1945), p. 347.

[21] United Nations Commission on Human Rights, *Definition and Classification of Minorities* (New York: 1950), pp. 2–3.

[22] A different point of view has been taken by Melville J. Herskovits, *The Myth of the Negro Past* (Boston: The Beacon Press, 1958).

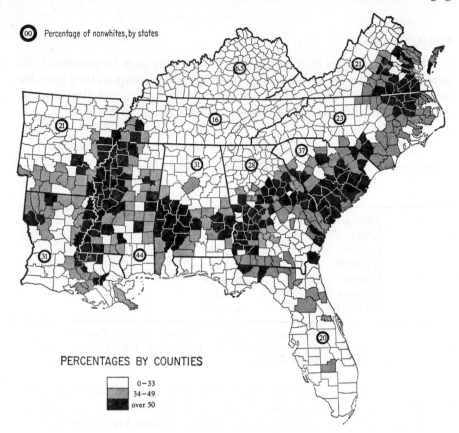

FIGURE 5.—*Percentage of Nonwhite Population in Counties of Southern States*

SOURCE: Adapted from "Next Steps in the South: Answers to Current Questions," *New South,* Vol. II, Nos. 7, 8 (July–August, 1956). Used by permission of the Southern Regional Council, Inc.

century had a status generally inferior to that of the so-called Anglos, was until recently the larger group, and still is in many communities.

Minorities in the United States

The United States has been called a "nation of nations." [23] It should more aptly be called a nation of races, nations, and religions. The heterogeneity of the population is so great that it is difficult to think of a stereotyped "typical American." Minority groups in the United States may be divided into three types, with primary emphasis on race, ethnic background, or religion.

[23] Louis Adamic, *A Nation of Nations* (New York: Harper & Row, Publishers, 1944).

RACIAL MINORITIES

Racial minorities in America represent slightly over 10 percent of the population. Negroes constitute the largest minority group, as they have for over a century, followed by the Indian, the Japanese, and the Chinese. Table 17.1 shows the racial minorities as they were in 1960.

Table 17.1. Racial Minorities in the United States, 1960

	Number	Percent of total population
Total population	179,323,175	100.00
Negro	18,871,443	10.5
Indian	523,591	0.29
Japanese	464,332	0.26
Chinese	237,292	0.13
Filipino	176,310	0.098
All other	218,087	0.12

SOURCE: United States Census of Population, 1960, *General Population Characteristics,* United States Summary, Final Report PC (1)-1B (Washington, D.C.: Government Printing Office, 1961) pp. 1–144 and Table 44.

The American Negro. The "Negro" is more of a cultural than a biological concept. He cannot always be physically identified, for in American society, in the North as well as in the South, persons known to have *any* Negro ancestry, no matter how small, are considered to be Negroes. United States census enumerators, for example, are given the arbitrary instruction that persons of mixed white and Negro "blood" should be classified as Negroes regardless of the proportion of Negro "blood." In some southern states this distinction has sometimes raised complicated legal questions. In those states where the question has been raised the courts have not been unanimous as to the proportion of Negro "blood" a person must have to be classified as a Negro.[24] In Virginia, for example, a person is considered a Negro for legal purposes if he is one sixteenth Negro, even though he is fifteen sixteenths white.

This cultural norm can be contrasted with that of Brazil, where there are also millions of Negroes but where status is not based to any extent on color. Whereas in the United States one drop of known Negro "blood" makes a person a Negro, many Brazilians whose grandmothers were Negroes of pure African descent are listed in the census as white and are so

[24] Charles S. Mangum, *The Legal Status of the Negro* (Chapel Hill: University of North Carolina Press, 1940), p. 1.

considered by others.[25] Thus many individuals are considered as white who have definitely Negroid physical features. Cultural norms define the Negro differently in the United States and in Brazil.

Beginning with the twenty Negroes who were first sold at Jamestown in 1619, the American Negro population has increased enormously as a result of natural increase and slave trade. Today there are 18,871,443 Negroes; or one in every ten Americans is a Negro. About one of every five Southerners is a Negro, whereas only one in twenty of the population in the Northeastern and North Central states and only one in thirty-three in the West are Negroes. (See Table 17.4.) The distribution of the Negro population in states with the largest percentage is shown in Table 17.2. In 1960,

Table 17.2. Number and Percentage of Nonwhite Population in Some Southern States and the District of Columbia, 1960

State	Number nonwhite	Percentage of total population
District of Columbia	418,693	54.8
Mississippi	920,595	42.3
South Carolina	831,572	34.9
Louisiana	1,045,307	32.1
Alabama	983,131	30.1
Georgia	1,125,893	28.6
North Carolina	1,156,870	25.4
Arkansas	390,569	21.9
Virginia	824,506	20.8

SOURCE: United States Census of Population, 1960, *General Population Characteristics*, pp. 1–164 and Table 56.

54.8 percent of the population of the District of Columbia was nonwhite, 42.3 percent of the population of Mississippi was nonwhite, as was 34.9 percent of South Carolina.

Although the Negro population has steadily increased, it has declined in proportion to the total population. The highest proportion of Negroes to whites occurred in the first census of 1790, when there were 757,000 Negroes, or 19.3 percent. The Negro population of the South has continued to decline, while that of the North and the Far West has increased. As late as 1910 almost 90 percent of the Negro population lived in the South, but during World War I the "Great Migration" of southern Negroes to the larger northern cities began. Manpower demands had increased in the North, as a result of war production, and at the same time immigration

[25] Donald Pierson, *Negroes in Brazil* (Chicago: The University of Chicago Press, 1942), pp. 127–128.

from other countries had decreased to almost nothing. The needed labor supply came, therefore, chiefly from southern Negroes.

The high prosperity of the 1920's continued this northward movement to the cities, and although the depression of the 1930's temporarily reduced it, World War II brought about a great increase in migration not only to the North but to the West and the industrial cities of the South. By 1940 the Negro population residing in the South had declined to 77 percent of the total Negro population; after the extensive population movements of World War II it continued to decline, reaching 59.9 percent in 1960. At that time nearly all the 6,474,536 Negroes in the North, and the 1,085,688 Negroes in the West, resided in large cities. Harlem, the largest Negro city in the world, has around a million people, and the so-called Black Belt of Chicago has over half a million in population. (See Table 17.3 for the nonwhite populations of the large cities of the United States.)

Table 17.3. Number and Percent of Nonwhite Population in Selected Large Cities, 1960

City a	Total Population a	Number nonwhite	Percentage nonwhite of total population
New York City	7,781,984	1,143,952	14.7
Chicago	3,550,404	837,895	23.6
Philadelphia	2,002,512	534,671	26.7
Detroit	1,670,144	487,682	29.2
Washington, D.C.	763,956	418,648	54.8
Los Angeles	2,479,015	416,475	16.8
Baltimore	939,024	328,658	35.0
St. Louis	750,026	216,008	28.8
Birmingham	340,887	135,332	39.7

a Data above refer to the 1960 census definition of "urban places." Roughly speaking, the area included in this definition corresponds to the central city and excludes the urbanized but unincorporated areas surrounding or lying adjacent to the city limits.

SOURCE: United States Census of Population, 1960, *General Population Characteristics*, pp. 1–176 and Table 63.

The migration of the rural Negro to the cities has brought many problems. He finds barriers at every turn, and he is shunted into the most disreputable areas of the city where he often lives under crowded, unhygienic conditions. This urban physical and social situation in which the Negro migrant finds himself has resulted in extremely high rates of death, particularly from tuberculosis, and in high rates of such forms of deviant behavior as delinquency and crime.

Because of these difficult conditions the majority often tends to view the Negro as if they constituted a single class. Negroes are socially stratified, and class relations within the group are important as well as those

Table 17.4. Location of the Negro Population, by Region, 1790–1960

Year	North a		South		West	
	Number	Percent	Number	Percent	Number	Percent
1790	67,424	8.9	689,784	91.9	—	—
1860	340,240	7.7	4,097,111	92.2	4,479	0.1
1910	1,027,674	10.5	8,749,427	89.0	50,662	0.5
1940	2,790,293	21.7	9,904,619	77.0	170,706	1.3
1950	4,246,058	28.2	10,225,407	68.0	570,821	3.8
1960	6,474,536	34.3	11,311,607	59.9	1,085,688	5.8

a Includes Northeastern and North Central states.

SOURCE: Bureau of the Census, *Historical Statistics* (Washington, D.C.: U.S. Government Printing Office, 1949), and *Characteristics of the Population*, Pt. I., 1960 Census, *op. cit.*

between its members and the majority group. For example, social class among Negroes is important in predicting the behavior in a given race-relations situation. The institutions and other activities of the Negro community can be understood only when studied in relation to the Negro class structure. Lower-class, middle- and upper-class Negroes differ markedly not only in social characteristics but in behavior as well. For example, delinquency, criminal behavior, and sexual promiscuity are comparatively rare among middle-class Negroes. The Negro class system of northern cities has been thus described by Frazier:

THE LOWER CLASS

At the bottom of the class structure in the Negro community in the northern city is the lower class, which comprises about two-thirds of the Negro population. In the lower class are found the great body of unskilled workers who earn a precarious living and those who subsist on irregular employment and relief. In this class are many of the most recent migrants from the South, especially those who have little education or are illiterate. However, this class is set off from the middle class not merely because of occupation and low income or even illiteracy. The lower class is distinguished from the middle class because of certain forms of behavior which are associated with lower-class status.

The shiftlessness and irresponsibility of lower-class Negroes are due partly to their lack of education and partly to the lack of economic opportunity for the great masses of Negro men. Since emancipation the masses of Negro men have constantly been drawn from the southern plantations into a fluctuating labor market. Because of the uncertainty and seasonal nature of work in lumber and turpentine camps, many of them have become footloose wanderers. In the towns and smaller cities of the South, they have provided the cheap and casual labor which was needed. Their position in northern cities has scarcely been better except where there has been a demand for large numbers of unskilled workers. But usually the lower-class husband and father must share the economic burden with his wife, who often finds more secure employment in domestic service.

In the northern city the lower class tends to be concentrated in those areas where the Negro first gains a foothold in the city. In these areas the lower-class Negroes are crowded into tenements and dilapidated houses which are held for speculative purposes. In these deteriorated slum areas are found second-hand clothing stores, taverns, cheap movies, and the lighter industries. Moreover, these areas are characterized by the absence of what constitutes a real neighborhood. The public schools located in these areas not only reflect in their physical appearance the general deterioration but have scarcely any relation to the life of the residents. Even the church which plays such an important role in the life of the middle class is absent or is represented by the numerous "store front" churches. Consequently, the behavior of the lower class is free from the control of neighborhood influences and the control of other institutions.

The absence of neighborhood controls is associated with a general lack of participation in the institutions of the community. Various studies have shown that Negroes of lower-class status are not affiliated with many forms of organized activities. Even in their religious affiliations they tend to become associated with the "store front" churches and churches outside the regular denominations. In those churches they find escape from their poverty and frustrations in a highly emotionalized type of religious service. But such church affiliations have little influence on their morals and manners. The shiftlessness and lack of ambition which characterize lower-class behavior are generally associated with a lack of race pride. For the lower-class Negro, as opposed to the middle class, tends to accept the estimation which whites place upon the Negro's ability and racial characteristics.

There is an element among the lower class that is quiet and exhibits good manners in public. There are lower-class families that struggle to maintain stable and conventional family life. They may humbly accept the fact that they are poor in worldly goods as a part of God's plan but they believe that even the poor may live righteously. Or they may believe that by living honestly and justly and rearing their children properly, their children because of education will rise to a higher status.

THE MIDDLE CLASS

The emergence of a clearly defined middle class of any size and significance in the Negro community has coincided with the growing occupational differentiation of the population. Consequently, it is in the large urban communities of the North that a fairly large, well-defined middle class has appeared. In the northern city there is a large group of clerical workers, skilled industrial workers, responsible persons in the service occupations, and firemen, policemen, and other types of workers in protective service. There has thus come into existence a relatively large group of workers with a background of stable family life, a good elementary or high school education, and an income adequate to support a respectable way of living. Since the class structure in the Negro community is fluid, the upper layers of the middle class merge with the upper class, while the lower layers are hardly distinguishable from the lower class.

Because of their fairly secure and adequate incomes, Negroes of middle-class status are able to maintain what they regard as a desirable mode of life. This desirable mode of living includes, first, certain standards of home and family life. In the larger cities the middle class constantly struggles to escape from those neighborhoods inhabited by the lower class. This is often difficult because of rents and the restrictions upon the mobility of the Negro population. Nevertheless, the middle class endeavors to isolate itself from the environment of the lower class by moving into apartments occupied by people with similar standards. Since in middle-class families there is often a tradition of homeownership, which may have its roots in the South, Negroes of middle-class status endeavor to buy homes out of their savings. This ambition is generally thwarted because of the multiple dwellings in the large cities.

Even when Negroes of middle-class status cannot escape from an undesirable physical environment, they endeavor to maintain a stable and conventional family life. In the middle-class family, the husband and father assumes responsibility for the support of the family. He often takes pride in the fact that his wife does not have to aid in the support of the family. Both parents are usually interested in the welfare and future of their children. They are not simply interested in the physical welfare of their children but they want their children to conform to conventional moral standards. They want their children to avoid the behavior associated with lower-class status. Moreover, they want their children to take advantage of the educational opportunities which they themselves did not enjoy.

The stability of the middle-class family is often tied up with its affiliations with the institutions in the Negro community. The vast majority of Negroes of middle-class status are affiliated with the church. Although some of the more emancipated upper layers of the middle class may scoff at religion, they usually come from families which were closely identified with the church. But the religion of the middle class is different from that of the lower class. The middle class takes its religion seriously and believes that religion and morality are inseparable. At the same time Negroes of middle-class status believe that religious services should be decorous and that people should avoid the more extravagant forms of religious ecstasy. For the middle class the lodge also is an important form of associated activity. In the large cities the more secular Elks lodge becomes more attractive than the more sacred types of fraternal organizations. Likewise, for many of the middle-class families in the larger cities, affiliation with various social clubs where card playing and dancing are the chief forms of recreation represents a new outlook on life. But the middle class will seldom go in for "society," which is the prerogative of the upper class.

Just as the middle class looks down upon the ways of the lower class, it attempts to discover flaws in the behavior of the upper class. The flaws which it attempts to discover in the upper class are moral lapses. Perhaps the chief value of the middle class is respectability; and respectability in not only correct public behavior but moral conduct. The moral conduct and respectability of the middle class is bound up to some extent with its race consciousness. For the middle class is extremely race conscious. Failure to maintain respectability and moral conduct is a reflection upon the "race," i.e., the Negro. The race consciousness of the middle class is also tied up with the desire to rise in the world. Middle-class Negroes are ambitious for their children to get an education and rise in the Negro world. At the same time they are ambitious to prove the ability of Negroes to rise in the white man's estimation if not in the white man's world.

THE UPPER CLASS

In the northern cities, the Negro professional man, especially the doctor or dentist, figures prominently in the upper class. Members of these two professional groups find in the large Negro community in the North a rich source of income as well as a relatively free environment. Likewise, the Negro lawyer, the more successful at least, will be found in the upper class. It is in the border and especially the northern cities that the Negro lawyer will find the most fertile field for the practice of his profession. Moreover, the position of the Negro lawyer in the northern city is supported by the political power of the Negro, whereas in the South his practice is restricted because of the traditional status of the Negro. Public school teachers are likewise found in the upper class. Where the Negro public school teachers are not numerous, they gain a certain prestige by the uniqueness of their position. But as their numbers have increased, their class position has been determined by a complex of factors involving family, color, income, personal factors, and style of living. The same is true of the growing number of social workers. Negro public administrators who have recently made their appearance in the northern cities derive their social prestige partly from their occupations and partly from economic and social distinctions.

. . . The Negro businessman in the northern city has appeared in response to the varied needs of the large Negro communities in the North. . . . Although the more successful businessmen are at the top of the upper class, many of those in clerical occupations have gained admission to the upper class because their occupational status involves high educational qualifications and they are able to maintain certain standards of living. As among whites, in order to gain access to the upper class in northern cities, a Negro must have an income which will enable him to maintain a certain standard or style of living.

. . . The standards of consumption which the upper class regards as appropriate for its position in the Negro community are generally set by the wealthiest members of the upper class. They include the type of home which one should occupy or own and the manner in which it should be furnished. In the southern and border cities homeownership is high among the upper class. Ownership of homes in the northern city is determined, of course, to some extent by the general character of the city. But in recent years, even in New York City, the more prosperous among the upper class have bought homes outside the city. The furnishings of the upper-class homes generally reflect the desire for comfort and luxury, while taste in the selection of furnishings varies according to the general culture of the family. Likewise, in the matter of clothes, the cost of one's clothes and the amount of clothes which one possesses are regarded as an indication of upper-class status. Sometimes whites who work or associate in other ways with Negroes in professional and clerical occupations are at a loss to understand why their colored fellow workers dress better than they themselves. The same tendencies are apparent in the make of an automobile which a member of the upper class buys.

Since income and pecuniary valuations are beginning to play such an important role in upper-class status, there has naturally arisen a conflict between economic and social distinctions, as a basis of upper-class status. In Negro communities, especially in the North, there has appeared a class of Negroes who are eligible for upper-class status from the standpoint of income but who have gained their wealth through "rackets" or other unlawful means and lack the family or educational background associated with upper-class status. Shut out from the legal areas of competition, some of the more enterprising and intelligent Negroes find an outlet for their abilities in such outlawed activities as gambling. These so-called "upper shadies" engage in all types of conspicuous consumptions, involving expensive clothes and automobiles and luxury in food and drink, and expensively furnished homes. At the same time they are often conscious of their failure to achieve the respectability which would make them eligible for inclusion in the upper class. Some of them observe the social ritual, at least, which characterizes upper-class-status behavior.

Social ritual plays an important role in the life of the upper class. This social ritual, which is usually characterized as "social life," is focused upon entertaining and involves considerable expenditures. The numerous social clubs, in some of which there is much duplication of membership, are organized about cliques. These clubs are constantly breaking up and re-forming in order to eliminate members who do not represent the exclusiveness which they attempt to maintain. But most of these clubs are similar in that they undertake to provide lavish entertainment in expensively equipped homes. . . .

The social position of the upper class in the Negro community is indicated by its institutional affiliations. Its members are generally affiliated with the Episcopal, Presbyterian, or Congregational church. As among whites, the church affiliation of the upper class is due partly to the traditional association of their families with these churches, and partly to the tendency of Negroes of middle- or lower-class status to become affiliated with these churches when they achieve a higher status. Sometimes professional and businessmen maintain their membership in the Baptist and Methodist churches for economic reasons. Usually, the upper class prefers membership in the Congregational, Episcopal, or Presbyterian church because the sermons and mode of service accord with their general outlook on life and their ideas of decorum in public worship. For the same reason some members of the upper class have been turning to the Catholic Church in recent years.[26]

---

[26] Reprinted by permission of the publisher from *The Negro in the United States* by E. Franklin Frazier. Copyright 1957 by The Macmillan Company. Also see his *Black Bourgeoisie* (New York: The Free Press of Glencoe, 1957).

The Negroes' historical background of slavery and plantation living is different from that of other minorities. Both elements in this background have left a mark on contemporary race relations. In 1860, slaves constituted 89 percent, or approximately 4 million, of the Negro population, the ancestors of many of these having also been slaves. Many families in the South did not have slaves, and most of those who did owned only a few. For example, only one third of the southern families in 1850 had slaves, the average number of slaves being 8.6. In 1850, of the families who had slaves in the United States, about 17.4 percent had 1 slave, 29.5 percent had 2 to 5 slaves, 24.4 had 5 to 10, 17.4 had 10 to 20, and 11.3 had 20 or more slaves.

The position of the Negro in the United States cannot be understood without reference to the plantation, which, for centuries, was the home of nearly all members of this minority. In many ways the plantation was a forerunner of the present-day emphasis on mass production. With the use of a considerable amount of land, specialization in a commodity, a cheap labor supply, and an elaborate division of labor, it was possible to produce fairly cheaply certain agricultural products, chiefly for European export.

The complex division of labor on plantations involved the master or landowning class, the "poor-white" overseers, and the Negro slaves, who were divided into household or personal and domestic servants, skilled artisans, such as blacksmiths and shoemakers; and field hands, who were at the bottom of the social structure. The members of this biracial group lived a largely isolated existence on the plantation, but at the same time were in close physical proximity. In order to maintain a degree of separation, a system of social relationships developed, increasing social distance. These included beliefs about the racial superiority of the master class and the inferiority of the Negro, beliefs which were largely accepted by both groups, distinctive ways of addressing one another to indicate subservience on the part of the slaves, separate living quarters, a benevolence on the part of the master class toward the slaves, and legal penalties which, although infrequently employed, were there to guarantee obedience and the separation of the races. Each generation inducted the other into the philosophy of rule by the master class and subservience on the part of the young slaves born into slavery, new slaves from Africa taking from older slaves the patterns of being "good slaves." Slavery was upheld by institutional norms in the South and was supported by most organized religions as being natural and decreed by God. Since slaves were not allowed to read or write, were seldom allowed to gather in large groups, to leave the plantations at night, or to have their own ministers, it was evident, however, that this accommodation or acceptance of servile status was not complete. After the Reconstruction period harsh laws or "Black Codes" were put into effect in most southern states in order to guarantee the separation of the races and the segregation of the Negro.

This long history of slavery on plantations affected the Negro people in many ways. As an authority on the Negro has written, "The pattern of race relations which developed on the plantation provided the traditional basis of future race relations in the South." [27] Plantation life, which broke the Negroes into small groups and maintained close physical proximity to the whites, destroyed the African cultures of the slaves within a relatively short period of time. This process was aided by the diversity of backgrounds of the slaves and their lack of a common culture. Consequently, African cultures have almost completely disappeared among the Negroes. The languages, religions, and other customs are no longer there, and the Negro is fully "American." This has meant that, as compared with other minorities, the Negro has lost his cultural identity. He is not discriminated against because of his religion—practically all Negroes, for example, are Protestants —or because of his customs, but because of his biological background.

Life on the plantation affected Negro and white relations in other ways. It left patterns of speech and manners, "tones of command" on the part of the whites, and a tendency on the part of the Negro to be servile and dependent. A large part of the hostility of many southern poor whites to the Negro is a carry-over from plantation days. The plantation often had the best land, and the cultivation of land on plantations was more efficient as a result of the division of labor. To the poor whites the Negro represented a cheap competitive labor supply, household servants were often cared for better than they were, the artisan slaves often had mechanical skills which they did not possess, and the sick and aged Negro had a degree of security on the plantation. At the same time, the Negro, as a group, represented something for the poor white, despite a status lower than that of other whites, to look down upon.

The stereotype of the Negro as a poor, unskilled, superstitious, illiterate agricultural field hand came from plantation days and has been carried over today despite the large-scale movement of the Negro into industry. Finally, the slave and rural background of the Negro has handicapped him in his adjustment to urban life. He did not have experience with urban life. During slavery marriage was largely impossible, for as slaves Negroes could not make a legal contract. As a result, conditions of illegitimacy and sexual promiscuity were common, and the mother rather than the father was largely the center of what family there was. These patterns have been difficult to eliminate in modern society, imposed as they have been upon the instability of large-scale migrations. In 1959, for example, of the registered illegitimate live births in the United States, 134,100 were by nonwhite mothers, as compared to 74,600 for white mothers.

The Negroes in America have come a long way since plantation slave

---

[27] Frazier, *The Negro in the United States*, p. 44. Also see Edgar T. Thompson, "The Plantation: The Physical Basis of Traditional Race Relations," in Edgar T. Thompson ed., *Race Relations and the Race Problem* (Durham, N.C.: Duke University Press, 1939), pp. 180–218.

days and the largely penniless condition into which they were thrust after the Civil War. Practically all of the nearly 6 million Negroes of the North and West live under urban conditions and are engaged in industrial work. Approximately one half the southern Negroes now live under similar conditions. Between 1940 and 1944 alone a million Negroes moved from farming to urban industrial work. In 1960 over a million and a half Negroes belonged to labor unions, and increasingly they are moving from unskilled labor into positions of semiskilled and skilled employment. They are also making increasing use of the ballot. In spite of the fact that pressures from whites, apathy, lack of leadership, and low economic and educational status keep the number of Negroes who register smaller than it should be, legislative changes and other factors have made it possible for the Negro to participate in primaries and to vote in all elections in increasing numbers in the South. In Florida, for example, whereas only 5.5 percent of the adult Negro population was registered to vote in 1944, in 1956 37.5 percent had registered.[28]

Leading the spearhead of this rising Negro militancy are the general organizations of the National Association for the Advancement of Colored People (NAACP), which dates from 1909 and has over 350,000 members, and the National Urban League, established in 1910, which has as its chief goal the adjustment of Negroes to urban life.

The American Indian. America's half a million Indians have long captured the imagination of the world. They have been both heroes and villains in literature and song out of all proportion to their actual numbers. A majority of the Indians are still members of 200 reservations located in twenty-six states, most of them in the Far West. Half of them, however, live away from the reservation and are in the process of gaining title to land. Thirteen states, including Alaska, contain the bulk of the Indian population. Arizona has the largest number, with 83,387, Oklahoma second with 64,689, and New Mexico third with 56,255. (See Table 17.5.)

It is difficult to generalize about the American Indian. Some Indians are almost completely assimilated, whereas others, with their witchcraft, poor hygiene, and opposition to Western European ways, are almost as "Indian" in their customs as they were in 1870. Nearly all of them are still farmers or livestock raisers, eking out additional incomes by selling curios or acting as tourist attractions and guides. Most of their reservations are marginal lands, and the Indians on them must often be supported by special governmental appropriations and relief. This governmental help amounted to $87 million in 1953.

Most of the Indians are unbelievably poor, although a few tribes are well-to-do. The average family income of the Sioux on the Standing Rock

[28] H. D. Price, *The Negro and Southern Politics* (New York: New York University Press, 1957), p. 33.

Reservation in North Dakota was $767 in 1955; it ranged from $730 to $855 among the Navahos. During the same year the average national family income was about $5300. Living conditions and health standards among the Indians are also far below the national average. On the Turtle Mountain Reservation in North Dakota, for example, as many as fifteen people live in a one-room cabin. The life expectancy for Papago Indian children in southern Arizona is seventeen years, as compared with sixty-nine years for the United States as a whole.

Table 17.5. States with Largest Indian Populations, 1960

State	Indian population	Percentage of total state population
Arizona	83,387	6.4
Oklahoma	64,689	2.8
New Mexico	56,255	5.9
California	39,014	0.25
North Carolina	38,129	0.84
South Dakota	25,794	3.8
Montana	21,181	3.1
Washington	21,076	0.74
New York	16,491	0.098
Minnesota	15,496	0.45
Alaska	14,444	6.4
Wisconsin	14,297	0.36
North Dakota	11,736	1.9

SOURCE: United States Census of Population, 1960, *General Population Characteristics,* pp. 1–164 and Table 56.

The difficulties which many present-day Indians face result from past policies and past contradictions. The original policy that "the only good Indian is a dead Indian" found expression in campaigns to exterminate them in many parts of the country. The program to place Indians on reservations began about 1850, and Indians were removed, often by force, to certain specified areas, to which they were given title. When land- and gold-hungry whites wanted these lands, the Indians were often moved farther West, from one reservation to another, until, finally, most of them had such poor lands that they had to be partially supported by government subsidies.

In 1887 the Dawes Allotment Act was set up to make "white men" out of the Indians by giving each an individual allotment of 160 acres from the reservations which had previously been commonly held by the tribe. After a certain number of years this land was finally to become the Indian's property. There was a provision that surplus reservation land could be homesteaded by whites. The Indians often sold these individual land rights, usually for very little, and between 1887 and 1928 they lost title to 87 million out of 137 million acres of land.

In 1934 a new policy was instituted under the Indian Reorganization Act, which provided for the purchase of additional lands, for irrigation projects, and for self-government. Although these provisions strengthened the reservations, they continued segregation and expenditures of public funds for the special care of the Indians.

About 1950 a new program was begun which will eventually mean the discontinuance of federal supervision over Indians and the gradual assumption of necessary services by the states. In addition, efforts are being made to eliminate reservations entirely by granting them complete autonomy over a period of years and by assisting Indians to leave the reservation permanently and to relocate in other areas, particularly large cities. The Menominee Indians of Wisconsin, after some delay, were first to be affected by this program, federal supervision ending in 1961.

Two alternative ways of dealing with the Indian situation are available.[29] One aims at a quick and intensive attempt to break down the special status of Indians and integrate them into the mainstream of American life. The other aims at maintaining Indian tribal integrity and special rights until such time as the Indians are ready and willing to dispense with federal supervision and control.

On the whole, various Indian groups are so divided in their aspirations that they have not been too effective in working out a single national program. Some degree of pressure for an improvement in their situation, however, has been exerted on Congress and the general public through tribal representatives, the National Congress of American Indians, and an organization of persons interested in the Indian: Association on American Indian Affairs, Inc.

Japanese-Americans. Of the 464,332 persons of Japanese ancestry in the United States, 43.8 percent live in Hawaii and 33.9 percent life in California. Five states have 11.2 percent: in order, Washington, Illinois, New York, Colorado, and Oregon. The other forty-three states have only 11.2 percent.

These Japanese are immigrants or descendants of immigrants who came to the United States largely between 1870 and 1920. La Violette has divided the history of Japanese immigration into (1) the frontier period, from 1870 to 1908, (2) the family-building period, from 1908 to 1920, and (3) the second-generation period, from 1921 to 1941.[30] Although most of the immigrants were single, middle-class farmers who could afford the

---

[29] See Oliver La Farge, "Termination of Federal Supervision: Disintegration and the American Indian," *The Annals*, 311:41–46 (May, 1957).

[30] Forrest E. La Violette, *Americans of Japanese Ancestry: A Study of Assimilation in the American Community* (Toronto: Canadian Institute of International Affairs, 1945), p. 10.

passage, they first worked as laborers in this country. Between the period from 1908 to 1920 the general practice was to write home for a bride, "picture brides," as they were called. A so-called Gentleman's Agreement with Japan in 1907 had strictly limited the emigration of men to the United States, but some women were allowed to enter the country. The arrival of these women stabilized the Japanese family system in the United States.

The Japanese Exclusion Act of 1924 eliminated all immigration. Their exclusion was based on the erroneous belief that their industry, aggressiveness, and high birth rate constituted a threat to the numerically superior dominant group. One writer thus summarized this opposition to them.

> An anti-Japanese movement has been developing in the United States leading to differential race legislation. It has taken acutest form in the California Anti-Alien Land Law. Without attempting to characterize this movement adequately I may describe it as a movement partly economic, implicitly confessing fear of Japanese superior efficiency; partly racial, expressing scorn, disdain, and arrogance at the ambition and success of a people "instinctively" felt to be essentially inferior; partly political, furnishing opportunity to certain individuals and political groups to gain personal and party advantage by appealing to selfish interest and race prejudice against sections of the community politically helpless; and partly natural and inevitable, arising from numberless mistakes, misunderstandings, and misdeeds of individuals of different race groups speaking different languages and acting under different customs, ideas, and ideals.[31]

The Japanese in America have been characterized as having "a highly developed disposition of obedience and obligation, heavy self-demands involving the giving up of free impulse, a pride in name and the bringing of honor to one's family, an unusual cohesive organization of the group," and a generally dynamic aggressiveness.[32] In many ways, as Robert E. Park stated, the Japanese minority resembles the Jewish minority, for it is small in numbers, intimate, compact, and well organized. Both groups have great advantages in competition with a larger and less-organized community.[33]

The Japanese culture affects this minority group in different ways, according to whether its members are Issei, Nisei, or Sansei. The Issei are those born in Japan, who, prior to 1952, were aliens because laws prevented their naturalization and, in the past, in California their ownership of land. The Nisei and the Sansei, who make up about two thirds of all Japanese, are the children and the grandchildren of the Issei. Although they are a

---

[31] Sidney L. Gulick, *American Democracy and Asiatic Citizenship* (New York: Charles Scribner's Sons, 1919), p. 22.

[32] R. A. Schermerhorn, *These Our People* (Boston: D. C. Heath and Company, 1949), p. 206.

[33] See J. F. Steiner, "Some Factors Involved in Minimizing Race Friction on the Pacific Coast," *The Annals*, 93:117 (1921).

part of both Japanese and American cultures, their acculturation is generally not complete.[34] The social separation of the Issei from the Nisei is very great because of differences in the degree of language facility and in the extent of participation in American institutions. The Nisei, however, more than the Sansei, are a part of both cultures while not fully a part of either.[35]

At the time of World War II, nearly half of the Japanese in continental United States were engaged in agriculture.[36] Truck farming predominated, about 1600 farms being owned by Nisei, since the Issei were not then permitted to own land under California law. The Japanese produced about a third of all truck crops grown in California. About two fifths of the nonagricultural Japanese workers were in business, a like proportion of these being in personal and commercial services.

During World War II, the Japanese, most of whom were United States citizens, were subjected to one of the most extreme forms of discrimination in American history when they were ordered evacuated from the Pacific Coast and transferred to relocation centers. Several factors accounted for this action. The military officials in charge of the West Coast had a curious notion of the relations of race and culture; moreover, certain newspapers and politicians were opposed to the Japanese, many of whom were technically "enemy aliens." [37] These people were hurriedly uprooted and given only limited opportunities to protect their property, which many of them had to sell at a heavy loss when they could find no non-Japanese person to take care of it. The Japanese were incarcerated in camps behind barbed wire and under armed guards, in crowded institutional conditions and subject to tremendous psychological tensions.[38] During the war a large proportion were eventually released from the camps and relocated in states away from the Pacific Coast. After the war some 80 percent of them returned to the West Coast, three fourths of them to California. Actual income and property losses because of forced sales and damage during their absence have been estimated at $350 million.[39] Some 24,000 claims totaling $130

---

[34] Before World War II there was a small group of Nisei called the Kibei, American-born Japanese who had been sent to Japan for part of their education and who were, therefore, often closer than the others to Japanese culture and traditions.

[35] Jitsuichi Masuoka, "Race Relations and Nisei Problems," *Sociology and Social Research*, 30:456–457 (July–August, 1946).

[36] Dorothy Swaine Thomas and Richard S. Nishimoto, *The Spoilage: Japanese-American Evacuation and Resettlement* (Berkeley: University of California Press, 1946).

[37] *Ibid*. Also see Morton Grodzins, *Americans Betrayed* (Chicago: The University of Chicago Press, 1949).

[38] Alexander Leighton, *The Governing of Men* (Princeton, N.J.: Princeton University Press, 1945).

[39] Leonard Broom and Ruth Riemer, *Removal and Return* (Berkeley: University of California Press, 1949), pp. 201–203. Also see Dorothy S. Thomas, *The Salvage* (Berkeley: University of California Press, 1952).

million were filed, and congressional legislation was passed permitting claims up to $100,000 to be settled without court litigation.

Since World War II a great many of the handicaps caused by relocation have been overcome, and Japanese-Americans are encountering less discrimination. The elevation of Hawaii to statehood in 1959 ended a long delay which was due, in part, to the many Orientals in its population.

Their chief organization is the Japanese-American Citizens League (JACL), a militant association which attempts to remove discrimination.

Chinese-Americans. Most of the Chinese now living in America are descendants of immigrants who came here from about 1850 to 1882, when the Exclusion Law barred further legal immigration. During the California gold rush few people would do the necessary menial tasks, and Chinese were imported as unskilled laborers. As the gold rush subsided and the whites returned to the cities, however, they competed with the Chinese for available jobs. As a result of a series of disturbances, the Chinese withdrew to segregated living in Chinatowns. This ghetto method of living kept the possibility of hostilities with the white population at a minimum, gave the Chinese certain limited specialized occupations, and enabled them to maintain their cultural unity. Their numbers were greatly increased from 1860 to 1882, when the western part of the transcontinental railroad was built and there was a need for cheap labor on the Pacific Coast. In some instances the Chinese laborers later returned to China. Although all immigration was officially banned until 1943, when a quota of 105 was permitted, some Chinese have illegally entered this country from Mexico and other places.

The number of Chinese in this country is still small, 237,292, as compared with 464,000 Japanese, largely because few Chinese women came here. Most of the Chinese immigrants came as young men, remained single, and often returned to China to live out their last years on the money made in the United States. Since they could not be citizens in California they, like the Japanese, were not allowed to own land there. Sixty years ago the Chinese population was considerably larger than it was in 1940. A large proportion of the Chinese in the United States is therefore American-born, as has been true of several generations.

With the passage of years Chinatowns appear to be declining. Several factors have accounted for this trend.[40] (1) Generally a Chinatown today must be part of a city of at least 50,000 people in order to exist. A smaller community could not support the different typical Chinese enterprises: restaurants, laundries, and curio shops. In 1940, 71 percent of the Chinese lived in the larger metropolitan cities. (2) The increasingly diversified employment opportunities for American Chinese, originally denied them through discrimination or legislation, have resulted in a decline in the

---

[40] Rose Hum Lee, "The Decline of Chinatowns in the United States," *American Journal of Sociology*, 54:422–433 (March, 1949).

number of persons living in Chinatowns. (3) In those smaller Chinatowns where there are extensive family and clan interrelationships, intermarriage in the community is difficult and thus many of the inhabitants move to larger Chinese communities. (4) Depressions and wars have weakened the economic structure of Chinatowns within cities and redistributed their population. (5) The movement of the central business districts is pushing Chinese inhabitants out and thus eliminating Chinatowns as distinct cultural entities. Probably only those in San Francisco and New York will remain. As Chinatowns disappear and the Chinese-Americans become acculturated, their dispersion will be much like that of other small minority groups who have become integral parts of the American society. Rose Hum Lee has summarized the situation as follows:

> In summary, Chinatowns go through various stages of development and decline: from an immigrant ghetto to a tourist-attracting centre, then to a shopping centre for the Chinese. While residents may live around it, more and more of them move outward and they return to it for special goods and services. The larger society's members travel there on special occasions. What distinguishes it from another community is its attempt to maintain a set of distinctive institutions, such as Chinese churches, *tongs* or Merchants' Associations, stores selling curios from various countries, shops handling the few items of Chinese merchandise they can import from "Free China," and restaurants catering to a dwindling clientele. Chinatowns have lost much of their exotic quality and uniqueness.[41]

With the exception of San Francisco's Chinatown, where generation after generation live in the same area and maintain their Old World culture, American-Chinese of successive generations live in a cultural setting which is more American than Chinese today.[42] The Old World culture gradually is lost, their ability to speak and write the Chinese language is usually lost by the third generation, and they become Americans in all but physical appearance. They want to be considered as Americans rather than as "marginal men" and assigned a minority status, but the possession of distinctive racial features adds to their difficulties. Because of these physical distinctions they may be treated as Chinese in one situation and as American in another. Thus they acquire a dual set of responses and are never wholly free from the possibility of differential treatment. Incidents of prejudice and discrimination, although perhaps not frequent, do arise, evoking feelings of marginality, resentment, and dormant fears.

---

[41] Rose Hum Lee, *The Chinese in the United States of America* (Hong Kong: Cathay Press, 1960, p. 68.
[42] *Ibid.* Lee points out (p. 410) that "the Chinese as a group are no longer economically depressed; their annual median incomes exceeded those of the Negro, Puerto Rican, Mexican, poor white, and those of other Asian groups, except Japanese, in 1950."

ETHNIC MINORITIES: SPANISH-SPEAKING AMERICANS

Most immigrants to the United States prior to 1890 were minority groups at one time, such as the Swedish and German groups in the nineteenth century, but they have now become part of the majority group. On the other hand, many of the groups in the New immigration, such as the Italians and the Poles, might still be regarded as ethnic minorities today. They are rapidly changing their minority status as they move into the second and even third and fourth generations. The status of these groups is chiefly dependent on their social class and on the part of the country in which they reside.

One ethnic minority, the Spanish-speaking Americans, has a unique position. This group includes Mexican immigrants and Puerto Ricans, who are American citizens, and those persons descended from them, as well as those persons of Spanish-American and Mexican descent in the Southwest who have been part of the United States for a century and whom one can hardly regard as immigrants. Their number has been estimated at about 3.5 million, as of 1950, or somewhat less than 2 percent of the total population of the United States.[43] This minority group thus comes after Negroes and Jews in size. Most of the Spanish-speaking minority is concentrated in five southwestern states, Texas, California, New Mexico, Arizona, and Colorado, but many are found in the Middle West and the Northeast, chiefly in such cities as Chicago, Detroit, Kansas City, and New York. (See Table 17.6.)

Spanish-Americans. The Spanish-Americans, or "Hispanos," are primarily descendants of the early Spanish colonists who settled mainly in what is now New Mexico, ceded to this country in 1848 after the Mexican War. They have lived in the Southwest for over three hundred years, and most of them are subsistence farmers in small communities. For the most part they have remained as Spanish in custom as many persons in Spain or in South America. They are unusually attached to the small, sleepy, isolated communities in the Southwest not only because of their cultural background and language but because of the discrimination on the part of Anglos. They are generally poor, and their illiteracy rates and death rates are very high. Some refer to them as the Forgotten People because so few Americans outside the Southwest have much knowledge of them or their problems.[44] Although most of them are still in these areas, there has been a recent movement to cities where, together with persons of Mexican an-

---

[43] Paul A. F. Walter, Jr., *Race and Culture Relations* (New York: McGraw-Hill Book Company, Inc., 1952), p. 325.

[44] George L. Sanchez, *The Forgotten People: A Study of New Mexicans* (Albuquerque: University of New Mexico Press, 1940).

cestry, they have generally set up a Spanish city within a city. Their adjustment to urban life has been a complicated one.

It is not the visibility of the Spanish-American minority that separates them from the majority group but their social and cultural differences. Although it is a heterogeneous group, it is largely a combination of a rural, folk way of life and a Spanish and sometimes an Indian culture. Between them and the Anglos or non-Spanish population there are a difference in language (the state documents in New Mexico are still being published in two languages), a difference in religion (the Spanish-Americans are nearly all Catholics), and frequently a difference in outlook on life. Their background is nonindividualistic, is family- and village-centered, and has a relatively low technological development.

Table 17.6. Estimated Spanish-Speaking Population of the Southwest, 1950

State	Total population	Spanish-speaking population	Percent Spanish-speaking
Texas	7,500,000	1,150,000	15.3
California	10,500,000	500,000	4.8
New Mexico	650,000	250,000	38.5
Arizona	750,000	160,000	21.3
Colorado	1,350,000	50,000	3.7
Total	20,750,000	2,110,000	10.2

SOURCE: By permission from *Race and Culture Relations* by Paul A. F. Walter, Jr., p. 329. Copyright, 1952, McGraw-Hill Book Company, Inc. Figures are approximate, to indicate roughly the proportion of Spanish-speaking people in each state. Since there are no precise statistics on the Spanish-speaking group, pretense at greater accuracy would be meaningless.

The world of the twentieth century is rapidly moving in on the Hispanos, who have found that their way of life of three hundred years ago cannot cope with it. The frequent feeling of futility is intensified by awareness of poverty, ignorance, poor diet, inadequate landholdings, and discrimination. Although they and government agencies are making efforts to improve this situation, the road will not be short or easy for a people who have resisted change for so long a time.[45]

Mexican-Americans. A hundred years ago, when the Southwest became part of the United States, it was peopled largely by Spanish-Americans and Mexicans. The descendants of those Mexicans and of many others who came later, together with Mexican nationals living in the United States, will be discussed here as Mexicans. The largest part of the Mexican migra-

[45] John H. Burma, *Spanish-Speaking Groups in the United States* (Durham, N.C.: Duke University Press, 1954).

tion came during the period of World War I to the time of the depression, and again during World War II, when there was a great demand for labor but little opportunity for European immigration. Over half the Mexicans and persons of Mexican descent in the United States live in Texas, but over 600,000 live in California and 100,000 in Arizona. Los Angeles has 120,000 Mexicans; Chicago, about 25,000.[46]

Although Mexicans are increasingly being employed in industry, they are still mainly migratory laborers, planting and harvesting beet sugar and cotton, and picking the fruit crops of the West. Most of them are unskilled laborers, few are in business or the professions. They are a comparatively poor and illiterate people, usually living in segregated and poor slum areas. As a source of cheap harvest labor, the Mexican migratory workers in one area have been described as being a "necessary evil."

> Generally speaking the Latin American migratory worker going into West Texas is regarded as a necessary evil, nothing more or less than an unavoidable adjunct to the harvest season. Judging by the treatment that has been accorded him in that section of the State, one might assume that he is not a human being at all, but a species of farm implement that comes mysteriously and spontaneously into being coincident with the maturing of cotton, that requires no upkeep or special consideration during the period of its usefulness, needs no protection from the elements, and when the crop has been harvested, vanishes into the limbo of forgotten things—until the next harvest season rolls around. He has no past, no future, only a brief and anonymous present.[47]

The discrimination against persons with a Mexican background arises from a number of factors. Although some of the Spanish-Americans and most Mexicans have a mixed Spanish and Indian ancestry—mestizos—this statement applies more to the Mexican group. As a result, they are often physically visible enough to be distinguished from the non-Spanish population. Many have dual nationalistic ties which Spanish-Americans do not have, and in the Southwest, particularly in Texas, they often encounter the latent century-old hostility of Anglos for Mexicans. Discrimination can also be explained by the fact that there is also often a difference in language, culture, and religion. Most of the Mexicans are poor. Many persons also tend to associate them with petty theft, personal violence, delinquency, and drunkenness, in all of which their rates are high but probably no higher than those for persons in a similar economic and cultural situation.

---

[46] During a year in the United States there are estimated also to be at least 40,000 "Wetbacks," Mexicans who enter illegally. Although they were for a long time a rural, agricultural people both in Mexico and in this country, over half of them now live, for at least part of the year, in urban areas. They often leave these urban areas for migratory agricultural work during the spring or summer.—*Ibid.*, p. 37.

[47] Pauline R. Kibbe, *Latin Americans in Texas* (Albuquerque: University of New Mexico Press, 1946), p. 176.

Several organizations set up by Mexicans and Spanish-Americans in recent years to help solve their problems have been concerned with discrimination against their group and other problems of adjustment which they encounter. The League of United Latin-American Citizens (LULACS), established in 1929, is their principal organization.

Puerto Ricans. By the end of 1956 there were an estimated 577,000 Puerto Ricans living in New York City, or about 95 percent of all Puerto Ricans in the United States. Nearly three fourths of them live in "Spanish Harlem." Most Puerto Ricans have emigrated in the last fifteen years because of overcrowding and poor economic conditions in Puerto Rico. But they have taken up residence in some of New York's worst housing areas. Although many Puerto Rican workers have improved themselves economically, most of them have a marginal existence and many come to the attention of the welfare authorities. Their background in language and culture is largely Spanish, but some, because of their mixed white and Negro racial background, encounter the same types of prejudice as do American Negroes. Consequently, these Puerto Ricans try to emphasize their Spanish language and customs. Their problems, particularly juvenile delinquency, will continue as long as the areas in which they reside contribute to deviant behavior and until, through cultural assimilation, they become more Americanized.[48]

Puerto Ricans on the whole are a youthful population, the median in 1950 being 24.3 years of age as compared with 35.0 years for New York City. The sexes are about equally divided as compared with previous migrant groups, and they tend to marry much earlier. Their birth rate is considerably higher than that of the general population of New York City. Their educational level is much lower than the level of New Yorkers in general, only one fifth of the adults over twenty-five having an eighth-grade education, as compared with three fourths of the New York population.

Unemployment among them is high. Generally they are employed as semiskilled "operatives," sewing machine operators or service tradesmen, and not as domestic servants. In fact, these first two classifications accounted for two thirds of employed Puerto Rican men as compared with approximately one third of all men. Four fifths of the women were "operatives" as compared with one third of nonwhite and one fourth of white women.

Despite these conditions, Puerto Ricans as a whole do not feel that they are discriminated against; in fact, in one survey only 5 percent thought so, and 98 percent thought their families had been treated fairly well in New York City.[49] There are several reasons for this rather unusual attitude:

---

[48] Burma, *op. cit.*, pp. 176–187. Also see Morris Eagle, "The Puerto Ricans in New York City," in Nathan Glazer and Davis McEntire eds., *Studies in Housing and Minority Groups* (Berkeley: University of California Press, 1960), pp. 144–177 and Clarence Senior, *Strangers Then Neighbors: From Pilgrims to Puerto Ricans* (New York: Freedom Books, 1961).

[49] Eagle, in Glazer and McEntire, *op. cit.*, p. 186.

(1) compared with wages, housing, and other living conditions in Puerto Rico, to them the situation is not too bad, (2) pride among Puerto Ricans prohibits them from admitting discrimination, (3) there is little contact with others than Puerto Ricans, and (4) they are so concerned with economic matters that discrimination means little to them.

RELIGIOUS MINORITIES: THE JEWS

The United States Census does not enumerate a person's religious beliefs any more than it does his political affiliation. Thus the only statistics on religious groups must be obtained through the religious denominations, generally from church memberships. These figures are often misleading, particularly in the case of the Jew, for some persons are regarded by others and by themselves as Jews even though they may not attend any church, or may even belong to some Christian denomination.

The Jews are classified here as a religious minority, although they are not clearly a religious group. Having been discriminated against for two thousand or more years, they are the classic minority group of Western civilization. Christ was a Jew and the Bible contains the history of the Jewish people and a large part of their traditional philosophy. Hence a Jewish author, Lewis Browne, wrote with irony, "How odd of God" to choose the Jews.[50] They have endured generations of persecution in many lands and under many rulers, from Herod to Hitler.

Many people believe it is impossible to speak of Jews as a group because of the diversity among them in the United States and throughout the world. No concept would include all Jews, even in the United States. They are certainly not a race. Most Jews are white and so mixed that they constitute no distinctive subgroup; there are also Negro Jews and Chinese Jews. Nor are they a religion. Many persons are called Jews who are not Jews at all; moreover, there is considerable variation within each religious group. Some people feel that Jews do not have a distinctive culture because of the cultural and linguistic variations which distinguish those from America, Germany, Iraq, Yemen, Algiers, India, and other countries. Studies of Israel, which has become a haven of Jews from all lands, indicate that it is one of the most diverse cultural groups existing today.[51] As one Jewish periodical has said: "We have not yet determined whether we are to use the term 'race,' 'religion,' 'nation,' or 'culture' to clarify the nature of our Jewish entity and identity." [52]

In sociological terms a Jew is simply a person who says he is a Jew or is considered by others to be a Jew. Several characteristics, however, give

---

[50] Lewis Browne, *How Odd of God* (New York: The Macmillan Company, 1936).

[51] Rafael Patai, *Israel: Between East and West* (Philadelphia: Jewish Publication Society, 1953).

[52] *Reconstructionist*, June 23, 1944, as quoted in Schermerhorn, *op. cit.*

some unity to the Jews as a group despite the many exceptions: the nature of the Jewish religion, the high regard for learning, the biculturality or dual culture of many Jews, their long ghetto existence, and their urban and commercial background.[53] Many of these characteristics, if considered individually, would apply equally to groups other than the Jewish.

1. The religion of the Jews has been at the same time different from and similar to that of the Christians, among whom they have lived since A.D. 70, when the people of Jerusalem were dispersed by the Roman legions. The Old Testament, on which their religion is based, is also a part of the Christian religion; yet in their belief that Christ was not divine they have been almost the only distinctive religious group residing in Western European countries. This denial of the divinity of Christ was one reason for their persecution.

2. Learning has always been highly regarded among Jews. A large part of Jewish education has been based on the study of the books of the Talmud, in which the role of the scholar has been stressed: "Turn all thou hast into money and procure in marriage for thy son the daughter of a scholar, and for thy daughter a scholar." As a result of this emphasis, the medical, legal, and teaching professions, as well as the ministry and philosophy, have probably meant more to Jews as a group than to gentiles.

3. Jews can frequently be characterized by their possession of a somewhat dual culture. While usually taking on the customs of the people with whom they have lived, the Jews retained some of the customs of ancient Israel. This biculturality has meant a dual set of customs of education and etiquette. Because they have long had a dual culture the loyalty of many Jews to a national state has often been doubted.

4. The Jews' long ghetto existence constituted a severe form of segregation which has affected even those Jews who have never been forced to live in a ghetto.[54] These areas in medieval days, and even recently, were surrounded by walls and gates which were closed at night. Armed guards watched the gates but only a few Jews ventured out even on weekdays to transact business. Inside the ghetto were the synagogue, the burial place, and the tenements. Often there were pogroms and other invasions of the ghetto in which the Jews were slaughtered:

> Forced by these circumstances to shun the Christians, the group within the ghetto became more provincial, narrow, ignorant, and superstitious, and the religion of the masses, as well as that of many rabbis, became more rigidly set than ever. The social effects of enforced segregation gave rise to an exaggerated cohesiveness and solidarity of the community (to outsiders, clannishness). It meant a temper of mind increasingly uneasy when too far from the organized forms of Jewish institutions and communal activities. Just as it has

---

[53] Schermerhorn, *op. cit.*, pp. 381–387.
[54] Louis Wirth, *The Ghetto* (Chicago: The University of Chicago Press, 1928).

been remarked that one can take a girl out of the country but not the country out of the girl, so it would be equally true that it might be comparatively easy to take the Jew out of the ghetto but not the ghetto out of the Jew. In times of persecution—even though it affected their fellows in far distant lands—the lines within the Jewish community tightened so that an unbroken front was presented to the host society.[55]

Few other white Europeans have so suddenly in recent times been moved from segregation and economic and political subordination to freedom as were the Jews following their emancipation from the ghetto. Moreover, the Jew was probably the last such group to gain his freedom. Emancipation of the Jew followed the French Revolution and, beginning in France in 1806, was part of Napoleon's program in his conquest of Europe. This period of emancipation of only a century and a half is actually much shorter when one considers that it was not in effect in eastern European countries until fifty years ago. The ghetto was restored by Hitler in Germany and the occupied countries only thirty years ago.

This sudden change had a powerful and in some ways a disruptive effect upon the Jewish people as a whole. Even today the emancipation is only a century old, and for many members of the community less than that. The extent of the new-found freedom has been spotty and uneven. Late entrance into Western society has meant a sudden adjustment to the scientific and political revolutions which required centuries of adjustment to become assimilated into the thought patterns of the Christian world. Thus the full impact of the Copernican, Newtonian, and Darwinian world views struck the Jewish community at a single blow.[56]

A study of Jews in three small communities in the United States has revealed the effect of this past and the difficulties of acceptance by the gentile community which make the Jew "the eternal stranger."

As a group the Jews find it very difficult to break with their past nor are they ever quite accepted into the larger society. Thus they remain, par excellence, the eternal strangers. In general, they live in two worlds—a little disillusioned in both. They have no real world of their own because the ideological system of the ghetto, which was responsible for the survival of the Jewish world in the first place, fails to solve the intellectual and moral perplexities by which the modern American Jew is beset. On the other hand, the world of the larger community is not quite their own because despite the fact that it may admire and tolerate them, it feels eternally irritated at their stubborn persistence in being different and treats them, at best, as guests. Being loyal and neighborly has not helped, living together in the same town for a hundred years has not helped, speaking the same language and venerating the same national heroes and institutions have not helped. Even

---

[55] From R. A. Schermerhorn, *These Our People* (Boston: D. C. Heath and Company, 1949), p. 384. Extracts from this work are reprinted by permission of the publisher.
[56] *Ibid.*, p. 385.

when the lines between the Jewish and the Gentile communities become very thin, the Jews still find themselves far from constituting full-fledged members of the general community and their positions remain one of ambivalence.[57]

5. The Jews have traditionally been city persons from the time they left Israel, where they were pastoral nomads, until their present re-emergence as farmers in that country. Several factors account for this city background. During medieval times they were forbidden by law to own land, they could not take the oath of fealty, and their religious customs did not permit their serving in armies, service which might have enabled them to acquire land. Consequently, over the centuries the Jew has been limited to an urban, commercial way of life which has affected his approach to social relationships. Of all immigrant groups in the United States, he was not only the most urban; he was the only one with such an exclusively urban background. So pronounced has been this characteristic that Rose has tried to explain anti-Semitism as an outgrowth of everyone's unconcious dislike of the frustrations and problems of urban life.[58] Since he is the most closely identified with city life, the Jew has received the overt expression of this dislike for the city.

6. The proportion of Jews engaged in commerce is, and has been, probably larger than that of any other group, as would be expected from their urban background. Moreover, during medieval times Christians were generally not permitted to lend money at interest; hence it was logical that some Jews assumed the banking function. Aware of this commercial background of the Jew, anti-Semites have often charged that Jews dominate the economy. Several studies of the occupations of Jews in the United States, although not conclusive because of the difficulties of making such studies, do not support any general Jewish dominance of the economy out of proportion to their numbers.[59] A few occupations do have disproportionate numbers of Jews. They are not, however, occupations of any particular power, being largely in light industries, such as the manufacture and distribution of clothing. Jews do not occupy a strong position in newspaper publishing; banking and investment; rubber, chemicals, and petroleum; transportation; or public utilities.

The Jews have come to the United States in approximately four more or less distinct groups: the Sephardic Jews of colonial days; the German Jews, from about 1800 to 1880; the east European Jews, from 1881 to 1924;

---

[57] Benjamin Kaplan, *The Eternal Stranger: A Study of Jewish Life in the Small Community* (New York: Bookman Associates, Inc., 1957), p. 156.

[58] Arnold M. Rose, "Anti-Semitism's Part in City-Hatred," *Commentary*, 6:374–378 (October, 1948).

[59] William M. Kephart, "What Is the Position of the Jewish Economy in the United States?" *Social Forces*, 28:153–164 (December, 1949).

and the refugees from the Nazis and the effects of World War II from all over Europe from 1933 to the present.[60]

The Sephardic Jews, who came during the period before 1800, were largely the descendants of those Spanish Jews who had fled from Spain and Portugal after Ferdinand and Isabella had ordered their expulsion in 1492. During colonial times some of these Jews came to America, beginning in 1654 with the arrival in New Amsterdam (later New York City) of twenty-three Jewish men, women, and children who had been exiled when the Portuguese conquered the Dutch colony of Recife on the coast of Brazil. During the American Revolution a number of Jews achieved considerable status. Sephardic Jews have almost disappeared as an identifiable group.

There were proportionately few Jews in the United States until 1848, when they numbered about 20,000 in a population of 20,000,000. A few German Jews—in general, small tradesmen and peddlers—started emigrating between 1800 and 1848; in the years following the revolutionary movements which swept Germany in 1848, some 200,000 sought the political and economic freedom of the new land. They were chiefly political liberals as well as religious liberals who belonged to the Reform or liberal Jewish synagogue. On the whole, they did not tend to believe, as compared with Orthodox Jews, that kosher and other dietary laws were binding, that religious services need be conducted primarily in Hebrew, or that men and women need be seated separately during services.

Since these Jews had enjoyed considerable freedom in their home country, they thought of themselves more as Germans than as Jews. Their political, religious, and social liberalism, which was not as strongly opposed to intermarriage with gentiles, together with their largely middle-class, educated background, made the German Jew assimilate American ways more readily. Although some German-Jewish groups were traditionalists or German separatists, by the time the eastern Jews began emigrating they were well on the road to economic prosperity and a considerable degree of assimilation and amalgamation.

Eastern Jews from Poland and Russia began coming in large numbers in 1881, eventually numbering approximately 2 million immigrants and now with their descendants constituting the majority of the American Jews. As a result of the pogroms in Russia and Poland begun by the czarist government as a political policy, various European Jewish groups outside Russia and Poland arranged to bring thousands of Jews, mostly as family units, to this country. These eastern European Jewish immigrants differed greatly from the German Jews because they had been confined to an almost medieval ghetto existence. The majority were poor, Orthodox even

---

[60] Jews from Germany and eastern Europe entered the United States during all these periods.

in style of dress, and almost a quarter of them were illiterate. The German Jews had dispersed to the smaller cities and many to the Midwest, but the eastern Jews concentrated in New York City, which today has almost half the Jews in the United States. Many of the Polish and Russian Jews, although poor, had been skilled laborers—tailors, hatmakers, milliners, and shoemakers—and their services were needed in the garment industry in New York.

The eastern Jews, emancipated suddenly from the ghetto, have had tremendous difficulties in adjustment. Thrown into a large industrial metropolis after living in small cities and towns, many of them were able to move from extreme poverty to extreme wealth. These changes in economic status greatly strained their family system, which was traditionally closely organized and patriarchal, and produced friction between the generations. They also resulted in conflicts between German and eastern Jews, the former often tending to look down upon the eastern Jews and avoid them. Despite its problems, the eastern Jewish group, on the whole, has been able to maintain a considerable degree of solidarity through its organization and centers. Some modifications of the Orthodox Jewish religion have been made, members of this movement being called Conservative Jews. Their modifications, however, have not gone as far as those of the liberal or Reform group.

The last wave of Jews came with Hitler's persecutions and the subsequent postwar adjustment. In *Mein Kampf* Hitler set forth the battle cry of the Nazis against the Jews, who were regarded as a "race" personifying all evil.[61] The resultant Nazi purge reduced the Jewish population of Europe from 1939 to 1950 by two thirds, or more than 6 million. (See Table 17.7.) Most of the European Jews were killed, but some escaped to other countries, mainly to the United States and Israel. Between 1933 and 1944, about 160,000 to 200,000 Jews were admitted to the United States, almost all from Germany and Austria. In 1960 almost half of all the Jews in the world, 5,780,000, were in the United States and Canada, as contrasted with one third in 1939. (See Table 17.7.) The countries with the largest estimated Jewish populations in 1960 are the United States, 5,370,000; Soviet Union, 2,268,000; Israel, 1,880,000; Great Britain, 450,000; Argentina, 400,000; France, 350,000; Rumania, 220,000; Morocco, 200,000; Algeria, 135,000; and Brazil, 125,000. New York City and Los Angeles are the American cities with the largest Jewish populations, with 1,940,000 and 400,000 respectively. (See Table 17.8.)

The Jewish immigrants who fled the Nazis were largely older people with primarily a middle-class, skilled, or professional background. After

---

[61] For an account of the persecutions of the Jews under Hitler and of the results of the extermination policies, see William L. Shirer, *The Rise and Fall of the Third Reich* (New York: Simon and Schuster, Inc., 1960).

Table 17.7. Jewish Population, by Continents

Continent	1939	1950	1960	Percent increase or decrease, 1950–60
United States and Canada	4,965,620	5,198,000	5,780,000	+8.0
South and Central America	524,000	621,930	681,150	+9.5
Europe	9,739,200	3,550,000	3,714,300	+4.6
Asia (including Israel)	771,500	1,374,350	2,057,650	+46.7
Australia and New Zealand	33,000	44,000	68,500	+55.6
Africa	609,800	702,400	543,180	−21.5
World Total	16,643,120	11,490,680	12,836,790	+10.1

SOURCE: Figures for 1939 and 1950 secured from *Monthly Bulletin of Statistics,* Office of the United Nations, August, 1950. Figures for 1960 are from the Jewish Statistical Bureau, as presented in *The World Almanac 1962,* p. 258. (New York: New York World-Telegram and the Sun, 1962), p. 258.

the war another Jewish group of about the same size, principally displaced, poorer eastern Jews, came to the United States.

Because of these four distinct immigration periods, the American Jewish community has many differences, cultural and religious. An outstanding example of the latter is the division into Orthodox, Conservative, and Reform or liberal synagogues. The Orthodox membership, by families, is estimated to be 30,000; the Conservative, 250,000; and the Reform, 250,000.

Despite their differences in background and religious customs, Jewish groups are well organized. In fact, they are probably the most effectively

Table 17.8. Jewish Population by Cities of the World, 1960

City	Jewish population
New York City (greater)	1,940,000
Los Angeles (greater)	400,000
Tel Aviv-Jaffa	383,000
Philadelphia (greater)	330,000
Chicago	282,000
London (greater)	280,000
Paris	175,000
Haifa	174,000
Jerusalem	160,000
Boston	150,000
Montreal	102,000

SOURCE: Estimates given by the Jewish Statistical Bureau, as presented in *The World Almanac 1962,* p. 258.

organized minority group. Some of their associations are the American Jewish Congress, established in 1917 to defend the political rights of Jews and active among middle-class persons interested in militant Jewish efforts; the Anti-Defamation League of B'nai B'rith, organized in 1913 to oppose discriminatory articles in the press; the Jewish Labor Committee; Jewish Welfare Board; the Young Men's Hebrew Association; the Jewish War Veterans; the United Jewish Appeal; and many others devoted specifically to the aid of the Jewish state of Israel.[62]

Summary

A fully developed minority group is one which is discriminated against by a certain group. This treatment clashes with other values in the culture which would tend to give the group equal status. Both the minority and the majority group recognize this situation as discrimination, and the minority group organizes itself to remove the discrimination. On the basis of this analysis there are a number of minorities in the United States. Some are racial minorities, such as the American Negro, the American Indian, the Japanese-American, and the Chinese-American. Others are religious minorities, such as the Jew, and still others are ethnic minorities such as the Spanish-speaking American. The present status of all these groups can be understood only in terms of a long series of historic relations among various groups.

Selected Readings

BARRON, MILTON L., ed. *American Minorities*. New York: Alfred A. Knopf, Inc., 1957. A collection of readings in intergroup relations covering a wide range of topics.

BURMA, JOHN H. *Spanish-Speaking Groups in the United States*. Durham, N.C.: Duke University Press, 1954. A discussion of the background and problems of the Hispanos, Mexican-Americans, Filipino-Americans, and Puerto Ricans in the United States.

DAVIS, ALLISON, BURLEIGH B. GARDNER, and MARY R. GARDNER. *Deep South*. Chicago: The University of Chicago Press, 1941. A study of whites and Negroes in a southern city and their relations with one another.

DOLLARD, JOHN. *Caste and Class in a Southern Town*. New Haven, Conn.: Yale University Press, 1937. The relations of whites and Negroes in a southern town.

DRAKE, ST. CLAIR, and HORACE R. CAYTON. *Black Metropolis*. New York: Harcourt, Brace & World, Inc., 1945. A study of the Negro area of Chicago and in particular the differences in social classes.

---

[62] For further discussions of the social characteristics of American Jews, see Marshall Sklare, *The Jews* (New York: The Free Press of Glencoe, 1958) and Albert I. Gordon, *Jews in Suburbia* (Boston: The Beacon Press, 1959).

FRAZIER, E. FRANKLIN. *The Negro in the United States*. Revised edition. New York: The Macmillan Company, 1957. An analysis of the American Negro. Chapters 2 and 3 deal with slavery and the plantation as a social institution.

GREENBERG, JACK. *Race Relations and American Law*. New York: Columbia University Press, 1959. A comprehensive discussion of the legal aspects of race relations and their sociological implications.

KING, MARTIN LUTHER, JR., *Stride toward Freedom*. New York: Harper & Row, Publishers, 1958. A detailed chronological account of the steps and strategy used in the Montgomery bus strike by the leader of the Negro group.

LEE, ROSE HUM. *The Chinese in the United States of America*. Hong Kong: Cathay Press, 1960. An analysis of the Chinese in the United States today: their culture, social organization and personality, institutions, and their economic organization and social structure.

MYRDAL, GUNNAR. *An American Dilemma*. New York: Harper & Row, Publishers, 1944. Probably the best-known book on minorities in America. It is a detailed study of the Negro by a large staff under the direction of the Swedish economist Gunnar Myrdal. The first chapter deals with the American Creed.

SCHERMERHORN, R. A. *These Our People*. Boston: D. C. Heath and Company, 1949, Chap. 16. A discussion of the Jewish community and its bicultural status.

SHOEMAKER, DON, ed. *With All Deliberate Speed*. New York: Harper & Row, Publishers, 1957. Eleven members of the staff of the Southern Education Reporting Service, publisher of the *Southern School News,* analyze various aspects of the school-desegregation process. Particularly useful is the chapter dealing with communities where there was violent resistance to integration.

Southern School News. Southern Education Reporting Service, Nashville, Tenn. A monthly publication providing a comprehensive coverage of developments in the school integration picture in all the southern and border states. Its reporting is objective and factual. In addition to its regular reports, it reproduces some of the more important documents, speeches, and proposals relevant to public school segregation and desegregation. Extremely useful in following current developments.

These Rights and Freedoms. United Nations Department of Public Information. New York: United Nations, 1950. Contains the full text of the University Declaration on Human Rights adopted by the General Assembly of the United Nations in 1948 as well as the various drafts of this declaration.

WIRTH, LOUIS. *The Ghetto*. Chicago: The University of Chicago Press, 1928. A well-known study which traces the ghetto historically and shows its effect on the contemporary Jew.

WOODWARD, C. VANN. *The Strange Career of Jim Crow*. New York: Oxford University Press, 1957. An outstanding American historian shows that racial segregation in the South is of relatively recent origin and describes the social and political mechanism of its establishment.

Chapter

18

Discrimination and Prejudice

Discrimination can be defined as the denial of equality of treatment to an individual or to groups of persons who desire this equality.[1] Often it involves restrictions on social participation and on occupying positions of social status which give a degree of power in a society.

Although there can be many kinds of discrimination, such as by sex or social class, the discussion here will be limited to discrimination on the basis of race, ethnic background, or religion. Several forms of discrimination can be described and analyzed: (1) restrictions on general social participation, (2) discriminations affecting health and life expectancy, (3) exclusion from organized groups, (4) discrimination in public accommodations, (5) discrimination and segregation in educational facilities, (6) discrimination in employment and business, (7) discrimination in suffrage, public office, and immigration, (8) discrimination in administration of justice, and (9) other forms of discrimination.

Several rather widespread misconceptions exist about the nature of discrimination against minority groups. Many people associate discrimination only with lynching, "Jim Crow" or segregated seating arrangements in public transportation, poor housing, menial positions, and the poor quality of segregated education among the Negroes. Many other forms are less overt and thus there is less awareness of them. Although the exclusion of a member of a minority group from voting would generally be recognized as discrimination, for example, not so readily regarded as discrimination is the fact that even though that individual has a vote it might be virtually impossible for one of his group to be elected to public office.

Discrimination is often thought of chiefly as a problem of the Negro, whereas many other minority groups are subject to it. Another misconception is to think of discrimination in the United States as existing chiefly in the South. Actually there is frequent discrimination in many forms against nearly all minority groups from coast to coast and from North to South. As it has been observed more than once, "The Northerner is all for

---

[1] Gordon W. Allport, *The Nature of Prejudice* (Reading, Mass.: Addison-Wesley Publishing Company, 1954).

equality for the Negro, provided it is in the South." In 1960 more than half of the Negroes in the country lived outside of the Confederate states, primarily in the Negro ghettos of the large cities of the North. As one writer has stated, the second half of the twentieth century will find solutions of Negro discrimination in the United States primarily hinging on the success of integration in the northern and western metropolises.[2] So far Negro citizens largely live as second-class citizens in these cities.

Forms of Discrimination

RESTRICTIONS ON GENERAL SOCIAL PARTICIPATION

Probably the most serious forms of discrimination for a society are those restrictions which affect the general social participation of minority groups. They include a wide range of customs involving social conventions, segregated living, and media of mass communication. All of them represent restrictions on the full participation of certain minority members in the society.

Social Conventions. Certain social conventions may prohibit full social participation of members of minority groups. For example, they are often referred to as "nigger," "Injun," "Chink," "darkey," "boy," or "uncle." Children learn to associate degrees of acceptance with such verbal symbols which are considered "bad." Such words become categories of ideas with emotional effect and are difficult to overcome by later relearning or by contact with the real objects.[3] Frequently members of minority groups are called by their first names only and are not accorded such terms of formal address as "Mr." and "Mrs." Jokes about them also represent a subtle form of discrimination, for they tend to reinforce the social discrimination barrier.[4] Such characters as Rastus, Mandy, Abie, Ikie, and Mike are familiar examples of stereotypes.

Members of minority groups are often required to use rear entrances, to remove their hats in the presence of a member of the dominant group, and to use the term "sir" freely in speech. Numerous social taboos further restrict social participation. In certain parts of the South, Negroes and whites do not eat together, swim together, or participate in professional or nonprofessional sports together. One Negro has described what these restrictions mean:

---

[2] Harry S. Ashmore, *The Other Side of Jordan: Negroes Outside the South* (New York: W. W. Norton & Company, Inc., 1960).

[3] H. H. Smythe and Myrna Seidman, "Name Calling a Significant Factor in Human Relations," *Human Relations,* 6:71–77 (Autumn, 1958).

[4] Milton Barron, "A Content Analysis of Intergroup Humor," *American Sociological Review,* 15:88–94 (February, 1950). Also see John H. Burma, "Humor as a Technique in Race Conflict," *American Sociological Review,* 11:710–715 (December, 1946).

I recall a trip I made in the Deep South with a famous sociologist and his wife. We rode on that trip as conspirators in an enemy country. Each meal presented itself as a challenge, a battle to be fought, and each success was greeted by us as a victory over the enemy. As lunch time grew near we were all silent with a tension which descended over the entire car. Would we, under some pretext, be able to eat together? If not, could I find a Negro restaurant? If there were no Negro restaurants, should I go to the kitchen of the white hotel and pretend to be their chauffeur or should I remain in the car and have them bring sandwiches to me? At night came the question of finding a place to sleep. Should I again pretend to be their servant and attempt to get servant quarters at the hotel? Could I find a Negro family who might have a clean guest room? Should I sleep in the car or should we all travel on, in spite of fatigue, until we could find a city where I could obtain lodging?

Even normal body functions presented a problem. They could be performed, to quote Belden, "only with considerable opposition, delay, annoyance and irritation." Could I drink from the water fountain at the filling station? Would there be provisions for washing my hands or face? If a toilet is not marked "white" or "colored," dare I use it? [5]

There may also be restrictions on entertaining members of minority groups or inviting them to dances, parties, picnics, or other informal activities. Even more prevalent are restrictions on such social relationships as dating, courtship and marriage. In some states a member of a minority group seen in the company of a member of the majority group of the other sex may be arrested for disorderly conduct. There are more anti-miscegenation laws (laws prohibiting marriage between certain races), in fact, than any other kind of discriminatory statute.[6] Several states have only recently repealed such laws: Oregon, 1951; Montana, 1953; North Dakota, 1955; Colorado and South Dakota, 1957; and Idaho, 1959. The California Supreme Court held its antimiscegenation law unconstitutional in 1948. Such laws not only prohibit Negro-white marriages but often also forbid the marriage of whites with Mongolians, Malayans, Hindus, Koreans, and others, and often declare the marriage void, with criminal penalties which may be quite severe. The couple might be ordered to leave the state, and their children might be declared illegitimate.

Segregated Living and Inadequate Housing. Minority groups usually reside in poor housing and in segregated parts of towns, in "Niggertown," "Chinatown," or "Japtown," or on Indian reservations, or in Spanish-speaking areas. Housing, stores, motion-picture houses, taverns, and other facilities are often separate from the dominant group. One of the most

---

[5] Horace R. Cayton, "The Psychological Approach to Race Relations," *Reed College Bulletin*, 25:8–27 (November, 1946).

[6] Jack Greenberg, *Race Relations and American Law* (New York: Columbia University Press, 1960), p. 343.

difficult problems for a Negro, for example, is to try to live in a white neighborhood.[7]

Living in segregated areas has generally meant, for minority groups, poor housing conditions as well as high disease and infant mortality rates. Minority groups tend to live chiefly in the slums of such cities as New York, Birmingham, San Antonio, Phoenix, and San Francisco, or in shacks in rural areas. The 1950 census showed that 60 percent of all urban Negro families lived in substandard dwellings which were either dilapidated or lacked proper sanitary facilities. Only 20 percent of the white population lived in a comparable situation.

In addition to poor physical surroundings, the slum is often characterized by deviant norms, the presence of gambling, prostitution, and "honky-tonks," all of which create a hazardous moral atmosphere in which to raise families. Segregated living areas also interfere with free lines of conversation and social participation between minority and majority groups. One writer has described this restriction on social participation in reference to the Spanish-speaking people in Texas.

> It has been my observation that everywhere in the state the Spanish-speaking and Anglo groups have trouble in communicating with one another. It is an oversimplified but nonetheless accurate statement of the situation to say that Latins tend to talk mainly to other Latins and Anglos to other Anglos. There are many reasons why this is so. One is the "we" and "they" identification which I have already mentioned. All of us feel more comfortable with people like ourselves than we do with those we consider different. Another is the physical separation of the two groups resulting from separate residential and business sections, and, heretofore, separate schools. Still another is occupational separation which comes about because the Latins are channeled into relatively few occupations in which they make up the numerically dominant group. But whatever the reasons, it is an observable fact that, by and large, Spanish-speaking people tend to associate with other Spanish-speaking, English-speaking tend to associate with other English-speaking. There are few organizations in any community with mixed membership, few in which members of the two groups have an opportunity to talk across ethnic lines about matters of common concern. There are Anglo churches and Latin churches; Anglo Parent-Teachers Associations and Latin Parent-Teachers Associations; Anglo fellowship organizations and Latin fellowship organizations; Anglo veterans' groups and Latin veterans' groups.[8]

---

[7] Although minorities live in segregated areas because of low income and other reasons, there are also restrictive covenants of property owners, city zoning laws, and real-estate boards that seek to restrict the minority groups from living areas occupied by the majority group. The Supreme Court has outlawed restrictive covenants but the ruling has not put an end to their informal existence.

[8] Lyle Saunders, Address Delivered at the National Convention of the League of United American Citizens, San Antonio, June 11, 1949. (Report on the Study of Spanish-Speaking People, University of Texas.)

For minority group members whose education and income have improved it is often difficult to move into areas of better housing in suburban areas. Landlords will often not rent to them, and real-estate agents will not sell housing. In addition, the residents will often not welcome them. Although Jewish discrimination in housing is less a problem in suburbia than it was ten years ago and several hundred thousand Jews have moved into these areas, discrimination is still a problem.[9] A 1957 survey of the policies of the real-estate agents in suburban Detroit showed that one third indicated they did not wish to sell or rent to Jews and discriminated against them in one way or another.[10] The living situation in suburbia is partly a product of anti-Semitic attitudes and partly a product of Jews having their closest friendships among other Jews of the same community, class, synagogue, and organizational interests.

Such discrimination against the Japanese-Americans, an economically successful, highly educated, upwardly mobile group, is a constant source of unhappiness, irritation, and deprivation. One writer has said this about the California situation:

> Discrimination against the Japanese in California has diminished greatly since the end of the war. Partly as a result of this decline in discrimination, the economic and occupational status of the nisei has risen. Paradoxically, this economic progress has intensified the discriminatory situation in housing. For, before the war, very few nisei had the money or the inclination to seek independent housing. Most of them lived in the Japanese communities and many with their parents. The increase in income and in status of occupants have led many of them to search actively for better housing in better neighborhoods. And there they have often encountered discrimination.[11]

The situation is uneven in different cities, and among various minorities. For example, Negro housing is much better in Atlanta than in Birmingham.[12] In 1950, 17 percent of the Negro households in urban areas were classified as overcrowded, as compared to 4 percent of the white. Areas where Negroes live in Chicago, for example, which were built to house 20,000 persons per square mile now have 90,000.[13] It is common for several families to use the same toilet and kitchen facilities. In general, housing conditions of the Negro and Spanish-speaking minorities are

[9] Albert I. Gordon, *Jews in Suburbia* (Boston: The Beacon Press, 1959).

[10] Anti-Defamation League, *Reports on Social, Employment, Educational, and Housing Discrimination*, Vol. 2, No. 5 (January–February, 1959).

[11] Harry H. L. Kitano, "Housing of Japanese-Americans in the San Francisco Bay Area," in Nathan Glazer and Davis McEntire eds., *Studies in Housing and Minority Groups* (Berkeley: University of California Press, 1960), pp. 195–196.

[12] Robert A. Thompson, Hylan Lewis, and Davis McEntire, "Atlanta and Birmingham: A Comparative Study in Negro Housing," in Glazer and McEntire, *op. cit.*, pp. 13–84.

[13] Harry J. Walker, *The Negro in American Life* (New York: Oxford Book Company, 1959), p. 22.

similar to those which have been found for the Puerto Ricans in New York City.[14]

1. A very high proportion of families live in furnished rooms and apartments.
2. Families have insufficient space.
3. They live mainly but not entirely in the more deteriorated areas.
4. They live in old buildings in poor condition.
5. They have inadequate service and facilities.
6. They pay high rents, as compared with those paid by comparable groups.[15]

Media of Mass Communication. An important form of exclusion of minorities from participation in society is their relative omission from media of mass communication. Negroes, Spanish-speaking people, or those of Oriental descent are seldom cast as actors in motion pictures, television, or the radio except in stereotyped inferior roles. Magazine fiction also reflects majority and minority status. In an analysis of some two hundred stories, about 84 percent of the characters were identified simply as Americans, which usually implied white, Protestant, English-speaking, and Anglo-Saxon.[16] Of nine hundred identifiable characters, only sixteen were Negroes and ten were Jews. Typically, minority characters were described as the "amusingly ignorant Negro," "the Italian gangster," "the sly and shrewd Jew," and "the emotional Irish." Articles about Negro citizens who are not celebrities, or about Negro social gatherings, weddings, and other activities seldom appear in widely read newspapers, and advertisements seldom picture Negro families or individuals, except for an occasional Negro singer or athlete.[17]

Most school textbooks contain little deliberate bias, but there is often subtle discrimination through the omission of certain materials dealing with minorities. The history of America, at least in school textbooks, is largely the history of the majority group.[18] Although the situation is improving, this constitutes a basic form of discrimination.

HEALTH AND LIFE EXPECTANCY

Minority groups, such as Negroes, Spanish-speaking peoples, and Indians, generally have a higher death rate than has the white population

---

[14] Morris Eagle, "The Puerto Ricans in New York City," in Glazer and McEntire, *op. cit.,* pp. 144–178.

[15] *Ibid.,* p. 156.

[16] Bernard Berelson and Patricia J. Salter, "Majority and Minority Americans: An Analysis of Magazine Fiction," *Public Opinion Quarterly,* 10:168–190 (Summer, 1946).

[17] Consequently, some two hundred Negro newspapers and magazines are published whose contents, including advertisements, are almost exclusively Negro and whose advertisements usually show Negroes. One magazine, *Ebony,* has a circulation of over 500,000.

[18] Report of the Committee on the Study of Teaching Materials in Intergroup Relations (Howard E. Wilson, Director). *Intergroup Relations in Teaching Materials* (Washington, D.C.: American Council on Education, 1949).

in the United States. The higher death rate among Negroes is due to several factors, including poor health practices, insufficient medical care, poor living conditions, and their low economic level. In 1956 the death rate for whites was 9.3 (number of deaths per 1000 population) while the nonwhite rate was 10.1. The nonwhite death rate in 1930 was 16.3, as contrasted with 10.8 for the whites, which indicates the great health gains made by the nonwhites during the last two decades. Another indication of these gains is the fact that the life expectancy of the nonwhite population increased 5.7 years from 1940 to 1955, while the increase was 2.4 years for the white population. In 1959, the deaths under one year, per 1000 live births, were 23.2 for white babies, and 44.0—almost double—for nonwhite babies.

The higher death rate for the nonwhite population, which consists chiefly of Negroes, is predominantly in the communicable disease categories and nonmotor-vehicle accidents, primarily in industry. One example illustrates this differential. In 1959 in the United States approximately 30 percent of all deaths from pneumonia and influenza were among the Negroes.

Better hospital and health facilities are an obvious need to correct these conditions, but segregation and exclusion from hospitals is widespread in the South as well as in parts of the North. Hospital regulations, and even state laws which support them, often bar Negroes from medical association membership. Greenberg has written on this situation:

> Where there is discrimination in hospitals against Negro doctors they frequently must lose their patients to white physicians, for "white" hospitals are by far the best equipped. This bias is usually connected with medical society and hospital arrangements. Hospitals will admit only society members and the societies often will not accept Negroes, although this restriction has been waning in some places. Inability to participate in medical association meetings and to work in the best hospitals also impairs professional training. This discrimination has had a striking impact. Dietrich Reitze's study, *Negroes and Medicine,* reveals that while the Negro populations of New Orleans, Atlanta, and Nashville are increasing at a rapid rate the number of Negro doctors in these cities is decreasing substantially. This has been caused by the inability of Negro doctors to secure postgraduate training there along with their white peers and by the bar against Negro doctors' treating their patients in the best hospitals.[19]

EXCLUSION FROM ORGANIZED GROUPS

Nearly all organized groups have certain criteria for membership, such as occupation and education, and many persons who do not have these qualifications might often consider them discriminatory. The term "dis-

---

[19] Greenberg, *op. cit.,* pp. 168–169.

criminatory" will be restricted, however, to those members of racial, ethnic, and religious groups who are still not permitted to join even when they possess the necessary occupational or educational qualifications. Many organizations of a recreational nature have practiced discrimination, and some still do. Private golf clubs generally exclude Negroes, and often Jews.

A 1961 survey of 1152 clubs in forty-six states and the District of Columbia found that 781, or 67 percent, practice religious discrimination.[20] Of the 781 discriminating clubs, 691 excluded or limited Jewish membership, and 90 were Jewish clubs which excluded or limited Christian membership. The 1152 clubs represent a total membership of approximately 700,000 persons. Particular attention in the survey was paid to those clubs which were evaluated as enjoying maximum prestige in their communities. Of the 693 top American clubs, 60 percent practice religious discrimination, and of these discriminatory clubs more than 90 percent discriminate against Jews. The survey concluded: "If the thesis is accepted that many prestige clubs are factors in the power structures which influence greatly the political and economic life of the community, then the fact that 60 percent of the prestige clubs of the United States discriminate against Jews has serious implications for the Jewish group." [21] It was also pointed out that this type of discrimination against Jews is far greater than the levels of discrimination against them in other areas such as education, employment, housing, and public accommodations.

Although the situation is changing, many national college social fraternities and sororities exclude from membership those who are non-Christian or non-Caucasian. The exclusion may be explicitly stated in the constitutions; if there are no constitutional provisions, the exclusion is just as real—students from these minority groups are not asked to join.[22] Consequently, this is one reason why Jewish and Negro students have separate fraternities and sororities. Several universities within the past few years have taken a strong position against this discrimination, and it is becoming a subject of frequent discussion among fraternities and sororities. Occasionally a fraternity or sorority may defy the national organization and pledge a member of a minority group.

Many professional fraternities and associations either exclude certain minorities from membership or discriminate against them. In 1949 the American Bar Association had only 13 Negroes among its 41,000 members. Several national law fraternities exclude Jewish students as well. The American Medical Association and the American Dental Association has no national policy, but leaves the question of discrimination up to local

[20] "A Study of Religious Discrimination by Social Clubs," *Rights* (Publication of the Anti-Defamation League of B'nai B'rith), 4:83–86 (January, 1962).

[21] *Ibid.*, p. 86.

[22] See Alfred McClung Lee, *Fraternities without Brotherhood* (Boston: The Beacon Press, 1955).

groups, with the result that many qualified Negro doctors and dentists do not belong; hence Negroes have their own separate national medical, dental, and legal associations. Even where members of minorities are accepted in the organization they are seldom elected or appointed to positions of leadership. In 1949 the American Medical Association, for example, named a Negro to its policy-making body for the first time in its 103-year history.

About 98 percent of all Negroes attend exclusively Negro churches. Consequently, some Negro church organizations are very large, as is the African Methodist Church. Other Negroes may belong to separate Negro religious sects. Some of this separation is the choice of the Negroes and is a result of other forms of segregation, principally segregation in housing. In other instances separation in worship is the result of a church's not allowing Negro attendance, or failing to encourage it, or requiring separate seating arrangements. Various church groups have opposed these discriminatory practices and some have made a positive effort to end them.

The exclusion of minorities from formal organizations hinders general social communication with other groups. It may also mean exclusion from groups with high social status and consequently the denial of opportunities for "prestige" membership in the society. This exclusion often indirectly results in serious economic discrimination in certain occupations. Membership in certain social and professional fraternities, and even clubs, may mean associations and contacts which may furnish a definite business or professional advantage.[23]

PUBLIC ACCOMMODATIONS

Widespread discrimination against Negroes still exists in many parts of the South, as well as in some parts of the North, in the use of public accommodations—restaurants, hotels, resorts, and beaches, for example. Public facilities in the South, such as libraries, parks, drinking facilities, and toilets, are often marked "For Colored" and "For Whites," and in one state until recently there was even a law providing for separate telephone booths. Not only are these public accommodations segregated; in most areas of the South, where Negroes often outnumber whites, the

---

[23] "The exclusion of Jews from 'Greek letter' fraternities and sororities parallels their exclusion from social clubs and is similarly motivated [for social power]. It is silly to speak of college fraternities as though they were the end-product of some instinctive process by which like-minded individuals are sorted into special categories. Freshmen are rushed for the most specific and tangible reasons: social standing, wealth, family connections, special talents, athletic ability, and so forth. Fraternities, like clubs in later years, are the pools and generators of social power and prestige: those with it enter them, those entering them, heighten their potency. Social alliances formed in college naturally tend to carry over into adult life."—Carey McWilliams, "Does Social Discrimination Really Matter?" *Commentary*, 4:411 (November, 1947).

facilities for the white population exceed those for nonwhites. In 1952 nine southern states, for example, had 12 parks for Negroes, as compared with 180 for whites. In addition, most cemeteries in the South are segregated.

Before 1899 just three states required or authorized Jim Crow waiting rooms, but within a decade almost all aspects of rail travel in the South had come under segregation laws. Later, interstate busses followed in the 1930's, until, finally, only the airplane escaped. As one historian has written, "even to the orthodox there was doubtless something slightly incongruous about requiring a Jim Crow compartment on a Lockheed Constellation or a DC-6." [24] Busses, streetcars, and trains throughout the South have had separate seating arrangements for white and colored passengers; in addition, custom has also required that Negroes wait until all white persons have boarded a bus or a streetcar before they themselves could enter. In 1959 thirteen southern states had laws requiring or authorizing segregated travel. In 1961, however, the Interstate Commerce Commission ordered the elimination of all segregated facilities in waiting rooms and eating places in railway and bus terminals serving interstate passengers. Also within the last few years the bus companies of several southern cities, beginning with Montgomery, Alabama, and Tallahassee, Florida, have been forced, through widespread boycotting of the services by Negroes, to integrate passenger seating.[25]

Discrimination has also taken the form of prohibiting Negroes access to certain hotels, motels, restaurants, resorts, and the like, throughout most of the South as well as in parts of the North. Some of the self-styled better restaurants throughout the United States discourage the patronage of Negroes, Indians, Orientals, or Spanish-speaking persons. Discrimination may be accomplished by refusing admittance to these patrons, by asking them to leave, by refusing or delaying service, or by serving them unpalatable food. In the South Negroes may not be allowed to attend a public theater, a concert, or a motion picture or drive-in theater, or they are permitted to occupy only the least desirable section. Otherwise they must attend separate motion-picture theaters for Negroes, a discrimination which often represents a considerable financial burden to maintain in some of the smaller southern cities. In the South, and sometimes in the North, parks, playgrounds, swimming pools, and beaches are operated on a segregated basis. This discrimination is not limited to Negroes, for the Mexicans and Mexican-Americans in the Southwest encounter difficulties in such things as being refused

---

[24] C. Vann Woodward, *The Strange Career of Jim Crow* (New York: Oxford University Press, 1957), p. 103.

[25] See Martin Luther King, *Stride toward Freedom* (New York: Harper & Row, Publishers, 1958); and C. U. Smith and Lewis M. Killian, *The Tallahassee Bus Protest* (New York: Anti-Defamation League of B'nai B'rith, 1958).

service in barbershops, soda fountains, cafes, drive-ins, beauty parlors, hotels, bars, and recreation centers; segregation in housing, movies, schools, churches, and cemeteries, as well as in public buildings and public toilets; reluctant service in hospitals, colleges, social welfare offices, and courts; and even refusing to permit Mexican-American hostesses in USO's. Sometimes there will be signs "No Mexicans Allowed," "Mexicans Will Be Served in Kitchen Only," or "We Do Not Solicit Mexican or Negro Trade"; more often it is the less obtrusive but equally well understood "We Retain the Right to Refuse Service to Any Customer." [26]

Discrimination in vacation resorts may involve many minority groups, including Jews. Members of all these minority groups have even encountered difficulty in finding hotel or motel accommodations on the highways. The denial of the opportunity to take a vacation in a particular area or place because of an individual's or a family's race, religion, or ethnic background is a severe type of discrimination. A study of a midwestern vacation state has given us more specific information on at least one area. In this state a nationwide automobile association in 1946 listed 341 hotels, cabins, and tourist camps and houses as being restricted to gentiles only. According to a resort association official, in 1950 at least 80 percent of the state's resorts would not admit Jews or Negroes: "As for Negroes, I know of absolutely no top grade or even medium grade resort in the state which will accept a colored person." [27]

In 1959, twenty-six states had enacted laws forbidding bias in public accommodations, such as restaurants, hotels, and motels. These states are Alaska, California, Colorado, Connecticut, Illinois, Indiana, Iowa, Kansas, Maine, Massachusetts, Michigan, Minnesota, Montana, Nebraska, New Hampshire (covering advertising only), New Jersey, New Mexico, New York, Ohio, Oregon, Pennsylvania, Rhode Island, Vermont, Washington, Wisconsin, and Wyoming, as well as the District of Columbia.[28] Changes are taking place in other states also. In 1961, for example, Atlanta department stores' eating facilities, as well as many other restaurants, were opened to Negro patronage.

EDUCATIONAL FACILITIES

The accumulated knowledge of a culture is principally transmitted through its educational institutions, and discrimination in the extent and quality of any group's education may affect the cultural adjustment, social status, and personal enjoyment of its members. As groups, Negroes,

---

[26] John Burma, *Spanish-Speaking Groups in the United States* (Durham, N.C.: Duke University Press, 1954), pp. 107–108.

[27] Through the work of a state commission on human rights considerable improvement has been made in this situation since then.

[28] Jack Greenberg, *Race Relations and American Law* (New York: Columbia University Press, 1959), p. 101.

Spanish-speaking people, and Indians receive less education than members of the majority group, the dollar cost of their education is less, the quality of their school buildings is poorer, and their teachers are often less educated and more poorly paid than other teachers. Negro children in many parts of the South, as well as children of Spanish-speaking migratory workers, have fewer required days in school per year than do white children. This situation has improved considerably, and even more can be expected in the future because of the Supreme Court decision of 1954 ordering the end of segregation in education.

At the time of the 1954 decision seventeen southern and border states, in addition to the District of Columbia, had complete segregation in their elementary and secondary schools, with the exception of a few communities with only a few Negro children to educate. Four states outside this region—

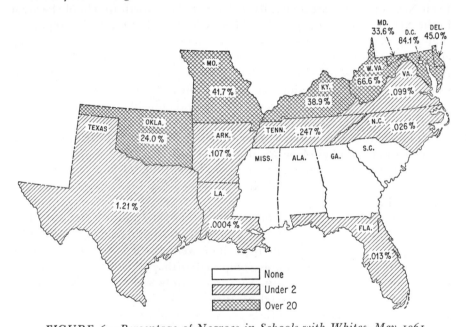

FIGURE 6.—*Percentage of Negroes in Schools with Whites, May 1961*

SOURCE: Southern Education Reporting Service, Nashville, Tenn., May 1961.

Arizona, Kansas, New Mexico, and Wyoming—allowed some local segregation contrary to law. Sixteen states prohibited by law any segregation, although not all of them enforced these statutes. Eleven other northern and western states had no laws on this matter. Figure 6 shows the present status of school segregation-desegregation in the southern and border states in May, 1961, exactly seven years after the Supreme Court decision.

As of May, 1961 in the southern region—that is, the states of Alabama, Arkansas, Delaware, Florida, Georgia, Kentucky, Louisiana, Maryland,

Mississippi, Missouri, North Carolina, Oklahoma, South Carolina, Tennessee, Texas, Virginia, West Virginia, and the District of Columbia—the Negroes in the 783 desegregated districts (out of a total of 6663 school districts) represented 22.9 percent of the region's total Negro enrollment. However, of these 706,163 Negroes in the desegregated districts, only 30.2 percent actually attended desegregated schools. The South in May, 1961, had 213,534 Negroes attending the same schools with whites, representing 6.9 percent of the region's 3,088,261 Negro students.[29]

Segregated schooling is not always a consequence of laws, however, for residential segregation in large cities generally means that, in both the North and the South, many schools are in fact segregated without laws. Since pupils are required to attend schools in the neighborhoods in which they live, the schools in Negro areas will virtually have all Negro pupils. Even Negro teachers are generally assigned in the North to schools located in the Negro areas. In 1959 the New York City Board of Education reported that 56.7 percent of the students in elementary schools throughout the city were attending segregated schools, defined as 90 percent or more from the same race.[30] This situation had improved, however, by 6.5 percent since 1957. Thus until residential segregation is markedly changed, segregated schooling, whether by law or otherwise, is not likely to affect a large proportion of Negro students in the North or the South.

The effects of segregated schooling have been amply demonstrated through special studies of pupils in schools which have been desegregated. In Washington, D.C. and elsewhere it was found that when Negro students were integrated with whites their educational level, in many cases, was generally inferior.

The majority of Negro college students, either from the North or the South, still attend Negro colleges. Although figures are difficult to obtain and the picture is changing, in 1948 there were about 3000 Negro college students in northern colleges, as compared with 75,000 at the 108 Negro colleges primarily in the South. In a 1957 study southern Negro college students attending an interracial northern university placed general social participation (Negro fraternities, sororities, dances, and so on) as the greatest asset of their college.[31] On the other hand, the greatest handicap was the inferiority of their college as measured by reputation, faculty, and their own performance at the northern university.

Another form of discrimination exists under the quota system by which only certain percentages of a given minority are accepted by an educa-

[29] "Statistical Summary of School Segregation-Desegregation in the Southern and Border States," *Southern Education Reporting Service*, Nashville, Tennessee, May, 1961, p. 3.

[30] Ashmore, *op. cit.*, p. 122.

[31] Marshall B. Clinard and Donald L. Noel, "Role Behavior of Students from Negro Colleges in a Non-Segregated University Situation," *Journal of Negro Education*, 27:182–188 (Spring, 1958).

tional institution. In a study of 10,000 high school seniors who applied for college admission, 72 percent of the applications of Protestant students were accepted, as compared with only 56 percent of the applications of Jewish students: "If we use the term 'discrimination' solely as an objective label for a difference in application success rates, leaving out any over- tones concerning the social attitudes of responsible college admission officers, we can certainly say on the basis of these data that discrimination against Jewish high school students appears evident." [32] This study indi- cated, moreover, that the bright Jewish student was handicapped even more than those Jewish students whose grades were lower. A Connecticut study, involving 1381 questionnaires sent to students with equivalent grades, also revealed similar discriminatory college admission practices against the Jewish students. Some 41 percent of the Jewish applications, and 71 percent of the Protestant applications were accepted.[33] Quota systems also appear to apply to some professional and other graduate schools. The quota system is being abolished by many colleges and universities, because of public attitudes and the pressures of governmental agencies.

EMPLOYMENT AND BUSINESS

Members of the Negro, Indian, and Spanish-speaking minorities are disproportionately employed in such unskilled or semiskilled jobs as com- mon labor, farm labor, housework, gardening, fruit picking, and shoeshin- ing. Usually they do not receive equal pay for equal work, a white man often receiving more pay than a Negro, and an Anglo more than a Spanish-speak- ing person. On this subject Saunders remarked: "If one were to attempt to characterize the condition of the Spanish-speaking Texans, he would be forced to say that, in general, and for nearly any index of socioeconomic status that might be devised, the Spanish-speaking people are found to occupy a less desirable position than the Anglos or the population as a whole." [34]

Many unions have extensive restrictions on Negroes. Some discriminate by ritual and others by constitutional provisions, tacit agreement, or segregated auxiliary status. Certain unions bar Negroes from many posi- tions. Although no constitutional provisions affecting Negroes exist, it is difficult for a Negro, for example, to become admitted to full membership in a union as a carpenter, painter, or bricklayer in many areas of the North and South. He may sometimes, however, become a member of a subordinate

---

[32] A. C. Ivy and Irwin Ross, *Religion and Race: Barriers to College* (New York: Public Affairs Pamphlets, No. 153, 1949), p. 11.
[33] Henry G. Stetler, *College Admission Practices with Respect to Race, Religion, and National Origin of Connecticut High School Graduates* (Hartford: Connecticut State Inter- racial Commission, 1949).
[34] Saunders, *op. cit.*, pp. 7–8.

affiliated union. It is equally hard for a Negro in the North or the South to become an electrician or a plumber. Some unions put Negroes in a sort of Jim Crow status by allowing them to pay dues but to have little voice in the organization.

This situation has improved with the advent of the industrial union, the short labor supply in some trades from the beginning of World War II, and the pressure of state Fair Employment Practices Commissions and the FEPC laws. In 1960 Negro union members numbered 1.5 million.[35] The average wages of nonwhite males have increased in the past twenty years from 41 to 58 percent of what white workers get. In this same period the percentage of Negroes in professional and skilled work doubled. These improvements, however, have not necessarily meant complete equality for the Negro workers, for one of the most persistent forms of discrimination in employment involves opportunities for advancement.[36] Sometimes advancement is contingent upon union membership, which cannot be secured; an example is a Negro brakeman who cannot become a railroad conductor. Discrimination may affect promotion to supervisor, foreman, salesman, buyer, or junior executive. According to Ashmore, in 1960 only six of the AFL–CIO unions had Negroes in positions of elected national leadership.[37]

Contrary to popular opinion, economic discrimination against non-whites increases systematically with their age and education.

> Many barriers to the education of non-whites will probably be taken down in the future, and this will increase their education relative to that of whites. This would also increase their income relative to that of whites if there were no discrimination; but, since discrimination rises with education, an increase in the education of non-whites may increase only slightly their incomes relative to those of whites. Hence it is important to investigate the cause of the greater market discrimination against older and better-educated non-whites.[38]

SUFFRAGE, PUBLIC OFFICE, AND IMMIGRATION.

Several million Negroes in the South are still restricted in their use of the ballot. Poll tax provisions still remaining in certain southern states curtail suffrage rights, for each voter must annually pay approximately $1.50 in order to vote, a large sum for low-income families. This voting prerequisite is also directed at poor whites and often serves to keep certain

---

[35] Ashmore, op. cit., p. 78.
[36] Robert C. Weaver, "Negro Labor Since 1929," Journal of Negro History, 35:20–38 (January, 1950).
[37] Ashmore, op. cit., p. 81.
[38] Gary S. Becker, The Economics of Discrimination (Chicago: The University of Chicago Press, 1957), p. 130.

social classes and political machines in power. Other restrictive devices have included registration requirements or literacy tests, the passage of which has often been subjectively determined by white poll workers, as well as various forms of intimidation at the polls or before elections.[39] Interestingly enough, large numbers of Negro voters were registered to vote in the various southern states before the turn of the century; the effectiveness of the various disfranchisement measures can be illustrated by what happened in Louisiana. Here 130,334 Negroes were registered voters in 1896, but there were only 1342 in 1904, after the passage of literacy, property, and poll tax qualifications. Also, in 1896 there was a majority of Negro registrants in twenty-six Lousiana parishes, but by 1900 there was a majority in none.[40]

There has been a tremendous growth in Negro voting during the past two decades. These advances have resulted from improved intergroup relations, state legislation, and various decisions of the United States Supreme Court. These decisions have outlawed a number of the various devices which had earlier been passed to prevent the exercise of the ballot. One of these devices, the so-called grandfather clause, stated that one's grandfather had to have been capable of voting; another, the exclusive "white primary" provisions, outlawed in 1944, kept a Negro from joining the Democratic party and thus virtually prevented him in some places from casting a meaningful vote. The poll tax is also gradually being removed throughout the South, although it is still in force in five states.[41] One study indicated that whereas in 1940 only about 2 percent of the total number of Negroes of voting age in twelve southern states qualified to vote, in 1947 some 12 percent, or more than 600,000, did so. In 1952 there were 1,200,000 Negroes registered to vote, and the number has been growing rapidly.[42]

Even if all minorities could vote freely, a wide and significant area of discrimination would exist if qualified members of minority groups could not be freely appointed to important governmental positions or run for political office without the possibility of discrimination. These positions are largely held by the older native white stock, and a relatively minor role in national and state politics is played by millions of citizens from minority groups. No Negro has ever been a cabinet member or a Supreme Court justice, but in 1961 Robert Weaver was appointed the first Negro to head a federal government agency, the Federal Housing and Home Finance Agency. Negroes have seldom held high subordinate positions in

---

[39] Ralph Bunche, "The Negro in the Political Life of the United States," *Journal of Negro Education*, 10:547–584 (July, 1941).

[40] Woodward, *op. cit.*, p. 68.

[41] These states are Alabama, Arkansas, Mississippi, Texas, and Virginia, although their poll tax laws are not uniform.

[42] Woodward, *op. cit.*, p. 127.

the federal government, although such appointments are increasing. Within recent years Negroes have been appointed directors of large state agencies in such states as Illinois and New York.

Members of minority groups are seldom elected to high state or national offices. In 1961 there were no Negro senators and only 3 Negro representatives. In 1956 there were but 1 senator and 2 representatives with a Spanish-American background, although this group is numerically large in several states.[43] Herbert Lehman, in 1949, was the first Jew ever elected to the Senate by popular vote, the last Jewish member having been appointed to the Senate in 1915. No person of American Indian ancestry occupies an elective position of political importance in the United States. Even the long opposition to Hawaii's statehood came, in part, from the fear that Hawaii might possibly be represented in Washington by Oriental senators and representatives, which is now the case.

At the local and state level of government, however, there has been increasing recognition of the right of minority members to be freely appointed or elected to public office. In 1949 a Mexican-American was elected for the first time since 1881 to the City Council in Los Angeles, and in 1950 for the first time in Chicago a Negro became a Cook County judge. Negroes are occupying an increasingly significant place in the local political communities, being appointed or elected to school boards in several southern cities, serving on the state boards of education, and securing places on city councils.

American immigration laws have almost consistently discriminated against some minorities: first, the Chinese Exclusion Act of 1882; later, the 1924 act, which outlawed Japanese immigration.[44] The 1952 immigration law, the McCarran Act, allowed the entrance of 185 Japanese annually; another act passed during World War II permitted the entrance of 105 Chinese, but it also provided for a total "Asia-Pacific triangle" quota of 2000 Orientals regardless of nationality. Laws also formerly prohibited naturalization of persons of Japanese or Chinese ancestry. This discrimination in immigration and naturalization reflects on immigrants of such ancestry and gives them the status of second-class and unwanted Americans.

ADMINISTRATION OF JUSTICE

It is a generally established fact that Negroes, as well as Spanish-speaking peoples, on the whole, are arrested, tried, convicted, and re-

---

[43] Some of these difficulties are described in Beatrice W. Griffith, "Viva Royal—Viva America," *Common Ground*, 10:61–70 (Autumn, 1949).

[44] This immigration act established quotas based on the proportion of the United States population which each country had in the 1890 Census, and thus discriminated against persons from Eastern and Southern Europe. The 1952 immigration act based quotas on the 1920 census instead of substituting the 1950 census, as advocated by many persons.

turned to prison more often than others who commit comparable offenses.[45] They appear to be more frequently subjected to the illegal "third degree" and other forms of police brutality. During 1949, for example, thirty-four Negroes were killed and thirty-three were injured while in police custody. A Negro or a Spanish-American offender may be dealt with more harshly by a judge than will a member of a majority group. Part of this situation in the past has stemmed from discrimination in the appointment of members of minority groups to police forces and the courts or in their limited service on juries.

Mob lynchings are still a blight on the American scene, but their extent has been exaggerated. From 1900 through 1960, altogether 1992 persons have been lynched. In the 1890's, when the population was only about 40 percent of what it is today, lynchings averaged 154 a year; in the 1930's, 13 a year; and in the 1940's, 4 a year. In some recent years no lynchings have been recorded: 1952–1954, 1956, 1958, and 1960. Many attempted lynchings still occur, and it has been estimated by Tuskegee Institute that lynchings of about 200 Negroes were prevented from 1937 to 1946.[46] Most lynchings occur in isolated rural areas, according to a 1930 study, which also found that most of the participants were young and unemployed, many with police records.[47]

Race riots involving Negroes and whites have occurred in several large cities, including Chicago in 1919 and Detroit and New York during World War II. During the last few years, as school integration has proceeded slowly in the South, there has also been some rioting and other acts of violence, but on the whole the fight against segregation throughout the South has been pushed largely by other means. Efforts to prevent rioting and violence have been made in several notable instances by the calling out of the National Guard, for example, in Clinton, Tennessee, and later in Nashville, Tennessee. By order of the President, federal troops were used in Little Rock, Arkansas to restore order.

In addition to rioting, many acts of vandalism have been directed against various minorities. Their property has been damaged or destroyed, and, in the case of the Jews, their cemeteries and synagogues have been defaced. In the first two months of 1960 there was an epidemic of 323 anti-Semitic acts directed against Jews in the United States.[48] About half of these acts involved the painting of a Nazi swastika, and other acts included, in order, anti-Jewish slogans, threats, physical damage, bombings,

---

[45] See, for example, Edwin M. Lemert and Judy Rosberg, "The Administration of Justice to Minority Groups in Los Angeles County 1948," (Publications in Culture and Society, Vol. 2, No. 1; Berkeley: University of California Press, 1948).

[46] President's Committee on Civil Rights, *To Secure These Rights* (New York: Simon and Schuster, Inc., 1947), p. 24.

[47] Arthur F. Raper, *The Tragedy of Lynching* (Chapel Hill: University of North Carolina Press, 1933).

[48] David Caplovitz and Candace Rogers, *Swastika, 1960: The Epidemic of Anti-Semitic Vandalism in America* (New York: Anti-Defamation League of B'nai B'rith, 1961).

Nazi flags, cross burnings, and ambiguous markings. Not all rioting and acts of vandalism have been directed against Negroes and Jews. One such example is the Los Angeles "Zoot Suit Riot" in 1943, which involved brutality to young adult Mexican-Americans.[49]

PAST DISCRIMINATION IN THE ARMED FORCES

Since World War II segregated service in the armed forces has largely been eliminated.[50] Even peacetime service in the army in any numbers, or on a nonsegregated basis, is a fairly new experience for the Negro. As late as 1949 California, Connecticut, Illinois, Massachusetts, Wisconsin, and Minnesota ended segregation in the National Guard. In 1939 there were 4500 Negro enlisted men in the United States Army and 5 Negro officers. Although, because of lack of racial identifications since complete integration, it is not possible at the present time to report the exact number of Negroes now in the armed services, it has been stated with some assurance that "for the total service personnel, approximately 2,500,000 for all the Services, ten percent are Negro." [51] The last tabulation of service personnel by race which was issued on a percentage basis as of July 1, 1954, gave the following percentages of Negro personnel against total personnel in the military services:

Army officers	3.0
Army enlisted men	13.7
Navy officers	0.1
Navy enlisted men	3.6
Air Force officers	1.1
Air Force enlisted men	8.6
Marine Corps officers	0.1
Marine Corps enlisted men	6.7

The highest ranking Negro officer in the United States Armed Forces in 1961 was Maj. Gen. Benjamin O. Davis, Jr., Chief of Personnel, Office of the Deputy Chief of Staff for Operations, Headquarters, United States Air Force. He was confirmed as a major general by the Senate in 1959, thereby becoming the highest ranking Negro ever to serve in the Armed Forces. His father, Brig. Gen. B. O. Davis, when he retired after fifty

[49] Carey McWilliams, *North from Mexico* (Philadelphia: J. B. Lippincott Company, 1948), pp. 244–258. Also see Ralph H. Turner and Samuel J. Surcase, "Zoot-Suiters and Mexicans: Symbols in Crowd Behavior," *American Journal of Sociology*, 62:14–20 (July, 1956).

[50] Lee Nichols, *Breakthrough on the Color Front* (New York: Random House, Inc., 1954).

[51] This information was obtained, in a letter to the author, from the Manpower Office, of the Office of the Assistant Secretary of Defense in Washington, D.C., July 20, 1961.

years of Army service, served as a member of the American Battle Monuments Commission.[52] The highest ranking Negro line officer in the navy in 1960 was a lieutenant commander, although there have been full commanders in such professional specialties as medicine and engineering. In 1962 a Negro was appointed, for the first time, to be the commander of a United States warship.

Although West Point was established in 1802, the first Negro was graduated in 1877; five had been graduated by 1942; twenty-two by 1953; and thirty-eight through 1960. During the year 1959–1960, nine were attending the Military Academy, and two were graduated in 1961. The first Negro was graduated from Annapolis in 1949, the year in which the first Japanese-American entered the Naval Academy. From 1949 through 1959, fourteen Negroes were graduated from the Naval Academy, and three were graduated in 1961. For the academic year 1959–1960 three Negroes were enrolled at the Air Force Academy. Until recently, Negroes have been assigned chiefly to the transportation and engineering corps rather than to the combat infantry. As a result, they have not generally been associated with military traditions either as units or as officers and, of course, this fact has an important bearing on their national military status.

Relation of Discrimination to Prejudice

Thus far minority groups have been described and the extent and nature of the discrimination against them analyzed. To complete this discussion the basic sources of prejudice toward minority groups must be understood. As it is used here, prejudice is a negative emotional attitude of prejudgment toward a group of people. The "prejudgment" aspect of this definition means that prejudices exist only when they cannot be changed by new knowledge.[53] It is the quality of prejudgment and rejection of contrary evidence which indicates the emotional nature of prejudice.

Although prejudice and discrimination are generally associated, one can have prejudice without showing it by discrimination, either because there is no opportunity or because other attitudes may prevent the free expression of prejudice. Also, some people practice discrimination without necessarily being prejudiced, simply because the situation may call for it. This is particularly true in parts of the South, where a relatively unprejudiced person may still generally follow the discriminatory pattern. In fact, there are some five possible relations of prejudice and discrimination:

---

[52] "The Negro Officer in the Armed Forces of the United States of America," Memorandum for James C. Evans, Civilian Assistant Office, Assistant Secretary of Defense (Manpower, Personnel and Reserve) from Lt. Col. John T. Martin, Executive to the Civilian Assistant, Washington, D.C., June 30, 1960.

[53] Allport, *op. cit.*, p. 9.

1. There can be prejudice without discrimination.
2. There can be discrimination without prejudice.
3. Discrimination can be among the causes of prejudice.
4. Prejudice can be among the causes of discrimination.
5. Probably most frequently they are mutually reinforcing.[54]

In fact, as Rose has indicated, the history and process of change in intergroup relations involving discrimination and segregation may be quite distinct from prejudice.[55] Since 1940, for example, intergroup relations between majority and minority groups have drastically changed, but prejudice has not necessarily done so. The explanation appears to be in the differences in the legal, economic, political, and social forces that are operating.

Thus it can readily be seen that prejudice is not a simple concept. It is a complex social psychological state involving various degrees of negative attitudes toward minority groups. One does not, for example, have a single attitude toward Negroes, Jews, and foreigners, but one's opinions vary with respect to their social, political, and economic rights and aspirations. The same individual, too, may hold different kinds and degrees of prejudice toward the various minority groups.[56]

Prejudice is not limited to members of the majority group. Minority groups also have their prejudices. Negroes in America may be prejudiced against whites. Some white people may be prejudiced against Indians, but the latter also have strong dislikes for many whites. Many Jews are prejudiced against gentiles, and some Jews even have anti-Semitic attitudes toward other Jews.

Three sources of prejudice are analyzed here: the cultural heritage, the personality needs of the individual, and the extent to which economic factors exclude a minority group in a certain way. Finally, the effect that members of minority groups have on prejudice among the majority will be discussed.

Cultural Factors and Prejudice

Studies of infants and preschool children indicate that they typically do not exhibit prejudice toward racial or ethnic groups. This finding is of great significance, for it was at one time believed that human beings were by nature negatively disposed toward those who were biologically different. Prejudice is learned and appears to develop when definitions of the nature of subgroups (racial, ethnic, and religious) become more precise. Although

---

[54] George E. Simpson and J. Milton Yinger, *Racial and Cultural Minorities* (rev. ed.; New York: Harper & Row, Publishers, 1958), p. 21.

[55] Arnold M. Rose, "Intergroup Relations vs. Prejudice: Pertinent Theory for the Study of Social Change," *Social Problems*, 4:173–176 (October, 1956).

[56] Brewton Berry, *Race Relations* (2d ed.; Boston: Houghton Mifflin Company, 1958), p. 375.

some studies have reported finding marked prejudice against Negroes in children of five,[57] others indicate that children do not begin to withdraw from Negroes until about the fourth grade, do not think of themselves as a separate group until the fifth grade, and even in the eighth grade have many associations across race lines.[58]

Prejudice in its early stages of development is quite vague. The child begins with a rather undefined awareness of racial and religious differences, then develops hostility and avoidance of certain groups which later become more specific, and he may even, by ten or eleven, totally reject a minority group. Later this total rejection may be modified by democratic and other pressures in the society.[59] The child acquires prejudice in a gradual and subtle manner, so gradual that when he later finds he has antipathetic feelings toward certain groups he does not know why he feels in this way. From his culture the child learns many things which are related to prejudice, and he acquires from his culture beliefs about the nature of race and racial characteristics or marks. He learns the ways in which members of minority groups are supposed to act and what they are permitted and not permitted to do. He likewise learns that members of minority groups are supposed to exhibit fairly uniform negative characteristics or stereotypes. He early learns linguistic tags such as "nigger," "kike," "Jap," "Chink," and "greaser" which carry with them the idea of power for him and rejection and avoidance of members of minority groups. Lasker has stated that the pressures which mold the child's prejudicial beliefs are those which make for social conformity, namely, the attitudes of the parents, playmates, and such social institutions as the school and the church.[60] The child learns that certain groups, such as Negroes, have a lower status, that he should not play with them, and that there are other restrictions on their social participation. This lower status is often indicated to the child by the shabby appearance of members of minority groups, their poor housing, and their relative absence from white-collar positions in stores, banks, and similar places. He also notices that members of minority groups are not invited into the intimacy of the family. These patterns of minority and majority group behavior soon become accepted by the child as "natural," and even by the age of ten or eleven he may ascribe all favorable qualities to whites and none to Negroes, although at a later age he may modify this exclusiveness somewhat.[61]

---

[57] E. L. Horowitz, *The Development of Attitudes toward the Negro* (New York: Archives of Psychology, No. 194, 1936).

[58] Joan H. Criswell, "Racial Cleavage in Negro-White Groups," *Sociometry*, 1:81–89 (1937).

[59] Allport, *op. cit.*, pp. 297–310.

[60] Bruno Lasker, *Racial Attitudes in Children* (New York: Holt, Rinehart and Winston, Inc., 1929). Also see Mary Ellen Goodman, *Race Awareness in Young Children* (Redding, Mass.: Addison-Wesley Publishing Company, 1952).

[61] Allport, *op. cit.*, p. 309.

CULTURAL STEREOTYPES

Many things that the child learns about minority groups are learned through stereotypes, which are accepted as evidence that all members of any group have the same characteristics. Some of the common stereotypes which are culturally transmitted are these: "Certain minorities are lazy, irresponsible, and immoral"; "Certain minorities are more hard working and shrewd and get ahead too fast [e.g., Orientals and Jews]"; "People of minority groups are incapable of holding important positions in our society without the risk of a decline of our civilization"; "Negroes are Africans at heart, are a 'primitive, childlike people,' and expect to be treated as inferiors"; "Orientals are by nature crafty and cruel and cannot be trusted"; "Jews control business, banking, the press, motion pictures, and other important segments of our society"; "Jews cannot be trusted like other people, for they crucified Christ"; "Jews are noisy, vulgar, and aggressive in behavior."

Some cultural stereotypes are mutually exclusive, although this fact does not prevent some prejudiced persons from believing both. For example, the cultural stereotypes that Jews are Communists and at the same time "international capitalist bankers" are mutually exclusive. Some minorities are also looked down upon because they are thought to be indolent and incapable of full participation in our society, whereas others, like the Jews, may be discriminated against because they are all thought to be excessively aggressive. Merton has referred to this illogical approach to ingroup values as the "damned-if-you-do and damned-if-you-don't process of ethnic and racial relations." [62]

Although some aspects of a stereotype may be supported by facts, they are largely unscientific. In reality, they cannot be applied to all members of a minority group for a number of reasons, outlined by Simpson and Yinger:

1. The stereotype gives a highly exaggerated picture of the importance of some few characteristics—whether they be favorable or unfavorable.
2. It invents some supposed traits out of whole cloth, making them seem reasonable by association with other tendencies that may have a kernel of truth.
3. In a negative sterotype, personality tendencies that are favorable, that would have to be mentioned to give a complete picture, are either omitted entirely or insufficiently stressed.
4. The stereotype fails to show how the majority of other groups share the same tendencies or have other undesirable characteristics.
5. It fails to give any attention to the cause of the tendencies of the minority

---

[62] Robert K. Merton, "A Social Psychological Factor," in Arnold M. Rose ed., *Race Prejudice and Discrimination* (New York: Alfred A. Knopf, Inc., 1951), p. 515.

group—particularly to the place of the majority itself, and its stereotypes, in creating the very characteristics being condemned. They are thought of rather as intrinsic or even self-willed traits of the minority.

6. It leaves little room for change; there is a lag in keeping up with the tendencies which actually typify many members of a group.

7. It leaves no room for individual variation, which is always wide in human groups. One does not deal with a group average, but with specific individuals. One of the functions of stereotypes is shown by this failure to adjust to individual differences—to do so would be to destroy the discriminatory value of the stereotype.[63]

CULTURAL MISCONCEPTIONS ABOUT RACE

Racial beliefs and stereotypes are extremely important, for they not only give rise to prejudice and discrimination against minority groups, but also help to support both. These beliefs and stereotypes are of a number of types and include the concepts that the majority group must defend its values, that subordination to the majority group is natural, that the minority has some biological or other inferiority, and that discrimination against members of the minority is in their best interests.[64]

Such rationalizations to help one avoid subjective conflict are extremely powerful instruments for maintaining prejudice and discrimination. The individual can call on a ready-made stockpile of rationalizing beliefs which the culture provides. If one erroneously believes that Negroes innately have a body odor he can also believe that any close social contact or intermarriage with Negroes is impossible. If a minority group is believed to be mentally inferior, it would be only a mockery to place persons belonging to it in places of political or economic power where they would endanger American society. If a minority group, on the other hand, is believed to have a higher intelligence and to be excessively competitive, it would be detrimental to society if educational quotas and other restrictions were not imposed.

A major source of prejudicial attitudes are the numerous culturally transmitted misconceptions about race. As the child grows up in a culture he is certain, sooner or later, to hear frequently many such statements as the following: "Racial prejudice is innate"; "Certain races are pure, ordained by God, and should not be mixed"; "Races are distinct groups and over the years have not changed"; "All mixtures of racial groups result in biologically and socially inferior human beings"; "Certain peoples are markedly inferior in their native intellectual qualities"; and "Certain peoples are more or less emotional than others." These beliefs, and many

---

[63] George E. Simpson and J. Milton Yinger, *Racial and Cultural Minorities* (rev. ed.; New York: Harper & Row, Publishers, 1958), pp. 166–167. Reprinted by permission of the publishers.

[64] Berry, *op. cit.*, p. 118.

similar ones, represent folklore which has been transmitted in our culture without scientific evidence and largely below the level of conscious understanding. They often arise out of scientific half-truths or the misinterpretation of some actual historical facts. The evolution of man, for example, is expanded to include the false belief that the Negro is closer to the ape than is the white man. The historical fact that in many parts of the world slaves have been chiefly Negroes rather than Indians or Asiatics is enlarged to the belief in the world-wide natural inferiority of the Negro peoples.

Most of the beliefs about minorities are based on a misunderstanding of the scientific relation of race and culture. Race refers simply to biological subgroups distinguishable by certain physical characteristics, whereas culture refers to social norms and values which are nonbiological. There are Caucasian, Negroid, and Mongoloid races and various subgroups under each of these races.[65] Racial groups have few clearly distinguishable race marks, for there are no sharp and stable lines of demarcation. Rather, each race is a hypothetical average of certain physical features, including skin color, head shape, facial angle, nasal index, lip form, body proportions, and other characteristics. Although skin color is of great cultural importance, it is one of the most unreliable indices of race. Many "white men"—for example, most of the people of India and Pakistan—are actually not white in skin color at all.

Strictly used, the term "race" refers to biological processes and is distinct from culture. The two differ not only in terms of process but also in unit, transmission, method of change, and product, as indicated in the following outline.

	Race	Culture
Unit	genes and chromosomes	norms and values
Transmission	fertilization	communication
Method of Change	by mutation or amalgamation	by invention and diffusion
Product	biological individual	person (personality)
Examples	hair color, eye color, skin color, height, etc.	attitudes toward objects and ways of believing

Today there are no "pure" races. Through thousands of years, and as a result of trade, wars, and migrations, there has been a constant mixing of the races. Linton pointed out in his *Study of Man* that it seemed "slightly ludicrous" for the main exponents of the theory of superiority of pure

[65] "A race is a sub-group of peoples possessing a definite combination of physical characters, of genetic origin; this combination serves, in varying degree, to distinguish the sub-group from other sub-groups of mankind, and the combination is transmitted in descent, providing all conditions which originally gave rise to the definite combination remain relatively unaltered; as a rule the sub-group inhabits, or did inhabit, a more or less restricted geographical region."—W. M. Krogman, "The Concept of Race," in Ralph Linton ed., *The Science of Man in the World Crisis* (New York: Columbia University Press, 1945), p. 49.

strains to come from Europe which is one of the "most thoroughly hybridized regions of the world." "Tribes have marched and countermarched across the face of this continent since before the dawn of history, and the ancestry of most of the present population is not even pure white. . . . The result of all this has been an extreme mixture of heredity in Europe and a perfect hodgepodge of varying physical types." [66]

By varying one or the other of these components in different situations it is relatively easy to show that racial and cultural characteristics are independent of one another, and not correlated.[67] On the one hand, there are situations where the culture is fairly homogeneous but the racial groups constituting the culture are quite diverse. This is the case in the United States and in Brazil where, in addition to the white race, there are large Negro groups and an Oriental population.

On the other hand, there can be *relative* homogeneity of biological type and great cultural diversity. Before his Europeanization, the American Indian, who is biologically a subtype of the Mongoloid race, exhibited enormous cultural differences. The variations ranged from the Arctic and sub-Arctic culture of the Indians of northern Canada to the tropical culture of the Amazon jungles, and from the culture of the Plains and Forest Indians to the stone houses of the Pueblo Indians of the Southwest. Finally, there were the great cultures of the Aztecs, Mayas, and Incas, which were undoubtedly more advanced than those of the Britons and Gauls of the time of Caesar's *Commentaries*. Today in nearly every continent of the world the Negro exhibits enormous cultural diversity. There are American, British, Spanish, Portuguese, French, Belgian, and Dutch Negroes, besides those who belong to a host of native African cultures. Another example of cultural diversity is found in the white race, which exhibits considerable cultural variety in Western Europe; moreover, the Arabs, the Egyptians, and the people of India and Pakistan, all of whom are white men, also have greatly differing cultures.

In other situations the racial group can remain relatively constant while great changes take place in its culture. The difference between the type of culture of Japan at the time of Commodore Perry's visit a century ago and modern Japan, with its Western industrial type of culture and its fondness for baseball, is an example. Furthermore, although no culture ever really dies out completely, there are a number of instances where the racial group has continued even though there has been little or no understanding of the meanings of the previous culture. Until certain scientific discoveries were made, neither modern Egyptians nor Mayans could read the hieroglyphics on their ancient buildings. The descendants of the Car-

[66] Ralph Linton, *The Study of Man* (New York: Appleton-Century-Crofts, Inc., 1936), p. 35.

[67] See Edward B. Reuter, "Race and Culture" in Robert E. Park ed., *An Outline of the Principles of Sociology* (New York: Barnes & Noble, Inc., 1939), p. 188.

thaginians, Babylonians, and Assyrians live on; their cultures are largely dead.

The cultural misconceptions of racial characteristics have made it possible to associate all types of cultural factors with certain biological features. Sometimes a group is even defined as a race when it is not a race at all biologically. The Jews, for example, are generally referred to as a separate race when actually they are members of the white race. They may have had more physical homogeneity when they inhabited ancient Israel, but it is impossible to tell today, in a large proportion of cases, whether a person is a Jew.[68] The so-called Jewish nose existed among non-Semitic peoples and only a relatively small proportion of Jews today have such a nose. Today there are so many variations in measurable characteristics among Jews in various parts of the world that they have no racial identity. In parts of Germany, for example, as much as half the Jewish population have blue eyes and appear as fair as their neighbors.[69]

A culture defines certain physiological traits as being superior or inferior, in addition to defining certain supposed biological marks as constituting a "race." Actually a hooked nose is not inferior to a straight nose, thin lips are not superior to protruding lips, and wavy hair has no natural advantage over kinky or straight hair, although many societies may think so. A white skin is not "better" than a black or yellow skin, the Mongolian slanting eye, which is actually only a fold of skin over the eye, is just as good as the straight Caucasian eye, and a narrow head is neither inferior nor superior to a round one.

Beauty and ugliness are also seen in terms of the culture, for there is nothing "natural" about the aesthetic qualities of certain physical characteristics. Gleaming black skin and kinky hair, almond eyes and fat, tubby bodies are all regarded as being beautiful in particular cultures.[70] Livingstone is said to have remarked once, after having resided in Africa for some time among black-skinned people, that he felt almost ashamed of the paleness of his white skin.

Through the centuries various peoples have boasted of their biological superiority over others. Greeks, Egyptians, Romans, Arabians, Chinese, Incas, Tibetans, Vikings, Teutons, Anglo-Saxons, and Slavs have all pro-

---

[68] A recent book on race relations concluded that "Jews are a mixed people derived originally from Caucasoid stocks in the eastern Mediterranean area. Insofar as the original stock remains the basis of their inheritance, they can sometimes be identified as eastern Mediterranean peoples, but not as Jews. Since there are very few eastern Mediterranean peoples in the United States except Jews, their identification with this wider stock is not usually made."—Simpson and Yinger, op. cit., p. 59.

[69] R. A. Schermerhorn, These Our People (Boston: D. C. Heath and Company, 1949), p. 32.

[70] A Malay story of creation illustrates this point. In the beginning, so the story goes, man was created out of dough and baked in an oven. The first one was cooked too much, and he was a Negro. The second was pale and not done enough, and he was a white man. The third was cooked just right, a golden brown, and he was a Malayan.

claimed their superiority. There are a number of reasons, however, why no race or ethnic group can be shown to be superior over another.

1. No one has yet been able to demonstrate the innate mental, temperamental, or emotional superiority of one racial group over another, even though many of the results have indicated a lower intelligence for Negroes and American Indians.[71] This comparative testing has usually been based on a biased unrepresentative sample of the minority group with its differences in socioeconomic backgrounds, schooling, language, motivation, and rapport.[72] All groups have superior and inferior individuals. The differences among groups as a whole can probably be explained in terms of social and educational opportunities.

2. Superiority would have to be defined. Does it mean physical strength, military power, technological development? Or does it mean human happiness and the relative absence of social deviations? Does superiority imply the development of great religious philosophy, art, and literature? Although many nonwhite races cannot equal the development of machines and public sanitation, they may still have developed an emphasis on moral values, art forms, and cooperative living that may excel the technological developments of Western European civilization. The question of superiority in itself is an issue involving value judgments which, by their nature, may be incapable of solution. Can modern machines be compared with the complex system of reckoning kinship among the so-called inferior Australian aborigines? Can religious beliefs or art forms be compared in terms of any universal standards?

3. Superiority cannot be considered without regard to time. In different historical periods every racial group and most European national groups have excelled in warfare. At other times the Mongoloid peoples have been technologically superior to the white people. In fact, the idea of the superiority of a people is based on the belief that a given race actually produced all its culture. This assumption is contrary to the scientific position that most culture has been borrowed and spread by diffusion. As Linton has indicated, little of the average American's daily activity is exclusively a Western European invention or development.[73]

Prejudice and Personality Needs

Various attempts have also been made to explain prejudice almost exclusively in terms of personality needs. These explanations have taken two forms: that prejudice arises from frustrations and aggressions; and that

---

[71] Otto Klineberg, *Characteristics of the American Negro* (New York: Harper & Row, Publishers, 1944), p. 35.

[72] Otto Klineberg, *Race Differences* (New York: Harper & Row, Publishers, 1935), pp. 167–168.

[73] Linton, *The Study of Man*, pp. 325–327.

there is a general prejudiced personality pattern, often referred to as a "conformist" or "authoritarian personality." Although some of these explanations appear useful if accompanied by proper emphasis on the cultural heritage, they are not complete explanations of prejudice.

According to the first explanation, feelings of hostility arising within the individual may be freed at one level or all three. First, the individual may exhibit hostility in the form of free-floating aggression toward anyone or anything. Second, he may attach his hostility to the behavior of specific individuals and attribute his own inadequacies to their behavior. A common way to release hostilities is, however, the third type, wherein the aggression is deflected toward certain larger social categories, usually minority groups.[74] Dollard has probably developed this explanation more than anyone, particularly with reference to Negro-white relations in a southern town.[75] The frustrations of whites, arising out of the repressions placed by their culture on their free social and sexual relations, for example, serve to make them overtly and psychologically aggressive toward the Negro.

One form of the frustration explanation of prejudice, the "scapegoat theory," has had wide support among many writers on anti-Semitism who have sought to explain the centuries' old hatred for the Jew as a product of the frustrations of the gentile world. The Jew has been blamed for political failure, economic misery, and religious strife. In various historic periods other "safe goats," as Carey McWilliams has called them, have been scapegoats. According to Allport, a good scapegoat should have five characteristics: (1) The group should be highly visible in physical appearance, manners, or customs. (2) It should not be a weak group; yet (3) it should be an accessible one which is not strong enough to retaliate. (4) There must be some latent hostility toward the group. Finally, (5) the group should represent some ideological principle which the people resent.[76]

The frustration-aggression theory sounds extremely plausible, but it is too simple an explanation for minority prejudice in general. The political, economic, and social positions of some groups, such as the Indian and the Spanish-speaking peoples, are so inferior that it would be difficult to attribute prejudice toward these minorities as a scapegoat mechanism. Likewise, as one author has indicated, the Negro's social and economic status has been historically so inferior that one could hardly blame our troubles on him.[77] Many cultural and competitive factors other than frus-

[74] Robin Williams, Jr., *The Reduction of Intergroup Tensions* (Bulletin 57; New York: Social Science Research Council, 1947), p. 52.

[75] John Dollard, Neal Miller, Leonard Doob, *et al.*, *Frustration and Aggression* (New Haven, Conn.: Yale University Press, 1939), and John Dollard, *Caste and Class in a Southern Town* (New Haven, Conn.: Yale University Press, 1937).

[76] Gordon W. Allport, *ABC's of Scapegoating* (rev. ed.; New York: Anti-Defamation League of B'nai B'rith, 1948), pp. 42–43.

[77] Bohdan Zawadski, "Limitation of the Scapegoat Theory of Prejudice," *Journal of Abnormal and Social Psychology*, 43:127–141 (April, 1948).

tration and aggression enter into the explanation of prejudice. Aggression may well intensify prejudice, but this is not the same thing as saying that it causes prejudice. This theory, moreover, does not adequately explain why one group rather than another is the object of prejudice. Most prejudice has a long cultural history independent of the frustrations of given individuals or of historical situations. Simpson and Yinger have concluded that even though this theory helps to explain some of the forces behind prejudice, the "need" for it, it does not explain the "direction" prejudice takes.[78]

A somewhat different approach in terms of personality needs is the more recent work by psychologists and psychiatrists in the field of racial and religious discrimination which has sought to discover the general personality characteristics of prejudiced persons. This new approach has been based on the hypothesis that a certain constellation of personality traits characterizes the prejudiced person and that there is a "prejudiced personality." In 1938 Murphy and Likert reported that prejudiced college students tend to be prejudiced toward all minorities, and that these students were usually conservative and reactionary about other social issues.[79]

The most comprehensive attempt to discover a basic prejudiced personality pattern is reported in *The Authoritarian Personality* by Adorno, Frenkel-Brunswik, Levinson, and Sanford.[80] The purpose of this study was to reveal the characteristics of the "authoritarian personality," i.e., a specific syndrome which includes anti-Semitism, general ethnocentrism, and political-economic conservatism. Their sample consisted of 2099 persons, primarily professional, middle-class people. The total sample included, however, a mixed group from West Coast service clubs, patients of psychiatric clinics, inmates of San Quentin Prison, men at the Merchant Marine Officer School, parent-teacher association members, university students, and working-class men and women. A smaller group of the most prejudiced and the least prejudiced was then selected for comparative study. They were given an elaborate set of questionnaires consisting of a scale to measure anti-Semitism, one to measure ethnocentricism, and one to measure conservative and fascist tendencies. Approximately 80 of the highly prejudiced were chosen for intensive interviews and projective testing.

This research study revealed marked differences in the characteristics of the least and the most prejudiced persons. The least prejudiced were liberal, whereas the most prejudiced tended to be authoritarian and conservative. The former were cooperative, permissive, and flexible in social relationships, whereas the latter were power-oriented, looked up to the strong, disclaimed the weak, and had a conventional rigid fear of new situa-

---

[78] Simpson and Yinger, *op. cit.*, p. 84.
[79] Gardner Murphy and Rensis Likert, *Public Opinion and the Individual* (New York: Harper & Row, Publishers, 1938).
[80] T. W. Adorno *et al. The Authoritarian Personality* (New York: Harper & Row, Publishers, 1950).

tions. The least prejudiced had had an affectionate childhood and had an equalitarian marriage, whereas the most prejudiced had had an exploitative parent and had a dependent attitude toward their wives.

This theory of a prejudiced personality pattern may be useful if it is interpreted only in terms of the possible intensification of group prejudice. It has limitations, however, if it is suggested as a universal or basic explanation of all prejudice. The few such studies which have been made have been almost entirely concerned with anti-Semitism, and they have been based largely on samples of prejudiced persons who are probably unrepresentative of the general population.

Such theories have also not dealt sufficiently with the differential exposure to cultural norms concerning minority groups. It is possible that "authoritarian" and "liberal," rather than simply representing basic personality trait structures, actually denote certain norms which groups of persons display. It is likely that in many cases it is no more necessary to use psychological factors to explain prejudice toward Negroes than it is to explain certain habits in eating or dress. Even the selection of groups for prejudicial treatment has a cultural explanation and may vary from society to society. It is likely that many persons with an "authoritarian personality" or something resembling it are not excessively prejudiced. Conversely, in instances of excessive prejudice where such psychological theories may contribute an understanding, all such persons need not be explained in this way. Exposure to extremely anti-Semitic attitudes in the family or in other intimate social groups, with no unique psychological traits being present, could probably make a person a Jew-baiter.

> Before we can explain antiminority feelings in terms of a harsh, capricious, and unloving childhood, we must be aware of group structure and of variation in values among the subcultures of a society. If residents of Mississippi have a higher anti-Negro score than those of Minnesota, this does not prove that they are more authoritarian—i.e., more intolerant of ambiguity, more cynical, more rigid, less self-accepting. It may be that they simply express different cultural influences. Differences in agreement with the idea that there are two kinds of people in the world, the weak and the strong, may simply indicate differences in actual experience.[81]

Prejudice and Economic Factors

The previous discussion has emphasized the cultural and personality factors in prejudice. Attempts have also been made to attribute prejudice

---

[81] George E. Simpson and J. Milton Yinger, "The Sociology of Race and Ethnic Relations," in Robert K. Merton, Leonard Broom, and Leonard S. Cottrell, Jr., *Sociology Today* (New York: Basic Books, Inc., 1959), p. 379. Also see William J. MacKinnon and Richard Centers, "Authoritarianism and Urban Stratification," *American Journal of Sociology*, 61:610–620 (1956).

and the minority problem exclusively to economic competition and class conflict. It has been suggested that prejudice arises from unfair competition or the tendency of one group to exploit another.[82] One writer has stated that American history and our contemporary life clearly reveal the "stark, material profit-seeking core from which all of the varied forms of anti-Negro discrimination and oppression emerge." [83] Another Negro writer has concluded, after a lengthy study, that race prejudice is a social attitude engendered by certain classes who stigmatize a group as inferior in order that they might justify their exploitation of the group or its resources.[84]

There can be little doubt that economic competition does intensify prejudice. History has demonstrated that for centuries prejudice has been used as a weapon in religious and political struggles in Europe, including particularly the numerous anti-Semitic purges and pogroms. At various times there have been groups in America who have sought to eliminate certain minorities from economic and social competition. They have included the Native American party of the 1830's, the Know-Nothing Order of the 1850's, and a variety of more recent groups.

The great differentiation of groups and social roles in our modern society has made possible extensive areas of conflict over social and economic status. Under these conditions, therefore, it is sometimes possible for one group to try to restrict the economic position of another group entirely, or even to eliminate it. These intergroup tensions are more likely to develop in situations where there are more rapid and far-reaching social changes, changes that have resulted in increased culture conflict between groups. Migrations of groups with different physical and social characteristics often increase prejudice, for these newcomers exert pressures on housing facilities, transportation, schools, jobs, and even general social status. The pressures vary according to the size of the migration in relation to the existing population and the rapidity of the influx of the migrants. This type of pressure, with the resulting tensions, appears to have been an important factor in the famous Chicago race riot of 1919 and the Detroit race riot during World War II.

Open conflict between groups also seems to vary according to how direct and successful the minority competition is for wealth and prestige. The prejudice toward the Japanese exhibited in California by certain vested farming interests is an illustration of this point, and it contributed greatly to their removal from the West Coast at the outbreak of World War

---

[82] Alexander Lesser, "Anti-Semitism in the United States," *Journal of Negro Education*, 10:545–556 (July, 1941). See also Oliver C. Cox, *Caste, Class and Race* (New York: Doubleday & Company, Inc., 1948).

[83] Doxsey Wilkerson's Introduction to Herbert Aptheker, *The Negro People in America* (New York: International Publishers Co., Inc., 1946), pp. 8–10.

[84] Oliver Cox, "Race Prejudice and Intolerance—A Distinction," *Social Forces*, 24:216 (December, 1945). See also his *Caste, Class and Race*.

II.[85] Much of United States immigration policy has been directed toward excluding first the Chinese, then the Japanese, later people from Southern and Eastern Europe, and, finally, the Mexicans from competition with various groups in the society.

Certainly minorities experience discrimination in employment, wage scales, and occupational opportunities. The generally low status of unskilled labor, held at one time or other by most minority groups, has added to the prejudices against them, and interferes with their social participation in society.

This role of the competitive and individualistic nature of modern society in prejudice cannot be overlooked. An economic explanation of prejudice is far too simple, however, for such an explanation does not consider the varied role of cultural definitions nor the possible role of personality factors. Actually it does not explain prejudice; it only suggests an explanation of intensity in some cases. More specific arguments against such an explanation can be cited. As they grow older, children, for example, often exhibit prejudice under circumstances where there is little competition. Likewise, individuals of all groups may exhibit prejudice toward a given minority, whereas only a small number are in direct competition with the group. Upper-class southern whites, for example, may be prejudiced toward Negroes with whom they are in little competition, although they may benefit from having Negro servants. There may even be prejudice where there is almost no competition, as demonstrated by the attitudes of the whites of Australia toward the native aborigines. Simpson and Yinger have indicated the limitations of the competitive theory of prejudice as follows:

> Many contradictory forces are at work in any given expression of prejudice. Which one will predominate depends upon their relative strength and the setting in which they work. The "economic" element in prejudice is *least* likely to predominate where traditional definitions of roles are most stable, where economic classes are least self-conscious and organized, where the "intellectual climate" encourages the interpretation of individual frustrations in terms of personal opponents. The "economic" element in prejudice is most likely to predominate where traditional definitions of roles are being challenged, where large-scale organizations along class lines are most highly developed, and where group differentiation tends to correspond with differences in economic functions. The careful student will not accept a blanket statement of the *general* role of group conflict in prejudice, whether it be a statement that stresses or one that minimizes that role. He will, rather, seek to find the role of group conflict in *specific* situations as it interacts with the other forces at work in those situations.[86]

---

[85] Carey McWilliams, *Prejudice—Japanese-Americans: Symbol of Racial Intolerance* (Boston: Little, Brown & Company, 1944).

[86] Simpson and Yinger, *Racial and Cultural Minorities*, p. 148. Reprinted by permission of Harper & Row, Publishers.

Prejudice and the Minority

Prejudice can be related to the minority group as well as to the majority group. In the first place, it is likely that some relation between the behavior of the minority and prejudice exists. To many who are prejudiced this is a satisfactory explanation of their prejudices, and Allport has referred to it as the "earned reputation" theory.[87] Although it is far too simple an explanation, one writer has suggested that pronounced differences in behavior may cause prejudice and that prejudice is much more a product of interaction than solely a result of majority attitudes.[88] As yet there has been little research in this direction, but the approach looks feasible provided that proper weight is given to the likelihood that the majority attitudes are far more important in establishing prejudice.[89]

More evident is the effect of prejudice and discrimination on the behavior of minority members. First of all, prejudice and discrimination are interpreted by members of minority groups in different ways according to the nature of the contact, the cohesiveness of the minority, the region of the country, and the education, income, occupation and social class, personality, skin color, and the individual's early training for minority-majority relations.[90] In general, discrimination results in a feeling of inferiority on the part of the individual minority member, but may be expressed in other ways as well.

Minorities may deal with prejudice and discrimination by acceptance, avoidance, or aggression.[91] Some minority members may avoid difficulties by accepting their lot in life completely, as have "folk" or subservient Negroes.[92] They do not challenge their role and may look with disfavor on those who do. Such acceptance may arise from a real feeling of inferiority or it may give the person a feeling of security, acceptance, and pride in the approval with which he is received by an employer or other member of the majority group.

Avoidance can come in a number of ways. The member of the minority group may simply withdraw from it as do some mulattoes who pass as white persons or some Jews who hide their identity. There are indications that there even exists self-hatred among minority members, particularly anti-Semitism among some Jews.[93] Upper-class members of a minority —as do some Negro professional people—may simply isolate themselves

[87] Allport, *The Nature of Prejudice*, p. 217.

[88] Zawadski, "Limitation of the Scapegoat Theory of Prejudice," *loc. cit.*

[89] Allport, *op. cit.*, p. 217.   [90] Simpson and Yinger, *op. cit.*, p. 189.

[91] *Ibid.*, pp. 229–258.

[92] Charles S. Johnson, *Patterns of Negro Segregation* (New York: Harper & Row, Publishers, 1943), pp. 256–257.

[93] Kurt Lewin, *Resolving Social Conflicts* (New York: Harper & Row, Publishers, 1948), pp. 186–200.

from the problems of the lower-class members of their group. Another way to avoid some forms of discrimination is by living, for example, in all-Negro or all-Jewish communities. This withdrawal is only partly successful, simply because Harlem and similar segregated parts of a city are not completely self-contained and the minority member encounters prejudice in the outer world. Migration is a similar way of avoiding difficulties. Others may simply go out of their way to avoid contacts or incidents with members of the majority group.

Adjustment to prejudice and discrimination may take a pattern of aggression and hostility. Some may become aggressive group leaders who try in various ways to achieve equal status with the majority. Sometimes these attempts may involve physical aggression on the majority, but this is more apt to occur among children, as in juvenile gang warfare. Others may show their defiance of an accepted role by adopting the style of dress and acquiring the accouterments, such as an expensive automobile, of the majority. Some minority members may withdraw their patronage from business concerns operated by one of the majority group or refuse to patronize some individual belonging to it.

Summary

Discrimination is the denial of equality of treatment to an individual or group of persons who desire this equality. Discrimination may take several forms, including the following: (1) restrictions on general social participation; (2) health and length of life; (3) exclusion from organized groups; (4) segregation in public accommodations; (5) segregated and unequal educational facilities; (6) unequal opportunities in employment and business; (7) denial of the right to vote, to hold public office, to enter the country; (8) biased administration of justice; and (9) other forms of discrimination.

Prejudice is a negative emotional attitude of prejudgment toward a group of people. Although prejudice and discrimination are generally associated, one may be prejudiced without discriminating or discriminate without being prejudiced. There are three sources of prejudice: the cultural heritage, the personality needs of the individual, and, to a limited extent, the need for competitive advantages. The cultural source is basic to prejudice, and personality needs, as well as competitive advantage, appear merely to intensify it. Prejudice tends to affect the personality of minority members, but more research is needed to determine the extent to which their response accounts for the existence of prejudice in the majority.

Selected Readings

ADORNO, T. W., ELSE FRENKEL-BRUNSWIK, DANIEL J. LEVINSON, and R. NEVITT SANFORD. *The Authoritarian Personality.* New York: Harper & Row, Publishers, 1950. The most important study which has attempted to show that prejudice is primarily a result of a certain type of personality. The methodological sections are particularly good.

ALLPORT, GORDON W. *The Nature of Prejudice.* Reading, Mass.: Addison-Wesley Publishing Company, 1954. A comprehensive analysis of the group differences and psychological and sociocultural factors dealing with prejudice. Part V discusses the manner in which the child acquires prejudice.

ASHMORE, HARRY S. *The Other Side of Jordan: Negroes Outside the South.* New York: W. W. Norton & Company, Inc., 1960. It is the thesis of this writer and journalist that in the second half of the twentieth century the race problem in America is approaching its final focus in the great cities outside the South —New York, Detroit, Chicago, and San Francisco—where more than one third of the Negroes now live.

BARRON, MILTON L., ed. *American Minorities.* New York: Alfred A. Knopf, Inc., 1957. A collection of readings in intergroup relations covering a wide range of topics.

BERRY, BREWTON. *Race Relations.* Rev. ed. Boston: Houghton Mifflin Company, 1958. An analysis of the concept of race and race differences as well as an excellent critique of the various theories of prejudice.

BOYD, WILLIAM C. *Genetics and the Races of Man.* Boston: D. C. Heath and Company, 1950. A discussion of race and racial differences.

GREENBERG, JACK. *Race Relations and American Law.* New York: Columbia University Press, 1959. A comprehensive discussion of laws affecting race relations and their sociological implications. Includes public accommodations, interstate travel, elections, earning a living, education, housing and real property, the criminal law, and domestic relations laws.

JOHNSON, CHARLES S. *Patterns of Negro Segregation.* New York: Harper & Row, Publishers, 1943. A study of the different ways in which Negroes react to discrimination and segregation. Contains material from personal documents.

LEE, ALFRED MC CLUNG. *Fraternities without Brotherhood.* Boston: The Beacon Press, 1955. A study of racial and religious prejudice among fraternities.

ROSE, ARNOLD M., ed. *Race Prejudice and Discrimination.* New York: Alfred A. Knopf, Inc., 1951. A collection of readings on intergroup relations. Particularly good is the section dealing with prejudice and discrimination.

SIMPSON, GEORGE E., and J. MILTON YINGER. *Racial and Cultural Minorities.* Rev. ed. New York: Harper & Row, Publishers, 1958. Chapters 3–5 deal with the cultural, competitive, and personality functions of prejudice.

WILLIAMS, ROBIN, JR. *The Reduction of Intergroup Tensions.* New York: Social Science Research Council, Bulletin 57, 1947. A general survey of research on prejudice and discrimination and the techniques for their reduction.

The Effect of War on
Deviant Behavior

War today affects the incidence and nature of several forms of deviant behavior. Some forms decrease whereas others increase when a country is at war, and if these changes can be anticipated a country should be able to plan its national programs more adequately. Before discussing the effects of war on deviant behavior, however, it is important to understand the effects of modern warfare on a nation's economy and the relationship of war to social change.

In order to distinguish it from a number of other forms of armed conflict, war is usually defined as a conflict involving armed force between two sovereign nations.[1] War involves the use of force to subdue a nation or nations to the point where they will either surrender unconditionally or agree to concessions. As "instruments of national policy," wars have become a part of cultural mechanisms. War actually is a massive game conducted according to certain prescribed procedures which embrace the methods adopted, the instruments employed, and the rules governing its conduct.[2]

Modern warfare differs greatly from wars of a century or more ago. Instead of being largely a conflict of armies and navies with some demands on the civilian population, contemporary wars can now be characterized as "total war." Today entire nations mobilize for war, for the destruction of an enemy's military potential behind the lines has become as important for victory as the destruction of its armed forces. A nation's fighting strength depends upon how well and to what extent its entire resources have been mobilized and managed toward the ends of war.[3]

President Wilson once said that it is not an army that must be shaped

---

[1] Alvin Johnson, "War," *Encyclopedia of Social Sciences* (New York: The Macmillan Company, 1934), VIII, 331–342.

[2] James Wilford Garner, "Laws of Warfare," *ibid.*, p. 359. These rules include declarations of war, white flags of truce, the care of the wounded and prisoners, treatment of spies, the powers of an occupying commander, and even the outlawing of certain weapons such as the dumdum bullet and poison gas. An 1868 international agreement on war stated: "There are technical limits at which war ought to yield to the requirements of humanity."

[3] United States Bureau of the Budget, *The United States at War* (No. 1 of the Historical Reports on War Administration; Washington, D.C.: Government Printing Office, 1946), p. 3.

and trained for war but a nation. This complete mobilization of manpower and resources for war thus has great consequences for all the people of a nation. A wartime economy cannot rely on voluntary military or industrial manpower. Men are drafted for the armed services. Industrial plants are told what goods must be produced and how much, and the earnings and hours of workers in essential industries are controlled. In addition, heavy taxes must be levied to pay for the tremendous wartime expenditures, and efforts must be made to control dangerous wartime inflation.

War and Social Change

War creates a crisis situation which is favorable to social change. When a nation is fighting for survival, changes in the political, economic, and social framework are more likely to occur. An important aspect of war, and one which must be understood in relation to the changes which come about, is the way in which the inventive genius of the people is stimulated in order to overwhelm the enemy.[4] War has brought forth enormous advances in technology, in industrial development, and in such physical sciences as chemistry and physics.

During World War II total war mobilization produced a crisis situation which resulted in great changes in American society. Millions of new jobs meant the incorporation into the working force of many persons who had not previously participated in industrial production, and millions of men and women entered the armed services and government employment. These expanded opportunities for employment and positions with higher status meant increased social mobility. Between the summer of 1940 and April, 1944, the number of persons employed either as civilians or as members of the armed forces increased by 16 million. This number consisted of 7 million previously unemployed and 9 million additional persons, mostly young people, women, and older persons.

War also increases the number of families broken by temporary separation, desertion, and death. During World War II an estimated 3 to 4 million families were temporarily broken, chiefly because the man in the home had been taken into the armed forces. Hasty and often ill-considered marriages contributed to a postwar divorce rate nearly twice the usual one. Family tensions frequently developed, in part because of the shift of family roles. When women suddenly became independent wage earners or had to assume the role of both father and mother it was sometimes hard to re-establish a former and perhaps more compatible family role.

Millions of civilians and soldiers move to new residences during wartime. During World War II 27 million such moves were made, the most extensive shift of population in a short time in our entire history. The

---

[4] Waldemar Kaempffert, "War and Technology," *American Journal of Sociology,* 46:431–444 (January, 1941).

Bureau of the Census estimated that in March, 1945, 12 percent of the civilian population (15,300,000) were living in a county different from their residence at the outbreak of World War II. The white population in ten major war production areas increased 27 per cent. The Detroit–Willow Run industrial area increased 250,000, or 10.3 percent, in its resident white population; Hampton Roads, Virginia, 91 percent; and San Diego County, California, 110 percent. Much of this migration was from the farms to the cities, in some cases thousands of miles away. People from small towns and farms, between one fourth to one half of them from southern states, constituted the majority of the population that came to work in the bomber plants at Willow Run.[5]

This migration of millions of people, who would probably not have moved otherwise, meant the increase of impersonality, individualism, and norm conflicts. The loss of relatives and friends, in addition to housing difficulties, further increased the various tensions of people living under wartime conditions. As people moved to areas of insufficient housing, the crowded, congested conditions became more or less typical of wartime housing in many areas. Trailer housing developed in boom towns, and families often doubled up in tenements, thereby adding to already existing tensions.

Any wartime period produces other broad social consequences. So many have referred to these positive benefits of war in establishing common values that William James suggested the need for a "moral equivalent for war" to give people a common purpose. The conflict of war usually increases consensus among all groups in a society and consequently means less antagonism among various segments of the social structure. Intergroup tensions between majority and minority groups generally decline in the face of a common enemy, thus increasing the participation of minorities in wartime.[6]

Wars tend to unite the continuity of a nation in time by linking together its past, present, and future historic values. Even suicide seems to decline under such feelings of identification. During wartime many more groups and individuals are concerned with social issues which affect the general welfare of the people than are in time of peace.

War and Social Deviation

The waste of human life, natural resources, and civilian goods during war and the miseries of the vanquished are so obvious and have been enu-

---

[5] Lowell Juillard Carr and James Edson Stermer, *Willow Run: A Study of Industrialization and Cultural Inadequacy* (New York: Harper & Row, Publishers, 1952).

[6] In certain areas, however, where there has been a rapid increase in a minority group and limited housing and other facilities, there may be increased tension and in some cases even outbreaks of violence.

merated so often it is unnecessary to go into them here.[7] Instead, the discussion will deal with the effect of war on juvenile delinquency, ordinary and white-collar crime, prostitution and sexual promiscuity, mental disorder, suicide, family maladjustment, and discrimination. War affects the incidence and nature of these various forms of deviant behavior; yet it actually does not "cause" them. Rather, social trends present in a society become intensified and shifted during war. Social change and mobility, which are characteristic of an urban society, are simply increased by a war situation. Writing about World War II, one writer has stated: "Many of the social problems arising from wartime maladjustments were thus much the same as those apparent in peacetime, with their severity enhanced by accelerated wartime change." [8]

WARTIME JUVENILE DELINQUENCY

War brings with it a great increase in the number of children who get into trouble. In Great Britain, for example, during the first year of World War II, delinquency among children increased 41 percent in the under-fourteen age group, and 22 percent in the group aged fourteen to seventeen.[9] At the same time the crime rate of those over twenty-one decreased 12 percent. The high rate for the under-fourteen age group may have been the result of evacuation from their homes in areas under bombing attack, for all British children of this age were eligible for removal.

In the United States juvenile court cases increased 67 percent between 1938 and 1945. Cases disposed of in 56 counties serving areas with populations of 100,000 or more increased from 47,816 in 1938 to 79,748 in 1945. (See Table 19.1.) Boys' cases increased by the large figure of 65 percent in this period, but girls' cases increased by the even larger figure of 79 percent. Wartime delinquency among girls was chiefly related to sexual promiscuity.

A number of reasons for this increased wartime delinquency can be mentioned. Merrill has suggested the many dislocations—population, community relationships, economic relationships, employment relationships, educational opportunities, and family life.[10] The wartime dislocation of population and community relationships has already been referred to in our general discussion. Carr has stated that during wartime "in general, the greater the disruption of normal living and ordinary familial and other

---

[7] See, for example, Quincy Wright, *A Study of War* (Chicago: The University of Chicago Press, 1942), and L. L. Bernard, *War and Its Causes* (New York: Holt, Rinehart and Winston, Inc., 1944).

[8] Francis E. Merrill, *Social Problems on the Home Front* (New York: Harper & Row, Publishers, 1948), p. 10.

[9] Victor H. Evjen, "Delinquency and Crime in Wartime," *Journal of Criminal Law and Criminology*, 33:138 (July–August, 1942).

[10] Merrill, *op. cit.*, pp. 151–159.

Table 19.1. Number of Juvenile Delinquency Cases Disposed of by
56 Courts Serving Areas with Populations of
100,000 or More, 1938–1945

Year	Total cases	Index	Boys' cases	Index	Girls' cases	Index
1938	47,816	100	40,149	100	7,667	100
1939	52,800	110	44,981	112	7,819	102
1940	50,700	106	42,355	105	8,345	109
1941	55,064	115	45,474	113	9,590	125
1942	59,316	124	47,675	119	11,641	152
1943	78,692	165	63,972	159	14,720	192
1944	76,058	159	61,813	154	14,245	186
1945	79,748	167	66,047	165	13,701	179

SOURCE: Computed from United States Department of Labor, Children's Bureau, *Juvenile Court Statistics, 1945*, Preliminary Statement (Division of Statistical Research; Washington, D.C.: March 8, 1946). It is often difficult to compare statistics on juvenile delinquency because of changes in official policies and reporting. See, for example, Peter P. Lejins, "American Data on Juvenile Delinquency in an International Forum," *Federal Probation*, 25:18–22 (June, 1961).

social controls, the greater will be the amount of deviant behavior per unit population of youth exposed." [11]

There is evidence that delinquency increased more in areas of increased population than in those with decreases in population. Where areas had increased in population, juvenile cases had increased 55 percent, as compared with a 44 percent increase in areas of decreased population.[12] The movement of rural children into heavily urbanized wartime areas meant their exposure to different, and often deviant, values. It has also been pointed out that the rapid dislocation of economic relationships has an effect on children.[13]

During wartime many juveniles are employed who otherwise would be in school. It has been estimated that in April, 1944, 2.8 million boys and girls aged fourteen to nineteen were new to the work force. This rapid increase in employment was often correlated with the disruption of regular school programs, crowded schools, and shortages of teachers in heavily populated war areas. In addition, many of these adolescents were employed in activities which were not always inherently desirable.

War conditions produce tensions under the most normal family conditions. Few families can maintain their prewar status; hence tensions are increased at this critical period. Many fathers enter the armed forces or

[11] Lowell J. Carr, *Delinquency Control* (rev. ed.; New York: Harper & Row, Publishers, 1950), p. 116.
[12] Merrill, *op. cit.*, p. 164.
[13] David Bogen, "Trends in Juvenile Delinquency," *Federal Probation*, 9:25–28 (January–March, 1945).

go into defense work in other areas, and millions of mothers are engaged in full-time industrial or other work. As a result, children are given less supervision than usual. During World War II, such terms as "doorkey children" or "latchkey children" were frequently used to describe these youngsters.[14] Young boys, expecting to be drafted into military service, became more restless, more anxious about their future, and probably less concerned about the restrictions of traditional norms on their behavior. All these factors were added to the normal situations which tempt young people to engage in delinquent behavior.

WAR AND ORDINARY CRIME

Ordinary crime decreases during wartime. Sutherland studied criminal convictions during World War I in England, Germany, and Austria and to some extent in other countries. He concluded that the absolute number of convictions for crime in civilian courts decreased in all countries he studied except Canada, and that the absolute number of convictions of the male population decreased in all countries at war.[15] During World War II in the United States there was a decline in the rate of crimes reported to the police, arrests, and commitments to correctional institutions.[16] Even the large new industrial community around the bomber plants at Willow Run had little crime.[17]

This general decrease in crime appears to have been due primarily to the entrance of millions of young men into the armed forces. In the United States, from 1941 to 1944, arrests of men from eighteen to twenty-one, charged with all crimes, decreased 33.7 percent. This decline should not be attributed to any great increase in anticriminal norms or to the decline of criminal norms generally in our society. Since most ordinary crime is committed by persons in the younger age groups, their removal from the civilian population would obviously result in the decrease of wartime property offenses. One writer has stated that we should look for the effects of war "to be strained through intervening changes in conditions, regulations, and policies, and we should not expect war to have a predetermined or a direct effect on criminal and delinquent behavior." [18]

In the past, wars have had such different effects that it is often impossible to generalize about their relation to certain types of crime.[19] During World War II, property crimes in general decreased in the United

[14] Henry L. Zucker, "Working Parents and Latchkey Children," The Annals, 236:43–50 (November, 1944).

[15] Edwin H. Sutherland, "Crime," in William F. Ogburn ed., American Society in Wartime (Chicago: The University of Chicago Press, 1943), p. 186.

[16] Merrill, op. cit.   [17] Carr and Stermer, op. cit., pp. 273–274.

[18] Walter C. Reckless, "The Impact of War on Crime, Delinquency and Prostitution," American Journal of Sociology, 48:378 (November, 1942).

[19] Hermann Mannheim, War and Crime (London: C. A. Watts & Co., Ltd., 1941).

States. There was a 13.2 percent decline in the rate for robberies reported to the police from the 1939–1941 average to 1944 as well as a decrease in larceny of 13.3 percent.[20] Burglaries during 1944 had declined 8.9 percent over the prewar average. Automobile theft, however, increased by 15.2 percent, largely because of the scarcity of cars. After the first few months of 1942 few new automobiles were produced, and they became increasingly valuable commodities worth, at times, over twice their original cost. The automobile had become almost indispensable to some people, and thus there was a better market for them than before the war.

Personal offenses, as a group, increased during World War II, but individual offenses varied greatly. The rate for rape increased by 27 percent over the previous average, and assault went up 19.9 percent. On the other hand, manslaughter by negligence remained about the same and, curiously, murder and nonnegligent manslaughter declined during the war by 7.5 percent. The increase in rape, largely statutory, that is, relations with girls under the legal age with or without consent, was due in part to what appears to have been a general increase in promiscuity. The greatest increase in rates occurred in those areas with the largest increase in population where there may have been more wartime public awareness of these offenses and thus more careful reporting.

The prison population appears to decrease markedly during a war. Between 1940 and 1944 the number of prisoners in American correctional institutions declined from 180,002 to 127,076, and new admissions to prison declined by 25 percent. A similar decline occurred in Canada and Great Britain. The decrease in prison population during wartime is almost immediate. Although there was an increase in the prison population of the United States from 1937 to 1939, beginning with the defense period, there was a decrease in 1940 of about 4.0 percent and in 1941 a decrease of 6.0 percent.[21]

This decline in the prison population seems to result from a number of other factors in addition to the general decline in the crime rate. Since over half of the men committed to prison are under thirty years of age and a large proportion of them are single, there is a tendency during a war situation for the courts to be more lenient and to consider the national interest in additional manpower. Consequently, probation is used more extensively, particularly if the offender is subject to draft and enlists voluntarily in the armed forces. During the last war, for example, the Army did permit the enlistment of men who had committed even two felonies, if the crimes were not of certain types. The public generally approved this practice because it felt that a person should not be allowed to avoid mili-

---

[20] Merrill, *op. cit.*, pp. 184, 186.
[21] Marshall B. Clinard, "Wartime Trends in the Prison Population," *Proceedings of the American Prison Association, 1942* (Boston: The Association, 1942), pp. 359–360.

tary service by committing a crime. As a result, many men were released from prison to enlist in the armed forces. More than one warden and reformatory superintendent complained that it was difficult to operate their institutions properly because the number of new admissions declined and other prisoners were paroled to the armed forces.

WAR AND WHITE-COLLAR CRIME

Although most ordinary crime appears to decline during a time of war, there is evidence that white-collar crime increases. This might be expected because opportunities for such violations increase during a total war. Laws regulating a much larger part of the economy are enacted, including production and labor controls as well as price and rationing laws, and there is an increase in the possibility of illegal activities in connection with government contracts and income tax regulations.

War Contract Frauds. War contracts provide a fertile field for illegal activities. War frauds and illegal profiteering were so extensive in World War I that for as long as fifteen years after the war Congressional committees continued to expose them. Similar large frauds on war contracts occurred during World War II. A postwar report of the United States Comptroller General stated that overpayments or frauds were involved in more than 5 percent of all war contracts. The investigations of the Truman Committee,[22] later the Mead Committee,[23] revealed that there were extensive violations, although by no means were all concerns at fault. Committee reports revealed that many substandard and defective products were manufactured, expense accounts were padded, and public officials were bribed.

Allocation of Scarce Materials. During World War II, there were serious violations of the War Production Board's orders on the allocation of priorities on scarce materials. During 1944, for example, in a total of 26,434 investigations the board found violations in three of five cases. In one case, for example, a concern used the scarce nylon allocated for military parachutes to make nylon hosiery. Another corporation was convicted of securing on false grounds a scarce material, an air-conditioning apparatus, ostensibly for its company hospital. The corporation in question claimed that its hospital was the only one in the community and that it could not be kept clean without the air-conditioning apparatus; but this equipment was actually installed in an exclusive country club of which many of the com-

---

[22] *Investigation of the National Defense Program,* S.R. 10, Additional Report of the Special Committee Investigating the National Defense Program Pursuant to S.R. 71, Pts. 1–14, 78th Cong., 2d Sess., 1943; and Pts. 15–20, 78th Cong., 2d Sess., 1944 (Washington, D.C.: 1944).

[23] *Investigation of the National Defense Program,* S.R. 110, Additional Report of the Special Committee Investigating the National Defense Program Pursuant to S.R. 71, Pts. 1–4, 79th Cong., 1st Sess., 1945; and Pts. 5–8, 79th Cong., 2d Sess. (Washington, D.C.: 1946).

pany's officers were members. This same corporation also fraudulently obtained such scarce items as ornamental stair rails, plumbing fixtures, and a new kitchen for the pampered country club.

Tax Violations. In spite of generally increased profits, some business concerns attempted to avoid their heavy wartime taxes. One popular method of avoidance was the submission of padded reports of costs in order to reduce taxable profits. Others were the excessive increase of salaries and bonuses for executives, the inclusion of interest on investments as costs, the placing of fictitious values on raw materials, the manipulation of inventories, the increase of reserves for depreciation, and the concealment of profits by intercompany transactions.[24] Taxes were also avoided through the manipulation of financial data.

Many income tax violations were revealed in connection with the government's efforts to deal with the black market in price-fixed and rationed commodities during World War II. Black-market profits were often not reported, or prices paid in black-marketeering transactions were allowed as a business expense in computing taxes, even though this was prohibited by the income tax laws. The government often could not collect other wartime taxes because of the illegal practice of keeping false accounts of transactions to avoid prosecution by government investigators trying to discover price and rationing violations.[25] These false bookkeeping practices were also violations of internal revenue laws. In 1947 revenue agents were still seeking persons who had not reported wartime black-market profits. "These include black-market deals on automobiles, liquor, textiles, sugar, poultry, meat and many other products. One man was found to have bought 3,900,000 pounds of rationed sugar for a fictitious candy manufacturing company. He resold the sugar at a huge black-market profit. Agents recently assessed him $310,000 for taxes, interest, and penalty on those profits." [26]

Black-Market Violations. The black market which existed throughout the United States in World War II is a good example of white-collar crime. It covered a wide range of violations of laws regulating the prices of commodities, the rationing of supplies of certain commodities, and the control of rents. Congress labeled violations of these laws as socially injurious, constituting a serious threat to our national security, and specified certain punishments by the state. Uncontrolled prices and rents could easily result in inadequate production of war commodities and facilities, profiteering from abnormal wartime market conditions, dissipation of defense appro-

---

[24] Federal Trade Commission, *Report on Wartime Profiteering*, Sen. Doc. 248, 65th Cong., 2d Sess. 1918 (Pt. 2 of the Nye Committee's Report; Washington, D.C.: 1935).

[25] Marshall B. Clinard, *The Black Market: A Study of White-Collar Crime* (New York: Holt, Rinehart and Winston, Inc., 1952), pp. 24–27, 272.

[26] "Hunt for Income Tax Evaders," *U.S. News & World Report*, 23:23–24 (December 5, 1947).

priations by excessive prices, undue impairment of the standard of living of persons on fixed incomes, and a possible postwar collapse of economic values. Compulsory rationing was necessary to avoid the unequal distribution of commodities in limited supply, such as meat, canned foods, gasoline, shoes, and tires. With millions of men in the armed services and unable to produce for themselves, and with many of our allies in need of large quantities of our supplies, rationing became a wartime necessity.

Price and rationing violations occurred in almost all commodities, from heavy industrial materials to such items as clothing, gasoline, potatoes, onions, cigarettes, and alcoholic beverages.[27] These actions involved mainly manufacturers, wholesalers, and retailers, and, in the case of rationing, consumers. There were also violations of rent regulations by landlords. Serious black markets occurred in the following: coffee, meat, poultry, potatoes, onions, sugar, grains, cigarettes, liquor, apparel, lumber, wastepaper, consumer durables, gasoline, fuel oil, used cars, tires, building materials, industrial materials, and scrap metal.

Black-market violations consisted of several types of activities: (1) over-ceiling price violations, (2) evasive price violations, (3) rationing violations (including the theft and counterfeiting of ration currency), (4) violations of rent ceilings, and (5) record keeping and reporting violations. Most of them were evasive in nature, and nearly all were subject to criminal prosecution because of the definite element of willfulness. There were "cash-on-the-side" payments, payments for goods which were never delivered, tie-in sales, short shipments, and quality deterioration. Sometimes cash payments above the legal price were treated as "loans" which the person making the sale never repaid the buyer. Illegal profits were secured by making an invoice for goods and simply not delivering them. In other cases a bill might be made out for a certain weight of goods—for example, a hundred pounds—but only part of it would be delivered. Desirable commodities often were sold "tied" to another and undesirable one. For example, when onions were scarce it was quite common for buyers of onions to have to purchase another item which was plentiful, in much the same way wholesalers sold beef to retailers only if they agreed to purchase such hard-to-sell items as hearts, tripe, and the like. Commodities were upgraded beyond their true value to secure extra illegal profits. Black-market beef graded "good" was often upgraded and sold as "choice," thus adding several cents a pound to the cost to the consumer. In other instances the size or the quality of a commodity was reduced without a change in the price, as when heavy "sizing" was added to cheesecloth to make it look like broadcloth. Violations of rent control orders included not only charges in excess of the legal rent ceilings but violations through side payments and through charges for rental services which were not provided.

[27] Clinard, op. cit., pp. 39–48.

For the first time in its history the United States government undertook the tremendous task of equalizing the distribution of goods in scarce supply through a compulsory rationing program. The rationing of goods for a large civilian population is indeed difficult. During a single year of World War II, for example, there were 30 million applications for gasoline, 18 million for tires, and 17 million for sugar for canning. Ration currency was similar in many ways to regular money, for it constituted a demand on a certain available supply in the nation-wide "bank." The violations of these rationing regulations constituted one of the most serious aspects of the black market.

The most common rationing violation involved illegal use of ration stamps and coupons, but there were also falsifications of applications for rationed goods based on need and previous use. In particular, there were widespread cases where invalid currency was used or valid stamps were not collected when they should have been. In some cases consumers did transfer their ration currency illegally to others, but in general the major violations consisted of the purchase by dealers of counterfeit and stolen currency from individuals and then the sale of a rationed commodity without requiring currency. Professional counterfeiters made, in most cases, the forged currency; other persons, many with criminal records, stole coupons from war rationing boards. Illicit gasoline coupons, selling from eight to fifteen cents a gallon, were easy to sell. A sheet of five-gallon coupons worth several thousand dollars could be carried in an overcoat pocket. In 1944 the Administrator of the Office of Price Administration reported that there had been over 650 robberies of local rationing boards in which coupons for 300 million gallons had been stolen. At least one in sixteen filling stations had severe sanctions instituted against it for accepting such currency during the war, although the figure was probably much higher because violations reported by investigators ran as high as 60 percent of such concerns. While our armed forces were burning 25 million gallons of gasoline a day during 1944, the black market in gasoline was also using up an estimated 2.5 million gallons a day, an amount which would have increased legitimate civilian supplies by 25 percent.[28]

Estimates of the extent of these black-market activities varied widely; yet, strangely enough, business estimates exceeded those of government agencies. One government estimate stated that "unofficial figures place as much as 20 percent of the meat supply going into black markets," and the OPA estimated that some 5 percent of the gasoline supply in 1943 and early 1944 was passing in illegal channels through the trafficking in counterfeit or stolen gasoline coupons on the part of filling station operators. In 1945 the Greater Cincinnati Meat Packers' Association estimated that 50 to 75 percent of all civilian meat was passing in black-market chan-

[28] Clinard, op. cit., pp. 163–165.

nels, and in 1946 the American Meat Institute, after a survey of eleven major cities, concluded that five in six stores were in the meat black market. In March, 1944, a random sample group of 145 food retailers interviewed in Washington, D.C., revealed that at least one fifth (21 percent) of them believed that wholesalers did not observe their ceilings.[29]

Some estimate of the extent of the black market can be gained from a study of the actions taken by the Office of Price Administration. From the beginning of the OPA in 1942 until its termination on May 31, 1947, a period of slightly over five years, the limited OPA staff conducted over 1 million investigations and turned up 259,966 cases which resulted in the institution of some action leading to possible serious punishment.[30] By March 31, 1947, action had been completed on 170,708 of these cases, of which only 8465 were lost by the government, while 31,469 were withdrawn.[31] Approximately 1 in 15 of the 3 million business concerns in the country was punished by some serious sanction. Between 1943 and 1947, price, rent, and rationing civil cases amounted to as much as 54.2 percent, and criminal cases, 12.8 percent, of all cases brought before the federal courts.

In addition to these actions—the formal sanctions of the OPA— volunteer citizen price panels handled thousands of violations at the retail level; moreover, tens of thousands of actions were taken under local ordinances against the black market, ordinances which were similar to the national law in the five states and seventy-five municipalities which had them. In New York City alone, for example, there were 18,875 prosecutions of retailers and 4000 prosecutions of wholesalers in 1944. Uncounted black-market cases were also dealt with by other federal agencies. During the three years from June, 1942, to June, 1945, the OPA received a total of 784,147 tenant complaints which resulted in adjustments and settlements of some form, many, of course, being minor difficulties. In 1944 alone, a total of 6855 serious rent cases were referred to the Enforcement Department for formal action.

Large as the numbers of these cases are, they are mostly cases involving fairly serious action and barely scratch the surface of the total violations. In general, less than a fourth of the cases where the government found violation resulted in any serious action. In other cases warnings were sent, informal adjustments were made, or the case was dismissed with no

---

[29] "Grocer Experiences with the Price Control System," Special Memorandum No. 113, Surveys Division, Bureau of Special Services, Office of War Information, May 10, 1944, p. 11.

[30] For all its investigative work the government investigative staff consisted, on the average, of less than 3000 investigators and some 600 attorneys.

[31] The large number of cases withdrawn, for the most part, were those in which the defendants made a settlement or adopted some other compromise action, or they were cases in which the government suspended action in the closing days of price and rationing controls.

action. Consequently, a conservative estimate of serious violations during the five-year OPA period, instead of being 259,966 cases, should probably be at least three times this figure.

PROSTITUTION AND SEXUAL PROMISCUITY

Wars have generally been associated with increased prostitution and sexual promiscuity. One could hardly expect anything else when large numbers of unmarried young men are away from home in the armed forces at an age when sexual tensions are greatest. In addition, industrial workers, many of whom are married but away from home, are often well paid and living in congested areas, conditions which are sometimes conducive to sexual promiscuity.

Table 19.2. An Analysis of 1912 Studies Made by the American Social Hygiene Association, January 1, 1940, to March 31, 1945, in Communities Adjacent to Military Installations

Year	Percentage "good"	Percentage "bad"
1940 (82 communities)	36.6	32.9
1941 (364 communities)	44.5	24.9
1942 (517 communities)	44.7	12.7
1943 (401 communities)	47.4	9.0
1944 (415 communities)	46.8	6.2
1945 (First quarter, 133 communities)	47.3	3.8

SOURCE: "Social Protection—A Summing Up," Journal of Social Hygiene, 31:304 (May, 1945). Journal of Social Hygiene, copyright 1945, American Social Hygiene Association.

During World War II, however, the armed services, as well as national and local committees, worked so hard on this problem that organized prostitution was kept under more effective control than it had been in World War I. "Red-light" districts were closed in 650 communities during the war. The American Social Hygiene Association made 1912 studies of communities where there were large numbers of military and naval personnel, and classified conditions as "good" or "bad."[32] A community was "bad" if there was public solicitation by prostitutes; if bellboys, bartenders, taxicab drivers, and others worked as solicitors; and if hotels, taverns, and other places allowed prostitutes. Between 1940 and 1945 "good" communities increased from 36.6 percent to 47.3 percent, and the percentage

[32] "Social Protection—A Summing Up," Journal of Social Hygiene, 31:303-307 (May, 1945).

of "bad" communities declined phenomenally from 32.9 in 1940 to 3.8 in 1945. (See Table 19.2.)

Sexual promiscuity presented a different problem. Although prostitution decreased in World War II, sexual relations on an unorganized and noncommercial basis increased. As has been indicated, delinquency among girls increased by 79 percent during the war. Likewise, cases of rape, primarily statutory, reported to the police went up by 27 percent. In both instances the evidence suggests that an increase in sex relations with girls was characteristic of the last war. Some 50 to 75 percent of all women held for sex offenses in 1944 were under twenty-one years of age, and in one state 41.5 percent of all hospital cases of venereal disease involved girls under nineteen.[33] Arrests of girls under eighteen reported to the FBI increased 117.8 percent between 1941 and 1944. Arrests of all girls under twenty-one during this same period increased 134 percent. All the evidence —local observations, studies of various communities, Army and Navy findings, and juvenile court cases—indicated that the problem generally concerned the promiscuous and inexperienced young girl rather than the experienced prostitute.

Communities near service camps and other boom towns were particularly high in the incidence of promiscuity. Young girls were attracted to these areas for adventure, and there were few possibilities of social control because so much of the male population consisted of strangers. The reasons for this increase in sexual promiscuity during wartime, in communities within fifty miles away from service camps, have been summarized as follows:

> Among these conditions were the tendency of young persons to take less interest in their school work, especially the young girls who were subject to the attentions of the soldiers on leave; the tendency of many such young people to condone or accept new standards of behavior, particularly in the field of sex relations; an inordinate increase in the social activities of young girls of high school age who were "drafted" by local committees for dances and other entertainments; and finally the interchange of veneral disease between the youth of the local community and the military personnel, with uniformly unfortunate results.
>
> The effect of such modifications in the customary relationships of young persons was most clearly evident with the girls. Many of the problems of sexual promiscuity on a nonremunerative basis were the most obvious results of the changed community relationships. . . . As one high school superintendent remarked, with commendable understatement, "I must say that the near-by camp for more than 30,000 men has made this a very undesirable place in which to bring up boys and girls." [34]

---

[33] Eliot Ness, "Sex Delinquency as a Social Hazard," *Proceedings of the National Conference of Social Work, 1944* (New York: Columbia University Press, 1944), p. 280.

[34] Merrill, *op. cit.*, pp. 152–153.

WAR AND MENTAL DISORDER

War may be expected to affect the rate of mental disorder of various sections of the population differently. Children, women, adolescents, industrial workers, and those in the armed forces face war situations under different stresses.[35] Likewise there are differences when a civilian population is under attack and evacuations are necessary, and when it is not under attack.

There is no evidence of any marked increase in neuroses among the civilian population in World War II, although there was a marked increase in psychoses. First admissions of psychoneurotics to hospitals for mental illness increased from 4423 in 1939 to 5809 in 1944. Although the number so hospitalized constitutes only a minor part of neurotic behavior, it is still possible to use it as some sort of index. After studying neuroses during World War II, Merrill concluded that, for whatever they were worth, the figures did not indicate a widespread increase in neurotic behavior during World War II.[36]

This general mental state, as far as neuroses are concerned, was due in large part to the general participation in the war by all parts of the population, the mentally stable and the unstable. Those with neurotic behavior had an opportunity to divert their anxiety into a common, unified, and, to some, ideologically satisfying cause. Individual sentiments were replaced by national ones.

Of course, not all potentially neurotic persons shared these goals, and some experienced difficulties if they could not measure up to the expectations of others or if they could not develop sufficiently aggressive patterns to meet wartime conditions. As a result, some developed a "civilian war neurosis." [37] Some of these difficulties also appear to have been associated with fears about members of the family in service.

Psychotic behavior took a different trend during the war and increased, at least as measured by hospital first admissions. Schizophrenia appeared to account for the greatest increase. In 1939, there were 20,876 first admissions, or 22.4 percent of total admissions; by 1944 this number had increased to 29,010, or 26.1 percent of the total. However, this figure probably should be even larger because of the millions in the armed forces.

Mental disorder of a psychotic nature develops over a long period of time, and it is likely that these additional breakdowns were borderline cases and would have occurred in any event. The accelerated pace of life and

---

[35] H. Warren Dunham, "War and Personality Disorganization," *American Journal of Sociology*, 48:387–395 (November, 1942).

[36] Merrill, *op. cit.*, pp. 207–208.

[37] Felix Deutsch, "Civilian War Neuroses and Their Treatment," *Psychoanalytic Quarterly*, 13:300–312 (July, 1944).

more intense personal relationships during wartime probably widened, for example, the gap between the schizophrenic and other persons. In fact, it is likely that war simply aggravates in a society certain conditions which result in schizophrenia.[38] The wider opportunities for social participation in the war may account for the fact that the manic-depressive psychoses did not increase greatly. Between 1939 and 1944 there was a national increase of only 679 new cases committed to mental hospitals. The trend was considerably different from that of the schizophrenic cases.

It is difficult to determine whether the incidence of neuroses and psychoses would increase if the civilian population of the United States were subjected to heavy bombardment. There are indications, however, that mental illness did not materially increase in Great Britain under the German air attacks of 1940 and 1941. One British psychiatrist has written that "one of the most striking things about the effects of war on the civilian population has been the relative rarity of pathological mental disturbances among the civilians exposed to air raids. . . . The patients who do come, with few exceptions, present mainly the same problems as in peacetime." [39]

So far the discussion of mental disorder has been with reference to the civilian population. From 1942 to 1945 over 1,000,000 neuropsychiatric cases were admitted to Army hospitals, or between 6 and 7 percent of all hospital admissions.[40] Undoubtedly many of these cases were repeaters, and thus the figures probably were not quite this high. Neuropsychiatric disorders accounted for about half of all the discharges from the Army during the war, or a total of 545,000.

This high rate of mental breakdown, some of brief duration and others for a long period, appears to have resulted largely from a number of factors influencing a soldier's life. These included the demands of a new life, discipline, the lack of privacy, uncertainty, separation from home, privations, fatigue, danger, and difficulties in interpersonal relations—for example, inequalities in privileges, barracks life, and anxiety about problems at home.

There is no indication that particular factors in the previous background of soldiers made them more liable to mental disorders. On the contrary, it appears that group factors rather than individual inadequacies were the most important determinants in explaining variations in susceptibility to mental illness. The quality of leadership was particularly important, as well as the degree of group motivation and identification with a military group, whether it was a platoon, a company, or a bomber crew. The loyalty and the gripes that a man shared with his fellow members, no

---

[38] H. Warren Dunham, "War and Mental Disorder: Some Sociological Considerations," *Social Forces,* 22:137–142 (December, 1943).

[39] R. D. Gillespie, *Psychological Effects of War on Citizen and Soldier* (New York: W. W. Norton & Company, Inc., 1942), pp. 106–107.

[40] William C. Menninger, *Psychiatry in a Troubled World* (New York: The Macmillan Company, 1948), pp. 58–72. Menninger was Chief Consultant in Neuropsychiatry to the Surgeon General of the Army, 1943–1946.

matter what the danger and privation, and his confidence in leadership were important elements of his mental health.

SUICIDE AND WAR

Durkheim noted some sixty years ago that suicide tends to decline during wartime.[41] This same trend occurred during World War II, when the suicide rate per 100,000 declined by about one third, from 15.3 in 1938 to 11.2 in 1945. The number of suicides per year decreased to 14,782, which meant that many more failed to take their lives, possibly as many as 25,000 during World War II. Moreover, there was a steady decline from year to year until the postwar years, when the rates increased. (See Table 19.3.)

Table 19.3. Suicide Death Rates per 100,000 Population, United States, 1938–1947

Year	Rate per 100,000	Year	Rate per 100,000
1938	15.3	1943	10.2
1939	14.1	1944	10.0
1940	14.4	1945	11.2
1941	12.8	1946	11.5
1942	12.0	1947	11.5

SOURCE: "Mortality from Suicide," *Epidemiological and Vital Statistics Report* (Geneva: World Health Organization, 1956), IX, No. 4, 250–253.

Several factors probably accounted for this decline. The feeling of unity in wartime is the opposite of the social isolation of the typical suicide. National solidarity and the "we feelings" of wartime probably make personal difficulties of less importance to the individual. War also brings increased economic opportunities, and it has already been indicated that the rate of suicide is related to the business cycle. Wartime is a period of full employment, as well as high wages and profits, and thus less economic insecurity. Perhaps it would not be facetious to add that many persons would like to live to see the outcome of a war. At least, following the war there was a slight increase in the suicide rate.

WAR AND MARITAL CONFLICTS

Wars bring a number of changes in family relationship. The separation of wives and husbands, the new role suddenly assumed by some work-

---

[41] Émile Durkheim, *Suicide* tr. by John A. Spaulding and George Simpson (New York: The Free Press of Glencoe, 1951). Durkheim's original book was published in Paris in 1897.

ing wives, the movement of families to new locations, and the frequent crowded living conditions strain family relationships. In addition, hundreds of thousands of marriages are contracted in wartime without adequate preparation or understanding. In spite of these situations, the divorce rate did not increase much during the war years. The rate per 100 marriages increased only 10 percent: from 17.3 in 1942 to 27.5 in 1944.

The divorce rate did not increase appreciably during the war years for several reasons. Some persons solved their marital difficulties by entering the armed forces or moving to war industries in other areas in what might almost be termed desertion in peacetime. Others delayed divorce action until after the war because of the dependency checks which wives and children received while the husband was in the armed services. As Burgess has stated: "Wives who might otherwise sue for separate maintenance or divorce postpone such action until after the war, a prudential course in view of compulsory allowances to dependents of men in the service." [42] In June, 1944, 2,485,908 wives were receiving benefit checks from the Army.

The divorce rate remained stationary for two other more subtle social psychological reasons, morale and emotional factors. It was generally considered unpatriotic even to threaten to divorce a man who was defending his country, for if the individual soldier's morale were undermined the morale of the armed forces in general might be affected. It was considered a patriotic duty in wartime to retain family ties; consequently, many divorces were temporarily postponed. Probably some wives wanted a divorce, but were unable to obtain it because of the legal difficulties involved in divorcing a soldier who did not also want one. A soldier was not required to answer a divorce summons.

In the dangers of wartime for soldier and civilian alike marriage gave some sense of emotional security to both partners. There was a tendency even to idealize the absent partner: "The same deep desire for human assurance that increases the marriage rate in wartime helps also to maintain the solidarity of the family once it is established. In the immensity of war, men and women often hesitate to break the one human relationship which promises to give them sanctuary in a chaotic world. They may cling desperately to the form of the relationship, although the substance may long since have departed." [43]

On the other hand, war may have increased difficulties in postwar adjustments between persons who had been separated. Separations and other requirements of the wartime situation, with its interruption of established continuity, bring out conflicts and tensions between wives and husbands which had previously been covered up by the conventions of their immediate environment: "It often happens that a man realizes only in wartime what he did not notice in the routine of settled bourgeois exist-

---

[42] Ernest W. Burgess, "The Family," in Ogburn, *op. cit.*, p. 25.
[43] Merrill, *op. cit.*, p. 43.

ence, that his wife cannot or is unwilling to participate in his life. In the army he may need help he did not need before. Several men realize with shock that their wives loved their prestige, their social standing rather than themselves as persons." [44]

After the war all this changed. Divorces temporarily postponed were obtained. Many of the hastily contracted marriages did not last when the marriage was resumed under more normal, peacetime conditions. These divorces, added to the usual divorce rate, meant a steady postwar rise, with 1946 having the highest rate in history. In fact, it was not until 1952, seven years after the war, that the divorce rate became comparable with that of the prewar years.

DISCRIMINATION AND WAR

Now that wars have become world-wide in scope, discrimination against minorities has taken on even greater ideological significance than formerly. Media of mass communication make it possible to use discrimination within a country against some racial, religious, or ethnic group as a device for winning the support of other countries whose relation to the discrimination is only one of indirect identification.

If one were to choose one of the most positive results of World Wars I and II it might well be the general advancement of the position of minority groups in the United States. In a total war of today three things accounted for this advance: the urgent need for all available manpower, regardless of the racial, ethnic, or religious background of the person; the movement up the socioeconomic scale of the minority group due to the expansion of production and the opportunities in other areas for advancement; and, finally, the threat of a crisis situation in which the possibility of defeat made it possible and even desirable to grant more equality to certain groups than could be done in peacetime. Unfortunately, there were exceptions in discrimination against identifiable minorities who were closely associated with the belligerents, such as persons of German origin in World War I and of Japanese origin in World War II.

It would be impossible to describe the improvement of each minority group's position during and after World War II. Instead, the discussion will be limited here to the position of the Negro. At the beginning of the defense preparations his position in industry was weak in comparison with that of the white man. There was still a disproportionate amount of unemployment among Negroes, who were generally employed as unskilled or semiskilled labor. Many industries observed a color line in hiring and in making promotions.

---

[44] R. C. Anderson, "Neuropsychiatric Problems of the Flyer," *American Journal of Medicine*, 4:637–644 (May, 1948).

The first defense efforts helped the white industrial workers considerably, but did so little for the Negroes that their leaders organized a protest march on Washington in 1941. Discrimination in hiring continued to exist in many communities, even where there were labor shortages. Conditions improved in 1942, partly because of the upgrading of whites and the general labor shortage, but mainly because of the creation by executive order of the Fair Employment Practices Commission (FEPC) in 1941.[45] This order, issued by President Roosevelt, stated that discrimination because of "race, creed, color or national origin" was to be abolished in defense industries, and it forbade the granting of government contracts to those who did not obey it. Although the order could not be completely enforced, a large part of industry faced with shortages of labor honored it.

As the war progressed, another large migration of Negroes to industrial centers took place. This was similar, in general, to the urban migration during and after World War I; but this time there was also a movement of rural Negroes to the cities of the South where industrial production had increased. An estimated one million Negroes moved from the farm to industrial positions between 1940 and 1944. During this period the proportion of Negro labor in the skilled positions—as well as in the unskilled and semiskilled—doubled, and the income of Negroes increased materially.[46] They also entered new industries where they were able to demonstrate new skills, some of which had been acquired in expanded vocational training programs.

All this progress was reflected in the wider participation of Negroes in the armed forces, in improved public housing, and in attempts to remove other forms of discrimination. The Negro became militant in his demands for more social action. So much has changed in Negro-white relations since 1940 that some speak of it as a "Revolution." Perhaps these changes would have occurred anyway, but the war greatly accelerated them. In fact, the changes were so rapid and the Negro influx so fast that in certain areas during the war there was increased resentment, particularly because of pressures on limited housing. In several areas, such as Detroit and New York, there were brief race riots of considerable violence.

Summary

Modern warfare between industrial societies is referred to as total war and is accompanied by extensive social change, the regulation of all aspects of the economy, the separation of families, the movement of populations, a large increase in the labor force, and the organization of the

[45] Louis C. C. Kesselman, *The Social Politics of F.E.P.C.* (Chapel Hill: University of North Carolina Press, 1948).

[46] Robert C. Weaver, "Negro Labor Since 1929," *Journal of Negro History*, 35:20–38 (January, 1950).

members of a society into a force with a common purpose of increased nationalism and morale. It brings about many changes which are, however, largely a reflection and an intensification of trends already present in a society: an increase in the rates of juvenile delinquency, in white-collar crime, in sexual promiscuity, and in the psychoses.

On the other hand, during a war there appears to be a decrease in the incidence of ordinary crime, in the neuroses, in suicide, and in discrimination against minorities. Marital conflict during a war, as measured by divorce, does not increase materially, but during the postwar period divorce rates are far greater than those before the war. Whether these trends would occur in a nuclear war is another question. Large parts of the civilian population would be under attack, and there would probably be evacuation of large numbers of urban people to other areas, with different norms and values and at the same time an increase in impersonal relationships.

Selected Readings

CARR, LOWELL J. *Delinquency Control.* Rev. ed. New York: Harper & Row, Publishers, 1950, Chap. 5. This chapter deals with a survey of available information on the relation of war to juvenile delinquency.

CLINARD, MARSHALL B. *The Black Market: A Study of White Collar Crime.* New York: Holt, Rinehart and Winston, Inc., 1952. A study of price and rationing violations in the United States during World War II.

MANNHEIM, HERMANN. *War and Crime.* London: C. A. Watts & Co., Ltd., 1941. A study of the effect of war on crime by probably the leading authority on this topic.

MERRILL, FRANCIS E. *Social Problems on the Home Front.* New York: Harper & Row, Publishers, 1948. The most comprehensive analysis of the relation of war to various forms of deviant behavior, using primarily data from World War II.

OGBURN, WILLIAM F., ed. *American Society in Wartime.* Chicago: The University of Chicago Press, 1943. A series of essays by leading sociologists on the relation of war to various aspects of American life. Edwin H. Sutherland discusses the relation of war and crime.

PART

III

Deviant Behavior and

Social Control

The Reduction of Deviant
Behavior: General Programs

Over a period of time a society may adopt a number of alternative ways of dealing with negatively regarded deviant behavior. Sometimes social deviations may produce continuous tension in a society. In other cases the society may come to accept the deviations, establish an uneasy equilibrium, or, in the more usual cases, try to eliminate the deviations by increased pressure.

It might be argued that reduction of deviant behavior must be delayed until the nature and causes of deviations have finally been scientifically established, and ways of dealing with them found. Yet in a democratic society this is not feasible, for both policy and action depend ultimately on public decision, and when practical problems present themselves, public decision cannot always await the scientist. There is generally a period in which public action takes the form of trial-and-error efforts to combat the perceived threat of deviancy, a belief that "something must be done." But this action, however "unscientific" its foundation, ties in directly with the efforts of scientists. It is through such action, regardless of its success or failure in reducing deviation, that public interest and concern are aroused. One notable consequence of this is that funds for scientific research are often made available to scientists concerned with deviation. Eventually, the results of such scientific study may contribute to the fabric of understanding with which legislators and citizens arrive at more adequate policy decisions.

On the other hand, within a social system there may ultimately be acceptance of deviations, as has occurred countless times in Western European society. Women's use of cosmetics and their smoking and drinking a century or less ago among certain social classes were almost infallible signs of immorality, and for many justified the assumption that a woman who indulged in any of these practices was a prostitute.

Deviations may constitute a condition of equilibrium such as exists with regard to certain deviant sex practices or gambling in the United States. Although many people may realize that gambling, for example, is an expensive and, for society, an unproductive form of behavior, their attitude is complicated by the fact that most people have, at some time or other, gambled. "Drawing up legislation which will penalize the unwarranted deviation without jeopardizing the status of the numerous casual participants is exceedingly difficult." [1]

Societies may try energetically to eliminate deviations. Such a reaction more often occurs "when the norms violated are highly compulsive and universal in the culture." [2] Such deviations as incest, witchcraft, and adultery, for example, have almost always been treated harshly among primitive societies. On the other hand, in frontier days of a century ago horse stealing was regarded as a much more serious crime than is automobile theft today. In modern societies there is strong reaction against brutal murders, kidnaping, and sex crimes of violence, particularly those involving children.

One method by which strong societal action can be taken against deviation from norms is to cut the deviant off from communication with the group. Generally, this takes the form of rejection and decreased interaction, denial of privileges which the group controls, lowering of status, and, eventually, ostracism. As a result of this action, the deviant may leave the group voluntarily, or the group will collectively push him out.[3] Thus the individual who, as a member of a group, develops ideas or engages in behavior at variance with the group norms may be ostracized if initial communications directed at him are not successful in causing him to conform. If the individual perceives the group as at least as satisfying as his deviant ideas, and if he believes that the group will reaccept him if he renounces his ideas or behavior, he may do so.[4]

In a complex society, even though communication among members is not as direct and personal, there is still a considerable amount of collective hostility expressed toward deviants. Some of this is evidenced by societal stereotypes concerning deviants, such as the "delinquent," "sex deviate," "ex-convict," "chronic drunk," "dope fiend," "criminal," or "insane" person. These stereotypes are also communicated through newspapers, radio, television, and movies. For example, newspaper accounts seize upon such terms in their headlines, and mass media, in effect, play up the societal image of the deviant or law violator as one with defects of character, mentality, or intelligence. These stereotypes reflect societal attitudes concerning deviation, and the tendency to reject, label, ostracize,

---

[1] Edwin H. Lemert, *Social Pathology* (New York: McGraw-Hill Book Company, Inc., 1951), p. 60.

[2] *Ibid.*, p. 63.

[3] Stanley Schacter, "Deviation, Rejection, and Communication," *Journal of Abnormal and Social Psychology*, 46:190–207 (April, 1951).

[4] For further discussion of this process, see John W. Thibaut and Harold H. Kelley, *The Social Psychology of Groups* (New York: Holt, Rinehart and Winston, Inc., 1959), especially Chap. 13, and George W. Homans, *Social Behavior: Its Elementary Forms* (New York: Basic Books, Inc., 1961), section on conformity, pp. 116–119 and 339–358.

and isolate the deviant. These same stereotypes form the base of many traditional methods of dealing with deviants. This is evident from the manner in which deviants are "cut off" or isolated from respectable society through consignment to prisons, mental hospitals, treatment institutions for drug addicts or alcoholics, reformatories, or other "protective" institutions.[5] In some instances, of course, deviants are not physically isolated, but are socially isolated through relegation to a degraded status. When this occurs, the deviant's opportunities for finding employment and enjoying other societal privileges are markedly limited. He may, at this point, feel forced to seek the support of a deviant organization or subculture. Some suggest that this is one reason underlying the development of deviant groups, such as subcultures.[6]

If deviations become a subculture the difficulties of controlling such behavior are increased. Deviants of this type communicate knowledge among themselves about disapproved ways of conduct, and there is rapport among them. The members develop their own set of norms, distinct social roles, and a status system apart from that of the larger society. Some systematic deviation may have less organization, as is true of many delinquent gangs, than that of others, for example, organized and professional crime or traffic in drugs. Some types of deviant behavior—professional pickpocketing, begging, or prostitution, to name a few—have a long history. Many forms of professional crime, such as the techniques and language of pickpockets, can be traced back to Elizabethan times and earlier. Among such highly organized forms of deviant behavior "a definite professionalization of conduct by deviant group members develops, along with craft pride similar to that found among integrated occupational groups." [7] It is easier for members of such groups to indoctrinate others and more difficult for society to deal effectively with behavior which is supported by a highly organized subculture.

Some people feel that efforts to reduce deviant behavior should be concentrated, not on specific programs, but on broader attacks on a society's excessive mobility, impersonal relations, individualism, materialism, and norm conflicts. However, the general attack can be effective only if it is implemented by specific programs. The extensive spatial mobility of the American population, for example, may be reduced by a number of indirect measures. Some legislation, usually enacted for other purposes, has

---

[5] Lemert, op. cit., pp. 44–47. These will be discussed in the next chapter.

[6] Ibid. See also Austin L. Porterfield, "The We-They Fallacy in Thinking about Delinquents and Criminals," Federal Probation, 21:44–47 (December, 1957). Also see Harold Garfinkel, "Conditions of Successful Degradation Ceremonies," American Journal of Sociology, 61:421–422 (1956). He points out that criminal judicial processes may be regarded as "status degradation ceremonies" from the prisoner's point of view. Two aspects of such ceremonies are the destruction of the person's identity, and the assignment of a new identity that is lower in the social scheme.

[7] Lemert, op. cit., p. 44.

helped to keep people from moving to other areas. The government has attempted to stabilize the economy through measures to prevent depressions and inflations, and through unemployment insurance, social security legislation, and minimum-wage laws. More adequate housing has probably kept some persons from desiring to move, and mental hygiene clinics, as well as counseling agencies, family and individual, have kept others from changing their residences because of difficulties in interpersonal relations. Finally, the gradual elimination of racial discrimination is keeping certain people from migrating to other areas in the hope of removing inequalities in citizenship. A reasonably stable population would make it possible to deal more effectively with the norm conflicts of groups and reduce difficulties in interpersonal relations.

Moral and Ameliorative Problems

Difficulties in dealing with deviant behavior are often complicated by the lack of public agreement over whether certain deviations constitute a problem and also by disagreement about the norms and values involved in the solution. In this connection Fuller and Myers have distinguished between ameliorative and moral problems.[8] Ameliorative problems include deviations such as the conventional crimes of robbery, burglary, and murder, as well as drug addiction, mental illness, and alcoholism. The existence of an ameliorative problem implies that if the situation were eliminated the deviant behavior would be "ameliorated" or made better. Although in ameliorative deviations there is more general agreement that the situation is undesirable, there is disagreement as to the value of the corrective means or proposed solutions. This situation exists because the corrective means either interfere with other values of individuals or groups, or are believed to be inefficient. The solutions proposed frequently involve habits and attitudes which might have to be altered, and which currently provide a source of satisfaction for the individuals concerned. For example, few would say that mental illness or such ordinary crimes as burglary and larceny are other than "bad." The solution to these problems, however, presents a different issue entirely, for it might mean changing, for example, some aspects of urban life.

In moral problems there is not only disagreement over the proposed solution to the problem but there is disagreement as to whether or not the situation is undesirable and should be changed. There may be disagreement over whether such "moral" conditions as divorce, discrimination against minority groups, white-collar crime, gambling, and political cor-

---

[8] Richard Fuller and Richard R. Myers, "Some Aspects of a Theory of Social Problems," *American Sociological Review*, 6:24–32 (February, 1941). Also see John F. Cuber, Robert A. Harper and William F. Kenkel, *Problems of American Society: Values in Conflict* (3d ed.; New York: Holt, Rinehart and Winston, Inc., 1956).

ruption actually constitute social problems. To some, divorce is a serious moral transgression; to others, it is a solution to a problem which would be infinitely more serious if divorce were not permitted. Racial and religious discrimination is not "bad" to some people. They see the protection of vested interests, and preservation of so-called biological superiority or white supremacy, "natural law," and a host of others as reasons why it is, if not necessarily a good thing, certainly not a social problem. Others believe that it is a serious contradiction of the American Creed of human rights, democracy, and freedom of opportunity. Some people regard white-collar crime as real crime and a serious form of deviant behavior in society, whereas others do not. Gambling and political corruption have been similarly looked upon by some; by others they are regarded not as social problems but as "normal" situations in contemporary urban life. Obviously there are similar difficulties about solutions when there is disagreement over the existence of a problem.

Organized Public Education

Many people feel that public education is basic to any program dealing with certain types of deviant behavior. The underlying factors which account for the problems confronting modern society must be sought and dealt with on a broad basis. As some have noted, in order to find ways of combatting crime and delinquency, a necessary first step is to provide the public with more information about present problems and the successes and failures of methods used to deal with them.[9] Since in a democratic society operation of correctional and preventive measures rests ultimately on public support, it is imperative that the public be adequately informed. This information may be communicated not only through radio, television, the press, films, pamphlets, and books, but also through discussion. It is the type of education which seeks to provide such information which will be discussed here.

DELINQUENCY AND CRIME

The public has been educated about delinquency and crime through those national, state, and local conferences and various legislative commissions or committees which have wide publicity. In 1959, for example, the investigating subcommittee authorized by the Senate Judiciary Committee conducted widely publicized public hearings on the problem of juvenile delinquency. The objectives of the investigation were to examine: (1) the extent of delinquency, its causes and contributing factors;

---

[9] Hugh P. Reed, "The Citizens' New Role in Combatting Crime," *Federal Probation*, 24:31–36 (December, 1960).

(2) the adequacy of existing laws; (3) sentences and correctional action employed by federal courts; and (4) the extent of juvenile violation of federal narcotics laws.[10] The committee focused public attention upon the problems it brought to light, and recommended measures considered to be helpful both in preventing juvenile delinquency and in rehabilitating delinquents and youthful offenders. The publicity which the findings of this subcommittee have received helped to arouse the public about the gravity of existing conditions and the difficulty of dealing with them.

One of the most famous of all Congressional investigations of crime was the Special Committee to Investigate Organized Crime in Interstate Commerce, which was headed by Senator Estes Kefauver and which held nation-wide hearings during 1951.[11] These public hearings, the first senatorial hearings to be televised, enabled millions of Americans to see members of the Senate committee questioning organized criminals and their political allies about their activities.

In the past thirty years several Congressional investigations have influenced public opinion about white-collar crime: the investigation of the Teapot Dome scandals of the mid-twenties; the various committees investigating business ethics during the 1930's; and the Truman Committee, which investigated graft and corruption in connection with war contracts during World War II.[12] Senator Paul H. Douglas headed a well-known committee which, in 1951, went into the question of preventing graft and corruption in government. This committee made several proposals to avoid corruption in government, including the disclosure of income and other transactions by government officials, the definition of improper or unethical conduct, and the imposition of specific penalties. Douglas also proposed that a commission on ethics in government be set up.[13]

Congressional investigations which have received much attention within recent years have dealt with unethical conduct in the labor and management field, and with manipulation of prices by business executives in a number of major industries. The Senate inquiry of 1956 into labor corruption revealed the penetration into manufacturing concerns of racketeers and gangsters known to be connected with several large labor unions. Further inquiry documented a succession of collusive arrangements between business organizations and some unions. In addition, numerous improper and illegal activities were revealed in some labor unions, including collusion with organized criminals, violence and beatings, pay-offs, black-

---

[10] Senate Report of Juvenile Delinquency Hearings, 86th Cong., 1st Sess., S.R. 54, *Investigation of Juvenile Delinquency in the United States* (Washington, D.C.: Government Printing Office, February 12–13, 1959). See also reports dated during subsequent months.
[11] See pp. 274–283.   [12] See p. 577.
[13] Report of the Commission on Ethics in Government, Committee on Labor and Public Welfare, to accompany Senate Joint Resolution 107, October 9, 1951. Also see Paul H. Douglas, *Ethics in Government* (Cambridge, Mass.: Harvard University Press, 1952).

mail, padded expense accounts, speculation in gambling, and other forms of vice.[14] These investigations led to the passage of laws requiring labor unions to make full reports of their administrative and financial affairs, and to hold fair election proceedings with secret ballots. Also, these laws restrict the use of union funds by providing criminal penalties for their misappropriation. Yet one of the most significant results of these investigations was the arousal of public attention and concern, and the recognition by lawmakers of the need for legal restrictions as well as their adequate enforcement. As Attorney General Robert F. Kennedy has noted, an active interest on the part of citizens in public affairs is necessary: "Crime, corruption, and delinquency will continue to spread as long as people remain disinterested and lax and apathetic." [15]

In more general terms, people appear to need to be educated to realize that a democratic society rests fundamentally on the premise that laws are to be obeyed. This concept differs somewhat from the currently accepted idea that it is the responsibility of government to force the citizens to obey the law through fear of being apprehended if they disobey it. Organized crime, for example, cannot be successfully controlled unless there is some agreement on the immoral consequences of widespread commercialized gambling by the public and its relation to the bribery of public officials and police officers. The public's definition of a criminal needs to be changed so that it will include not merely those who violate the criminal law but those who violate any law. Society cannot expect to control ordinary crime with one set of standards while at the same time allowing violations of law such as organized or white-collar crime to take place under another set of standards. The citizen's responsibility for society's laws can be strengthened through his wider participation in neighborhood, community, and welfare activities which will help him to understand social objectives.

An important area in the control of white-collar crime is the development of more effective ethics among the professional groups and various organizations.[16] More ethical standards need to be developed among politicians and government officials as well as among professional men and businessmen. There needs to be some agreement among the various groups in society as to what is proper conduct, how new members are to be indoctrinated with such a code of ethics, and how deviations are to be treated. This relationship of ethics to white-collar crime is illustrated by the difficulties encountered in controlling "sharp" practices in business:

---

[14] Robert F. Kennedy, *The Enemy Within* (New York: Harper & Row, Publishers, 1960), pp. 17–25.

[15] *Ibid.*, p. 300.

[16] Marshall B. Clinard, "Corruption Runs Far Deeper than Politics," *The New York Times Magazine*, August 10, 1952, pp. 20–21. Also see the special issue entitled "Ethical Standards in American Public Life," *The Annals*, Vol. 280 (March, 1952).

Control of sharp, evasive, and fraudulent practices in business will have to develop externally, that is, by boycotting and the reporting of white-collar violators by their victims (other businessmen, buyers, and consumers) as well as internally, that is, within the world of business and its various organizations and associations. The reporting of white-collar violations and bringing of action in the regular law enforcement channels rather than through investigations and action of administrative commissions and regulatory bodies is a matter of vital concern to crime control. Crystallized public sentiment against white-collar crime would be more of a preventive force, since one of the reasons that so much white-collar violation in the business world exists is that the public is really not vitally interested in the ethics of its businessmen just so long as it gets good service from them. Businessmen, through their own organizations and associations, must also become vitally concerned with the ethics of doing business and the ways of rendering service to the public. In several quarters of well-established and highly organized business, strong internal controls over members by associations are developing, whereby businessmen through their own collective pressure can hold their colleagues in line. Ethical business practices are what is needed to combat white-collar crime, although it is realized that this is difficult to bring about in some highly competitive enterprises, in wildcat operations, and in businesses that have not developed a strong association.[17]

EDUCATION ABOUT MENTAL DISORDERS

During the past decade, great strides have been taken toward educating the public about mental disorder. Such education is carried out largely through the mass media and through the efforts of three agencies—citizens' mental health organizations, federal and state agencies, and professional groups. The National Institute of Mental Health, an agency created by an act of Congress in 1946, is responsible for coordinating work dealing with mental disorder, including the dissemination of information to the public, community programs, research, and training of psychiatric personnel. State agencies generally function to assist public education through community services.

Voluntary citizens' organizations are chiefly concerned with educating themselves and other members of the public about mental health. The work of these groups consists of such activities as gathering and documenting information about conditions affecting mental health, encouraging research on mental health, and trying to improve the number and quality of personnel in the field of mental health.[18] Much of their work is done through public speakers, motion pictures, radio and television programs,

---

[17] Walter C. Reckless, *The Crime Problem* (2d ed.; New York: Appleton-Century-Crofts, Inc., 1955), pp. 678–679.

[18] George D. Stevenson, "Citizens Mental Health Movement," *The Annals*, 286:92–99 (March, 1953).

and pamphlets. The professional organizations of certain applied disciplines, such as social work, medicine, and psychiatry, have assumed some of the responsibility for informing the public about mental disorder.

Despite such efforts as those described above, research evidence shows that the public generally continues to associate mental disorder with the stigma of public disgrace. A two-year poll of Americans' opinions of their own mental health showed that although one in four believed they had problems serious enough to seek help, only one in seven sought such help.[19] A 1960 study, for example, found that relatives of former mental patients tend to expect that friends and neighbors will respond to them with rejection and disapproval.[20] Other studies and national opinion surveys have revealed similar attitudes.[21]

There is also evidence that public ideas about mental disorder are highly stereotyped. To the public, the term "mental disorder" often connotes bizarre, highly disturbed behavior.[22] Some suggest that such stereotypes may be fostered by mass media information which tends too often to present an oversimplified, distorted view of the subtleties involved in mentally disordered behavior.[23] It has also been shown that information distributed to the public about mental disorder is biased in the direction of middle-class values and norms, and that the picture the public receives may not represent the norms of mental disorder or mental health in the other social classes.[24]

One of the most significant proposals of the Joint Commission on Mental Illness and Health (which was authorized by Congress in 1955 to conduct a five-year study on aspects of mental health in the United States) was for public information of a *specific* kind on mental illness.[25] The commission noted that the continuing lag in treatment of the mentally ill reflects a basic pattern of social rejection. It stated that information to

[19] Gerald Gurin, Joseph Veroff, and Sheila Feld, *Americans View Their Mental Health* (New York: Basic Books, Inc., 1960). Also see Charles D. Whatley, "Social Attitudes toward Discharged Mental Patients," *Social Problems*, 6:313–320 (Spring, 1959), and Howard E. Freeman and Ozzie G. Simmons, "Feelings of Stigma among Relatives of Former Mental Patients," *Social Problems*, 8:312–322 (Spring, 1961).

[20] Freeman and Simmons, "Feelings of Stigma among Relatives of Former Mental Patients," *loc. cit.*

[21] Charlotte Green Schwartz, "Perspectives on Deviance: Wives' Definitions of Their Husbands' Mental Illness," *Psychiatry*, 20:275–291 (August, 1957); and Robert H. Felix, "Social Psychiatry and Community Attitudes," *World Health Organization Technical Report* (Series 177; Geneva: World Health Organization, 1959).

[22] Shirley A. Star, "The Public's Ideas About Mental Illness." Paper presented to the annual meeting of the National Association for Mental Health, November 5, 1955.

[23] John Clausen, "Mental Disorders," in Robert K. Merton and Robert R. Nisbet, *Contemporary Social Problems* (New York: Harcourt, Brace & World, Inc., 1961), pp. 127–180.

[24] Orville R. Gursslin, Raymond G. Hunt, and Jack L. Roach, "Social Class and the Mental Health Movement," *Social Problems*, 7:210–217 (1960).

[25] Report of the Joint Commission on Mental Illness and Health, *Action for Mental Health* (New York: Basic Books, Inc., 1961), pp. 275–282.

the public should aim specifically to counter this societal pattern of rejection of the mentally ill. Such information should focus on the major difference between physical and mental illness, e.g., the differences in the reactions and attitudes toward the person by *others*. The commission report further stated that there is a tendency for persons to react to the mentally ill person with revulsion and ridicule. Public information should therefore make clear that public stereotypes of mental illness, as characterized by violent behavior, represent an exceedingly small proportion of all those who are mentally ill, and that these stereotypes inaccurately represent the overwhelming majority of the mental patients.

MARRIAGE AND FAMILY EDUCATION

Extensive work is being done now to dispense scientific information about marital and family relations. Many schools, particularly those dealing with higher education, have introduced courses in family relationships. High school courses are generally not designated as courses in family problems, but the subject is treated in health, home economics, and social science subjects. The first college course on marriage was given in 1926 at the University of North Carolina; marriage and family courses are now a regular part of the curriculum of many colleges and universities.

Numerous national and local organizations are interested in family relationships—so many, in fact, that it is sometimes referred to as "the family life movement." Some are interested only in education, whereas others include counseling and discussion of proposed legislative changes in their programs. Utah, for example, has passed legislation requiring marital counseling for couples who have filed for divorce. Most national organizations have a large number of local chapters. Some work is done by the YMCA and the YWCA and by many church groups.

The National Council on Family Relations, organized in 1938, is probably the best known of the national private family organizations. Other national private organizations not affiliated with religious groups include the American Association of Marriage Counselors, the American Eugenics Society, the American Social Hygiene Association, the Family Service Association of America, and the Planned Parenthood Federation of America.

ALCOHOL EDUCATION

Some of the most effective work in public education has already been done with alcoholism.[26] The accomplishments made in this area have

---

[26] Marty Mann, "The Challenge of Alcoholism," *Federal Probation*, 24:18–23 (March, 1960).

been fairly recent but they have encouraged similar work in other areas of deviant behavior. Considering that extensive scientific efforts in this field are hardly more than twenty years old, the progress has been remarkable. As early as 1949 a study found that nationally about one in five persons had come to believe that alcoholism is a "sickness" and that alcoholics should not be punished.[27] There are indications that this belief is held even more widely today. Some suggest that this indicates progress in the field of alcohol education. This change in attitude on the part of the public has been largely due to the work of Alcoholics Anonymous, state bureaus of alcoholism, Yale University's Section on Alcohol Studies (now at Rutgers University), the National Committee on Alcoholism, which has many local chapters, school educational programs, industrial in-plant programs, as well as the fullest cooperation of all types of media of mass communication.

Since the work of Alcoholics Anonymous will be discussed in the last chapter the remarks on alcohol education will be limited here to a few other programs. In 1956 there were state programs on alcoholism in forty-one states and the District of Columbia, many of which helped coordinate work in this area, furnished information on the subject to the public, and developed treatment and education programs. Practically all the states and the District of Columbia now require the teaching of alcohol education at some level in their school programs. More than sixty cities have information centers dealing with the problems of alcoholics, but many more are needed. Trained persons staff these centers, which are sources of information on alcoholism, including data on available treatment facilities—hospitals and sanatoria, medical specialists, Alcoholics Anonymous groups, and so on. Staffs not only help alcoholics work out some sort of treatment program but also help other persons who are interested in the problems of the alcoholic. Manuals devised for the use of schoolteachers cover many of the important aspects of what has been learned about alcohol and alcoholism.[28] These school manuals have adult counterparts in a large number of books, pamphlets, and audiovisual programs, which have been developed for the adult citizen.

The public attitude, held increasingly by many, that alcoholism is a "sickness" may enable the alcoholic to receive sympathy and social support for his temporary occupancy of a "sick role." [29] To this extent, the alcoholic's rehabilitation may be enhanced, since his compulsive drinking

---

[27] John W. Riley, Jr., "The Social Implications of Problem Drinking," *Social Forces*, 27:301–305 (March, 1949).

[28] See, for example, Joseph Hirsh, *Alcohol Education: A Guide Book for Teachers* (New York: Abelard-Schuman Ltd., 1952). For a general discussion of these programs see Raymond McCarthy and Edgar M. Douglass, *Alcohol and Social Responsibility* (New York: Thomas Y. Crowell Company and the Yale Plan Clinic, 1949).

[29] Lemert, *op. cit.*

seems to be due largely to perceived social rejection, ostracism, and isolation stemming from experiences of drinking of a noncompulsive nature.[30]

EDUCATION ABOUT DRUG ADDICTION

Recent information on the extent of drug addiction among young
people has so disturbed the general public that immediate frontal attacks
on the problem, including educational programs, have been instituted.
Teaching concerning narcotics is required by New York State law. On
the other hand, it is argued that information about the use of drugs may
pique the curiosity of some teen-agers to the point that they will desire
to experiment themselves.

There are some doubts as to the value of public information now
distributed about drug addiction. For the most part, this information
is communicated in a sensational manner and with heavy moralistic
overtones which create an erroneous conception of the drug addict.[31] Like
some of the information on mental disorders, this information tends to
reflect and exploit public stereotypes concerning drug addicts. Ideally,
educative efforts should be directed at what some suggest is the basis of
the addiction problem in America—namely, public attitudes toward addiction and the drug addict. So long as addicts are ostracized, rejected,
stigmatized, and isolated from respectable society, their rehabilitation and
the reduction of the drug problem is impeded. As the experience of Britain
suggests (see the discussion in Chapter 11), reduction of drug addiction
will be possible only when the response of the public to addiction is
directly approached.

DISCRIMINATION

Efforts to reduce discrimination are now so extensive that it is possible to do little more than to list them.[32] Educational methods include
such a variety of approaches as intergroup education in the schools, community self-surveys on the extent of discrimination, and work camps where

---

[30] See Edwin H. Lemert, "Alcoholism and the Sociocultural Situation," *Quarterly
Journal of Studies on Alcohol*, 17:306–317 (June, 1956) for some comments relating to the
above. Also see David Mechanic and Edmund A. Volkart, "Stress, Illness, and the Sick
Role," *American Sociological Review*, 26:51–58 (February, 1961).

[31] H. J. Anslinger and William F. Tompkins, *The Traffic in Narcotics* (New York:
Funk & Wagnalls Company, 1953). These authors suggest (see p. 213) that information
in the form of articles, speeches, discussions, pictures, and programs have bombarded the
public in the last few years, yet by and large this information has fostered an image of a
"dope fiend" and has tended to present inaccurately the picture of drug addiction.

[32] For a more detailed discussion see the special issue of *The Annals*, "Controlling
Group Prejudice," 244:1–182 (March, 1946) and George E. Simpson and J. Milton Yinger,
Racial and Cultural Minorities (rev. ed.; New York: Harper & Row, Publishers, 1958),
Chaps. 22, 23.

members of different racial groups can associate freely, as they do in the well-known camps conducted by the American Friends Service Committees. These camps bring together young people from various racial, religious, and national groups around a task—such as building a new rural schoolhouse or repairing housing in a slum area—not primarily concerned with majority-minority relations but which often influences them indirectly in a marked way.

An increasing number of workshops in intergroup relations have been held since the end of World War II. Most of these workshops are held on college and university campuses, with the cooperation of such agencies as the National Conference of Christians and Jews or the Anti-Defamation League, the city community relations boards, state agencies, the American Jewish Committee, the American Jewish Congress, and a number of the colleges and universities themselves. These workshops have averaged between thirty to forty students, who are often community leaders, and they have varied in length from one day to a summer term of six weeks or longer. In April, 1957, one report listed sixty-six workshops in twenty-five states for the summer of that year.

Many church groups, labor unions, and similar groups have been active in developing an interest in discrimination and its consequences for American society. Most colleges now have a course in minority problems, and many secondary schools deal with this topic in their social science or civics courses.

In 1956 there were 491 public or private national, regional, state, and local agencies, with paid staffs, exclusive of agencies of the federal government, working in the area of intergroup relations: 61 national private agencies, 63 regional agencies, 23 state public agencies, 48 state private agencies, 30 municipal agencies, and 266 local private agencies. In addition there were a large number of other groups with voluntary staffs.[33]

Of the national private agencies working in this area the most important are the American Friends Service Committee, the American Jewish Committee, the American Jewish Congress, the Anti-Defamation League of B'nai B'rith, the Japanese-American Citizens League, the Jewish Labor Committee, the National Association for the Advancement of Colored People, the National Community Relations Advisory Council, the National Conference of Christians and Jews, and the National Urban League.

Most significant of the post–World War II developments in intergroup relations have been not only the enactment of state laws against discrimination in the fields of public accommodations, employment, housing, and education but the creation of governmental civil rights agencies to administer these laws. According to the latest information available,

[33] Material furnished by the Research Department, National Association of Intergroup Relations Officials.

twenty-eight states have enacted laws prohibiting discrimination in one or more of these fields. Twenty-five of the states have public agencies with authority ranging from purely advisory powers, as in Kentucky and Florida, to full-fledged regulatory powers, including the issuance of enforceable orders, as in sixteen of the northern states. The public accommodations laws of some states, such as Massachusetts, date back to the post–Civil War period.

New York and Wisconsin were among the first states to enact fair employment practices (FEPC) laws in 1945. In 1961 Illinois passed fair employment practices laws to become the twenty-first state with such legislation. The first state fair-housing laws prohibiting discrimination in the sale, lease, and rental of dwellings were adopted by such states as New York, New Jersey, and Wisconsin in the late 1940's. All of these early laws applied only to public or publicly assisted housing. In 1959, Colorado, Connecticut, Massachusetts, and Oregon passed the first fair-housing laws applicable to private housing as well. Similar comprehensive fair-housing legislation has been enacted by three of the fifteen states which had such bills before their 1961 legislatures.[34]

Depending upon many complex factors, such as the population make-up and the climate of opinion toward human rights, state civil rights agencies vary considerably in organization, powers, functions, and budgets. The Wisconsin Governor's Commission on Human Rights, for example, with thirty governor-appointed nonsalaried commissioners, a civil service director, and a staff of two, was created by the legislature in 1947 with a broad mandate: ". . . to disseminate information and to attempt by means of discussion as well as other proper means to educate the people of the state to a greater understanding, appreciation and practice of human rights for all people. . . ." Without specific administrative responsibility or regulatory powers, the commission's program includes fact finding, education, community organization and relations, the handling of cases of discrimination, and recommendations of needed legislation. A broad approach utilizing existing agencies and resources and "tailor-made" techniques is employed to remedy specific problems and to promote a climate of opinion favorable to equal opportunity for all disadvantaged groups, such as Negroes, Indians, and migrant workers. The commission also has initiated and/or supported legislation which is now law, relating to non-discrimination in public accommodations, the National Guard, public housing, employment, migrant camps, and Indian affairs.

Twenty states also have private agencies in intergroup relations. About twelve of them are councils on human relations in southern states or-

---

[34] "State Laws and Agencies for Civil Rights: A Comparative Study of 28 States," (mimeographed; Madison, Wisc., Governor's Commission on Human Rights), February, 1960.

ganized through efforts of the Southern Regional Council to help particularly with tension growing out of school desegregation.

There are over thirty municipal intergroup relations agencies with paid staffs located in twenty-seven cities. Some have fair employment practices responsibilities, and others work for the improvement of relations between various groups through education, persuasion, and consultation. Most are in larger cities, such as Boston, Chicago, Cincinnati, Cleveland, Denver, Detroit, Kansas City (Missouri), Los Angeles, Milwaukee, Minneapolis, New York City, Philadelphia, Pittsburgh, Toledo, and St. Louis. In addition, there are 117 cities with local private agencies.

It is difficult to say how effective these public and private programs of public education actually are. The very organization of these official and unofficial bodies is an indication that more citizens are assuming a larger share of the responsibility for these problems. This widespread awareness of group prejudices is evident in the results of surveys and in the extent to which the subject of racial and cultural relations has been featured in the press, television, the radio, and motion pictures. "The fact that discussion of these problems is increasingly open and frank is in itself an indication of a more wholesome state of affairs." [35]

Preventive Agencies

It is often difficult for the public to see that it is easier and less expensive, in the long run, to prevent the development of deviant attitudes and antisocial behavior than to try to modify them later. In preventive work it is necessary to get to a situation before the person has been organized in a certain manner and a deviant conception of self has been formed. Several different types of preventive agencies have been, or are in the process of being, established. Some represent a general approach and apply to many problems, whereas others deal only with one.

LOCAL COMMUNITY PROGRAMS OR NEIGHBORHOOD COUNCILS

One of the most promising efforts to deal with the unsatisfactory features of urbanization and to reduce social deviation has undoubtedly been the greater citizen participation in attempts to change the local community. Local community programs or neighborhood councils, as most of these groups have been called, are becoming increasingly widespread and appear to have a sound theoretical basis, both in accomplishing group redefinitions and situations and in giving the individual a feeling of belong-

[35] Louis Wirth, "The Unfinished Business of American Democracy," *The Annals*, 244:6–7 (March, 1946). Also see Robin M. Williams, Jr., *The Reduction of Intergroup Tensions* (New York: Social Science Research Council, 1947).

ing in the larger social structure. They are used not only in the United States but also in many countries, including Great Britain and even India.[36]

This approach stresses the neighborhood as an important area of first-line action in combating deviant behavior. It is an attempt to deal with conditions in the environment which contribute to delinquency. An impressive amount of evidence in certain areas of social deviation indicates that often the neighborhood, rather than the individual or the family, is the locus of the problem. Research by social scientists in a number of cities has revealed that some neighborhoods have higher rates of deviations than others. This does not mean that deviations are nonexistent in some areas, but rather that if they are controlled in certain selected areas the total incidence can be materially reduced. As has been indicated, the rate of delinquency may be as much as five times greater in certain neighborhoods than in others. There are great variations in the rates for ordinary crime. Likewise, the amount of sexual promiscuity and family maladjustment may vary with neighborhoods. Similar variations have been found in the amount of suicide, discrimination against Negroes, and anti-Semitism. Although alcoholism and certain forms of mental illness have not been characterized by such wide ecological differences, the incidence of mental illness may be several times greater—and the chances of getting early treatment much less—in certain areas.

"Problem neighborhoods," as those areas generally characterized by high rates of deviant behavior are often termed, appear to exhibit a number of social characteristics. They are areas of great diversity in social norms and values, considerable spatial mobility, and little stability of the population. People migrate there from rural and urban areas, and from other countries and cities. Social contacts in the entire area are often less numerous or intimate, and although there is more tolerance, there is less concern for the welfare of neighbors. Shared activities of the entire neighborhood are less frequent and seldom involve common problems.

The neighborhood is an area in which the family functions. To a large extent the kind of neighborhood determines the type of family life which will develop. Often what a middle-class neighborhood claims as the personal virtues of the family are the reflection of groups of families and other institutions surrounding it. Conversely, there is a limit to what a single family with one set of norms can do if it is surrounded by other families with deviant norms and is in an area where the institutions also cater to

[36] Arthur Hillman, *Neighborhood Centers Today* (New York: National Federation of Settlements and Neighborhood Centers, 1960), and B. Chatterjee and Marshall B. Clinard, *Organizing Citizens' Development Councils* (Delhi: Delhi Municipal Corporation, 1961). Also see Marshall B. Clinard and B. Chatterjee, "Urban Community Development in India: The Delhi Pilot Project," in Roy Turner, ed., *India's Urban Future* (Berkeley: University of California Press, 1962), and Marshall B. Clinard, "Perspectives on Urban Community Development and Community Organization," *Social Welfare Forum*, 1962.

deviant norms. The family may come to reflect neighborhood approval or disapproval of conditions of marital infidelity, excessive drinking, or discrimination against certain groups. Neighborhoods and the children of neighbors help, more than is realized, to raise one's children.

The neighborhood is the child's world. It is largely the area of his social participation during afternoons, evenings, week ends, holidays, and vacation periods. His informal neighborhood education is frequently at odds with his more formal school education. There is often conflict between the neighborhood and the school in the definitions of what constitutes proper use of leisure time, sportsmanship, and moral codes.[37] Often the neighborhood play group can enforce more conformity than the school, and school programs which attempt, for example, to deal with juvenile delinquency cannot be effective without the active cooperation of the neighborhood. If there is a cleavage between school norms and neighborhood norms, the problems of dealing with delinquency are greatly increased. Similarly, child guidance clinics and law enforcement must depend on neighborhood support. The people of a neighborhood can support or ridicule the work of psychiatrists and police officers. What their neighbors think is often the really important thing to people. Where they have no neighbors only formal agencies are able to influence them.

Neighborhood programs usually involve a symbiotic relationship between local leaders and professional personnel, usually social workers or sociologists, who serve as catalysts for stimulating local desires for social reintegration. These professionally trained people generally do not carry out the programs and do not desire to do so. Rather, they find the leadership and suggest various possible ways in which to execute the programs, but they leave the decisions to local leadership.

> Outside leaders have a definite but limited role. This approach to area reorganization places principal emphasis on the role of natural community leaders who are carriers of conventional conduct norms. Not only do such leaders serve as nondelinquent models for emulation by youngsters attracted to programs offered by projects of this type, but because these indigenous leaders have prestige in the local area, they easily attract adults, as well as children and youths, to project programs in the first instance. It is around natural community leaders, then, that legitimate social structures can be germinated and multiplied in delinquency-prone areas. And it is in relationship with such leaders and within such structures that youngsters can develop the close and intimate attachments with conventional models, achieve the satisfactions, and acquire the sense of personal worth and purpose necessary to counter the drift toward delinquency characteristic of their life situations.[38]

---

[37] Henry D. McKay, "The Neighborhood and Child Conduct," *The Annals*, 261:33 (January, 1949).

[38] John M. Martin, "Three Approaches to Delinquency Prevention: A Critique," *Crime and Delinquency*, 7:23 (January, 1961).

The so-called Area Project work in Chicago has been one of the best known of these efforts. This neighborhood approach began a few years before 1934 and was incorporated in that year as the Chicago Area Project. Although primarily organized to counteract delinquency, it has indirectly stimulated many efforts to solve other problems. Initially the project was instituted to reduce the high delinquency in three areas of the zone in transition in the city; since then the work has been expanded to include seven other areas. The Area Project has the same purpose as have other agencies—the control of delinquency—but its methods are different:

> (1) It emphasizes the development of a program for the neighborhood as a whole. (2) It seeks to stress the autonomy of the local residents in helping to plan, support, and operate constructive programs which they may regard as their own. (3) It attaches special significance to the training and utilization of community leaders. (4) It confines the efforts of its professional staff, in large part, to consultation and planning with responsible neighborhood leaders who assume major roles in the actual development of the program. (5) It seeks to encourage the local residents to utilize to the maximum all churches, societies, clubs, and other existing institutions and agencies, and to co-ordinate these in a unified neighborhood program. (6) Its activities are regarded primarily as devices for enlisting the active participation of local residents in a constructive community enterprise, for creating and crystallizing neighborhood sentiment on behalf of the welfare of the children and the social and physical improvement of the community as a whole. (7) It places particular emphasis upon the importance of a continuous, objective evaluation of its effectiveness as a device for reducing delinquency, through constructive modification of the pattern of community life.[39]

More specifically, programs of this type try first to develop a civic pride in the activity of its residents. The degree of participation in community activities seems, in part, to be a product of the individual's conception of his responsibility for improving social conditions. Second, the local committees try to develop recreational programs for the neighborhood children and to reach natural groups of children, such as gangs. Being citizen-led, members of these groups often have the advantage of knowing the delinquents personally, and they can enlist the support of persons with similar racial and ethnic backgrounds. Third, community groups assist in the rehabilitation of delinquent and criminal offenders by encouraging them to adopt conventional norms. This is often done by asking such people to serve on community committees: "By this method the parolee or ex-offender is introduced into a conventional group, his role in

---

[39] Clifford R. Shaw and Jesse A. Jacobs, "The Chicago Area Project: An Experimental Community Program for Prevention of Delinquency in Chicago," "Mimeographed; Chicago: Institute for Juvenile Research, undated). Also see Anthony Sorrentino, "The Chicago Area Project after 25 Years," *Federal Probation:* 23:40–45 (June, 1959); and Solomon Kobrin, "The Chicago Area Project—A 25-Year Assessment," *The Annals,* 322:19–29 (March, 1959).

the community is thus redefined, which, in turn results in a redefinition of his own conception of himself. The vigor with which parolees and others with criminal records have worked to improve their own communities and to keep boys out of delinquency has been one of the most encouraging aspects of the Area Project program." [40] Programs of this type have now been developed in a number of communities in Illinois, patterned after the Chicago project. In Quincy, for example, such programs have been set up in five low-income neighborhoods. Variations of these projects, some with less citizen responsibility and more direction by the professional staff, have been adopted in other parts of the country.[41]

In an evaluation of the Chicago Area Projects by Witmer and Tufts, these conclusions were enumerated:

1. Residents of low-income areas can organize and have organized themselves into effective working units for promoting and conducting welfare programs.
2. These community organizations have been stable and enduring. They raise funds, administer them well, and adapt the programs to local needs.
3. Local talent, otherwise untapped, has been discovered and utilized. Local leadership has been mobilized in the interest of children's welfare.[42]

Some area projects go beyond a single neighborhood and become an association of neighborhoods, as in the Southside Community Committee in the large Negro area of Chicago. Between 1934 and 1940 eighteen in every hundred boys in this highly deteriorated area were brought before the court, a rate almost four times that of the city as a whole. In an attempt to reduce this high delinquency rate and to develop closer community integration, the local citizens set up committees, organized community centers and summer camps, and planned a variety of other programs. They have written about their work: "Each neighborhood organization attempts to deal with these problems as vigorously as possible. . . . Police were exceptionally cooperative with the neighborhood organizations, responding eagerly, and in some cases with ill-concealed surprise, to the novel spectacle of residents in vice-ridden neighborhoods taking action against disreputable elements in the community." [43]

---

[40] "Report of the Chicago Area Project, 1947–48" (Mimeographed; Chicago: Institute for Juvenile Research, 1949), p. 6.

[41] See Hillman, *op. cit.*

[42] H. L. Witmer and E. Tufts, *The Effectiveness of Delinquency Prevention Programs,* Children's Bureau, U.S. Department of Health, Education, and Welfare, Publication 350 (Washington, D.C.: Government Printing Office, 1954), p. 15.

[43] Southside Community Committee, *Bright Shadows in Bronzetown* (Chicago: South Side Community, 1949), p. 104. See Julia Abrahamson, *A Neighborhood Finds Itself* (New York: Harper & Row, Publishers, 1959), for a detailed description of how other Southside citizens in Chicago united in an effort to save their neighborhood from deterioration into a slum.

Martin has summarized the importance of a local community approach to delinquency prevention:

> Students of delinquency are becoming increasingly aware of the necessity of reaching out beyond the child and his family in their efforts at prevention. It is submitted that the most efficacious approach for modifying the operating milieu of the bulk of our delinquents is through the widespread establishment of community-centered programs of prevention. Supported by continued improvement in the collective welfare—particularly in terms of the successful assimilation of low-status groups—and incorporating the best of "corrections" and individual treatment, the community-centered approach offers the most hope for reducing law-violation by our children and adolescents.[44]

STREET CORNER PROJECTS

Another type of preventive program involves semiparticipant work with a group of deviants. This approach has been used particularly with delinquent gangs by various groups, such as the Boys Club of New York City and, more dramatically, by the Central Harlem Street Clubs Project of the Welfare Council of New York City. This project worked intimately with four Harlem street gangs from 1947 to 1950 in an effort to divert their activities into legitimate channels. The gangs varied from thirty-five to over a hundred boys, ranging in years from nine to nineteen, all of whom had been engaging in such behavior as fighting in gangs, stealing, committing sex offenses, smoking marihuana, drinking liquor, and gambling:

> The boys tended to see adults as authorities, hoodlums, or suckers. Authorities pushed them around, told them what to do and what not to do, moralized, made demands, threatened, condemned, and meted out punishments. Some boys regarded their parents and teachers in this light. According to the boys, the cops chased them from the streets in which they played, picked them up without reason, and subjected them to humiliating verbal abuse and brutal beatings. (On several occasions the workers observed actual instances of mistreatment on the part of the police.)
>
> According to the boys, hoodlums were the smart guys who got along in the work by exploiting, cheating, and outwitting the other fellow. The numbers man, the pimp, and the racketeer were outstanding examples. They were admired because they were "in the know," knew the "ins" and "outs," and could get around the law. One always had to be on guard with an adult because any adult might be a hoodlum at heart. The boys were especially suspicious of "nice" adults.
>
> The boys had little, if any, community identification. They hated living in Harlem. They hated the filth, the lack of decent places to play, the overcrowding. They felt that the community had no place for them. They were pushed around by the janitor. They were chased out of the candy store

---

[44] Martin, "Three Approaches to Delinquency Prevention," *loc. cit.*, p. 24.

by the store-keeper. They were hounded off the street by cruising patrol cars. As far as they were concerned adults had no use for them and this feeling was mutual! Many boys felt that their fellow club members were the only persons in the world for whom they cared or on whom they could count.[45]

A project worker was attached to each gang. As the project workers established relationships with the boys in the gang, gradually won their confidences, and became accepted by them they played several roles. One was a neutral role of observing and seeking information without displaying approval or disapproval; another was that of stimulating changes. They used such techniques as example-setting, delaying antisocial acts, and insight-inducing to make the boys aware of feelings they did not recognize. Through their associations they tried to encourage self-direction along the lines of new programs. They used various means to divert the boys' activities:

> 1. They organized baseball and basketball teams, obtained the use of school and church gyms for practice sessions, and participated in tournaments with the teams of former enemy gangs.
> 2. They held a number of dances and block parties at which they sold refreshments and raffled off gifts. With the profits from these ventures some of the clubs were able to buy uniforms and equipment for their teams.
> 3. They organized a series of movie programs for their members and friends. The Project supplied the movie projector, but the boys ran the shows themselves—choosing the films, setting up chairs, collecting tickets at the door, and cleaning up afterwards.
> 4. They went on a number of overnight hikes, camping trips, and fishing and crabbing outings.[46]

A more recent project has been the study of street corner groups and patterns of delinquency in connection with the program for detached workers of the YMCA of metropolitan Chicago.[47] Workers are assigned to make contacts with, and to try to change the delinquent patterns of, juvenile gangs. A preliminary report has stated that "we can say with a big degree of confidence that *gang fighting* virtually has been eliminated on the part of gangs with which the program has worked intensively. We want to know a good deal more about *why* this is true, however, and why other forms of delinquent behavior apparently are much more resistant to change than is gang fighting." [48]

---

[45] Paul L. Crawford, Daniel I. Malamud, and James R. Dumpson, *Working with Teen-Age Gangs,* A Report on the Central Harlem Street Clubs Project (New York: Welfare Council of New York City, 1950), pp. 18–19.

[46] *Ibid.,* pp. 39–40.

[47] James Short, Jr., "Street Corner Groups and Patterns of Delinquency," A Progress Report from National Institute of Mental Health Research Grant, M-3301 (Mimeographed; March 1, 1961).

[48] *Ibid.,* p. 28. Italics in the original.

THE SCHOOL

More and more schools have been recognizing that their duties extend beyond the transmission of knowledge. As the schools have taken over many responsibilities for character development which were formerly left entirely to the family and the church, some families have tended to attribute to them the difficulties which their children develop. Teachers can have a beneficial effect on children. The training of teachers has increasingly emphasized problems of mental health, and they have learned to recognize many incipient behavior difficulties of children in the classroom situation.[49] Such children are referred to the counseling staff for guidance if the school has one, or to any other appropriate community agency.

> Few would deny that the family is the best of all possible settings for the promotion of mental health. Here are concentrated the crucial influences and relationships that shape the development of the child and young adult, for better or for worse. Unfortunately, the family is a rather isolated unit of modern society; its members go forth from the home as individuals but may return to it as components of a different group. The family is not readily accessible to outside help, except as it seeks it, and society has no pervasive mental health resources that encompass the family within their structure.
>
> The school, however, comes remarkably close to achieving this relationship with the family. At least it is in a position to do so. In an era of universal compulsory education, the school is one institution of society through which each of us must pass. During our formative years we are influenced to varying degrees by this educational experience, which takes place against the background of the family, yet apart from it. Here, then, is a ready-made setting with a potentiality for directing, reinforcing, or correcting mental health. The school may not only guide, strengthen, and even treat the mental health of the pupil but also, through the role of the pupil as a family member, seek means of improving home situations for the sake of all members of the family.[50]

In some localities, schools have also done some work in antidiscrimination programs. The best known of such programs has been the Springfield Plan, where for many years in this Massachusetts community the school has attempted to teach a constructive program of intergroup relations from the lowest grades.[51] At the same time there are similar programs in adult classes, PTA's, churches, labor unions, and teachers' training courses to change the attitudes of adults.

---

[49] For a discussion of these issues see Wesley A. Smith and G. W. Goethals, *The Role of the Schools in Mental Health* (in preparation), as cited in *Action for Mental Health*.

[50] Joint Commission on Mental Illness and Health, *Action for Mental Health* (New York: Basic Books, Inc., 1961), pp. 123–124. Reprinted by permission.

[51] Alexander Alland and James Waterman Wise, *The Springfield Plan* (New York: The Viking Press, Inc., 1945).

Unfortunately, some school situations add to behavioral difficulties and to intergroup tensions, and may even contribute to truancy and to more serious delinquency. Many professional educators agree that schools are often places where juveniles, during the school day, are bored, subjected to monotonous routine, crushed when they try to express any individuality, or thrown into needless competition with others instead of learning how to cooperate with them.[52] In many urban areas the relation of teacher and pupil is impersonal. Nevertheless, the school situation is one of personal interaction, and too frequently those selected to educate others are themselves uninspiring and may even be seriously maladjusted. Teachers too often silence inquisitive, creative students by demands for obedience. As a result, "it is no wonder that part of the function of juvenile gangs engaging in delinquency is to furnish new experience, the thrill of the cleverly executed act of vandalism or auto theft." [53]

The National Education Association recently sponsored a project in juvenile delinquency which was initiated by the question, "What can the school do to prevent and control norm-violating behavior of children?" The project committee offered suggestions as to how the school may more effectively serve as a preventive agency from which the following were selected.[54]

1. The classroom teacher assumes the major responsibility for early identification of the potential norm-violating youngster. He maintains records and anecdotal reports of every pupil he teaches, thus ensuring that accurate and up-to-date information about individual students and their backgrounds will be readily available to himself and to other professional personnel.

2. The teacher maintains an attitude toward all his students which recognizes and upholds the dignity and worth of every individual, including that of the norm violator. As an instructional motivator and guide in the learning experience, he makes every effort to enable each pupil to achieve a level commensurate with his ability, despite norm-violating behavior arising from emotional or cultural problems.

3. The school develops an integrated system of special services, adequately and professionally staffed, to help the norm violator. These services generally are designed to assist the individual classroom teacher as she works with any pupil needing help. The school periodically assesses its unique needs for such services in the present and future, and it adopts long-range plans for meeting these needs.

---

[52] "Education for Our Time," Special Issue of *Survey Graphic*, 36:565–653 (November, 1947).
[53] Marshall B. Clinard, "Secondary Community Influences and Juvenile Delinquency," *The Annals*, 261:45 (January, 1949).
[54] See William C. Kvaraceus, *Delinquent Behavior: Principles and Practices*, Vol. II; and *Delinquent Behavior: Culture and the Individual*, Vol. I (Washington, D.C.: National Education Association, 1959).

4. For the extremely disturbed or disturbing youngster the school provides special facilities with special personnel in which remedial and rehabilitative services are available. The special class or center should be conceived of as, or allowed to become, a custodial or a hospital facility.

5. The school recognizes and accepts the fact that the family is one of the most important influences in the life of an individual, that few parents are willfully negligent or have any wish to raise a delinquent youngster, and that parents are in a strategic position to understand and evaluate the growth and development of their own children. The school, having recognized and accepted the responsibilities of identifying potential or actual delinquent behavior in the school situation, works with the family in a common endeavor to achieve what is best for the youngster.

6. The school and law-enforcement and court personnel develop a co-ordinated and cooperative program in all common areas related to juvenile norm-violating behavior.

7. The school recognizes that delinquency prevention and control is a community problem and requires action on the part of all citizens. The school studies, evaluates, understands, and makes use of the peer, ethnic, racial, and religious systems at work in its community. Utilizing and working with the resources of all available agencies and institutions, the school has a leadership role in the formation and continuation of a community-wide effort for the prevention and control of norm-violating behavior.

THE CHURCH

Churches of all types are increasingly recognizing their community responsibilities for attempting to improve interpersonal relations. Like the medical doctor, the clergyman is in a favorable position to detect potential problems in the early stages. A recent study found that 42 percent of Americans turn for help for problems to clergymen, 29 percent to physicians in general, 18 percent to psychiatrists or psychologists, and 10 percent to social agencies or marriage clinics.[55] Numerically there are far more clergymen than psychiatrists in the United States. Many theological students are now receiving training in counseling persons with problems of various types. In 1960 there were 343 programs in clinical pastoral training, counseling, or psychology offered by 212 Protestant seminaries; training is also provided in Catholic and Jewish theological schools. It is estimated that between 8000 and 9000 clergymen have taken formal training courses in clinical pastoral training.[56] Some even spend some time studying the problems of patients in mental hospitals and clinics. This study enables them

---

[55] Gurin et al., Americans View Their Mental Health.

[56] R. V. McCann, The Churches and Mental Health (in preparation) as cited in Action for Mental Health, pp. 132–140.

to supplement the work of the limited number of psychiatrists by counseling their parishioners.[57]

It has been suggested that clergymen's efforts in the area of mental health should be chiefly those of prevention. In particular, the clergyman can provide intervention during times of crises, partly by the use of religious rituals and partly by direct support and action. In order to accomplish this the clergyman should be readily accessible to his parishioners. "Finally the effectiveness of clergymen as psychological counselors appears to depend much more on their capacity for understanding human behavior and on the warmth of their personalities than it does on their professional training and orientation. This may also apply to mental health personnel, and with more cogency than many of us in the field are willing to admit." [58]

A similar development has been the increasing activity in pastoral premarital and marital counseling. Traditionally the church has also been the refuge of the aged in their loneliness. For many years there has been a large interdenominational program to deal with discrimination. This has included particularly the work of the National Conference of Christians and Jews. Programs to make the church a center for community activities, particularly youth programs, have also helped to deal with many of the problems created by urbanism. For example, the boxing programs of the Catholic Youth Organization (CYO), founded in Chicago in 1930, have been particularly effective in the zones of transition of larger cities. Some suggest that churches can play a more important role in forestalling juvenile delinquency. This might be accomplished through the church's effort in providing "education for living" and in providing social activities with other young persons or with families.[59]

CLINICAL AND COUNSELING FACILITIES

Many difficulties in interpersonal relations which might eventually lead to more serious problems have been treated in the early stages by outpatient clinics of various types, the chief ones being mental health clinics, child guidance clinics, alcoholic clinics, and marriage and family counseling agencies. Mental health facilities provide outpatient services with a full- or part-time psychiatrist and usually a psychologist and a social worker who help with diagnosis and treatment. In 1956 there were only 1294 such facilities in the entire United States; 750 for children and adults, 400 for children only and 144 for adults only. Of this number one third were in

---

[57] Thomas A. C. Rennie and Luther E. Woodward, *Mental Health and Modern Society* (New York: The Commonwealth Fund, 1948), p. 239.

[58] Joint Commission on Mental Illness and Health, *Action for Mental Health* (New York: Basic Books, Inc., 1961), p. 140. Reprinted by permission.

[59] Robert and Muriel Webb, "How Churches Can Help in the Prevention of Delinquency," *Federal Probation* 21:22–25 (December, 1957).

New York and Massachusetts alone. In the entire country during 1956 there were only 379,000 mental health clinic patients, 182,000 of these being adults. With the present staff in many cases the facilities were often unable to give treatment or to do follow-up work.

Child guidance clinics are of several types.[60] Some are general clinics which take all types of children with behavioral disorders. Some are affiliated with hospitals; others in larger urban areas are often set up in connection with school programs. There are few adequate evaluations of clinics such as these, and their effectiveness in reducing deviant behavior is not definitely known. However, one of the few studies evaluating the effect of such clinics on reducing delinquent behavior concluded that there was no indication of any effect.[61]

Special facilities for the treatment of alcoholics have been established in many cities. Some of the first clinics for alcoholics were established in Connecticut by Yale University in 1944. Although for most of the patients alcoholism has been a long and persistent difficulty, many are helped before it can become even worse. The recommended staff consists of a part-time psychiatrist, two full-time psychiatric social workers, an internist, and a psychologist. Such a clinic can deal with about 350 cases annually at a cost which represents but a fraction of the cost of untreated alcoholism in most communities.[62]

The first marriage clinics were established in Austria in 1922 and about eight years later in this country in New York City, Los Angeles, and Philadelphia. Today there are many such counseling centers which deal with problems of marriage and family relations. In general, their work is diagnosis and treatment, and they use the services of such specialists as psychiatrists, psychologists, sociologists, urologists, and gynecologists. Many other agencies, such as family service, are performing similar work along with their other activities.

COMPREHENSIVE PROGRAMS

Several attempts are now being made to deal with deviant behavior through more comprehensive programs. One of the largest, which began in 1962, involves an expenditure of $12.6 million to deal with juvenile delinquency on the lower East Side of New York City.[63] The project area of 107,000 persons has one of the worst juvenile delinquency records in the city despite recent public and private housing for 60,000 residents. The three-year project, called Mobilization for Youth, involves community de-

[60] George E. Gardner, "American Child Psychiatric Clinics," The Annals, 286:129–135 (March, 1953).
[61] H. Warren Dunham and LeMay Adamson, "Clinical Treatment of Male Delinquents: A Case Study in Effort and Result," American Sociological Review, 21:312–320 (June, 1956).
[62] McCarthy and Douglass, Alcohol and Social Responsibility, p. 114.
[63] The New York Times, June 1, 1962, pp. 1, 14.

velopment, recreation, school programs, clinical facilities, and the creation of new jobs for youths.

The community development and recreation programs include: neighborhood councils to create and guide the programs; neighborhood service centers, or helping stations, to offer casework facilities for families with special problems; coffee shops, furnished and staffed by young people, to serve refreshments and feature folk music, art, sculpture, and other cultural activities; and an adventure corps, for boys 9 to 15, to provide marching bands, educational programs, athletics, and vocational training.

Another phase of the project will be to meet the problems of "slum children in slum schools" through these programs: home visits by teachers; a planning committee to develop a curriculum for slum schools; reading centers in all elementary schools and reading clinics in two elementary schools; experimental classes for retarded children; and a homework helper program, with 300 good high school students being paid to tutor failing elementary school pupils.

One other phase of the project will seek to create new jobs and find existing work through these special programs:

1. Urban Youth Service Corps, to hire about 1000 unemployed, out-of-school youths and pay them $1 an hour for up to 35 hours a week. They will repair tenements, construct playgrounds, manufacture toys, repair furniture, beautify the neighboring areas, and serve as aides in public and nonprofit private institutions.

2. Youth Jobs Center, a central employment agency for counseling and job placement.

3. Exploratory work course, to be offered in junior high schools to inform students of job possibilities and requirements.

Summary

There are a number of ways to deal with negatively regarded deviations, including acceptance, a condition of equilibrium, and the elimination of the deviation, particularly through social isolation of the deviant. Norm and value conflicts are involved not only in the definition of various forms of deviant behavior but in proposals for their solution. Much can be done through public education to develop consensus on deviations. Agencies to prevent deviant behavior include local community programs or neighborhood councils, street corner projects, the school, the church, and clinical and counseling agencies.

Selected Readings

Action for Mental Health. Joint Commission on Mental Illness and Health. New York: Basic Books, Inc., 1961. Includes a detailed discussion of the role of public education in the prevention of mental disorder. Also a discussion of the part the school, church, and clinical and counseling facilities can play in the prevention of mental disorder.

Annals, The. Usually each year *The Annals* of the American Academy of Political and Social Science devotes one or more issues to some form of deviant behavior, considering it not only from theory but from social action as well.

BARTON, REBECCA CHALMERS. *Our Human Rights.* Washington, D.C.: Public Affairs Press, 1955. A detailed description of how a governor's Commission on Human Rights in a midwestern state operates to reduce discrimination. Contains numerous case materials.

CRAWFORD, PAUL L., DANIEL J. MALAMUD, and JAMES R. DUMPSON. *Working with Teen-Age Gangs.* A Report on the Central Harlem Street Clubs Project. New York: Welfare Council of New York City, 1950. A description of an attempt by the Central Harlem Street Clubs Project to change the behavior of delinquent gangs. Contains case materials.

CUBER, JOHN F., ROBERT A. HARPER, and WILLIAM F. KENKEL. *Problems of American Society: Values in Conflict.* Third Edition. New York: Holt, Rinehart and Winston, Inc., 1956. A discussion of the role of value conflicts in defining certain behavior as deviant. Includes a discussion of the distinction between ameliorative and moral problems.

DEAN, JOHN P., and ALEX ROSEN. *A Manual of Intergroup Relations.* Chicago: The University of Chicago Press, 1955. A manual of principles and techniques for reducing racial and religious discrimination in a community.

DOUGLAS, PAUL H. *Ethics in Government.* Cambridge, Mass.: Harvard University Press, 1952. A series of lectures given at Harvard University by the chairman of the Senate Commission on Ethics in Government. Contains proposals for the improvement of government ethics.

KOBRIN, SOLOMON. "The Chicago Area Project—A 25-Year Assessment," *The Annals,* 322:19–29 (March, 1959). An evaluation of the work of Chicago Area Projects in preventing juvenile delinquency.

Law and Contemporary Problems. "Narcotics," Vol. 22, No. 1 (Winter, 1957). Contains articles dealing with public attitudes and different methods of dealing with drug addiction.

MC CARTHY, RAYMOND G., ed. *Drinking and Intoxication.* New York: The Free Press of Glencoe, 1959. Discusses public attitudes toward problems arising from the use of alcohol, programs of alcohol education, and alcoholic clinics.

RECKLESS, WALTER C. *The Crime Problem.* Third ed. New York: Appleton-Century-Crofts, Inc., 1961. Chapter 21 is a discussion of delinquency prevention measures, including psychiatric clinics, the Chicago Area Project, the New York City Youth Board, and detached workers for street-corner groups.

SUTHERLAND, EDWIN H., and DONALD R. CRESSEY. *Principles of Criminology.* Sixth ed. Philadelphia: J. B. Lippincott Company, 1960. Chapter 29 is a discussion of the prevention of crime and delinquency, including the use of local community organizations, organized recreation, case work with near delinquents, group work with near delinquents, coordinating councils, and institutional reorganization.

Chapter

21

The Reduction of Deviant
Behavior: The Use of Institutions

Many people think that, in order to deal more effectively with certain deviant behavior, it is necessary to build more and better institutions to which delinquents, criminals, mentally ill persons, and alcoholics can be sent to be "cured." Actually, institutional treatment has limited possibilities. In the first place, the sheer size of the deviant population is so great that the cost of institutionalizing more than a fragment of all deviants would be prohibitive. For example, the prisoner population of state and federal institutions, on December 31, 1959, was 213,709 (206,013 males and 7696 females), with about 97,000 new admissions each year. Yet in most cases the facilities in prisons were overcrowded.[1] This prison investment, antiquated as it often is, represents a capital outlay of hundreds of millions of dollars and a large annual operating cost. Second, it is difficult to change the attitudes of a human being in a setting as artificial as those an institution provides. Moreover, the mere fact that a person has received institutional treatment, in a prison or a mental hospital, for example, may be sufficient to stigmatize him for life and make ultimate rehabilitation even more difficult.

Prisons

Although many people think that prisons are the only way to treat law violators, prisons as they are known today are a relatively recent invention, being hardly more than a century and a half old. Serious offenders—thieves, burglars, and robbers—except for those sent to the galleys, were formerly not imprisoned. Either they were executed or they were punished by being subjected to physical torture, branded, maimed, sent to the pillory, or transported to a penal colony, usually in another hemisphere. Penal servitude in the galleys was used from about 1500 until early in the eighteenth century.

---

[1] U.S. Department of Justice, *National Prisoner Statistics* (No. 25; Washington: February, 1961).

Many factors affected the development of prisons—imprisonment in castle dungeons, the use of cell confinement by the church, houses of correction, and, most significant of all, the attitudes of the Quakers toward capital punishment. A few persons were held for periods of time in castles or fortress structures, but they were chiefly noblemen or persons awaiting trial or punishment. The Catholic Church, whose clergy could not be punished by the state by the use of the death penalty for criminal offenses, used confinement in cells. It also maintained institutions in which the sick, aged, and the mentally ill, as well as delinquents and criminals, sought refuge. Houses of correction, which came into use in several European cities during the sixteenth century, were used for petty offenders, including vagabonds, family deserters, prostitutes, and some juveniles.

In America toward the end of the eighteenth century the Quakers of Pennsylvania became appalled at the brutal methods being used on ordinary criminals, particularly the use of capital punishment for hundreds of crimes. The Pennsylvania legislature reduced the number of capital offenses to four, substituting fines, hard labor, and a relatively new idea for serious offenses—imprisonment—for all other offenses. The Walnut Street Prison in Philadelphia, built in 1790, was used for these offenders, who served their sentences in solitary confinement. This concept of using imprisonment as a punishment for crime spread throughout the world, and although there have been many modifications of the original idea, a sentence to prison is still one of the chief means of dealing with criminal offenders.

Today prisons are widely used in every country in the world. In 1959 there were approximately 230 state and federal prisons, for adult offenders, in the United States.[2] This number of prisons and reformatories does not include other places of incarceration, such as prison camps, workhouses, or farms, nor does it include the number of prisons in Alaska and Hawaii. There are also approximately 1500 municipal jails, workhouses, and farms for offenders convicted of misdemeanors and 2500 county jails, workhouses, farms, and camps for misdemeanants. There are also 177 juvenile correctional institutions, of which 117 are state, 30 county or municipal, 4 federal, and 25 private.

OBJECTIVES OF IMPRISONMENT

Originally the Quakers believed that meditation in prison would bring about reformation, but today public attitudes are extremely confused about the purpose of incarceration. Prisons seem to exist for such widely divergent purposes as retribution, deterrence, incapacitation, and rehabilitation. Some people regard the function of prisons as one of exacting retribution, *lex talionis*, "An eye for an eye and a tooth for a tooth."

---

[2] Of the approximately 214,000 prisoners confined in state and federal prisons and reformatories, about 25,000 are federal prisoners, under the Federal Bureau of Prisons.

This principle, based on the concept that an individual is completely responsible for his actions, presumes that the punishment of an offender is in proportion to the injury to society that he has committed. Those who hold such an attitude regard prisons as places in which society may exact vengeance upon the wrongdoer.

Many persons regard prisons as places whose very existence deters others from committing crimes. They assume that the knowledge that some are imprisoned for their crimes deters other citizens from committing crimes. Tappan has raised a number of objections to any belief that the mere threat of punishment has a uniform effect on individuals: (1) The restraining influences on crime are not as rational as punishment would suggest. (2) Deterrence from crime is not merely the result of punishment but also of many other factors, such as prestige in the community, moral training, attitudes toward authority, and the like. (3) The threat of punishment is probably greatest before a person is first convicted or incarcerated and declines thereafter. This is because the stigmata and ostracism associated with conviction and incarceration destroy the basis of this threat— a person's status as a "respectable citizen" or his self esteem. (4) The certainty and speed of punishment seem to have a more deterrent effect than merely the fact that punishment exists. (5) Finally, in many offenses of a circumstantial type the threat of punishment has slight deterrent effects.[3]

Still other persons look upon prisons as methods of getting offenders out of the way. Being imprisoned, they are unable to inflict further injury on society. This belief has two main flaws. Most of the people sentenced to prison not only are not dangerous but in all probability need more community participation rather than social isolation. A small proportion of men generally in prison, perhaps as little as 5 and not over 25 percent, are serious offenders. In the second place, nearly all prison inmates today are now released within from five to ten years, and it is highly unlikely that society would tolerate any incarceration for the actual life of many offenders, particularly since so many are committed when they are relatively young men. Thus prisons can only temporarily incapacitate persons from continuing their criminal activities.

For those who believe that the purpose of prisons is to rehabilitate, and these include practically all persons scientifically trained in correctional work, the idea of punishment is felt to be inconsistent. These people believe that prisons should be places where—after the social and psychological characteristics of prisoners have been studied by specialists, such as psychi-

[3] Paul W. Tappan, "Objectives and Methods in Correction," in Paul W. Tappan ed., *Contemporary Correction* (New York: McGraw-Hill Book Company, Inc., 1951), pp. 8–9. For further discussion of this problem, see Donald R. Cressey, "Limitations on Organization of Treatment in the Modern Prison," in *Theoretical Studies in Social Organization of the Prison* (New York: Social Science Research Council, March, 1960), pp. 78–110.

atrists and psychologists, sociologists, and others—offenders are classified into various types and a program is devised for their institutional treatment. Confusion in the minds of the public, the nature of prisons as they exist after a century or more of punitive methods, and, in fact, the whole idea of incarcerating men like animals, however, have all worked against much success in this direction. Here and there can be found examples of an effective use of prisons as instruments of rehabilitation. Even in those rare places where theory is applied to practice, however, there are often so many negative factors present, including the artificial nature of prison life and the stigma of society, that much progress in reformation would appear difficult. Probably prisons should serve primarily to prevent repetition of crime, by attempting to change prisoners' attitudes toward crime and their self-conceptions. The programs of such institutions should be directed toward changing offenders from law-violating to law-abiding persons, rather than providing custodial care as the majority of prisons presently still do.

Most prisons today do not appear to rehabilitate a very large proportion of their prisoners, although they may perform some other functions more effectively. Between 40 and 70 percent of most prison inmates have been previously incarcerated in some correctional institution, the national average being about one in two men. Leading prison officials are almost unanimously skeptical about the failure of the contemporary prison to rehabilitate, as are scientific observers and ex-inmates. There is abundant evidence that prisons are, in fact, excellent places for tutoring in crime.

CHARACTERISTICS OF PRISON LIFE

Prisons provide little or no freedom comparable to that of the civilian life to which nearly all the inmates return. A prisoner cannot generally go where he wants to go, eat what and when he pleases, tune in on as many radio or television programs as he desires, or even take a bath at any time, let alone when he needs one. Although there is some choice of work, it is limited, and where a man is fortunate to have full-time employment his pay is rarely more than from ten to fifty cents a day. Few opportunities are given him to make decisions, and permission to go anywhere is granted on much the same terms that it is granted a closely supervised child. In most prisons, inmates are marched everywhere, at night they are confined in cells hardly as large as lions' cages in the zoo, and at all times men on gun towers have lethal weapons ready to shoot. The attitude of some guards is impersonal, for they often operate almost mechanically in terms of the rule books and are interested in their work only for the security the jobs bring. Where the custodial officers are ignorant, untrained political appointees, their relationships with the inmates are likely to be even worse. Life for the inmates becomes dull, monotonous, and often a bitter, repetitious experience.

What particularly lengthens the social distance between prison officials and the inmates and negates rehabilitation are the endless prison rules which have been built up in the history of prisons. Once a rule has been put into effect, it is changed only with difficulty. Some of the rules result from the incarceration of thousands of men under maximum security in our larger prisons. The numerous rules of most prisons completely circumscribe the inmate's behavior, prescribing such things as the care of cells, personal hygiene, eating, going to chapel, respect for officers, and obedience. Many of these rules interfere with essentially human behavior and cause particular resentment among young men—rules about not talking in the dining room, from cell to cell, and in the corridors, or those regulating what is called "boisterous conduct." Most rules are so petty that they could not be generally enforced in a free society, in an industrial plant, or even in a military establishment. A few are necessary for the maintenance of order in any institution, but most prison rules are for the sake of rigid discipline or a display of authority, or are due to some situation the need for which may have disappeared a long time ago. Guards may display unwarranted authority over inmates because of the vague nature of many rules and the wide latitude with which they may be interpreted.[4]

In modern institutions infractions of rules largely result in the withdrawal of certain privileges, in counseling, and in rare cases, in the use of solitary confinement. Some institutions, however, use more severe methods to secure compliance.

The artificiality and social isolation of prison life and the multiplicity of rules are great hindrances to any program which attempts to deal with criminal attitudes. As long as prisons in general do not allow more social relations with the outside world it is unlikely that institutional treatment can achieve much in the way of attitude changes or satisfactory emotional adjustment. To change attitudes there must be opportunities to assimilate conventional cultural attitudes. Prison confinement allows only rare outside social contacts; visits from the outside are infrequent and rigidly supervised, the general practice being only once a month; letters are limited in number and censored; and often choices of reading materials, radio programs, and movies are restricted. The one-sex nature of prison communities results in great mental suffering and excessive discussion of sex, and the impossibility of heterosexual intercourse encourages homosexual practices among some inmates. The difficulties connected with the sex problem in prison communities make it one of the most serious and demoralizing features of prison life.

---

[4] See Vernon Fox, *Violence behind Bars* (New York: Vantage Press, 1956); and John Bartlow Martin, *Break Down the Walls* (New York: Ballantine Books, Inc., 1954).

The institutional system is not the only reason why it is difficult to rehabilitate inmates through imprisonment. Even if prisons were more successful, it would still be necessary to contend with the public's "convict bogey." [5] The public holds against a man not so much the crime for which he was convicted as the fact that he has been in prison. Perhaps if prisons were not the places they are, the public's reaction to imprisonment would not be as negative as it is. It is the prison experience which sets men apart and changes them, in the eyes of the public, into "dangerous convicts." Society vents its indignation against crime not on criminals but on "convicts." Once a man has been in prison the public attitude today is to stigmatize him in much the same way as a person who had been in a tuberculosis sanitorium was often formerly stigmatized. Ex-inmates frequently find it so difficult, after having left prison, to help their families face the stigma of the neighborhood, to get and hold a job, to participate in community activities, and even to have the right to vote again, that even those who at one time had intended to go "straight" return again to criminal activities, thanks to their post-prison experiences.[6]

THE PRISON SOCIAL SYSTEM

The prison community and the prison code also work against reformation. Every prison has its subculture and a complex social system of officers and inmates; within the latter group is a social structure in which some inmates have higher status than others.[7] For example, some have found that prisoners and staff members differ markedly in whom they consider to be a "leader." [8] This inmate subculture exists alongside the formal prison system. The informal rules which reflect this subculture generally exert a greater effect on the prisoner's actual behavior than does the system of formally prescribed rules. "The value system of the prisoners commonly takes the form of an explicit code, in which normative imperatives are held forth as guides for the behavior of the inmate in his relations with fellow

---

[5] Harry Elmer Barnes and Negley K. Teeters, *New Horizons in Criminology* (Englewood Cliffs, N.J.: Prentice-Hall, Inc., 1951), pp. 420–422.

[6] For further discussion, see Donald R. Cressey ed., *The Prison: Studies in Institutional Organization and Change* (New York: Holt, Rinehart and Winston, 1961), Chaps. 1–3.

[7] Donald Clemmer, *The Prison Community* (rev. ed.; New York: Holt, Rinehart and Winston, Inc., 1958), and S. Kirson Weinberg, "Aspects of the Prison Social Structure," *American Journal of Sociology*, 47:717–726 (March, 1942). For a general article and bibliography, see Morris G. Caldwell, "Group Dynamics in the Prison Community," *Journal of Criminal Law, Criminology and Police Science*, 46:648–657 (January-February, 1956). Also see Edwin H. Sutherland and Donald R. Cressey, *Principles of Criminology* (6th ed.; Philadelphia: J. B. Lippincott Company, 1960).

[8] Clemmer, *op. cit.*, pp. 134–137, and Clarence Shrag, "Leadership among Prison Inmates," *American Sociological Review*, 19:37–42 (February, 1954). Also see Erving Goffman, "On the Characteristics of Total Institutions: The Inmate World," in Cressey, *The Prison*, pp. 15–67.

prisoners and custodians." [9] Violation of these norms, or informal rules, by any inmate evokes sanctions ranging from ostracism to physical violence. Some of these informal inmate rules are described in the following general maxims:

a. Don't interfere with the interests of inmates. Concretely, this means that inmates "never rat on a con," or betray each other. It also includes these directives: "Don't be nosey," "Don't put a guy on the spot," and "Keep off a man's back." There are no justifications for failing to comply with these rules.

b. Keep out of quarrels or feuds with fellow inmates. This is expressed in the directives, "Play it cool," and "Do your own time."

c. Don't exploit other inmates. Concretely, this means, "Don't break your word," "Don't steal from the cons," "Don't welsh on debts," and *"Be right."*

d. Don't weaken; withstand frustration or threat without complaint. This is expressed in such directives as, "Don't cop out" (cry guilty), "Don't suck around," *"Be tough,"* and *"Be a man."*

e. Don't give respect or prestige to the custodians or to the world for which they stand. Concretely, this is expressed by "Don't be a sucker," and "Be sharp." [10]

In addition to these informal rules of behavior, inmates share a prison argot which expresses their code or value systems. By means of this argot, they communicate to one another stereotypes of prison officials and of the prison world. Guards are known as "hacks" or "screws," and are to be treated with distrust and suspicion. Inmates who conform to the values of the prison officials (by accepting the ideal of hard work and of submission to authority) are labeled "suckers." In addition, there is great preoccupation with "rats" who "squeal" on another inmate to gain favors. The "yard" serves as a place to talk about prison life, about crime, and about the vagaries of society. The inmate who tries to be part of the inmate sub-culture and at the same time tries to benefit from the professional and administrative staff generally finds himself playing contradictory social roles.[11] The control of the inmate subculture, as one writer has described, is in the hands of "politicians" and "right guys."

The prison population is largely in the control of a small group of men which has two divisions. There are the "politicians," "shots," or whatever they

---

[9] Gresham M. Sykes and Sheldon L. Messinger, "The Inmate Social System," in *Theoretical Studies in Social Organization of the Prison* (New York; Social Science Research Council, 1960), p. 5.

[10] Sykes and Messinger, *loc. cit.,* pp. 6–8. See also Gresham M. Sykes, *The Society of Captives: A Study of a Maximum Security Prison* (Princeton, N.J.: Princeton University Press, 1958); and for a more recent treatment of this same problem, see Goffman, "On the Characteristics of Total Institutions: The Inmate World," *loc. cit.*

[11] Lloyd E. Ohlin, *Sociology and the Field of Corrections* (New York: Russell Sage Foundation, 1956), pp. 34–37.

may be called in varying institutions, who hold key positions in the administrative offices of the prisons. They wield a power to distribute special privileges, to make possible the circulation of special foods or other supplies. They in frequent instances become "racketeers" and use their positions to force money and services from less powerful inmates. These men are seldom trusted by the top level of the prison hierarchy, are frequently hated by the general population because of the exclusiveness and self-seeking behavior characteristic of them. Yet the fact remains that in their position they are able to demand adherence to the behavior code of the community.

The other section of this controlling power is held by the so-called "right guys." These men are so known because of the consistency of their behavior in accordance with the criminal or prison code. They are men who can always be trusted, who do not abuse lesser inmates, who are invariably loyal to their class—the convicts. They are not wanton trouble-makers but they are expected to stand up for their rights as convicts, to get what they can from the prison officials, to never permit an opportunity to pass from which they might secure anything from a better job to freedom. . . . These men, because of their outright and loyal behavior, are the real leaders of the prison and impose stringent controls upon the definitions of proper behavior from other convicts.[12]

In recent years, studies of prison social structure have initiated interest in the possibility of harnessing informal inmate groups in modifying prison culture. As yet, there is insufficient knowledge of the kinds of social interactions occurring among prisoners, or of the specific mechanisms by which prison life alters inmate attitudes and loyalties.[13] In order to reintegrate offenders effectively the informal system of relationships and controls needs to be utilized and directed toward conformity with conventional norms.

Some rudimentary beginnings toward modifying prison culture have been made in creating "honor systems," a kind of prison self-government in which prisoners are given responsibility and allowed to make choices. Honor systems have been used in prison camps for smaller groups of prisoners, and are presently used in the California Institution for Men, a minimum security, honor type of institution.[14] Evidence suggests that prisoners released from such institutions have lower recidivism and parole violation rates; yet this may be due in part to the careful selection of prisoners for such institutions.[15]

Programs which effectively utilize all aspects of the inmate social sys-

---

[12] Hans Reimer, "Socialization in the Prison Community," *Proceedings*, American Prison Association, 1937 (New York: The Association, 1937), pp. 152–153. In order to make this study, Reimer, a sociologist, arranged to have himself voluntarily committed to prison.

[13] Sutherland and Cressey, *op. cit.*, p. 497. See also Clemmer, *op. cit.*

[14] Walter C. Reckless, *The Crime Problem* (3d ed.; New York: Appleton-Century-Crofts, Inc., 1961), pp. 524–528; Sutherland and Cressey, *op. cit.*, p. 492. Also see Kenyon Scudder, *Prisoners Are People* (New York: Doubleday & Company, Inc., 1952).

[15] Sutherland and Cressey, *op. cit.*

tem have not yet been devised, and promising programs which have been suggested have not been adequately applied. Some suggest that penal institutions, by their disciplinarian character, obviate the success of any such programs. Others suggest that though there are many obstacles to such programs, they are nevertheless possible, provided bold and imaginative steps are taken toward restructuring the formal system in such a way as to utilize the informal system. Cressey's "group relations approach," using programs involving groups, suggests a possible way of accomplishing this.[16]

THE FUTURE OF PRISONS

The predominance of certain bad features in prisons today raises questions about their future. Unfortunately, it appears that, because of society's attitude toward the offender, prisons will continue to exist for a long time. Meanwhile the main effort needs to be concentrated on keeping people out of prison by preventing delinquency and crime and by the wide use of adequately supervised probation. It is generally agreed that, from the standpoint of crime prevention, it is much wiser to concentrate on the widespread and effective use of probation than to attempt to change an offender's attitudes within the artificial confines of a jail or prison. Probation is a suspension of sentence after conviction in which the offender is allowed, with some restrictions, to remain in free society rather than being imprisoned. Probation, of course, should be well supervised and administered by a trained staff. If this situation exists it would be wise even to place an offender several times on probation rather than incarcerate him in a jail or prison. Not only is well-supervised probation likely to be more effective than prison treatment in preventing further crime; it is far less expensive even if carried out by well-paid professional persons. It is estimated that one probation officer carrying a recommended case load of fifty cases can adequately supervise this number at about the cost of maintaining three or four men in a prison for a single year.

Prisons generally would be more effective, however, under these conditions: [17]

---

[16] For discussions of prison social structure and group-centered programs, see Sykes, *The Society of Captives: A Study of a Maximum Security Prison;* Johan Galtung, "The Social Functions of a Prison," *Social Problems,* 6:127–140 (Fall, 1958); Lloyd E. Ohlin and William Lawrence, "Role of Inmate Systems in Institutional Treatment Procedures," *Proceedings,* National Association of Training Schools and Juvenile Agencies (1958), pp. 115–136; and Oscar Grusky, "Organizational Goals and the Behavior of Informal Leaders," *American Journal of Sociology,* 65:59–67 (July, 1959).

[17] See, for example, Marshall B. Clinard, "Prevention of Crime," *Journal of Correctional Work* (India), 7:1–12 (1960). Also see Marshall B. Clinard, "Prison Systems," *Encyclopedia of Criminology* (New York: Philosophical Library, Inc., 1949), pp. 384–385. See also Sutherland and Cressey, *op. cit.,* Reckless, *op. cit.,* and Richard R. Korn and Lloyd W. McCorkle, *Criminology and Penology* (New York: Holt, Rinehart and Winston, Inc., 1959).

1. An institutional setup is directed at a program of changing norms so as to make the offender into a law-abiding person. Wider use of group therapy should be promoted with a small group of offenders of similar type, discussing such topics as the nature of criminal behavior and how it might be changed, a technique which will be discussed in the next chapter. In a limited number of cases there should be individual therapy in the form of case work.

2. Institutions should be so diversified that the treatment program of a correctional institution can concentrate largely on offenders of a similar general type. Within each type, institutional treatment programs should be worked out for specific types of offenders. There should be institutions for the ordinary type of offender, for the more hardened and sophisticated type, for those with markedly inferior intelligence, and for others.

3. Correctional institutions should be of such size that an intensive treatment program can be worked out and the impact of the staff can be personal. The smaller the institution the fewer rules are necessary and the less rigorous the discipline. Generally a correctional institution should not be larger than 100 inmates although, if that is financially too difficult, the prison population might be as large as 500.

4. If correctional institutions are to be effective in changing a prisoner's attitudes, they should be relaxed and as much like normal living as possible. Less emphasis should be placed on discipline, rules, military programs, and an artificial institutional setting. Often the conceptions of themselves of persons subjected to this become even more criminal.

5. One new type of approach which has great promise is a combination of an institutional program with participation in free society. Nearly all offenders sooner or later return to free society, most of them, in fact, after less than five years. In prisons and jails criminals should associate with noncriminals. Relations with their families must also continue to be as normal as possible if they are not to become even more isolated and bitter against society. These objectives might be secured in several ways: (1) A program of home furloughs might be instituted. (2) Another way to encourage the outside contacts of the offender is to confine him to the institution during the evenings and week ends but allow him to work in free society during the day. This would mean that the noncriminals with whom he works would have a greater effect in changing his attitudes and criminal self-conception than his former criminal associates. This type of program is being tried in a number of countries. (3) Some kind of work camps might be set up for young persons, primarily nonoffenders, but judges could allow offenders to join them in place of institutional treatment. This procedure was used during the 1930's in the United States by the Civilian Conservation Corps camps, which carried out work in forests and on road construction programs.

6. In any institutional setup the staff should be stressed. The members

should be selected primarily in terms of how effective they can be in changing the attitudes of offenders. Of all the persons in authority in a correctional institution, probably the guard plays the most strategic role in that he is more frequently in contact with the offender. The guard is too frequently thought of as a custodial officer rather than as potentially a highly effective member of the treatment staff. Since his social background is generally much like that of most offenders he has an advantage in communicating with them that a more highly educated officer does not have. In any event, all the staff members of the correctional institution should have had training in criminology and in their role of changing the attitudes of prisoners. Those, of course, in higher administrative and welfare posts should have had college training that included advanced courses in the behavioral sciences.

7. Finally, there should be an effective selection of persons for parole and effective parole treatment.

California has developed a number of modern correctional programs in its Youth and Adult Authority, its forestry camps, and particularly its program at the California Institution for Men at Chino.[18] Here about 1500 men, of all ages and convicted of almost all types of offenses, have been in a rather unique program since 1941. The inmates of this farm-ranch of several thousand acres are carefully selected minimum security risks with good potential rehabilitative qualities. The institution has a trained staff and offers extensive educational and vocational programs. The inmates are housed in open dormitories having no walls or guns, they wear no uniforms, they do not march to the dining room, and they are allowed to take more leisurely meals than are permitted in most correctional institutions. Informal receptions for groups of inmates are often held at the superintendent's home, and an inmate council participates in the administration of the institution. Mail is not censored, except on an occasional sample basis. A most significant rehabilitative feature is the three-hour family picnic allowed each Saturday, Sunday, and holiday in a designated area.

After discovering that traditional methods did not work, Sweden in 1945 adopted a new comprehensive program including small correctional institutions of usually not more than a hundred inmates in order to promote a high degree of group interaction with the staff, something that is virtually impossible in larger prisons.[19] Most institutions are open, with

---

[18] Scudder, *op. cit.*

[19] Almost all these features have been included in the Swedish Prison Act of 1945. See Thorsten Sellin, *Recent Penal Legislation in Sweden* (Stockholm: Isaac Marcus Book Publishers, 1947). Thorsten Sellin, "The Treatment of Offenders in Sweden," *Federal Probation*, 12:14–18 (June, 1948). Also see Wilfred Fleisher, *Sweden: The Welfare State* (New York: The John Day Company, Inc., 1956), Chap. 11; Ola Nyquist, "How Sweden Handles Its Juvenile and Youth Offenders," *Federal Probation*, 20:36–42 (March, 1956); Torsten Eriksson, "Postwar Prison Reform in Sweden," *The Annals*, 293:152–162 (May, 1954); and Gösta Rylander, "Treatment of Mentally Abnormal Offenders in Sweden," *British*

no walls, armed guards, or gun towers. In addition, the Swedes allow most offenders short furloughs home every four months, in addition to special emergency furloughs and frequent visits and contacts with the outside world in order to change attitudes and reduce sexual tensions.[20]

Since men in prison spend a great deal of time in their cells or rooms, Swedish inmates are allowed to furnish their rooms in a homelike way, with rugs, drapes, pictures, bedspreads, individual radios, as well as many flowers, plants, paintings, books, electric hot plates, and cups and saucers for coffee. Swedish inmates work in diversified and skilled employment and are paid a fairly adequate wage, amounting to between 80 cents and $2.50 a day. All members of the staffs of correctional institutions are highly trained.

Mental Hospitals

Mental hospitals appear to have two functions: the treatment of patients so that they will recover sufficiently to return to normal society and the provision of custody and care so that both patients and society are protected. Too often the function of custody appears to take precedence over treatment in public mental hospitals.

The custodial aspect of mental institutions primarily serves to protect the patient from those of the outside world who might not understand him and his problems and also to protect him from harming others or himself. Most patients have not constituted a public menace. More often they are merely persons who have bizarre ideas, depressions, or suspicions of others. Few patients will actually harm others, in spite of the societal stereotype that mental patients are dangerous and to be feared. Some patients who have become accustomed to institutional life feel happier in custody than in free society because decisions are made for them, and life is routine. Where their care is good, they are often better fed and are cleaner and neater in dress and manners than they would be outside, and they usually do get some recreation and entertainment in institutions. In fact, it is these very features of custody which some people consider sufficient. Moreover, some patients become so accustomed to the hospital routine that it is difficult to prepare them for the changes in their interpersonal relationships which are necessary for a return to normal society.

EXTENT AND COST OF MENTAL HOSPITAL CARE

Today almost 88 percent of all patients are in state and local mental hospitals. Nearly 10 percent are in veterans' hospitals, and slightly over

---

Journal of Delinquency, 4:262–268 (April, 1955). During 1954 the author studied delinquency and crime and their treatment in Sweden.

[20] In Wisconsin, many jail prisoners, under the Huber Law, are allowed to work in private employment during the day.

2 percent are in private hospitals. Whereas admissions to state and local mental hospitals have increased during the past few years, releases have also increased, reflecting a shortened length of stay for many patients. From 1955 to 1960 there was a consistent decline in the resident population of these hospitals. (See Table 21.1.) In 1960 there were 235,231 admissions

Table 21.1. Resident Patients by Type of Hospital, 1955–1959

Year	All hospitals	State, county, and city hospitals	Veterans' hospitals	Public Health Service hospitals	Private hospitals
1955	632,551	557,969	57,991	2,001	14,590
1956	626,567	550,456	60,080	1,935	14,096
1957	620,544	545,796	59,240	1,965	13,543
1958	620,289	544,008	59,855	1,955	14,471
1959	616,964	540,662	60,779	1,827	13,696

SOURCE: Department of Health, Education, and Welfare, *Trends* (Washington, D.C.: Government Printing Office, 1961), p. 27. These are hospitals for long-term psychiatric care.

to state and local hospitals, 192,351 releases, and 49,846 deaths.[21] One study has concluded that this decline is not reflected in other types of hospitals, that it only represents a "shift in the flow and whereabouts of mental patients, possibly reflecting in part the readily accepted conviction that, if at all possible, it is better for the patient and his prospects to keep him out of State hospitals" and also represents a policy of increased discharge rates, which is in part a reflection of savings in maintenance costs.[22] Much of the increase in discharge rates has been possible through the use of tranquilizers.

The cost of caring for the mentally ill is enormous. During 1950 state governments spent, in tax funds, about $520 million on capital costs and maintenance of their state mental hospitals and about $45 million for other mental health services. Yet the amount spent for patients in state mental hospitals is meager when compared with the amount spent for care in general or private hospitals. In 1961 the Joint Commission on Mental Illness and Health reported that the average amount spent for patients in state hospitals is $4.44 daily, whereas the average daily amount for patients in community general hospitals, largely private, is $31.16, and for those in veterans' psychiatric or tuberculosis hospitals, $12.00.[23]

[21] Department of Health, Education, and Welfare, *Trends* (Washington, D.C.: Government Printing Office, 1961), p. 27.
[22] *Action for Mental Health*, The Final Report of the Joint Commission on Mental Illness and Health (New York: Basic Books, Inc., 1961), p. 20. This commission was appointed by Congress to make a five-year study.
[23] *Ibid.*, Chapter 1.

The Joint Commission reported in 1961 that overcrowding characterizes state hospitals in the United States today. Most state hospitals have from 2000 to 4000 patients.[24] They also found that the ratio of personnel to patients in state mental hospitals today is 0.32, as compared to a ratio of 2.1 for community general hospitals. In general, there is a shortage of psychiatrists in public mental hospitals. Although in 1956 there were 8713 psychiatrists in the United States, only about 1400 were employed full time in public mental hospitals.[25]

METHODS OF HOSPITAL TREATMENT

Because of their large size, it is extremely difficult for state hospitals to give effective treatment to their patients. Thus, the majority of patients receive either no treatment, or receive somatic treatments, usually in the form of drugs or electric shock. These latter treatments can be administered to large numbers of patients in a minimum of time and with little effort on the part of the staff.[26] These treatments help to reduce anxiety and the symptoms of the illness, but rarely deal with the "causes." Group psychotherapy, psychodrama, individual counseling, and occupational therapy, on the other hand, require a much greater effort on the part of the staff. The 1961 report of the Joint Commission on Mental Illness and Health concluded that 80 percent of the 277 state hospitals in the United States today are seriously lagging in the use of modern advances in the treatment of the mentally ill, and were providing custodial care rather than treatment. In only 20 percent of these hospitals was there evidence of some effort to take advantage of these new techniques. The commission found that more than half of all patients in state mental hospitals receive "no active treatment of any kind designed to improve their mental conditions." [27]

The use of the shock therapies, electric and insulin, has been largely a development of the past fifteen to twenty years. Electric shock therapy, which produces temporary convulsions or coma, can be administered to many patients in a relatively short period of time. Although various

---

[24] The Commission strongly recommended that present state hospitals of 1000 patients or more "add not one" additional patient, and that no additional hospitals of more than 1000 beds be built. The Commission further recommended a major reorganization of the existing method of treating the mentally ill, rather than simply increasing the size and population of hospitals, as has been customary in the past.

[25] *Action for Mental Health,* pp. 8–9, 144. In 1960 the American Psychiatric Association had 11,787 members, which, although insufficient for the demand, were nearly three times the 4000 members in 1946.

[26] M. Greenblatt, D. J. Levinson, R. H. Williams, *The Patient and the Mental Hospital* (New York: The Free Press of Glencoe, 1957). Also see Alfred H. Stanton and Morris S. Schwartz, *The Mental Hospital* (New York: Basic Books, Inc., 1954), p. 69, and S. Kirson Weinberg and H. Warren Dunham, *The Culture of the State Mental Hospital* (Detroit: Wayne State University Press, 1960).

[27] *Action for Mental Health,* p. 23.

theories, biological and psychological, have attempted to explain what happens in the shock therapies, so far none has been generally accepted. It has been difficult to come to a general theory in view of the fact that the results of this type of therapy vary greatly. The original claims of high success have been revised in more limited terms. Some patients do recover after a series of shock treatments and others are greatly improved. Most recoveries, however, are only temporary, and the relapse rate is high.

In general, relapse is greater where there is little follow-up treatment with individual psychotherapy. In one study of 380 patients who were given electric shock over a six-month period, 64.8 percent improved or recovered and 35.2 were unimproved.[28] Other studies which have used well-matched experimental and control groups and have employed rigorous research designs have found a much smaller percentage of improvement.[29] Studies of treatment methods in hospitals have found that the choice of treatments for given patients by the physician in charge is not related to the patient's diagnosis so much as it is to his social characteristics, principally his social class. It was found that upper-class patients were much more likely to receive psychotherapy, whereas somatic or physical treatments were used primarily with the lower-class patients.[30] One sociological study has suggested that the extent of prior social participation is favorably associated with this treatment.[31]

Beginning in 1953, tranquilizing drugs, including chlorpromazine and reserpine, have been widely used to relieve some of the symptoms of mental illness. In 1961 it was estimated that as many as one third of all public mental hospital patients received these drugs. One report, in fact, refers to the present situation in treatment as "the tranquilized hospital." [32] Being used to tranquilize those patients who are excited, hyperactive, unmanageable, highly disturbed or highly disturbing, these drugs have changed somewhat the management of psychotic patients in mental hospitals. They have helped to reduce shock treatments and have given more freedom to the patients. In addition, they have made possible greater communication and, consequently, closer relations between staff and patients.

The debate still continues, however, regarding the physiological and

---

[28] S. Kirson Weinberg, *Society and Personality Disorders* (Englewood Cliffs, N.J.: Prentice-Hall, Inc., 1952), p. 435.

[29] See George H. Alexander, "Electroconvulsive Therapy: A Five-Year Study of Results," *Journal of Nervous and Mental Diseases*, 117:244–250 (March, 1953) and Ugo Cerletti, "Electroshock Therapy," *Journal of Clinical and Experimental Psychopathology*, 15:191–217 (July–September, 1954).

[30] See Eugene B. Gallagher, Daniel Levinson, Iza Erlich, "Some Sociopsychological Characteristics of Patients and Their Relevance for Psychiatric Treatment," in Greenblatt *et al., op. cit.,* pp. 371–373.

[31] Malak Guirguis, "Interpersonal Relationships as a Prognostic Factor in Electric Shock Therapy of the 'Functional Psychoses.' " Unpublished doctoral dissertation, University of Wisconsin, Madison, Wisconsin, 1951.

[32] *Action for Mental Health.*

sociological results of these drugs. Some have predicted they would empty mental hospitals, while others have called them "clinical strait jackets." [33] A four-year study in New York State of the use of tranquilizers in state public hospitals between 1955 and 1959 gives some partial, but by no means complete, answers.[34] It was concluded that restraint and seclusion of patients decreased markedly, and that, by 1959, 60 percent of all cases were given freedom of the grounds, or ten times the number who had this freedom in 1956. Whereas first admissions had in previous years exceeded discharges, there was a reversal in 1959. About half of the patients continued on drug therapy after leaving the hospital. The relapse, or rate of return to the hospital, was 35 percent, which was no higher than that of predrug days. The greatest gain in the release of patients was in the age group twenty-five through forty-four; there was little change in the rate of release of those over sixty-five. The drugs had little effect on the senile psychoses, which is the primary cause for admission to mental hospitals. Schizophrenic patients showed far greater benefit than did patients with other types of psychoses or organic brain disease, and these drugs may help to reduce chronic schizophrenic cases.

THE SOCIAL STRUCTURE OF THE MENTAL HOSPITAL

The social structure of mental hospitals may work for or against success in treatment, for a mental hospital is a unique community with its own special social structure in terms of status and power to make decisions. (See Figure 7.) It is organized with the superintendent and professional staff, including psychiatrists, psychologists, occupational therapists, social workers, and similar personnel at the top of the prestige hierarchy. Next come the clerical staff and, following it in social status, the attendants and utility workers. The patients make up the "lowest" group. One of the major difficulties of this social system of status and power relationships is that in the treatment of the mental patient there is often a breakdown in formal and informal communication between staff members and between staff and patients.[35] This breakdown in the communication of information may lead to misunderstanding and interfere with the recovery of a patient.

Patients may be classified behaviorally in terms of the expectations of hospital staff members that they will or will not recover. "Hopeful" patients

[33] Ibid.

[34] H. Brill and R. E. Patton, "Analysis of Population Reduction in New York State Mental Hospitals during the First Four Years of Large-Scale Therapy with Psychotropic Drugs," American Journal of Psychiatry, 116:495 (1959). According to the authors there was no change in the methods or standards for admitting or discharging patients during this period. Unfortunately, a control group was not used, so that their findings cannot be accepted as conclusive.

[35] Alfred H. Stanton and Morris S. Schwartz, The Mental Hospital (New York: Basic Books, Inc., 1954), pp. 193–243.

are those whom the staff regards as having high chances of recovery and discharge. "Chronic" patients are those assigned lower chances of discharge, and who are expected to remain in the hospital for a long time. "Agitated" patients are those regarded as temporarily preoccupied with their illness and in need of special care, usually custodial. Patients may vacillate from "hopeful" to "agitated" and, conversely, from "chronic" to "agitated." [36]

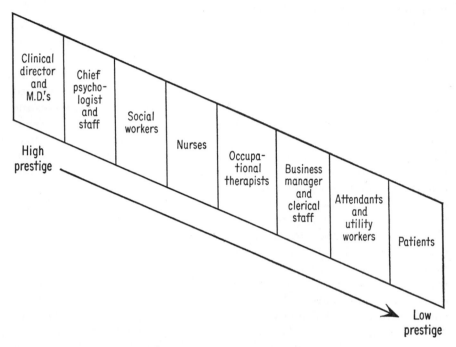

FIGURE 7. Hospital Status Hierarchy

SOURCE: Derived from Martin B. Loeb and Harvey L. Smith, "Relationships among Organizational Groupings within the Mental Hospital," in Milton Greenblatt, Daniel J. Levinson, and Richard H. Williams, *The Patient and the Mental Hospital* (New York: The Free Press of Glencoe, 1957), p. 16.

Patients of these three types are generally assigned to a ward with others of the same type. Each of these wards—the hopeful, the chronic, or the agitated—has its own culture, with a set of norms and values which differs from those of other wards. For example, for patients in the hopeful ward, "going home" is a value highly esteemed. Thus, the ward norms prescribe behaviors which will achieve this value. There is great disapproval of patients who show childish or disturbed behavior, but approval of those who

[36] S. Kirson Weinberg and H. Warren Dunham, *The Culture of the State Mental Hospital* (Detroit: Wayne State University Press, 1960).

give evidence of "making it on the outside." On the other hand, patients in the chronic wards (called the "back wards" by patients) often seem resigned to remaining in the hospital for the rest of their lives. Many, after numerous disappointments and setbacks, have given up hope of achieving some life on the outside. In the chronic wards, therefore, behavioral norms are directed toward accepting and making the best of hospital life. This involves keeping out of trouble with attendants or other patients, doing their work, and making some sort of life *within* the hospital.[37]

Patients in mental hospitals may not have quite the same attitude toward the professional staff as have patients who are being treated by private psychiatrists or in public clinics. The reason is that the contacts between patients and staff in the mental hospital are quite different in character. In the first place, patients have relatively little contact with their assigned physician, since as many as a hundred or more patients may be under the same physician's care. Thus, for the most part, contacts between patients and doctors are impersonal and highly superficial. As one patient stated, "The doctor just comes through one door and goes out the other. He spends no time with the patients." [38] Other patients believe that because doctors can shorten or prolong an inmate's stay, in a sense doctors have entire control over their future. Patients try to cultivate the friendships of doctors and even learn to feign symptoms of recovery.

Social class factors also are related not only to the etiology of mental disorders but to their treatment.[39] Class IV and V patients—those from the lower socioeconomic groups—are generally not as cooperative, as compared with Class I and II, in their treatment and not as highly motivated to become well.[40] They have little scientific knowledge about mental disorders and tend to think of them as a physical illness, wanting not therapy but "pills and needles." They are even secretive about giving knowledge about mental illness in the family, associating it with "bad blood," "a bump on the head," "too much booze," or some physical defect. On the other hand, Class I and II patients stress fatigue and overwork, which tend to make them more amenable to treatment.

Even more important, Class V patients tend not to think in the terms used by the psychitarist and other professional workers, who are middle and upper class and frequently have middle- and upper-class family origins. Frequently these difficulties even involve differences in indicating the meaning of what is said because of the differences in the language used. To the psychiatrist such patients with limited education often appear to be dull and stupid. They are worlds apart socially, and it is difficult for the profes-

---

[37] Weinberg and Dunham, *op. cit.*   [38] *Ibid.*, p. 41.
[39] August B. Hollingshead and Frederick C. Redlich, *Social Class and Mental Disorders* (New York: John Wiley & Sons, Inc., 1957). A partial replication of this study revealed a similar finding.—Robert H. Hardt and S. J. Feinhandler, "Social Class and Mental Hospitalization Prognosis," *American Sociological Review,* 24:815–821 (December, 1959).
[40] See pp. 396–398.

sional to think of them as friends in the same manner in which he might regard patients from Class I or II. Psychotherapy becomes difficult, and shock therapy often seems to be the simplest form of treatment. When the lower-class patient fails to cooperate he is regarded as a "bad patient," particularly when he displays lower-class violence. Whether or not a patient is a "good patient" depends on the sensitivity, intelligence, and the social and intellectual standards of the psychiatrist.

Much has been written about some of the attendant staffs of public mental hospitals: the inadequacy of their numbers, the frequent lack of proper motivation, insufficient training, and extensive turnover, largely because of poor pay. Fortunately, this situation has been improving. By far the greatest amount of contacts of patients is their contact with attendants. The relationship of many attendants to patients, unfortunately, appears still to be largely a custodial one. The patients learn to comply with the demands of the attendants and to know which ones are friendly or unfriendly. The patient who stands up for his rights is all too often likely to be classified as an "agitated person."

Sometimes attendants have favorites who are given preferred treatment: "These favorites may include the informal 'ward leaders,' the functionaries, or the 'stool pigeons.' Generally, the favorites are disliked by the other patients, although the exceptions are those who remain 'loyal' to the patients." [41] Strict enforcement of rules is often defended on the ground that the staff is too limited in size for other methods. One study found that resistance to the introduction of reform measures within a mental hospital came primarily from the attendants. Despite in-service training, unscientific rationalizations and beliefs about patients and mental disorders persisted. They included, for example, the belief that patients are "children" and in reality are happy, and that female patients are wilder and stronger than male patients.[42]

Too frequently much of the mental patient's life in a public mental hospital is spent either in aimless boredom in the wards or in performing menial tasks around the institution, tasks which have no connection with therapy. Although there may be some therapy in it, most of the maintenance work around a public hospital is done by patients, whether or not it is good for them. Some resent this subordinate role, but others become so habituated to it that they become incapacitated for the outside world. As one patient said: "This hospital has been home to me for eleven years. I'm used to it. The work isn't hard and I know how to get along. It wasn't easy the first two years, but after being in and out three times, I can call this home." [43]

[41] Weinberg and Dunham, *op. cit.*, Chaps. 3 and 4.
[42] Thomas J. Scheff, "Control over Policy by Attendants in a Mental Hospital," *Journal of Health and Human Behavior*, 2:93–105 (Summer, 1961).
[43] Weinberg, *Society and Personality Disorders*, p. 430.

THE FUTURE OF THE MENTAL HOSPITAL

In spite of these various limitations, mental hospitals would be more effective in treatment if patients had more visitors, more letters, and other social relationships. Often, in fact, a patient's chance of discharge does not depend on the state of his "illness," but on whether there is someone interested in him—and willing to help him—on the outside.[44] Visits particularly mean a great deal to mental patients; yet generally the longer a patient stays in a mental hospital the less likely is he to have many visitors. Visiting appears to vary according to the type of ward, those on the hopeful ward receiving the most. The patient who has few visitors often loses prestige on the ward, feels he is forgotten, and misses this way of breaking up the hospital routine. One patient has written:

> Many patients are thrilled to have visitors. It takes their mind off the drabness of the hospital and off their own thoughts. It brings them closer to the world of which they so anxiously want to be a part. Pleasant conversation with company brings an assurance to patients that they may be treated affectionately and warmly by their family and friends.[45]

The trial home visits of hopeful patients before release are crucial experiences for most mental patients. This is the test period of adjustment in the interpersonal relations of the patient with his family, friends, and neighbors, and unless they and the patient have been sufficiently prepared by the professional staff, particularly the psychiatric social workers, a relapse may occur. The readjustments necessary because of institutional living and the stigma of having been in a mental hospital are often too much for the patient unless he has help from others.

The stigma of having been in a mental hospital presents one of the most serious difficulties. Many released mental patients are conscious of this stigma, and it interferes with recovery because it makes them feel that a barrier exists between themselves and others. To the public institutional treatment often implies that the patient is different from others. The past reputation of public hospitals has not helped the conception that "insane persons" are confined much as prisoners are. Consequently, few persons wish to admit confinement in a mental hospital, although people may increasingly admit, without too much fear of the stigma, having been under treatment, outside a mental hospital, by a psychiatrist or a psychoanalyst. It may be some time before a person feels like talking as fully about hospitalization for mental difficulties as about hospitalization for some operation.

---

[44] See Simon Dinitz, Mark Lefton, Shirley Angrist, and Benjamin Pasamanick, "Psychiatric and Social Attributes as Predictors of Case Outcome in Mental Hospitalization," *Social Problems*, 8:322–328 (Spring, 1961).

[45] Weinberg, *Society and Personality Disorders*, p. 445.

Although there is no question that the long-term goal of society must be largely one of prevention and early treatment of mental illness rather than extensive reliance on mental hospitals, the present plans of state mental hospitals, where most patients are treated, need to be altered. In this connection, the Joint Commission on Mental Illness and Health in 1961 made the following recommendations which are designed to reorganize our present system of dealing with the mentally ill:

1. Doubling federal, state, and local expenditures for public care of mentally ill within the next five years (1961–1965).
2. Ending the present state mental hospital program, and replacing it with specialized intensive treatment hospitals and community clinics. This would involve:
   a. Establishing a community mental health clinic for every 50,000 population.
   b. Establishing regionally located, non-isolated, intensive psychiatric treatment centers of 1000 beds or less.
   c. Discontinuing addition of patients to state mental hospitals of 1000 or more, and discontinuing construction of hospitals of more than 1000 beds.
   d. Converting existing state hospitals of 1000 beds or more into centers for long-term treatment of physically ill as well as some mentally ill.
3. Extensively expanding after-care and rehabilitation services.
4. Using non-medical hospital personnel with aptitude (attendants, nurses, etc.) to do psychotherapy since this essentially involves listening to patients talk about their troubles. Physicians would be given priority with specifically medical tasks, such as neurological examinations.
5. Greatly increasing the amount of money spent for research into human behavior. As compared to the amount spent on biological problems, such as polio, research on mental illness is in the 1908 era.
6. Increasing aid, in the form of loans, scholarships, etc., to persons entering the mental health field.[46]

An unusual program to prevent admissions to mental hospitals has been developed in Amsterdam, as a municipal government service, and involves the treatment of patients in their own homes wherever possible.[47] Prospective admissions are seen by a city psychiatrist immediately, or within twenty-four hours, after a patient has been reported as disturbed by such persons as the family doctor or the police. By seeing the patient in his own home the psychiatrist can better determine the circumstances and assess the contributing causes more effectively. If clinical observation is necessary the patient may be sent to one of the psychiatric wards in Amsterdam. Amsterdam is divided into four sectors, and a "team," consisting of a psychiatrist and several social workers, is responsible for supervision in

[46] *Action for Mental Health*, pp. vii–xxiv.
[47] A. Querido, "Social Psychiatry and the Legal Issue," *International Journal of Social Psychiatry*, 1:3–8 (Autumn, 1955).

each sector. Supervision is carried out by visits to patients' homes, the frequency of the visits depending on the particular case. The number of cases per team is about four hundred. In addition, the psychiatrist visits clinics about four times weekly and mental hospitals less frequently. Each team is part of the "Consultation Bureau," a sort of central agency with a personnel of about forty-five. It may also give advice to other public agencies, such as public assistance departments, and may give other help, including aid in finding jobs. About 8000 patients are dealt with by this Bureau each year.

It is reported that the program has succeeded in reducing the Netherlands mental hospital population. At present the program meets the needs of about a third of all patients who would otherwise require hospitalization. Dr. Querido, who has done much to develop the Amsterdam program, points out the extreme importance of the patients' *first* contact with societal representatives. Because of the nature of the program he has felt that it has had an effect in changing the public's attitudes toward mental illness and also in changing the psychiatrists' approach to the nature of mental disorder.

Summary

Institutions treat individuals who have developed some type of deviant behavior. It is difficult, however, to treat deviant behavior adequately through institutions because of the large number of those needing treatment and its cost, the limited professional personnel available, the artificiality of institutional life, and the stigma associated with institutional confinement.

Selected Readings

Action for Mental Health. The Final Report of the Joint Commission on Mental Illness and Health. New York: Basic Books, Inc., 1961. This report contains an analysis of the state of mental hospitals, with recommendations for improvement. The Joint Commission on Mental Illness and Health was set up by Congress to make a five-year study of the United States and make necessary recommendations.

Annals, The. "Prisons in Transformation," Vol. 293 (May, 1954). This issue presents various aspects of the problem of prisons and some suggestions for possible solutions.

CLEMMER, DONALD. *The Prison Community*. New York: Holt, Rinehart and Winston, Inc., 1958. A study of the prison as a social system, with particular emphasis on the inmates and their social relationships.

CRESSEY, DONALD, ed. *The Prison: Studies in Institutional Organization and Change*. New York: Holt, Rinehart and Winston, Inc., 1961. A series of articles on the organization of the prison, particularly its social system.

SCUDDER, KENYON J. *Prisoners Are People.* New York: Doubleday & Company, Inc., 1952. The story of the California Institution for Men, one of the most advanced prisons in the United States, by its first superintendent.

STANTON, ALFRED H., and MORRIS S. SCHWARTZ. *The Mental Hospital.* New York: Basic Books, Inc., 1954. A study of the mental hospital as a social system by a psychiatrist and a sociologist.

SYKES, GRESHAM M. *The Society of Captives: A Study of a Maximum Security Prison.* Princeton, N.J.: Princeton University Press, 1958. A sociological study of a prison, particularly the way informal rules of the inmate subculture control the behavior of its members.

TAPPAN, PAUL W., ed. *Contemporary Correction.* New York: McGraw-Hill Book Company, Inc., 1951. A series of articles on various aspects of modern correctional work by some of the leading men in this area.

WEINBERG, S. KIRSON, and H. WARREN DUNHAM. *The Culture of the State Mental Hospital.* Detroit: Wayne State University Press, 1960. A sociological study of a large midwestern public mental hospital. Contains much case and interview material.

Chapter

22

The Group Approach to
Social Reintegration

Throughout the previous chapters the importance of the group in the development of deviant behavior has been emphasized. The group has been related to the acquisition of deviant norms and to difficulties in interpersonal relations, self-concept, and role conflicts. It has been seen that the deviant is a member of various types of social groups; that he plays a certain role in each of these groups; and that role conflicts may arise if participation in these groups exposes the deviant to competing demands and obligations. In addition, the deviant develops certain desires and attitudes through his group experiences which may conflict with the demands of the larger group, or "society." This recognition of the importance of group relationships is not confined to sociologists:

> The group factor in our civilization is receiving increasing attention. During the past decade there has been much interest in, and more understanding than previously of, the impact of the group on the individual, on the community, and on problem solving. The group in its various attributes—educational, therapeutic, recreational, and actional—is the object of study not only by social group workers but by educators, psychologists, and psychiatrists. Anthropologists and sociologists who have long been interested in the group as an institution are gaining new insights into the power of the group factor in present-day culture.[1]

The importance of group relationships was revealed, for example, in studies of neuroses among members of the armed services during World War II. It was learned that integrating or nonintegrating forces in the immediate social environment of the soldier were far more important than either his personality make-up, his family structure, or his previous history of personal maladjustment. The presence or absence of group supportive

---

[1] Dorothea F. Sullivan ed., *Readings in Group Work* (New York: Association Press, 1952), p. v. Also see Louis Wirth, "Clinical Sociology," *American Journal of Sociology*, 37:60 (July, 1931); Stuart A. Queen, "Social Participation in Relation to Social Disorganization," *American Sociological Review*, 14:252 (April, 1949), and his "The Concepts of Social Disorganization and Social Participation," *American Sociological Review*, 6:307–316 (June, 1941).

elements in the army, particularly identification with a group under conditions of stress, was found to be one of the most important keys to the development of mental disorder even among those who were supposed to have few tendencies in that direction.[2]

One commission of civilian psychiatrists who studied combat neuroses during World War II found that when "an individual member of such a combat group has his emotional bonds of group integration seriously disrupted, then he, *as a person,* is thereby disorganized. The disruption of the group unity is, in the main, a primary causal factor, not a secondary effect of personal disorganization."[3] William Menninger stated: "We seemed to learn anew the importance of the group ties in the maintenance of mental health. We were impressed by the fact that an individual who had a strong conviction about his job, even though his was a definitely unstable personality, might make remarkable achievement against the greatest of stress."[4] Such information, although limited, has suggested that neurotic symptoms may occur among ordinarily stable persons if the group situation is disturbed and that it might be well to analyze similar situations in civilian life which cause mental breakdowns.[5]

Primarily during the past twenty years numerous developments have recognized the importance of the group and have applied group methods in the prevention and treatment of social deviation. Still other work has combined theory and application in the study of group dynamics in problem areas.[6] Although some group psychotherapy existed as early as 1906, much of the recent increase in this work resulted from its use during World War II, when the number of civilian and military neurotic and psychiatric casualties, as well as the need to rehabilitate military offenders, made it impossible to treat cases on an individual basis.

The group approach differs sharply from the relationship of a pro-

---

[2] See Arnold M. Rose, "Factors in Mental Breakdown in Combat," in Arnold M. Rose (ed.), *Mental Health and Mental Disorder* (New York: W. W. Norton & Company, Inc., 1955), pp. 291–313. It was found that the rate of neuropsychiatric casualty in army units during World War II was higher in units with low morale, and lower in units with high morale.

[3] L. H. Bartemeir *et al.,* "Combat Exhaustion," *Journal of Nervous and Mental Diseases,* 104:370 (October, 1946). In order to minimize mental breakdowns among members of the armed forces in Korea an army psychiatrist in 1952 suggested that squads rather than individuals be rotated. The loss of a squad leader or disruption of friendships contributed to the breakdown of members left behind.

[4] William C. Menninger, "Psychiatric Experience in the War, 1941–1946," *American Journal of Psychiatry,* 103:581 (March, 1947). Also see his *Psychiatry in a Troubled World* (New York: The Macmillan Company, 1948), Chaps. 5–6.

[5] See S. Kirson Weinberg, "The Combat Neuroses," *American Journal of Sociology,* 54:465–478 (March, 1946).

[6] See Kurt Lewin, *Resolving Social Conflicts* (New York: Harper & Row, Publishers, 1948). See also Dorwin Cartwright, "Achieving Change in People: Some Applications of Group Dynamics Theory," *Human Relations,* 4:381–392 (1951) and J. Douglas and Marguerite Grant, "A Group Dynamics Approach to the Treatment of Nonconformists in the Navy," *The Annals,* 322:126–135 (March, 1959).

fessional person with an individual patient: the psychiatrist, for example, the clinical psychologist, and the social worker and their clients, where the emphasis is on a person-to-person relationship rather than on a group-person therapy. Moreover, not all forms of "group work" can be described as applying a *group* orientation to the treatment of social deviation. Many forms of so-called "group work" are actually *individually* oriented and are based upon the assumption that deviation is a consequence of a personality trait which is unique to an individual and not a kind of behavior developed in group relationships. Since this is assumed, the individual approach attempts to correct psychological malfunctions, believing that they, and not self-other relationships, are the causes of deviation.[7]

It is not the objective of the group approach merely to assist or supplement other forms of treatment, however. In essence, in the group approach, it is the *group* which is the instrument of change. The group approach views the *individual* as part of a broad stream of human relationships and within a complex network of roles and statuses. In a sense, any deliberate action which alters the relation of the individual to others in this network in an effort to change his behavior is an example of the group approach.[8]

There is evidence of growing recognition that the group approach is not distinguished by the number of persons involved, but by its particular perspective and theory.[9] There are today several variations of the group approach to social reintegration, all of which conform to our definition above. One type consists of group therapy, or group discussion sessions, which are usually employed with from four to twenty deviants, such as a group of prison inmates, in an effort to change attitudes and other behavior. This method has been employed both with deviants in institutions and in communities. In some cases role-playing techniques, such as psychodrama and sociodrama, have been used. Another type consists of activity or interest groups which have been employed primarily with delinquents and older persons. In some instances, groups in their "natural settings," such as delinquent street groups, have been the focus of reintegrative efforts.[10] Still other forms of the group approach include community reorganization,

---

[7] See Donald R. Cressey, "The Nature and Effectiveness of Correctional Techniques," in *Law and Contemporary Problems* (Durham, N.C.: Duke University Press, 1958), pp. 754–771.

[8] For further discussion of this approach, see Edwin H. Sutherland and Donald R. Cressey, *Principles of Criminology* (6th ed.; Philadelphia: J. B. Lippincott Company, 1960), pp. 322–327.

[9] This concept of the group approach agrees with our definition of the group in Chapter 1, page 4. See also Dorothy Fahs Beck, "The Dynamics of Group Psychotherapy Seen by a Sociologist, Part I: Basic Processes," *Sociometry*, 21:98–125 (June, 1958).

[10] See M. Stranahan, C. Schwortzman, and F. Athens, "Activity Group Therapy with Emotionally Disturbed Delinquent Adolescents," *International Journal of Group Psychotherapy*, 7:425–436 (1957); Walter B. Miller, "The Impact of a Community Group Work Program on Delinquent Corner Groups," *Social Service Review*, 31:390–406 (December, 1957); Lloyd W. McCorkle and Albert Elias, "Group Therapy in Correctional Institutions," *Federal Probation*, 24:57–63 (June, 1960).

of which the Chicago Area Project is a classic example.[11] The essential features of a "therapeutic community" have been applied to a number of institutions, such as mental hospitals.[12] Reports of these attempts suggest that they hold considerable promise.

Another type of group approach is the assumption by citizen groups of the major responsibility for dealing with a common problem with which the members are personally concerned. They are known by such names as Alcoholics Anonymous, Narcotics Anonymous, Recovery Incorporated, and Golden Age Clubs. Such groups have been formed to aid in the rehabilitation of the alcoholic, the drug addict, former mental patients, and delinquents, and to overcome the loneliness of old age. In each instance the group helps to integrate the individual, to change his conception of himself, to make him feel again the solidarity of the group behind the individual, and to combat social stigma.[13] These group processes, it is felt, replace the "I" feelings with "we" feelings, give the individual a feeling of being a member of a group, and redefine certain norms of behavior.

Group Approaches to Alcoholism

ALCOHOLICS ANONYMOUS

Alcoholics Anonymous is probably the most widely known and presumably the most successful of all informal group approaches to social reintegration. There are more than 7000 chapters—groups of alcoholics or "arrested" alcoholics—in the United States, in addition to chapters in many other countries. The total membership in the United States consists of about 300,000 persons; in the approximately 700 foreign groups there were 15,000 members. "In 1957 there were 257 hospital groups with 6000 members and 296 groups with 15,000 members holding meetings in jails, reformatories, prisons, and workhouses. Approximately 1000 seamen and 'lone' members in remote areas maintain a contact with each other by mail." [14]

Alcoholics Anonymous was founded in Cleveland less than thirty years ago by two alcoholics who felt that their mutual fellowship helped both of them with their drinking problems.[15] It is not an association or society in

[11] See Solomon Kobrin, "The Chicago Area Project—A 25-Year Assessment," *The Annals*, 322:19-29 (March, 1959).

[12] C. E. M. Harris, L. B. Brown, J. E. Cawte, "Problems of Developing a Group-Centered Mental Hospital," *International Journal of Group Psychotherapy*, 10:408-418 (October, 1960); and F. Knobloch "On the Theory of a Therapeutic Community for Neurotics," *International Journal of Group Psychotherapy*, 10:419-429 (October, 1960).

[13] Marshall B. Clinard, "The Group Approach to Social Reintegration," *American Sociological Review*, 14:257-262 (April, 1949).

[14] Harrison M. Trice, "Alcoholics Anonymous," *The Annals*, 315:111 (January, 1958).

[15] For a history of this organization see *Alcoholics Anonymous Comes of Age: A Brief History of A.A.* (New York: Alcoholics Anonymous Publishing, 1957).

the accepted sense of the word, for it does not have a formal organization with officers or dues. However, it maintains a central office in New York and publishes a journal called *A.A. Grapevine*.

It is difficult to ascertain definitely the degree of success of Alcoholics Anonymous, but there is considerable evidence that there has generally been a high rate of recovery among the members.[16] One writer, for example, has stated that A.A. claims it has a recovery rate of 75 percent for those who really try their methods.[17] Such statements are impossible to verify, for A.A. has no complete set of records, many A.A. members have a number of "slips" during the program, and many persons associate themselves with A.A. who are totally unsuited for it. There are also indications that those who associate themselves continuously with the A.A. program view their problem somewhat differently from those who have been exposed to A.A. but did not join it. In a study of 111 A.A. members compared with 141 non-members, a significant difference was found in that A.A. members tended to regard themselves, even before they ever attended a meeting, as persons who often shared their troubles with others. They tended less frequently to have known persons whom they "believed" stopped drinking through will power. They had lost longtime drinking companions, and they had had exposure to favorable communications about A.A.[18]

Alcoholics Anonymous is run by members only. No psychiatrists or other professional persons are directly associated with it. A potential new member must seek the help of the organization by admitting that he cannot deal with his drinking unaided. If he has been drinking unusually heavily for some time attempts are made to get medical help for him and to tide him over the aftereffects of his excesses.

The emphasis is on mutual help. When norms and values conflict there is a tendency to achieve some unanimity as to the goals and purpose of life and the relationship of alcoholism to them. The routine nature of life is diminished by participation in an outside activity in which the human element is stressed. Finally, and most important of all, the individual has a place to go and a group with whose members he can talk, where he can give and receive support.

The A.A. program breaks down the alcoholic's social isolation that

---

[16] Oscar W. Ritchie, "A Socio-historical Survey of Alcoholics Anonymous," *Quarterly Journal of Studies on Alcohol,* 9:149 (June, 1948); and J. Alexander, "Drunkard's Best Friend," *Saturday Evening Post,* 222:17–18, 74–79 (April 1, 1950).

[17] H. M. Tiebout, "Therapeutic Mechanisms of Alcoholics Anonymous," *American Journal of Psychiatry,* 100:468–473 (May, 1944). For a discussion of the use of A.A. techniques in correctional work, see Joseph A. Cook and Gilbert Geis, "Forum Anonymous: The Techniques of Alcoholics Anonymous Applied to Prison Therapy," *Journal of Social Therapy,* 3:9–13 (First Quarter, 1957). See also H. M. Tiebout, "Alcoholics Anonymous—An Experiment of Nature," *Quarterly Journal of Studies on Alcohol,* 22:52–68 (March, 1961).

[18] Harrison M. Trice, "The Affiliation Motive and Readiness to Join Alcoholics Anonymous," *Quarterly Journal of Studies on Alcohol,* 20:313–321 (June, 1959).

has resulted from the stigma of his excessive drinking, by drawing him into a group in which he is accepted on face value as a past drunkard. This group is an intimate, primary one in which members can more easily re-orient themselves. An alcoholic feels at home with other alcoholics who, like himself, have known degradation and the stigma of being an alcoholic.[19] The life stories told at meetings are helpful to the members, as well as is the reading of their basic book, *Alcoholics Anonymous*, which contains many stories of ex-alcoholics. The organization even has a common argot, including, for example, words like "slip" to describe a person who has returned to drinking, "twelfth-stepping" for working with other alcoholics, and "dime therapy" for a member who uses the telephone to help someone in the group avoid a "slip." [20]

Each new A.A. member is assigned to a sponsor, perhaps an old friend or drinking companion, although more often a complete stranger, who refers to him as his "baby." This sponsor is someone who has been successfully coping with an alcohol problem, and is ready at all times to help his charge. He often asks the man's wife or his employer to give their support and understanding to the new A.A. member, and he may even visit persons to whom the alcoholic may have given worthless checks or from whom he may have borrowed money, asking them to give the alcoholic an opportunity to get back on his feet.[21]

As soon as possible the sponsor will take his "baby" to A.A. meetings several nights a week. These meetings are of two types, the open meetings which family, friends, and other outsiders may attend, and the closed ones attended only by alcoholics. At open meetings a number of alcoholics may speak of their experiences and of their rehabilitation; in closed meetings experiences and problems are told in a more intimate situation. In these meetings the alcoholic takes up separately the so-called twelve steps which are discussed and interpreted by other alcoholics. These twelve steps are briefly outlined as follows:

Step One: We admitted we were powerless over alcohol—that our lives had become unmanageable.
Step Two: Came to believe that a Power greater than ourselves could restore us to sanity.
Step Three: Made a decision to turn our will and our lives over to the care of God "as we understood Him."
Step Four: Made a searching and fearless moral inventory of ourselves.

---

[19] John F. Lofland and Robert A. LeJeune, "Initial Interaction of Newcomers in Alcoholics Anonymous: A Field Experiment in Class Symbols and Socialization," *Social Problems,* 8:102–111 (Fall, 1960).

[20] Simon Dinitz, "The Therapeutic Effects of Alcoholics Anonymous." Unpublished master's thesis, University of Wisconsin, Madison, 1948.

[21] See H. S. Ripley and J. K. Jackson, "Therapeutic Factors in AA," *American Journal of Psychiatry,* 116:44–50 (1959), for a discussion of the roles of "sponsor" and "baby" and their importance. Sometimes the word "pigeon" is used in place of "baby."

Step Five: Admitted to God, to ourselves and to another human being the exact nature of our wrongs.

Step Six: Were entirely ready to have God remove all these defects of character.

Step Seven: Humbly asked Him to remove our shortcomings.

Step Eight: Made a list of all persons we had harmed, and became willing to make amends to them all.

Step Nine: Made direct amends to such people wherever possible, except when to do so would injure them or others.

Step Ten: Continued to take personal inventory and when we were wrong promptly admitted it.

Step Eleven: Sought through prayer and meditation to improve our conscious contact with God "as we understood Him," praying only for knowledge of His will for us and the power to carry that out.

Step Twelve: Having had a spiritual awakening as the result of these steps we tried to carry this message to alcoholics, and to practice these principles in all our affairs.[22]

These twelve steps, which are greatly emphasized in the program, can be roughly summarized in four principles: (1) reliance on a power greater than themselves, (2) making an inventory of their problems, (3) making amends to others, and (4) carrying the message to others. The "power greater than themselves" is not specifically related to a particular religion, for A.A. accepts men of all faiths and does not tolerate discussion of religious doctrines. However, such a belief tends to reduce the isolation of the alcoholic, which has involved building all sorts of glass houses filled with rationalizations.[23] This "something" helps the individual to identify with the group, in fact, so great is the identification that "the so-called religious emphasis in A.A. may be explained in terms of Durkheim's thesis that religion represents essentially the group and the feeling of getting outside of one's self by identification with others."[24] The concept of a greater power constitutes a symbol of future resources and hope for the individual.

The moral inventory of the twelve steps represents a sort of self-analysis and is closely related to the procedure of making amends to others for things done while drinking. The inventory helps alcoholics discover some of the sources of their problems: making amends is a way to resolve problems because it helps to bring about their reacceptance into society. Relating their life stories at meetings enables the alcoholics to review their past experiences in the presence of the group. In this way they are able to assert their new role as nondrinkers.[25]

---

[22] *Alcoholics Anonymous* (13th ptg.; New York: Works Publishing Company, 1950), pp. 71–72.
[23] Tiebout, "Therapeutic Mechanisms of Alcoholics Anonymous," *loc. cit.*
[24] Clinard, "The Group Approach to Social Reintegration," *loc. cit.*, p. 262.
[25] For an excellent discussion of the group processes in A.A., see Sutherland and Cressey, *op. cit.*, p. 496.

In addition to these meetings, the alcoholic spends a great deal of time with other A.A. members, in the evenings or during lunch hours, in the late afternoon, and during week ends. Special programs are arranged for long week ends and holidays when the temptation to drink may be extreme. Coffee and "cokes" are served in the clubhouse, where card games and other recreational activities are common. There are also picnics for the families and sometimes auxiliary group meetings for the wives.

Carrying the message of A.A. to others is particularly important. In fact, Bales considers it the most important therapeutic aspect of the program. The relation of sponsor and "baby" and that of one member to another tends to create a series of reciprocal obligations toward others which result in greater solidarity or identification with the group. Alcoholics Anonymous involves a network of personal relationships and in this network each person is a focal point of interpersonal relations. This network of obligation is strengthened by the "carrying of the message." Bales has described it in this way:

> Further, his relationship to those whom he has brought into the group is strengthened by the expectation of each of his converts that he, who persuaded them that the program would work, will remain abstinent. He is, in fact, under obligation to each of these converts because of their dependence upon him. If he fails in his example to them, they may fail also. His failure cannot be a matter of purely personal concern, but involves the repudiation of accepted obligations. The success of each is to a peculiarly high degree contingent upon the success of the others in the group.[26]

The A.A. program allows the sponsor to see himself as he was before, in the image of the recently drunken "baby," or "pigeon," as the new members are sometimes called. Each is an image to the other, and the "baby" can call on his more successful sponsor for help on a twenty-four-hour basis. The "baby" is not only integrated into the group, "but he is integrated in a sympathetic but nevertheless strongly 'anti-alcohol' group in which status is clearly assigned according to the amount of anti-alcohol behavior which is exhibited." [27] In this way the attitudes and motives of the alcoholic about the use of alcohol are replaced with new attitudes and motives, for "A.A. redefines self and role as that of an ex-alcoholic who cannot stand liquor." [28] By associating with other teetotalers the member is not under pressure to drink alcohol. The frequent stories told in A.A. meetings of the alcoholic binges of others remind the alcoholic of his former self and role. The

---

[26] Robert F. Bales, "Types of Social Structure as Factors in 'Cures' of Alcohol Addiction," *Applied Anthropology*, 1:8 (April–June, 1942) and his "Therapeutic Role of A.A. as Seen by a Sociologist," *Quarterly Journal of Studies on Alcohol*, 5:267–274 (September, 1944).

[27] Sutherland and Cressey, *op. cit.*, p. 496.

[28] Edwin M. Lemert, *Social Pathology* (New York: McGraw-Hill Book Company, Inc., 1951), p. 367. Alcoholics Anonymous does not take any stand on the general consumption of alcohol by others, but it does as far as alcoholics are concerned.

A.A. Grapevine, their national official publication, contains chiefly stories and cartoons relating to the problem of alcoholics, and they serve as constant reminders of success and the dangers of failure. Mottoes supply additional social pressures to conform and include the "24-Hour Plan" of keeping sober only for the day, and such clubhouse slogans as "But for the Grace of God," and "This Clubhouse Keeps Us on the Beam."

The group therapy of A.A. appears to help overcome the forces which produced and reinforced the continuance of alcoholic drinking. As has been indicated, the alcoholic, through his drinking experiences, has built a conception of himself as a compulsive, uncontrolled drunkard. He has lost his self-respect, his friends have avoided him, and he himself has avoided groups except possible drinking groups. He wants acceptance, but conventional groups will not accept him. The A.A. member, through others' acceptance of him as he is, is offered an opportunity to learn new skills in interpersonal relationships. In addition, he acquires new goals: to keep sober and to reform other alcoholics. Thus, "the member sees in his prospective convert himself as he once was, and by teaching the other, becomes his own therapist." [29]

To turn again to the problem of why some persons become affiliated with A.A. and others do not, Trice found initial experiences at the first meetings to be important.[30] The chances were greater if the problem drinker had a clear understanding of what the meetings would be like, if he had a sponsor and group ties to keep in touch with him, if he had firm convictions about his drinking, and if he was not unduly sensitive to the social class differences found in A.A.[31] The effectiveness of these factors is increased if after a few weeks he finds that he can adjust to small informal and spontaneous groups, if his wife or his girl friend goes along with the program, and if he is aware of the symptoms of alcoholism.

RESIDENTIAL TREATMENT CENTERS

Hospitals have long been used for alcoholics. However, they are not of primary interest here, for their approach has often been typically individualistic and physiological. The type of center which is of interest here is generally called a "halfway house." The first were established several years ago in New York City, Long Island, and Boston. At present there are twenty such programs in different sections of the United States.[32] Halfway houses were begun in an attempt to rehabilitate the allegedly hopeless Skid Row type of alcoholic. These houses were established on the premise

[29] Cook and Geis, "Forum Anonymous," *loc. cit.*

[30] Trice, "The Affiliation Motive and Readiness to Join Alcoholics Anonymous," *loc. cit.*

[31] One study reports that initial activity is greatest where the A.A. group is relatively high and the newcomers are relatively low in social class.—Lofland and LeJeune, "Initial Interaction of Newcomers in Alcoholics Annoymous," *loc. cit.*

[32] E. Rubington, "The Chronic Drunkenness Offender," *The Annals,* 315:65–72 (1958).

that the deviant subculture of the Skid Row alcoholic and its meanings to him must be considered if rehabilitation were to succeed. The halfway house was thus seen as a social milieu offering social support halfway between the deviant subculture and conventional society.

After entering a halfway house the alcoholic is expected to get a job, pay for his room and board, assist with maintenance tasks, and to stay sober. The staff, which frequently consists of recovered alcoholics, conducts counseling sessions with new residents. Perhaps the most powerful rehabilitative force is the group pressure from both staff and group members. In the halfway house group pressures operate to produce sobriety, whereas on Skid Row they operate to produce inebriety. The halfway house is a good example of the modification of the alcoholic's system of social relationships in an effort to change his behavior.[33] Preliminary reports of the reintegrative success of the halfway house program suggest that it provides an essential transitional period that allows the alcoholic to prepare to abandon his old ways of life for new ones. Yet complete success seems to depend upon the opportunities he has of being reaccepted into conventional society.

GROUP PSYCHOTHERAPY

Other group methods, such as group psychotherapy, have been employed with alcoholics. They have involved group discussions of a small number of alcoholics, usually led by a professional person.[34] Group therapy has also been used with the wives of alcoholics.[35] Some persons have suggested that "therapeutic communities" or changes in hospital orientation, such as have been developed for mental patients, be organized in institutions for alcoholics.[36] (See pages 660–661.)

Group Methods with Drug Addicts

NARCOTICS ANONYMOUS

Narcotics Anonymous was established in 1948 by Danny Carlson, a former drug addict. Similar to Alcoholics Anonymous in both its activities and its structure, it uses an informal organization in combating drug addiction.

---

[33] *Ibid.*

[34] E. M. Scott, "A Special Type of Group Psychotherapy and Its Applications to Alcoholics," *Quarterly Journal of Studies on Alcohol,* 17:288–290 (1956).

[35] D. E. MacDonald, "Group Psychotherapy with Wives of Alcoholics," *Quarterly Journal of Studies on Alcohol,* 19:125–132 (1958); and W. W. Igersheimer, "Group Psychotherapy for Non-Alcoholic Wives of Alcoholics," *Quarterly Journal of Studies on Alcohol,* 20:77–85 (March, 1959).

[36] See Lorant Forizs, "Therapeutic Community and Teamwork," *Research Conference on Problems of Alcohol* (New Haven, Conn.: Laboratory of Applied Biodynamics, Yale University, 1958), pp. 591–595; and Florence Powdermaker and Jerome D. Frank, *Group Psychotherapy* (Cambridge, Mass.: Harvard University Press, 1953), pp. 62, 67–69.

Carlson was fully aware of the difficulties faced by former addicts in keeping off drugs, and he founded Narcotics Anonymous in the belief that addicts would be more likely to stay off them if they could join some sort of group comprised of ex-addicts who could understand and help each other in dealing with their difficulties.[37] The strength gained from the mutual support of those interested in keeping away from drugs was felt to be the best answer to the problem of addiction.[38] During the first year there were eighty members in this group. Although handicapped by financial problems, due to minimal outside support, it has grown in size. At present branches exist in most large cities in the United States and Canada.[39]

Members of Narcotics Anonymous hold meetings twice a week. New members are recruited by getting in touch with addicts while they are hospitalized for withdrawal of the drugs, or while they are still in prisons or reformatories. As in Alcoholics Anonymous, new members are assigned to an older member upon joining the group, and the new member can call upon his "partner" when he is having a difficult time.[40]

The process in Narcotics Anonymous is similar to that of A.A., in that norms and attitudes favoring the use of drugs are replaced by norms and attitudes opposed to their use. This is evidenced by the fact that members who are actively on drugs are not retained in the group. They are given the assurance, however, that once they are off the drugs, they will be accepted. In this way group processes operate to change behavior from that of an addict to that of an ex-addict. In addition, N.A. members adhere to a set of prescribed steps similar in content to those of A.A. The first step, for example, requires that members admit that they are addicts and reads as follows: "We admit that we were powerless over drugs—that our lives had become unmanageable." [41] The N.A. steps, like those of A.A., seem to provide members with a kind of formal "guide" which assists them in making the difficult transition from addiction to postaddiction.

In general, Narcotics Anonymous has not been as successful as A.A. in terms of effecting permanent change. However, this group is still not highly developed, and accurate judgment of its potential value must await systematic investigation. Some believe that the comparative ineffectiveness of N.A. is due to the absence of public and community support. Others suggest that the public attitude toward addiction in the United States is responsible for the tremendous handicaps an addict faces in being reac-

---

[37] Marie Nyswander, *The Drug Addict as a Patient* (New York: Grune & Stratton, Inc., 1956), p. 144.

[38] See Jerome Ellison, "These Drug Addicts Cure One Another," *Saturday Evening Post,* 227:22–23, 48–52 (August 7, 1954).

[39] Nyswander, *op. cit.*

[40] *Ibid.* Also see John M. Murtagh and Sara Harris, *Who Live in Shadow* (New York: McGraw-Hill Book Company, Inc., 1959), pp. 178–179.

[41] Murtagh and Harris, *op. cit.,* p. 178.

cepted by society.[42] There is no doubt that the public attitude toward drug addiction is much more negative than it is toward alcoholism.

OTHER GROUP METHODS

Doubt has been expressed by some persons as to whether the kind of group therapy afforded by N.A. would have a permanent or even a marked effect on drug addicts.[43] Such skepticism is probably due, however, to the prevailing view among many authorities that the drug subculture and the "personality traits and psychological needs" of the drug addict make change by informal methods difficult. Yet the findings of one study definitely show that group-oriented methods were effective in reforming drug addicts.[44] In this study the prodrug subculture of the treatment ward was significantly changed to an antidrug subculture by reorganizing the status system and by reassigning prestige to those showing signs of abandoning drug use. As a result, addicts on this ward reformed, in contrast to other treatment wards where reorganization was not attempted.

This method has thus far been employed on a small scale; yet it is possible that its use will increase. Some persons, in fact, believe that drug addicts present special problems which may be resolved by changes in hospital orientation rather than by changes in individual addicts. One therapist reports a situation where the creation of a "therapeutic community" in a hospital for drug addicts resulted in a noticeable change in patients' attitudes.[45]

Group psychotherapy has been employed to some extent with addicts.[46] Generally, however, such attempts have used an individual approach, so that the effect of the group, if any, has been incidental. Until specifically *group*-oriented psychotherapy is attempted on a wider scale, a definitive evaluation of its effectiveness will not be possible.

Group Methods in Reintegrating the Mentally Disordered

Until recently the only major form of group treatment of mental patients was group psychotherapy. Within recent years there has been a fertile expansion of group approaches to reintegrating psychotic and neurotic deviants.

---

[42] See Nyswander, *op. cit.*, pp. 145–146 and Murtagh and Harris, *op. cit.*, pp. 179–181.

[43] Walter C. Reckless, *The Crime Problem* (2d ed.: New York: Appleton-Century-Crofts, Inc., 1955), p. 376.

[44] James J. Thorpe and Bernard Smith, "Phases in Group Development in the Treatment of Drug Addicts," *International Journal of Group Psychotherapy*, 3:66–78 (January, 1953).

[45] See Arnold H. Zucker, "Group Psychotherapy and the Nature of Drug Addiction," *International Journal of Group Psychotherapy*, 11:209–218 (April, 1961).

[46] Nyswander, *op. cit.*, pp. 143–144.

RECOVERY, INCORPORATED, AND OTHER
INFORMAL ORGANIZATIONS

In existence at the present time are a number of informal groups which function to assist former patients in becoming socially reintegrated. One of these organizations, called Recovery, Incorporated, was founded in 1937 by thirty recovered mental patients of the Psychiatric Institute of the University of Illinois Medical School to help mental patients adjust to society in a satisfactory manner after their release from the hospital.[47] This organization emphasizes self-help, and the members mutually support each other in the problems of their daily lives. Most of the social activities of the ex-patients are of an informal nature. Families of the recovered patients often become closely identified with each other, and there are group visits, picnics, and other activities.

Formal group meetings are usually scheduled three times a week. On Monday, discussion sessions are held at the headquarters; on Wednesday, subgroups have neighborhood meetings in private homes; Saturdays are set aside for open meetings which patients, relatives, and friends attend. These meetings help the families to become familiar with the symptoms and behavior of mental illness, and learn how they can help the ex-patients. Since no formal meetings are held during four days of the week the new member is then alone without group support. If he should suffer a setback, however, he is instructed to call a veteran Recovery member, who will come to help him at any hour. If the illness becomes worse a neighborhood panel leader is summoned, and if he cannot help, psychiatric help may be suggested. In order that they will not be overly concerned, former patients are instructed not to indulge in self-diagnosis of their symptoms.

Clubs whose membership is composed of former mental hospital patients, sometimes known as "social therapeutic clubs," have been established in many sections of the United States in recent years, and are growing in number and variety.[48] Such organizations provide patients with an opportunity to gain confidence in social situations through participating in group activities with others who have similar problems. In this way groups such as these function as "steppingstones" to permanent community reintegration. This type of organization is much more common in England, where these groups have been in operation for many years.[49]

---

[47] A. A. Low, "Recovery, Incorporated: A Project for Rehabilitating Postpsychotic and Long-Term Psychoneurotic Patients," in W. H. Soden ed., *Rehabilitation of the Handicapped* (New York: The Ronald Press Company, 1949), pp. 213–226.

[48] Milton Greenblatt, "The Rehabilitation Spectrum," in M. Greenblatt and Benjamin Simon eds., *Rehabilitation of the Mentally Ill* (Washington, D.C.: American Association for the Advancement of Science, 1959), p. 19. See also pp. 229, 243.

[49] See J. Bierer ed., *Therapeutic Social Clubs* (London: H. K. Lewis, 1948).

GROUP THERAPY

Group therapy became generally recognized as an acceptable method of treatment during World War II, and since then the number of persons who have experimented with various forms of group therapy has increased. The success of the armed forces with group treatment of neuropsychiatric patients, the greater awareness of the overcrowding in mental hospitals, the shortage of psychiatrists, and the high cost of individual therapy resulted in the adoption of group therapy as a part of the general treatment program. In addition, many feel that group therapy methods are more effective with many mental patients than individual therapy.

There are several different types of group therapy. In some cases lectures dealing with difficulties of adjustment are given to the patients, and are often followed by discussions. In the usual method of group therapy, however, a psychiatrist and from four to twenty patients hold frequent discussions as a group in which all participate and in which there is group sharing of experiences. Sometimes additional tools are employed, for example, the psychodrama in which conflict situations are acted out by a group on a stage.[50]

In some instances, hospitals have found it advantageous to provide special group therapy sessions for close relatives of their patients.[51] These group sessions are held for about an hour or two once or twice a week, and are limited to approximately ten people. Such relatives often have a feeling of isolation, disgrace, hopelessness, and even guilt, and the purpose of group therapy is to discuss such feelings and to provide a more positive approach to the problem. Some therapists take a passive role, encouraging the relatives to talk about their feelings and at the same time allowing relatives of the other patients to discover the resemblances to their own feelings. As a group, the relatives of mental patients often try to help one another and sometimes develop strong feelings of group identification. Other therapists, however, take a more active role, explaining the principles of psychiatry to relatives and talking about the care given to the patients.

Psychodrama is somewhat similar to discussion therapy, but it is carried out in a different setting. It had its origin in Vienna in 1922, when Moreno founded the psychodramatic theater to treat various mental disorders. As a result of his establishment of a psychodramatic institute later at Beacon, New York, this technique has been increasingly used in mental

---

[50] Powdermaker and Frank, *op. cit.*, pp. 4, 5.

[51] W. D. Ross, "Group Psychotherapy with Psychotic Patients and Their Relatives," *American Journal of Psychiatry*, 105:383–386 (November, 1948). Also see H. P. Peck, R. D. Rabinovitch, and J. B. Cramer, "A Treatment Program for Parents of Schizophrenic Children," *American Journal of Orthopsychiatry*, 19:592–598 (October, 1959); and Erika Chance, *Families in Treatment* (New York: Basic Books, Inc., 1959).

hospitals.[52] The essence of psychodrama and sociodrama [53] is the acting out of behaviors in imaginary situations which have previously proved difficult for patients. In this sense both psychodrama and sociodrama are role-playing techniques, which offer an opportunity to acquire the social skills necessary to cope with certain situations. These techniques have been used in mental hospitals by both staff and patients, as means of fostering communication and understanding. They have also been used to assist patients in acquiring social skills, both in relation to the hospital group and in relation to anticipated real-life situations with friends, family, and employers.[54] The usual procedure employed in psychodrama is to have patients and staff—usually but not always a small group—meet together and choose a problem situation to enact, members of the group assuming the necessary roles. The group may be seated in a semicircle, with or without a stage, and usually there is a "leader" appointed to take charge of the meeting. The problem situation may be drawn from some past or anticipated hospital occurrences: the recovering mental patient may be urged to re-enact some of the episodes leading to hospitalization. By re-enacting these experiences the patient is able to anticipate new behaviors which will enable him to cope more effectively with the recurrence of such experiences. A patient may have walked away from his work assignment, for example, and this incident may be enacted. Or a new staff member may have arrived on the ward, and the feelings of patients toward his reception might be dramatized.

In psychodrama various imaginary scenes with family, friends, and employers may also be enacted, so that the patient may be able later to cope with difficult situations outside the hospital. After the initial enactment of the problem the roles may be reversed, with the patients assuming the roles of staff members and staff members the roles of the patients. The audience in attendance acts as a sort of "jury" or "discussion panel," for after the enactment, criticism and comments are invited. These comments may suggest how the problem might have been more adequately dealt with, and how the skills of the role players could have been improved. Frequently, these criticisms are difficult for both staff and patients, yet they seem to be helpful in enabling staff members to overcome professional blind spots and in assisting patients to grapple with situations which previously they have met with psychotic or neurotic deviation.[55]

---

[52] Jacob L. Moreno ed., *Group Psychotherapy* (New York: Beacon House, Inc., 1945).

[53] There is no clear distinction between these concepts in the literature.

[54] M. Greenblatt, Richard H. York, Esther L. Brown, *From Custodial to Therapeutic Patient Care in Mental Hospitals* (New York: Russell Sage Foundation, 1955), pp. 180–183.

[55] See Greenblatt, York, and Brown, *op. cit.*, pp. 180–190, and Knobloch, "On the Theory of a Therapeutic Community for Neurotics," *loc. cit.* Also see Robert H. Hyde and Richard H. Williams, "What Is Therapy and Who Does It?" in M. Greenblatt, D. Levinson, and Richard H. Williams, *The Patient and the Mental Hospital* (New York: The Free Press of Glencoe, 1957), pp. 173–196.

Evaluations of group methods have challenged the traditional psychoanalytic view of the treatment of mental disorders. It has been suggested that the role of the therapist does not call for special medical or psychiatric training, that the therapist's role may be assumed by nurses, aides, and attendants.[56] Indeed, it has been suggested by some that the social distance between psychiatrists and patients creates a barrier to therapy of a nonorganic sort. In addition, it has been pointed out by others that group therapy can, and does, result in changes in attitudes, motives, and self-concepts. A sociologist has described group psychotherapy as the "deliberate creation of an artificial subculture and the manipulation of a special social system" to effect changes in behavior patterns.[57] The key to effectiveness of group therapy is seen sociologically to result from experience in playing new roles, and learning to deal with situations previously met with inappropriate role behavior.[58]

Although few really carefully controlled experiments have as yet been made of the results of group therapy in mental disorders, there is almost unanimous opinion among those who have been engaged in this work that group therapy is effective. Little fundamental research has been done on what takes place in such group sessions, but it seems possible that the encouraging results are explained not by the theoretical scheme of the group analysts but by the process of informal group adjustment. In group therapy with mental patients, "should an individual member express misgivings about his prospects of improvement, or about the need for resolving his problems, or about the worth of the group itself, he will be resisted by other members, for any group that strives to survive evolves a set of objectives. . . . In effective group psychotherapy the identity of the collectivity and its survival center around the improvement of its members." [59]

In group psychotherapy mentally disturbed patients appear to develop an identification with one another and a degree of group integration; sometimes the opinion of the group appears to change the personality pattern and attitudes of one of its members; and each member secures an opportunity to play new roles and to acquire a new conception of himself. In the light of the problems of others it is possible for the patient to see his own difficulties and to relieve his feelings of social isolation. As one psychiatrist states the problem, "It is the group itself that becomes the therapeutic agent as a result of the interaction between the individuals who form

[56] Hyde and Williams, "What Is Therapy and Who Does It?" *loc. cit.*
[57] Beck, "The Dynamics of Group Psychotherapy . . . ," *loc. cit.*
[58] *Ibid.,* Also see George Psathas, "Phase Movement and Equilibrium Tendencies in Interaction Process in Psychotherapy Groups," *Sociometry,* 23:177–194 (1960) and "Interaction Process Analysis of Two Psychotherapy Groups," *International Journal of Group Psychotherapy,* 10:430–445 (October, 1960).
[59] S. Kirson Weinberg, *Society and Personality Disorders* (copyright, 1952, by Prentice-Hall, Inc., Englewood Cliffs, N.J.), p. 343. Reprinted by permission of the publisher.

the group." [60] Weinberg has summarized the result of such a treatment program in this way: "He finds that other persons have problems somewhat similar to his own, that all want to be socially accepted and all want to improve. The collective morale and identity that emerge encourage the isolated and timid person to increase his confidence, to become more socially active, and to feel that the therapeutic context is more real than in individual therapy." [61]

OTHER GROUP METHODS

Certain other methods, such as dance and music therapy, have been used to engage otherwise isolated patients in group activities. Often square dancing and other group dances are used. It has been found that even catatonic patients, who were given special rhythmic exercises if they were seriously withdrawn, would stay together and participate in the program if they held hands in a circle, but would scatter immediately if they dropped their hands. Music therapy has involved singing and similar activities involving rhythm. It is felt that songs have personal meanings, are an outlet for self-expression, revive memories, and are therefore useful in the treatment of mental patients. Patients may be given wooden blocks or sticks and encouraged to clap them together in time with a march music in two-four time. The music sessions also include the singing or humming of the national anthem, folk songs, or familiar new songs. Group discussion often goes along with these activities. These methods seem to have had some success. It has been suggested that whatever value these activities have depends on their ability to foster interpersonal relationships, and that there is little intrinsic value in the activities themselves.

THERAPEUTIC COMMUNITIES

In recent years several mental hospitals both here and abroad have attempted reorganizing their social structure in an effort to create what have been called "therapeutic communities" or "group-centered hospitals." The rationale behind these attempts has been that the social environment or the system of social relationships imposed by the hospital structure is so overwhelming that therapy of any kind cannot succeed in reintegrating patients unless this environment is itself "therapeutic." Thus, the general changes attempted have been to "level" the rigid hierarchical status structure by giving patients more responsibility for themselves, giving attendants and other lower-status personnel greater status-giving roles, redefining the

---

[60] Bruno Solby, "Group Psychotherapy and the Psychodramatic Method," in Moreno, *op. cit.*, pp. 50–51.
[61] Weinberg, *op. cit.*, p. 357.

roles of doctors and psychiatrists so as to give them less power in making decisions for patients, creating "patient governments" and establishing hospital-wide discussion meetings, and introducing greater use of psychodrama, for both staff and patients, and group therapy sessions led by nurses, attendants, and other nonmedical personnel. Important corollaries of these changes have been greater interaction between staff and patients and between patients, and greater ease of communication.[62]

In general, creation of a therapeutic community changes the hospital into a more "democratic" organization, where all may participate in what goes on. This contrasts to the highly authoritarian climate of the great majority of mental hospitals, where power of decision is vested in the few at the top of the prestige hierarchy.

In an Australian mental hospital, for example, reorganization took place after community group discussions were introduced.[63] In these discussions patients and staff of all levels were expected to suggest changes to improve hospital functions and relationships. If people were able to defend their suggestions these were tried out experimentally in the hospital. When it became recognized that changes could be initiated by people at all levels, a change in the rigid hierarchical role and status system of the hospital became necessary. Such changes were implemented, to some extent, in later staff policy meetings. Some of these changes consisted of allowing patients of both sexes to mix, beginning group therapy sessions led by attendants and nurses where patients were allowed to answer their own questions, and increasing interaction between patients, and between staff and patients.

FAMILY CARE AND HALFWAY HOUSES

Some procedures have attempted to reintegrate the mental patient under more "normal" group situations. The treatment for the mentally ill in Gheel, Belgium, for example, consists chiefly of incorporating mental patients into a small city. Here they are allowed, in the majority of cases, to live as part of the community rather than under the general scheme of institutionalization.[64] The people of Gheel have cared for the mentally ill since the medieval ages, when a shrine there became the object of frequent visits by mentally ill persons. A government mental hospital was

---

[62] See Greenblatt, Levinson, and Williams, op. cit., Chaps. 4 and 36.

[63] D. Barker, L. B. Brown, J. E. Cawte, J. Riley, "Revising the Patients' Day in a Mental Hospital," Medical Journal of Australia, 45:700–702 (1958); and C. E. M. Harris, H. L. Brown, and J. E. Cawte, "Problems of Developing a Group-Centered Mental Hospital," International Journal of Group Psychotherapy, 10:408–409 (October, 1960). Also see H. Wilmer, Social Psychiatry in Action (Springfield, Ill.: Charles C Thomas, Publisher, 1958).

[64] See John D. J. Moore, "What Gheel Means to Me," Look Magazine, May 23, 1961, pp. 24–39 and Marvin E. Opler ed., Culture and Mental Health (New York: The Macmillan Company, 1959), pp. 4–5. The author visited Gheel in 1955.

established later. Among the 22,000 inhabitants of Gheel there are today over 2000 patients living with foster families. The town is divided into four wards, each with medical and nursing facilities, and the physician calls on the patients generally in the home. The mental hospital in the town is usually only a last resort. The objective of this plan is to absorb patients into both the home and the community. In addition, patients often perform various types of work, such as the care of children or farm work. Families receive a small remuneration for this patient-care from the Belgian government. It is believed that the value of this type of treatment lies in integrating patients into a normal, useful life, and freeing them from the social isolation of hospital wards. In addition, because Gheel residents are accustomed by tradition to caring for them, they are able to accept patients without fear or mistrust. This latter fact is believed to remove the stigmata of mental illness so that patients can be reintegrated.

This method of placing patients in individual homes has been practiced in several other European countries extensively for some years. In Denmark, for example, there are as many patients living outside the hospital at Aarhus as within it. The United States does not have a history of family care programs comparable to those of Europe, and generally, when employed, they have been used only for chronic patients. At present family care programs are in operation in Maryland, Massachusetts, and a few other states.[65] Experience with family care programs in this country indicates that they have great, but unexploited, potential.

Halfway houses for mental patients are similar to those described for alcoholics. The objective of such houses is to provide a transitional living unit for ex-patients who need an opportunity to regain the social and vocational skills necessary for "life on the outside." Such houses as these are more common in Europe than in the United States, and in 1960 there were less than ten such houses.[66] Houses differ in the degree to which they are autonomous: some are run almost wholly by the former patient residents, and others are dependent on hospital or social agencies. In 1956 a hospital in Vermont established a halfway house for 35 women, all chronic schizophrenics who had been hospitalized on an average of four years.[67] A housemother and a case worker were appointed, but the greater portion of responsibility for house maintenance and care was given to the patients themselves. Patients were able to make their own decisions and, as a group, were permitted to deal with the problems that arose. Many patients were

[65] M. Greenblatt and T. Lidz, "Some Dimensions of the Problem," in Greenblatt, Levinson, Williams, op. cit., p. 515. Also see Greenblatt and Simon, op. cit., p. 242.

[66] Greenblatt and Lidz, "Some Dimensions of the Problem," loc. cit., p. 514, and Greenblatt and Simon, op. cit., p. 240.

[67] George W. Brooks, "Opening a Rehabilitation House," in Greenblatt and Simon, op. cit., pp. 127–139, and Donald M. Eldred, "Problems of Opening a Rehabilitation House," Mental Hospitals, 8:20–21 (September, 1957).

assisted in finding employment. In addition, they were encouraged to participate in community social functions, in this way gradually regaining their place in the "outside." At the time of the study, twenty-seven of the thirty-five patients initially in the house were out of the hospital. Of them, eleven were completely free of psychotic symptoms, were employed and socially active, and were thought to be making a superior adjustment. Another ten were making a satisfactory adjustment, were employed, less active socially, but retaining some delusions and other symptoms. Five patients were making marginal adjustments, most of them living with their families. Only one patient was reported to be relapsed, but living in the community.[68]

These various group treatments of mental disorders seem to suggest that mental illness cannot be adequately explained by individualistic theories which attribute mental illness to early childhood experiences, such as those often advanced by psychiatrists and psychoanalysts. Rather, mental illness may develop out of difficulties that arise in relating to groups in adult life without necessarily having experienced exceptional difficulties early in life. One psychiatrist, in discounting the individual or personal problems of the patient, has stated that "since he [the patient] worked up his psychosis in the group, he can never be cured until he has worked out his recovery in a group." [69] As a research statement on the relation of mental disorder to socioenvironmental factors indicated, "the possible existence of group character structures, the stresses put on many by changing conditions or by the excessive demands of the culture, the sources of and the effect of loneliness and social isolation, and the techniques and effects of social esteem and social punishment on personality, these and many other problems need careful and continued investigation." [70]

Group Methods in Reintegrating the Aged

OLD PEOPLE'S CLUBS

One of the most prominent group approaches to reintegrating aged persons consists of informal groups or social clubs. Many clubs run by and for older persons have been organized within the last twenty years. Some, such as the Townsend Clubs, grew out of the depression and the need for

---

[68] Brooks reports that the thirty-five patients in this house had formerly been "dilapidated derelicts on the disturbed and semi-disturbed wards of the hospital—denuditive, smearing the walls of the seclusion rooms." He also reports that, as a result of this experiment, there had occurred in the hospital a marked increase in the status-value of the diagnosis "chronic schizophrenia," many hoping that they might be candidates for the halfway house.

[69] L. Cody Marsh, "Group Treatment of the Psychoses by the Psychological Equivalent of the Revival," *Mental Hygiene*, 15:341 (April, 1931).

[70] R. H. Felix and R. V. Bowers, "Mental Hygiene and Socio-Environmental Factors," *The Milbank Memorial Fund Quarterly*, 26:134 (January, 1948).

political organization to secure larger pension grants, but now they emphasize social relationships among old people. Some groups have originated around social activities, such as Golden Age Clubs or Three-Quarter-Century Clubs, and for the most part they have been concerned with group activities for the aged. Some but not all of the Golden Age Clubs are directed by professional workers and financed by Community Chests or other groups.

Regardless of the original purpose of the clubs, they provide a place for old people to gather, to meet others of their own age, and to enter into activities in which they are mutually interested. They play games, talk, sing, or sew, and, in the case of the Townsend Clubs, have engaged in political activities to promote their interests. All these activities give them something to do, a feeling of belonging, and also help to change their conception of themselves and their own problems because they see themselves through the eyes of others with similar, and perhaps even greater, difficulties.

Group Methods with Delinquent and Criminal Offenders

Although sociologists have used the group approach in their explanation of delinquents and criminals in criminology perhaps more than in any other field, the verification of the findings through the practical manipulation of the social world of offenders, using group methods, has not been as extensively investigated. The use of group therapy in correctional programs has increased in recent years.[71] Yet most of these programs are of relatively recent origin and have not been adequately evaluated as to their effectiveness.

Individual clinical methods of treating potential or actual offenders, although quite commonly used, are often assumed to be effective, in spite of the fact that their success has not been demonstrated. One study of the effectiveness of clinical treatment with male delinquents in Detroit found, for example, that there was no significant difference in percentages of arrest for those receiving psychiatric treatment as compared with those not receiving such treatment. These researchers concluded that "psychotherapeutic treatment of juvenile delinquents in varying degrees does not serve to prevent them from becoming adult offenders." [72] In view of the question about the ineffectiveness of clinical and individual methods, some persons have suggested that rehabilitative efforts in correctional institutions should be more on a group basis.

---

[71] Lloyd W. McCorkle and Albert Elias, "Group Therapy in Correctional Institutions," *Federal Probation*, 24:57 (June, 1960).

[72] H. Warren Dunham and LaMay Adamson, "Clinical Treatment of Male Juvenile Delinquents: A Case Study in Effect and Result," *American Sociological Review*, 21:320 (June, 1956).

INFORMAL GROUPS IN CONVENTIONAL SETTINGS

As yet little on the order of Alcoholics Anonymous or Recovery, Incorporated, has been developed for juvenile and criminal offenders. Efforts have been made to work on problems of deviant attitudes on an informal group basis, incorporating, for example, an entire delinquent group within a conventional framework. In one of these attempts the California Youth Authority, in cooperation with the War Department, in 1944 placed two groups of about 150 seriously delinquent boys in Army arsenals to work side by side with several thousand civilian men and women. The Army furnished barracks and provided otherwise for the boys. Efforts were made to change their roles by incorporating them into the norms and objectives of conventional society. The program seems on the surface to have made marked changes in the work habits of the boys, in their conception of themselves, and in group objectives.[73]

In India a similar though community-based approach has been used in an effort to achieve social reintegration of the formerly "criminal tribes" of India. These groups consist of people who for centuries have lived by criminal means such as stealing, robbery, and some types of pickpocketing. Frequently they sell women for prostitution, make alcohol illicitly, and fight with knives. Children born into the tribes acquire the deviant behavior patterns of their elders, with the result that the criminal traditions have been perpetuated. In recent years the Indian government has undertaken a rehabilitative program with these tribes. This program was begun when it was recognized that traditional methods, such as imprisonment, were largely ineffective. The objective of the present program is to achieve change in the behavior of these tribes by placing them in communities where they may gradually acquire noncriminal attitudes and norms. This is done by relocating groups within noncriminal villages or communities, and arranging special services to foster social interaction between local community members and members of the formerly criminal tribes.[74] A new experimental program has been started near Lucknow, India, where young children of these tribes are placed in a resident school on a voluntary basis. Here they receive a normal school program and have frequent associations with school children in the nearby noncriminal community. An effort is made to change not only attitudes but also self-conceptions by insulating them from their former associates.

---

[73] Described in John R. Ellingston, *Protecting Our Children from Criminal Careers* (Englewood Cliffs, N.J.: Prentice-Hall, Inc., 1948), pp. 95–118. Also see J. Douglas and Marguerite Grant, "A Group Dynamics Approach to the Treatment of Nonconformists in the Navy," *The Annals*, 322:126–135 (March, 1959).

[74] B. H. Mehta, "Ex-Criminal Groups in India," *Indian Journal of Social Work*, Vol. 16 (June, 1955); and P. N. Saxena, "Rehabilitation Work among Ex-Criminal Groups in India," *Social Welfare in India* (New Delhi: Planning Commission of the Government, September, 1955), pp. 505–516.

In Wisconsin, inmates of the county jails are permitted, under the Huber law, to work in free society during the day, as "day parole," returning to the jail in the evenings and on week ends, and deductions are made for their "lodging." The 1772 prisoners employed outside the jail during 1956 under this law earned $364,282.[75] In the Model Prison at Lucknow, India, a similar program is followed.

GROUP THERAPY

During World War II group therapy of a more specific nature was used with British military offenders. Later it was used in the United States at the Service Command Rehabilitation Center at Fort Knox, where the necessity for rehabilitating large numbers of persons far exceeded the supply of professional men available. In this group therapy work the "belligerent, over-assertive, anti-social rehabilitee is brought into line by his fellows and the asocial, shy, withdrawn person is drawn into the conversation." [76] Since World War II, more and more civilian correctional institutions have established group therapy as an aid to rehabilitation. For example, group therapy is extensively used at present in New Jersey prisons and reformatories as well as in many other states. In California, a group counseling program has been in operation since 1944.[77] Although there has been some use of sociodramas and psychodramas, for the most part the therapy has been mainly of the discussion-group type. These discussions may be guided by either a professionally trained leader, such as a sociologist, a psychologist, a social worker, or a psychiatrist, or by nonprofessional personnel with some in-service training. In New Jersey group therapy in correctional institutions is called "guided group interaction" in an effort to avoid confusion with group therapy as practiced by psychiatrists, as well as the implication that inmates are "mentally abnormal." The following excerpt is taken from a discussion in a New Jersey correctional institution in which an inmate comes to see that his difficulties in living in various cell blocks are primarily from his own actions and not from those of other inmates.

> S: Well, I might. But he wants me to adjust myself to the people in A Wing [cell block] and learn to get along in A Wing.
> J: Why can't you get along in A Wing?
> S: Because I can't.

---

[75] Sanger B. Powers, "Day-Parole of Misdemeanants," *Federal Probation*, 22:42–46 (December, 1958).

[76] Joseph Abrahams and Lloyd W. McCorkle, "Group Psychotherapy of Military Offenders," *American Journal of Sociology*, 51:458 (March, 1946).

[77] Sutherland and Cressey, *op. cit.*, pp. 492–493; Norman Fenton, *A Brief Historical Account of Group Counselling in the Prisons of California* (Sacramento: State Department of Corrections, 1957); and G. Sterna, "The Correctional Officer as a Treatment Figure," *Group Counseling Newsletter*, California Department of Corrections, June, 1958, pp. 9–10.

J: What makes you think you can get along in another wing?

S: Because I'd be by myself then.

A: Can't you be by yourself in A Wing?

S: No.

J: Why can't you make those fellows leave you alone? You want to stay by yourself.

S: That is not the point. The point is they'll turn around and bother you anyhow. At least in one of the lock-up wings, if you don't want nobody around, you go in your cell and lock the door, and the hell with them. Right?

O: Sure.

B: Do you mean to tell me people bother you, S_____?

S: Yeah.

J: I think S_____ bothers people if I know S_____. I locked with you for three and a half months. If you come over to E-2 and pull the s_____ you pulled on B-3.

S: Well, anyhow, that's what he said. I am just stating what he said, that's all.

Leader: Well, I think S_____ made a point. He said that really what determines whether or not a guy is ready to go out depends on his ability to get along in any kind of situation.[78]

Such therapy seems to set in operation group forces directed toward socially accepted goals, and which partially counteract the antisocial group conniving that goes on so extensively in correctional institutions. This process does not occur automatically; and it extends over a long period of time. If the group atmosphere is one of true acceptance, respect, and non-censure, offenders seem to feel free to express their feelings and to share experiences of which conventional society would disapprove. Group acceptance of mutual feelings thus enables offenders to examine their experiences and the reasons for their confinement. In addition, if in the therapy group the offenders are trusted and expected to abide by anti-criminal norms, they may come to regard themselves as nonoffenders, or at least as potential nonoffenders. If such changes in self-concepts do occur, it is probable that offenders will then aspire to the lives of "respectable" law-abiding persons. If this point is reached, criminal attitudes and motives will have been replaced by noncriminal attitudes and motives.[79]

. . . . there seems to be an assumption that free discussion of an inmate's problems and personality characteristics by and with an inmate group and a therapist will both enable him and force him to "face the facts" of his case. . . . Inmates who have had experiences similar to his will not let him lie,

---

[78] F. Lovell Bixby and Lloyd W. McCorkle, "Guided Group Interaction in Correctional Work," *American Sociological Review*, 16:458–459 (August, 1951).

[79] Sutherland and Cressey, *op. cit.*, pp. 494–496. Also see Richard R. Korn and Lloyd W. McCorkle, *Criminology and Penology* (New York: Holt, Rinehart and Winston, Inc., 1959), Chaps. 23 and 24.

bluff, or provide *ex post facto* justification for his criminal behavior. Presumably, the inmates . . . will accept his fellow inmates' friendly denunciations of his behavior and rationalizations more readily than he would accept the rejections and denunciations of the same behavior and rationalizations by an outsider.[80]

A variation of group therapy which has been employed in some correctional institutions consists of "role training" or role playing as part of the therapeutic technique. One institution conducted an experiment in "role training" as a means of preparing inmates for the problems which would be encountered after release from the institution.[81] According to these experimenters, if an offender upon release is to play the role of a nonoffender and a law-abiding citizen, he must have experienced (1) knowledge of the expectations of the role, generally through intimate contact with nonoffenders which allows identification with persons occupying the role; (2) rehearsal in the role, either imaginal or incipient; and (3) actual practice in the role.[82] Results indicated that role training was successful in improving role-playing skills and attitudes. There were highly significant differences when these offenders were compared with a control group.

It is unfortunate that, instead of changing the attitudes of the inmate about various *social norms,* most correctional group therapy work is still directed at attempts to modify personality traits and allowing the individual to release some of his aggressions. The approach used may, of course, help the inmate adjust to the frustrations of prison life, but often it does not get at the basis of his criminal behavior. Because the inmate's attitudes are derived from the social groups to which he has belonged, and because he has not had normal relationships with more conventional groups, it is important that group therapy programs be based on a group, rather than on an individual, theory of criminality.[83]

---

[80] Sutherland and Cressey, *op. cit.,* p. 494. In a rather unusual experiment in group therapy, two small groups of incorrigible prisoners in a North Carolina prison, one from security isolation and the other from the yard, were selected for discussion therapy.—Richard McCleery, *The Strange Journey* (Chapel Hill: University of North Carolina Extension Bulletin, Vol. 32, No. 4 [March, 1953]). A more recent study of fifty prison "rats," or prisoners at odds with their fellow inmates, has examined some of these circumstances. —Elmer H. Johnson, "Sociology of Confinement: Assimilation and the Prison 'Rat,' " *Journal of Criminal Law, Criminology and Police Science,* 50:528–533 (January–February, 1961).

[81] Martin R. Haskell and H. Ashley Weeks, "Role Training as Preparation for Release from Correctional Institutions," *Journal of Criminal Law, Criminology and Police Science,* 50:441–452 (January–February, 1960).

[82] *Ibid.,* p. 441.

[83] Donald R. Cressey, "Contradictory Theories in Correctional Group Therapy Programs," *Federal Probation,* 18:20–26 (June, 1954); also his "Changing Criminals: The Application of the Theory of Differential Association," *American Journal of Sociology,* 61:116–212 (September, 1955) and his "The Nature and Effectiveness of Correctional Techniques," in *Law and Contemporary Problems.*

One interesting recent group experiment in dealing with juvenile delinquency is known as the Provo (Utah) Experiment.[84] A group of habitual offenders, aged fifteen to seventeen, is assigned by the local court to join twenty others in daily group discussions. A control group is either placed on probation or sent to a correctional institution. The group discussions assume that delinquency is primarily a group phenomenon and the task of rehabilitation is one of changing shared delinquent characteristics. It involves discussions which (1) permit delinquents to examine the role and legitimacy of authorities in the treatment system; (2) give them the opportunity to examine the ultimate utility of conventional and delinquent alternatives for them; (3) provide the opportunity to declare publicly a belief or disbelief that they can benefit from a change in values; and (4) make peer group interaction the principal rehabilitative tool because it permits peer group decision making and grants status and recognition, not only for participation in treatment interaction, but for willingness to help others.

RESIDENTIAL TREATMENT CENTERS

A well-known experiment in a residential treatment center has been carried out at Highfields, which is part of the New Jersey correctional system and makes extensive use of group therapy and informal associations between staff and inmates in a fairly permissive, nonauthoritarian atmosphere.[85] It is a short-term detention facility located on the former estate of Charles Lindbergh in New Jersey, without bars or walls. The impact of the guided group interaction sessions, which are held five nights a week, appears to be reinforced by the group living experience.[86] In both guided group interaction and the living experience, the influence of the group is directed toward freeing the boys from delinquent associations and changing their conceptions of themselves from lawbreaking to law-abiding persons.

An evaluation made of the Highfields Project indicates that the delinquent boys aged sixteen and seventeen sent to Highfields have a lower rate of recidivism than those in the control group sent to the Annandale Reformatory.[87] In this study a control group of offenders, matched as to age, previous commitments, and so on, was sent for more conventional treatment to the New Jersey Reformatory at Annandale. A much lower percentage of boys from Highfields became delinquent after returning to

[84] LaMar T. Empey and Jerome Rabow, "The Provo Experiment in Delinquency Rehabilitation," *American Sociological Review*, 26:679–695 (October, 1961).

[85] Lloyd W. McCorkle, Albert Elias, and F. Lovell Bixby, *The Highfields Story* (New York: Holt, Rinehart and Winston, Inc., 1958).

[86] H. Ashley Weeks ed., *Youthful Offenders at Highfields* (Ann Arbor: University of Michigan Press, 1958).

[87] *Ibid.*

the community than did the boys from Annandale, even when such factors as age, parents' marital status, race, parents' occupation, residence, and so on, were held constant. Also, comparison of Annandale boys with the Highfields boys on a number of scales designed to measure attitudes and value orientations reveal favorable changes among the latter. The conclusion of the evaluating committee was that Highfields had demonstrated greater success than the traditional type of institution in reintegrating delinquents.[88]

Summary

Since evidence shows that deviant behavior is developed through group processes, group methods should help to bring about the social reintegration of deviants. Primarily during the past fifteen years, several different applications of group methods have been developed to treat mental disorders, delinquency and criminality, alcoholism, and old-age adjustment. These group methods have included more group therapy limited though it is; group counseling and discussion sessions; psychodrama and sociodrama; clubs for former deviants in communities; and, more recently, the creation of therapeutic communities in some mental hospitals and some correctional institutions. There have also been many informal applications through Alcoholics Anonymous and similar informal groups of mental patients, narcotic addicts, and old people who are working out their problems more successfully together than they can alone.

Group methods appear to be more effective in reintegrating many social deviants than the individualized approach. The group approach to social reintegration affects the deviant in a number of ways which can be summarized as socialization into nondeviant behavior patterns through taking the role of a nondeviant person, sharing feelings and examining problematic past experiences in a permissive, noncensuring group setting, identifying with others who are beginning to regard themselves as nondeviants, establishing loyalty and allegiance to new group norms and values, and eventually reorienting attitudes and overt behavior. As the individual is socialized, or resocialized, a network of new interpersonal relations is established. Group identification is enhanced and a "we" feeling is developed by noting that others have similar problems. The group becomes an important link in helping its members to adjust. The individual is thus enabled to gain a new conception of himself through group interaction. Finally, the operation of social pressures aids the establishment and mainte-

---

[88] The Highfields Project actually is not evaluating group therapy alone, but is also evaluating the difference between a small treatment institution with a permissive atmosphere and a reformatory. Although this study has shed some light on the value of group therapy, a more specifically directed research project is needed which would take inmates in the same institution and compare results in a group under such therapy with a control group which does not have such therapy.

nance of new social norms and values. This approach to the treatment of deviant behavior appears to offer unlimited possibilities for reintegrating deviants.

Selected Readings

Alcoholics Anonymous. New York: Works Publishing Company, 1950. This is the basic book used by members of Alcoholics Anonymous. It contains the stories of the founders, the general program, including the twelve steps, and a series of personal stories.

BALES, ROBERT F. "The Therapeutic Role of A.A. as Seen by a Sociologist," *Quarterly Journal of Studies on Alcohol,* 5:267–274 (September, 1944). The dynamics of Alcoholics Anonymous as seen by a sociologist who has studied it.

BIXBY, F. LOVELL, and LLOYD W. MC CORKLE. "Guided Group Interaction in Correctional Work," *American Sociological Review,* 16:455–459 (August, 1951). A theoretical analysis of the use of "guided group interaction" in the New Jersey correctional institutions. Contains several extracts from actual sessions.

CLINARD, MARSHALL B. "The Group Approach to Social Reintegration," *American Sociological Review,* 14:257–262 (April, 1949). An analysis of the entire area of group approaches to reintegration. Indicates the theoretical implications of this work, particularly for sociology.

CRESSEY, DONALD R. "Contradictory Theories in Correctional Group Therapy Programs," *Federal Probation,* 18:20–26 (June, 1954). A criticism of the present use of group therapy in prisons as placing too much emphasis on modifying personality traits and not enough on changing the attitudes and social roles of criminal offenders.

KORN, RICHARD R., and LLOYD W. MC CORKLE. *Criminology and Penology.* New York: Holt, Rinehart and Winston, Inc., 1959, Chaps. 23 and 24. Contains a discussion of group methods in prisons.

MC CORKLE, LLOYD W. "Group Therapy," in Paul W. Tappan ed., *Contemporary Correction.* New York: McGraw-Hill Book Company, 1951. A general statement on the use of group therapy in correctional institutions by one of the leaders in this area.

MC CORKLE, LLOYD W., ALBERT ELIAS, and F. LOVELL BIXBY. *The Highfields Story.* New York: Holt, Rinehart and Winston, Inc., 1958. A description of the plan, procedure, and operation of the experimental project for the group treatment of youthful offenders at Highfields.

POWDERMAKER, FLORENCE B., and JEROME D. FRANK. *Group Psychotherapy.* Cambridge, Mass.: Harvard University Press, 1953. A research study of the therapeutic effect of group therapy on neurotic and schizophrenic patients of the Veterans Administration hospitals. Contains extensive material from actual group therapy sessions.

VON MERING, OTTO, and STANLEY H. KING. *Remotivating the Mental Patient.* New York: Russell Sage Foundation, 1957. A description of efforts to treat patients by restructuring the social milieu of the hospital, with discussions of results in terms of patient improvement.

Author Index

Abrahams, Joseph, 666
Abrahamsen, David, 129
Abrahamson, Julia, 611
Adamic, Louis, 503
Adamson, L., 618, 664
Addams, Jane, 100
Adorno, T. W., 563, 568
Albrecht, Ruth, 488
Alexander, Franz, 137
Alexander, George H., 635
Alland, Alexander, 614
Allardt, Eric, 349
Allen, D. D., 277
Allen, F. L., 319
Allen, George N., 403
Allport, G. W., 534, 555, 562, 567, 569
Alpert, Harry, 403
Anderson, Nels, 60, 65, 68, 97, 103, 355
Anderson, R. C., 588
Anderson, Theodore R., 450
Andics, Margarethe von, 420
Angell, R. C., 115
Angrist, Shirley, 640
Anshen, R. N., 125, 430, 442, 457
Anslinger, H. J., 297, 299, 309, 317, 604
Apfelberg, B., 243
Appleby, Lawrence, 381
Aptheker, Herbert, 565
Asbury, Herbert, 328
Ashley-Montagu, M. F., 43
Ashmore, Harry S., 535, 546, 548, 569
Athens, F., 646
Aubert, Vilhelm, 165
Auden, W. H., 75
Aveling, E., 100

Babcock, J. O., 173
Bacon, Selden D., 102, 115, 325, 327, 336, 337, 346

Badgley, Robin F., 450
Bailey, D. S., 247
Bailey, Percival, 138, 140
Bales, R. F., 356, 358, 458, 651, 671
Balistrieri, James, 15, 219, 229
Banay, R. S., 44, 232, 234
Barer, Naomi, 112
Barker, D., 661
Barnes, H. E., 106, 626
Barnett, M. L., 359
Barron, Milton, 486, 532, 535, 569
Bartemeir, L. H., 645
Barton, R. C., 620
Bastide, Roger, 496
Bates, A., 431
Bateson, Gregory, 364, 383
Baur, E. Jackson, 336
Beach, F. A., 247
Beccaria, Cesare, 146
Beck, Dorothy Fahs, 646, 659
Becker, Gary S., 548
Becker, H. S., 65, 69, 304, 317
Beegle, Allan J., 83
Beesley, T. Q., 282
Belknap, Ivan, 483
Bell, James, 218
Bell, W., 66
Bellin, Seymour S., 362
Bellow, Barbara, 224
Benedict, Ruth, 247
Bennett, George K., 464
Berelson, Bernard, 539
Berezin, F. C., 327
Berg, I. A., 234
Berman, Louis, 42
Bernard, Jessie, 436, 439, 440
Bernard, L. L., 573
Berreman, Gerald D., 348
Berry, Brewton, 494, 554, 557, 569

Beshoar, Barron, 175
Bierer, J., 656
Bierstedt, Robert, 150
Birren, James E., 461, 464, 468, 486, 487, 488, 489
Bixby, F. L., 667, 669, 671
Black, Hillel, 268
Blackstone, William, 407
Blalock, H. M., Jr., 86
Blau, Zena S., 48, 484, 485, 487, 488
Bloch, H. A., 193, 202, 277, 290, 327
Blomberg, Dick, 195
Blumenthal, Albert, 75, 79
Blumer, Herbert, 180
Bogen, David, 574
Bogue, Donald J., 186
Bohannan, Paul, 235, 411, 419, 420
Bonger, William, 100, 101
Böök, J. A., 398
Booth, Charles, 100
Bott, Elizabeth, 431, 432, 450, 451, 457, 458
Bowers, R. V., 663
Bowerman, Charles F., 450
Boyd, William C., 569
Brancale, Ralph, 240, 241, 242, 243
Branham, V. C., 132, 217
Brearley, H. C., 235
Bredemeier, H. C., 65
Breen, Leonard Z., 460, 461, 463, 465
Brill, H., 636
Bromberg, Walter, 243
Bronner, Augusta, 180, 184, 197, 199
Brooks, George W., 662, 663
Broom, Leonard, 376, 518, 564
Brown, Esther L., 658
Brown, H. L., 661
Brown, L. B., 647, 661
Brown, L. G., 37, 374
Browne, Lewis, 525
Buerkle, Jack V., 450
Bühler, Charlotte, 117
Bullock, H. A., 15, 236
Bunche, Ralph, 493, 549
Bunzel, Bessie, 82, 406, 412, 414, 416, 418, 419, 424, 426, 429
Burchardt, H. H., 80
Burgess, E. W., 29, 79, 87, 88, 90, 97, 186, 273, 431, 432, 433, 444, 446, 447, 448, 450, 451, 452, 453, 456, 459, 467, 472, 477, 483, 485, 487, 489, 587
Burma, John H., 522, 524, 532, 535, 544

Burt, Cyril, 222
Byrd, Admiral R. E., 5–6

Cadwallader, Mervyn, 271
Caldwell, Morris, 626
Calhoun, A. W., 456
Calkins, R., 329
Calverton, V. F., 394
Cameron, Norman, 59, 366, 375, 378, 380, 381, 385, 386, 388, 389, 393, 401, 482, 483
Cannon, Kenneth, 438
Cantor, Donald J., 292
Caplovitz, David, 551
Carlson, A. J., 461
Carlson, G. G., 278
Carr, Lowell J., 572, 574, 575, 590
Carrothers, J. C., 394
Carstairs, G. M., 366
Cartwright, Dorwin, 645
Cason, Halsey, 218
Cavan, Ruth S., 259, 403, 413, 415, 419, 421, 425, 429, 453, 467, 468, 484, 485, 489
Cavanagh, J. R., 179
Cawte, J. E., 647, 661
Cayton, H. R., 532, 536
Cerletti, Ugo, 635
Cervantes, Lucius F., 432, 436, 450, 458, 459
Chance, Erika, 657
Chandler, Margaret K., 331
Chapin, E. Stuart, 112
Chatterjee, B., 77, 608
Chein, Isidor, 306, 307, 308
Christensen, H. T., 439
Clark, Alexander, 441
Clark, R. E., 354, 396
Clark, Walter Houston, 223
Clausen, J. A., 67, 301, 307, 308, 362, 369, 376, 380, 394, 401, 402, 601
Cleckley, Hervey, 217
Clemmer, Donald, 11, 176, 626, 628, 642
Clinard, M. B., 15, 59, 72, 77, 80, 85, 86, 97, 105, 138, 148, 149, 163, 165, 168, 185, 186, 202, 209, 213, 219, 230, 258, 266, 268, 290, 321, 327, 331, 332, 360, 546, 576, 578, 579, 580, 590, 599, 608, 615, 629, 647, 650, 671
Cloward, Richard A., 11, 17, 181, 191, 193, 195, 202, 307, 308
Cohane, Tim, 171

Cohen, A. K., 11, 13, 14, 17, 191, 193, 203, 213, 214, 223, 271
Cohen, J., 431
Coleman, James S., 12, 14
Coleman, Richard, 445
Confrey, Eugene A., 481, 483
Connor, Ralph, 351
Cook, Joseph A., 648, 652
Cook, S. W., 35
Cooke, A., 218
Cooley, Charles, 106
Cooper, M., 369
Corsini, Raymond J., 123
Corson, J. W., 472
Cory, D. W., 248
Cotton, H., 43
Cottrell, L. S., Jr., 376, 444, 447, 449, 450, 453, 459, 564
Coughlan, R., 120
Cox, Oliver, 565
Cramer, J. B., 657
Crawford, P. L., 613, 620
Crecraft, H. James, 299
Cressey, D. R., 11, 19, 40, 55, 59, 138, 140, 153, 157, 172, 176, 177, 183, 204, 215, 216, 230, 269, 270, 290, 620, 623, 626, 628, 629, 642, 646, 650, 651, 666, 667, 668, 671
Cressey, Paul, 253
Criswell, J. H., 555
Cromwell, W. O., 334
Cuber, J. F., 22, 596, 620
Cumming, John, 381
Cushman, J. F., 117

Dai, Bingham, 303
Daric, Jean, 412
Davis, Allison, 532
Davis, Kingsley, 13, 60, 61, 65, 250, 251, 254, 255, 365, 384, 437, 446
Day, Barbara R., 450
Dean, J. P., 620
Delaney, Lloyd T., 224
Demareth, N. J., 394
Deutsch, Felix, 584
Deutsch, M., 35
Deveraux, George, 394
Dewey, Richard, 44, 68
Dewhurst, Henry S., 222
Diethelm, Oskar, 359
Dietrik, D. C., 195
Dinitz, Simon, 213, 215, 329, 342, 640, 649

Dollard, John, 50, 352, 353, 532, 562
Donahue, Wilma, 461, 462, 464, 469, 483
Donne, John, 5
Doob, L., 562
Dorcus, R. M., 43, 372
Dorfman, Robert, 485, 488
Doshay, L. I., 244
Douglas, J., 645, 665
Douglas, P. H., 172, 203, 598, 620
Douglass, E. M., 319, 322, 361, 603, 618
Drake, St. Clair, 532
Driver, Edwin D., 239
Dubin, Robert, 16, 468
Dublin, L. I., 82, 406, 412, 414, 416, 418, 419, 424, 426, 429
Dumpson, J. R., 613, 620
Dunham, H. W., 15, 93, 97, 103, 211, 230, 297, 364, 393, 401, 483, 584, 585, 618, 634, 637, 638, 639, 643, 664
Dunn, Marie S., 443
Durea, Mervin A., 221
Durkheim, Emile, 16, 84, 403, 409, 429, 586
Dyer, Dorothy T., 450

Eagle, Morris, 524, 539
Eastman, Harold D., 72, 80
Eaton, J. W., 364, 395, 396, 401
Eberhart, John C., 221
Eddy, Nathan B., 293
Efron, Vera, 333, 339, 341
Eldred, Donald M., 662
Elias, Albert, 646, 664, 669, 671
Elkin, Frederick, 226
Ellingston, J. R., 225, 665
Elliott, Mabel, 436, 437, 438, 440
Ellis, Albert, 240, 241, 242, 243
Ellis, Edward R., 403
Ellison, Jerome, 654
Empey, LaMar T., 669
Engels, F., 100
Erikson, Erik, 194
Eriksson, T., 631
Erlich, Iza, 635
Evans, James C., 553
Evjen, V. H., 573
Eynon, Thomas G., 184

Faigenbaum, David, 219
Fanshel, D., 487
Farberow, Norman L., 415, 418, 422
Faris, Ellsworth, 10, 297

Faris, R. E. L., 15, 27, 80, 93, 96, 394, 409
Feder, Sid, 211
Fein, Rashi, 28
Feinhandler, S. J., 638
Feld, Sheila, 385, 601
Felix, R. H., 368, 370, 483, 601, 663
Fenichel, Otto, 132
Fenton, Norman, 666
Ferracuti, Franco, 418
Ferrero, G. L., 147
Field, Eugene, 328, 329
Fine, Benjamin, 227
Finestone, Harold, 296, 307, 308, 311, 313
Firebaugh, W. C., 328
Fleisher, Wilfred, 631
Folsom, J. K., 456
Foote, Nelson N., 449, 459
Ford, C. S., 247
Forizs, Lorant, 653
Form, William H., 77
Fox, Vernon, 234, 625
Foxe, A. N., 132
Frank, J. G., 653, 657, 671
Frankel, E., 238
Frazier, E. F., 111, 495, 507, 511, 513, 533
Freedman, Lawrence Z., 392
Freeman, Howard E., 601
Frenkel-Brunswik, Else, 568
Freud, Sigmund, 135
Fried, Jacob, 396
Friedmann, E. A., 468, 489
Friedsam, Hiram J., 483
Frohlich, M. M., 482
Frosch, Jack, 243
Fuller, Richard, 276, 596
Fuller, Richard C., 165
Futterman, Samuel, 350

Galbraith, John Kenneth, 114, 115
Gallagher, Eugene B., 635
Galpin, Charles, 78, 80
Galtung, Johan, 629
Gardiner, Gerald, 158
Gardner, Burleigh B., 532
Gardner, G. E., 618
Gardner, Mary R., 532
Garfinkel, Harold, 595
Garner, J. W., 570
Garrity, Donald L., 211, 230
Gebbard, Paul H., 246
Geis, Albert, 148
Geis, Gilbert, 648, 652
George, Henry, 100

Gerard, Donald, 301
Gibbons, Don C., 211, 230
Gibbs, Jack P., 407, 409, 418, 419, 428
Gibney, Frank, 161, 290
Giering, Elsie, 148
Gillespie, R. D., 585
Gillin, J. L., 6, 232, 233
Gillin, J. P., 6, 394
Gilmore, H. W., 104, 115
Gingery, S. L., 222
Ginsberg, Eli, 442, 445
Glad, D. D., 358
Glaser, Daniel, 213
Glazer, Nathan, 524, 538, 539
Glick, P. C., 439
Glueck, Eleanor, 123, 140, 184, 185, 197,
    198, 199, 200, 203, 209, 223, 252
Glueck, Sheldon, 140, 185, 197, 198, 199,
    200, 203, 209, 223, 252
Goddard, H. H., 116
Goethals, G. W., 614
Goffman, Erving, 53, 59, 72, 75, 373, 626,
    627
Golder, Grace, 348, 361
Goldhamer, Herbert, 28, 370
Goldman, Nathan, 228
Goldmann, F., 483
Goldstein, Marcus S., 481, 483
Goode, W. J., 34, 437, 438, 439, 448, 452,
    467, 489
Goodrich, H. F., 440
Gordon, Albert I., 532, 538
Gordon, C. Wayne, 352, 355, 361
Gordon, Margaret S., 472
Gordon, Raymond, 224
Gorham, Maurice, 329
Goring, Charles, 147
Gottlieb, David, 332
Gough, H. G., 217
Grant, Marguerite, 645, 665
Green, A. W., 13, 90, 398
Greenberg, J., 498, 533, 536, 540, 569
Greenberg, Leon A., 323, 324
Greenblatt, M., 378, 634, 637, 656, 658,
    661, 662
Griffith, B. W., 550
Grimshaw, Allen D., 86
Grine, R. J., 327
Grodzins, Morton, 518
Grosser, George H., 11
Gruener, J. R., 76, 480
Grünhut, Max, 421
Gruenberg, Ernest M., 362

Grusky, Oscar, 629
Gudeman, Jon, 358
Gueneau, Monique, 195
Guirguis, Malak, 635
Gulick, S. L., 517
Gurfein, M. L., 282
Gurin, Gerald, 385, 601, 616
Gursslin, Orville R., 365, 601

Hackwood, F. W., 328
Haer, J. L., 350
Haggard, H. W., 322, 324
Hakeem, Michael, 138, 140
Halbwachs, Maurice, 82
Haley, Jay, 383
Hallowell, A. Irving, 364
Halpern, Florence, 117
Handel, Gerald, 445
Hardt, Robert H., 638
Harlan, Howard, 239
Harlan, W. H., 478
Harper, Robert, 22, 38, 596, 620
Harris, C. D., 96
Harris, C. E. M., 647, 661
Harris, George, 175
Harris, Sara, 654, 655
Hartung, F. E., 11, 22, 92, 162, 164, 166
Haskell, Martin R., 668
Hathaway, Starke, 216
Hatt, P. K., 34, 65, 68
Hauser, P. M., 180
Havighurst, R. J., 465, 467, 468, 480, 485, 486, 488, 489
Hayner, Norman S., 211
Healy, William, 137, 148, 180, 184, 197, 199
Heath, R. G., 355
Hecht, C. A., 327
Henry, A. F., 417, 426, 427, 429
Herling, John, 262, 290
Herman, Abbott, 73, 107
Herskovits, Melville J., 502
Hilgard, E. R., 45
Hill, H., 498
Hill, Reuben, 431
Hillman, Arthur, 608, 611
Hirsh, Joseph, 603
Hoch, Paul H., 373
Hollingshead, A. B., 14, 15, 366, 373, 376, 388, 397, 400, 401, 638
Homans, George, 7, 9, 21, 34, 594
Honigmann, J. J., 453
Hooton, E. A., 119

Hopkins, E. J., 174
Horney, Karen, 134, 392, 401
Horowitz, E. L., 555
Horton, Donald, 349
Hoskins, R. G., 43
Hostetter, G. L., 282
Howell, Rapelje, 147
Hoyt, Homer, 87
Humber, W. J., 44
Hunt, J. McV., 80
Hunt, Raymond G., 365, 601
Hunt, W. A., 369
Hunter, W., 44
Hurvitz, Nathan, 441
Hurwitz, S., 148
Hutchinson, B., 465
Hyde, Robert H., 658, 659
Hyde, R. W., 330, 353

Igersheimer, W. W., 653
Ivy, A. C., 547

Jackson, Charles, 345
Jackson, Don D., 383, 399, 400
Jackson, J. K., 351, 649
Jaco, E. Gartly, 81, 370, 395, 396
Jacobs, H. Lee, 486
Jacobs, J. A., 610
Jacobson, P. H., 436, 437, 439
Jahoda, Marie, 35, 364, 402
Jaspan, Norman, 268
Jefferson, Thomas, 492
Jellinek, E. M., 40, 82, 341, 342, 360
Jerome, Edward A., 464
Johnson, Alvin, 570
Johnson, C. S., 567, 569
Johnson, Elmer H., 668
Johnson, Malcolm, 162, 281
Johnson, Nora, 442
Johnson, Ronald, 201
Jolliffe, Norman, 325
Jones, E., 127
Jones, Harold E., 464
Judges, A. V., 288

Kaempffert, Waldermar, 571
Kahl, Joseph A., 13, 35
Kahn, R. L., 468
Kahn, Roger, 278
Kallman, F. J., 398, 399, 400
Kaplan, Benjamin, 528
Kaplan, O. J., 463, 464, 481, 483, 490
Kaprio, L. A., 483

Karpman, Ben, 129, 131
Katz, C. J., 123
Kay, Barbara, 215
Kefauver, Estes, 274, 280, 290
Keller, Mark, 333, 338, 339, 341
Kelley, Harold H., 594
Kenkel, W., 22, 596, 620
Kennedy, Robert, 162, 282, 290, 599
Kephart, W. M., 436, 439, 528
Kesselman, L. C. C., 589
Khalifa, A. M., 78, 205
Kibbe, P. R., 523
Killian, Lewis M., 543
Kinberg, Olof, 148
King, Martin Luther, Jr., 533, 543
King, Stanley H., 671
Kingsley, L. V., 353
Kinsey, A. C., 13, 42, 117, 170, 171, 246, 247, 250
Kirchheimer, Otto, 157
Kirchwey, G. W., 152
Kitano, Harry H. L., 538
Kitsuse, J. I., 195
Kleemeier, Robert W., 461, 468, 483
Klineberg, Otto, 561
Kluckholn, Clyde, 398
Knobloch, F., 647, 658
Kobrin, Solomon, 104, 185, 203, 223, 610, 620, 647
Kohn, M. L., 380, 394
Kolb, Lawrence, 299
Koos, E. L., 446
Korn, Richard R., 629, 667, 671
Kornetsky, Conon, 301
Kramer, Morton, 368, 370
Kretschmer, E., 119
Krogman, W. M., 558
Kuhlen, Raymond G., 486, 487, 488
Kutash, S. B., 132, 217
Kutner, B., 487, 488
Kuusi, P., 349
Kvaraceus, W. C., 94, 191, 192, 615

La Farge, Oliver, 516
Landesco, John, 275, 283
Landis, B. Y., 320
Landis, Carney, 117
Landis, P. H., 71, 82, 149
Lane, R. E., 267, 268
Lane, Robert A., 161
Lang, Olga, 476
Langner, T. S., 487
Larrabee, E., 468

Larson, O. F., 485
Lasker, Bruno, 555
Laubscher, B. J. F., 394
Lavers, G. R., 331
LaViolette, F. E., 516
Lawrence, William, 629
Lawton, George, 473, 481
Leacock, Eleanor, 67, 81, 369
Leavy, Stanley A., 392
Lebeaux, Charles N., 76, 77, 98
Lecky, W. E. H., 405
Lee, A. McC., 541, 569
Lee, E. S., 97
Lee, Rose Hum, 60, 63, 70, 519, 520, 533
Lefever, D. W., 117
Lefton, Mark, 640
Leighton, Alexander H., 67, 307, 362, 369, 374, 402, 518
Leites, Nathan, 75, 447
LeJeune, Robert A., 649, 652
LeMasters, E. E., 439
Lemert, Edwin, 21, 22, 35, 36, 38, 51, 59, 250, 253, 255, 258, 348, 349, 390, 551, 594, 595, 603, 651
Lemkau, P. V., 369
Lendrum, F. C., 414, 415
Lesser, Alexander, 565
Levin, Yale, 90
Levinson, D. J., 378, 568, 634, 635, 637, 658, 661, 662
Levy, Marion J., Jr., 65
Lewin, Kurt, 430, 567, 645
Lewis, Hylan, 538
Lewis, N. D. C., 481
Ley, H. A., 333
Leznoff, Maurice, 249
Lidz, T., 662
Likert, Rensis, 563
Lind, A. W., 496
Lindesmith, A. R., 39, 46, 50, 59, 90, 211, 230, 283, 292, 301, 302, 309, 313, 315, 316, 317
Lindner, R. M., 132
Linton, Adelin, 225
Linton, Ralph, 225, 502, 558, 559, 561
Lisansky, Edith S., 340
Litwak, Eugene, 450, 458
Locke, H. J., 29, 103, 351, 434, 435, 441, 446, 447, 451, 452, 456, 459
Locke, John, 492
Loeb, Martin B., 637
Loeser, L. H., 247
Lofland, John F., 649, 652

Lolli, G., 348, 358, 359, 361
Lombroso, Cesare, 146
Lorge, Irving, 463
Low, A. A., 656
Luton, F. H., 81, 369
Luckey, Eleanor B., 450
Luzzatto-Fegis, Pierpaolo, 348, 358, 361
Lyle, Jack, 178, 203
Lynd, R. S., 76

McCann, R. V., 616
McCarthy, R. G., 318, 319, 320, 322, 325, 331, 335, 351, 353, 361, 603, 618, 620
McCleery, Richard, 11, 668
McCluggage, Marston M., 336
McConnell, J. W., 472, 480
McCord, Joan, 339, 341, 354, 358
McCord, William, 339, 341, 354, 358
McCorkle, L. W., 629, 646, 664, 666, 667, 669, 671
MacDermott, W. R., 93
MacDonald, D. E., 653
McDonald, J. F., 272, 291
McDunnett, M., 329
McEntire, Davis, 524, 538, 539
McGraw, R. B., 482
McKay, H. D., 91, 98, 184, 185, 198, 223, 224, 272, 291, 609
MacKinnon, William J., 564
McLean, H. V., 131
Macrory, B. E., 320, 330, 331, 335
McWilliams, Carey, 542, 552, 566
Malamud, D. I., 613, 620
Malinowski, Bronislaw, 174, 411
Malzberg, Benjamin, 80, 81, 97
Mangin, William, 348
Mangum, C. S., 504
Mann, Marty, 342, 602
Mannheim, Ernest, 222
Mannheim, Hermann, 9, 148, 221, 575, 590
Marden, C. F., 332, 333, 334, 336, 356
Marsh, L. C., 663
Marshall, Alfred, 99–100
Marshall, Andrew, 28, 370
Martin, C. E., 117, 170, 246
Martin, J. B., 96, 625
Martin, John M., 221, 230, 609, 612
Martin, John T., 553
Martin, Walter T., 428
Marx, H. L., 280
Marx, Karl, 100
Maslow, A. H., 224

Masuoka, Jitsuichi, 518
Mathews, M. T., 80
Matza, David, 195
Maurer, D. W., 254, 285, 290
Maxwell, M. A., 320, 333, 335, 336, 351, 352
Mays, John Barron, 225
Mead, G. H., 47
Mead, Margaret, 174, 394
Mechanic, David, 367, 604
Mehta, B. H., 665
Menninger, Karl, 129, 364
Menninger, W. C., 585, 645
Mercer, J. D., 248
Merrill, Francis E., 436, 437, 438, 440, 455, 573, 574, 575, 576, 583, 584, 587, 590
Merrill, Maud A., 180, 223
Merton, Robert K., 15, 16, 125, 213, 251, 376, 380, 401, 407, 409, 428, 437, 440, 452, 556, 564, 601
Messinger, Sheldon L., 11, 627
Meyersohn, R., 468
Middendorff, Wolf, 148, 194, 219
Middleton, Russell, 457
Miles, Arthur P., 138
Miller, Donald E., 82, 333, 335, 336, 338, 340
Miller, J. L., 335
Miller, Neal, 562
Miller, Walter B., 13, 14, 35, 94, 191, 192, 203, 646
Mills, C. Wright, 75
Moir, John B., 219
Monachesi, E. D., 106, 216, 217
Monahan, T. P., 436, 438, 439
Monroe, R. L., 140
Moore, E. C., 329
Moore, John D. J., 661
Moore, Merrill, 359
Moore, S., 100
Moore, Wilbert, 474, 479
Moorthy, M. V., 104
Moreno, Jacob L., 658
Morris, Norval, 159
Morris, Terence, 14, 91, 98, 113, 115
Moser, Alvin, 443
Motz, A. B., 431, 432, 445
Mouchot, Gabriel, 331
Mowrer, E. R., 92, 326, 403, 415, 420
Moynihan, Daniel P., 275
Mueller, J. H., 107, 115
Mulford, Harold A., 82, 333, 335, 336, 338, 340

Mumford, Lewis, 110
Muncie, Wendell, 392
Murphy, Gardner, 48, 563
Murphy, H. B. M., 395
Murphy, J. P., 220
Murphy, Lois, 48
Murray, Ellen, 213, 215
Murray, Henry A., 398
Murtagh, John M., 654, 655
Myers, Jerome K., 15, 394, 397
Myers, R. R., 276, 596
Myerson, Abraham, 43, 80
Myrdal, Gunnar, 30, 491, 533

Nadel, S. F., 50
Ness, Eliot, 583
Neustadt, R., 43
Newcomb, T. M., 39, 46, 48, 54
Newman, Donald J., 154, 162, 166
Nichols, Lee, 552
Niederhoffer, Arthur, 193, 202
Nielsen, J. M., 42
Nimkoff, M. F., 53, 87, 106, 454
Nisbet, Robert A., 16, 213, 251, 380, 401,
    407, 409, 428, 437, 440, 452, 601
Nishimoto, R. S., 518
Noel, Donald L., 546
Nye, F. Ivan, 198
Nyquist, Ola, 631
Nyswander, Marie, 313, 654, 655

Ogburn, William F., 53, 87, 106, 107, 128,
    575, 587, 590
Ohlin, L. E., 11, 17, 181, 191, 193, 195,
    202, 307, 308, 627, 629
Opler, Marvin, 364, 394, 395, 396, 661
Orbach, H. L., 466, 469, 486
Orlansky, Harold, 135, 136, 140
Osborn, L. A., 364, 380

Packard, Vance, 72
Page, J. D., 82, 90
Panakal, J. J., 78, 205
Park, R. E., 65, 87, 88, 494, 559
Parker, Edwin B., 178, 203
Parrot, Philippe, 195
Parsons, Talcott, 8, 16, 37, 430, 431, 442,
    457, 458
Partridge, Eric, 286
Pasamanick, Benjamin, 374, 640
Patai, Rafael, 525
Patrick, C. H., 321, 361
Patton, R. E., 636

Peck, H., 657
Pescor, M. J., 218, 294, 297, 298, 311, 313
Peterson, V. W., 175, 269, 275, 280, 291
Peterson, W. Jack, 351, 352
Pfautz, Harold W., 330
Pfeffer, A. Z., 243
Phillips, B. S., 466
Piaget, J., 48
Pierson, Donald, 496, 505
Pittman, David J., 321, 352, 355, 360, 361
Ploscowe, Morris, 241, 242, 317
Pollak, Otto, 206, 469, 490
Pollock, H. M., 426
Pomeroy, W. B., 170, 246
Porterfield, A. L., 169, 236, 418, 595
Potter, Robert J., 352
Powdermaker, F. B., 653, 657, 671
Powers, Edwin, 221
Powers, Sanger B., 666
Price, G. M., 350
Price, H. D., 514
Psathas, George, 659
Putney, Snell, 457

Queen, S. A., 76, 80, 480, 644
Querido, A., 641

Rabinovitch, R. D., 657
Rabow, Jerome, 669
Rabuck, A. J., 110
Rachlin, H. L., 117
Radzinowicz, L., 244, 245
Rainwater, Lee, 445
Ranck, K. H., 115, 453
Randall, O. A., 473
Raper, A. F., 551
Rasch, P. J., 120
Rasor, Robert W., 299
Reckless, W. C., 90, 155, 168, 184, 210,
    212, 213, 215, 225, 230, 252, 254, 255,
    260, 271, 284, 291, 313, 575, 600, 628,
    655
Redden, Elizabeth, 269
Redlich, F. C., 15, 363, 365, 366, 376, 397,
    400, 401, 638
Reed, Hugh P., 597
Rees, P. S., 320
Reimer, Hans, 628
Reiss, Albert J., Jr., 14, 15, 65, 68, 242
Reitman, B. L., 249
Renborg, Bertil A., 314
Rennie, T. A. C., 378, 383, 617
Reuter, Edward B., 559

Rhoades, Albert Lewis, 14
Ricardo, David, 99
Richmond, A. H., 494
Riemer, Ruth, 518
Riesman, David, 74, 98, 352, 442, 445, 468, 469
Riis, Jacob, 100
Riley, John W., 332, 333, 334, 336, 356, 603, 661
Ripley, H. S., 649
Ritchie, O. W., 648
Roach, Jack L., 365, 601
Roberts, Bertram H., 15, 394, 397
Robinson, Duane, 353
Robinson, Kenneth, 408
Robison, Sophia, 203
Robson, R., 431
Roe, Anne, 322
Roebuck, Julian, 201, 271
Rogers, Candace, 551
Rogler, Lloyd H., 388
Rolleston, J. D., 328
Rosberg, Judy, 551
Rose, A. M., 69, 76, 98, 130, 396, 402, 466, 528, 554, 556, 569, 645
Rose, Arnold, 13
Rose, Caroline, 130
Rosen, Alex, 620
Rosen, George, 483
Rosenfeld, Eva, 306, 307, 308
Rosenfeld, L. S., 483
Rosengren, William R., 386
Ross, Irwin, 547
Ross, W. D., 657
Rossi, Peter H., 77
Roth, N. R., 327
Roth, W. F., Jr., 81, 369
Rothrock, S. E., 327
Rothschild, David, 481
Roucek, Joseph, 138, 148, 154
Rousseau, 492
Rowntree, B. Seebohm, 331
Rubington, Earl, 352, 652
Ruedi, O. M., 106
Ruesch, Jurgen, 364
Rusche, G., 157
Rylander, Gösta, 631

Safrin, Ranate, 298
Sainsbury, Peter, 15, 82, 419, 429
Salter, P. J., 539
Samuel, M., 130
Sanchez, G. L., 521

Sanders, S. E., 110
Sanford, R. N., 568
Saunders, Frank, 221
Saunders, Lyle, 537, 547
Saxena, P. N., 665
Schaap, Richard, 278
Schacter, Stanley, 594
Scheff, Thomas J., 639
Schepses, Erwin, 229
Scher, Jordan M., 381
Schermerhorn, R. A., 517, 525, 526, 527, 533, 560
Schlapp, Max, 42
Schmalhausen, S. D., 394
Schmid, C. F., 92, 94, 95, 98, 414, 424
Schmidt, Emerson P., 106
Schmidt, J. E., 309
Schmidt, J. F., 486
Schneidman, Edwin S., 415, 418, 422
Schneider, David M., 398
Schoeppe, Aileen, 226
Schramm, Wilbur, 178, 180, 203
Schroeder, C. W., 80
Schroeder, H. C., 138, 347
Schroeder, W. W., 83
Schuessler, K. F., 138, 140, 216
Schur, Edwin M., 316, 317
Schwartz, Charlotte Green, 601
Schwartz, M. S., 634, 636, 643
Schwortzman, C., 646
Scott, E. M., 653
Scudder, Delton L., 486
Scudder, K. J., 628, 631, 643
Sears, R. R., 135, 137, 141
Segerstedt, T. T., 10
Seidman, Myrna, 535
Seliger, R. V., 132
Sellin, Thorsten, 20, 21, 31, 35, 631
Selye, Hans, 461, 462
Senior, Clarence, 524
Serianni, E., 348, 361
Sewell, W. H., 135, 141, 381
Shaffer, G. W., 43, 372
Shah, Jyatsna H., 414
Shalloo, J. P., 43
Shanas, Ethel, 486
Shannon, Lyle, 85, 137, 141
Shaw, C. R., 91, 98, 184, 185, 198, 209, 223, 224, 272, 291, 610
Shaw, D. M., 466
Sheldon, H. D., 461, 479
Sheldon, W. H., 119, 120, 121, 122, 123
Sheppard, Harold L., 480

Sherif, Muzafer, 10, 53
Shevky, E., 66
Shibutani, Tamotsu, 5, 18, 37, 49, 50, 51, 52, 59
Shirer, William L., 530
Shock, N. W., 463, 479, 490
Shoemaker, Don, 533
Short, J. F., Jr., 190, 196, 212, 213, 214, 271, 417, 426, 427, 529, 613
Shraq, Clarence, 626
Shulman, H. M., 222
Simmel, Georg, 65
Simmons, L. W., 474, 475, 490
Simmons, Ozzie G., 348, 601
Simon, Benjamin, 656, 662
Simpson, G. E., 16, 403, 429, 554, 557, 560, 563, 564, 566, 567, 569, 586, 604
Sjoberg, Gideon, 60, 76, 98
Sklare, Marshall, 532
Skolnick, Jerome H., 356
Slavick, Fred, 471
Smith, Adam, 99–105
Smith, Bernard, 655
Smith, C. U., 543
Smith, E. H., 42
Smith, Harvey L., 637
Smith, Joel, 77
Smith, Lynn, 476
Smith, Richard A., 262, 263
Smith, T. L., 80
Smith, Wesley A., 614
Smythe, H. H., 535
Snyder, Charles R., 321, 348, 356, 360, 361
Solby, Bruno, 660
Solomon, Ben, 221
Sorokin, Pitirim, 78, 80
Sorrentino, Anthony, 104, 610
Sower, Christopher, 326, 336
Spaulding, John A., 16, 403, 429, 586
Spiro, Melford E., 396
Srole, Leo, 369
Stanton, A. H., 634, 636, 643
Star, Shirley A., 601
Steiner, J. F., 517
Steiner, Peter, 485, 488
Stermer, J. E., 572, 575
Sterna, G., 666
Stetler, H. G., 547
Stevens, S. S., 120
Stevenson, G. D., 600
Stewart, Charles T., Jr., 68
Stieglitz, E. J., 461, 462
Stoddard, G. L., 118

Stone, Gregory, 77
Stranahan, M., 646
Straus, Jacqueline, 235
Straus, Murray, 235
Straus, Robert, 102, 115, 327, 336, 337, 350, 351, 356
Strauss, A. L., 39, 46, 50, 59
Sugar, C., 243
Sullivan, D. F., 644
Sullivan, H. S., 380
Surcase, Samuel J., 552
Sutherland, E. H., 15, 19, 34, 35, 40, 55, 102, 103, 115, 117, 124, 138, 141, 148, 153, 157, 161, 162, 163, 164, 165, 166, 172, 176, 177, 183, 185, 203, 204, 215, 217, 218, 230, 236, 240, 243, 246, 256, 263, 265, 266, 267, 284, 286, 287, 291, 347, 350–351, 575, 590, 620, 626, 628, 629, 646, 650, 651, 666, 667, 668
Svalastoga, Kaare, 239
Sykes, Gresham M., 11, 195, 627, 629, 643
Symes, Leonard, 138, 347, 361
Szabo, Denis, 84
Szasz, Thomas S., 138, 141, 363

Taft, D. R., 95, 168, 182, 199
Taietz, Philip, 485
Talbert, R. H., 236
Tannenbaum, Frank, 175
Tappan, P. W., 166, 218, 623, 643, 671
Tarde, Gabriel, 147
Teeters, N. K., 626
Terman, L. M., 29, 449, 451, 452
Thibaut, John W., 594
Thomas, D. S., 518
Thomas, Dorothy I., 97
Thomas, W. I., 22, 52
Thompson, E. T., 513
Thompson, G. N., 42
Thompson, Robert A., 538
Thorman, George, 73
Thorpe, James J., 655
Thrasher, F. M., 91, 179, 186, 188, 203, 227
Tibbitts, Clark, 460, 461, 462, 463, 464, 469, 471, 472, 479, 480, 481, 483, 490
Tiebout, H. M., 648, 650
Tietze, Christopher, 369
Toby, Jackson, 199
Togo, Alice M., 487
Tompkins, W. F., 297, 309, 317, 604
Toolan, James, 298
Tordella, C. L., 138, 347

Toro-Calder, Jaime, 235
Trice, Harrison M., 320, 341, 342, 349, 350, 647, 648, 652
Truxal, A. G., 455
Tucker, W. B., 120
Tufts, E., 104, 611
Tulchin, S. H., 117
Turkus, B. B., 211
Turner, Ralph H., 552
Turner, Roy, 61, 77, 608

Ullman, A. D., 348, 350

Van Arsdol, M. D., Jr., 414
Van Den Berghe, Pierre, 496
Van Vechten, C. C., 20
Veblen, Thorstein, 72
Verkko, Veli, 235
Veroff, Joseph, 385, 601
Vold, G. B., 235
Volkart, Edmund A., 604
Voltaire, 492
Von Hentig, Hans, 120, 239
Von Mering, Otto, 671

Wade, Andrew L., 219, 230
Wahl, J. R., 335, 341, 342
Walker, Charles R., 108, 115
Walker, Harry J., 538
Waller, Willard, 431, 443
Wallerstein, J. S., 169
Wallin, Paul, 29, 171, 431, 432, 433, 441, 444, 446, 448, 451, 452, 453, 456, 459
Wallis, W. D., 109
Walter, P. A. F., Jr., 521
Warner, W. L., 398
Watson, Jeanne, 352
Wattenberg, W. W., 15, 219, 221, 222, 229
Weakland, John, 383
Weaver, R. C., 548, 589
Webb, Muriel, 617
Webb, Robert, 617
Webber, I. L., 485
Weber, Max, 74, 476
Wechsberg, Joseph, 381
Wechsler, Henry, 86
Weeks, H. A., 668, 669
Weil, J. R., 285
Weil, R. J., 395, 396, 401
Weinberg, S. K., 21, 381, 383, 387, 391, 402, 438, 466, 484, 626, 634, 635, 637, 638, 639, 640, 643, 645, 659, 660
Weiss, R. S., 468

Weller, C. V., 479
Wellman, Marvin, 350
Wertham, Frederic, 179
Westermarck, Edward, 409
Westley, William, 174, 226, 249
Westwood, G., 248, 256
Whalen, Thelma, 350
Whatley, Charles D., 601
Wheeler, Stanton, 241, 245, 246
White, R. C., 110
Whitman, H., 162
Whyte, W. F., 23, 74, 76, 77, 89, 90
Wilensky, Harold L., 76, 77, 98
Wilkerson, Doxsey, 565
Williams, G. L., 403, 408
Williams, J. E. Hall, 241
Williams, R. H., 634, 637, 658, 659, 661, 662
Williams, R. M., Jr., 9, 12, 23, 378, 493, 562, 569, 607
Williams, Roger J., 325
Wilmer, H., 661
Wilson, H. H., 173
Wilson, Howard E., 539
Wilson, Robert N., 67, 307, 362, 369, 402
Winck, R. F., 443, 448, 449, 457, 459
Winick, Charles, 299, 300, 309
Winterbottom, Miriam, 356
Wirth, Louis, 65, 66, 67, 68, 69, 79, 80, 85, 86, 98, 502, 526, 533, 607, 644
Wise, J. W., 614
Witmer, H. L., 104, 611
Witmer, Helen, 221
Wittels, D. G., 217
Wittman, P., 123
Wittson, C. L., 369
Wolfbein, Seymour L., 471
Wolfenstein, Martha, 75, 447
Wolfgang, Marvin, 15, 201, 231, 237, 239, 256, 421
Wood, Arthur, 235
Wood, E. F., 112, 113
Woodward, C. Vann, 497, 533, 543, 549
Woodward, L. E., 617
Wootton, Barbara, 138, 141
Wortis, S. P., 298
Wright, G. C., 282
Wright, Quincy, 573
Wyle, C. J., 169

Yap, P. M., 411, 412, 419
Yinger, J. M., 554, 557, 560, 563, 564, 566, 567, 569, 604

York, Richard H., 658
Young, K., 43

Zawadski, Bohdan, 562, 567
Zeleny, L. D., 117
Ziegler, Benjamin Munn, 498
Zilboorg, Gregory, 129

Zimmering, Paul, 298
Zimmerman, C. C., 78, 80, 432, 436, 450, 456, 458, 459
Znaniecki, Florian, 22, 52
Zorbaugh, Harvey, 89
Zucker, Arnold H., 655
Zucker, H. L., 575

Subject Index

Abnormal behavior (*see* Deviant behavior)
Abortions, 20
Accomplice in crime, 155
Achieved status, 6
Achievement, 9
Addiction (*see* Drug addiction)
Addicts, drug (*see* Drug addicts)
Adrenal glands, 42
Age, drinking and, 335–337
   drug addicts, 297
   of offenders, 207–209
   suicide and, 415–417
   vandalism and, 221–222
   See also Old Age
Aged (*see* Old age)
Aging, physiological changes and, 460–463
   psychological changes and, 463–464
   See also Old age
Aggravated assault, 24, 79, 84, 120, 153, 169, 205, 208, 210
Aggression, suicide as, 426
Alcohol, physiological effects of, 321–325
Alcohol drinking, 318–361
   age and, 335–337
   as a social phenomenon, 325–327
   attitudes toward, 321
   conflict of values and, 318–320
   crime and, 200–201
   excessive (*see* Excessive drinking)
   extent of, in the U.S., 332–334
   frequency of, 334–335
   types of drinkers, 337–341
Alcoholic process, 341–346
Alcoholic psychoses, 27, 40, 371, 372
Alcoholics, chronic, 26, 339
   defined, 26, 338
   residential treatment centers, 652–653

Alcoholics (*continued*)
   statistics on, 26
   subculture of, 11
Alcoholics Anonymous, 104–105, 647–652
Alcoholism, 318–361
   age-old problem of, 318
   anomie and, 17
   body-type theory and, 119, 123
   chronic stage in, 344–346
   city size and, 85–86
   comparison of, in rural and urban areas, 81
   defined, 24, 339
   frustration as cause of, 16
   general discussion of, 26
   excessive drinking state in, 343
   glandular dysfunctions and, 43
   group and subcultural factors in, 347–359
   group approaches to problem of, 647–653
   heredity and, 40–41
   homosexual drives and, 131
   infantile regression and, 132
   intelligence and, 117
   middle drinking stage in, 343–344
   norms and, 19
   process of, 341–346
   psychiatric theory and, 129, 133
   public education concerning, 602–604
   residential treatment centers, 652–653
   "visibility" of, 21–22
American Creed, 30, 491–501
   discrimination and the, 493–501
   segregation and the, 497–501
   sources of the, 492–493
American Friends Service Committee, 605
American Indians, 31, 514–516

American Jewish Committee, 605
American Jewish Congress, 532, 605
Anomie, 16, 17
Anti-Defamation League of B'nai B'rith,
    532, 605
Anti-Semitism, 31
Antisocial behavior (see Deviant behavior)
Arson, 92, 132
Ascribed status, 6
Assault, aggravated, 24, 79, 84, 120, 153,
    169, 205, 208, 210
Associates, as source of criminal attitudes,
    184–186
    criminals and, 213
    drug addicts and, 303
    drinking and, 349–352
    juvenile delinquency and, 200–201
Association on American Indian Affairs,
    Inc., 516
Atomic energy, 4
Attempted crime, 155
Attitudes, defined, 53
    delinquent and criminal
        general culture and, 168–178
        sources of, 167–203
    development of, 52–57
Auto theft, 12, 14, 24, 79, 84, 92, 132, 169,
    170, 205, 208, 228–229

Baumes Laws, 159
Beating, wife, 29
Beggars, 103–104
Behavior (see Criminal behavior; Deviant
    behavior; Social behavior)
Behavior systems of deviants, 210–216
Bicycle theft, 92
Bigamy, 9
Biology, social behavior and, 38–45
Black market, 578–582
Blackmail, 20, 241
Body type, deviant behavior and, 119–125
Bookmakers, 278, 279
Broken homes, as source of criminal at-
    titudes, 198–199
    statistics on, 29
Burglary, 9, 15, 19, 24, 79, 84, 85, 92, 120,
    132, 153, 169, 205, 208
Business, discrimination and, 547–548
    organized crime in, 281–283
Business-cycle, fluctuations and deviancy,
    105
    suicide and the, 427

Call girls, 252
Capital punishment, 157–159
Car theft (see Auto theft)
Career criminals, 257–291
    behavior system of, 210
    habitual petty offenders as, 258–261
    ordinary, 270–272
    organized, 273–284
    progression in crime, 215–216
    white-collar offenders as, 261–270
Childhood experiences, deviant behavior
    and, 125–126
Chinese-Americans, 31, 519–520
Christophobia, 130
Chronic alcoholism defined, 26
Churches, reduction of deviant behavior
    through, 616–617
Cities (see Urbanism; Urbanization)
City size, social deviation and, 83–87
Class status (see Social class; Social status)
Clinics, reduction of deviant behavior
    through, 617–618
Clubs, aged and, 663–664
Cocaine, 25, 292, 293–294
Comic books, 38, 178–181
Communication, discrimination and, 539
    urbanization and, 74–76
Companions (see Associates)
Companionship, in marriage, 541
Competence and crime, 154
Compulsive behavior, 27, 375
Compulsory psychiatric examinations of
    offenders, 156
Concealed weapons, 21, 169, 208
Confidence games, 284–285
Conflicts in marital and family roles, 430–
    459
Conformity, 16, 36, 37
Constitution, U.S., 31
Control group in scientific method, 33
Controlled drinking, 26, 338
Corruption, political, 23, 25
Counseling facilities, reduction of deviant
    behavior through, 615–618
Crime, accomplice in, 155
    alcohol and, 200–201
    anomie and, 17
    as criminal-law violation, 152–160
    attempt to convert, 155
    body-type theory and, 120, 121
    city size and, 84–85
    competency and, 154

Crime (continued)
  defined, 152–165
  differentials in treatment of, on basis of class, race, and sex, 155–156
  distinction between felonies and misdemeanors, 153–154
  distribution of, within a city, 92
  drug addiction and, 310–313
  infantile regression and, 132
  intent and, 154
  motion pictures and, 178–181
  neighborhood and, 181–183
  newspapers and, 177–178
  occupations and, 181–183
  organized, 273–284
  professional, 284–289
  progression in, 215–216
  public education concerning, 597–600
  punishment for (see Punishment)
  radio and, 178–181
  reduction of, 597–600
  rural, compared with urban, 79–80
  social control and, 148–152
  social status and, 15
  sources of, 167–203
  television and, 178–181
  type of, classification of offenders by, 204–206
  war and, 575–577
  See also Criminals; White-collar crime
Crimes, personal, 25, 205
  property, 24–25, 80, 205, 210
  types of, 204–206
  See also names of crimes
Criminal behavior, personality traits and, 216–218
  scientific study of, 145–148
Criminal law, crime as a violation of, 152–160
  federal, extension of, 159–160
  in practice, 153–156
  trends in, 156–160
Criminals, associates of, 213
  attitudes, sources of, 167–203
  behavior systems of, 210–216
  body-type theory of, 119, 120
  conception of self and, 213–215
  glandular dysfunction and, 42
  group methods used in treatment of, 664–670
  heredity and, 40–42
  identification with crime, 213

Criminals (continued)
  personality traits of, 216–218
  professional (see Professional offenders)
  progression in crime, 215–216
  scientific study of, 145–148
  sex ratio, 206–207
  social roles of, 212–213
  subculture of, 11, 23
  See also Career criminals; Crime; Offenders
Cultural change, urbanism and, 69–70
Cultural lag, deviant behavior and the, 105–110
Cultural norms (see Social norms)
Culture, characteristics, 8–9
  defined, 8–9
  general, criminal attitudes and, 168–178
  social norms and, 8–10

Dawes Allotment Act (1887), 515
Death penalty, 157–159
Declaration of Human Rights, 30
Declaration of Independence, 31
Defects, physical, behavior and, 43–44
Definitions of situations, 52–53, 56
Delinquent attitudes, sources of, 167–203
Delinquent gangs, 17, 186–196
Delinquent subcultures, types of, 190–191
Dementia paralytica (see Paresis)
Democracy, 9
Deviant behavior, anomie and, 16
  approved, 17, 18
  as social behavior, 36–59
  attitudes toward, 17–20
  body type and, 119–125
  business-cycle fluctuations and, 105
  city size and, 83–87
  comparison of, in rural and urban areas, 78–83
  cultural lag and, 105–110
  defined, 22
  distribution of, within a city, 87–96
  economic factors and, 99–105
  effect of war on, 570–590
  feeble-mindedness and, 116–119
  frustration and, 16, 17
  glands and, 42–43
  heredity and, 39–42
  housing and, 110–113
  intelligence and, 44, 116–119
  physical characteristics or defects and, 43–44

Deviant behavior (*continued*)
  poverty and, 99–105
  psychiatric theory of, 125–126
  psychoanalytic explanation of, 126–139
  punishment for, 17–19, 156
  reduction of, 593–643
  scientific study of, 31–34
  social problems distinguished from, 22
  social roles and, 49–52
  social stratification and, 13–17
  social visibility of, 20–22
  societal reaction toward, 17–20
  technological factors and, 105–110
  theories of, controversial, 116–141
  toleration of, 17–20
  types of, 23–31
  urbanism and, 60–98
Deviation, primary, 51
  secondary, 51
Differential association, and criminal attitudes, 215
Differentiation, social (*see* Social differentiation)
Discrimination, 534–569
  administration of justice and, 550–552
  American Creed and, 493–501
  business and, 547–548
  city size and, 86–87
  communication and, 539
  defined, 534
  educational facilities and, 544–547
  employment and, 547–548
  exclusion from organized groups, 540–542
  forms of, 535–553
  housing and, 536–539
  immigration and, 550
  misconceptions about, 534
  norms relating to, 12
  public accomodations and, 542–544
  public education concerning, 604–607
  public office and, 550
  reduction of, 604–607
  relationship to prejudice, 553–554
  restrictions on general social participation, 535–536
  segregated living and, 536–539
  statistics on, 31
  suffrage and, 548–550
  war and, 588–589
  See also Minority groups; Prejudice
Disease and antisocial behavior, 43
Disorganized society, 22–23

Desertion, 29, 435–436
Delinquency (*see* Juvenile delinquency)
Differential association, white-collar offenders and, 264–266
Disorderly conduct, 21, 25, 154, 169
Divorce, 436–441
  disapproval of, 29
  extent of, in U.S., 436–438
  rates, factors in, 438–441
  statistics on, 430, 436–438
  steps leading to, 434
Dreams, analysis of, 127–128
Drinking (*see* Alcohol drinking; Alcoholism; Excessive drinking)
Drinkers, types of, 337–341
Driving while intoxicated, 208
Drug addiction, 292–317
  anomie and, 17
  argot in, 302, 308–309
  associates and, 303
  control of, 314–316
  crime and, 310–313
  culture of, 305–310
  extent of, 295–297
  frustration as cause of, 16
  general discussion of, 25–26
  group treatment methods, 653–655
  juvenile delinquency and, 307, 310–313
  length of, 298
  opiate, process of, 301–303
  public education concerning, 604
  subculture and, 11
  subgroups and, 24
  teen-age, 306
  treatment, 313–314
Drug addicts, age of, 297
  attitude of public toward, 292
  defined, 293
  education of, 298
  effect of drugs on, 293–295
  group treatment methods, 653–655
  number of, in U.S., 295
  occupation of, 298–301
  personality traits, 301
  self-concept of, 303
  sex ratio, 296
  treatment of, 313–314, 653–655
  urban areas and, 296–297
  withdrawal distress and, 294–295, 302
Drugs, effect of, 293–295
  depressant, 293–294
  illegal, profits in, 305
  legislation concerning, 292

Drugs (*continued*)
  stimulating, 293, 295
Drunkenness, 21–22, 26

Economic factors, deviant behavior and, 99–105
Economic problems, marital stability and, 452–453
Education, public, and reduction of deviant behavior, 397–407
Educational facilities, discrimination and, 544–547
Ego, 128
Electra complex, 133, 134
Embezzlement, 25, 132, 164, 268
Emotional security, family and, 199–200
Employment, discrimination and, 547–548
  old age and, 468–472
Endocrine glands, 43
Equality, 9
Ethnic groups, 520–525
  excessive drinking and, 357–359
  Mexican-Americans, 522–524
  Puerto Ricans, 524–525
  Spanish-Americans, 521–522
Excessive drinking, class differences in, 352–353
  companions and, 349–352
  defined, 26
  ethnic differences in, 357–359
  false assumptions concerning, 36
  occupation and, 354–356
  personality traits and, 346–347
  religious differences in, 356–357
  See also Alcoholism
Exhibitionism, 210, 241, 245
Experimental group in scientific method, 33

Family, as a social institution, 7, 8, 430
  conflicts within, 29, 430–459
  distintegration process, 433–435
  emotional security and the, 199–200
  interpersonal relations within, 431
  public education concerning, 602
  source of criminal attitudes, 196–200
  structure, changes in, 454–456
  traits, 42
  urban life and the, 454–458
Federal laws, crime and, 159–160
Federal Narcotics Control Act (1956), 293
Feeble-mindedness and deviant behavior, 116–119

Felonies, defined, 153–154
Forgery, 120, 132, 205
Formal controls, 148–152
Fraud, 92, 120, 164
Free association, 127
Frustration, deviant behavior and, 16, 17
Functional mental disorders, 362–402
Functional psychoses, 27, 376–379
Funds, misappropriation of, 161–162

Gambling, 25, 92, 169, 170, 205, 209, 276–281, 593–594
  subgroups and, 24
Gangs, delinquent, 17, 186–196
Glands and deviant behavior, 42–43
Gonads, 42
Gossip, 149
Government, as a social institution, 7
Groups, attitude development and, 54
  based on interests, 6–7
  characteristics of, 4
  control, 33
  defined, 4
  dependence on, man's, 5
  ethnic (*see* Ethnic groups)
  experimental, 33
  membership, 54
  organization of, 6
  peer (*see* Peer groups)
  primary, 54
  racial (*see* Racial minority groups)
  reference, 54, 57
  religious (*see* Religious groups)
  secondary, 55
  social differentiation and, 9–13
  social norms and, 9–10
  social reintegration through, 644–671
  teen-age, subculture of, 11, 23
  See also Minority groups

Halfway houses, 662–663
Happiness, marital, companionship and, 451
  psychological characteristics and, 448–450
  sexual relationship and, 451–452
  social participation and, 450
Health, antisocial behavior and, 43
  mental, problems of definition, 363–367
  minority groups and, 539–540
Heavy drinkers, 26
Heredity, alcoholism and, 40–41
  criminals and, 40–42

Heredity (*continued*)
  deviant behavior and, 39–42
  schizophrenia and, 398–401
Heroin, 25, 292, 293, 294, 296, 305, 306, 307
Heroism, 17
Habitual offenders, 258–261
Harrison Act (1914), 292
Homeless men, factors contributing to, 103
Homicide, criminal, *see* Murder
Homosexuality, 247–248
  alcoholism and, 131
  body-type theory and, 121
  glandular dysfunctions and, 42–43
  norms and, 19
  Oedipus complex and, 133
  prisons and, 625
  social visibility of, 20
  subculture and, 11, 23, 24
Hormones, sex, 42
Horse races, 279
Hospitals, mental (*see* Mental hospitals)
Housing, deviant behavior and, 110–113
  discrimination and, 536, 539
  juvenile delinquency and, 38, 111–113
  minority groups and, 536–539
Human behavior, theory of, 28
  See also Deviant behavior; Social behavior
Human rights, 491
Humanitarianism, 9
Hypochondria, 27
Hypothesis, 32, 33
Hysteria, 27, 375

Id, 128–130, 134
Immigration, discrimination and, 550
Imprisonment, 159
  objectives of, 622–624
Incest, 24
Income tax returns, falsified, 25
Incorrigibility, 25
Indecent exposure, 92
Indeterminate sentences, 156
"Indian hemp," 293
Indians, American, 31, 514–516
Individualism in urban society, 73–74
Infantile regression, 131–132
Informal controls, 148–150
In-law problems, 446–447
Innovation, 16
Instincts, 39

Institutional norms, 9
Institutions, social, defined, 6
  function of, 8
  reduction of deviancy through, 620–643
  structure of, 7–8
Intelligence, behavior and, 44–45
  deviant behavior and, 116–119
  limits of, 44
  tests of, 44
Intent, criminal, 154
Interests, groups and, 6–7

Japanese-American Citizens League, 519, 605
Japanese-Americans, 31, 516–519
Jewish Labor Committee, 532, 605
Jewish War Veterans, 532
Jewish Welfare Board, 532
Jews, 525–532
  discrimination and, 31, 130
Juvenile delinquency, alcohol and, 200–201
  anomie and, 17
  associates and, 184–185
  attitudes of delinquents, sources of, 167–203
  auto theft, 228–229
  behavior covered by term, 154–155
  behavior systems and, 210–216
  body-type theory and, 121, 123
  broken homes as source of, 198–199
  class status and, 17
  combating, group methods used in, 664
  comic books and, 38, 178–181
  defined, 25, 219
  distribution within a city, 91
  drug addiction and, 307, 310–313
  family and, 196–200
  gangs and, 186–196
  housing and, 38, 111–113
  movies and, 178–181
  neighborhoods and, 181–183
  newspapers and, 177–178
  nongang companions and, 185–186
  occupations and, 181–183
  personality traits in, 216–218
  public education concerning, 597–598
  radio and, 178–181
  reduction of, 597–598
  residential treatment centers, 669–670
  rural, compared with urban, 79–80
  social class and, 14–15
  social roles and, 212

Juvenile delinquency (*continued*)
  statistics on, 25
  subgroups and, 24
  television and, 178–181
  vandalism as type of, 219–228
  wartime, 573–575

Kidnaping, 20, 24

Labor unions, racketeering in, 281–283
Language, as unique characteristic of man, 45–46
Larceny, 24, 79, 84, 169, 205, 208
Law, general disobedience to, 168–172
  selective obedience to, 172–174
  suicide and the, 407–408
  violation, in U.S., 24
  See also Criminal law
Law-enforcement officers and agencies, behavior of, 174–176
League of United Latin-American Citizens (LULACS), 524
Legal norms, defined, 9
  penalties for violation of, 24
Lewdness, 92
Life, protection of, 9
Life expectancy, among minority groups, 539–540
Life imprisonment, 159
Life organization, defined, 58
  behavior and, 58
Lotteries, illegal, 278
Lynching, 20, 551

Mala in se, 152
Mala prohibita, 153
Man, social nature of, 45–49
Manic depressive behavior, body-type theory and, 120
  characteristics of, 27, 378–379
  distribution of, within a city, 93–94
Manic-depressive psychoses, 376
Manslaughter, 9, 24, 25, 79, 84, 205, 208, 231
  negligent, 231
Marihuana, 25, 292, 293, 296, 300, 306, 307
  using, process of, 303–304
Marital happiness (*see* Happiness, marital)
Marriage, adaptability in, 432
  companionship in, 451
  conflicts in, 29, 430–459
  cultural background and, 447–448
  economic problems and, 452–453

Marriage (*continued*)
  happiness in, 450–452
  in-law problems, 446–447
  interests and, 447–448
  interpersonal relations in, 431–433
  psychological characteristics and, 448–450
  public education concerning, 602
  sexual relationship and, 451–452
  social participation and, 450
  social structure and, 453–458
  stability in, 452–458
  war and, 586–588
Masculinity-femininity conflict, 131
"Mass Society," 60
Materialism, urbanism and, 72
Membership groups, 54
Mental disorders, cultural factors in, 394–396
  developmental process in, 379–383
  extent of, in U.S., 27–28, 367–370
  functional, 362–402
  group treatment methods and, 655–663
  inappropriate role playing and, 389–394
  old age and, 480–483
  organic, 371–372
  problems of definition, 363–367
  public education concerning, 600–602
  social stratification and, 396–398
  stress and, 383–386
  suicide and, 425–426
  war and, 584–586
  See also Mental illness
Mental health, problems of definition, 363–367
Mental hospitals, 632–642
  extent and cost of care in, 632–634
  functions of, 632
  future of, 640–642
  group therapy and, 657–660
  reduction of deviancy through, 632–642
  social structure of, 636–639
  therapeutic communities, 660–661
  treatment methods in, 634–636
Mental illness, anomie and, 17
  body types and, 119, 121
  distribution of, within a city, 93–94
  economic costs of, 28
  extent of, in the U.S., 27–28, 367–370
  family care and, 661–662
  general discussion of, 26–28
  halfway houses and, 662–663

Mental illness (continued)
  intelligence and, 117
  norms and, 24
  rural and urban areas compared, 80–81
  self-conception and, 386–389
  social status and, 15
  statistics on, 27–28
  therapeutic communities, 660–661
  trends in, 370–371
  visibility of, 21
  See also Mental disorders
Mexican-Americans, 522–524
Minority groups, 491–533
  American Creed and, 491–501
  concept of, 501–503
  discrimination against, 30–31
  ethnic, 520–525
  health and, 539–540
  housing and, 536–539
  in the U.S., 503–532
  life expectancy among, 539–540
  mass communication and, 539
  norms relating to discrimination against, 30
  prejudice and, 567–568
  racial, 504–520
  religious, 525–532
  segregated living and, 536–539
  vandalism and, 551–552
  See also Discrimination; Prejudice
Misappropriation of funds, 161–162
Misdemeanors, 153–154
Mobility, urbanism and, 70–72
Morphine, 25, 292, 293–294
Motion pictures, as source of criminal attitudes, 178–181
Motives, acquisition of, 57
Murder, 9, 15, 19, 20, 24, 25, 79, 80, 84, 110, 120, 129, 131, 156, 205, 208, 210, 211, 231–240
  as a behavior system, 234–237
  statistics on, 231–232
  types of, 232–234
  victims of, 238–240
Murder, Inc., 211
Murderers, 231–240

Narcotics (see Drug addiction; Drug addicts; Drugs)
Narcotics Anonymous, 653–655
National Association for the Advancement of Colored People (NAACP), 514, 605

National Community Relations Advisory Council, 605
National Conference of Christians and Jews, 605
National Congress of American Indians, 516
National Institute of Mental Health, 600
National Urban League, 605
Nationalism, 9, 23, 30–31
Natural process, human nature studied as a, 32
Negroes, American Creed and, 491–501
  as minority group, 504–514
  class structure among, 507–511
  prejudice against, and psychoanalytic theory, 130–131
  See also Discrimination; Minority groups; Prejudice
Neighborhood, as source of criminal attitudes, 181–183
Neighborhood norms, 12
Neighborhood programs, for reduction of deviant behavior, 607–612
Neuroses, 375–376
  cause of, 123
  class status and, 15
  defined, 27
  extent of, in the United States, 28
  See also Mental disorders; Mental illness
Newspapers, as source of criminal attitudes, 177–178
Noncareer offenders, 210, 211
Nonconformity, 37
  attitudes toward, 17
Nongang companions, as source of delinquent attitudes, 185–186
Nonorganic mental disorders (see Functional mental disorders)
Normative standards, 8
Norms (see Legal norms; Neighborhood norms; Social norms; Subcultural norms)
Numbers racket, 171, 278

Observation in scientific method, 33
Occasional property offenders, 257–258
Occupation, as source of criminal attitudes, 181–183
  excessive drinking and, 354–356
  suicide and, 418–419
Oedipus complex, 133, 135
Offenses against public order, 25

Offenders, age of, 207–209
  behavior systems and, 210–216
  career, 210, 211
  classification of, 204–230
  conception of self, 213–215
  differential association, 215
  group methods, used in treatment of, 664–671
  habitual, 258–261
  identification with crime, 213
  murderers, 231–240
  noncareer, 210, 211
  occasional, 257–258
  personality traits of, 216–218
  professional (see Professional offenders)
  progression in crime, 215–216
  psychiatric examination of, 156
  sex (see Sex offenders)
  sex ratio, 206–207
  social roles of, 212–213
  types of, 204–291
  white-collar (see White-collar offenders)
  See also Criminals
Old age, changes in social rules and status, 464–468
  employment and, 468–472
  group methods in dealing with, 663–664
  mental disorders and, 480–483
  nonurban societies and, 474–476
  physiological changes and, 460–463
  population, increase in, 476–480
  psychological changes and, 463–464
  role and status conflict in, 30
  social adjustment and, 486–488
  social participation and, 484–486
  statistics on, 30
  urban family and, 472–474
Old-age psychoses (see Senile psychoses)
Opium, 25, 292, 293
Ordinary criminal careers, 270–272
Organic mental disorders, 371–372
Organic psychoses, 27
Organized crime, 273–284
  areas of, 276
  as a career, 283–284
  features of, 273
  feudal structure of, 273–274
  gambling as, 276–281
  politics and, 274–276
  widespread operations, 274

Paranoia, 376
  characteristics of, 27, 379

Parents, role conflicts between children and, 445–446
Paresis, 27, 371–372
Patriotism, 9
Peeping Toms, 92
Peer groups, defined, 12
  norms and values of, 12
Personal crimes, 25, 205
Personality, individual, 9
Personality traits, criminal behavior and, 216–218
  excessive drinking and, 346–347
  juvenile delinquency and, 216–218
Phobias, 27
Physical characteristics and defects, behavior and, 43–44
Physical punishment, 156–159
Physique, deviant behavior and, 119–125
Pickpocketing, 284
Police, behavior of, as source of criminal attitudes, 174–176
Policy, 278
Politics, corrupt, 23, 25
  organized crime and, 274–276
Population (see Urbanism; Urbanization)
Poverty, deviant behavior and, 99
Prejudice, cultural factors and, 554–561
  economic factors and, 564–566
  minority groups and, 30–31, 567–568
  personality needs and, 561–564
  psychoanalytic theory of, 130–131
  relationship to discrimination, 553–554
  See also Discrimination
Press, as source of criminal attitudes, 177–178
Primary deviation, 51
Primary groups, 54
Prisons, 621–632
  future of, 629–632
  life in, characteristics of, 624–626
  objectives of, 622–624
  social system in, 626–629
  subculture in, 11
Probation, 156
Professional offenders, 284–289
  argot of, 286–287
  defined, 284
  role skills of, 287
  social role of, 285–287
  status of, 287–288
Progress, 9
Property, protection of, 9
Property crimes, 24–25, 80, 205, 210

Prostitutes, backgrounds of, 253–254
  false assumptions concerning, 36
  types of, 251–253
Prostitution, 249–255
  appeals of, 250–251
  class status and, 15
  defined, 249
  drug addiction and, 26
  extent of, 25, 249–250
  feeble-mindedness and, 177
  norms and, 19, 20
  patrons, 250–251
  process of, 254–255
  psychoanalytic theory of, 133–134
  societal reactions to, 251
  subculture and, 11, 23, 24
  war and, 582–583
Protection of life and property, 9
Psychiatric examination of offenders, compulsory, 156
Psychiatric theory, of deviant behavior, 125–126
Psychic development, 133
Psychoanalytic theory of deviant behavior, 126–139
  criticisms of, 134–136
  evaluation of, 136–139
Psychodrama, 657–658
Psychogenic traits (see Personality traits)
Psychoneuroses (see Neuroses)
"Psychopaths," defined, 217–218
Psychoses, alcoholic, 27, 40, 371, 372
  body-type theory and, 120
  distribution of, within a city, 93–94
  extent of, in the U.S., 27–28
  functional, 27, 376–379
  manic-depressive, 27
  organic, 27
  senile, 27, 30, 371
  social class and, 15
  types of, 27
Psychotherapy, group, alcoholics and, 653
  mental disorders and, 659–660
Public accomodations, discrimination and, 542–544
Public drinking houses, society and, 327–332
Public education, alcoholism and, 602–604
  crime and, 597–600
  discrimination and, 604–607
  drug addiction and, 604

Public education (continued)
  family life and, 602
  juvenile delinquency and, 597–598
  marriage and, 602
  mental disorders and, 600–602
  reduction of deviant behavior through, 597–607
Public office, discrimination and, 550
Public order, crimes against, 205
Puerto Ricans, 31, 524–525
Punishment, capital, 157–159
  deviant behavior and, 17–19, 156
  physical, 156–159
  solitary confinement as form of, 5
  white-collar crime and, 164–165

Race, cultural misconceptions about, 557–561
Race riots, 551
Racial discrimination (see Discrimination)
Racial minority groups, 504–520
  American Indian, 514–516
  Chinese-Americans, 519–520
  discrimination against, 30–31
  Japanese-Americans, 516–519
  Negroes, 504–514
Racketeering, 281–283
Radio, as source of criminal attitudes, 178–181
Rape, 9, 20, 24, 80, 84, 92, 120, 205, 208, 210
  forcible, 240
  statutory, 240
Rebellion, 16
Recovery, Incorporated, 656
Reduction of deviant behavior, 593–643
  churches and, 616–617
  clinics and, 617–618
  comprehensive programs for, 618–619
  counseling facilities and, 617–618
  institutions and, 621–643
  local community programs and, 607–612
  moral and ameliorative problems in, 596–597
  preventive agencies and, 607–619
  public education and, 597–607
  schools and, 614–616
  street corner projects and, 612–613
"Reefers," 293
Reference group, 54, 57
Regression, infantile, 131–132

Reintegration, social, group approach to, 644–671

Religious groups, excessive drinking and, 356–357
Jews, 31, 525–532
suicide and, 417–418

Representative sample in testing hypothesis, 33

Research techniques in scientific method, 33

Retreatism, 16

Ritualism, 16

Robbery, 19, 20, 24–25, 79, 84, 85, 92, 120, 132, 152, 170, 205, 209

Role conflicts, between marital partners, 441–444
between marital partners and other relatives, 446–447
between marriage and other activities, 444–445
between parents and children, 445–446

Role playing, defined, 50
family and, 430–433, 441–447
inappropriate, mental disorders and, 389–394
marriage and, 430–433, 441–447

Role taking, 50, 52

Rural areas, deviant behavior in, compared with that in urban areas, 78–83

Saloons (see Public drinking houses)

Schizophrenia, 376
body-type theory and, 119
characteristics of, 27, 376–378
distribution of, within a city, 93–94
etiology of, 132
heredity and, 398–401
self-conception and, 387
social class and, 15
subtypes of, 377

Schools, reduction of deviant behavior through, 614–616

Science, 31–34
man's achievements in, 3

Scientific method, 4, 31–34

Scientific study of deviant behavior, 31–34

Secondary deviation, 51

Secondary groups, 55

Security, emotional, family and, 199–200

Segregation, American Creed and, 497–501

Segregation (continued)
elimination of, 31

Self-conception, development of, 46–49
drug addicts, 303
of offenders, 213–215
schizophrenia and, 387
white-collar offenders and, 263–264

Self-control, 50

Senile psychoses, 27, 30, 371

Separation, in marriage, 29, 435–436

Sex codes, 23

Sex hormones, 42

Sex offenses, classification of, 240
social visibility of, 20

Sex offenders, 240–255
intelligence and, 117
misconceptions about, 36, 242–245
subcultural factors and, 245–247

Sex ratio, drug addicts, 296
of offenders, 206–207
vandalism and, 221

Sexual deviation, class status and, 15

Sexual promiscuity, war and, 583

"Sexual psychopath," 243

Sexual relationship, and marital happiness, 451–452

Shelter-house men (see Homeless men)

Shoplifting, 92, 284

Situations, defining, 52–53, 56

Skid Row, 351

Slums, 88

Smoking, change in attitudes toward, 18, 19

Social behavior, biology and, 38–45
deviant behavior as, 36–59
glandular dysfunctions and, 42–43
heredity and, 39–42
instincts and, 39
intelligence and, 44–45
physical characteristics or defects and, 43–44
social roles and, 49–52
See also Deviant behavior

Social change, war and, 571–572

Social class, defined, 13
deviant behavior and, 13–17
mental disorders and, 396–398
vandalism and, 222–223

Social control, 8, 18, 50
crime and, 148–152
urbanism and, 74–76

Social differentiation, 10–13

Social disorganization, 22–23
Social drinking, 26, 338
Social groups (see Groups)
Social institutions (see Institutions)
Social interaction, defined, 4, 46
Social nature of man, 45–49
Social norms, city life and, 68–69
    culture and, 8–10
    defined, 9
    diversity of, 10–13
    social values distinguished from, 9
    sources of, 12–13
    tolerance limit of, 20
    transmittal of, 9–10
Social problems, deviant behavior compared with, 22
Social reintegration, group approach to, 644–671
Social relationships, defined, 4
    social norms and, 9
Social research, 31–34
Social roles, city life and, 68–69
    defined, 4
    deviant behavior and, 49–52
    development of, 49–52
    diversity of, 49–52
    family and, 430–459
    marriage and, 430–459
    mental disorders and, 389–394
    of offenders, 212–213
    old age and, 460–490
    white-collar crime and, 267–268
    See also Role playing
Social status, achieved, 6
    ascribed, 6
    defined, 6
    deviant behavior and, 13–17
Social stratification, deviant behavior and, 13–17
Social structure, deviant behavior and, 13–17
Social values, defined, 9
    social norms distinguished from, 9
    See also Social norms
Social visibility of deviant behavior, 20–22
Socialization, defined, 10
Societal reaction, deviation and, 17–20
Society, differentiated, 10–12
    drinking houses and, 327–332
    group relationships and, 4–8
    Mass, 60
    modern, 10–12

Society (continued)
    types of, suicide and, 408–412
Sociology, defined, 4
Sodomy, 92
Solitary confinement, 5
Solitude, 5–6
Spanish-speaking Americans, 521–525
Standards, normative, 8
Status (see Economic status; Social status)
Stealing (see Theft)
Street corner projects, and reduction of deviant behavior, 612–613
Stress, mental disorders and, 383–386
Subcultural norms, 10–13
Subcultures, contributions of, 23
    defined, 11
    delinquent, types of, 190–191
    norms of, and social differentiation, 10–13
    organized, 23
    teen-age, 12
Subprocesses, differences in, 37, 58
Success, 9, 15–16
Suffrage, discrimination and, 548–550
Suicide, 403–429
    age and, 415–417
    aggression and, 426
    anomie and, 17
    business cycle and, 427
    city size and, 86
    cultural norms and, 404–406
    defined, 403
    extent of, in U.S., 403
    forms of, 403
    general discussion of, 28–29
    law and, 407–408
    marital status and, 417
    mental disorders and, 425–426
    occupation and, 15, 418–419
    process of, 419–425
    psychiatric theory and, 129
    race and, 415
    religious groups and, 417–418
    rural and urban areas compared, 82–83
    sex ratios, 412–415
    social class and, 15
    social differentials in, 412–419
    statistics on, 28–29
    status and, 426–428
    type of society and, 408–412
    variations and rates by countries, 406–407
    varieties of, 129

Suicide (*continued*)
  war and, 586
Superego, 128–130
Suspended sentence, 156
Swindling, 132
Syndicates (*see* Organized crime)
Syphilis, 27, 371

Taverns (*see* Public drinking houses)
Technological development, 3, 105–108
Technological factors, deviant behavior
  and, 105–110
Teen-age gangs (*see* Gangs)
Teen-age subculture, 12
Television, as source of criminal attitudes,
  178–181
Tests, intelligence, 44
Theft, 9, 12, 14, 16, 20, 92, 120, 132, 153,
  169, 208
  auto, 12, 14, 24, 79, 84, 92, 132, 169, 170,
    205, 208, 228–229
  bicycle, 92
  drug addiction and, 26
Therapeutic communities, 660–661
Therapy, group, criminals and, 666–669
  delinquents and, 666–669
  mental disorders and, 657–660
Thymus gland, 42
Tolerance limit of norm, 20
Toleration, of deviant behavior, 17–19
Traffic cases, 25
Tramps (*see* Homeless men)
Truancy, 25

Unconscious mind, 127
Unethical practices (*see* White-collar
  crime)
Unions, racketeering and, 281–283
United Jewish Appeal, 532
Universal Declaration of Human Rights,
  30
Urbanism, as a way of life, 65–74
  characteristics a matter of degree, 76–
    78
  city size and deviant behavior, 83–87
  communication problem, 74–76
  comparison of deviant behavior in rural
    and urban areas, 78–83
  cultural change and, 69–70
  deviant behavior and, 60–98
  distribution of deviant behavior within
    a city, 87–96
  individualism and, 73–74

Urbanism (*continued*)
  materialism and, 72
  mobility and, 70–72
  norm and social role conflicts and, 68–
    69
  social control and, 74–76
Urbanization, in the U.S., 63–65
  world, growth of, 60–63

Vagrancy, 21, 25
Values, social, 9
  See also Social norms
Vandalism, 12, 25, 169, 219–228
  age group involved, 221–222
  cost to public, 220
  defined, 219–220
  group nature of, 223–224
  minority groups and, 551–552
  predatory, 227–228
  relation of, to other delinquency, 223
  sex ratio, 221
  social class of offenders, 222–223
  subtypes of, 227–228
  typology of, dimensions in a, 224–227
  vindictive, 227, 228
  wanton, 227, 228
Verification of hypothesis, 33
Violations of trust, 268–270
"Visibility" of deviant behavior, 20–22

War, crime and, 575–577
  discrimination and, 588–589
  effect on deviant behavior, 570–590
  marital conflicts and, 586–588
  mental disorders and, 584–586
  prostitution and, 582–583
  sexual promiscuity and, 583
  social change and, 571–572
  suicide and, 586
  white-collar crime and, 577–582
White-collar crime, 261–270
  compared with conventional crime,
    162–163
  defined, 25, 160–161
  different punishment of, 164–165
  distribution of, within a city, 92
  nature and extent of, 160–161
  offenses considered as, 161–164
  organization of, 267
  reduction of, 599–600
  social status and, 15
  social visibility of, 20

White-collar crime (*continued*)
  subculture of, 23
  violations of trust as, 268–270
  war and, 577–582
White-collar offenders, 261–270
  differential associations, 264–266
  role orientations, 267–268

White-collar offenders (*continued*)
  self-concept of, 263–264
Wife beating, 29
Withdrawal distress, drug addiction and,
  294–295, 302

Young Men's Hebrew Association, 532